5-2-80

Life Forces

"Browse, enjoy, take whatever you find useful." So suggests Louis Stewart (a pseudonym) in this massive compendium of the spiritual sciences. Yet *Life Forces* is so much more than a reference book to the occult. Writing in an anecdotal, breezy, and at times tongue-in-cheek style, Stewart has produced a highly readable and enjoyable book which, in its almost hypnotic fascination, cannot easily be put down.

The first part of the book deals with the practice of the spiritual sciences. Aimed toward both the skeptic and the believer, this section leads the reader through the ascending levels of the spiritual hierarchy — from the physical and etheric planes of being (yoga, oriental healing, martial arts) to the astral plane of out-of-the-body experiences (seances, demonic possession, reincarnation) to the mental plane (hypnosis, astrology, meditation). Stewart winds up this section with accounts of bizarre experiences of voodoo and witchcraft and brief biographies of gurus, mystics, and charlatans (Buddha, Don Juan, Jesus Christ, Charles Manson).

In Part Two, "The Occult Bible," Stewart investigates the various sacred texts and tenets of occultists — from the story of Atlantis to the influence of extraterrestrial visitations on human life. Even works of convoluted madness are presented deadpan by Stewart in a convincingly reverential tone.

Finally, there is "The Dissenting Viewpoint" which reveals surprising, little-known accounts of occult history and occult fiction.

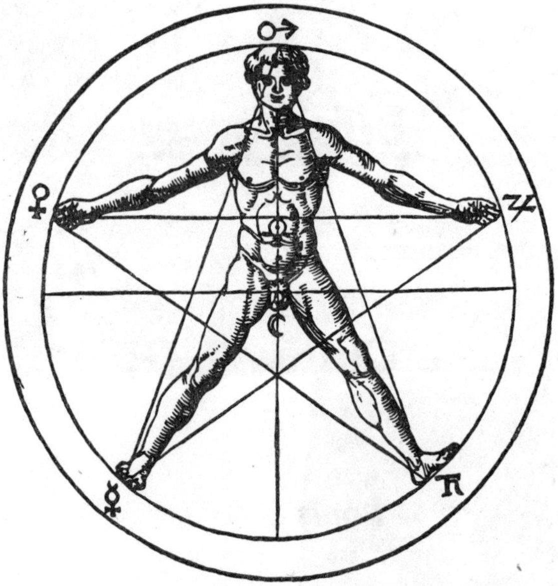

In *Life Forces* the entire realm of the occult is made accessible, perhaps for the first time, to the general reader while providing the serious enthusiast with sources for further information on each subject. For the curious outsider it is a delightful invitation into the mysterious world of the occult.

LIFE FORCES

A Contemporary Guide to The Cult and Occult

Louis Stewart

Andrews and McMeel, Inc.
A Universal Press Syndicate Company
Kansas City • New York • Washington

Printed in the United States of America.

For information write Andrews and McMeel, Inc.,
a Universal Press Syndicate Company,
Time & Life Building, Suite 3717
1271 Avenue of the Americas,
New York, New York 10020

Library of Congress Cataloging in Publication Data
Stewart, Louis, 1950–
Life forces.
Includes index.
1. Occult sciences. 2. Psychical research.
I. Title.
BF1411.S83 133 79-20402
ISBN 0-8362-7903-4

Acknowledgments

Grateful acknowledgment is made to the following for permission to quote excerpts from their material:

The Book of Ceremonial Magic, by A.E. Waite. Published by Citadel Press, a division of Lyle Stuart, Inc.

Mumbo Jumbo, by Ishmael Reed. Published by Doubleday & Company, Inc.

Voodoo in New Orleans, by Robert Tallant. Copyright © 1946 by Robert Tallant. Copyright © renewed 1974 by Minnie Magruder Gibbs. Published by Macmillan Publishing Company, Inc.

The I Ching or Book of Changes. The Richard Wilhelm translation rendered into English by Cary F. Baynes. Bollingen Series XIX. Copyright © 1950, 1967 by Princeton University Press. Copyright © renewed 1977 by Princeton University Press. Excerpts reprinted by permission.

The Mask of Cthulhu, by August Derleth. Excerpts reprinted by permission of Arkham House Publishers, Inc.

Hostage to the Devil, by Malachi Martin. Excerpts reprinted by permission of the author.

The author wishes to thank John Robey for the invaluable contributions he made to the chapter on magic, both through his research and through his generous advice. His work gave the chapter a depth it otherwise would not have had. Thanks are also due to Martha Wyatt for her many suggestions concerning "The Occult Bible," to J. J. Canavia for help in preparation of "A History of the Occult," and to M.A. Evans for inspiration in the chapter "Occult Fiction."

Any errors are of course my own.

Contents

Introduction

In this book, I have tried to make the spiritual sciences (occultism, if you prefer) accessible to the general reader. The job has not been easy. As a glance at the contents page will show, the subject is enormous. The subject is confusing as well—more than once I have had to bring conflicting viewpoints into accord (more for the sake of brevity than harmony). So a few preliminary paragraphs are in order by way of a guide to the guidebook.

First, I have a few words about the principle of selection at work here. How does one define occultism? The word *occult* denotes something secret or hidden, and that usually serves as a starting point, albeit an unsatisfactory one. Astrology, though undeniably occult, is as public a mystic art as one could imagine. Its secrets are more widely known than the facts of astronomy. After puzzling over the matter for a while, I finally decided that the characteristic feature of occultism is its claim to being a spiritual science.

Occultism does not claim to be a set of beliefs. It claims to be a system of knowledge. The distinction is important, since it lets us rule out religions on one hand and mysticism on the other. Religions, though they are codified to some extent, ultimately rest on faith. Mysticism, though it claims direct knowledge of the Divine, is not systematic. Occultism alone claims to give a detailed, verifiable map of the Absolute. It is a spiritual science.

Therefore, you will not find little-known Christian sects in this book, nor will you find biographies of the great mystics. You will find information on certain Eastern religions, but only because they have made a contribution to occultism. You will also find some slightly extraneous material (such as an article on Wilhelm Reich and a discussion of the Unification Church). This material is included because it bears on occultism and sheds light on certain of the occultists' claims.

As to the method of organization, I have divided the book into three parts: "The Practice of the Spiritual Sciences," "The Occult Bible," and "The Dissenting Viewpoint."

"The Practice of the Spiritual Sciences" serves as an initiation into occultism. The chapters, when read in order, will lead the reader through the ascending levels of the spiritual hierarchy. Thus, chapter one ("The Body") concerns the physical and etheric planes of being. Chapter two ("Out of the Body") concerns the astral plane. Chapter three (the tools of occultism—

astrology, Tarot, meditation, and so forth) takes the reader to the mental plane. The fourth chapter ("Magic") discusses in practical terms the mastery of all the planes of being. Finally, chapter five gives brief profiles of various gurus, people who have attained the very highest level in the spiritual hierarchy.

"The Occult Bible" is a synthesis of occult beliefs. It presents as briefly as possible what occultists know about the evolution of the universe and of humankind, the history of Atlantis, the Earth's geography, the influence of extraterrestrial visitation on human life. I have tried to make this material entertaining as well as informative.

Finally, there is "The Dissenting Viewpoint," a review of occultism as seen from the historical and literary perspective. Elsewhere in the book, I have, for the most part, tried to present the spiritual sciences sympathetically, as they are seen by a practitioner. In "The Dissenting Viewpoint," I have stepped outside of occultism and asked questions about the origins of occult beliefs, the conditions in which they developed, and the succeeding forms they took. I hope the reader will be as open-minded about this section as about the others.

The best advice I can give to the reader is: Browse, enjoy, take whatever you find useful. The ragpicker's approach is best. If you find something here to make you marvel at the variety of the human imagination, then this book will be worthwhile.

Part One

The Practice of the Spiritual Sciences

Chapter One

The Body

(The Physical and Etheric Planes)

• *Yoga* • *Wilhelm Reich* • *Bodywork*
• *Gadgets* • *Oriental Healing* • *Martial Arts*
• *Psychic Surgeons*

Yoga

On March 7, 1952, the great teacher Paramahansa Yogananda died. His friends and followers let him lie in state for twenty days. They made no attempt to preserve the corpse; despite that, many came to pay their last respects. The mortician at Forest Lawn Cemetery did not receive the corpse for burial until March 27. When he examined it before laying it in the casket, he found that Yogananda's body was perfectly intact—there was no decay, no smell, no putrefaction whatever.

People react to this story in different ways. Students of yoga say, "Of course." Materialists express disbelief. Perhaps the moral, if there is one, is simply that if you treat your body like a slab of meat, it will become a slab of meat; treat it as something better, and it will become something better.

In this chapter I will be writing about some systems that treat the body as something better than meat. They all have in common the concept of *biological energy*, the idea that there is a universal life force flowing through each of us. This life force can be used for healing, psychotherapy, self-defense (as in the martial arts), or to reach a state of spiritual enlightenment, as Paramahansa Yogananda did. No one system owns a monopoly on biological energy, so in reading each section in this chapter, please bear the others in mind. They all have something to contribute. I have given yoga precedence only because it's the oldest.

Yogananda had spent his life purifying his body, so at death the body did not decay. But that was merely a side effect of his way of life. Yogananda knew that the body is literally a small-scale model of the universe and that whoever realizes the true nature of the body also realizes the nature of God.

Origins of Yoga

Yoga is a means toward union with God. The word comes from an Indo-European root, *yuj*, meaning to bind together. Later that root became the Sanscrit word *yoking*, meaning a union, and finally *yoga*.

Yoga has played an important role in the development of two major religions—Brahmanism and Buddhism—and it is an element of the esoteric tradition of Tantrism. Nobody knows how old yoga is or exactly how it developed, but we can trace its origins to some extent.

In the last quarter of the second millennium B.C., a seminomadic people settled in India. These people developed (or perhaps brought with them) the oldest body of religious literature in the world, the Veda. In the Veda, these people set down their belief in an eternal conflict between *sat* (order) and *asat* (chaos), between gods (*devas*) and demons (*asuras*). Their highest god was Indra, who alternately took martial and agricultural forms. Indra fought against the snake demon Vṛtra and so organized the universe from chaos.

Brahmanism. The priests of the Vedic religion were called Brahmins. They eventually developed a highly organized system of ritual and their own body of literature, the Upanisads, the earliest of which date from around the sixth century B.C. In the Brahmin cosmology, which is the one commonly used in yoga, the universe is a manifestation of one force, eternal and infinite, called Brahman. Brahman is a force rather than a person. Its body is the universe, and the portion of Brahman that is in every living thing is called Ātman. The Ātman is your true self; as soon as you realize that self, you become one with Brahman. Free from the cycle of reincarnation called *saṃsāra*, or bondage, you achieve the state the Brahmins call *mokṣa*—final emancipation.

To put it more succinctly, the universe—everything we see, hear, touch, smell, and taste, and the mind itself that perceives those objects—is entirely an illusion. Yet the universe exists because we believe in it. We create it, sustain it, and destroy it moment by moment. When you realize your true self, the world stops existing for you. When the last human ceases to believe in the world, the world will simply end.

Brahmanism and yoga share these ideas about illusion and reality, but it is not known whether yoga got the ideas from Brahmanism or vice versa. We do know that yoga has historically been one of the paths of Brahmanism. The *Bhagavadgītā* (*The Lord's Song*), written around 200 B.C., presents the three traditional paths, or *mārga*, leading to emancipation. These are:

1. *Karma-mārga*, the path of duties (i.e., rituals and social obligations);
2. *Jñāna-mārga*, the path of knowledge (i.e., meditation and yoga); and
3. *Bhakti-mārga*, the path of devotion to a personal God.

But the *Bhagavadgītā* comes late in the history of yoga. By the time that book was written, the influence of yoga already had spread far beyond Brahmanism.

Buddhism. Gautama Buddha (ca. 560-ca. 480 B.C.) was a yogin, and he studied under the yogins Ālāra Kālāma and Uddaka Rāmaputta. Therefore, yoga has always been a strong element in Buddhism, particularly in *Yogācāra* (yoga practice) or *Vijñānavāda* (mind-only) Buddhism. It's usual to say that this school was founded by the brothers Asaṅga and Vasubandhu (fifth century A.D.) and by Sthiramati (sixth century A.D.). Perhaps it would be truer to say that these men reorganized and formalized very old teachings that had always been present in Buddhism. They taught that each person inherits a storehouse of potential perceptions. These are like seeds that develop into the five modes of perception and the mind itself. The illusion of the world arises because the mind comes to see the flowers of the other five seeds as different from itself, as external.

As yoga spread, it also became part of Tantrism (see below). Later still,

Patañjali wrote his *Yoga Sutras*, which are the earliest yogic texts. Scholars date the *Sutras* anywhere from the second century B.C. to the fourth century A.D. In any case, we can be sure that yoga was very old by the time Patañjali wrote his texts.

Today, yoga is more widely practiced than ever before. It remains a strong influence on Buddhism, Brahmanism, and Sufism (an Islamic mystical sect). Millions of people in the West practice it for its physical benefits. And it exerts an influence on occult thought through Theosophy and related schools.

The Eight Stages of Yoga

The full and correct name of yoga is *astāṅga-yoga*—eight-membered yoga. The adept, or *yogin*, must proceed through eight stages on the way to union with God. These stages are:

1. *Yama*, or restraint. The most important of these is *ahīmsa*, restraint from doing violence of any kind. The yogin must also abstain from greed, theft, lying, and incontinence.
2. *Niyama*, or observance. The yogin must observe rules of cleanliness and ritual purification. The yogin studies, diets, and surrenders his or her life to God.
3. *Āsana*, a seat or a posture. The yogin practices techniques of physical development and control.
4. *Prānāyāma*, or breath control. Because the breath is intimately connected with the universe's vital energy, or *prānā*, breath control is a separate stage from practice of the *āsanas*.
5. *Pratyāhāra*, or withdrawal. The yogin begins to turn away from the world of the senses. The yogin looks toward things but not at them, hears sounds but does not listen.
6. *Dhārana*, holding on. The yogin learns to concentrate for long periods on a single object.
7. *Dhyāna*, concentrated meditation. The yogin learns to direct his or her thought on consciousness itself.
8. *Samādhi*, or self-collectedness. The yogin achieves release from the world and oneness with God.

The first four stages are called *hatha yoga*, meaning "union by violence"; the name comes from the fact that hatha practices are strenuous and at times painful. There is a deeper meaning to the name, also. The word comes from two roots: *ha* (sun), and *tha* (moon). *Hatha* therefore means the joining of the sun and moon, or of the male and female principles. By the practice of the first four stages of yoga, one can resolve all the oppositions within the body.

The last four stages are called *dhyāna*; *dhyāna* combined with the practice of *hatha* makes *rāja yoga*. *Rāja* means royal, best, highest, and shining; it is what most yogins mean by the term *integral yoga*. According to ancient texts, yogins who subordinate themselves to powers of nature or to past *avatars* (incarnations of God) thereby keep themselves in the cycle of reincarnation. Therefore, hatha yoga and devotional practices are lower forms. To reach union with God, the *yogin* must concentrate on the meditative stages and especially upon the freeing of *kuṇḍālinī*, the divine creative force within you. (See p. 10 for details about the *kuṇḍālinī* power.)

The Practice of Yoga—Hatha

Before the body can be used as an instrument toward union with God, it must be pure. Yoga therefore prescribes a series of cleansing techniques called *kriyas*, which are part of the *niyama* stage. These may seem severe, but they are usually recommended by teachers. Please do not try to do them (or any other yoga exercise) without the supervision of a good teacher.

Purifications. The six basic types of *kriya* are called *dhauti, neti, nauli, tratak, kapalabhati,* and *basti*—cleansing of the upper alimentary tract, the nose, the abdominal muscles, the eyes, the respiratory organs, and the colon.

Dhauti. Some *dhauti* practices are simple: brushing the teeth, keeping the ears clear of wax, gargling to keep the throat clean, massaging the tongue with your fingers. Others are more rigorous. One method of cleaning the stomach requires you to swallow a large quantity of salt water, shake it around inside of you, and then vomit it out. Another method involves the use of a long piece of cloth, usually muslin, fifteen feet long and three inches wide. The cloth should be clean and sterile, with no loose threads hanging from it. Dip it into tepid salt water, then wring it dry. Put one end of the cloth in your mouth, drink a bit of salt water, and start to swallow the cloth. Get it down inch by inch, leave it in place for about two minutes, and then draw it back out very slowly. Drink a cup of milk afterward. This *kriya* should be done in the morning on an empty stomach.

Neti: There are two common ways of cleaning the nasal passages. Pour a little lukewarm salt water into a nostril, tip the head back, and let the water run into the back of your mouth; spit it out, and exhale whatever water has remained in your nose. Or take a sterile string or rubber catheter, insert it in a nostril, and draw it out through the mouth by reaching into the back of the mouth and pulling it through with your fingers.

Nauli: Breathe out forcibly and completely. This will raise your diaphragm to its highest point. With your lungs still empty, pull in your stomach so that your intestines and navel go as far back and up as they can. Put your hands firmly on your thighs and bend forward from the waist. This should be done from a standing position, with the feet slightly apart.

Hold the posture only as long as it is comfortable.

Tratak: Stare at the flame of a candle for a few minutes; close your eyes and visualize the candle's flame; repeat.

Kapalabhati: Breathe out by raising the diaphragm and pulling in the stomach muscles. Inhale by allowing the muscles to relax. Perform ten sharp exhalations in a row, each followed by a brief inhalation. On the tenth time you inhale, hold the breath as long as you can. Beginners usually do only two or three rounds of this.

Basti: This is essentially an enema performed with the aid of the *nauli* technique. Insert a small rubber tube about four inches into the rectum. Then sit in a tub of water and perform the *nauli* contraction. The *nauli* causes a vacuum in the colon, which draws the water upward. As soon as the water goes into your colon, remove the tube. By proper churning of the stomach muscles, you can then expel the water. Again, please do not attempt this *kriya* without competent supervision.

Postures. Tradition has it that there are 840,000 postures, or *āsanas*, in hatha yoga. Most yogins deal with only 84 of them, and I shall mention only a few of those.

There are five meditative postures. The best-known is the lotus position, or *padmasan*, a sitting posture in which the yogin crosses the legs so that the feet rest on the upper thighs and the knees stay on the ground. In an easier version of the lotus, *sukhasan*, the yogin sits with feet crossed on the floor and knees up. The adept's position, or *siddhasan*, is more difficult. The yogin sits with the left heel pressed against the perineum (the space between anus and genitals); the right heel rests against the pubic bone. An easier and usually more comfortable version of *siddhasan* is called *mukthasan*; in this posture it isn't necessary to press a heel against the perineum. *Swastikasan* resembles the lotus position, but the soles of the feet rest against the insides of the thighs. A sixth posture, *vajrasan*, is used by people who cannot perform the other meditative postures. In *vajrasan*, the yogin simply kneels and then sits on the heels.

Postures for concentration. There are certain exercises in hatha yoga called *mudras* that aid concentration. For example, in *khechari mudra* the yogin gradually severs the tongue from its base by cutting it a few hairsbreadths at a time and rubbing in an astringent so the wound won't heal. At the same time, the yogin lengthens the tongue by pulling it. Eventually the yogin can reach the tongue all the way to the back of the mouth and use it to close the nasal cavity, thereby aiding in the enjoyment of the nectar of *kundālinī*. Westerners don't show much inclination toward these practices.

There are two *mudras*, though, that are in common use in the West. The first is *shāmbhi mudra*. The yogin sits in *siddhasan*, thereby closing the anus and urethra by pressing against them with the heels. Then the yogin puts the thumbs over the ears; the index fingers over the eyes; the third and fourth fingers against the nostrils; and the little fingers over the lips. Now the nine doors of the senses are shut, and the yogin is in an excellent posture for meditation.

Yoga mudra is used to awaken the energy at the base of the spine and to direct it upward. Sit in the lotus position. Put your fists between your heels and stomach. Then exhale and bend forward till your forehead touches the floor.

What is the purpose of the *āsanas*? They tone the muscles, relieve stress, promote good circulation, cure various disorders, and prolong life. All that is reason enough to practice hatha yoga; but these benefits, though real, are short-term. The *āsanas* are designed principally to prepare the yogin for the development of *prānā*, the life force. Therefore, the next of yoga's eight stages is *prānāyāma*, or the control of *prānā* through breathing.

Breath Control. First, what is *prānā*? In a sense, it's life itself. It is the energy that streams through the universe and is concentrated in each living being. If you want an illustration of what *prānā* is, imagine a person a moment before death and a moment after death and ask yourself what is the difference between the two states. The body hasn't changed materially—the nerves, skeleton, tissues, and organs are the same. Even on a molecular level, the body remains pretty much as it was. But the *prānā* is gone, and the body is dead.

So *prānā* is a universal energy, one that we can develop and control. The principal method for doing so in hatha yoga is breath control.

Prānā has five major forms. Yogins picture each form as having a different color, function, and location.

1. *Prānā*: This form is red and is associated with the heart. It functions in

---

KILLING TIME

Well-authenticated cases are on record of masters of *hatha yoga* who have been able to arrest the vital processes of the body to such a degree as to become like unto one dead. A famous case of this sort, which was made a test case, is that of the Sādhu Haridās, who was buried for four months and afterward disinterred living, under the careful supervision of the Mahārāja of Lahore, Ranjett Singh, early in the last century. Over the grave of the Sādhu, who lay therein in a chest sealed by the Mahārāja with the royal seal, barley seed was sown and grew up, in a place enclosed by a wall and guarded incessantly by armed sentinels. On the day of the interment, the *yogin*'s face had been shaven clean, and when he was revived, after the expiration of four months, his face was as smooth as on the day of his burial.

From *Tibetan Yoga and Secret Doctrines*, arranged and edited by W.Y. Evans-Wentz.

---

respiration and controls the verbal centers and the respiratory muscles.

2. *Apāna*: This form is a mixture of white and red and is associated with the anus. It functions in excretion and controls the genitals as well as the organs of excretion.

3. *Samāna*: This form is shining and milky white and is located at the navel. It controls the digestion.

4. *Udāna*: This form is plain white and is located at the throat. It controls the swallowing of food. It is also the force that puts one to sleep and that separates the astral body from the physical body at the time of death.

5. *Vyāna*: This form is colorless, like a ray of pure light, and moves all over the body. It controls the muscles and joints.

In the practice of breathing exercises, the first two forms of *prānā*, *prānā* and *apāna*, are of the most importance. You generate *prānā* when you inhale; you generate *apāna* when you exhale. When you hold in your breath, these two forms meet and interact around the solar plexus. Their meeting is of prime importance in the awakening of *kundālinī*, as I will describe below.

In practicing the breathing exercises, you should sit in any of the meditative *āsanas*. Your spine should be straight, and you should feel relaxed. The best time to practice *prānāyāma* is before breakfast. If you've had a snack, wait two hours before practicing; if you've eaten a meal, wait four hours.

The following three exercises are examples of breathing techniques. The exercises work together. The first activates the muscles and sets up the rhythm of breathing; the second clears the nasal passages and deepens the breath; the third fills the whole body with *prānā*.

Kapalabhati: This was described above as one of the six purification techniques; it is also a beginning exercise in *prānāyāma*. Exhale sharply through the nose while drawing in the stomach. This will make you inhale automatically. Expel the breath at once. You should exhale about once a second; do five or six repetitions, rest for awhile, then go on to another set of five or six exhalations until you've done the exercise for ten minutes. You can work up to two exhalations per second and thirty-minute periods.

Bhastrika (the bellows): You begin by shutting both the nostrils. Press your right thumb against the right nostril. Bend the index and middle fingers into your palm. Extend the ring and little fingers and use them to close the left nostril. Now, release the thumb and exhale through the right nostril only. Inhale sharply through the same nostril, then close it again with your thumb. Exhale the breath through the left nostril. Inhale through that nostril, close it again with your last two fingers, and exhale the breath through the right nostril. Continue in this fashion. Beginners should do this exercise ten times, rest, and then repeat it once. You can work up to sixty sets.

Ujjayi: Exhale completely, and then inhale slowly through both nostrils.

As you inhale, let yourself make a low, sobbing sound in your throat. (Some *yogins* concentrate here on the first syllable of a *mantra*: *hang*.) When you've finished inhaling, contract your anus, drop your chin to your chest, and hold the breath for as long as you can. Then relax the anus and chin and exhale very slowly through the left nostril. (At this point, some *yogins* pronounce the second syllable of the *mantra*: *sa*.)

In these three exercises, as in all of *prāṇāyāma*, rhythm is of primary importance. The ratio of in-breath to retention to out-breath should be 1:4:2.

At the risk of becoming tedious, I will repeat: Do not try to do this or any other yoga exercise unless you have a teacher. Sometimes students of hatha yoga overexert themselves in *prāṇāyāma* and black out. If that happens to you, you run the risk of smashing your head on the floor, which is always a dangerous accident. So please be cautious.

Postures for concentration. There are certain exercises in hatha yoga called *mudras* that aid concentration. For example, in *khechari mudra* the yogin gradually severs the tongue from its base by cutting it a few hairsbreadths at a time and rubbing in an astringent so the wound won't heal. At the same time, the yogin lengthens the tongue by pulling it. Eventually the yogin can reach the tongue all the way to the back of the mouth and use it to close the nasal cavity, thereby aiding in the enjoyment of the nectar of *kundālinī*. Westerners don't show much inclination toward these practices.

There are two *mudras*, though, that are in common use in the West. The first is *shāmbhi mudra*. The yogin sits in *siddhasan*, thereby closing the anus and urethra by pressing against them with the heels. Then the yogin puts the thumbs over the ears; the index fingers over the eyes; the third and fourth fingers against the nostrils; and the little fingers over the lips. Now the nine doors of the senses are shut, and the yogin is in an excellent posture for meditation.

Yoga mudra is used to awaken the energy at the base of the spine and to direct it upward. Sit in the lotus position. Put your fists between your heels and stomach. Then exhale and bend forward till your forehead touches the floor.

The Practice of Yoga—Awakening *Kuṇḍālini*

Everything up to this point has been preparation. Now the yogin proceeds to the last four stages of development, the meditative exercises.

An adept can practice meditation in relation to various objects: parts of the body, emotions, even something as abstract as the barrier between subject and object. This is the way to develop occult powers, called *siddhis*, such as knowledge of the time of one's own death, knowledge of the thoughts of others, the ability to go without food or drink, powers of levitation and invisibility. These powers, though marvelous, must never be desirable to the yogin for then they become a trap, another way of attaching the yogin to the world. True yogins regard the *siddhis* as little more than sideshow tricks, entertainments for their disciples. The true goal of yooic meditation is the awakening of *kundālinī*.

Kuṇḍālinī means "the earringed one," and it is one of the names given to the Hindu goddess Kālī. She is one of the chief aspects of the divine energy called *śakti*. She is also the consort of Śiva, the highest yoga god. The power of *śakti*, the *kuṇḍālinī* force, lies coiled like a snake at the base of the spine.

The *kuṇḍālinī* is not simply at the base of the spine. It is also at the bottom of a hollow tube, or *nadi*, called the *sushumna*. The *sushumna* runs through the spinal cord and up to the top of the head. Two other tubes, the *ida* and *pingala*, run on either side of the *sushumna*. In yogic tradition, there are 72,000 *nadis* running through the body; but the *ida*, *pingala*, and *sushumna* are by far the most important.

Through the practice of hatha yoga, the yogin begins to awaken *kuṇḍālinī*. When the two types of breath, *prānā* and *apāna*, meet at the base of the spine, they stimulate *kuṇḍālinī*. If they should meet with enough force, they will block the *ida* and *pingala* tubes. At that moment, the *sushumna* opens, and *kundālinī* begins to rise.

The Seven Chakras. There are seven special points along the *sushumna*. These are called *chakras*; yogins compare them to lotuses, or wheels of fire. The *kuṇḍālinī* power has lain dormant at the bottommost of the seven; the yogin, through meditation, must make it rise to the uppermost. Yogic texts go into great detail about the *chakras*; the following is a very brief summary of their characteristics.

Muladhara chakra: A yellow, four-petalled lotus at the base of the spine. Its deity is Brahman; its element is earth; its mantric syllables are *sam, sham, sam, vam*. A triangle of energy lies in the lotus's center, and *kundālinī* lies within the triangle.

Swadhisthana chakra: A white, six-petalled lotus at the genitals. Its deity is Vishnu; its element is water; its mantric syllables are *bam, bham, nam, yam, ram, lam*. A crescent moon lies in its center.

Manipura chakra: A red, ten-petalled lotus at the navel. Its deity is Rudra; its element is fire; its mantric syllables are *da, nda, na, ta, tha, de, dhe, ne, pa, pha*.

Anahata chakra: A smoke-colored, twelve-petalled lotus at the heart. Its deity is Isa; its element is air; its syllables are *ka, kha, ga, gha, ge, cha, chha, ja, jha, je, ta, tha*. There are two interlocking triangles in its center, one facing up, the other down.

Vishudha chakra: A sixteen-petalled lotus the color of pure sea water, located at the throat. Its deity is Sada Śiva; its element is *prānā*; its syllables are *a, aa, e, ee, u, uu, ri, ree, lre, lree, ye, yai, o, ow, am, ah.*

Ajna chakra: A snow-white lotus of two petals located between the eyebrows at the place of the third eye. Its element is mind; its syllables are *ham* and *ksham*. A triangle of energy lies in its center, and within the triangle is the syllable *AUM*.

Sahasrara chakra: The thousand-petalled lotus at the top of the skull. Its deity is Śiva. When the female energy of *kuṇḍālinī* reaches this lotus and reunites with the male energy of Śiva, the yogin attains complete liberation.

This state, the goal of yoga, is called *samādhi*. What is it like? Ramakrishna said, "In *samādhi*, nothing external remains. One cannot even take care of his body any more; if milk is put into his mouth, he cannot swallow. If he remains for twenty-one days in this condition, he is dead. The ship puts out to sea, and returns no more."*

The system of *chakras* outlined above is accurate, as far as it goes. However, it is not only too brief, it is also a composite. There are as many systems of *kundālinī* yoga as there are teachers, and to say that the outline above is the system of *chakras* would be like saying that all flowers are American Beauty roses. To give you an idea of the variety of yogic systems, here is a method that teaches meditation on twelve points rather than the usual seven.

The Rāja Yoga of Sabhapathy Swami. Sabhapathy believed that *prānā* runs down the body through a hollow tube called the *sukhmana*. The *sukhmana* starts at the top of the skull, passes by the eyes and nose, and then joins with the alimentary canal near the throat. It runs down to the navel, makes a loop by the genitals, and then runs back up the spine to the top of the skull. The part that runs up the spine is called the *kumbhaka*.

The *sukhmana* and *kumbhaka* are threefold tubes. In the *sukhmana*, the first vessel conveys sensations, the second conveys subconscious images, and the third conveys the five elements of nature—fire, air, water, earth, and mind. In the *kumbhaka*, the first vessel conveys intellect, the second consciousness, and the third ideas. The downward flow of *prānā* through the *sukhmana* is active and has the threefold function of creating, preserving, and destroying. The upward flow of *prānā* through the *kumbhaka* is nonactive and has the functions of blessing, embracing, and becoming.

As it descends through the *sukhmana*, *prānā* takes on twelve forms. These forms, from the highest to the lowest, are emanations of Brahman. Their locations and functions are:

1. Top of the skull—wisdom (passive and pure)
2. Top of the brain—intelligence (active)

*Translation by Edward C. Dimock, Jr. Quoted in *The Complete Illustrated Book of Yoga*, by Swami Vishnudevananda.

3. Middle of the brain—knowledge
4. Bottom of the brain—prudence and the love of passing pleasures
5. Center of the forehead—memory
6. Space between the eyebrows—poetic imagination
7. Tip of the nose—self-love
8. Center of the tongue—will and goodness
9. Center of the throat—intellect (emotions, doubts, pride)
10. Heart—lusts, desires, impulses, attachments
11. Navel—the five senses
12. Base of the spine—the five elements

The yogin begins meditation on the twelfth point, directing his or her attention on that point, in order to examine its nature, question it, and understand why it is not the Absolute. Once the yogin has realized detachment from it by means of mantras and meditation, he or she goes up to the eleventh point and does the same for it. The yogin proceeds upward in this fashion to the top of the skull. Once the yogin transcends the first point, wisdom, he or she attains *samādhi*.

Tantra

Tantra is an esoteric tradition that has followers among both the Hindus and the Buddhists. The name comes from the root *tan*, meaning to extend, continue, or multiply. Thus Tantra is that which extends knowledge. *Tantra* also means "a loom." It symbolizes the interweaving of male and female energies.

Most people think of Tantra as sexual yoga, a cult of orgasm and drugs leading to supreme physical and spiritual ecstasy. However, yoga (includ-

---

TANTRIC MANTRAS

Bīja-mantras, or seed *mantras*: These have no denotation; they are pure sound. Examples: *hrīṃ, phaṭ*.

Ahaṃ Brahmāsmi—I am Brahman.

Ahaṃ devī na cānyosm—I am the Goddess, none else.

Oṃ āḥ hūṃ—Body, speech, mind (a *mantra* for the unification of the three with the Absolute).

Oṃ maṇipadme hūṃ—An invocation to the goddess Manipadmā, who is a female counterpart to Buddha. (*Om*________*hūm mantras* are usually invocations.)

Hrīṃ klīṃ hrīṃ—A seed *mantra* for identification with Kālī.

Krīṃ krīṃ krīṃ hūṃ hūṃ hrīṃ hrīṃ dakṣiṇe—Another mantra for identification with Fālī in her form as Dakṣiṇā.

Oṃ hrāṃ hrīṃ hrūṃ hreṃ hraiṃ hroṃ hrauṃ hraḥ dātarasya mama śāntiṃ kuru kuru padmāvatyay namaḥ svāhā—Confers mental peace and readiness for higher meditation. This *mantra* must be repeated either 108 or 12,000 times.

---

ing the sexual kind) is only one element of Tantra. Tantric texts treat four categories: philosophy, ritual (including the making of icons and the building of temples), social obligations, and finally yoga techniques. The ritual practices are very involved. They include the use of sacred pictures (*yantras*) and sacred chants and syllables (*mantras*). The *mantras* are aids in meditation and devotion.

There is a strong element of nonconformism in Tantra, an attempt to free the adept quickly and violently by liberating him from social conventions. (I write *him* because Tantric texts are addressed exclusively to the male; see below.) You can see an element of this social revolt in the Tantric list of the eight fetters that keep the adept from liberation: hatred, doubt, fear, shame, slander, pride in family, conformity, and pride in caste. The first five of these are attitudes that Hindu adepts traditionally try to overcome. The last three, though, take us into another tradition altogether. The adept in Tantra must cut the most basic ties to his society and seek liberation *as an individual*.

Tantric ritual shows the same reaction against conventions. A Brahmin who carried out the ritual would automatically become an outcast; nor are there many Buddhist groups that would permit their monks to participate in these acts. The ritual eating of meat is itself an outrage, to say nothing of ritual sex.

There are supposedly two types of ritual: the left-handed (*vāmācāra*) and the right-handed (*dakṣiṇācāra*). In the right-handed ritual, the adept treats the ritual acts in a symbolic, internalized way. There are some authorities, though, who claim that the right-handed ritual is a hypocritical sham—the only Tantra is *vāmācāra*.

The practice of Tantra. Here is an abbreviated version of the ritual, addressed, according to tradition, to the male.

The day before the ritual, fast and go to bed alone. On the day of the ritual, awaken yourself thoroughly, sit up in bed, and immediately begin a devotion to your guru. Offer a flower to your guru and to your consort in their absence. Murmur the seed *mantra aiṃ* one-hundred times. Worship your patron deity.

Get out of bed with the left foot first. Move your bowels, brush your teeth, and take a ritual bath.

For the next stage in the devotion, you will need a meditation mat. Purify it, and identify it in your mind with the abode of the goddess Śakti. This is of prime importance. The ritual as a whole is a sacrifice to Śakti, who is divine, creative energy. For the purpose of the sacrifice, your consort will be the embodiment of Śakti. Therefore, you must put your whole mind into the devotions to come.

Draw an equilateral triangle on the meditation mat (you can use flour, rice powder, or any other suitable offering). Purify the triangle with an invocation to the goddess, and place a bowl of marijuana in the triangle. The marijuana should be in a form in which you can eat it. Consecrate the marijuana to the goddess and eat it.

The next stage of the ritual should take about an hour, or until the marijuana takes effect. Before your meditation mat, trace a symbol of Śakti with rice powder: the symbol is two interlocking triangles. The triangle pointing up represents the male principle; the triangle pointing down represents the female principle.

Worship the six-limbed goddess in each corner of the figure. The form of the devotion is: *Hraṃ*, adoration to her heart—*hrīṃ*, *svāhā* to her head—*hrūṃ*, *vaṣeṭ* to her hair—*hraiṃ*, to her amulets, *hūṃ—hrauṃ*, *vaṣaṭ* to her three eyes—*hrāḥ*, to her palms and backs of her hands, *phaṭ*.

Next, worship the aspects of Śakti: *Dhūṃ* worship to Dhūmrā (the smoke-colored one); *aṃ* worship to Acciṣā; *jvaṃ* worship to Jvālinī (the flamelike one); *viṃ* worship to Visphuliṅgiṇī (the emberlike one); *suṃ* worship to Suśrī (the blessed Srī); *sūṃ* worship to Sūrapā (the liquor-drinking one); *kaṃ* worship to Kapilā (the reddish-colored one); *haṃ* worship to Havyakavyavahā.

Now take a bowl containing five kinds of flowers and meditate on them. Visualize the sperm of Śiva's eternal copulation with Śakti caught in the bowl and mingling with the essence of the flowers. Pick up a stick of sandalwood incense and a flower and place them near your heart. Meditate on your patron deity. Imagine the *kuṇḍālinī* power rising along your spine to your brain. When you feel the power growing within you, the preparatory period is over.

The next part of the ritual is often communal. The adepts sit in a circle with their partners on their left. You must now consecrate the five essentials of Tantra, the *pañcatattva*: wine, meat, fish, parched grain (any aphrodisiac grain), and sexual intercourse. Before you, place bowls containing four of the five. The bowl of flowers that you consecrated earlier served as a symbol of sexual intercourse.

Draw the *kuṇḍālinī* from the base of your spine to the tip of your tongue. Offer the meat to the goddess, who now sits on the tip of your tongue. Do the same for the fish, the wine, and the grain.

Now you are ready for the fifth offering. Go alone to your bed; it should be in a separate room or alcove. Draw a triangle on the bed and recite the *mantra Om āḥ vajra hūṃ phaṭ svāhā*. Meditate on Śakti, who is present now in the triangle, and worship her.

Sit down on the bed and meditate. Your partner will then enter. You must see her as the embodiment of Śakti; she must *be* Śakti to you.

Whisper the *mantra hrīm* into her ear three times to consecrate her. Bathe her, put oil on her hair, comb her hair, dress her in a red robe, and seat her on the bed. Sprinkle purifying water over her. Touch your right hand to her forehead, eyes, nostrils, mouth, arms, and thighs. Then touch her vulva with your right thumb and mutter *aiṃ* one-hundred times. *Aiṃ* is the most intimate of the goddess's seed *mantras*. When you touch your partner's vulva and recite this *mantra*, you have already reached union with the goddess.

Now begin copulation, the ritual sacrifice to Śakti. Keep in mind at all times that your partner is the goddess; your penis, according to the Tantric texts, is a sacred ladle, an instrument of sacrificial oblation. The copulation must be as long-lasting as possible. Some Tantric adepts insist that neither of the partners should move during intercourse. When this is the method used, the woman sits on the man's penis in such a way that it can't slip out of the vulva.

At the moment of orgasm, say: "*Oṃ* with light and ether as my two hands, I, the exulting one, relying on the ladle, I, who take *dharma* and non-*dharma* as his sacrificial ingredients, offer this oblation lovingly into the fire, *svāhā*."

If you ejaculate, do so at *svāhā*. You may not choose to ejaculate, though. Buddhists don't. (The Tantric scholar Agehananda Bharati says that's because the Buddhists have no interest in sacrifice as such.) In some other sects, the man does not ejaculate but draws energy into himself from the woman's orgasm. There are also techniques by which the man draws the semen up into his own body. In some cases, the man first ejaculates and then by urethral control draws the fluid back into his penis.

Since Tantric texts are all written by men and to men, there is no scriptural record of what the woman is supposed to think of all this.

Tibetan Yoga

This is the most miraculous branch of yoga. It is also the most esoteric—indeed, very few people know anything about it. The student can get a glimpse of the system from the works of W.Y. Evans-Wentz, who has made public the Six Doctrines of Tibetan Yoga (see bibliography next page).

The first doctrine is *tūmmō*, the idea that the body can accumulate *prānā* and redirect it. Tibetan yogins regularly practice *tūmmō* to generate heat. This is properly regarded as part of hatha yoga, though a very advanced part. The technique requires much meditation, exercise, and complete sexual continence.

Gurus sometimes hold contests in *tūmmō* for their disciples. The students go at night to a frozen river or lake. They cut a hole in the ice, dip sheets into the water, and then cover themselves with the sheets. They must dry the sheets by means of their prānic heat. As soon as a sheet is dry, the student must soak it again in the icy water and once more cover himself. The student who has dried the most sheets by morning wins the competition. One must be able to dry at least three sheets to be considered proficient in *tūmmō*. Students also test their proficiency by seeing how much snow they can melt simply by sitting and emanating *prānā*.

The second doctrine is that of the illusory body (*māyāvi-rūpa*). This doctrine says that the body is merely an appearance, a form.

The third doctrine is that of the dream state. All sense experiences are as illusory as the body. The world is a dream of Brahman.

The fourth doctrine is that of clear light. At the moment of death, all people attain a moment of pure consciousness called "clear light." Yogins can attain clear light at will. Buddhas experience it constantly.

The fifth doctrine is that of the after-death state. The Tibetan yogins believe that after death one is in a prolonged dream, an illusion, that leads back to the illusion of life.

The sixth doctrine is that of transference of consciousness, or *pho-wa*. This states that the yogin can enter a deathlike state for set periods by making his consciousness fly out of his skull "as a bird flies out of a skylight." The yogin thus learns to conquer death; he also can give spiritual aid to those who have died recently.

A related phenomenon is called *trongjug*. This is the ability to discard one's own body and enter that of another person, either with or without permission. The body doesn't have to be alive, either. *Trongjug* is considered to be black magic, and yogins disapprove of its practice.

For Further Reading

The standard historical and philosophical work on yoga is Mircea Eliade's *Yoga: Immortality and Freedom* (New York: Pantheon, 1958). The standard work on Tantra is *The Tantric Tradition*, by Agehananda Bharati (London: Rider and Company, 1965). A beginning student cannot do better than to read these two books. See also *Tantra of the Great Liberation*, by Arthur Avalon (New York: Dover, n.d.), and *Tantric Mysticism in Tibet: A Practical Guide*, by John Blofeld (New York: Dutton, 1970). There are many guidebooks for hatha yoga; you should buy whichever one your teacher recommends. As a reference work for hatha, I prefer *The Complete Illustrated Book of Yoga* by Swami Vishnudevananda (New York: Pocket Books, 1972). It's cheap, generally available, clearly written, and complete. Sabhapathy's system is available in a pamphlet titled *The Philosophy and Science of Vedanta and Raja Yoga*, by Sabhapathy Swami (Bombay: Chaitanya Prabha Mandali, 1950). For Tibetan yoga, see *Tibetan Yoga and Secret Doctrines*, arranged and edited by W.Y. Evans-Wentz (London: Oxford University Press, 1958).

Wilhelm Reich

Occultists have always believed in the existence of a universal energy. Yogins believe in such an energy; the Chinese and Japanese believe in it, and so do the members of virtually every tribal cult. Do Western scientists believe in it? The answer is that they once did.

Up through the nineteenth century, physicists commonly believed that there was no such thing as purely empty space. Rather, they thought that the whole universe was permeated with an energetic substance called ether. At the same time, biologists believed in the existence of a life force. Not many biologists were willing to speculate on whether this life force was related to ether; but they did think the force existed. Pasteur, for example, placed great emphasis on the role of this force, which he called *élan vital*. Ironically, it was Pasteur's experiments in spontaneous generation that gave the theory of the life force its greatest single setback.

By the beginning of the twentieth century, both ether and the life force were pretty much dead concepts for scientists. Biologists were convinced they could explain life entirely in physio-chemical terms.

Today they have a different attitude, largely because of the work of Wilhelm Reich.

Early Years

Reich was the son of a farmer. He was born in 1897, grew up in the Ukrainian part of Austria, and served in the Austrian army from 1915 to 1918. After the war, he moved to Vienna and entered the Faculty of Medicine of the university. There he began to read Freud. In his enthusiasm he organized psychoanalytic study groups; then he began to correspond with members of Freud's circle. These people soon recognized Reich's talents, and at the very young age of twenty-three, he became a member of the Vienna Psychoanalytic Society.

One of the things that had most excited Reich about psychoanalysis was Freud's libido theory. This was the concept of a specific sexual energy, something like an electric current. Freud had spoken of this biological energy as the source of all activity, indeed as the basis of human personality.

Reich took all this literally. He believed that the origin of anxiety lay in sexual stasis, a block in the flow of libido. Such a block could exist even in people who seemed to be sexually active. Neurotics (especially neurotic males) are often able to achieve orgasm, but they cannot feel genuine, comptete pleasure. Something is always lacking for them, and so they go on repeating the same actions joylessly and habitually in search of satisfaction.

Photo of Wilhelm Reich courtesy of the Bettmann Archive, Inc.

Nobody can be happy, Reich said, without orgastic potency. This is the ability not merely to reach orgasm but to enjoy it fully. As Reich's biographer David Boadella explains, orgastic potency is the "capacity for surrender to the flow of biological energy without any inhibition, the capacity for complete discharge of all dammed-up sexual excitation through involuntary pleasurable contractions of the body."

Reich presented this theory well. He argued persuasively and clearly for it, drawing on many fine clinical observations. But he put forward the theory at a very bad time. Just as he was insisting on the literal biological truth of Freud's theory, Freud was moving away from biology toward a theory of instincts. The Psychoanalytic Society went along with Freud. When Reich insisted on holding to his own theories, he met not only indifference but hostility. The animosity that grew against him in the Society would eventually be ruinous to him.

All this time Reich was still working as a psychoanalyst. In 1928 he became vice-director of the Psychoanalytic Polyclinic. The clinic offered free treatment to the poor, and so Reich began to treat people who were vastly different from the usual psychoanalytic patients. He became intimately acquainted with the troubles of working people, especially their sexual troubles.

And he began to ask questions that no other psychoanalyst had bothered to ask. What exactly do you do when you make love? How do you start? How long does it last? What do you feel? What do you think about when you're doing it? Do you masturbate? Right-handed or left-handed, and in what room of the house?

Eventually Reich began to give counselling to poor people on everyday problems, partly because of his political convictions—during this period he was a member of the Communist Party. To carry out his goals, he set up the Socialist Society for Sex Consultation and Sexological Research, where he gave advice on birth control, sexual problems, marital problems, and methods of child rearing. The clinic was open to unmarried people and adolescents—a scandal at the time.

More and more his colleagues in Vienna snubbed him; he had become a great embarrassment to them. So Reich moved to Berlin. In 1931, with the help of the German Communist Party, he set up the German Association for Proletarian Sexual Politics. His program included the abolition of antiabortion laws, distribution of free contraceptives, the abolition of legal distinctions between married and unmarried people, and a drive to eliminate prostitution and venereal diseases.

This was the period of Reich's greatest political activity. He had perceived that sexual repression and political repression go together, that capitalism keeps working people not only economically impoverished but sexually impoverished. The working people whom he treated often could not fully enjoy sex because they were worn down from laboring to make a subsistence wage. As for the politicians and businessmen, they preached that sex was bestial and shameful and quietly made their profits from the pornography trade. Nor did it look as if things would get better—the Nazis and Fascists were ten times worse then the old capitalists.

The Nazis, for their part, did not like Reich, either. He was a Jew, a Communist, and he wanted people to enjoy sex. In March 1933, Reich had to flee to Austria. Now the full burden of hostility of the Vienna Psychoanalytic Society came down on him. His colleagues did not regard him as a hero and a refugee—they thought him a bother, and some went so far as to bait him publicly. The International Psychoanalytic Press, which had contracted to publish Reich's book on character analysis, cancelled its contract. Reich had to borrow money and have the book printed privately.

He could not go on living in such a situation; besides, the Nazi threat to Austria was too great. On May 1, 1933, he left Vienna; for the next year he wandered homelessly in Denmark, Norway, and Sweden. His colleagues ostracized him; the police harassed him; for a while he had to live under an assumed name. Finally he found refuge in Oslo. He lived there until 1939, when he emigrated to America.

In 1931 he began the research that would occupy him for the rest of his life; his findings would be so extraordinary that they would cause Albert Einstein to say that they threatened to overthrow all of physics.

Bions and the Orgone

Through his clinical work, Reich had developed the concept of muscle armor. Every emotional block, he said, has a corresponding physical block. Certain sets of muscles become tense and inflexible; they restrict movement, breath, feeling. No biological energy can flow through them.

It seemed to Reich that if this theory was true, he should be able to test it. He would set up a device to measure the electrical current of the skin. He went to considerable trouble and expense to build such an apparatus, but it was worth it—he confirmed that the body has a continuous bioelectric field that varies with different emotional states.

What might be the next step in the study of this flow of energy? Reich thought he ought to study the flow of protoplasm in one-celled organisms. So he obtained the necessary equipment and began to prepare a culture of amoebae and paramecia in the textbook fashion. He left some hay soaking in clear water for ten to fourteen days. Protozoal spores were supposed to float from the air into the hay infusion and grow there.

Something in that procedure bothered Reich. There were no protozoa in the hay; there were none in the water. How could he be sure that the protozoa really came from the air? To check on it, he put the hay infusion under a high-powered microscope, rigged a camera to the eyepiece, and took time-lapse photos while the hay soaked. He discovered that little sacs formed on the hay and then broke away and floated into the water. The sacs tended to gather in a heap, in which they would move rhythmically, pulsating as a group. Were these elementary life forms?

For his next infusions, Reich carefully sterilized all his materials. The results actually increased. He added protein and cholesterol to his infusions; there was still more activity. He removed the little sacs from the water and put them onto culture media. They grew. By now Reich was convinced that he had come across a primitive life form. He called it the bion.

In 1939, Reich took up residence in Forest Hills, Long Island, and joined the New School for Social Research as associate professor of medical psychology. And he continued his research into the bion.

He'd found that bions of a certain shape would cause cancer when injected into mice. When he cut open the tumors of these mice, he found them swarming with bions of the same shape. He called these bions T-baccili (*T* for *Tod*, death). Certain other bions were luminescent—they gave off a radiation that seemed to counteract the T-baccili. Obviously his next task was to investigate this radiation. In so doing, he stumbled upon his most important discovery, the existence of orgone energy.

The story of this discovery is one of the strangest in the history of science. Reich wanted to have an insulated box in which to put his sample groups of radiating bions. So he built a sheet-metal box and lined it on the outside with wood. The materials were quite ordinary, and the design was plain. The only thing unusual was that the box glowed in the dark.

Reich was not the sort of man to let a phenomenon like that go unexamined. He called in other observers; they saw a glow in the empty box as well. Perhaps, he thought, the light was in their eyes rather than in the box. So he performed a simple control experiment—he had them spend some time staring at a completely dark room. They saw what they would expect to see—nothing.

This was still not enough for Reich. He wanted a completely reliable observer. He chose Albert Einstein. Einstein went to Reich's lab, saw the box glow in the dark, and confirmed that he, too, saw the light. But Einstein would neither comment nor speculate on the phenomenon; it was at this time that he said Reich's discovery threatened to overthrow physics.

But Reich wasn't all that concerned with the theoretical implications of his finding. He was now certain that the box concentrated a universal energy—he called it orgone energy—and that this force could help people. He built an orgone accumulator large enough for someone to sit in, and he began to study its effects.

He found that his subjects' body temperatures rose when they were in the box. Some said it gave them pins and needles. Others experienced an increased sensitivity to light. One woman said that the experience was comparable to orgasm. In all cases, a period of sitting increased the strength and flow of biological energy.

This was a breakthrough. Reich felt that the picture was now complete. There was a universal force, orgone energy, that strengthened biological energy (or perhaps that *was* biological energy). This same orgone energy was what made bions form from organic compounds.

Furthermore, orgone energy was useful in the treatment of diseases, including cancer. When Reich added that piece of information to his other findings, he was ready to formulate his general theory that the blockage of bioenergy causes:

1. Lack of sexual interest and satisfaction
2. Emotional emptiness
3. Deep muscle tension, areas of which may become cancerous
4. Poor respiration
5. Devitalized skin, with the skin's electrical charge lowered
6. Tendency of blood to disintegrate in certain clinical tests

In 1948, Reich published his findings in *The Cancer Biopathy*. At this stage he had independent, positive confirmation of his findings. There had been such confirmation of his research all along. He had, in fact, completely fulfilled the prime rule of scientific research—his experiments were repeatable and had veen verified. *The Cancer Biopathy* received very favorable reviews. From this time on, Reich, who had proved that he deserved serious attention and respect for his contributions to science, received only persecution, and it gradually destroyed him.

Starting in 1947, inaccurate, and at times slanderous, articles about Reich's work began to appear in such periodicals as *Harper's, The New Republic,* and the *Journal of the American Medical Association*. A typical claim of these articles was that the orgone accumulator was designed to "activate

---

HOW TO BUILD AN ORGONE ACCUMULATOR

An orgone accumulator is just a cabinet with a door. You can build it to any dimensions you like; bear in mind, however, that it's most effective when the walls are close to the body.

In a typical accumulator, the inside walls are 1/16-inch-thick steel sheets. The outer walls are wood. You will need to put insulation between the two sets of walls. The standard insulation is layers of glass wool and steel wool. The glass wool goes against the inner, steel walls; then comes the steel wool. Use three layers of this double insulation. (There are boxes with as many as ten layers.)

Cut a hole in the door for ventilation. You might want to attach a light to the box so you can read while sitting in it.

---

masturbation." At first these attacks were merely an annoyance. But then investigators from the Food and Drug Administration began to visit Reich's research institute. They were already convinced that Reich was doing something dirty, and they seemed to get cheap thrills by poking around the institute. They asked whether patients sat in the orgone box naked and how many women used the box. One investigator blurted, "What do you do with the women?"

Eventually, the Food and Drug Administration's hard work had its effect. A court ordered Reich to stop giving orgone treatments and to stop accepting money for the sale of his literature or rental of his accumulators.

Reich had fled the Nazis, faced opposition from his closest colleagues, and finally established a whole new life in America. Now the United States government, in which he believed deeply, was persecuting him, and he broke under the strain.

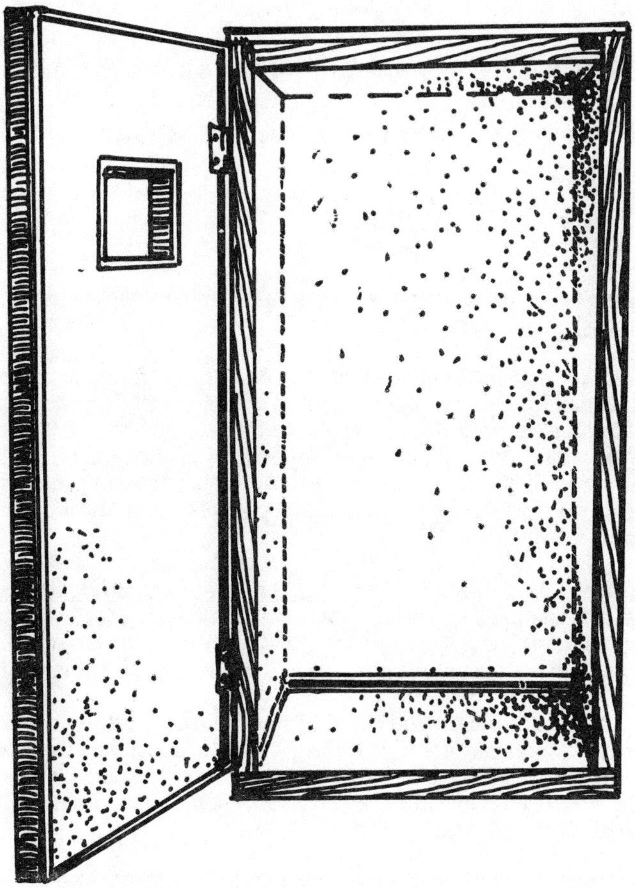

He'd begun experimenting with devices for weather control early in the 1950s. Now he converted one of those devices into what he called a space gun. He did so because he knew UFOs were visiting us. The UFOs were powered by orgone energy, and they carried CORE men (Cosmic Orgone Energy Men). The UFOs were poisoning our air, he said, and he was firing at them with his space gun.

The question of the existence and mission of UFOs is irrelevant here. (UFOs are discussed in more detail in chapter six, "The Occult Bible.") The plain fact was that Reich had become paranoid. In 1956, he began to speculate that he was himself from outer space. He wondered if his children were the beginning of a new interplanetary race.

That same year, Reich was tried for contempt of court for having ignored the injunction against his work. His violation of the injunction had been minor—some materials had gone out of his institute, and rental money for accumulators was still trickling in. For this infraction, the Wilhelm Reich Foundation had to pay a fine of $10,000, and Reich was sentenced to a jail term of two years. The FDA destroyed all the orgone accumulators they found at the institute; they burned all of Reich's books that they could get their hands on.

Reich died in Danbury Federal Correctional Institution on November 2, 1957.

THE POWER OF ODIN

Wilhelm Reich was not the first modern Westerner to stumble upon the existence of universal life energy. In the middle of the nineteenth century, a German industrialist and scientist named Baron Karl von Reichenbach encountered the same phenomenon. He named it the Od Force, after the Norse god Odin.

Reichenbach said that there was positive Od, which was a yellowish-red, and negative Od, which was blue. People radiate positive Od on the left sides of their bodies and negative Od on the right.

You can feel the effects of Od quite easily. Get a bar magnet, and hold your left hand over one end of it for a few minutes. The hand should be from two to six inches over the magnet. Then hold your hand over the magnet's other pole. You may find that the magnet's north pole (negative Od) gives your left hand a cool, refreshing feeling; the positive south pole will feel warm and somewhat unpleasant.

There's also an experiment you can try if you have access to a completely dark room. Place a bar magnet or a flowering plant in the room; then wait. Very sensitive people usually have to sit in the dark for only an hour; less sensitive people must wait up to four hours. Eventually, though, you will see Od flaming from the magnet or the plant.

For Further Reading

Reich's books are generally available in editions by Farrar, Straus & Giroux. The principal titles are *The Cancer Biopathy; Character Analysis; The Function of the Orgasm; The Mass Psychology of Fascism; Selected Writings: An Introduction to Orgonomy*; and *The Sexual Revolution*. Most of these are available in paperback as well. Vintage paperback publishes a good selection of Reich's writings, called *Sex-Pol*. The best biography of Reich is *Wilhelm Reich: The Evolution of His Work*, by David Boadella (London: Vision Press, 1973) published here in paperback by Henry Regnery Company.

Bodywork

In this section I will discuss some of the therapies, or techniques, designed to release tension and free the body's energy.

Alexander Lowen and Bioenergetics

Bioenergetics has been the most successful offshoot of Reich's work. It was developed by Alexander Lowen, who studied under Reich on and off from 1940 to 1952. Lowen was analyzed by Reich, and he worked as a Reichian therapist from 1945 to 1953. There could hardly be a closer relationship between the two therapists and their work.

Lowen graduated from the medical school of the University of Geneva in 1951. He returned to the United States and found Reich in the final, agonizing stage of his life. In 1953, with his mentor for all purposes gone, Lowen began to develop his own methods of therapy, with the help of Dr. John C. Pierrakos and Dr. William B. Walling.

What Lowen did was go back to Reich's ideas on muscle armor, or character armor. As the emotions become blocked, so do groups of muscles; moreover, they do so in a characteristic way. Lowen learned to type people by their way of blocking and discharging energy. He found that in general, impulsive types will discharge energy any way they can and as soon as they can. Compulsive types tend to discharge energy in rigidly patterned ways; they feel anxious about spontaneous discharges. Depressives, since they have no energy, don't do anything with it. They just sit there. Lowen also started to devise exercises that would release muscle tension. His aim was both to get the bioenergy flowing properly and to overcome his patients' repressions, their emotional amnesia.

Think of the body as a coded document. Each muscle block tells the history of an emotional disturbance; but neither the patient nor the therapist can easily read that history. As the muscles loosen, though, the coded history becomes plain. Lowen had learned this for himself when he was in analysis with Reich; at the age of thirty-three, he'd relived experiences he'd had as young as nine months old. In practice, such recall usually does not have the shattering intensity that it does on television and in pulp novels. Rather, it comes as a full emotional understanding of something one has always known. The experience is no less deep for being quiet.

The first stages of bioenergetics are straightforward. There is an interview in which the patient discusses the usual biographical information. Then the therapist will have the patient strip to his or her underwear, and begin to read the patient's body. Is he balanced on his heels instead of on the balls of his feet? He's a pushover. Are her knees knocking together? She must be afraid. Some patients wobble when they stand—they're weak-kneed, or can't stand on their own two feet. Some women look as if they're encased in stone from the waist down—they're on a pedestal. Many of the therapist's conclusions are based on such common-sense readings of the body and such commonplace phrases.

Most important of all, the therapist will be watching how the patient breathes. People maintain and increase their bioenergy through breathing, and when there's a disturbance it almost always shows in the breathing. (Think of the role the emotions sometimes play in asthma, for example.) One of the first things the patient does in bodywork, then, is learn to breathe properly. The breath should be deep, even, and relaxed. It must go all the way down to the belly on in-breaths; on out-breaths, the stomach must come in and the diaphragm must rise. When one breathes naturally, the pelvis goes back on the the in-breaths and comes forward on the out-breaths. Of course, the patient may not start breathing naturally at the first session; natural breathing is one of the therapy's goals, and it takes time.

The therapist might try a couple of exercises with the patient. Among the most common are a pair called the Bow and Grounding.

For the Bow, plant your feet at about shoulder-width with the toes pointing to each other. (In bioenergetics the toes always point toward each other, or at the very least the feet should be parallel. No pointing the toes outward.) Now bend your knees, arch your back, and put your fists against your buttocks. Try to push through the buttocks with your fists. This is a stress position (hence the name—the body is like a drawn bow). It's useful for letting the therapist read blockages. Some people can hardly arch their backs; others bend over backward; others arch their backs well enough but can't seem to bend their knees. While the therapist is studying your body, you should be paying attention to how you feel. Where do you feel tense? Which parts of your body most want to get out of the position? Is it hard to breathe? Why is the therapist staring at you like that?

From the Bow you will usually go to Grounding. Simply bend forward from the waist, bring your feet a bit closer together, and let your fingertips dangle on the floor. Don't lock your knees—keep them bent, but allow them a little up-and-down play. Let your back round out as much as it can. A lot of people have rigid spines, so they feel some tension or even pain as they stretch forward in this position. Tension in the legs will show up, too; you will feel your legs tingling as if they're going to sleep. That is just the flow of bioenergy trying to get past muscle blocks. Above all, remember to breathe. This is a good position for getting back in touch with reality; hence the name.

When you feel as if you have done Grounding long enough, start to straighten up. Take your time. It's pleasant to come up from the position, so savor it. Then simply stand erect for a while and pay attention to how you feel. You might start vibrating. That's the bioenergy breaking through.

You can try this series of positions on your own. It will be more fooling around than therapy, but you might just learn something new about your body.

There are two more notable exercises that I might mention here. The first is kicking. Lie on your back on a bed; make sure it's large enough for you and that it is sturdy. Then start kicking your heels down into the mattress. Again, do not lock the knees. Alternate the feet, rather than kicking them both down at once. Use your fists, too—pound the mattress. If you are in a fairly soundproof room, or if you're not self-conscious, try screaming "No, I won't" as you kick. (As Lowen puts it, "Everybody wants to say no about *something*.")

The second exercise involves a prop, the handle of a broom. Put the handle on the floor, and in your bare feet walk very slowly over it, first forward and then back. This is very good for stimulating energy. Some people say they can feel the flow come right up to their faces.

Of course, bioenergetics is not simply a system of exercise. All the time the therapist is taking the patient through these exercises, he or she is also encouraging the patient to talk about them. There are often rest periods as well, during which the patient might fantasize on material brought up by the exercises.

What is the goal of all this? It is a change in habits, new growth, renewed vitality. Ultimately, one hopes for a stronger flow of energy and better methods of directing that flow. However, success depends on the patient. The key word is self-regulation. Reich believed that the healthy individual—the one who is sexually, emotionally, and politically

SEEING AURAS

One of the more interesting aspects of Lowen's work is his demonstration that the bioenergetic field gives off visible light. There's nothing new in the concept of auras; but Lowen has devised an easy method whereby anybody can see auras.

Have someone stand against a blank wall. The wall should be painted a flat, light color, and the person should be in soft, diffused light. Now simply look at the person through a cobalt-blue filter. (These filters can be found at scientific supply houses or photo studios.) Don't stare—just keep the eyes relaxed and look at the person. You should see the aura. It will pulsate, flaring out every two seconds or so and then contracting again. Its color will depend on the person's emotional state. In relaxed, peaceful states, the aura is blue. When one is angry, the aura flashes red. When one is speaking or acting from deep conviction, the aura turns golden.

You can also see auras without a filter. Try holding your hand up to the sky sometime when the sky is clear and the light is even. If you can relax your eyes sufficiently, you will see the aura of your hand. Trees have noticeable auras, too.

For more on this subject, see the section on Kirlian photography later in this chapter.

healthy—is the one who finds direction from within. You must choose what you want to do, and then in doing it, you must control your energy, limiting it if necessary. That ideal remains basic to bioenergetics.

For Further Reading

Alexander Lowen has published extensively. His principal books are *The Betrayal of the Body* (New York: Collier, 1969); *The Language of the Body* (New York: Collier, 1971); *Depression and the Body* (New York: Penguin, 1973); *Pleasure: A Creative Approach to Life* (New York: Penguin, 1975); *Love and Orgasm: A Revolutionary Guide to Sexual Fulfillment* (New York: Collier, 1975); and *Bioenergetics* (New York: Penguin, 1977).

Rolfing

Rolfing, a method of bodywork that involves deep massage of the muscles, has become more and more popular in recent years. It, too, is based on the idea of muscle armor, but it's a faster, more rough-and-ready therapy than bioenergetics.

The method, more properly known as structural integration, was the invention of a New York biochemist, Dr. Ida P. Rolf (1896–1979). In 1940, Dr. Rolf began to use yoga for therapeutic purposes. She believed that muscle armor pulls the body out of its natural alignment. In a healthy body, there should be a straight line from the middle of the ear down through the shoulder, hip, knee, and ankle. The pelvis should be relaxed and horizontal, providing support for the abdominal muscles and a smooth link between the spine and the legs. Above all, a person should be able to stand and walk with a minimum of exertion. Unhealthy people seem to be pulled down by gravity. Their shoulders slump, their rib cages collapse onto the pelvis, and they have to fight to pick their feet up off the ground.

To correct these misalignments and release muscle tension, Rolf prescribed a course of structural integration. This involves a basic set of ten, one-hour sessions. During these sessions (which are often extremely painful) the therapist works directly on the muscles and the connective tissue around the muscles (called the fascia).

Here is an outline of a typical ten-session course of structural integration.

Session one: The patient lies on a massage table or on the floor. Rolf had the patient strip as far as the underwear; other therapists prefer their patients to be naked. In this session, the therapist tries to stretch the torso to give more room between the rib cage and the pelvis. This gives the abdominal muscles more freedom, deepens the breathing, and improves circulation. The therapist begins by manipulating the fascial layer that lies just under the skin. There may also be deeper work on the muscles around the rib cage, hips, and upper legs. Finally, the therapist works on lengthening the lower back. This session releases very pleasant feelings, especially around the heart.

Session two: The therapist works on the feet and ankles. This helps the patient distribute his or her weight properly and evenly. The result is better contact with the ground (and therefore with reality). Work on the feet has an effect on the pelvis, upper back, and shoulders as well. At the end of the hour, the therapist works again on lengthening the back.

Session three: This session concerns the sides of the torso, including the arms and shoulders. In particular, the therapist works on a muscle called the quadratus lumborum. This muscle connects the bottom rib to the top of the pelvic bone. When relaxed and lengthened to its natural state, it maintains the proper distance between the ribs and pelvis. Breathing becomes deeper, and the patient gains a revitalized appearance. The therapist also tries to loosen the shoulders and widen the sides.

Session four: Up to now, the therapist has mostly been working with the layer of fascia between the skin and muscles. This layer tends to dry out as a result of tension; the flow of blood decreases, and so does flexibility. By the fourth session, the fascia should be revitalized. Now the therapist begins deeper work, on the legs, especially the adductor and hamstring muscles at the insides and backs of the thighs. By releasing tension in these muscles, the therapist frees the pelvis further.

Session five: The therapist returns to the torso. The work is on two main muscles: the large abdominal muscle (rectus abdominus) and the deep muscle that runs from the bottom of the spine to the top of the thighbone (psoas). As usual, this session improves the breathing. It also releases abdominal and genital tension and helps move the pelvis into a horizontal position.

Session six: In this session, the therapist works on the backs of the legs (especially the thighs), the buttocks, and the small of the back. A lot of people are insensitive to these areas, so work here can be especially stimulating. The muscles here are also the ones that were affected during toilet training; when they finally let go of their tension, they let go of a lot of shame and anxiety as well.

Session seven: This session is devoted to the face and neck. The therapist goes into the throat and nasal passages, gives the eyes a deep massage, and works on the scalp. Some people have said that this is the most painful of all the sessions.

Sessions eight and nine: Rather than working on specific muscles, the therapist begins to work on large groups of muscles. In a sense, the therapist sculpts the body. Session eight deals with the upper body; session nine, with the lower body. The emphasis is on the patient's particular physiological problems; no set sequence of work is required.

Session ten: As with eight and nine, this session tries to integrate the whole body. The therapist begins with the ankles and works right up to the head, shaping the body and working on problem areas.

Rolfing, like bioenergetics, involves more than just bodywork. The patient, aided by the therapist, has to deal with all the psychological material that comes up through the therapy. Will Schutz, a rolfer associated with the Esalen Institute, uses the technique of guided fantasy: the patient visualizes scenes associated with each emotion and to some degree acts them out.

There's one more important aspect in which rolfing differs from bioenergetics—you cannot experiment with it to feel what it's like. Do not try to rolf someone unless you have studied the techniques and know what you're doing.

For Further Reading

Ida Rolf had a book forthcoming from Viking Press; in the interim, the best book on her technique is *Body Fantasy*, by Will Schutz and Evelyn Turner (San Francisco: Harper and Row, 1977).

Alexander Technique

If rolfing seems too strenuous, try the Alexander technique. George Bernard Shaw, John Dewey, Aldous Huxley, and Lewis Mumford did, and they were all enthusiastic students of Alexander's. It involves no pain and as little exertion as possible.

Frederick Matthias Alexander is one of the more engaging figures in the history of bodywork. He was born in 1869 in rural Australia. At age seventeen, he took a job as clerk and salesman at a tin-mining company, but he was unhappy with his job. He wanted to be an actor. So he left for Melbourne and began to get minor roles.

However, he had a major problem. At times his voice would fail him during a performance. He sought medical help without success; so in 1888 he began to work the problem out for himself, through self-observation. After a very long period of staring into mirrors, he decided his problem was a tendency to pull his head backward and downward. The resulting tension choked his voice. He devised a series of exercises to correct this bad habit, and in 1894 he began to teach the exercises to others. At this stage, his technique was mostly an aid in voice production. Soon he gave up the stage and became a full-time teacher.

In 1904 he left for London, intending to establish a school there. He had little money, but he was one of those people who believe that something will always turn up. And it did.

Alexander loved to gamble on horse races. One day, early in his London stay, he ran into a bookie who gave him a hot tip. Alexander played it and won £750. With that money he set up his practice.

One of his first pupils was the great actor Sir Henry Irving. Soon he was teaching other prominent people. The great American philosopher and educator John Dewey was especially enthusiastic about the technique. Until he met Alexander, Dewey had assumed that it was somehow natural and proper to be clumsy. It was a revelation to him that he could be graceful instead.

Alexander returned to the theater for brief periods, producing Shakespearean plays with casts made up entirely of his students. He himself appeared as Shylock in one production. When asked about the relation of his technique to other disciplines, Alexander would express his contempt for yoga, hypnosis, calisthenics, deep-breathing exercises, relaxation techniques, meditation, and the occult. What he was after, he said, was natural movement, and that was all there was to it. He died in 1955 and was active almost to the end.

Alexander wanted his students to develop their kinesthetic sense, their awareness of their own movement. His technique seeks to correct psychophysical problems through motion.

According to this system, psychophysical problems, including lack of a kinesthetic sense, are due to subconscious bad habits, which need to be corrected. But Alexander found that every attempt to correct a defect leads to the introduction of another defect. If a student slumped and Alexander said, "Stand up straight," the student might then arch his back and stick his belly out, making things worse. The answer, then, was to correct bad habits *before* giving any direct instruction.

Alexander's method for doing this was ingenious. He would give his student an order—stand up, walk, sit down. The student's job was to disregard the order, and concentrate instead on the involuntary preparation to carry out the order, what Alexander called the "set." For example, when people go against gravity—when they prepare to get up from a chair or climb stairs—they have an unconscious tendency to pull the head down and back.

So when Alexander would say, "stand up," the student had to inhibit the desire to carry out the order; the set had to be eliminated. Then the teacher could gradually manipulate the student into the correct positions for motion.

What are the correct positions? In the simplest terms, the spine must be as long as possible, and the head and neck must be free. These two things go together, since there are no neck muscles that will raise the head. You can elevate the head only by lengthening the spine.

As the body comes into the natural, relaxed position, the breathing will naturally become deeper. But you must not *try* to breathe deeply. In fact, you must not try to do anything. Movement should be effortless.

There is a movie of Alexander taken when he was over eighty years old.

In it he performs a few simple movements, such as lifting one leg over a chair. At the time the movie was taken, he was recovering from an illness, but you'd never know it. His movements were effortless.

For Further Reading

The Resurrection of the Body: The Writings of F. Matthias Alexander, edited by Edward Maisel (New York: Delta, 1974).

Other Movement Therapies

Of the current methods for teaching awareness through body movement, three deserve mention. They are the techniques of Rudolf Laban, Moshe Feldenkrais, and the Arica group.

Laban, who is the person most responsible for dance therapy, was born in 1879 in Bratislava. He studied from 1900 to 1907 at the Ecole des Beaux Arts in Paris. He danced professionally under the name Atilla de Varalja; he also designed for the stage. In 1910 he began his teaching activities by opening what he called a "dance farm." By 1923 he had schools in Basle, Stuttgart, Hamburg, Prague, Budapest, Zagreb, Rome, Vienna, and Paris. His main idea was to use dance as a means of education and therapy, and he enjoyed great popular success. In 1929 he directed a pageant in Vienna involving ten thousand performers.

When the Nazis took power, they declared Laban's work inimical to the state. He fled to Paris and then London. He died in 1958.

One of Laban's great insights was that all of our senses are variations of the sense of touch. Hearing is the result of the action of sound waves on the eardrum; sight is the result of light rays touching the eye. All of our perceptions, then, come from our being in touch with environmental energies and responding to them.

Laban also believed that "empty space does not exist. On the contrary, space is a superabundance of simultaneous movements." These movements have a rhythm, and we vibrate to it constantly, whether we know it or not. (For information on the mathematic significance of this vibration, see chapter three, under numerology.) Laban thought that dance was the best way to become attuned to the world's vibrations, to realize one's place in the cosmos. Through education in movement, you can develop improved self-awareness and the ability to communicate more fully with others.

Among his other accomplishments, Laban developed a system for notating dance movements, based on his analysis of eight categories of physical effort. The categories are dabbing, flicking, floating, gliding, pressing, punching, slashing, and wringing. He characterized these efforts according to how they occur in time, space, and gravity. Efforts can be light or firm, sustained or sudden, direct, or flexible.

The Israeli teacher Moshe Feldenkrais has a somewhat similar system of training through movement, though his is more directly concerned with biological energy. Feldenkrais believes that "movement is the best clue to the activity of the nervous system. . . . Movement or its absence show the state of the nervous system, its hereditary endowment, and its degree of development."

Because very little comes naturally to humans, we must make an effort from infancy to learn to move. Almost all of us do so—we learn to walk, to run, to sit or to stand, to move our eyes, and to talk. But then we cut short the learning process. "The majority of us," Feldenkrais says, "achieve a happy-go-lucky mediocrity, just enough to make us one of the many." Furthermore, we have little awareness of our shortcomings, because our ability to judge movement develops at the same rate as our ability to move. In other words, we're both performers and critics, and our standards are very low.

Feldenkrais's answer to this problem was to develop a method for bringing about better maturation of the nervous system, using "the reversibility relationship of our muscular and nervous systems." This simply means that the nervous system usually gives orders to the muscles; but the muscles, when used in certain ways, can send messages to the nervous system and train it. This happens most effectively when you reduce movement to its simplest components. The smaller and simpler the movement, the greater your awareness of it.

Feldenkrais has devised a series of exercises to be done while lying down. When you lie down, your nervous system doesn't receive the usual stimuli from the soles of the feet; the ordinary skeletal pattern of stress is suppressed, too. Thus, this position helps break down muscular habits. The movements themselves are done slowly and lightly—after fifteen or twenty repetitions of a movement there should be no effort at all. An ordinary session of Feldenkrais exercises lasts about fifty minutes. When you stand up at the end, you discover that you have new responses, fresher reactions. You feel as if your body is hanging lightly from your head.

One very useful aspect of the Feldenkrais method is that you can work with it without a teacher. There's a book titled *Twenty-five Lessons by Moshe Feldenkrais*, annotated by Margalit Sonnenfeld and Michal Shoshoni (Holon, Israel: Movement Notation Society, 1971), and it contains a great many odd-looking charts filled with numbers and squiggles. After an hour's work, you can learn to decipher the charts. Then you can try the Feldenkrais method for yourself.

Finally, there is the Arica method of psychocalisthenics, a set of twenty-six exercises that may be done daily in a twenty-minute period. Oscar Ichazo, the founder of the Arica Institute, developed the exercises as part of his forty-day training method, which also includes dance, meditation, chanting, group exercises, and a special diet. But the psychocalisthenics can be practiced separately. For guidance, consult the illustrated text put out by the Arica Institute, *Psychocalisthenics* (New York: Simon and Schuster, 1977). The method promises to unify the mind, body, and emotions.

Laban's work is hard to summarize, but Samuel Thornton has done it in *Laban's Theory of Movement: A New Perspective* (Boston: Plays, Inc., 1971). The two major books by Feldenkrais are *Awareness Through Movement: Health Exercises for Personal Growth* (New York: Harper and Row, 1972); and *Body and Mature Behavior: A Study of Anxiety, Sex, Gratification and Learning* (New York: International Universities Press, 1966).

Gadgets

This section is about some of the devices that either use or explore the body's energy. Two of these gadgets—the pyramid and the dowser's pendulum—are ancient. The others—the machines used in biofeedback training and Kirlian photography—are contemporary. All are generally available for use.

Biofeedback Training

The term *biofeedback* applies to any cycle by which information goes to the brain so that the brain can in turn regulate the body. There are many simple examples of this process: scratching an itch, catching a china cup before it falls to the floor, recognizing and greeting a friend.

Biofeedback training (BFT) differs from these common cycles in that it concentrates on information that is not accessible to the conscious part of the brain. Two prime examples of such information are the electrical patterns of brain activity and the degree of blood pressure. BFT uses mechanical techniques to allow the individual to be aware of such information. It takes standard devices—the electrocardiograph, for example, or the electroencephalograph—and modifies them slightly so that their readings come out in lights or audible tones. The trainee can thus understand the readouts directly.

Then something strange occurs. The trainee learns to *control* the readouts. Nobody knows how this happens, but it does happen, rapidly and universally. Everybody can use BFT to learn to control basic bodily functions.

BFT explores four physiological areas: the skin, the muscles, the autonomic nervous system, and the brain. The monitoring techniques are somewhat different from area to area.

Everybody knows about one of the machines that monitors the skin—the lie detector. This device works because the skin is electrically active, and its activity is a primary indicator of emotional states and mental activity. The skin's activity depends on the sweat glands. Sweating affects the ability of the skin cells to absorb mineral elements, especially potassium, which occur in electrically charged forms called ions. This makes it possible for a researcher (or the police lab) to monitor two main measures of the skin's activity: its conductivity (resistance to electrical charge) and the voltage of its own current.

The police are not the only people interested in this type of bioenergy. Wilhelm Reich studied the skin's charge, and acupuncturists have used these monitoring techniques to map the meridians. (See the articles on Reich and acupuncture in this chapter.)

Some fascinating discoveries have been made about the skin's electricity. There is always more activity on the right side of the body than on the left, regardless of whether one is right- or left-handed. The skin's charge changes in response to color. Schizophrenics often show very low skin receptivity, as if signals from the outside world could not reach them. They seem to feel neither pleasure nor pain. Some doctors are now exploring the use of skin receptivity as an index of schizophrenics' potentials for recovery.

Biofeedback training of the muscles goes back to 1908, to the work of Edmund Jacobson at Harvard. Jacobson was studying techniques of muscular relaxation in the hope that they would prove useful in the treatment of psychosomatic illnesses. He discovered that there is residual muscle tension even when the body is at rest. Moreover, when someone thinks about doing work (lifting a weight, for example), the muscles show a burst of electrical activity. Jacobson published his findings in 1929 in his book *Progressive Relaxation*, where he outlined the exercises he had devised to teach awareness of muscle tension.

At the same time as Jacobson was doing his research, a German named J.H. Schultz was investigating physiological factors in self-hypnosis. He, too, developed a system, called Autogenic Training, which he began to teach in the 1920s. The autogenic system is still very much with us, as the basis of a system of memory expansion and learning acceleration developed by a Bulgarian, Doctor Georgi Lozanov. Lozanov teaches the method in his Institute of Suggestology in Sofia, Bulgaria. The method is used throughout the Soviet bloc, especially in the teaching of foreign languages, for which it supposedly cuts learning time by about one-fifth. (For information on the Lozanov method, see articles by Dr. W. Jane Bancroft in the *Canadian Modern Language Review*, Vol. XXVIII, No. 2, March 1972, and Vol. XXIX, No. 2, January 1973.)

The most widespread current use for BFT of the muscular system is in the treatment of tension headaches. The therapist attaches electrodes to the patient's forehead. The electrodes pick up electrical signals given by the small muscles in the forehead, notably the frontalis. These signals feed into a machine, an electromyograph, that translates them into audible tones. The higher the tone, the higher the level of electrical activty and the greater the tension. When the tone goes down, the patient knows that the tension has decreased. It's up to the patient to learn to reduce the tension through concentration.

There can be difficulties with this method. A tense, nervous person concentrates very hard on lowering the signal tone; nothing happens, and the patient becomes even more tense and nervous. At the beginning, then, the therapist might cheat. Since the machine gives a readout on a graph as well as by a tone, the therapist can see changes too small to be reflected in the tone. So at the first slight decrease in tension, the therapist will lower the tone. The patient thus gets a sense of accomplishment and can go on to profit from the training.

Perhaps the most startling aspect of BFT concerns its use in controlling the autonomic nervous system. Here researchers have learned just how precise our control of our bodies can be. BFT is useful in investigating the skills of yogins—indeed, the monitoring of pulse rate, breathing, and brain activity in meditation has become a routine experiment. But BFT also can tell us a lot about the potential of nonadepts.

John Basmajian set up biofeedback experiments on the spinal cord, monitoring the activity of nerve cells by means of a cathode ray oscilloscope or a loudspeaker. He found that his subjects would begin to identify certain patterns and give them pet names ("Oh, there goes Charlie again"). These patterns were characteristic of single cells. Once the subjects had identified these patterns, they would start to play with them. It seems that the subjects did this on their own, in a spirit of fun. Soon, of course, Basmajian was testing for the ability to do this. Nobody had ever expected that people could consciously control individual nerve cells in their spinal cords.

In summarizing his findings, Basmajian said that "Normal human beings can quickly, in a matter of fifteen or twenty minutes, isolate only one motor unit from the population of perhaps a hundred or two hundred which are within an area of pick-up of an electrode pair. They can suppress all of the units, fire single units, manipulate those units, turn them on and off easily, suppress the one they started with, pick up another one . . . "

Finally, there is BFT of the brain, which involves the study of brain waves, a subject currently of considerable interest.

Brain Waves. When researchers first monitored the brain's electrical activity, all they saw was a bewildering array of squiggles on graph paper. The first sign of order in all these squiggles was the similar wave patterns that they would see every time their subjects closed their eyes. These waves were not the largest or the most frequent; they were merely the ones most easily observed. They occurred eight to twelve times per second. The researchers called them alpha waves.

There are three other main kinds of waves: delta (one to three waves per second), theta (four to seven waves per second), and beta (around thirteen to twenty-eight per second). In general, alpha waves tend to be associated with relaxation and rest. They often accompany a loss of awareness of time and of one's surroundings. In alpha states, people may show an increased power of visualization and a greater susceptibility to hypnosis.

Beta waves are associated with alertness, intelligence, and anxiety. Theta waves are associated with drowsiness, dreaming, and the assimilation of new information.

People who show lots of alpha waves in their ordinary state tend to be passive, submissive, and dependent. People who show very little alpha in their ordinary state are overtly hostile.

These generalizations are not universally true, for brain waves are highly individual; people tend to have their own discernible patterns in the succession of their brain waves. For example, some people show more bursts of alpha during periods of work than during times of relaxation. This news disappointed people who had hoped to program Enlightenment through BFT. It seems as if the pattern for Enlightenment would have to be highly individual, like all brain patterns.

There is also a notable problem in the use of BFT for meditation. As I have said, one almost automatically gets alpha waves by closing the eyes. One almost always closes the eyes in meditation. The result is that a lot of people who have been seeking inner peace through BFT do not reach the depths of the self—they merely train their eye muscles.

For more information on BFT, write to: Bio-Feedback Research Society, c/o Department of Psychology CZ 68, University of Colorado Medical Center, Denver, Colorado 80220.

For Further Reading

The standard book on biofeedback training is *New Mind, New Body: Bio-Feedback: New Directions for the Mind*, by Barbara B. Brown (New York: Harper and Row, 1974). It will tell you the history of the technique, the scientific basis of all its aspects, and anything else you need to know about it. The book is clumsily written but informative.

Kirlian Photography

Kirlian photography, a technique invented by and named after the Russian scientists Semyon and Valentina Kirlian, is a method of photography that uses neither light nor a camera. It converts the nonelectrical properties of an object into electrical properties that can be filmed. It has thereby made it possible for the first time to photograph auras.

The human body has an electromagnetic field. The blood, lymph, and intestinal fluids are all electrically charged; the bioenergy—prānā, ki, orgone energy, or whatever names it may be given—also carries a charge. In some people the resulting energy field can be very strong indeed. In 1879 in Ontario, a nineteen-year-old girl developed an electromagnetic field so strong that metal objects stuck to her hands. In 1886, a sixteen-year-old boy in Maryland developed a similar ability (or problem). Metal objects had to be pried loose from him. Scientists at the Maryland College of Pharmacy studied the case. In 1895, a fourteen-year-old girl in Missouri developed such a powerful electrical current in her body that a doctor who tried to examine her was knocked unconscious on contact.

These, of course, were exceptional cases. For most people under most circumstances, the energy field could not be noticed, at least until the invention of Kirlian photography.

The basis of the method is the use of a high-frequency, alternating current generator in connection with photographic film. The film is placed over an oscillator plate connected to the generator. The film acts as a dielectric—that is, it stabilizes the plate's charge and distributes it evenly. Without the film (or a comparable dielectric), the plate's discharge would be in the form of sparks—unstable, irregular, and located at individual points. With the film, a stable flow of high energy is possible, and the flow is distributed over the whole surface of the plate.

Film, too, becomes charged when used in this manner. Therefore, when you put a grounded object against the film, you get a slow, stable discharge of electrons and ions. These make an impression on the film by distorting the electrical field. If the object against the film is alive, the result is a photograph of an aura.

It might seem as if the object (a human, let us say) would get a severe shock in the process, but the amperage is kept very low and this permits a safe flow of current. The great physicist Nikola Tesla, the developer of alternating current, used to give lecture demonstrations in which he would direct twenty thousand volts through his body, with the current alternating about a million times a second. He would explain to his audiences that if the current were directed in some other way, he would incinerate before their eyes.

The discoveries made possible by Kirlian photography have been extraordinary. Thelma Moss of UCLA and Kendall Johnson (her nonacademic coworker) have photographed human subjects under a number of physical and psychological conditions. They found no physical correlations to the auras they photographed, but they did find psychological correlations. Auras change when subjects are drunk, high on drugs, hypnotized, or in meditative states. Students of Reichian therapies showed an ability to extend their auras at will, as did students of yoga. Relaxation, they found, produces a brighter, wider aura; tension and emotional excitement make red blotches appear.

E. Douglas Dean has taken photographs of psychic healers. He found that red-orange flares appear in the fingers during healing. These flares are not present when the subject is at rest.

One of the strangest phenomena of Kirlian photography is the phantom-leaf effect. When a cut leaf is photographed, the picture may show the aura of a whole leaf.

Dennis Milner, at the University of Birmingham, England, has developed a similar apparatus. With it, he's taken photographs that give visual support to Wilhelm Reich's orgone theories. Milner took photographs of dark, vacuum chambers; he came out with photos of an energy field. Perhaps Milner's finding helps explain another phenomenon of Kirlian photography—the human aura is strongest at 7:00 P.M. Greenwich Mean Time and weakest at 4:00 A.M.

It's not too difficult or expensive to set up a Kirlian apparatus. For an outline of the method and a list of suppliers, see *Handbook of Psychic Discoveries*, by Sheila Ostrander and Lynn Schroeder (New York: Berkley Medallion, 1975). For Kirlian photography, see *The Kirlian Aura: Photographing the Galaxies of Life*, edited by Stanley Krippner and Daniel Rubin (New York: Anchor/Doubleday, 1974).

Other Gadgets for Auras. The simplest tool for seeing auras is the mirror. Sit in front of a light-colored, softly-lighted background. Look into the mirror at a point about six inches above your head and two feet behind you. Now relax and be patient. It may take a while, but you should see something.

Another method, developed by Dr. Walter Kilner of St. Thomas' Hospital, London, requires the use of glass screens stained with dicyanin dye. A more current version of this method uses goggles dyed with pinacyanole.

There is one more method of photographing auras, a nineteenth-century technique called the Schlieren method. For some time now scientists have used Schlieren photography to study the flow of air in supersonic wind tunnels. Now they are using it to study the body as well.

The body gives off heat energy as well as electromagnetic energy. The result is a flow of warm air around the body. When light passes through this flow of air, it breaks into colors, much as it does when it goes through a prism. The Schlieren technique is a means of photographing the resulting pattern of colors.

There's some question as to the nature of these patterns, whether they show the inner envelope of the aura or the interaction of the aura with the physical body. Whatever Schlieren photographs reveal, they are worth special mention because they're one evidence of auras that traditional scientists don't discount.

Finally, there is a complicated machine devised by Jack Schwarz, who is associated with the Aletheia Psycho-Physical Foundation in Grants Pass, Oregon. The machine is called the Integral Stimulating Intensity Stroboscope, or ISIS. When used in combination with training charts and eye exercises, it's been very useful in teaching people to see auras. It also seems to relieve glaucoma and improve the eyesight.

Pyramids

For centuries, people have speculated about the Pyramids, about how and why and by whom they were built, but one curious fact has escaped scrutiny. Pyramids seem to concentrate energy. Nobody knows what kind of energy, or how it's concentrated, but evidently they do it.

We owe this discovery to a French inventor named Antoine Bovis who visited the Great Pyramid early in this century. Bovis saw that various small animals had entered the pyramid and died there. The curious thing was that they had not rotted. They had mummified. Bovis was intrigued, and when he returned to France he built a scale model of the Great Pyramid. He put a platform inside of it, one-third of the way up, at the level of the King's Chamber, and on this platform he placed a dead cat. The cat dried out and mummified. In the 1930s, Bovis wrote a book about his findings.

That might have been the end of it, except that a Czechoslovakian engineer named Karl Drbal became interested in Bovis's research. Drbal learned, among other things, that dull razor blades become sharp when put in a pyramid. In 1959 he secured a Czech patent for a pyramid razor-blade sharpener, and that was the beginning of the current interest in pyramid power.

At present there are a number of ready-made pyramids on the market. If you'd rather make you own, it's easy. Any material will do; most people begin with cardboard. The pyramid can be built to any measure, but it should be as close as possible to the proportions of the Great Pyramid.

The easiest method for figuring the proportions is to start with the base. Draw a square to whatever measure you like. Now an isosceles triangle has to be erected on each of the four baselines. The sides of the triangles must be 4.855 percent shorter than the baselines. So if the sides of the base were 25 centimeters, for example, the sides of the triangles would be 23.786 centimeters.

What if you want to build a pyramid to a set height? Then you would use a formula offered by Valerie Ann Olin:

height x 1.5708 = base of triangle
height x 1.4946 = side of triangle

Thus, if you wanted a pyramid 30 centimeters high, the baselines would be 47.124 centimeters long and the sides 44.838 centimeters.

Once your pyramid is built, place it at least four feet from walls, radiators, fluorescent lights, and electrical appliances, with one side squarely facing north. Some people say it should face true north, but magnetic north is the more reasonable direction. Whatever sort of energy the pyramid focuses, it must be connected in some way with the Earth's magnetic field. That is why it should be kept away from electrical interferences, and that is also why it should not be set on a metal surface.

Now for the razor blades: Just put them one-third of the way up the pyramid and directly under the apex. Some people report that they have kept eggs, meat, and fish in pyramids for up to eight weeks and found that they stayed not only edible but tasty. The pyramid also seems to have a healthy effect on plant seedlings. Some people have built open-sided pyramids large enough to sit in; they use them for meditation.

A word of caution: Don't rely too much on your pyramid for keeping food fresh. Pyramid energy evidently depends to some extent on the attitude of the person using it, and as a result, pyramids sometimes fail.

For Further Reading

The *Handbook of Psychic Discoveries* (New York: Berkley Medallion, 1975) has information on pyramids and dowsing. For pyramids, see also *The First Practical Pyramid Book*, by Norman H. Stark (Kansas City: Sheed Andrews and McMeel, 1977).

Dowsing

In addition to pyramids, the ancient Egyptians had another device for focusing energy: a dowsing pendulum, called a *merkhet*. This was simply an ellipsoidal rock suspended from an L-shaped wooden beam. Priests used the tool for land surveying, astrological calculations, and to help establish the locations for temples.

How does a dowsing pendulum work? Essentially, it just monitors bioenergy—much as a biofeedback machine does. The work of divining is done by the energy currents flowing through the body. The pendulum is merely a convenient, visible sign of those currents.

There are many other kinds of dowsing instruments, but pendulums are the most popular. They can be made of various materials and in various shapes, depending on their intended use and the personality of the dowser. Christopher Hills, who does a good mail-order business in dowsing equipment from his University of the Trees in Boulder Creek, California, has a bewildering array of pendulums. Some are roughly conical, made of glass or polyethelene, and filled with mercury; these are for picking up thought waves. Some have a mirrored surface to insulate them from environmental vibrations; some have small quantities of radium inside to act as amplifiers. A spiral coil helps concentrate orgone energy in objects. A left-handed spiral with a mirrored surface is good for detecting the presence of negative energy, especially, Hills says, in spiritual hucksters.

The traditional dowsing tool, of course, is the rod used for locating water. You can make one by straightening out two wire coathangers and then putting an L-bend about one-quarter of the way down each. Grasp the short legs of the wires and hold the long legs straight out in front of you with your hands about three inches apart. Now you're ready to look for water. If you find it, that's because the friction generated by running water gives off an energy that your body picks up. As the energy enters you, your hands will involuntarily move the dowsing rod.

For more information write the American Society of Dowsers, Danville, Vermont 05828.

For Further Reading

Christopher Hills has taken the subject of dowsing about as far as it will go in *Supersensonics* (Boulder Creek, California: University of the Trees Press, 1975).

Oriental Healing

Acupuncture

Acupuncture is the oldest medical tradition in the world, developed by the Chinese well before the birth of Christ. In China today, acupuncture is still used as a relatively painless cure for disease and as a method of anesthesia for surgery. Acupuncture has now become common in Europe, particularly in France. It was introduced in the United States after James Reston of the *New York Times* underwent surgery with it in China in 1972.

Acupuncture is a method of regulating and harmonizing the body's flow of energy by the insertion of thin needles into the skin. The needles go into points that lie in the fatty layer between the skin and muscles. There are about one thousand such points in the body, each about one-tenth of an inch in diameter. When the body is diseased, these points are affected, either singly or in groups. An acupuncturist who stimulates these points in the proper way can cure the disease.

The Chinese believe that the acupuncture points lie along twelve primary lines, called meridians. Each meridian is associated with an internal organ. Each conducts bioenergy, which the Chinese call *qi* (sometimes spelled *ki*). Qi is either negative (*yin*) or positive (*yang*).

The system of meridians is very complex. There follows a summary of the twelve meridians, identified by their associated organs and their polarity, yin(−) or yang(+): This summary also shows you the order of the qi's flow, from the lung meridian to the liver meridian.

1. lungs (−)
2. large intestine (+)
3. stomach (+)
4. spleen (−)
5. heart (−)
6. small intestine (+)
7. bladder(+)
8. kidneys (−)
9. circulatory and sexual systems (−)
10. the triple warmer—functions of nervous energy and heat (+)
11. gall bladder (+)
12. liver (−)

With this scorecard, it is a little easier to follow the classification of meridians.

Meridians are either upper or lower, yin or yang. There are thus four major groups. The upper yin meridians (heart, lung, and circulation and sex) run from the fingertips along the inner arm to the chest. The lower yin meridians (spleen, kidneys, and liver) run from the toes up the inside of the legs and up the front of the body.

The upper yang meridians (small intestine, the triple warmer, and large intestine) run from the fingers along the outside of the arm to the face. The lower yang meridians (stomach, gall bladder, and bladder) go from the head down the back of the body to the toes.

The first question people ask about meridians is, "How can we know if they really exist?" There are now some good answers.

Kim Bong Han, a Korean acupuncturist, has invented a machine to measure small differences in the electrical resistance of the skin. Places that show sharp electrical distinctions turned out to be acupuncture points. Now, this could be nothing more than coincidence. But Han has also done an experiment in which he injected radioactive phosphorus into specific acupuncture points. He then traced the flow of the phosphorus. It travelled along the meridians.

There's another interesting confirmation of the meridians from experiments done by Hiroshi Motoyama of the Institute of Religious Psychology in Tokyo. He assembled a test group of one-hundred students of yoga. All of them had learned to stimulate individual *chakras* at will; the activity of the *chakras* showed up on a blood-pressure sensor. Thus, Motoyama was able to map the location of the *chakras*. They all lie on acupuncture meridians. Finally, researchers in Kirlian photography have been busy taking pictures of acupuncture points and meridians. In fact, the Soviets have invented a small device called a Tobiscope to help locate acupuncture points.

Theory and Therapy. When the body becomes diseased, a meridian (or part of one) becomes tender to the touch. White or purple streaks may appear along it. The meridian may also be affected by secondary diseases. That is to say, the liver meridian is affected by more than liver diseases. Hay fever will influence it as well.

Acupuncturists believe that the source of disease is always an imbalance of qi. There may be an excess or deficiency of qi in the body as a whole, in parts of the body, or along one or more of the meridians. Moreover, the imbalance will be not only of amount but of kind—too much or too little of either yin or yang. (These imbalances are no doubt similar to the energy blockages discussed by Wilhelm Reich, Alexander Lowen, and Ida Rolf.)

The time of year has a lot to do with these imbalances. Yang is relatively more active in spring and summer; yin, in autumn and winter. In the summer, yang tends to concentrate in the head and skin. In the winter, yin concentrates in the feet and internal organs. Yang is most active at the full moon; yin, at the new moon. In short, the natural rhythms of the year may upset the balance of qi. For this reason, astrology plays a large part in acupuncture diagnosis and treatment.

When an acupuncturist sees a patient, he or she must first decide the nature of the problem. For example, a weak pulse and low blood pressure are signs that the heart has too little yin. If the heart is pounding, it probably has too much yin. The acupuncturist can confirm the diagnosis by checking along the meridian for the sensitive points which indicate the presence of disease.

Now the acupuncturist must correct the problem by the placement of needles. In this there are a great many choices open to the acupuncturist. There are seven basic types of points for each meridian, and the acupuncturist is free to use them as he or she sees fit.

1. The points of tonification. These will stimulate the flow of qi.
2. The points of sedation. These will diminish the flow of qi.
3. The source points. These can either stimulate or diminish qi, depending on the nature of the problem. They have a very rapid effect.
4. The alarm points. These are points of yin disease that lie on the stomach and chest. They are useful for diagnosis.
5. The associated points. Each meridian has one of these points along the bladder meridian. They are yang points.
6. The points of entry and exit. These have special influence because they control the flow of qi from one meridian to another. They are, obviously, the points where qi goes into a meridian and where it leaves.
7. The Lo points. These connect meridians and introduce a new level of complexity to the treatment.

The meridians work in pairs. Lo points serve to connect the coupled meridians. Here is the system of coupling; yin meridians are given on the left, yang ones on the right.

lungs	large intestine
stomach	spleen
heart	small intestine
bladder	kidney
circulation and sex	triple warmer
gall bladder	liver

By skillful use of the Lo points, the acupuncturist can heal a meridian by remote control. There are other ways that the meridians work together, too. The three main ones are as follows:

Mother-son: In the flow of qi, the source meridian is called the mother, and the recipient is called the son. Thus, the lung meridian is the mother to the large intestine meridian, because qi flows from the first into the second. Therefore, you can control the qi in the second through proper stimulation of points on the first.

Husband-wife: In paired meridians, the yin is the husband, and the yang is the wife. Thus, the stomach meridian is husband to the spleen meridian; the heart meridian is husband to the small intestine. This provides another way of regulating and harmonizing qi.

Midday-midnight: The strength of the flow of qi to different meridians varies according to time of day. Again, the meridians work in pairs. The gall bladder will have the stronger flow at one time of the day, the liver at another.

Finally, there are points along each meridian for the basic elements. The Chinese recognize five such elements, rather than the four classical Western ones. These five are water, wood, fire, earth, and metal. Their interaction is complex; acupuncture helps balance them in the body. The diagram below shows their relationship. Note that each element creates another element and destroys an element; thus each element is yin in relation to one thing and yang in relation to another.

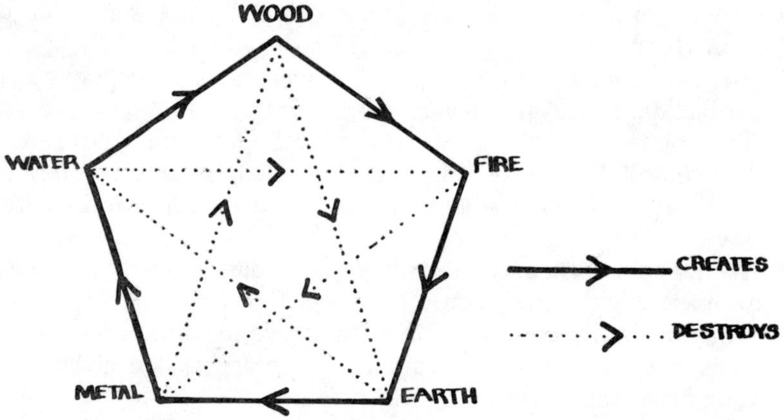

From *Acupuncture: The Ancient Chinese Art of Healing*, by Felix Mann, M.B.

A word of caution: Acupuncturists in the United States are not subject to the same sort of accreditation as medical doctors. So before you enter into a course of treatment, do some checking.

For Further Reading

The best popular introduction to acupuncture is *Acupuncture: The Ancient Chinese Art of Healing*, by Felix Mann, M.B. (New York: Random House, 1963). See also a book from the Academy of Traditional Chinese Medicine, *An Outline of Chinese Acupuncture* (San Francisco: China Books, 1975). Other books of interest are *Acupuncture and Maxibustion: A Handbook for the Barefoot Doctors of China*, edited by Martin E. Silverstein (New York: Schocken, 1975); *Acupuncture Therapy: Current*

Chinese Practice, by Leong T. Tan (Philadelphia: Temple University Press, 1976); and *Handbook of Medical Acupuncture*, by Frank Z. Warren (New York: Van Nostrand Reinhold, 1976).

Shiatzu

Not everybody can spend the time and effort to learn acupuncture. For this reason, you might want to study the Japanese technique of *shiatzu*, or healing by finger pressure. It's fairly easy to learn, and friends can practice it on each other without causing alarm.

Shiatzu therapy in its modern form was developed over the last forty-five years by Tokujiro Namikoshi, founder of the Nippon Shiatzu School. It is primarily a method of preventive medicine. By means of finger pressure exerted at different points on the body, a healthy flow of bioenergy can be maintained. Shiatzu is also good for relieving certain disorders, especially those caused by muscular tension. You can perform shiatzu on yourself or have someone do it for you.

Most of the pressing is done with the thumb. The main thing is to relax the thumb, not stiffen it. Leave it bent, and press with the pad rather than the tip. If you're tense while performing shiatzu, you will probably jab your patient, dig your nail into the skin, cut short any flow of energy, and tire out your arm. So take a few good breaths, make sure your back is straight, and lean into the patient with the thumb. Let your weight press the thumb into the skin—no muscle power is needed.

Here are some common shiatzu treatments.

Headache: Stand behind the patient and tilt his or her head to the left. You will see a muscle cord that starts in back of the ear and runs down the neck. Press down this cord at four or five spots, starting at the ear and working down. You should press each spot for about five seconds. Ask your patient how the pressure feels—that's the only way to know whether you're doing a good job. The pressure should be firm but not painful. When you reach the base of the neck, tilt the head to the right and go down the other side. Then press along the cord that runs from the neck to the shoulders. Start at the point directly below the ears and work across to the shoulders. Do not press on the bone—it's painful.

Backache: Have the patient lie prone. Kneel on the patient's left and put both thumbs on the left side of the spine. The thumbs should be diagonal to the spine, the left one pointing down the body, the right one pointing up. Press them down and toward each other. Start at the top of the spine and work down, exerting pressure for five second at each point. Again, don't press on the bone. Your thumbs should be immediately to the left of the spine but *not on it*. Be careful when you get to the area of the kidneys—press more gently and be sure to ask the patient how it feels. Then go to the right side and repeat.

Fever: Press along the back of the leg, starting at the back of the knee and going down to the Achilles tendon. Press a total of eight points; then go back and press them two more times. Now press three points along the inside of the Achilles tendon; don't try to press the tendon itself. Now press three points below the inside ankle and below the outside ankle. Do the same for the other leg. It's important to realize that this treatment is a stopgap measure, a way of relieving pain temporarily. If you have a fever, consult a doctor. Doctors tend to be more effective than do-it-yourself shiatzu.

For Further Reading

For an easy method of shiatzu, see *Shiatzu: Japanese Pressure Point Massage*, by Anika Bergson and Vladimir Tuchak (New York: Pinnacle, 1976).

Martial Arts

As he approached his eightieth birthday, the contemporary American master T. T. Liang wrote, "I must learn how to yield, to be tactful, not to be aggressive; to lose (small loss, small gain, great loss, great gain), not to take advantage of others; to give (the more one gives the more one will have). Life begins at seventy. Everything is beautiful!"

Liang wrote these words after thirty years of studying *t'ai chi ch'uan*. His vigor and openness of spirit are characteristic of the best elements of t'ai chi and the other martial arts.

In this section, I will discuss t'ai chi ch'uan and the related Japanese art of aikido. Both of these arts are very effective means of self-defense, which is, unfortunately, why they have become so popular recently. Self-defense is largely a by-product of the study of t'ai chi and aikido. Students practice self-defense techniques only as a means of training their energy. The main goal in t'ai chi and aikido is the unification of the mind and body. When the mind and body become one, they release energy; in Chinese the energy is called *chi*, and in Japanese it's called *ki*. The real objective for the use of this energy is expressed by Master Liang. Yield, be tactful, give to others; above all, appreciate life.

T'ai Chi Ch'uan

T'ai chi began around 250 A.D., when a physician named Hua-t'o developed a system of exercises based on the movements of five creatures: the tiger, deer, bear, ape, and bird. His aim was to improve people's health and coordination. The exercises became popular, and they still form the basis of t'ai chi ch'uan, especially in its nonmartial aspects.

The martial side of t'ai chi began with the boxing techniques called *shao lin ch'uan*. *Shao lin* means a young forest; it was the name of a monastery where the Buddhist monk Ta Mo taught. Ta Mo had come to China from India in 527 A.D. He found that the monks at the Shao Lin Monastery were slow and sluggish, so he taught them boxing. His methods are the basis of *kung fu*.

The two traditions of Ta Mo and Hua-t'o merged around 1350 A.D. A master of *shao lin* named Chang San-feng began to develop a martial art that was softer and slower than ordinary boxing. What inspired him in particular was the experience of watching a snake fight a bird. He studied the animals' movement, much as Hua-t'o had studied the movements of his creatures, and from them he developed t'ai chi ch'uan. The name means "grand ultimate exercise."

Chang San-feng wrote a text called *T'ai Chi Ch'uan Classic* in which he elucidated a system of thirteen postures: Ward Off, Roll Back, Press, Push,

Pull, Split, Elbow-Stroke, Shoulder-Stroke, Advance, Retreat, Look to the Left, Gaze Right, and Central Equilibrium. Gradually these thirteen postures became a series of forms. There are now 81, 108, 128, or 150 of them, depending in how they are counted.

The forms of t'ai chi must be practiced in a slow, even, continuous manner, with no breaks between the movements. By diligent practice, you attain perfect equilibrium. The head feels as if it is suspended from above; the lower back becomes straight; and most important of all, the vital energy, the chi, concentrates at a point about two inches below the navel. This point is called the *tan t'ien*. *Tan* means vital essence; it also means the color of blood. *T'ien* is a field or place. The *tan t'ien* is the natural place for your chi. From there, the chi can circulate effectively through the whole body.

Like everything else in Chinese philosophy, chi is both positive and negative, yang and yin. The forms of the t'ai chi exercise teach you to harmonize the yang and yin within yourself and to use them effectively.

The initial stance for the exercises is neutral and empty. The feet are parallel, about shoulder-width, with the weight evenly distributed. The hands hang at the sides, and the eyes look straight ahead. This state is called *wu chi* (the limitless).

As soon as you raise your hands and put your weight on one foot, you set up a polarity within the body. The weightbearing foot becomes yang; the nonweightbearing foot becomes yin. Thus, t'ai chi begins as soon as you start moving. You create yin and yang from the neutral state, and through the series of forms you play with yin and yang, as it were. Many of the forms require you to hold your hands as if you had a ball of energy between them; then you "roll the ball" from one side to the other and feel the continuous flow of yin and yang. At the end of the exercises, you return briefly to the neutral position.

There's a great affinity between the forms of t'ai chi and the hexagrams of the *I Ching*. The hexagrams, too, express polarity—their whole lines represent yang, and their broken lines represent yin. Eight of the original thirteen postures of t'ai chi are identified with the elementary trigrams of the *I Ching*. The trigrams also indicate the direction of the posture and its essential nature.

☰ *Ch'ien*: Ward off; south.
Turning, movement, and firmness.

☷ *K'un*: Roll back; north.
The belly; receptivity.

䷜ *K'an*: Press; west.
Water; the ears; dangers.

䷝ *Li*: Push; east.
Fire; crossed hands; empty inside, strong outside.

䷲ *Chên*: Split; northeast.
The feet; arousing thunder.

䷸ *Sun*: Pull; southwest.
Gentleness; penetration; the wind.

䷹ *Tui*: Elbow-stroke; southeast.
Hurting another.

䷳ *Kên*: Shoulder-stroke; northwest.
Legs and arms; a mountain.

The five other basic postures are related to the five Chinese elements: Advance (metal), Retreat (wood), Look to the Left (water), Gaze Right (fire), and Central Equilibrium (earth). (For a complete discussion of the *I Ching*, see chapter three.)

The use of t'ai chi ch'uan for self-defense begins only after the student has mastered the forms. Then comes a series of eight exercises based on *t'ui sho*—pushing hands.

Two students face each other with their right feet forward and their hands extended. They touch each other's right wrists; the palms remain turned inward toward their chests. Then they begin to push and pull gently, moving their hands in a small, horizontal circle. In this way, they learn to sense resistance in an opponent, and they learn how to make themselves yielding.

Eventually, the student will learn to "interpret energy." The student moves only when the opponent moves. Wherever the opponent focuses his energy, it is there that the student yields—there is literally nothing left to attack. At the same time, the student exerts force at the point that the opponent has left weak. The classic *T'ai Chi Ch'uan Treatise* of Wang Chung Yueh, as translated by T.T. Liang, says, "The fundamental point is to forget oneself and follow others."

Or, as another classic puts it, "The appearance is like a hawk seizing a rabbit; the spiritual insight is like a cat catching a rat."

For Further Reading

Translations of the t'ai chi ch'uan classics are in *T'ai Chi Ch'uan for Health and Self-Defense: Philosophy and Practice*, by Master T.T. Liang (New York: Vintage, 1977). For the forms of t'ai chi ch'uan, see *T'ai Chi Ch'uan: A Manual of Instruction*, by Lu Hui-Ching (New York: St. Martin's Press, 1973). The standard hippie-dippie approach to the subject is in *Embrace Tiger, Return to Mountain: The Essence of T'ai Chi*, by Al Chung-liang Huang (Moab, Utah: Real People Press, 1973).

Aikido

Aikido is a Japanese martial art developed some 300 years ago by Morihei Uyeshiba. To offer a simplified genealogy of the art, Uyeshiba applied the principles of t'ai chi ch'uan to the movements of Japanese sword-fighting and came up with a new method of unarmed self-defense. The art's name derives from three Japanese ideograms: *ai* (harmony), *ki* (vital energy), and *do* (a way). Aikido is thus "the way of harmonized ki."

There are a number of schools of aikido, all more or less alike. In this section I will describe the art as taught by Koichi Tohei. Tohei is the developer of a method called *shinshin toitsu aikido* (aikido with mind and body coordinated) and the founder of an organization called the Ki Society International (*Ki No Gai*). As of this writing, Tohei is approaching the age of sixty, and he has the suppleness and energy of a small boy. Among his other activities, he has acted as the special ki-coach of the Tokyo Giants baseball club.

Tohei places special emphasis on the teaching of mind-body coordination. He believes that not everybody can become a black belt in aikido, but everybody can learn to develop and use ki. To this end, he bases his instruction on four basic principles: keep one point, relax completely, keep weight underside, and extend ki. These principles are less mysterious than they sound, and anyone can understand them by trying a few simple tests.

By "keep one point," Tohei means what the t'ai chi masters mean when they speak of letting the energy concentrate in the lower abdomen. There is a point two inches below your navel, which Tohei calls the one point. It's the most concentrated point of ki in your body, and it is the point from which ki flows. To practice aikido, you must develop the habit of letting your mind settle to the one point. In that way, you become stable and unite your mind with your body.

Here's a test you can try. Stand in a natural position with your feet at about shoulder-width, and have a partner push you gently, but firmly, on the chest. If you are like most people, you'll fall backward. Now, stand in exactly the same way, but center your consciousness at the one point. This can be done without furrowing your brow or grimacing; just be aware of the point. Now have your partner push you again. You will probably find yourself more stable.

If the test does not work the first time, there's probably a reason. You might have locked your knees, or held your breath, or stiffened your spine, or tried to push against your partner in some way. Any of those actions will throw the body off the one point. Any strain, mental or physical, will make you unstable, which brings us to the second principle.

Relax completely—this does not mean go limp. It means be motionless but alert, ready for action but not anticipating it.

The third principle, to keep weight underside, simply means to let your weight settle naturally. The weight of a rock is always on the bottom surface; the weight of a cat is always on the pads of the feet. But humans, because we think a lot and get nervous, sometimes throw weight around in unnatural ways.

So try this exercise. Extend one arm, and think about the elbow as being heavy. Feel the weight along the bottom surface. Now have your partner try to lift the arm from the elbow. If you have succeeded in keeping weight underside, the arm will not go up. Now extend your arm in the same way, think about the weight being on the *topside*, and have your partner try to lift it. The arm will fly up.

By now it should be obvious that Tohei's principles go together. You can't keep one point unless you're completely relaxed; if you're relaxed, you will naturally have weight underside; if you have weight underside, you're also keeping one point. This is very useful for learning aikido—if you cannot get the right feeling by concentrating on one principle, try another. All three come together in the fourth principle—extend ki.

Ki flows into the body with every breath you take; it flows out every time you exhale. The first goal of aikido training is to learn to develop and control the flow of ki. One of the principal training methods is the practice called *Unbendable Arm*.

Stand with your right foot forward and extend your right arm as if shaking hands. Relax, let the weight settle to the underside, and keep your one point. Your fingers should be open and relaxed; the elbow should be slightly bent. Now imagine that a stream of water is flowing out of your arm, shooting out of your fingertips to the end of the Earth. When you have that feeling, let your partner try to bend your hand back to your shoulder. It should be difficult; when an aikido master extends Unbendable Arm, it's impossible. To check yourself, clench your fist and fight back with your muscles when your partner tries to bend your arm. You'll find the arm is much stronger when you're relaxed and have your ki flowing.

(Your partner should be pushing on the forearm. If your partner pushes on the wrist, your arm will indeed bend, and quite easily. That's because the ki is flowing out of your fingers very near the wrist; so that pushing on the wrist changes the direction of the flow. It works on the same principle as water flowing through a garden hose—you can bend the hose at the nozzle, but not at the middle.)

Once the four basic principles are understood, you practice them through a series of ki-development exercises. You also learn to tumble properly, to avoid being hurt on the practice mat. And you begin to study the throwing techniques.

The Self-Defense Techniques. The central principle of the aikido technique is freedom of movement. Whenever someone attacks, that person has limited his mind. If he's aiming a punch at the stomach, his mind stops at the point where he expects impact. If he's trying to grab the wrist, his mind stops at the wrist. In short, he's no longer free. He has bound himself by his own violence.

You, on the other hand, must not be bound by the attacker's violence. If he grabbed your wrist, fine—you can still move every other part of your body. You still have freedom of movement *so long as you don't stop your own mind at the point of attack.*

You can demonstrate this principle for yourself. You and your partner kneel and face each other. Extend one hand as if offering it and ask your partner to grab it. When your partner goes for your hand, pull it away at the last second. Your partner will fall forward. If he asks why you did such a dumb thing to him, explain that you didn't make him fall down—his desire to grab the hand made him fall down.

All aikido techniques are based on this principle. It's called *leading ki*. As the attacker comes at you, you must sense the direction of his energy and then harmonize with it. There are any number of ways of doing this—pivoting out of the way, stepping back out of the attacker's range, going toward the attacker so that you're safely inside the blow. All of these methods make the attacker overextend himself. At that point he's off-balance, and his ki is going nowhere. So you can join yourself with his aimless ki and give it a new direction.

There are five main categories of throw. Each one requires good timing, complete alertness, and above all, a strong sense of your own ki. If you can not direct your own ki, you surely can not direct an attacker's.

Kokyunage is the timing throw, or breathing throw. It has a great many varieties, all of which involve letting the attacker's momentum pull him off-balance. Then a light touch is enough to complete the throw.

Shihonage is the all-directions throw. You catch the attacker's hand and swing it back toward him, in effect completing a circle of ki. Because the direction of the ki has changed suddenly, the attacker must turn with it.

This makes it possible for you to throw him.

Kotagaeshi is changing direction. This technique is used most commonly against a punch to the stomach. You cover the attacker's hand with your own and lead him in a small circle; the feeling is much like walking down the street with a small child who has to hurry to keep up. Then you stop rather suddenly and turn the attacker's wrist so that the ki is going in the opposite direction. The attacker's wrist has only a little way to go when it changes direction; the attacker's body has quite a long way to go.

Kaiten-nage is the rolling throw. This is much like *kokyunage*. The difference is that you use the opponent's arm and head to swing him in a big circle, head over heels. This makes for quite a strong throw.

Ikkyo, nikkyo, sankyo, yonkyo are four wrist-lock techniques, all painful in varying manners and degrees. These are actually the most merciful of the aikido techniques. If you were to use *kokyunage, shihonage, kotagaeshi,* or *kaiten-nage* on an attacker on the street, you might crack his skull. Not many street-toughs know how to take a fall properly. There are throwing techniques for the wrist-locks, too; but they also give you the option of letting the attacker go with just a sore wrist and scraped knees.

These are only the basic categories of the technique. All the variations add up to about 100 techniques the student must learn before becoming a black belt. Then there are ten degrees of black belt to master. Ultimately, the number of aikido techniques cannot be counted, because a master goes beyond technique. Someone like Koichi Tohei merely keeps his own one point, goes with the flow of motion, and tries to look surprised when people fall down on all sides of him.

Aikido, like t'ai chi ch'uan, is finally a process of education. It teaches you that there are only a handful of ways to attack a person, but there are an infinite number of ways to respond. In that way, you come to learn something of what it means to meet people, to be free, and to use your energy.

For Further Reading:

You can read about Koichi Tohei's school of aikido in his book *This Is Aikido* (Elmsford, New York: Japan Publications, 1975). I also recommend the five volumes of Saito Morihro's *Traditional Aikido* (Elmsford: Japan Publications, 1973–1975). A. Westbrook and O. Ratti give an exceptionally clear account in *Aikido and the Dynamic Sphere* (Rutland, Vermont: Tuttle, 1970).

Psychic Surgeons

This chapter would be incomplete without some mention of the healers of Brazil and the Philippines. These people perform major surgery without benefit of anesthesia, sterile conditions, or rudimentary medical knowledge. Their patients not only survive, they actually get better.

The best known of the group was Arigó (José de Freitas), who worked for many years in the little town of Congonhas do Campo, Brazil. Arigó would perform surgery with rusty table knives and scissors. During the operations, small children and dogs would mill around on the dirt floor of Arigó's hut. He never bothered to wash his hands for surgery.

His method was quite simple—he would slash into people while they stood there unanesthetized. In one reported case of abdominal surgery, he slit his patient's belly, pulled out the colon, chopped off a section, shoved everything back inside the abdominal cavity, and closed the wound by waving his hand at it. Then he punched the patient in the gut and said, "That's it." There are movies of such operations.

The police have a way of catching up with such people as Arigó. He was arrested twice for practicing medicine without a license, so he grudgingly gave up surgery. He took up diagnosis instead.

Here again his method was simple. People would line up and walk by him. He sat at a table and looked at each patient briefly, then scribbled something on a scrap of paper. The scribbles were medical prescriptions written in either Portuguese or German. The patients would take them to pharmacists and have them filled. In 1968, a team of fifteen doctors and scientists from New York came to Congonhas do Campo to study Arigó. They checked his diagnoses and prescriptions and found they were faultless. The prescriptions were very detailed and gave generic and trade names of drugs, correct dosages, and complex (and medically sound) combinations of ingredients.

How did Arigó do it? He said a voice spoke to him in his right ear and told him what to write. The voice belonged to a German doctor named Fritz, who had died in 1918. Arigó said that Dr. Fritz got second opinions when needed from the spirits of a Japanese surgeon and a French specialist.

Arigó died in 1971. During the last fifteen years of his life he had treated over two-million people.

The most active current group of psychic surgeons practice on the island of Luzon in the Philippines. They have a curious connection with Arigó. Most of the Philippine healers belong to the Spiritist Society, an organization founded in 1857 by a Frenchman named Léon Denizarth Hippolyte Rivail (he usually used the name Allan Kardec). The area where Arigó lived also has a large and active Spiritist Society.

The surgeons from the Philippines differ from Arigó in that they are willing to use a few of the trappings of medicine. For example, they will dip cotton into a bowl of tapwater and swab the area of the incision. That does not make the area sterile, but it looks good.

They also differ from Arigó in that they don't bother with knives. They just push their fingers into the skin and pull open the body. Then they remove various strange objects from the patient's insides—bloody masses of flesh and tissue, or long strings of what looks like plastic wrap.

In 1973, a group of ten scientists led by George Meek went to Luzon with fifty of their own patients to test the psychic healers. The scientists concluded that the surgery was genuine and effective. What particularly astounded them was that despite the lack of anesthetics and sterile precautions, there were no cases of infection or postoperative shock.

The surgeon who is best known, and conforms most closely to the pattern, is Tony Agpao. Other healers tend to have their own variations. Josephine Sison will pull rusty nails, plastic bags, cans of film, and pieces of bushes from her patients. Juan Blance makes his incisions from a distance—he merely points a finger, and a cut appears, a clean one with no flow of blood. Jose Mercardo gives what he calls "spirit injections." These are like shots from a hypodermic needle; Mercardo gives them by pointing his finger at the patient's arm from a distance. The patient feels a prick, and most of the time a spot of blood appears at the spot of the injection.

The English biologist and author Lyall Watson devised a way to test Mercardo. Watson stood in line with other patients to receive an injection; he was wearing a sheet of polythene between his arm and his shirt. When he later took off the shirt, he found a neat hole drilled through the polythene. This, to him, ruled out the possibility of hypnotic suggestion. "Plastic is hardly susceptible to hysteria," he says.

Watson also reports an incident that gives some insight into the mental processes of the healers. Once, while Watson was on a boat trip through a remote part of the Philippines, one of his helpers developed a bad toothache. Some of the other Filipino boatmen said they were near the home of a great healer, so the party took a detour and went to the cabin of an old man. The old man didn't look like much, but Watson decided to wait judgment until he could see what he did.

The old man marched over to the patient, reached into the man's mouth with his fingers, and pulled out a molar. This surprised Watson, since he himself had given the tooth several good yanks with a pliers to no avail. But the strangest part was to come. The old man stepped back, pointed at the patient, and a column of army ants began to march out of the patient's mouth. They came by the dozens in orderly rows, trooping out of the man's mouth, down his body, and off into the jungle. Watson was aghast; the Filipino boatmen howled with laughter. This was the healer's idea of a joke—in the local dialect, the word for *army ants* is the same as the word for *pain*. The old man was a painless dentist.

For Further Reading

Arigo's story is given in *Arigó: Surgeon of the Rusty Knife*, by John G. Fuller (New York: Crowell, 1974). For the surgeons of the Philippines, see *Psychic Surgery*, by Tom Valentine (Chicago: Henry Regnery, 1972). David St. Clair gives an overview of the subject in *Psychic Healers* (Garden City: Doubleday, 1974).

Chapter Two

Out Of The Body

(The Astral Plane)

- *Astral Projection*
- *What Happens When You Die?*
- *Psychical Research: From Séance to Laboratory*
- *Great Mediums and Psychics*
- *Ghosts and Poltergeists*
- *Reincarnation and Possession*
- *How to Fake a Séance*
- *Psi Directory*

Astral Projection

In the first chapter of this book, I wrote about the energies associated with the body. Occultists call these energies the *etheric body*, by which they mean the form that animates the physical body.

Knowledge of the etheric body is the first step toward occult knowledge. It is the first step out of the physical. The second step is knowledge of the *astral body*.

The distinction between the etheric and astral bodies might seem frivolous at first glance. However, it comes from ancient yogic traditions that reached the West largely through the efforts of the Theosophical Society. (For the historical development of theosophy see chapter seven under Occult Sects.) According to these traditions, life takes place on no fewer than seven planes of existence.

The most basic plane is the physical—that one we all know about. The next plane is the etheric, to which I devoted chapter one. The third plane is the astral. Here the consciousness, in a body even more refined than the etheric body, can move to some extent in space and time. The etheric body is bound to the physical; the astral body, to a large extent, is not. The four highest planes, which transcend the limitations of time and space altogether, are called mental planes. This system of planes need not be taken literally, but it should indicate the size and complexity of occult systems.

Here is another way of looking at it. We live on a small planet, one of nine, orbiting a star we call the Sun. The Sun is one of some 250 billion stars in our home galazy, the Milky Way. The Milky Way is itself one of a local cluster of galaxies (a cluster being a few dozen). Astronomers say there are three or four billion such clusters of galaxies in the universe; the nearest important galaxy to our local cluster is about two-million light years away.

A yogin or a Buddhist or any sort of occultist would say that the universe thus described is an illusion. Maybe—but it's a very *big* illusion. And it illustrates how, by entering the astral and mental planes, you take the first steps away from your present, tiny corner of the universe (illusory or not).

If the thought of these vast spaces is frightening, remember that you travel in them every night when you go to sleep. It's natural for the astral body to dissociate slightly from the physical body during sleep, which means that you've already traveled astrally many times, although you haven't gone very far.

Some people *have* gone far. Sylvan Muldoon was one. In his book, *The Projection of the Astral Body* (written with Hereward Carrington), he gave the most reliable account we have of astral travel.

The Basic Experience

Muldoon was born in 1903 and grew up in the Midwest. He had his first out-of-the-body experience (OOBE) at the age of twelve, when his mother took him to a Spiritualist Association camp in Iowa one summer. Perhaps Muldoon's surroundings influenced him—he was in a boarding house with several well-known mediums. Perhaps his frail health was a factor in the incident. In any case, he left his body.

Muldoon awoke in the middle of the night and found himself in a "bewildering stupor," neither asleep nor fully conscious. When he tried to shift position, he could not move. He was lying supine (though he was not sure where) with his body rigid and paralyzed. He was rather frightened, of course, and what followed did not make him any more comfortable. His entire body began to vibrate, floating up and down very rapidly; he felt something pulling spasmodically at the back of his head. Given this chaos of sensations, he felt totally lost. But gradually his senses cleared, beginning with his hearing, and he saw that he was indeed lying in his bedroom at the boardinghouse. However, he was floating toward the ceiling.

For about two minutes he lay in midair in this cataleptic state. Then somehow he floated to an upright position and landed on his feet on the floor. Now, at last, he was free to move. With some difficulty—he had trouble keeping his balance—he turned and looked around the room. There was his physical body lying on the bed. A thin, elastic cable led from the physical body's forehead to the back of Muldoon's astral head. In a panic, Muldoon decided he was dead.

Like most twelve-year-olds caught in an extreme situation, he wanted help and reassurance. He decided to find his mother and try to awaken her. Going to his bedroom door, he reached for the knob and unwittingly propelled himself right through the door. He went through the house and tried to shake people awake, but his hands floated through them. Although he was fully aware of his surroundings—the ticking of the clock, the noises outside the house—he could not make contact. For fifteen minutes he moped around in this state; then he felt the cable tug at the back of his head. It had stretched until it was as thin as a thread. Now it began to contract and thicken, and Muldoon again became cataleptic. He floated back toward his physical body until he was hovering over it and the cable was only a few inches long and an inch-and-a-half thick. Then, with a painful shock, he rejoined his physical body and found he was awake and alive.

This was the end of Muldoon's first OOBE. There would be many more. In the spring of 1927, for example, he awoke in his astral body and travelled to a park he had never seen before. "I noted particularly a high rocky wall," he wrote, "and two small bridges crossing a stream. I had no memory of ever having visited this particular place, nor did I know where the place was. . . . It was two months later when, on a trip with a friend, I accidentally entered a park in a town about fifty miles from my home, and discovered it was the same place I had formerly visited in the astral!"

On another occasion, a moonlit summer night in Wisconsin in 1924, Muldoon felt himself propelled at a bewildering speed to a strange house. He found himself in a room with four people. One of them, an attractive teenage girl, was sewing a black dress. As was his habit, Muldoon observed the people and the room as carefully as he could. Then he willed himself back to his physical body. As he left, he noticed that he had been in a farmhouse. Six weeks later, he saw the teenage girl on a street in his town. He introduced himself to her. At first she was wary of him; but when he described her sitting room to her, she became intrigued and agreed to take him to her home. The home, a farmhouse, was fifteen miles out of town, and it was exactly as Muldoon had seen it on his astral trip.

Muldoon thought the easiest way of learning to travel astrally was to develop what he called "dream control." You must learn to remain conscious right up to the moment when you fall asleep. If you cannot focus your attention well enough for this—many people can't—try holding one arm in the air when you go to bed. As you drop off to sleep, the arm will sway and fall toward the bed. That should give you a slight jolt, enough to keep you aware, but not enough to awaken you entirely. Then, in this borderline state, concentrate on a dream. The dream should involve rising—flying in an airplane, for example, or going up in an elevator. The consciously controlled dream, combined with the astral body's tendency to dissociate from the physical with sleep, should help you lift off.

There are some interesting confirmations of Muldoon's experiences. His British contemporary Oliver Fox also began to have OOBE's as a result of sleep and dream experiences. In the first, he dreamed he was standing on the sidewalk outside his home. The dream was quite vivid, with all the details clear and colorful. Fox strolled around in his dream, enjoying the morning sunshine and the sight of some tall trees down the road. But then he noticed something strange. The pavement in front of his house, he knew, was made of small, rectangular stones set with their long sides perpendicular to the curb. In his dream, the long sides of the stones were parallel to the curb. When he saw that, Fox knew he was dreaming. Yet he did not awaken. He found, rather, that he could remain in the dream state and control the events of the dream. He could levitate, pass through walls, glide quickly over the ground, and move objects without touching them. He called such dreams, in which he knew he was dreaming, Dreams of Knowledge.

As a Dream of Knowledge wore on, Fox would begin to feel a pain at the back of his head. (Compare this to the cord Muldoon felt connecting him to his physical body.) As the pain increased, Fox would become aware of his physical body and its surroundings. At the same time, he remained aware of his dream surroundings. Before long, Fox would return to the physical.

He began to wonder what would happen if he resisted the pain in his head and tried to stay out of the physical. One night, he dreamed he was walking by the sea in the early morning. The pain came, and he fought it. Something clicked in his head, and he was free.

"It seemed to me," he wrote, "that the apparently solid shore and sunlit waves were not the physical land and sea; that my body was lying in bed, half-a-mile away at Forest View; but I could not feel the *truth* of this. I seemed to be completely severed from that physical body. At this point I became aware of a man and boy approaching. As they passed me they were talking together; they did not seem to see me, but I was not quite sure. A little later, however, when I met another man and asked him the time, he took no notice and was evidently unaware of my presence."

At this point Fox began to worry. Could he end the dream? Was he dead? With a great effort of will he forced himself to awaken in his bedroom. He was paralyzed. He lay there in panic, trying to move, and eventually managed to wiggle one of his fingers. Gradually, he regained the use of his other fingers, then his hands and feet, and finally he came back to his body.

What was the click he had felt in his head? Fox thought it was the astral body going through the pineal gland. With practice, Fox learned to project his astral body at will. He would concentrate on gathering his "incorporeal self" and forcing it to the pineal gland, which would open like a trapdoor, he said, and then click shut after the astral body had escaped.

Another interesting confirmation of Muldoon's and Fox's experiences comes from the English novelist William Gerhardi, who wrote about an OOBE in his book *Resurrection*, published in 1934.

THE THIRD EYE

Vedic literature says that the body's highest source of power is the space between the eyebrows. This space is called the third eye; it is the location of the next-to-highest *chakra* (see chapter one, under 'Yoga'.) It is also the location of the pineal gland.

For many years anatomists knew nothing about the pineal's function. They called it the pineal body. In 1886, German and English reserachers, working independently, discovered that the pineal had evolved from a light-sensitive spot still visible in some reptiles. The pineal was in fact a vestigial third eye.

It turns out to be more than that. In 1959, Aaron Lerner at Yale University discovered that the pineal is a gland that secretes a hormone called melatonin. The function of melatonin is not clear. We do know that melatonin is derived from serotonin, a chemical similar in molecular structure to LSD. Serotonin is naturally present in the brain.

Serotonin is also present in dates, plums, bananas, and the wild figs that grow from banyan and bo trees. According to tradition, Gautama Buddha attained enlightenment while sitting under a bo tree.

His experience, too, began in sleep. Gerhardi rose horizontally out of his body, as Muldoon had. He floated in that position for several minutes and then felt himself being pushed forward till he was standing. He was attached to the physical body in much the same way as Muldoon had been. A "coil of light," like the "strong broad ray of dusty light at the back of a dark cinema projecting onto the screen in front," ran from Gerhardi's astral body to his physical body. He saw that the light "illumined the face on the pillow, as if attached to the brow of the sleeper. The sleeper was myself, not dead, but breathing peacefully, my mouth slightly open." The coil of light, "like an umbilical cord," was the means by which the astral body kept the physical body alive.

Gerhardi wandered through his apartment, observing things carefully so that he could confirm upon waking that his experience had not been a dream. He found his senses were the same as usual, except for the sense of touch. He seemed to have no grip and would pass through objects when he tried to touch them. After a while, he was pushed "like a half-filled balloon" and flew outside. After a period of hovering around, he came back to the physical body with a jerk. When he checked the details he'd observed while in his astral body, he found they were all exact.

Other Cases

Not all OOBE's begin in sleep. Some are generated purely by an act of will. One outstanding case of this sort, known as the Verity Case, came to the attention of Edmund Gurney of the British Society for Psychical Research late in the last century. The astral traveller was a young man named S.H. Beard, who by force of will one Sunday night at 1:00 A.M. visited his fiancée, Miss L.S. Verity. He projected himself into the front bedroom on the second floor of her house, where she and her young sister slept. A few days after Beard's experiment, Miss Verity told him that at 1:00 A.M. on the night in question, she had suddenly awakened and seen him standing by her bed. Miss Verity screamed and awakened her sister, who also saw Beard. Then the figure vanished. Both women gave signed statements about the experience to Gurney.

About a year later, Beard performed his experiment again. Miss Verity was now living in a different house. (This was evidently one of those interminable Victorian engagements.) This time Miss Verity did not see Beard (she remained asleep), but her sister did. Beard approached the sister, stroked her hair, and held her hand. Gurney again got confirmation of the event, as he did in a third case. He discussed all this in a book he wrote with F.W.H. Myers and Frank Podmore, *Phantasms of the Living*.

Great stress also can trigger an OOBE. One of the most intriguing cases of this sort involved a man named Robert Bruce, who in 1828 was sailing as a first mate on a trading ship going from England to Canada. One day Bruce went into the captain's cabin on an errand and found a strange man sitting there, writing on a slate. The man looked up at Bruce; Bruce ran off. He reported the incident to the captain, and the two men went back to the cabin. The stranger was gone, but the slate was still there. On it were the words, "Steer to the Nor'west."

The captain, a skeptical man, assumed Bruce was playing a trick on him. He ordered Bruce to write the words "Steer to the Nor'west" on the other side of the slate. Bruce did so; the handwritings were completely different. So the captain ordered the ship searched for a stowaway, and meanwhile he had every member of the crew write the strange message. There was no stowaway on board; the handwritings did not match.

The captain was skeptical, but he also had a healthy curiosity. He ordered a change of course, to the northwest. After three hours, he came upon a ship, wrecked on an iceberg. He sent boats to rescue the survivors. In the third boat to return sat the man Robert Bruce had seen in the cabin. When the captain asked this man to write "Steer to the Nor'west" on the slate, the man's script matched the phantom handwriting. The man said he did not remember ever having been in the captain's cabin or writing those words; but that day he had fallen asleep in his exhaustion and dreamed about a ship that was coming to the rescue. On waking, he had given the other shipwreck victims a description of the ship he had seen. It matched Robert Bruce's ship.

Many cases of astral projection occur at moments of great physical danger. Of the various types of spontaneous OOBE, these are the ones that most interest researchers because they are the easiest to verify. Two well-known cases, which occurred during surgery, are all but conclusive evidence of the out-of-the-body state.

The first case was reported by the eminent British surgeon George Sava in 1953. He had performed an operation on an elderly woman, Mrs. Frances Gail. After the operation she lapsed into a coma. Dr. Sava rushed to the hospital and tried to save her life. Mrs. Gail recovered, and when she did she told Dr. Sava that she'd been out of her body and had watched the entire operation. Among other things, she told him that "You kept my body lying there under the anesthetic while you and the others discussed whether it was strong enough to withstand what you proposed to do. You took away some pieces of bone. You were chiefly troubled about the anesthetic and said to the anesthetist: 'Do you think she can stand three hours of it? Heart all right?' The anesthetist just nodded and said, 'She's okay, especially considering she's no chicken.' Is that right?" Dr. Sava admitted it was.

The second such case was reported by Dr. Russell MacRobert of the Lenox Hill Hospital in New York City. Dr. MacRobert was performing an ear operation on a clergyman who had been put under a strong anesthetic.

As Dr. MacRobert began the operation, he saw that one of his instruments was missing. The doctor swore, took off his gloves, and left the operating room. He came back a minute later with the necessary instrument. While a nurse sterilized it, the surgeon put on fresh gloves and a gown. Then he proceeded with the operation. Later, when the patient came out of the anesthetic, he described all these details to Dr. MacRobert. He even reproved the doctor jokingly for swearing in front of a clergyman.

Perhaps the most convincing story of this sort is one reported by F.J.M. Stratton, in 1957, in the *Journal of the Society for Psychical Research*. The story concerns a medical officer of the British Royal Flying Corps who crashed during take-off and was knocked unconscious. The doctor remembered looking down on the scene from a height of about 200 feet. He saw his body lying on the ground, face-up. He saw a brigadier and a pilot rush toward his body, and he saw the airfield ambulance start for the crash site and then stall. He then felt himself travelling through space away from the airfield and out over the Atlantic. The doctor awoke (if that is the right term) shortly thereafter, under treatment by an orderly. The others at the crash later confirmed everything he had seen while out of his body. The only way he could have been aware of all the details was from the position he said he was in, 200 feet up.

Contemporary research has turned up some useful facts about OOBE's. Celia Green, of the Institute of Psychophysical Research in Oxford, England, did a survey of 326 people who'd reported OOBE's. She gave her findings in a book titled *Out-of-the-Body Experiences*. Of this group, 12 percent reported the experience as having occurred during sleep, 25 percent at a time of psychological stress, 32 percent at a moment of physical danger or under an anesthetic. The remainder, an astonishing 31 percent, said they had had the experience while awake and going about their business. The majority of people—60 percent—claimed only one OOBE; most of these people were between the ages of fifteen and thirty-five. Another 21 percent reported six or more OOBE's. Among these people, the experience had been common since childhood. The vast majority of people surveyed said they had not experienced being in an astral body; they had simply become a "disembodied consciousness."

Researchers are also busy studying OOBE's in the laboratory. Among these scientists are Charles T. Tart at the University of California, Janet Mitchell at the American Society for Psychical Research, and Russell Targ and Harold Puthoff at the Stanford Research Institute. These researchers will take a talented subject—for example, the New York artist Ingo Swann—and put him through a test controlled in such a way that positive results can only be obtained through out-of-the-body travel. For example, they will lay drawings on a platform suspended over the subject's head and ask the subject to reproduce the drawings. Or they will name a geographical coordinate (49°20′S and 70°14′E, for example) and ask the subject what he sees. Swann, for one, has performed quite well on these tests. In the geographical test, Swann has scored 43 percent hits and 32 percent near-misses.

For Further Reading

For more information on these case histories, see *Astral Projection*, by Oliver Fox (New Hyde Park, N.Y.: University Books, 1962); *Resurrection*, by William A. Gerhardi (London: Cassell, 1934); *Out-of-the-Body Experiences*, by Celia Green (London: Oxford University Press, 1968); and *The Projection of the Astral Body*, by Sylvan Muldoon (London: Rider, 1968).

How to Leave Your Body

Robert A. Monroe has given the most detailed, practical advice yet on astral travel in his book *Journeys Out of the Body* (New York: Doubleday, 1971). This section will rely largely on his instructions.

Monroe, a businessman, first had an OOBE in 1958. Since then he has learned to control the process and has travelled astrally dozens, perhaps hundreds, of times. His book provides a useful summary of his experiences in three principal astral locales. Locale I is the world we ordinarily perceive with our senses, the one most casual, one-time astral travellers go through. Locale II is a nonphysical world, a place of thought rather than matter. Here Monroe learned about his past lives and met spirits, not all of them friendly. Some attacked him viciously; he says an astral traveller must always be prepared to deal with such attacks. (He has no specific recommendations for self-defense, saying just that one must fight back spontaneously and desperately.) Finally, Locale III is a world parallel to the one we know, particularly in its physical aspects, which are quite similar to those of our world (or Locale I). However, its history and customs are different, and the society there has a different and somewhat simpler technology.

In preparing for an OOBE, physical conditions are important. The air should be clear and dry, and the temperature should be fairly warm, at least 20° C (or 64° F—a warmer temperature is even better). Do not try the experiment during an electrical storm—there should be as few energetic interferences as possible. Some astral travellers "anchor" themselves by putting one hand into a bowl of water. This, too, is for purposes of controlling bioenergy—the water acts as a ground. Monroe recommends fasting before an OOBE, but if you must eat, make it fresh fruit and green vegetables, and eat as few of them as possible. Breathe deeply and evenly, and hold the breath in for a while each time. (Lyall Watson says these diet and breathing practices are useful in that they decrease the availability of oxygen to the brain, thereby slowing the mind and reducing activity in the forebrain.)

The most important preparation of all is to recognize and admit to the fact that you are afraid of leaving the body. Monroe says that even people who want very much to experience astral travel are afraid to try seriously. Once they succeed, they become afraid of dying, and they dive right back into the physical body. Then they're afraid to try again. This fear is nothing to be ashamed of, but it must be overcome.

You must also learn how to enter a borderline sleep state. This can be done through Sylvan Muldoon's technique, described earlier; Monroe recommends the practice of meditation or self-hypnosis. Or try concentrating on a single image as you go to sleep. If you can be right on the edge of sleep and still have the image in mind, you've made a start.

Now, go into a darkened room and lie along the north-south axis. Clothes should be loose, and you should wear no jewelry. Lie supine. Do not cross the arms or legs—that sets up a bioenergetic circuit with your own body, which will hold you back. Make sure there will be no interruptions, and do not set a time limit for the experiment. There should be no distractions.

Go into the borderline sleep state. Breathe evenly through your mouth. Now look into the blackness in front of your eyes. Try to see about six feet into the blackness; then direct your gaze upward about six feet. You should feel waves of vibration come into your head and enter your body. Some people panic when they feel the vibrations; others get excited by them and inadvertently shut them off. You must relax and learn to control the vibrations. If they make you uncomfortable, remember that you can break the connection just by willing yourself to sit up. If you are willing to go on with the experiment, you have to direct the waves through your body and get a feeling for their cycles and their strength. They should eventually be steady and rapid. As the vibrations accelerate, you will begin to leave your physical body.

At this point, you must keep all thoughts out of your mind. If necessary, concentrate on a single thought. Under no circumstances let your mind wander. This is a delicate business—you have to go with the experience, but at the same time, you must exert your will on the astral body. To help with this, Monroe has devised the following exercises.

First, imagine yourself reaching out with one hand to an object you know is nearby but out of reach. Do not strain, but extend your hand mentally until you touch the object. Feel the surface carefully, so you can check yourself later.

Next, raise the astral body's hands and bring the fingers together while your physical hands remain at your sides. Try to see both the physical and astral hands while your physical eyes remain closed.

Lastly, think of getting lighter, of floating. Or think of rolling over 180°. This should take you out of your physical body. Don't go more than three feet away from the physical body the first time. To return to the physical, just think of going back. You should feel a slight click when you return. Later, on longer trips, you will require a return signal for yourself, any gesture that will remind you of your physical body—clenching your fists, for example, or taking a deep breath.

You'll find that the astral body is subject to gravity to some extent, because it weighs 69.5 grams. Dr. Duncan McDougall in England and Dr. Zaalberg Van Zelst in The Hague, working independently, conducted tests in which they weighed people who were dying. Both doctors recorded the same results—a sudden loss of weight of 69.5 grams at death.

Astral travel can also be sexually stimulating. Monroe found this a terrible psychological trap. At first he never got very far in the astral body because he would immediately start thinking about sex. He'd go back to the physical body right away and try to do something about it. He had to train himself to control the impulse for a while. Monroe devotes a lot of attention to his sexual struggles; he is, however, the only astral traveller of note who complains about this problem.

If you succeed in having an OOBE with Monroe's methods, you should write to Dr. Charles T. Tart, P.O. Box 5366, New York, New York 10017. He would like to hear from you.

What Happens When You Die?

From all accounts, there's a great similarity between astral projection and death. One of the experiences all astral travellers report is a fear of dying. They want to know who's going to take care of their bodies while they're gone. Many travellers also believe the answer is that the astral body keeps the physical body alive through that strange umbilical cord, the coil of light, that runs between the two forms.

It would seem, then, that the difference between astral travel and death is that death severs the cord. What happens then?

The Findings of Researchers

Elisabeth Kübler-Ross and Raymond A. Moody, working independently, indeed without any knowledge of each other, have accumulated reports from hundreds of people who had been clinically dead or very near death and then came back. Their conclusions are virtually identical. There is a life after death, and it's not at all bad.

Here is what to expect. At the moment of death, you will hear a loud noise, a ringing or perhaps a buzzing. This is an unpleasant and disconcerting sound. At the same time, you will start to move through a long, dark tunnel, as if being pulled from the other side. Some people describe it as a funnel, or a tube, or a trough, or even a sewer. One of Moody's informants, one of the few who put his experience in conventional religious terms, said the tunnel was the Valley of the Shadow of Death. The tunnel seems airless, and you will move along it rapidly, headfirst. There will be just enough room for your astral body to fit.

You probably will not realize you're out of your physical body until the tunnel experience is over, and you find yourself hovering near your corpse. If you have died in a hospital, you may observe the staff's attempts to save your life; many people who have died and returned to life have expressed some contempt for these efforts. You might feel that you have become pure consciousness, but many people say they became astral bodies. With the astral body come astral senses—clairvoyance and telepathy.

More than one person reported a feeling of helplessness at this point. Where do you go? Usually other spirits begin to appear to you: friends and relatives who have died, or spiritual guides. The locale of your death begins to fade.

Then a light will shine, at first dimly, but it will grow brighter until it's dazzling. It will not become blinding, though, nor will it hurt the eyes. It is a person, a being, though one without a body as we know it, and it will draw you to itself by its warmth and evident love. It will speak with you telepathically, asking you if you're ready to die. And it will ask you what you think of your past life. Apparently, there is nothing judgmental in this question; the being asks it in a spirit of acceptance and love, as if each person had brought a precious gift to this being. The being's question will set off an immediate, intense review of your life, which you will see in three-dimensional, colored images.

Then you come to the barrier. This is a borderline, or a fence, or a curtain of mist. Moody's and Kübler-Ross's informants said that, at this point, the being sent them away from the barrier, back to their physical bodies. If it is in fact time for you to die, you will pass through the barrier.

From this point on, the testimony comes from mediums, and there are different versions. The account given by Seth, Jane Roberts's spirit control, has caught the attention of many occultists. Seth says that people get mostly what they expect when they die. People who are convinced the afterlife is mere oblivion may black-out for a while. People who expect pearly gates or hellfire will probably hallucinate accordingly. There are spirit guides whose special duties are to act out whatever afterlife the new arrival expected. Seth claims he once had a Muslim who believed Moses and Muhammad would fight over his soul; Seth had to arrange a whole battle for the man, complete with fiery armies clashing in the sky.

Why all the charades? Seth claims the spirit guides have to make sure that the new arrivals become used to death. Then the spirit guides explain to them, being careful not to go too slowly or too fast, the nature of reincarnation, and they explain to the souls their choices. They can reincarnate; go back over past lives and redo them, so to speak, living out variations of them and correcting old mistakes; or they can leave the world they've lived in and go to some different world. (The soul can't choose the third option unless it's lived out a complete reincarnational cycle.)

Those choosing to reincarnate may go about it in several ways. Some souls are specialists—they like to stay within one historical period, or have similar characteristics in each life. Some want to learn all they can about the physical world, and so they lead many short lives, spreading them through many historical periods and geographical areas. Some souls are on kind of a group tour, going through their reincarnational cycle with a few friends. Whatever plan the soul has, the spirit guides are there to give it counselling and help it make productive choices. (For more on Seth's beliefs, see the article on Jane Roberts in this chapter, under "Great Mediums and Psychics.")

The Lessons of the Bardo Thödol

There is an older and more respectable account that is more detailed and in accord with some of the reports we have from people who were clinically dead. This account is in the *Tibetan Book of the Dead*, or *Bardo Thödol*.

Translated literally, *Bardo Thödol* means "Liberation by Hearing on the

After-Death Plane." The book's origins lie in the very ancient Tibetan religion of Bonism. Followers of Bonism would study about life after death so they could be prepared for it. In their last moments and after their deaths, priests would read to them from the *Bardo Thödol* to help their spirits remember the teachings. The aim was to help them avoid reincarnation. If the spirit could succeed in remembering the *Bardo Thödol*'s teachings, it would not be deceived by the experience of the afterlife, and so it would escape the cycle of rebirth.

No one knows what the original, Bonist *Bardo Thödol* was like. The version we have was written down in the eighth century A.D. by the Great Guru Padma Sambhava, who introduced Tantric Buddhism to Tibet. (For more information on Tantric Buddhism, see chapter one under "Yoga.")

According to the *Bardo Thödol*, there are three stages of life after death. The first is *Chikhai Bardo*, in which the spirit that has just died loses all sense of ego and sees what is known as the Clear Light. (Compare this to the being of light seen by Moody's and Kübler-Ross's subjects.) This Clear Light is not a person. It is formless, uncreated, so primal that it cannot even be called a force. Souls that are very highly developed melt into the Clear Light. All others turn away from its blinding power and try to escape it. At that moment, the soul falls back into selfhood, and it must proceed to the next stage of the afterlife.

The second stage is *Chönyid Bardo*. The soul encounters seven peaceful deities (each of which has an opposite) and fifty-eight wrathful deities. The wrathful deities are truly fearsome; they torture the soul in terrible ways. And yet, no matter which deities the soul encounters, no matter what happens, the soul must remember that all these events are visions. If it succeeds in remembering that, it will not have to proceed any farther through the afterlife. Thus, it can escape the cycle of rebirth. (There's no reason to fear stopping at the level of the wrathful deities, by the way. According to Lama Anagarika Govinda, the wrathful deities are "only the former Peaceful Deities in changed aspect." So if you remember the teachings while in their company, you won't necessarily be tortured by them for eternity. And eventually, you can work your way back to the Clear Light.)

If the soul manages to go through the whole series of visions without understanding that all these events are illusory, it enters the third stage, *Sidpa Bardo*. On this level, the soul meets Yama-Raja, King and Judge of the Dead, who examines the souls with his karma-mirror and assigns them to their just places. The soul, now on its way to rebirth, undergoes the same process the world went through in its creation. Five elements emerge: fire, air, water, earth, and ether. Fire produces vital heat, lust, the emotions, and the Wisdom of Discrimination. Air produces breath, envy, the will, and the All-Performing Wisdom. Water produces the stream of life, anger, consciousness, and the Mirrorlike Wisdom. Earth produces the physical body, egoism, touch, and the Wisdom of Equality. Ether produces the mind and also enlightened consciousness.

Toward the end of *Sidpa Bardo* the soul attempts to return to its old body. However, as it sees whatever has become of the body, the soul will panic at its inability to return to it. The soul that comprehends this as only a vision will remain unborn. The soul that does not understand this has to undergo yet another incarnation.

There are six states of existence it sees as it approaches rebirth. These are: *devaloka* (great sages and enlightened people), *asuraloka* (heroes and powerful people), *manakaloka* (ordinary, competent humans), *tiryakaloka* (distorted people who resemble animals more than they do humans), *pretaloka* ("hungry ghosts," or neurotics), and *narakaloka* (hell, or the psychotic state).

The *Bardo Thödol* presents all this as a picture of what happens during the forty-nine days between death and rebirth. But, as Lama Anagarika Govinda explains, the *Bardo Thödol* is intended more as a way of teaching wisdom to the living. The book teaches you how to experience the death of the ego. Or, more precisely, it teaches you how to erase the distinction between the experience of life and that of death. Both are purely psychological, in the deepest sense. As C.G. Jung wrote in a commentary, "Not only the 'wrathful' but also the 'peaceful' deities are conceived as *sangsāric* projections of the human psyche, an idea that seems all too obvious to the enlightened European, because it reminds him of his own banal simplifications. But though the European can easily explain away these deities as projections, he would be quite incapable of positing them at the same time as real." (Jung's commentary is included in the edition of the translation by W.Y. Evans-Wentz, published by Oxford University Press, 1957.)

The gods of the *Bardo Thödol* are all in the mind. But they are no less real. The *Book of the Dead* is a map of the psyche, but it's a guide to the afterlife as well. This is the great lesson the *Bardo Thödol* can teach, not only about death but about all experience. Psychological reality is not only as important as external reality, but ultimately it *is* external reality.

The rest of this chapter will describe more strange and spooky things, which might make sense if you keep Jung's explanation in mind. Judge for yourself.

For Further Reading

For Elisabeth Kübler-Ross's theories, see *Death: The Final Stage of Growth* (Englewood Cliffs: Prentice-Hall, 1975). For Raymond Moody, see *Life After Life* (New York: Bantam, 1976).

Psychical Research: From Séance to Laboratory

Modern psychical research began in a shabby wood cabin in New York State and within a few years was being conducted principally by English lords and Cambridge dons. Its start was virtually contemporaneous with the development of the theory of evolution, and it was in large part a reaction against that theory. In its present form, it looks for support to the latest theories of physics and biology. It has spent more effort against fraud, and more often been defrauded, than any other branch of research. Here, as nowhere else, spiritual science has confronted traditional science by attempting to give hard evidence for its claims.

The First Spiritualists

The story begins with the Fox sisters, who in 1848 were living with their parents in a shack in Hydesville, New York. Margaret at the time was ten years old; her sister Kate was seven.

In March of that year, strange rattlings and rappings began to disturb the Fox family at night. On the night of March 31, the girls' father grew impatient with the noises, got out of bed, and rattled a window, thinking it might be loose. From somewhere in the room came an answering rattle. At this point Kate Fox decided to talk to the noises. "Do as I do," she said and clapped her hands. The same number of claps came back in reply. Margaret joined the game and counted aloud to four. Four raps sounded.

Soon the Foxes were communicating with whatever was making the noises. They would ask the presence questions that could be answered either yes or no; one rap meant yes, and two raps meant no. Eventually, they pieced together the presence's story. It was the spirit of a murdered peddler; its body lay buried beneath the cottage.

The noises in the house began to get worse. The Foxes heard what sounded like a death struggle, gurgling noises, the sound of a body being dragged across the floor. Finally the family left. Kate went to live with her brother David in Auburn, and Margaret and her parents joined her older sister Leah in Rochester. But the noises followed; in Leah's house there were poltergeist activities, too. Unable to stand the commotion, Leah tried to communicate with the spirit in her house. She recited the alphabet, and the spirit rapped at different letters; in this way it spelled a message for her. The message was, "Dear friends, you must proclaim this truth in the world. This is the dawning of a new era; you must not try to conceal it any longer. When you do your duty God will protect you and good spirits will watch over you."

Leah took this message to heart and organized the first meeting of Spiritualists on November 14, 1849, in Rochester's Corinthian Hall. On

November 28, she gave her first private séance. Margaret and Kate soon joined her as professional mediums.

They did not always have an easy time of it. There were accusations of fraud from the start; and no doubt some people feared the rapping came from demons. When the Foxes went on tour, their lives were threatened, and on one occasion they faced a lynch mob. In later life, relations among the sisters were strained; Margaret, widowed and ill, was living in poverty while Leah continued to perform as a successful medium. In an act perhaps intended to ruin Leah, Margaret wrote a letter to the *New York Herald* in 1888, confessing to fraud. She then gave a demonstration at New York's Academy of Music in which she claimed to show that the spirit rappings were nothing more than the sound of her snapping her toe joints, which she said she could do at will. Kate joined Margaret in making a confession. Later Margaret retracted her confession, claiming that it had been done to make money—perhaps so. Leah died in 1890, Kate in 1892, and Margaret in 1893. By then the movement they had started was far too large and strong for any one to hinder.

The Founders of Psychical Research

Spiritualism had spread rapidly to England; the first Spiritualist church there was established in 1853. Two years later, a clergyman's son named Henry Sidgwick went up to Trinity College, Cambridge, became interested in communication with the dead, and joined the Cambridge Ghost Society. Largely through his efforts, Spiritualism became psychical research.

Sidgwick was a brilliant scholar and a man of unquestioned moral integrity. He was elected a Fellow of Trinity College in 1859, but soon resigned his fellowship and assistant tutorship because he could not in conscience sign the Church of England's thirty-nine Articles of Faith, as all fellows were required to do. It was a mark of his colleagues' respect for him

---

HOW TO COMMUNICATE WITH SPIRITS ELECTRONICALLY

Just turn on a tape recorder, ask to speak with the spirits, and ask them questions. Leave enough time for them to answer each question, and make sure you've got the machine on record. Then play back the tape at high volume. It usually takes a number of playbacks before you can hear spirit voices. The better your tape equipment, the better the results will be (though some people say this is only a psychological factor). Be patient and listen carefully.

This is a method developed by Friedrich Jurgenson, Friedebert Karger, and Konstantin Raudive in experiments from 1959 to 1965. Raudive published the results in *Breakthrough: An Amazing Experiment in Electronic Communication with the Dead* (New York: Taplinger, 1971). In experiments conducted in England to test the method, the voice of Artur Schnabel addressed an old friend in attendance, Sir Robert Mayer, spoke to him in German, and mentioned many private matters.

---

that they still made a place for him in the college, appointing him Lecturer in Moral Science. He remained at that post till his death in 1900.

He also continued his psychical research. For this purpose he recruited an outstanding student of his, Frederic W.H. Myers, as well as a medical doctor named Edmund Gurney, the physicist Lord Rayleigh, and Arthur Balfour (who would later become prime minister). Myers and Gurney were also clergymens' sons. In 1882 Sidgwick became president of the Society for Psychical Research. He did not want the job, but he accepted it at the request of the Society's founder, Sir William Barrett, who said that no one else had the reputation or the moral authority needed.

Sidgwick and his colleagues spent a great deal of time collecting and evaluating evidence of psychic events. They also generated some evidence on their own, largely through research on Mrs. Leonore Piper, a medium whom they studied from 1889 to 1911. Piper had as her control a French doctor named Phinuit who spoke no French and had no medical knowledge. Nonetheless, Phinuit was useful to her—he helped her pass the Society's ESP tests. Once, for example, the physicist Sir Oliver Lodge obtained a watch that had belonged to an uncle of his who had died twenty years previously; he gave the watch to Piper. As soon as it was in her hands, Phinuit identified the owner and then contacted the uncle's spirit. The spirit gave Lodge information that Lodge had never heard but which he later verified to his satisfaction. Lodge, who'd been careful in devising this test, could think of no way Piper could have gotten that information or even known he would ask about his uncle. Nor, obviously, could she have gotten the information telepathically from Lodge.

Despite her talents, Piper produced a lot of nonsense and equivocation while in trance. She also developed a rather strange group of controls, including George Eliot. When the Society for Psychical Research had finished with her, she returned to America, where she had been born. She was not, however, finished with the Society. She began to get messages from Myers, who had died in 1901.

The strange thing about these messages was that somebody else was getting similar ones at the same time. Myers had had a friend from Cambridge, Mrs. A. W. Verrall, who was a lecturer in classics at Newnham. After Myers's death, Verrall had tried to contact his spirit by means of automatic writing. At first she would put pen to paper, close her eyes, and wait, while nothing happened. Eventually, though, the pen began to move and produce some curiously worded Latin and Greek texts signed "Myers." The texts came through at about the same time as Piper's messages from Myers, and they alluded to the same subjects.

This was only the beginning. Verrall's daughter Helen began to get similar messages before she had seen her mother's writing. A sister of Rudyard Kipling's, Mrs. Alice Fleming, wrote to Verrall from India to say that she, too, had received messages in automatic writing from Myers. Fleming had not known about Verrall's messages, but Myers had instructed her to write to Mrs. Verrall at 5 Selwyn Gardens, Cambridge. From 1908 to 1915, still more automatists joined: Mrs. Willett, Dame Edith Lyttleton, Mrs. Stuart Wilson. All the texts they were writing were full of classical allusions far above the level of any of the automatists except for the Verralls. Eventually there were three thousand texts, which are now in the archives of the Society for Psychical Research. Many of the texts are quoted in *Evidence of Personal Survival from Cross Correspondences*, by H.F. Saltmarch (London: G. Bell, 1938).

Upon examination, the texts work like a jigsaw puzzle. A word of Latin will appear one day; the next day another automatist will write a related word in English; on the third day, still another automatist will produce a line of poetry. Only when put together do the three clues become coherent. In these communications, Myers claimed that he had devised the texts in collaboration with Sidgwick and Gurney. Gurney had died in 1888; Sidgwick, in 1900. Their purpose was to provide mediumistic material that could have come only from those three scholars, thereby proving that they had survived death.

While Mrs. Verrall was busy taking dictation from Myers, her dead husband was giving his own dictation to Mrs. Winifred Coombe Tennant of Glamorganshire, Wales. From 1910 to 1915, Mrs. Tennant got joint spirit messages from Dr. Verrall and from his friend Henry Butcher, who had been Professor of Greek at Edinburgh. The communications form what is known as the Ear of Dionysius Case, since they were concerned in large part with a Sicilian grotto of that name. Again, the spirits claimed they had chosen an obscure subject to prove their identities. One has to judge their efforts a partial success at least, since the material they dictated was far beyond Tennant's comprehension. The spirits told her to keep the scripts secret from Mrs. Verrall until they were finished. Only when Mrs. Verrall examined the completed series of texts did their meaning become clear. (Mrs. Tennant, who was active in the Liberal Party, later became a British delegate to the League of Nations.)

The Coming of Parapsychology

Stories such as these were fascinating, but they did have shortcomings. They would not convince a skeptic, of course, nor did they offer any information as to the nature of psychic experiences. In addition, they seemed to indicate a degree of stagnation, or at least insularity, in psychical research: Myers had run the show while he was at Cambridge, and now that he was dead he was still running the show.

A much-needed new departure in psychical research came in 1927, when J.B. Rhine and his wife Louisa, both of whom had recently earned doctorates in botany, went to work at Duke University. Together with J.G. Pratt and a group of others, they developed the science of parapsychology.

As the Rhines explain it, parapsychology is that branch of natural science that investigates events that arise from the human personality and are not explicable wholly in physical terms. These events are of two main kinds: extrasensory perception (awareness by the subject of an object) and psychokinesis (action of the subject upon an object). Within the field of ESP there are further divisions: telepathy (thought transfer), clairvoyance (extrasensory awareness of objects or events rather than of mental states), and precognition and retrocognition (seeing forward and backward in time). Taken all together, these phenomena are called *psi*. The name is merely a convenient abbreviation, the Greek letter at the beginning of the word *psyche*, or soul. It should be pronounced *psee*. It is universally pronounced *sigh*.

Psi phenomena are universal. The Bible is full of psychokinesis and precognition—think of the prophetic dreams, the miraculous cures, the ascensions to Heaven. In the lives of the saints, too, there are angelic voices, levitations, stigmata, appearances of spirits. Nor is psi confined to that particular tradition. The Celts have spoken of Second Sight since pre-Christian times. The aborigines of Australia construct their entire world-view around the concept of the Dreaming. And, on a more everyday level, telepathy is common between twins. What the parapsychologists have done is to construct a method by which we can examine psi, rather than simply marvel at it.

How do you test for psi? Rhine and his associates at Duke have used games. They will test for clairvoyance by laying down cards and having the subject try to guess what they are. Rhine's cards (which are available from Haines House of Cards in Norwood, Ohio) are a deck of twenty-five with five suits: stars, circles, squares, crosses, and waves. S.G. Soal, who found those too boring, uses suits of penguins, lions, elephants, giraffes, and zebras. To test for psychokinesis (PK), Rhine sees if his subjects can affect the fall of dice. Experiments in telepathy involve rather complicated guessing games. In all these tests, there are strict controls.

In trying to establish parapsychology as a science, researchers run into certain problems of method. First, there is the possibility of fraud, either on the part of the subject or of the researcher. This is a widespread problem in scientific research; all you can do is guard against it. The second problem is verifiability. Ideally, any scientist anywhere should be able to duplicate the results of your experiments. In parapsychology this simply is not possible. First, the work is done with talented individuals; even if they were willing to travel and make themselves available to other researchers, the results might vary considerably. Second, parapsychologists, to some degree, elicit the results from their subjects. The atmosphere of the experiment is very important; another researcher might not be able to encourage the same results. Finally, there is the problem of the evidence itself. Many of the parapsychologists' findings are in the form of statistics. Researchers calculate the odds against something happening by chance, then show that the event *did* happen, even though odds against it were extremely high. However, this still leaves open the possibility, however small, that the event was random. Here the parapsychologist would answer that scientists must adapt their methods to the phenomena they're studying. Besides, for half a century physics too has been based on probabilities rather than certainties. Any student of physics now learns that on the most fundamental level it cannot be said that an event will occur, only that it is very likely to occur. (The corollaries to this are interesting. A physicist once told me, with a straight face, that he could calculate the probability of a given person's suddenly ceasing to exist. There is nothing to stop the subatomic components from all disappearing at once.)

Although there are methodological problems to parapsychology they are not insurmountable. Parapsychologists have now established beyond reasonable doubt that psi exists and have even begun to explain how it works.

Here are a few things we know about it:

Psi is strongest at the start of an experiment. The results tend to fall off as the subject continues to work. This yields a fatigue curve, which is fairly standard.

Psi requires effort, sometimes extreme effort. Some very successful subjects have fallen ill after tests. In other words, you can push yourself to show psi abilities.

People with positive attitudes toward psi show consistently higher scores than people with negative attitudes. (This is known in the field as the sheep-and-goats effect.)

Researchers get better results with socially adjusted subjects. There is no correlation between psi and intelligence. People who are feebleminded sometimes give significant results when tests are adapted for them. Psi also seems to be crosscultural—no group is outstandingly high or low in ability.

Animals have psi powers, too. Rhine has found some psi evidence in a horse; V. Bechterev has found it in dogs; and K. Osis has found it in cats (to no one's surprise).

In experiments in four cities (two in Holland, two in the U.S.), children in the fifth and sixth grades showed ESP abilities, whereas children in higher grades did not.

About 40 percent of the ESP cases investigated at Duke involve precognition.

Under certain conditions, some subjects give scores that are significantly *lower* than chance results would be. This is especially the case with people who have negative attitudes toward psi. They try so hard to repress their abilities that they end up proving they have them.

In tests for telepathy and clairvoyance, precognition sometimes shows up unexpectedly through what is called the displacement effect. At first the test results look negative; then they show that the subject consistently guessed ahead. For example, if cards are being used as targets, the subject will guess not the card that's up, but the card that's going to be up.

ESP is not affected by distance. There have been significant results in tests held between Durham, North Carolina, and Mufulira, Zimbabwe. And in a 1966 experiment, Yuri Kamensky sent telepathic messages 1,860 miles from Moscow to his colleague Karl Nikolaiev, who was in Siberia.

Soviet Research

This is a matter that's very hard to evaluate, since exchange of information between Soviet and American scientists is often restricted, especially in areas of research connected with espionage and state security (and this is the case with psychical research). As a result, we have very few sources for Soviet parapsychology. Moreover, these sources are themselves difficult to evaluate—standards of research and scholarship vary widely in the Soviet Union.

The Russians have been interested in mysticism since medieval times. The Revolution did not change that, but it did push them to seek materialistic explanations for their experiences. Soviet parapsychology goes back as far as 1919, when an electrical engineer, Bernard Kajinsky, began a study of telepathy. He concluded that "the human nervous system is capable of reacting to stimuli whose source is not yet known."

Much of what we know about Soviet parapsychology today comes from the writings of Dr. Leonid Vasiliev, who for years was the top Soviet researcher in the field. Vasiliev said that the Soviets began their earnest research into telepathy in the 1930s on orders "from a high authority." That probably means Stalin. We know that Stalin became interested in a stage telepathist named Wolf Messing, who allegedly performed various stunts privately for Stalin. The stunts all involved telepathic hypnosis (used for robbing a bank, or walking into Stalin's home past his guards).

For many years, according to Vasiliev, Soviet parapsychology concentrated mostly on telepathic hypnosis. One of Vasiliev's colleagues claimed to have knocked out a subject telepathically; the subject was in Leningrad, and the researcher was in Sevastopol. According to the Soviets, four people out of a hundred can be hypnotized telepathically.

In more recent years, the Soviets have somewhat reversed the direction of their research. Instead of using telepathy to impose hypnosis, they are using hypnosis to try to develop telepathy in their subjects. This information comes from one of the pioneers in this field, Dr. Milan Ryzl, who has emigrated from Czechoslovakia to the United States.

Evidently, the change in Soviet research came in the late 1950s as a result of an espionage rumor. The Soviets heard (probably incorrectly) that U.S. scientists were training submarine crews to communicate telepathically. The Soviets therefore began their own training program in ESP; they discovered that hypnosis was one of their best tools. Ryzl himself has been very successful in helping subjects develop ESP. But his most talented subject, Pavel Stepanek, has not undergone hypnosis. Stepanek's performance in laboratory tests has been unequalled. He performs well under a variety of conditions, and his results remain high throughout his tests—there's no fatigue curve.

The most popular work on Soviet parapsychology has been *Psychic Discoveries Behind the Iron Curtain*, by Sheila Ostrander and Lynn Schroeder (Englewood Cliffs: Prentice-Hall, 1970). That book publicized such discoveries as the psychokinetic abilities of Mrs. Nelya Mikhailova, a housewife from Leningrad who can move objects around on a table by looking at them. Dr. Gerady Sergeyev has measured the electromagnetic field around Mikhailova and found it to be fifty times stronger at the back of her head than at the front. (In most people, the field at the back of the head is three or four times stronger than at the front.) When Mikhailova uses psychokinesis, or PK, her electromagnetic field pulsates in rhythm with her heart and brain.

The common wisdom about Soviet parapsychology is that whereas the Americans are still trying to prove the existence of psi, the Soviets know it's there and are trying to work with it. This is something of a distortion. It would be truer to say that the Soviets started with an explanation for psi—that it's the result of measurable, physical energy given off by the brain—and have for years been trying to make all psi phenomena fit that explanation. In the process much valuable work has been accomplished.

As for the Americans, some genuinely exciting work has been done at the Division of Parapsychology and Psychophysics at Maimonides Medical Center in New York. In experiments there in dream telepathy and sensory deprivation, scientists have shown that ESP abilities are much more widespread than we had imagined. While subjects sleep or lie in a sensory-deprivation device, researchers concentrate on sending them telepathic images. Results so far have been very positive. If we are ever going to understand the nature of psi, it will probably be through experiments such as these.

A Glossary of Spiritualism

Automatic writing—A method by which the writer enters a dreamlike state, thereby giving up control of his hand to a spirit guide. The best-known communications by this method are the cross-correspondences of Mrs. Piper *et al*. (See above.) Goethe and Victor Hugo practiced automatic writing from time to time. Yeats based *A Vision* on his wife's automatic writing.

Control—A spirit who regularly speaks through a medium in trance and acts as go-between with other spirits who want to communicate with the living.

Direct writing—As distinguished from automatic writing, the messages are written by the spirits without the agency of the living, usually on small blackboards. Direct writing was at its most popular in the late nineteenth century.

Ectoplasm—A physical substance generated by some mediums when in trance. In its pure form, it is usually white and often resembles gauze.

Materialization—The production by spiritual means of physical objects, either of ectoplasm or of ordinary elements. The nineteenth-century English medium Agnes Nichol (Mrs. Samuel Guppy) was among the most gifted materializers. She took requests at her séances and on one occasion produced a large sunflower, roots and all, on very short notice.

Medium—A gifted living person through whom the spirits of the dead speak and act. Leah Fox was the first professional medium. She began her career on November 28, 1849.

Ouija Board—A board on which are printed the letters of the alphabet and the words *yes* and *no*. A heart-shaped pointer mounted on rollers comes with the board. One or more persons place their fingers on the pointer, which, guided by a spirit, proceeds to spell out messages. According to tradition, Pythagoras (sixth century B.C.) used a moving table and a set of symbols for the same purpose.

Planchette—The pointer from a ouija board with a pencil attached, used for automatic writing. It was invented in France in 1853.

Séance—A gathering held to contact the spirits of the dead. At least one medium must be present. The Fox sisters invented the séance as we know it; the practice is probably as old as the human species. See the story of the Witch of En-dor in 1 Samuel Chapter xxviii, verses 3-14.

Spirit photography—The appearance of inexplicable images in photographic prints. The images may be anything from blurs of light to clear pictures of people who were not present when the shutter snapped. The first spirit photographs were made in the United States early in the 1860s.

Trance—A state in which a medium loses consciousness, thus permitting a spirit to make use of his or her body.

Great Mediums and Psychics

Daniel Dunglas Home

Home was by far the greatest physical medium of the nineteenth century, and the only one who was never caught cheating in any way. Born in Scotland in 1833, he was an illegitimate child and lived with a childless aunt, Mrs. McNeill Cook, who took him to the United States when he was nine. He grew up in Greenville, Connecticut, and Troy, New York.

When Home was about seventeen years old, pieces of furniture began to rap in his presence. His aunt grew alarmed and told the young man to make them stop; he could not and so she called in Baptist, Methodist, and Congregationalist ministers to perform exorcisms on him. This rather feeble effort at ecumenism didn't work, and Mrs. Cook turned Home out of the house. From then on, he lived on the hospitality of whatever people he could impress. Since he impressed the likes of Elizabeth Barrett Browning and Napoleon III, he lived very well.

Home performed his most extraordinary stunt on December 13, 1868, in London. In a trance, he told the three witnesses to his séance to stay in their places for a moment. Then he left the room. A few moments later Home reappeared—standing upright in the air outside the window, three stories above the street. He opened the window, came in, and asked one of the sitters, Lord Adare, to go to the next room and close the window. Lord Adare did so; when he returned he said the window in the next room, through which Home had apparently escaped, had been open only a foot.

Lord Adare said he was baffled as to how Home could have gotten through such a small space. Home replied, "Come and see." He took Lord Adare to the next room and had him reopen the window about a foot.

As Lord Adare reported later, "He told me to stand a little distance off; he then went through the open space, head first, quite rapidly, his body being nearly horizontal and apparently rigid. He came in again feet foremost, and we returned to the other room." When Home came out of the trance a few moments later, he appeared to be very upset and nervous.

This was not Home's only successful levitation. He levitated quite often, and in well-lighted rooms before a goodly number of sitters. On one remarkable occasion, he made an entire ectoplasmic arm materialize on a table. The arm crawled over the tabletop, flowing from within. One of the sitters had the courage to touch it and said it felt soft and warm. The arm then dissolved. This also took place in a well-lighted room.

One of Home's most endearing traits was his love of music, which led him to make various instruments play tunes in his presence. In a test carefully conducted by Sir William Crookes, a highly respected physicist,

Home made an accordion play by itself; there was no possibility of cheating on Home's part. Perhaps none was needed. People on occasion heard music in Home's presence when there were no instruments in the room.

Home died in 1886, his reputation intact, and so it has remained.

Florence Cook

In 1871, when she was fifteen years old, Cook caused the ectoplasmic materialization of a young girl draped in white and wearing a white turban. The girl said her name was Katie King and that she would be with Florence Cook for the next three years. Katie looked a lot like Cook, but she was somewhat taller, her skin was more regular, and of course she was paler. Cook's ears were pierced; Katie's were not. Most curious of all, Katie's pulse rate was slower than Cook's.

Sir William Crookes, the scientist who had tested Daniel Dunglas Home, made tests on Florence Cook. Cook's practice, when in trance, was to sit in a draped cabinet, from which Katie King would emerge. Crookes's first test, then, was to tie Cook up in the cabinet. Katie King did indeed appear, but the test was not conclusive. Crookes felt he wouldn't know anything for sure until he saw Florence Cook and Katie King side by side. He got his wish in March 1874.

On March 12, Crookes had the medium hold her séance in his own home. (Usually Cook would only work in her own rooms.) Toward the end of the séance, Katie said to Crookes, "Come into the room and lift my medium's head up, she has slipped down." Crookes walked past Katie and into the room serving as Cook's cabinet. Cook had indeed slipped partially off the sofa where she was sitting. She was wearing a black velvet dress, and she was still deeply in trance. Crookes had seen the white-robed Katie only seconds before.

The conclusive sighting occurred on March 29. Again the séance was held in Crookes's home. Cook was in trance in the library; Crookes was with the other sitters in his laboratory. Katie King invited Crookes to follow her, and she led him into the library. The library was dark, but Crookes was carrying a phosphorus lamp. He went with it to Florence Cook, examined her, and held her hand. Katie King stood behind Cook. Crookes reported that he held his lamp up to Katie three separate times "until I had no doubt whatever of her objective reality."

After this séance, it became common for Katie and Cook to appear together, even for photo sessions. Then Katie announced that her three years were up and that she would leave.

Crookes's description of the leave-taking is rather moving. "Stooping over her [Cook], Katie touched her and said, 'Wake up, Florrie, wake up! I must leave you now.' Miss Cook then woke and tearfully entreated Katie to stay a little time longer. 'My dear, I can't; my work is done. God bless you,'

Katie replied, and then continued speaking to Miss Cook. For several minutes the two were conversing with each other, till at last Miss Cook's tears prevented her speaking. Following Katie's instructions I then came forward to support Miss Cook, who was falling onto the floor, sobbing hysterically. I looked around, but the white-robed Katie had gone."

For Further Reading:

For more of Crookes's writing, see his *Experimental Investigations of Psychic Force* (London: H. Gillman, 1871) and *Researches into the Phenomena of Modern Spiritualism* (Rochester, N.Y.: Austin Publishing Company, 1905).

More Ectoplasm

Where did Katie King come from? The most likely explanation (if one can speak of such things) is that Florence Cook produced her out of ectoplasm. The substance was named by Charles Richet, a French physiologist and winner of the Nobel Prize. Richet wrote, "I shall not waste time in stating the absurdities, almost the impossibilities, from a psycho-physiological point of view, of this phenomenon. . . . Nevertheless, it is a fact."

Even a Nobel science laureate could make a mistake, but there is evidence for the existence of ectoplasm, and the evidence should be examined.

A German physician, Baron A. von Shrenck-Notzing, obtained a sample of ectoplasm at a séance and analyzed it. He said it was mostly white blood cells and skin cells in "an organized tissue which easily decomposes—a sort of transitory matter which originates in the organism in a manner unknown to us. . . . " In separate studies of ectoplasm, Dr. W.J. Crawford of Queens University, Belfast, discovered that physical mediums lose weight in the course of a séance. One medium he studied lost almost fifty-five pounds, or half her normal weight.

Florence Cook was perhaps the most talented producer of ectoplasm, but she had her rivals. Marthe Beraud (known as Eva C.), the daughter of a French army officer, was also able to produce full-body materializations. There are photos of her with pasty-looking masses of tissue dripping from her body. There is some evidence of fraud in her case, but any number of her materializations seem to have been genuine.

A Polish banker and poet named Franek Klusky was more talented still. He discovered his abilities late in life, when he was fifty-six. The researcher Gustave Geley persuaded him to submit to tests, which he did with very good results. Klusky's specialty was the materialization of animals. He produced dogs, cats, birds, squirrels, once even a large buzzard that perched on his shoulders and let itself be photographed. Klusky did his sittings in 1920 with the International Metaphysical Institute. He worked without going into a trance. His researchers agreed that his most impressive stunt was the materialization of the protohominid *Pithecanthropus*, a hulking apeman that grunted a lot and tried to lick the sitters' faces.

Gladys Osborne Leonard

Leonard was born in England in 1882. While in her teens, she began to work as a singer in order to help her family, which had become impoverished. An attack of diphtheria put an end to her singing, and so she joined a touring theater company and appeared in bit parts.

Her control was named Feda; she was an Indian girl whom an ancestor of Leonard's had married. The conjugal relationship seems important—Feda was most active in the presence of Leonard's husband. Early in 1914, Feda told Leonard to set herself up as a professional medium, because "something big and terrible is going to happen to the world," and Feda had to help people through Leonard. The medium did as she was told.

In 1915, a young man named Raymond Lodge was killed in battle. He was the son of Sir Oliver Lodge, a renowned physicist, psychical researcher, and friend of the late Frederic Myers. Lodge and his wife were overcome with grief. Lady Lodge decided she would try to contact Raymond's spirit. Through an acquaintance, she got Mrs. Leonard's name and address, and she visited the medium anonymously. Working with no information from Lady Lodge, Leonard brought through a message from Raymond. Raymond mentioned that he had met a friend of his father's named Myers.

Soon Lodge himself was at Mrs. Leonard's house. He and Lady Lodge took great comfort in the communications from Raymond, which they considered genuine. At one point, Feda described in detail a photograph of Raymond and his fellow officers. Some time later, the mother of one of the officers in question sent Lodge a photograph. It fit Feda's description.

Feda was not Leonard's only control. Sometimes she stopped talking, and a new voice would come through Mrs. Leonard. The voice belonged to the Reverend C. Drayton Thomas, the father of one of Leonard's clients. The first time it spoke to Thomas, its first words were, "Charlie, Charlie, it is extraordinary, who would have thought it possible?" Thomas said that the turns of phrase, the vocal expression, and even Mrs. Leonard's physical attitudes were those of his father. It is almost certain that Mrs. Leonard had never met Thomas's father.

Mrs. Leonard showed extraordinary psi abilities while in trance. Professor E.R. Dodds arranged some tests for her that would take her telepathic abilities into account and control against them. He had a client contact Leonard through an intermediary; neither Leonard nor the intermediary knew the client. Dodds himself was the only link, and he carefully stayed in the background. Feda performed brilliantly. She gave an exact description of the spirit the sitter wanted to contact. Then she went on to tell family jokes and mention pet names. This was almost certainly mediumship. If it *was* telepathy, it's probably the strongest case on record.

Mrs. John H. Curran (Patience Worth)

Everybody thinks that Mrs. Curran was too stupid to be a fraud. She was a housewife in St. Louis, a woman with little education and a high level of boredom. The only interesting thing that ever happened to her was the development of a spirit control, Patience Worth; and Worth was so superior intellectually to Mrs. Curran that she regularly and impatiently insulted her unfortunate medium.

Sometime in 1913, a friend asked Mrs. Curran to try using a Quija board with her. Mrs. Curran went along with the experiment. Nothing happened, but she tried a few more times, and on July 8, 1913, Patience Worth took over the board.

Worth said she had lived in the seventeenth century on a farm in Dorset. She had emigrated to America and died at the hands of the natives. Worth wanted to use the board to write poetry, prayers, and novels, and she proceeded to do so at high speed. Among her productions were *The Sorry Tale*, a novel set in the time of Christ; *Hope Trueblood*, a nineteenth-century romance; and *Telka*, a story about medieval England. Worth's writing got good reviews. *The Athenaeum* published a favorable notice about *Hope Trueblood*; it had "definite and clear-cut characterization, good dialogue and arresting runs of expression, deep but restrained feeling. . . . "

It would be easy enough to claim that Mrs. Curran, like so many bored housewives, had abilities she had never been allowed to express, which could only emerge in this bizarre manner. Maybe so. But when a philologist examined Worth's medieval novel, he found that 90 percent of the words were of Anglo-Saxon derivation; moreover, Worth had used no words that had entered English after the seventeenth century. It would take a philologist a great deal of effort to write such a text. For Mrs. Curran, the project would have been impossible.

Mrs. Curran did get some comfort from her mediumship. She enjoyed Patience Worth's stories, and eventually she was able to imagine them as Worth dictated.

Eileen J. Garrett

On October 4, 1930, a huge dirigible called the R101 crashed on a hillside in Beauvais, France, killing its crew and forty-eight of its fifty-four passengers. Interest in the crash was high. The R101 had represented a major British effort to develop a dirigible for commercial use, and its unexplained crash was a setback for British aviation as a whole.

Two days after the disaster, a young medium named Eileen Garrett conducted a séance at the National Laboratory of Psychical Research in London. During the séance, the voice of the R101's captain, Flight-Lieutenant H. Carmichael Irwin, unexpectedly spoke through Mrs. Garrett. Irwin's spirit gave a detailed and highly emotional account of the last moments before the crash. A hired stenographer took down the information in shorthand and then rushed to publish it. Engineers who had worked on the R101 studied the newspaper account of the séance and admitted that Irwin (or Mrs. Garrett) had given more than forty highly technical details of the airship's construction.

This was not all. Major Oliver Villiers of the Ministry of Civil Aviation requested a séance with Mrs. Garrett. She was able to put him in contact with several other crew members who had died. Major Villiers interrogated these crewmen at some length and came away with highly detailed information.

The government convened a Court of Inquiry on October 28, some three weeks after Mrs. Garrett began to speak of the disaster. Only then did technical information about the airship become public. The Court of Inquiry's conclusions were virtually the same as Eileen Garrett's.

Garrett was born in County Meath, Ireland, in 1893. Her psychic gifts first became apparent in the most troubling way possible, when she foresaw the deaths of her two sons and her second husband. She determined to develop her psychic powers and did so with the help of J.H. McKenzie at the British College of Psychic Science. Moreover, she encouraged parapsychologists to test her and investigate her powers. She was probably the most trustworthy of all mediums; no one even suggests fraud about her work.

Garrett had two controls, called Uvani and Abdul Latif. She said she sensed things with her solar plexus rather than her brain. She also said she used her third eye while in trance (though she claimed to feel it at the back of her head rather than in the forehead). She knew Jung well and professed great respect for him, though she liked Freud's theories better. She also knew Aleister Crowley very well. "In the end," she said, "he really couldn't live with himself."

After Garrett's death in France in 1970, a writer named Archie Jarman came forward and said that soon after the R101 case was closed, Mrs. Garrett had come to him and asked him to investigate the matter thoroughly. She paid him no money and exerted no pressure—all she wanted was a complete record of the case. Jarman's conclusion after months of work: the only reasonable explanation of Garrett's part in the case was that Captain Irwin's spirit had indeed spoken through her. The technical data had simply not been available; as for Eileen Garrett's aeronautical knowledge, "she knew hardly enough to float a toy balloon."

Edgar Cayce

Cayce was born in 1877 in Hopkinsville, Kentucky, the son of a farmer. He had his first psychic experience when he was still a schoolboy. One day, while he sat under a tree, a shining figure appeared and spoke to him. Shortly thereafter, while he was at home studying for school, he fell asleep, laying his head on his spelling book. When he awoke, he knew every word in the book. This was fortunate, since Cayce had a lot of trouble in school. He finished only six grades.

As a young man, Cayce wanted to be a minister— he had always been deeply religious and read the Bible faithfully—but he decided the impediments of poverty and lack of education were too great. He became a salesman instead. But here, too, he encountered problems—every time he concentrated on making money, he would lose his voice. Cayce struggled on in this way until the age of twenty-four, when he finally got help from a friend named Al Layne.

Layne had taken a mail-order course in hypnosis, and he thought he could cure Cayce's vocal problem. So he put Cayce into a trance, using the stiff and solemn formulas the correspondence school had taught him, told Cayce to visualize his throat, and had him suggest a cure. The cure worked. Layne was so impressed that the next day he hypnotized Cayce and had him diagnose Layne's own problems.

This was the beginning of Cayce's career as a psychic. From then until his death in 1945, he gave medical readings for about thirty thousand people, in both their presence and absence. He predicted both World Wars, the years in which they would begin and end, the Crash of 1929, and the economic improvement of 1933. He also gave much information on geological disturbances. He said the Earth had begun tilting on its axis in 1936 and that there would be vast geological upheavals beginning in 1958 and lasting until 2000. In later years he spoke often of Atlantis, which he said had fallen into the sea ten thousand years ago and which would begin to rise again soon. (The Atlanteans had developed the use of crystals that drew energy from the stars when triggered by psychic concentration. It was an excess of this astral energy that destroyed Atlantis. For more on Atlantis see "Part Two: The Occult Bible.")

Cayce's wife Gertrude took over Layne's job as hypnotist. When Cayce wanted to go into a trance, he would go into his study with Gertrude and his secretary, Gladys Davis. He would remove his jacket and tie, loosen his collar, and lie on his back on the couch. Then Gertrude would give him the trance signal, a light touch on the cheek. She would repeat a modified version of Layne's mail-order hypnotic instructions. For example, if Cayce was doing a health reading on someone in another place, Gertrude would say, "You have the body of ———— before you, who is in ————. You will go over this body carefully, examine it thoroughly, and tell me the conditions you find at the present time. . . . You will speak distinctly at a normal rate of speech, answering the questions as I ask them." Cayce showed amazing clairvoyant powers in these readings.

Until 1923, Cayce would give only medical advice to people while in trance. Then he began to give readings of people's past lives. At first this disturbed him—he could find no support in fundamentalist Christianity for the theory of reincarnation—but the information kept coming. Eventually, past-life readings became something of a specialty for Cayce.

Over the course of many readings, he developed his own system of health and diet. He followed it himself for the most part, though he did violate one of his own key precepts—he ate pork. When someone would ask him about that, he'd say, "I wouldn't be worth much if I couldn't raise the vibration level of that poor little hunk of meat."

The archives of Cayce's readings are kept at the Association for Research and Enlightenment, P.O. Box 595, Virginia Beach, Virginia 23451.

Arthur Ford

Ford, a world-famous medium and founder of the Spiritual Frontiers Fellowship, was born in the 1890s in Titusville, Florida. His father was a steamboat captain. As an adolescent, Ford wanted to become a Baptist minister. But his ideas were too unorthodox for his church, and so he became a member of the Disciples of Christ. He was ordained in that church at the age of twenty-five.

He had his first psychic experience while serving as a second lieutenant in the army in World War I. He dreamed he saw a roster of the names of his men who had died of influenza; the next day he saw such a roster, with the names in the exact order of his dream. He also began to have dreams about men who would be killed at the front.

These experiences thoroughly unnerved Ford. At the same time, he felt he should face up to them. In 1924, he went to New York in hopes of finding a teacher who would help him develop his powers. He studied with Swami Yogananda and eventually made contact with a spirit control, a French-Canadian called Fletcher. Ford had known Fletcher as a boy; Fletcher had died in World War I and was now Ford's guardian. From time to time Fletcher would complain, "I wish he would die so I can get loose." Ford seemed remarkably tolerant of that attitude.

Ford first achieved fame in 1928 when he (or Fletcher) conveyed a message from the spirit of Harry Houdini. Houdini, who had died in 1926, had given a code word to his wife Beatrice so that she would know whether mediumistic communications from him were real or fake. Ford gave her the correct code message, and Beatrice Houdini issued a sworn statement that "the message, in its entirety, and in the agreed-upon sequence, given to me by Arthur Ford, is the correct message prearranged between Mr. Houdini and myself." The witnesses to Mrs. Houdini's statement were H.R. Zander of the United Press, Mrs. Minnie Chester (an old friend of Mrs. Houdini), and J.W. Stafford, the associate editor of *Scientific American*. This news, coming from the widow of one of the greatest debunkers of Spiritualism, caused a sensation.

Fame did not make Ford's life easy. Hospitalization after an auto crash turned him into a morphine addict. He was also an alcoholic. He fought bravely against both addictions for twenty years and finally mastered them.

His most famous séance in later life was one conducted on Canadian television for Bishop James A. Pike. In it, he apparently contacted the spirit of the bishop's dead son, James, Jr. After Ford's death in 1971, some private papers of his seemed to show he had faked the séance. He had a great many clippings of obituaries, and much of the information he had given Bishop Pike was in his files.

At worst, this incident means that Ford, like most other psychics and mediums, used trickery when his powers failed him. That he had powers is beyond doubt. Sir Arthur Conan Doyle called one of Ford's public performances "One of the most amazing things I have ever seen in forty-one years of psychic experience." Ford gave up his performances because, he said, "anything you say would fit *someone* in the crowd."

Sybil Leek

Sybil Leek is a witch. She is proud of being a witch, and she has probably done more than anyone alive to spread the good word about witchcraft.

She was born in the 1920s in England and had her first psychic experience at age two. This was nothing to her family—they all regarded psychic powers as normal. Leek claims that her mother's family had been witches as far back as the twelfth century, and her father's family had been psychics at the Russian court. Her family would presumably have been alarmed if she *hadn't* been psychic.

Leek had little formal education until she went to boarding school at age twelve. She married at age sixteen, was widowed at eighteen, and had a brief affair with the painter Augustus John. After her husband's death she became active in a coven. For two years she lived with gypsies in a Hampshire forest.

She opened an antiques shop in London when she was twenty-one and began her successful writing career. For a while she submitted to tests by parapsychologists, but then she revolted against them. She complains that "six hours in a trance are six hours I could be enjoying music." Once she did consent to levitate on camera for the British Broadcasting Company.

Leek does not have a control. She says she has found in recent years that she no longer needs to go into trance. Things just come to her now.

For Further Reading

Leek's writings include *The Complete Art of Witchcraft* (New York: NAL, 1973), *Diary of a Witch* (New York: NAL, 1972), *Guide to Telepathy* (New York: Macmillan, 1971), and many works on astrology, numerology, phrenology, herbs, and "successful living."

Jeane Dixon

Dixon was born Jeane Pinchert in a Wisconsin lumber town in 1918. Her parents, who were immigrants from Germany, moved to Santa Rosa, California, soon after Jeane's birth. While still a young girl, she began to show psychic abilities. She foretold the death of her grandfather (who was still in Germany). On another occasion, she knew in advance that her father, who was in Chicago on business, had bought her a black-and-white puppy. Her mother took her to a gypsy, who said Jeane had the gift of prophecy—the gypsy claimed there was a Star of David in her left palm and another star in the right. A Jesuit priest, Father Henry, taught her astrology and encouraged her to develop her gifts.

Jeane worked briefly as an actress and then married a realtor named James Dixon. She became a housewife in Los Angeles; later she and her husband moved to Washington, D.C., where they still live. She is a devout Catholic and attends mass daily. Her prophecies often come to her while she gazes into a crystal ball; she believes that they come directly from the Holy Trinity.

Dixon specializes in political prophecy. She claims that Franklin Roosevelt called her to the White House late in 1944, at which time she told him he had less than six months to live. In 1945, she predicted the partition of India. And in 1952, while in church, she had her most famous vision—that a tall, blue-eyed President, a Democrat who would be elected in 1960, would be assassinated while in office. Among her other accurate predictions were the launching of Sputnik, the suicide of Marilyn Monroe, the fall of Bulganin and Malenkov, the rise of Khrushchev, and the assassinations of Martin Luther King and Robert Kennedy.

She has had her mistakes too. She claimed that China would start a world war in 1958. She also said Nixon would win the 1960 Presidential election (despite her vision of a Democratic president). Dixon attributed the ghetto riots and campus revolts of the late 1960s to agitators sent by China and the Soviet Union.

Dixon believes her most important vision came to her in 1962. She says a world leader was born somewhere in the Middle East shortly after 7:00 A.M. (EST) on February 5. The child was born into a peasant family, but he is a descendant of Queen Nefertiti. Dixon calls him "the answer to the prayers of a troubled world." This man, who will bring all humankind together in Christianity, will begin to make himself known early in the 1980s. For some ten years there will be immense changes in the world until all war and suffering disappear. By 1999 this savior will have shown his full power and a new age will begin.

Irene Hughes

Irene Hughes was one of eleven children born to Joe and Easter Finger, who were farmers in Tennessee. Easter seems to have had psychic gifts—she used to give readings using coffee grounds—and perhaps she passed on her talent to Irene. As a child, Irene would give her mother advance notice of guests and letters.

Irene moved to New Orleans at age fifteen and found work in a hospital; later she became a secretary. She married Bill Hughes in 1945 and they moved to Chicago. She began writing a newspaper column in 1959, but she didn't develop her full gifts until 1961. In that year she made contact with her control, a Japanese man. The control gave Hughes the name and address of his daughter, who he said was a student at Cornell. Hughes followed up the information and got a letter back from the daughter. She said her father had died two months before Hughes first made contact with him.

Once, while doing a sitting with Senator Harold Hughes, she had a vision of John F. Kennedy, who told her that Robert would be joining him in six weeks. When Robert Kennedy was murdered six weeks later, Senator Hughes sent her a letter confirming that she had given him this information.

Hughes has also done police work, including murder cases. In her best-known case, the LaPorte-Cross kidnapping, she told Canadian police the location of the house where one of the victims was being held. She also predicted the murder of the other victim.

Peter Hurkos

One of the most famous psychic detectives, Hurkos was born Pieter Van der Hurk in Holland in 1911. As a young man he worked as a house painter and merchant seaman. He changed his name to Hurkos while working with the Dutch underground against the Nazis. Like many psychics, he grew up in an environment favorable to the development of his gifts—his mother was a talented card reader—but he did not show any abilities until the age of thirty.

In 1941 Hurkos fell from a ladder while painting a house. He lay unconscious in the hospital for three days; when he awoke, he had the gift of psychometry. When he touched an object, he would get mental images from it—"like a movie." He also heard information, mostly names. He became a professional psychic in 1946 and gained a considerable reputation for his work with police organizations. He accepts no money for police work, other than payment for his expenses.

Hurkos has received commendations from Pope Pius XII and Queen Juliana. In one of his biggest cases, he helped Scotland Yard retrieve the Scottish coronation stone (the Stone of Scone) when it was stolen from Westminster Abbey. He also caused a sensation in 1969 by solving the murder of six women students from the University of Michigan at Ann Arbor. In that case, Hurkos went on television in Detroit and gave the murderer's name and description.

Marinus Dykshoorn

Dykshoorn, an unusually talented psychic, says that he has extrastrong senses rather than extrasensory perception. He merely picks up more than most people do. He was born in Holland in 1921 and first gave evidence of his abilities at age five, when he told a woman she was pregnant. (Her doctor confirmed the diagnosis several days later.) Through adolescence, Dykshoorn was troubled by his powers—he was always at the mercy of other people's thoughts and emotions, and they disturbed him so much that he could barely stand to walk down the street. Eventually he learned to focus and control his impressions by the use of a piano-wire loop, which he also uses as a dowsing rod. When giving a reading or demonstration, Dykshoorn will twirl the piano wire like an antenna and pick up only the impressions he wants.

Like Peter Hurkos, Dykshoorn has done a lot of police work. He is licensed as a psychic by the Dutch police, and his passport is stamped CLAIRVOYANT. He has been especially successful in solving murders. His usual technique is to relive the victim's last five minutes. Police take him to the scene of the crime, he acts out the murder, and often enough he will then run off along the escape route taken by the murderer, while the police chase after him, just as if he were a bloodhound.

His most sensational case involved locating a boat that had been stolen in Germany. Dykshoorn, who was in Holland, did his work by long-distance telephone. He talked to the boat's owners and meanwhile twirled his loop of wire over a map of Germany. He traced the boat's exact route.

The Amazing Kreskin

Kreskin is of special interest because he insists he is not a psychic. He prefers to call himself a mentalist and freely admits the importance of hypnotic suggestion in his work. He is a stage and television performer rather than a consultant, and he takes pride in that fact.

He was born George Kresge in New Jersey in the 1930s. He has worked as a travelling magician since the age of nine; he incorporated hypnotism into his act when he was eleven. He also relies a great deal on automatic writing in his work.

Kreskin claims that hypnotism is a matter of rapport rather than control. He opens himself to the telepathic messages that come from his audiences, and at the same time he tries to send telepathic suggestions (hypnotic, if you will) to likely subjects. For example, Kreskin will write down a name from a phone book before his show. Then, during the act, he will choose a member of the audience to go to a stack of phone books, pick one, open it, seemingly at random, and point blindly to a name. He then produces his slip of paper with that name. Kreskin says the trick works because he mentally directs the subject to the name he has chosen.

Naturally, some people claim that Kreskin uses stooges. He has a standing offer of $20,000 to anyone who can prove that claim. So far, nobody has.

Rosemary Brown

When Rosemary Brown was a child, an elderly gentleman appeared to her in a vision and told her that one day he and other great composers would give her beautiful music. Young Rosemary didn't recognize the man; but years later she saw a picture of Franz Liszt and knew it had been he.

In 1964, when Brown was recently widowed and living in poverty, the prophecy came true. Bach, Beethoven, Chopin, Liszt, Brahms, Debussy, and Rachmaninoff began dictating music to her. Brown had a parlor piano and had taken a few lessons at one time in her life, but she was certainly not an educated musician. The music she began to take down from dictation—very rapidly but at times with difficulty—was beyond her ability to perform and almost certainly beyond her ability to compose. She has taken down not only piano works but full orchestral scores. At present, Beethoven is dictating his Tenth Symphony to her.

The composers speak to her in English, except when they get excited. Then Liszt will break into German or French, and Chopin will speak Polish. Brown has to take down the Polish phonetically and have a friend translate it.

A recording of the dictated music, titled "Rosemary Brown's Music," came out in 1970. The liner notes were by Sir Donald Tovey, the great musicologist (who is also dead).

Uri Geller

Everyone knows about Geller. He's the Israeli who bends doorkeys by psychokinesis. He also breaks metal objects, makes the hands of wristwatches go round, raises the temperature of thermometers, and sends and receives telepathic images with a clarity unusual even for famous psychics. Geller's detractors point out that he used to be a stage magician and that he seems to work best when the situation is loose ("rampant confusion" is what one critic called it). On the other hand, Ted Bastin, a physicist with a fairly skeptical turn of mind, tested Geller in his laboratory and reported that Geller dissolved half a crystal that was sealed in a container.

In 1949, when Geller was three years old, he saw a large bowl descend from the sky. A shadowy figure appeared in front of the bowl and directed a ray of light at Geller, which knocked him over and put him to sleep. When Geller awoke, the figure and the bowl were gone. He attributes his psi powers to this apparently extraterrestrial source.

His biographer and sometime sponsor, Andrija Puharich, goes along with this explanation. He says a spaceship named *Spectra*, which is stationed a few million miles away from Earth, is controlling Geller. The beings from this spaceship intend him to be a messiah. These are the same beings who made messiahs of Abraham and Pharaoh Imhotep.

Jane Roberts

The best-known living trance medium is Jane Roberts, a thin, dark-haired woman who lives in Elmira, New York, with her husband, Robert Butts. Before she began her career as a medium and teacher of ESP techniques, she wrote science fiction and verse. There is a certain clumsiness to her writing: "From the beginning, the obvious quality of the material intrigued us . . . "; "I do not mean to imply that we have any cornerstone on truth . . . " Psychic gifts do not necessarily go to the sophisticated.

Roberts had a spontaneous out-of-the-body experience in September 1963. Shortly thereafter she and her husband began to play with a Ouija board. They began receiving messages from a personality called Seth. After a while, Roberts knew what the board would spell before the indicator had begun to move; then she felt compelled to say what the board was going to spell. Within very little time, she was going into trance and speaking for Seth. She would sit in a rocking chair, remove her glasses, and speak in a deeper, more energetic voice than usual. The words came in a foreign accent, though an indefinable one that shifted from Russian to Irish to German to Italian. Her husband would take notes.

Roberts and Butts are in the habit of holding their trance sessions on Monday and Wednesday nights, usually between nine and eleven o'clock. Seth has given them a great deal of material at these sessions; often he gives advice to people who had written to Roberts asking for help. In January 1970, Seth began dictating a book through Roberts. He finished it in August 1971, and it has been published as *Seth Speaks: The Eternal Validity of the Soul*, by Jane Roberts (Englewood Cliffs: Prentice-Hall, 1972). A previous book of

Roberts's, *The Seth Material*, had been published in 1970, but it didn't attract as much attention as Seth's own book.

Seth is a teacher and lives in an astral world of teachers. He says the main activity on his astral plane is the creation of the plane's form. Everything there is fluid and evanescent—there are no permanent structures, no architecture or cities, but only mental forms. The inhabitants change shape at will. They also form separate personalities from their total selves and let the personalities go off on their own. Time does not exist on this plane. Seth says you have to die many times before you can get to his plane. Lesser souls see only confusion there and tend to get lost.

Our plane of existence is as fluid and unsettled as Seth's, but we habitually ignore the changes in us and around us, refusing to take responsibility for them. In fact, every part of the physical world, every atom, is conscious and wills its own existence. The atoms in a human, for instance, cooperate willingly to form a body. The moral is that "Consciousness creates form. . . . You create the world that you know."

In other words, we are all geniuses at psychokinesis, only we don't realize it. From moment to moment, we use our inner selves (which are beyond consciousness) to create ourselves and the world. Seth compares the process to the way a TV set works. As electron patterns form an image on a TV screen, so we form our bodies, thoughts, and emotions from atoms and electromagnetic waves. And, just as you have to tune a TV, so you have to be attuned to physical reality, or you simply don't see it. We poor humans are attuned *only* to the physical world. If we would change our habits of thought, we would see the other worlds and other beings all around us.

A human's consciousness is always flickering between the physical world (what we call life) and the nonphysical world (what we call death). The flickering is very rapid, and since we pay attention only to the physical world, we assume our consciousness of it is continuous. Thus we have the illusion that life is something steady, whole, and separate from death. Seth, who has died many times, knows better.

It is not quite accurate to say that Seth has died many times. Seth says that one's incarnations are simultaneous rather than successive. This idea is a logical extension of the notion that time does not exist in the nonphysical worlds. Seth himself has been a Hebrew courtesan at the time of David, a black Ethiopian, a Roman merchant named Millenius at the time of Christ, a minor Pope early in the fourth century, a seventeenth-century Danish spice merchant, and various monks, housewives, and husbands. Seth was all these people *at once*. They were earthly aspects of himself. At the same time, he had still other personalities living in nonphysical worlds. Seth calls the complex of one's personalities the *multidimensional self*. He likes to give a separate name to such a self to distinguish it from its component personalities. Thus, he calls Jane Roberts "Ruburt" and her husband "Joseph." Those are the names of their whole selves rather than their splinter personalities. (Seth knew Joseph and Ruburt back in the seventeenth century. Joseph was a painter then, as he is now. Ruburt was his son.)

In his most controversial application of this principle, Seth gives a new view of Christ as three separate personalities projected by a single soul. These personalities had first appeared and been recognized as Christ in Atlantis. The events of 4 B.C. to 29 A.D. were thus Christ's Second Coming. The three personalities projected by Christ were John the Baptist, Jesus of Nazareth, and St. Paul. The twelve disciples were fragment personalities created by the three Christs.

Seth claims that the crucifixion was a psychic rather than a physical event. Judas and some others formed a conspiracy to make it appear that Jesus had been crucified and thereby fulfill the prophecies. So they found a deluded man who believed he was the Messiah, drugged him, and handed him to the Romans. Peter denied this man three times because he could see the man was not Jesus (evidently Peter was not part of Judas's conspiracy). Jesus was actually in the wilderness with the Essenes at the time. (For more information about Christianity and occultism, see chapter seven.)

What we call the Second Coming (actually the Third Coming) will happen soon. The agent will be the third Christ personality, St. Paul, who will accomplish his mission by the year 2075 by reforming Christianity and starting a new religious system.

GHOSTS AND POLTERGEISTS

Ghosts are dead people with one-track minds. Their obsessions, usually the results of violence, are so great that they blind the ghosts to the very fact that they are dead. So they continue to loiter in the physical world, although it properly belongs to the living.

Typically, a ghost is either a murderer or a murderer's victim. Two of the world's most famous ghosts were wives of Henry VIII: Anne Boleyn, who walks through the Tower of London carrying her head beneath her arm, and Catherine Howard, whose shrieks still disturb Hampton Court Palace. Less distinguished murder victims may become ghosts as well. Nellie MacQuillie still haunts the North Carolina brook where natives killed her in the eighteenth century. A Civil War deserter regularly visits the bridge in southern Indiana where he was shot while trying to escape. Self-murderers run the risk of becoming unquiet spirits, too.

People who were violent and unsettled in life tend to be so in death as well. Lady Ferrars, who lived in Hertfordshire in the seventeenth century, used to enjoy dressing up as a highwayman. She haunted her own estates well into the 1800s. The ghost of Hermitage Castle in Roxburghshire, Scotland, is more spectacular—a laird who used to practice black magic. While living, he sacrificed children for his rites; now that he's dead, he still goes through the gestures of slaughter. And every year a ghost rides up to Wycoller Hall in Lancashire and enters it, whereupon people hear a woman's shrieks. The ghost is that of a man who murdered his wife in the castle in the 1600s. Sometimes a violent death will disturb a spirit so much that it, too, becomes violent. A Chicano who died while working on the construction of a bridge in Los Angeles now haunts the bridge. He tries to get people to jump off.

Apart from violence, the greatest factor in predisposing people to become ghosts is routine. Some people are so set in their ways that nothing disturbs them, not even death. There was a tall, spectral clergyman who faithfully attended services at a London church; one day in 1964 the vicar absentmindedly walked right through him. In 1965, a nondescript little man in a grey suit started showing up at a London bank.

There is some objective evidence for the existence of ghosts. They appear fairly often in photographs. Nobody sees them when the shutter snaps, but later they make a surprise appearance on the negative. Probably the most intriguing example is the photograph taken of the Brown Lady of Raynham Hall in September 1936. There are clearer photos of ghosts, but this one is special because the Brown Lady is something of a celebrity. She usually appears before deaths in whatever family owns the house.

Most of the evidence for ghosts, though, has been in the form of personal accounts. Enjoyable as such stories are, they leave something to be desired, even when told by experts.

For example, there's the case of Borley Rectory, a dismal house in Suffolk, built by the Reverend Henry Bull in the 1860s. It looks like the kind of place that deserves to be haunted, and indeed it was. For a time it was known as the most haunted house in England. The story was that a nun from a nearby convent had once tried to elope with a coachman; when her sisters caught her in the act, they walled her up alive in the convent. By the 1860s, when the Reverend Bull built his house, all that was left of the convent was the nun's ghost and that of the coachman. Eventually Bull returned to haunt the place, too.

Harry Price, a renowned ghost hunter, came to investigate the house in 1929 at the request of its residents, the Reverend and Mrs. Smith. The Smiths had grown disturbed at the way bells would ring in the house. Pebbles rolled downstairs; keys kept jumping out of locks. When Price first visited, he saw the nun's ghost pacing in the garden; he also held a séance attended by the spirit of the Reverend Bull. But he could not persuade the ghosts to leave, and so the Smiths moved out.

When new residents moved in, the ghosts' activities redoubled. Scrawled messages appeared on the walls addressed to the woman of the house (Price noticed that the ghosts were especially active in her presence). When this family, too, could take it no longer, Price himself rented Borley Rectory. He took a year's lease in 1935 and gathered a group of forty-eight assistants to help in the ghost hunt. But as so often happens in these cases, the prey vanished. After a year, Price had nothing to report about the ghosts and their doings.

The Borley ghosts are still of interest though, because they changed with the times, since they began as romantic, nineteenth-century ghosts and ended as common, twentieth-century poltergeists.

Nowadays, most ghosts are poltergeists. The name is German, meaning "noisy spirit," and it's somewhat dated. Parapsychologists now prefer to speak of them as manifestations of RSPK (recurrent spontaneous psychokinesis). In other words, ghosts as independent beings have disappeared. In their place, we now speak of unconscious, though spectacular, displays of psi, usually by an adolescent.

A typical case was that of the poltergeist that afflicted Mr. and Mrs. James Herrmann and their children, James, age twelve, and Lucille, age thirteen, who lived in Seaford, Long Island. This ghost was generally content to open bottles and spill their contents; it also threw glassware and moved the furniture. In 1958, J.G. Pratt and W.G. Roll came to Seaford to investigate. To help rule out the possibility of fraud, they worked with Nassau County Police Detective Joseph Tozzi. As for the possibility that the phenomena were hallucinations, they eliminated that from the start—the house was a mess. Pratt, Roll, and Tozzi found that the disturbances took place only when the whole family was at home and awake; the disturbances always centered on James. The researchers checked for every possible natural explanation of the phenomena; they even consulted specialists at Adelphi College and the Nassau Society of Engineers. After two months, they concluded that the phenomena were genuine.

A fascinating experiment done by George and Iris Owen with members of the Toronto Society for Psychical Research shows how powerful RSPK can be. This group has artificially created its own poltergeist. They call him Philip.

In 1972, the group decided to try an experiment in collective visualization. They would make up a ghost and then try to see it. So, one of the members of the group invented a story about a seventeenth-century English lord named Philip who killed himself over an unfortunate love affair with a gypsy. (The Toronto people obviously have a feeling for these things.) At first the experimenters sat around and stared at the floor, trying to make Philip appear through a collective hallucination. Then, for the sake of comfort, they started sitting around a table. Still nothing happened. Then one summer night, while they were taking a lemonade break, the table rapped. Instead of a group hallucination, they had produced a group PK phenomenon.

Philip the Table is now quite active. He moves around and at times lifts one or two of his legs. People talk to him, and he answers them by rapping. Dr. Owen explains that Philip is a very democratic poltergeist—he answers according to the majority opinion of the group. According to reports, he is most active when people tell him dirty jokes and cheap gossip.

If this seems unromantic, consider the horrors performed by poltergeists of the past, those who visited the Bell family, for example, and be glad that such ghosts have gone out of style.

John Bell was a successful farmer who lived with his wife and nine children in Robertson, Tennessee, in the early 1800s. The trouble started in 1817, when Bell's daughter Betsy was twelve years old. First there were knockings outside the house. Then there were gnawing sounds in the floors, ceilings, and bedposts. The house began to shake with the noise. Chairs flipped over; pebbles rained onto the roof. The younger children complained that they felt something pulling at their hair. The one most affected was Betsy. The ghost pulled her hair viciously and slapped her face till it grew red.

A neighbor, James Johnson, thought the family should try to communicate with the ghost. This only seemed to encourage the ghost, which intensified its attacks and threw rocks and sticks at the children as they walked to school. Betsy began to have fainting spells. And the ghost began to talk.

At first the family could scarcely hear it; then its voice grew to a distinct, insinuating whisper. The ghost started to repeat the sermons of the local parsons and imitate their voices. Later it began to curse and say it would torment "Old Jack Bell" for the rest of his life. Not surprisingly, Bell fell ill. His tongue swelled, he developed a nervous tic, and at last he became bedridden.

By this time the ghost had identified itself as a witch. It had a generous side—at times it showered Mrs. Bell with fruits and nuts. (Betsy, according to the reports, liked her mother.) Betsy did not like the boy she was engaged to, and the witch spent a great deal of time pleading with Betsy to break the engagement. She finally yielded to this outside pressure.

At last John Bell died, his health shattered by the witch. In his final crisis, it turned his medicine into a vile brown syrup. Nor would it leave his funeral undisturbed. As the family lowered Bell into his grave, they heard the witch singing, "Row me up some brandy, O."

Reincarnation and Possession

These two subjects can be discussed together because the evidence for reincarnation often resembles evidence for possession. Similarly, evidence for possession can often seem like evidence for reincarnation. The cases that follow show that, at the very least, there are some awfully strange stories going around.

First, there are the apparent cases of reincarnation discovered through hypnotic age-regression. The subject, in a deep trance, goes back in time to birth and then, on command, goes back even further to past lives.

The best-known case of this sort was that of Bridey Murphy. In 1952, an amateur hypnotist named Morey Bernstein tried an age-regression experiment on a friend named Virginia Tighe, a young housewife in Pueblo, Colorado. In trance, Tighe turned into Bridey Murphy, a woman who had lived in Cork, Ireland, from 1798 to 1864. Murphy spoke with a brogue and gave many details about Irish life in that period. Much of Murphy's description proved to be accurate; Virginia Tighe knew nothing about Ireland in that time. Bernstein wrote up the story of these hypnotic sessions in *The Search for Bridey Murphy*, which came out in 1956. The book was extraordinarily popular. It was also closely examined and discredited. There are still people who believe the case was genuine, but they are in the minority.

An English hypnotist named Arnall Bloxham has been more successful in the long run than Bernstein was. Bloxham has done age-regression experiments for many years now and has an impressive collection of material. One of his subjects tells about life at the court of Louis XIV. Another describes life as a naval gunner early in the nineteenth century. Bloxham's best subject was a schoolteacher named Ann Ockenden, who has regressed through eleven incarnations to her earliest appearance on this planet as a caveman. Bloxham gives the details in his book, *Who Was Ann Ockenden?* More recent (and convincing) data on hypnotic age-regression are in *Reliving Past Lives*, by Helen Wambach (New York: Harper and Row, 1978).

The most convincing case of hypnotic age-regression was reported by Ian Stevenson, professor of psychiatry at the University of Virginia, in an article titled "Twenty Cases Suggestive of Reincarnation." This was the case of a woman married to a Philadelphia doctor. When her husband tried hypnotic age-regression on her, she suddenly felt someone strike her on the head and attempt to drown her. She told her husband she was a man named Jensen Jacoby. Jacoby spoke mostly Swedish, a language the doctor didn't know. He held a few more hypnotic sessions with his wife, inviting Swedish-speaking people to help translate for Jacoby. They found that Jacoby's vocabulary was limited, but in a strange way—he had trouble naming twentieth-century objects, but he readily came up with the old

Swedish names for seventeenth-century museum pieces.

Stevenson's best stories don't involve hypnotism. Instead, they involve spontaneous awareness of a past life in circumstances in which a great many details could be confirmed. For instance, there was the case of Jasbir Jat, a child from the village of Rasulpur in India. In 1954, when Jasbir was three years old, he nearly died of smallpox; for a while his parents thought he *had* died. When Jasbir recovered, he started saying that his name was Sobha Ram and that he was a Brahmin from the village of Vehedi. His parents were distraught, especially when he refused to eat their food. He said he could eat only Brahmin food. Three years passed; then a woman from Vehedi came to visit Rasulpur. Although the two villages are only twenty miles apart, there is virtually no communication between them. This woman was the first visitor from Vehedi in years. Six-year-old Jasbir recognized her. She brought the family of Sobha Ram to see Jasbir, and he greeted them all by name. The boy told them how he, Sobha Ram, had died, and they confirmed the details. (Sobha Ram had fallen off a carriage at the same time that the infant Jasbir had come down with smallpox.) When Ian Stevenson heard this story, he visited both villages and listed thirty-nine facts about Sobha Ram that Jasbir had mentioned before ever visiting Vehedi. Stevenson corroborated thirty-eight of them.

Another case of Stevenson's is even more remarkable. It concerns a boy named Imad Elawar, who was born in Kornayel, Lebanon, in 1958. From a very early age, Imad talked about people his parents did not know and events they had never witnessed. He often mentioned a neighboring village called Khriby. His parents paid little attention to such prattling. But one day little Imad ran up to a stranger in the street and greeted him as an old friend and neighbor. Imad's parents began to pay attention. Stevenson heard of the story, and in 1962 he went to Kornayel. First he got as much information as he could from Imad and his parents, and then he went across the mountains to Khriby. The village was only fifteen miles away from Kornayel, but to the villagers it seemed quite remote.

The story he had from Imad was rather garbled, but with some effort and checking Stevenson straightened it out. Imad had once been Ibrahim Bouhamzy, a man who had died of tuberculosis in 1949. Ibrahim had a close friend named Said and a mistress named Jamile, both of whom Imad had mentioned constantly. Stevenson had a list of forty-seven details Imad had given about his past life and his village; of these, Stevenson confirmed forty-four.

As Stevenson implied in the title of his article, this case is *suggestive* of reincarnation. It doesn't prove it. Perhaps Imad had been possessed by Ibrahim Bouhamzy's spirit. Or perhaps Imad had extraordinary powers of retrocognitive telepathy, through which he saw Bouhamzy's life. In that case, Imad would merely have been identifying with Bouhamzy. We cannot say for certain that Imad *was* Bouhamzy.

The same three possibilities—reincarnation, possession, and telepathy—enter into the story of a young woman named Rosemary who lived in Blackpool, England. Sometime in 1927 she began to speak in an unidentified foreign language. She claimed she was saying things given to her by Telika-Ventiu, the Babylonian wife of Pharaoh Amenhotep III (1460–1377 B.C.). The queen said that Rosemary had been her favorite Syrian slave girl and that the two had drowned together in the Nile.

A local doctor, Frederick Wood, copied five thousand phrases and short sentences of Rosemary's and took them to an Egyptologist, Howard Hulme. Hulme became convinced that the ancient Egyptian Rosemary had spoken was grammatically correct, complete with peculiar popular terms and figures of speech. Hulme arranged a meeting with Rosemary and prepared for it by composing twelve questions in ancient Egyptian (an effort that took him twenty hours). In the course of a ninety-minute session with Hulme, Rosemary answered all twelve questions orally. No known living person can speak ancient Egyptian.

Finally, there is the case of Lurancy Vennums, a girl from Watseka, Illinois. In 1877, Lurancy went into a cataleptic state. For five years, from age thirteen to eighteen, she remained as if in a trance. When that period ended, she began to describe visions of angels and spirits; and she still lapsed into a trance from time to time. Her parents, deciding she was insane, sent her to an alienist, who hypnotized her and found that she was possessed by two personalities: an old hag, and a young man who had committed suicide. Under hypnosis, Lurancy said she would be free of these two personalities only if an angel came and possessed her. Did she know of such an angel? "Yes," Lurancy said. "Her name is Mary Roff."

Who was Mary Roff? She was a girl from the same town who had died at age eighteen in 1865, just fourteen months after Lurancy's birth. Mary had indeed seemed angelic to many of the townspeople; she had also been clairvoyant. Now she took over Lurancy Vennum's body. Lurancy went to live with Mary Roff's family and was very happy there. She knew all the details of family life and knew Mary's life history as well. After three months and ten days, Mary left Lurancy's body. Lurancy then went back to her own family. Her story was researched and authenticated by Richard Hodgson.

Being possessed by a devil is quite another matter, and one that deserves serious attention. Stories of demonic possession are universal. Every shamanistic culture has such stories to tell. The Japanese perform plays on the subject. Jews have their own tradition of casting out *dybbuks*. Jesus, too, cast out demons, and Christians have invoked his name ever since to drive away the Evil Spirit. Martin Luther flung an inkpot at Satan.

But for full-dress demonic possession and exorcism, you have to go to the Roman Catholic Church. In the discussion that follows, I have relied on the knowledgeable and quite orthodox account of Catholic exorcism given by Malachi Martin in *Hostage to the Devil: The Possession and Exorcism of Five Living Americans* (New York: Reader's Digest Press, 1976).

Demonic Possession

Demonic possession is one of the great themes of Western civilization. The early Church based much of its prestige on the power of its members to cast out demons in the name of Jesus Christ, and ever since the rite of exorcism has been in constant use. In literature, the subject of man's bargain with the Devil has been a central preoccupation since the Renaissance (witness Marlow, Goethe, Mann). As evidence of the continued vitality of the theme, we have a recent opera by the great Polish composer, Krysztof Penderecki, based on *Paradise Lost*. If there's one thing we've all been taught, ever since we heard of Adam and Eve, it's that Satan is ready to take over the soul of anyone he can get.

The Evil Spirit enters people gradually, and only with their consent. To the exorcist, this is the crucial fact about possession—it is a choice freely made. Even after the Evil Spirit has taken control of a person, some free will may be left, however weak and intermittent. The exorcist's task is to restore that free will with the aid of Jesus Christ.

In the first stage of possession, the devil will play upon the talents or preoccupations of its victim. Any strong interest or character trait can be of use. The devil offers the victim appropriate help of some sort—power, success, energy, knowledge—and the victim consciously accepts that help. The acceptance may be vague, it may be nonverbal, but it is there. And in return the Devil gets what it wants—a place to live.

The second stage of possession is a time of bad judgments, of drawing away from people once loved, of overthrowing everything that used to give life its meaning. The devil encourages the victim in this in the most direct way possible, by keeping its part of the bargain. It offered help, and it gives help. For a while the victim is deluded into thinking that everything is fine, scarcely noticing the destruction in most areas of his or her life.

Eventually the victim reaches a critical moment. The alien force within insists on taking control and demands obedience. The victim still retains free will up to this moment, but he or she may have become so corrupted that it is a pleasure, a relief, to give up control. The devil exerts great pressure, often threatening the victim in the harshest way imaginable. And the victim gives in.

From that moment, free will is gone. The devil orders, and the victim obeys. Words come to the victim's mouth; the body moves as if by its own will. The evidence of spiritual ruin is obvious to friends and family; and the victim, too, will retain one small corner of self-knowledge, or rebellion against the devil. That small corner will be there through God's grace, but the victim, unaware of that, will use it only as room to despair.

There may be physical signs of possession as well. The victim shows a repugnance toward all religious symbols and rituals. Poltergeist phenomena appear. Sometimes the victim's features become grotesquely distorted, or abnormally smooth. Catatonia sets in for periods. And there is a stench unlike any other smell. The popular book *The Exorcist* gives a vivid and fairly accurate picture.

The victim's family and friends will probably have sought medical and psychiatric help. If such help has failed, the family may then go to the Church. Each Roman Catholic diocese has access to an exorcist, and, following the authority of the church's hierarchy, that man must now examine the victim and determine whether he or she is actually possessed. The examination must be thorough. In the past, when people were eager to see the devil behind every personal aberration, the horrors inflicted in the name of God were themselves utterly demonic (See the "Occult Reformation" section in chapter seven). At present, people are more cautious, at least within the Church. Henri Gesland, a French priest and exorcist, says that three thousand cases came to him over a period of six years, and of that group, he believed only four involved demonic possession.

The Exorcism. If the priest determines that an exorcism is needed, he will begin the preparations by arranging for the victim to be placed in a comfortable room in some friendly place. Then the room must be stripped and carefully prepared, because during the course of the exorcism, the Evil Spirit may throw objects around the room, rip up the carpet, open and close the door violently, even try to push the exorcist or victim out of the window.

Before the ritual begins, the exorcist's lay-assistants (usually four in number) enter the room and tie down the victim. In some cases they leave the victim free, but only if they're sure they will be able to hold him down. Then the exorcist's assistant, a priest, enters the room. The assistant is usually an exorcist in-training. His function is to learn, to carry out the exorcist's orders immediately and unquestioningly, and to take over should the exorcist collapse, die, or be overcome.

The exorcist himself is the last to enter the room. He and his assistant wear black cassocks covered with white surplices and purple stoles. The exorcist has made confession beforehand and usually has said Mass; it is vital for the exorcist to have as clean a conscience as possible. The exorcist is most often a man of middle years, a pastoral rather than scholarly minister, sensitive but not brilliant, characterized above all by a sense of grace.

The importance of this combination of traits becomes obvious when you understand the exorcist's function. He must enter into direct, personal combat with the Evil Spirit. For the whole course of the exorcism—usually ten hours at least, often several days—he will face hatred and obscenity of inhuman power, all directed with vicious cunning at *him*. If he survives and overcomes the evil power, it will be through the strength of Jesus Christ. He cannot resist on his own.

As soon as the exorcist steps into the room, the Evil Spirit makes its presence felt. The presence seems to be everywhere at once, like an unseen pressure, a hissing in the ears, a threat hanging over everyone in the room. When the exorcist first speaks to the presence, though, it will speak in the victim's own voice and claim to be the victim himself. This is the Evil Spirit's first defense, the pretense that it is not there at all—only the victim is there. The exorcist must hammer at this pretense until it cracks. Meanwhile, the demon, through the victim, becomes more and more obscene, hideous, repulsive. The demonic smell grows heavier; unsecured objects hurl themselves at the exorcist; the victim claws at his restraints, or at anyone holding him down.

At the climax of this stage of exorcism, the priest and his assistants feel trapped in confusion. Their senses won't focus properly. A fear of insanity or death overcomes them, and they panic. If the exorcist can hold out, the demon will now stop using the victim's voice. For the first time, it will speak of the victim in the third person. It will call itself *I* or *we*.

As it does so, its voice becomes hideous, unbearable. Each syllable echoes in the exorcist's brain, and each echo is mocking, insulting, vile. The exorcist must strain not to lose himself in these echoes, which surround him with accusations of his every sin and pettiness. With a great effort of the will, and in the name of Jesus, the exorcist must silence the demon's voice. Then he will demand to know the demon's name and the ways it has misled the victim.

All the demon's violence and filth have been preliminaries till this point. Now the struggle truly begins. The demon is now within the exorcist as well as within the victim. It exploits every weakness of the exorcist's personality and faith; it shows him visions of horror and despair beyond his imagination. If the exorcist can summon the strength and protection of God, he will master the demon. Only then can he expel the Evil Spirit. The hideous presence leaves the room. The exorcism is over. Time and again at exorcisms, the Evil Spirit in departing will cry, "Where shall we go? We can't stay here any longer." We know, of course, where the demon has to go.

The following case is of special interest to students of the occult. It was reported by Malachi Martin, who claims to have based his account on interviews, videotapes, and the transcript of the exorcism itself.

The victim, Carl V., was a parapsychologist. As a child he showed psychic abilities, but his parents discouraged him from using them, and the abilities gradually fell into latency. The story of his possession begins when he was a teenager. One evening, just before dinner, he had a vision of a timeless, serene landscape. He not only saw the landscape, he *was* the landscape; he knew it from within. A voice said, "Wait." That was all. The material world looked very drab to him after that.

Carl went to Princeton, where he was a brilliant student of psychology. While there, he met a Tibetan student who taught him techniques of meditation. After much difficulty, Carl learned how to enter the state of no-mind, the pure awareness that is the starting point of Tibetan spiritual development. But his friend would no longer instruct him. When Carl demanded to know why, the Tibetan told him that when the soul achieves no-mind, it is like a lotus that has opened. Then a tiny silver urn, which is True Knowledge, is placed in the center of the lotus. But in Carl's case, the urn could not be put in the soul because something else was already there—"Filth. Materiality. Slime. Death." With that, the Tibetan sadly walked away.

Carl ignored this warning. His psychic abilities had begun to reawaken. He travelled, studied, and in 1958 took up residence as a professor at a Midwestern university. Soon he attracted a group of followers who shared his interest in parapsychology. More than that, they believed in his powers. Carl was now seeing auras, travelling astrally, exploring his past incarnations, even projecting an astral double. He told himself and others that all these powers were manifestations of God. What's more, by means of astral travel, he would go back in time and rediscover the true nature of Christianity.

All this came about through the agency of his "friend" within, a presence that called itself the Tortoise. One evening the Tortoise showed Carl a vision: The material world was growing greater and greater, and Carl himself was shrinking to nothing. Tortoise didn't have to speak to Carl—the vision was intself a threat and a message. Carl could either give in to Tortoise or be annihilated. Carl gave in.

The climax of the possession came on July 23, 1973. On that day, Carl and a group of his students and followers went to the cathedral in Aquileia, Italy, to perform a ceremony that Carl had seen during one of his astral voyages. He said it was an authentic early Christian ritual. He never performed it. He led his followers into the vaults of the old church beneath the cathedral and tried to carry out the ceremony; but on the word *Christum* he stuttered and went stiff. His friends had to carry him out.

Carl returned to his father's home in Philadelphia. He seemed lifeless and despairing. Finally he asked his father to call a priest who'd been in one of his classes years before, Father Hartney. Carl said Father Hartney was in Newark, New Jersey. Carl's father tried to call the priest long distance, but he wasn't in. The priest's housekeeper couldn't give any information about him. Carl's father hung up and was about to go back to his son when the phone rang. It was Father Hartney calling. He was in Philadelphia and wanted to speak with Carl.

Father Hartney was himself a psychic. He was born in Wales in 1905. It was a time and place where psychic gifts were considered normal, and Father Hartney never bothered to think much about his. He was born a Methodist but converted to Catholicism as a young man and was ordained in 1936. He began assisting at exorcisms in the early 1950s.

When he was in Carl's parapsychology class, Father Hartney was the only student to challenge Carl's basic assumption, that psychic abilities were gifts of God. Father Hartney maintained that there was both good spirit and evil spirit, and it was vital not to get them confused. Probably Carl would have ignored this argument, but there was something strange about Father Hartney. Carl could see into the minds of all his other students, but the priest was opaque to him. Carl didn't know that Father Hartney was psychic, he merely knew there was a fundamental barrier between him and the priest. Perhaps this was what made him think of Father Hartney years later.

After considerable preparation, the priest arranged for an exorcism. It lasted five days. The most remarkable thing about the struggle between priest and demon was that almost from the first it was internalized. At one point the demon knocked all the books off their shelves, but that was the only physical violence. Tortoise revealed itself and its name fairly early. After that, the exorcism was an uninterrupted psychic battle. "For as long as it lasted," Hartney said, "it was a brutal partial possession of me. All that remained finally free was my will. And even that . . ."

Tortoise showed Father Hartney a vision of a corrupted, ugly world, a place drained of meaning and love. The demon mocked and distorted every aspect of the priest's life; it even took over Father Hartney's mind so that he heard himself repeat all the accusations in his own voice. Through all this the priest was standing motionless, as if catatonic, clutching his crucifix. Gradually, weakly, he began to call on Jesus. As the name came from his lips, the demon's grip broke. The priest lifted his head and roared, "Murderer! Be murdered now! In your turn!"

From that moment, the exorcist was the demon's master. He compelled it to admit to everything it had done to Carl. Carl had never travelled astrally, had not experienced his past incarnations, had not projected a double. All these were delusions given him by the Evil Spirit. He had seen auras, visible signs of God's grace; but the demon had twisted and corrupted their meaning. The vision Carl once had as a teenager had been genuine as well, but Tortoise had crept into it and used it. He had told Carl, "Wait." And Carl had waited for him.

Carl's psychic powers left him with Tortoise. For a while he was distraught. He no longer is. In a letter he wrote after the exorcism, Carl said, "My advice for all who engage in the study and pursuit of the parapsychological is simple but vitally important: do not confound effects with causes, or systems with what maintains the systems. Do not take it that a photograph of Kirlian dots or auras is a photograph of spirit. Do not accept the feats of séance mediums as results of spirit from God. But do not, on the other hand, tamper with or treat parapsychological phenomena as if you could do this without ultimately impinging upon spirit. You cannot. And that fact will, depending upon what you do, be to your detriment or to your betterment—in spirit."

The Text for Exorcism. The following is a condensation of the Church's traditional text for exorcism as translated by Malachi Martin. It is important for you to remember that exorcism is not a sacrament; therefore, the priest is under no obligation to follow this text. In the course of an exorcism, the priest must in fact depart from this text many times in order to speak with the demon and command it. The Church provides a text only as a guide.

When a printed cross appears in the text, the priest makes a Sign of the Cross in the direction of the exorcee.

The priest who with the particular and explicit permission of his Bishop is about to exorcise those tormented by Evil Spirit, must have the necessary piety, prudence and personal integrity. He should perform this most heroic work humbly and courageously, not relying on his own strength, but on the power of God; and he must have no greed for material benefit. Besides, he should be of mature age and be respected as a virtuous person. . . .

Above all, he must not easily believe that someone is possessed by Evil Spirit. He must be thoroughly acquainted with those signs by which he can distinguish the possessed person from those who suffer from a physical illness. . . .

Let the exorcist note for himself the tricks and deceits which evil spirits use in order to lead him astray. For they are accustomed to answering falsely. . . . Innumerable are the stratagems and deceits which Evil Spirit uses in order to deceive men. The exorcist must practice caution in order not to be deceived by any of them. . . .

He should command the unclean spirit to keep silent and only to respond to what is asked of it. . . . Questions he must ask the possessing Evil Spirit are, for example: the number and name of the possessing spirits; when they entered the possessed; why they entered him; and other questions of the same kind. Let the exorcist restrain the other vanities, mockeries, and foolishnesses of Evil Spirit. . . .

The exorcist should perform and read the exorcism with command, authority, great faith, humility, and fervor. And, when he sees that the possessing spirit is being tortured mightily, he should multiply all these efforts at pressuring it. Whenever he sees some part of the possessed person's body moving or pierced or some swelling appearing, let him make the Sign of the Cross and sprinkle Holy Water. Let him pay attention also to the words and expressions which disturb Evil Spirit most, and repeat them very often. . . .

During Exorcism, the exorcist should use the words of the Bible rather than his own or somebody else's. Also, he should command Evil Spirit to state whether it is kept within the possessed because of some magical spell or sorcerer's symbol or some occult documents. . . .

If the possessed person is freed from Evil Spirit, he should be advised to be diligent in avoiding sinful actions and thoughts. If he does not, he could give Evil Spirit a fresh occasion for returning and possessing him. In that case, he would be in a much worse condition than before.

[The exorcism begins with an invocation to God to protect the possessed person, the exorcist, and the assistants. The exorcist makes the Sign of the Cross, sprinkles Holy Water, and recites Psalm 53. The exorcist then summons Evil Spirit.]

Unclean Spirit! Whoever you are, and all your companions who possess this servant of God. By the mysteries of the Incarnation, the Sufferings and Death, the Resurrection, and the Ascension of Our Lord Jesus Christ; by the sending of the Holy Spirit; and by the Coming of Our Lord into Last Judgment, I command you:

Tell me, with some sign, your name, the day and the hour of your damnation.

Obey me in everything, although I am an unworthy servant of God.

Do no damage to this creature (the possessed), or to my assistants, or to any of their goods.

[Gospel readings follow. These are usually John 1:1–12; Mark 16:15–18; Luke 10:17–20; and Luke 11:14–22.]

I exorcise you, Most Unclean Spirit! Invading Enemy! All Spirits! Every one of you! In the name of Our Lord Jesus +Christ: Be uprooted and expelled from this Creature of God. +He who commands you is he who ordered you to be thrown down from the highest Heaven into the depths of Hell. He who commands you is he who dominated the sea, the wind, and the storms. Hear, therefore, and fear, Satan! Enemy of the Faith! Enemy of the human race! Source of death! Robber of life! Twister of justice! Root of evil! Warp of vices! Seducer of men! Traitor of nations! Inciter of jealousy! Originator of greed! Cause of discord! Creator of agony! Why do you stay and resist, when you know that Christ our Lord has destroyed your plan? Fear him who was prefigured in Isaac, in Joseph, and in the Paschal Lamb; who was crucified as a man, and who rose from death.

(Then making the Sign of the Cross on the forehead of the possessed): Retire, therefore, in the name of +Father, and of the +Son, and of the Holy +Spirit. Give way to the Holy Spirit, because of this sign of the Holy +Cross of Our Lord Jesus Christ, Who lives and reigns as God with the Father and the same Holy Spirit, for ever and ever. . . .

Repel, O Lord, the power of Evil Spirit! Dissolve the fallacies of its plots! May the unholy tempter take flight. May your servant be protected in soul and body by the sign + of your name (on the forehead of possessed).

(Then he makes three signs of the Cross on the chest of the possessed, while pronouncing the following words):

+Preserve what is within this person.

+Rule his (her) feelings.

+Strengthen his (her) heart. . . .

I enjoin you under penalty, Ancient Serpent! . . . Surrender, not to me, but to the minister of Christ. His power forces you. He defeated you by His Cross. Fear the strength of him who led the souls of the dead to the light of salvation from the darkness of waiting. May the body of this man + (*on the chest of possessed*) be a source of fear for you. +God the Father commands you. +God the Son commands you. +God the Holy Spirit commands you. +The faith of the Holy Apostles, Peter and Paul, and the other saints commands you. +The blood of Martyrs commands you. +The purity of the Confessors commands you. +The pious and holy intercession of all the Saints commands you. +The strength of the mysteries of the Christian faith commands you. +Get out! Offender! Get out! Seducer! . . .

I, therefore, charge you solemnly under penalty, Most Evil Serpent, in the name of the Lamb +most immaculate who walked unharmed among dangers; who was immune to all Evil Spirit: Depart from this person + (*on forehead of possessed*). Depart from the Church of God +(*over the assistants*). Fear and take flight at the name of Our Lord whom the powers of Hell fear, to whom the Powers and Virtues and Dominations of Heaven are subject, whom the Cherubim and Seraphim praise with unceasing voices, saying: Holy! Holy! Holy! Lord God of Hosts!

The Word made Flesh + commands you. He who was born of a Virgin + commands you. Jesus + of Nazareth commands you. . . . [Further prayers to be repeated with devotion: the Pater Noster, Ave Maria, and the Credo, as well as the Magnificat and the Benedictus Canticle (ending the last two with a Gloria). At the expulsion of Evil Spirit, the recommended Psalms are numbers 90, 67, 34, 30, 21, 3, 10, and 12. Then comes the concluding prayer of thanks.]

We pray you, all-powerful God, that Evil Spirit have no more power over this servant of yours (*gives name of possessed*), but that it flee and not come back. Let the goodness and the peace of our Lord Jesus Christ enter him (her) at your bidding, Lord. For through Jesus we have been saved. And let us not fear any ill, because the Lord is with us, He who lives and reigns as God with you in the unity of the Holy Spirit, for ever and ever.

The assistants say, Amen.

How to Fake a Séance

All mediums are psychic to one degree or another, but even the most gifted medium has off-days and blind spots. Clients find that hard to understand or forgive; they want results, and so the medium had better be ready to perform, even if it means faking it. Faking is thus essential—but so is psi ability. Don't set up in business until you've developed yours to the point where you can get reliable impressions of people. Be ready to read moods, health, and overall emotional state; try to see auras.

While you're developing psi powers, you should also be assembling files of obituaries. Arthur Ford, who on the whole was quite reputable, had an extensive file, and when preparing for a séance, he would commit to memory a great many details taken from obituaries. I would recommend that you keep your information on index cards, which should be alphabetized and cross-referenced.

If at all possible, you should know something about your clients before their first visits. Don't rely exclusively on obituaries. Credit unions, banks, employers, and schools are often quite free with information about people if approached correctly. Send a stooge to gossip with neighbors and apartment-building managers.

The stooge, by the way, is important. Every fake medium needs one. When the clients come to visit you, your stooge must be the one to greet them, while you stay out of sight in another room. The stooge shows your clients into the waiting room, tells them he will announce their arrival, and takes their coats and purses. Then he goes into another room, locks the door, and rifles the clients' belongings for any information he can find. You, meanwhile, are listening to the clients by means of the microphone you've planted in the waiting room. People are invariably keyed-up before a séance. They're bound to say something that can be used.

When you're ready, have the stooge conduct your clients into the séance room. Feel free to use whatever stage manner suits you best—it's a highly individual matter. Some mediums like to be mysterious and a bit unsettling. However, a warm and unassuming manner can be more effective—once you establish rapport, the confidences will flow.

A trick helps to set the mood. One of the best involves spirit writing, which you can produce by means of a prepared envelope. Take an ordinary mailing envelope and trim it along the sides and bottom so that it comes apart in two pieces. Take the front piece, the one with the flap, and place it inside a second envelope; then seal the outer flap to the inner one. You now have an ordinary-looking envelope with a double front, very convenient for hiding any spirit messages you want to prepare.

To set up the trick, tell your clients as they enter that you've been getting impressions all evening—they're hard to explain, a sort of pressure within. Then turn to the client you've chosen for the trick and say that the pressure seems greatest around him. You would like to seek a sign. Hand the client a piece of paper of the sort you used for your planted spirit message. Ask him to write a brief note to someone (the spirit whose name you have signed to your note). Then bring out the prepared envelope. Hold it open and ask the client to breathe into it to magnetize its aura. This is a good way to show the client that the envelope looks empty—if you were to say, "You'll notice I'm giving you an empty envelope," you'd spoil the mood. Have the client fold his note to Aunt Louisa and place it in the envelope. Be sure to use full-size stationery and a business envelope, so that you can count on the client folding the paper in thirds. That, of course, is how you folded Aunt Louisa's reply when you planted it.

Now seal the envelope, put in on a desk, and forget about it. Make small talk with the other clients; give them some meaningless chatter about yourself. Their minds will all be on the envelope, and while they're distracted they might let more information about themselves slip out. When the trick has run on long enough, go to the envelope, tear it along the side, and remove Aunt Louisa's reply from the hidden compartment. Give the spirit message to the client at once, without looking at it. While the client reads Aunt Louisa's reply and the others gather around him, you should have time to pocket the prepared envelope. Quickly bring out another envelope with the flap sealed and the side torn—apparently identical to the first envelope—and give it to the client as a souvenir. That clinches the effect.

Now that everybody is in the right mood, you can start the séance. Turn off the lights. (The standard excuse for this is that the spirits are shy of light.) It's best to leave the room in total darkness, but even the most gullible clients grow suspicious at this. Therefore, you might want to burn a candle or an oil lamp. Used correctly, these can be even more deceptive than darkness.

Have the clients sit around the séance table and touch hands. You, too, must touch hands with the clients on either side of you—but not for long. You can gradually draw your hands together until the right hand is lying partially on top of the left hand. Then, at a distracting moment, pull back your right hand. The client on your left is still touching your left hand. The client on your right, who is also touching your left hand now, thinks he's still touching your right hand. This leaves you free to produce some poltergeist phenomena.

Another way of accomplishing the same thing: Sit away from the table, and have one of the clients sit facing you. Place your hands over his, explaining that he will be your control and assure the others that you're not faking. Lift your hands for a moment and say, "You can feel right away if I lift my hands, can't you?" The client will say that he can. Then put only your left hand down, laying it over both the client's hands. Babble for a moment longer about the importance of the control; then ask again, "Can you feel right away if I take away one of my hands?" Now tilt your left hand briefly; it will feel to the client as if you've lifted your right hand. Put your left hand down again, and he'll be convinced you're covering his hands with both of your hands.

Don't go into trance too soon. It's better if the clients are a little bored and impatient. At the critical moment, don't be afraid to overact. It can be very effective, especially if up to that point you have seemed dull and unassuming. Make sure that your voice, when in trance, sounds distinctly different from your ordinary voice.

Use your free hand to make the table rap. It would sound suspicious if the raps were to come from where you are sitting, so prepare the table by fixing a lever from your seat to under the table's center. Then, when you move the lever, the raps would sound a comfortable distance away from you. To make the table float around, simply lift with one knee—a transparent trick that usually works in the confusion of a séance.

Remember, you're in trance all this time. To all appearances you should be insensible, and you should be producing a constant patter from your control spirit. Use the control spirit to ask leading questions of the clients. For example, the control can say, "I see your uncle, Uncle Morris. Yes, it's Uncle Morris. There's a regret. Morris, regret. Something he left undone. The one thing he's sorry about." Most clients cannot resist blurting a suggestion as to what Morris's regret might be. Within a few minutes, a good medium can have the clients doing most of the work.

Once the right pitch of hysteria has been reached, the materializations begin. Here you are limited only by your budget. In the old days, mediums would bring out pieces of gauze soaked in luminous paint and wave them around at the appropriate moment, while tooting on toy trumpets. Today that would seem tacky. To give your clients their money's worth, invest in audio and holographic equipment. Spirits in 3-D Technicolor and quadrophonic sound can scare people out of their wits. If that is too expensive or too elaborate, there's a middle way.

Build a floor-to-ceiling partition in one corner of the séance room and call it your spirit cabinet. Invite your clients to examine it thoroughly before the séance begins. There's a trick to the cabinet, of course—it has a trapdoor in the ceiling. (In the floor it would be too obvious, and the clients might find it. It's very unlikely that they'll examine the ceiling.) At the right moment during the séance, your stooge will open the trapdoor and lower a black, padded ladder. Then, covered in luminescent gauze, he can emerge from the cabinet and spook the séance.

At the end of the evening, you may accept the clients' thanks, but be

CHAPTER THREE

Tools

(The Mental Plane)

• *Numerology* • *Astrology* • *Tarot*
• *I Ching* • *Meditation* • *Hypnosis* • *Drugs*

Numerology

Occultists and scientists hold one conviction in common, that there is nothing solid about physical reality. The smallest particles of matter are in constant motion. What's more, they're moving in pure nothingness—the distance between an atom's nucleus and electron cloud is vast (on the atom's scale, that is), and in that distance is empty space. In other words, any given physical object is more space than matter, and what matter it contains is spinning and whirling constantly.

Everything vibrates, as if the universe were one large musical instrument. The mathematical laws of this vibration are the basis of numerology.

Pythagoras, who lived in the sixth century B.C., is the source of our knowledge of numerology. He is also a major source of both occult and mainstream Western thought. Many of his ideas have been transmitted to us through Plato, who synthesized Pythagorean doctrines with Socratic ethics to form his own philosophy. Detailed information on Pythagoras's life and thought can be found in chapter seven. In this chapter, I will be concerned with Pythagoras's esoteric doctrines, the first and most important of which, for our purposes, is the theory of vibration.

Pythagoras reportedly was the first to discover the vibration ratios of the musical scale. You have him to thank for keeping your piano tuned. He compared the vibration rates of two strings tuned an octave apart and found that the octave string vibrated twice as fast as the tonic string; their vibration ratio is 2:1. The vibration ratio for the interval of the fifth is 3:2. The ration for an interval of a fourth is 4:3.

Now, the surprising thing about these relationships is that they're so simple. The ratio of notes in a musical scale could just as well involve such numbers as 8.37516 and the cube root of *pi*. But they don't—they involve simple, whole numbers, primarily 1, 2, 3, and 4.

Pythagoras regarded these numbers as the source of all other numbers. Their cross sum (1+2+3+4) is 10. You can see the relationship in a figure called the tetractys, which Pythagoras's followers used to draw on their walls:

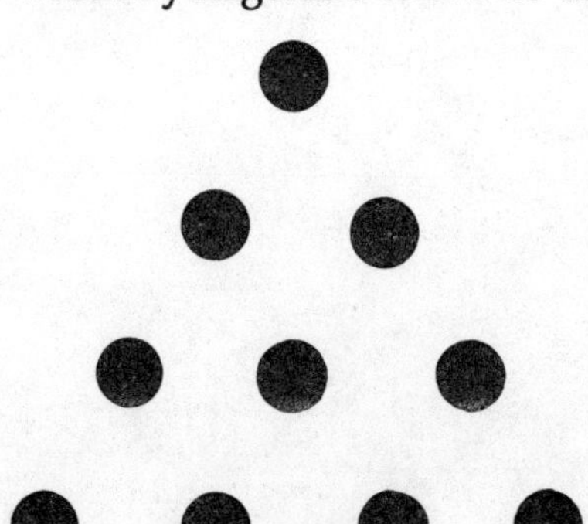

The numbers 1, 2, 3, and 4 generate the other numbers to 10. After 10, the numbers merely repeat themselves: the cross sum of 11 (1+1) is 2, the cross sum of 12 is 3, and so on.

What the Numbers Mean

The numbers 1 to 4 have their own generative symbolism. The Absolute, the beginning of all things, is 1. With 2 we have opposition and division, or polarity—for example, man and woman, or God and matter. But the two are static. Relationship begins with 3: Man plus woman plus sexual desire, or God plus matter plus creative will. The product of the relationship (lovemaking, or the created world) is 4.

The traditional symbolism of 1 to 10 is as follows:

1: The origin, God; the male principle.

2: The female principle. This is also the number of evil and the Devil, since it represents the first step away from 1. Contemporary numerologists gloss over this aspect of 2 (and with good reason). This is, unfortunately, the traditional interpretation.

3: Creation. One is divine, but it cannot create—a number multiplied by 1 remains the same. Two is feminine and therefore fecund, but it cannot create, either—a number multiplied by 2 will always be even, and therefore express an opposition. Three is therefore the basic generative number. It is, of course, the number of the Holy Trinity. Its symbol is the triangle, which also represents the male genitals.

4: An ominous number. It is both $2 + 2$ and 2×2. It is the number of the physical world—the four compass points, the four elements. It is also the number of the gospels.

5: The number of sex. It is the male (3) plus the female (2); God (1) plus the physical world (4). It is the number of our senses.

6: This is a tranquil number because it is perfect—that is, its divisors (1, 2, 3) add up to the number itself. It is traditionally the number of home and marriage.

7: This is a prime number—it can be divided only by 1. Unlike the other prime numbers under 10 (3 and 5), it cannot be multiplied by any other whole number and still yield 10 or less. Thus it is unique among the basic numbers. It is the number of the moon (since the moon's cycle is in four phases of seven days each). It is also the number that controls menstruation (a cycle of 4×7 days, with the menstrual period itself lasting about 3½ days). Thus, 7 is the number of life's rhythms. It is the most important number in the Book of Revelations, which mentions 7 a total of 54 times.

8: An intensified version of 4. As 4 stands for the physical world, so 8 stands for wealth and materialism. Some people say it stands for the afterlife as well, since it follows 7.

9: Because it is the highest of the basic numbers, 9 is an intensified version of 3. It is 3 × 3, and thus a number of special power. It is also the number of procreation, since pregnancy lasts 9 months.

10: The completion of the cycle, God (1) plus the original void (0); the number of the world.

Eleven begins a cycle of the higher world, of revelation and of martyrdom. Eleven is God (1) plus the world (10). It is the number of the faithful Apostles. In numerological analysis, 11 and 22 have special significance as master numbers, as the next section will reveal.

Practical Numerology

Numerology can be used for character analysis and prediction. Indeed, this is the most common current use of numerology, which as a characterological system can rival astrology.

As an example for study, I've made up a man with the improbable name of Satan Turk Laws, who was born on October 17, 1950. From these two pieces of information (arbitrary in this case), the numerologist can build up an entire character portrait.

Life Cycles. The first calculations derive from the birthdate. These are the numbers of the life path, the life cycles, and whatever problems and abilities the individual was born with.

To find the life-path number, add the month, day, and year of birth and then find their cross sum. In Mr. Laws's case, this would be 10 (for the month of October) + 17 (for the day) + 1950 (for the year) = 1977; 1 + 9 + 7 + 7 = 24; 2 + 4 = 6. So the life-path number is 6. (It's necessary to go through all the intermediate calculations in case there's an 11 or 22 hiding in the numbers. For example, if Mr. Laws had been born on October 15, 1950, his life-path number would be 22, and this would be highly significant.)

The life-path number illustrates the major theme of your life. The theme can be either a blessing or a burden; other numbers will reveal which. Here are the meanings of the life-path numbers:

1: An active life of individual accomplishment. This could mean satisfying self-expression, cold self-concern, or a desperate and unwelcome need to fall back on one's own resources.

2: A life of companionship and cooperation. This is usually a more conventional life than 1, and it can bring quiet, love, and fulfillment, or a constant struggle to overcome shyness and egotism.

3: A creative, sociable, generous, fortunate life. People born as 3 have an enviably easy time of it in life. Their chief difficulty is in learning to overcome jealousy—as much as they have, they're greedy for more.

4: A life of hard work, even drudgery. People born as 4 are reliable, good at detail work, and very hostile. Their lives aren't entirely grim;

for they derive satisfaction from their families, and they're usually content enough when left unbothered.

5: A life of adventure, travel, and sudden changes. There's often a strong emphasis on sex. Some 5 people become entirely too adventuresome and unattached; then there's a danger of alcoholism, drug addiction, and repetitious sex.

6: A life of leadership, public service, and marital concerns. The 6 person often has great success in life, but he or she tends to be a perfectionist, and this can interfere with marriages and love affairs, which are a major concern here.

7: A life of reclusiveness, often of scholarship or religious devotion. There's a threat of poverty and little chance for happy marriage. But the intellectual and spiritual benefits of a 7 life can more than offset its difficulties.

8: A life concerned with money, either with making lots of it or with worrying constantly about the lack of it. People with an 8 life path are generous when they have money, driven when they don't. The main concern here is power rather than pleasure.

9: A cosmopolitan life, full of achievement but also of sacrifice. People born as 9 are especially open-minded, but at the same time they tend to be ironic and cold. They can be sure that whatever happens to them will be intense.

11: A life of inspiration and great intelligence. People born as 11 usually have lived through many incarnations and are teachers by nature. For all that, they can be very hard on their companions and are not easy to live with.

22: The faculties of the 11, plus a global outlook and great moral integrity. People born with this number have great responsibilities. Under adverse conditions, those responsibilities become too much, and the individual relapses to a 4 life path.

Our fictional subject, Mr. Laws, has a 6 life path. He could be headed for worldly success and a happy marriage, or he could end up divorced, overloaded with responsibilities, and miserable. We will know more when we look at his other numbers.

The next calculation will tell us what special problems and advantages Mr. Laws will have. To find the area of his problems, take the day of birth (in his case 17) and subtract the smaller number from the larger. People born on the 1st through the 9th, the 11th, and the 22nd of the month have no specific problem expressed in their birthdate. Mr. Laws's problem is $7 - 1 = 6$. In brief, the nature of the problems attached to numbers follow:

1: To rely on oneself

2: To cooperate with others

3: To direct one's energies
4: To accept the burdens of one's work
5: To regulate oneself
6: To accept responsibilities
7: To find faith
8: To overcome greed.

Mr. Laws's problem is 6—to accept responsibilities. His life path is also 6. This tells us right away that he's going to have a hard time of it. Life will constantly be piling duties on him, and he will chafe at them all. He will have to devote a lot of energy toward keeping his love affairs going.

The birthdate also shows what advantage the individual has to compensate for his or her problem. To find the number of the advantage, subtract the problem number from 9. For Mr. Laws, the number is 9 − 6 = 3. The advantages for each number are as follows:

1: Worldly achievements
2: Intelligence
3: Creativity
4: Growth
5: Stability
6: Success
7: Knowledge
8: Material success

Mr. Laws's advantage is creativity. That will be of little help in offsetting his problem. People who are creative have enough troubles in life on that account alone; if they have to deal with unwelcome duties, too, they are almost sure to be miserable.

Now we have a pretty good idea of the main theme of Mr. Laws's life. But we can have even more exact information. Each life has three major periods: growth, maturity, and old age. By using the birthdate, we can characterize each of these periods. The number of the growth period derives from the month of birth; the mature period from the day; and the period of old age from the year. So for Mr. Laws, the three periods are 1 (October, 1 + 0), 8 (1 + 7), and 6 (1 + 9 + 5 + 0 = 15 = 6).

When do these periods come into effect? The best method of computation for this is the one given by Kevin Quinn Avery, using the method for finding what is called the *personal year*. For any given year (e.g., 1977), find the cross sum of the month and day of birth with the year. For Mr. Laws, this would be 10 + 17 + 1977 = 2004 = 6. The year 1977 is a 6 year for Mr. Laws. The year 1978 will be Mr. Laws's personal year 7, and so forth.

A person's first period ends and his second period begins in the 1 personal year closest to his twenty-eighth birthday. The second period ends and the third begins in the 1 personal year closest to his fifty-seventh birthday. In Mr. Laws's case, the second period will begin in 1981, and the third period will begin in 2008.

What have we learned so far? Mr. Laws's life as a whole will be dominated by the number 6, indicating concern with duties and domestic life. These concerns will seem a burden to him, a burden aggravated by his own creative abilities (shown in the 3 we found in his birthdate). For the first part of his life, he will be dominated by 1 (independence and self-reliance). Starting in 1981, when he will be thirty-one years old, his concern will switch to 8 (an indication of material success and high ambition). In 2008, when Mr. Laws will be fifty-eight-years old, he will enter the last phase of his life, in which his greatest concern will be with 6 (domestic burdens again).

In addition to the above, we can calculate three lessons to be learned in the course of the subject's life. One of these, the major lesson, will be present throughout life. The other two lessons are subsidiary, and each is in force for half the life cycle.

To find the numbers of the lessons, first reduce the birthdate to three digits. For Mr. Laws, these digits are 1, 8, and 6. The minor lesson in effect in the first half of life is the difference between the month and day digits, or $8 - 1 = 7$. The minor challenge in effect in the second half of life is the difference between the day and year digits, or $8 - 6 = 2$. To discover the major lesson, calculate the difference between the two minor lessons: $7 - 2 = 5$.

Here, in summary, are the natures of the lessons:

1: To develop a correct sense of oneself
2: To cooperate with others
3: To enjoy oneself with others
4: To integrate one's work with one's life
5: To avoid attachment to the world
6: To accept people as they are
7: To seek involvement in the world
8: To gain a proper attitude toward money

In Mr. Laws's case, it would seem, at first glance, that we have a contradiction. His major lesson is 5, to avoid attachment to the world; but the lesson for the first half of his life is 7 (to seek involvement in the world), and the lesson for the second half is 2 (to cooperate with others). Surely this is asking too much of the man.

But we have to coordinate these numbers with the numbers of his life cycle. The first period of his life, till age thirty-one, will be dominated by

1—independence and self-reliance. The presence of 7 as his lesson early in life tells us that Mr. Laws, when young, will be too independent, perhaps even withdrawn. We know he will come out of this phase, because the second period of his life (ages thirty-one to fifty-eight) will be dominated by 8, ambition and material success. Here we see the reason for the presence of 2 and 5 as his other lessons. Mr. Laws will indeed come out of himself and become involved in the world, but he will do so in terms of power, money, and personal achievement—he will leave no room in his life for other people. And at the same time, he will grow attached to his material success. Probably he will be forced to give up some or all of this success for the sake of others, and he will not like that at all. Here, perhaps, is the meaning of the 6 we've been finding throughout our reading on Mr. Laws. He will eventually have to sacrifice something of himself for others, and that will be the most important thing he will ever do (though he might never understand that).

So far we have been working exclusively with the birthdate, which reveals the structure of the subject's life, its overall shape. This is, of course, only half the picture. We now need to know something about the subject's character, and for that we have to look to the name.

Character. There's some disagreement among numerologists as to how to calculate with the name. Some people insist you must use the full name as given at birth; others say you should use whatever name the subject commonly uses. For a full reading, you should probably do calculations based on every name the person has ever used.

There's also disagreement as to the method of converting the name's letters into numbers. The most common system uses this chart:

1	2	3	4	5	6	7	8	9	
A	B	C	D	E	F	G	H	I	K=11
J	(K)	L	M	N	O	P	Q	R	V=22
S	T	U	(V)	W	X	Y	Z		

This is the method I'll be using for my calculations. The other method, which derives from Hebrew numerology, uses this chart:

1	2	3	4	5	6	7	8
A	B	C	D	E	U	O	F
I	K	G	M	H	V	Z	P
Q	R	L	T	N	W		
J		S			X		
Y							

I recommend that you try both systems. See which one suits you best.

To begin the study of the subject's character, substitute numbers for the letters and find their cross sum.

S	A	T	A	N	T	U	R	K	L	A	W	S	
1	1	2	1	5	2	3	9	11	3	1	5	1	= 45 = 9

Again, be sure to find the intermediate figure, since it could turn out to be an 11 or 22.

The figure just reached is called the digital root (or sometimes the expression number). It is the number of one's personality, the face one shows other people. The meanings of the digital roots are as follows:

1: Independent, ambitious, and aggressive. This person enjoys novelty and does not form deep friendships.
2: Even-tempered, well-balanced, shy, sometimes sneaky. This person is not self-assertive. Two sometimes indicates effeminacy in a male.
3: Imaginative, creative, outgoing, anxious for approval. This person is often highly successful.
4: Practical, steady, sometimes grim or melancholy. This is often a number of poverty and defeat.
5: Nervous, impatient, adventurous, unstable. This person is often highly charged sexually.
6: Domestic, kind, friendly, loyal, sometimes smug.
7: Scholarly and reclusive. Such people, despite their intellectual gifts, are not always able to explain themselves. They can be pessimistic and ironic.
8: Materialistic and selfish. Such people succeed, but they rarely do so easily.
9: Spiritual, romantic, charming, humanitarian—a number of high achievement.
11: The number of revelation and martyrdom. However, this only means you have potential. If you are an 11, you cannot count on revelation coming to you. You merely have the ability to earn it.
22: The master number, combining the strongest qualities of all the other numbers. Again, this is potential rather than actual.

Mr. Laws has a digital root of 9. This is very fortunate, especially given the problems we've found waiting for him in his life cycle. His personality is strong and well balanced; obviously he will have the resources to deal with his problems.

The second calculation from the name is called the heart number (or the soul urge). It is the indicator of inner desire and motivation. To find it, calculate the cross sum of the name's vowels.

S	A	T	A	N	T	U	R	K	L	A	W	S	
	1		1			3				1			= 6

Again, this is fortunate. We know that Mr. Laws will have a lot of problems with responsibilities and love affairs. His heart number shows that he has the willingness, even the desire, to deal with those problems.

The third calculation is of the latent self. This number indicates the inner personality, which may be unknown even to the subject. To find it, calculate the cross sum of the name's consonants.

S	A	T	A	N	T	U	R	K	L	A	W	S		
1		2		5	2		9	11	3		5	1	= 39	= 3

Here is a third fortunate number for Mr. Laws. He has within himself a reserve of creativity and imagination on which to draw.

But this is not the entire picture. There are certain significant gaps in Mr. Law's character, shown by the degree of frequency with which the numbers occur in his name.

Ideally, there should be an even distribution of numbers in your name. Most people show some imbalance; Mr. Laws shows a very large one. He has five 1's, only one 9, and no 4's, 6's, 7's, or 8's. The combination of the preponderance of 1's with the lack of 6's is telling. This is a man with a very strong ego; and though he yearns to accept responsibilities and love (as his heart number shows), he fails to do so—he simply lacks the means. In the calculations from his birthdate, the number 6 kept showing up as Mr. Laws's special problem; it is also the number of his inner desire. The fact that his name does not contain a single 6 is ominous.

Not that Mr. Laws should run out and hang himself. Rather, he should understand that the numerological analysis of his name is a reading of his karma.

Karma is the law of cause-and-effect that applies to our actions and their consequences. Everything we do, whether good or evil, will exert an influence on our lives—our present lives, or our future incarnations. Thus, it is possible for us to build up *karmic debts*, which we must work off in our future lives. In the case of Mr. Laws, what he can get from his present incarnation is plain to see. There is a hidden gap in his personality, but he has the desire to fill that gap, and the events of his life (as we have seen) will give him plenty of opportunity to do so. It looks as if there's a good chance for his karma to work itself out.

Incidentally, there are four important karmic numbers that may show up in a reading: 13, 14, 16, and 19. These may appear as hidden numbers in the life-path number, the digital root, the heart number, or the latent self number. They indicate unpaid karmic debts:

13: The subject did not do his share of work in a past life.

14: The subject could not control himself in a past life and was probably a sexual libertine. In this life he may have to face illness, accidents, and loss.

16: The subject hurt others in past lives, mostly through selfishness in love affairs. In this life he may face divorce and material loss.
19: The subject misused power in a past life. In this life he may face hard times.

If our fictional character were real, he would have just one further use for numerology, to predict the course of his life day by day.

Daily Life. In numerological prediction, the most important calculation is that of the personal year: the month and day of birth plus the present year. For Mr. Laws, for example, 1978 would be a 7 personal year: 10 + 17 + 1978 = 2005 = 7. The meanings of the personal years are as follows:

1: A time for new beginnings. There will be little interference from other people, either as help or hindrance.
2: A time for working with others. There will be emphasis on partnerships and love affairs.
3: A time for friendships, enjoyment, and self-expression. But old, unsolved problems may turn up.
4: A time for hard work. Ill health could be a problem.
5: A time for change, perhaps for moving to a new place. Projects started now may not be long-lasting. There's a possibility of adultery.
6: A time for adjusting to people (and also for paying debts in all senses).
7: A time for rest, study, and seclusion. Avoid taking risks with money.
8: A time for personal, material gain. The potential for loss is present, of course, but even so, this is the time to concentrate on money.
9: A time for finishing projects, taking care of your health, and reflecting on your life. This is a highly emotional time, and it could bring terrible losses. Try not to start new ventures.
11: A time for spiritual growth.
22: A time for serving others, on a large scale if possible.

You can extend this system to months and days as well. To find your personal month, add the number of your personal year (for example, 6) to the number of the month. For December, the personal month would be 12 + 6 = 18 = 9. To find the personal day, add the number of the personal year to the date. Thus, in a 6 year, December 5 would be a 2 day in a 9 month. In predicting your life's rhythms, all those vibrations must be taken into account. Of course, the year exerts the strongest vibration, with the month and day as overtones. If it seems confusing to keep those three numbers in your head, add the personal year, month, and day numbers to get a single number which expresses what your day will be. In this example, December 5, 1977, will be an 8 day: 6 + 9 + 2.

You can adapt this method to find out how you will get along with a given person on a given day. Calculate that person's personal year, month, and day numbers and add them to your own. The result will tell you what your interaction will be.

This has been only the briefest summary of numerology. Like all the topics in this chapter, numerology is too vast and elaborate to be discussed in further detail here. So please take the above as an outline offered with good intentions.

There is, however, a more important understanding to be gained from this chapter, and that is the relation of numerology to the other occult sciences. Numerology, astrology, the Tarot, and to some extent the *I Ching* all work together. The connections are too complex to trace, but remember that they exist, and as you read the next sections, keep what you now know about numerology in mind. It will be worth your effort.

For Further Reading

Probably the most complete contemporary book on numerology is Kevin Quinn Avery's *The Numbers of Life: The Hidden Power in Numerology* (New York: Doubleday, 1977). In my summary of the subject I have relied on Avery's work. For a less earnest, more historical introduction, see *The Black Arts*, by Richard Cavendish (New York: Capricorn Books, 1967). There's also a useful article in Cavendish's *Encyclopedia of the Unexplained* (London: Routledge and Kegan Paul, 1974). For a scholarly approach to the history of numerology, see J. Burnet, *Early Greek Philosophy*; V.F. Hopper, *Medieval Number Symbolism*; and G.S. Kirk, *The Pre-Socratics*.

Astrology

In this section, I shall consider three questions about astrology: Where did it come from, what does it mean, and how does it work?

Origins

Occultists generally believe that astrology is a very ancient science, probably dating back to Atlantis and transmitted with little change since then. This is certainly a wonderful theory, and there is no evidence against it. But there's no evidence *for* it, either. Therefore, I prefer to go along with the historians and say that astrology, as we know it, originated around the third century B.C.

Of course, people told fortunes according to the stars long before that. The ancient Mesopotamian court seers, the *bārus*, had a system for reading celestial omens. They first set down the system in the eighteenth century B.C. in a cuneiform text called the *Enūma Anu Enlil*. Our knowledge of these omens is sketchy, since the earliest surviving copies of the *Enūma Anu Enlil* date from the seventh century B.C. However, we do know that the *bārus* recognized four kinds of omens: lunar, solar, meteorological, and planetary. These included new moons, rings around the moon, lunar and solar eclipses, sightings of second suns, lightning storms, earthquakes, and sightings of stars. But this was not astrology. The interpretation of the omens was not organized by means of a horoscope, and it was a public, not private matter. The *bārus* believed that celestial omens were messages concerning God's will. By interpreting these omens for the king, the *bārus* helped prepare the kingdom for future events.

In the fifth century B.C., the Persians conquered Mesopotamia. The Persian empire was powerful and expanding rapidly; thus the Mesopotamian study of omens spread throughout the empire to Greece, Egypt, and India. Buddhist missionaries carried the omens still farther, from India to China and Japan.

The change from reading omens to casting horoscopes came around the third century B.C., when Babylonian seers began to use celestial omens for predicting individuals' lives. Meanwhile, Egyptian seers (living under the Greek rule of the Ptolemies) began to set up a mathematical system to correlate human experience with the stars' motions. The Egyptian system developed with borrowings from the Pythagoreans and evolved into the zodiac. Astrology settled into its present form around 100 B.C., although it had not yet reached its limits of expansion. It reached India in the second or third century A.D., and the Indians developed their own system, adding to the Hellenistic astrology their own ideas on caste and reincarnation. Astrology became important in the Islamic world around the seventh century A.D.

Meanwhile, astrology had lost its hold in Europe. Virtually all the astrological texts were in Greek, and after the fall of Rome the knowledge of that language all but disappeared. Through Moslem influence, astrology reentered Europe in Spain and Sicily in the twelfth and thirteenth centuries in translations from Arabic. However, the study of astrology did not truly revive until the Renaissance, when Europeans again began to read the original Greek texts. It has stayed more or less in fashion since that time.

What Does Astrology Mean?

Astrology is a way of mapping human experience against celestial events. The map is called a horoscope, and it is a double map, since it shows two kinds of time: the daily cycle, and the yearly cycle. The daily cycle (caused by the rotation of the Earth around its axis) yields a system of twelve *houses*. The yearly cycle (caused by the revolution of the Earth around the sun) yields a system of twelve *signs of the zodiac*. The horoscope superimposes these two cycles and thereby gives a complex, dynamic map of experience.

To begin with the daily cycle and the system of houses, imagine yourself standing at the South Pole and looking up at the Earth. (We're assuming for the moment that you can stand somewhat *under* the South Pole and see the whole globe.) How would you chart what you're seeing? You could draw a figure like this:

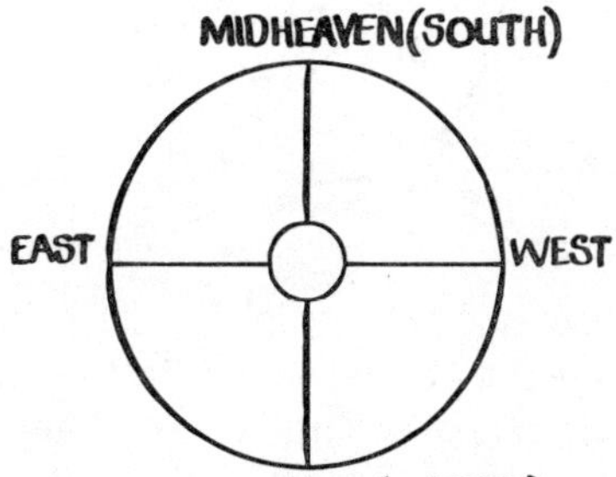

The small circle in the middle represents the center of the Earth. To help you see this diagram in three dimensions, imagine you're standing directly under the small circle at the South Pole. The top vertical line (the one marked "Midheaven") would be coming right at your nose; the Nadir line would be going away from you.

Now imagine that someone is standing on the Earth's surface at daybreak, watching the sunrise. On our chart, we would locate him this way (the arrow shows the direction in which he's looking):

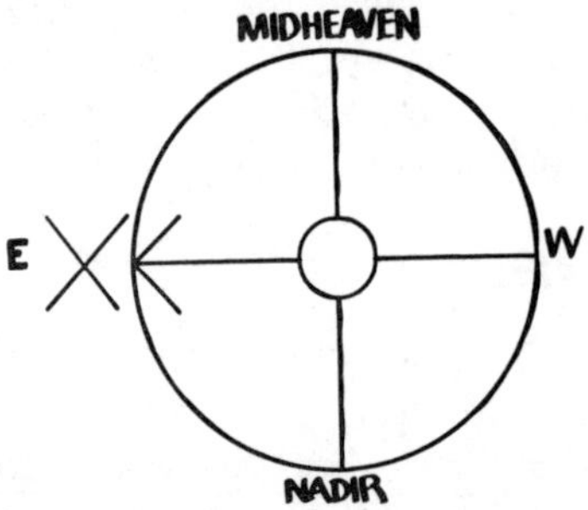

As the day progresses, this person stays in the same place on the globe (assuming he doesn't get onto a jet and fly away). But as the Earth turns, he faces different directions. At noon, he is facing the Midheaven (which we identify with South):

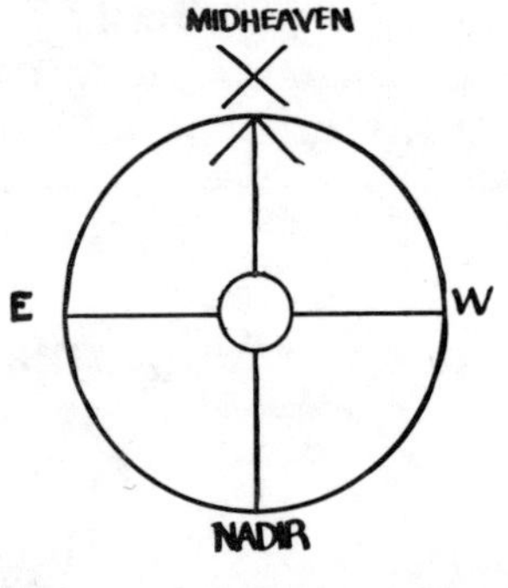

At sunset he faces West, and at midnight he faces the Nadir.

These four compass points, associated with the four principal times of day, have special importance in the horoscope. They are called the *angles*, and they generate the system of houses. The East-West line (or the horizon line) is the line of vital force. The North-South line (or meridian) is the line of spiritual energy. Between them, these lines divide the horoscope into quadrants, which we can in turn divide into twelve *houses*. So each house will represent two hours of the day. Each house will also have a symbolic meaning according to its relation to the four angles (see below).

The horoscope's yearly time is defined by the progress of the sun. As each year progresses through its seasons, the sun seems to change positions in the sky. As winter approaches, the sun rises farther and farther north each morning. Then, after the winter solstice, the sun creeps back south. It rises farther and farther to the south until the summer solstice, and then it begins its apparent journey back north again. (The reason for this is that the Earth's orbit is askew—we bob up and down as we travel around the sun.)

Ancient astrologers watched the apparent motion of the sun and divided it into phases. The most important, of course, were those of the South point (summer solstice), North point (winter solstice), and midpoint (vernal and autumnal equinoxes). These four phases are subdivided to yield a total of twelve—the signs of the zodiac.

The zodiac, properly understood, is *not* a group of twelve constellations. It's a measurement of the changing relationship between Earth and Sun over the course of the year. But for the sake of convenience, ancient astrologers matched the twelve divisions of the year to twelve constellations, each of which lay at a point along the sun's apparent course. This is an important point to keep in mind. It's not a modern apology for the zodiac—Ptolemy distinguished between the zodiac and the constellations in his *Tetrabiblos*, written in the second century A.D. (Claudius Ptolemy, the greatest ancient writer on astrology, flourished in Alexandria in the second century A.D. He is better known for having been the greatest ancient mathematical astronomer.)

These days, the sun no longer seems to enter the twelve constellations at the same time it used to. When this system was set up, the sun seemed to enter Aries on what we call March 21, the vernal equinox. Today, on the equinox, the sun is actually entering Pisces. The system has slipped back a whole 30 degrees. For this reason, some astrologers (led by Cyril Fagan) have adopted a system called the *sidereal zodiac*. When they say the sun is entering Pisces, they mean the *constellation* Pisces. Most astrologers, though, prefer to remain with the old system, believing that the use of the constellations was merely a convenience. The meaning of the beginning of spring is the same now as it was thousands of years ago, and that's what counts.

So we have the signs of the zodiac, as follows:

March 21	♈	Aries (ram)	September 23	♎	Libra (balance)
April 20	♉	Taurus (bull)	October 23	♏	Scorpio (scorpion)
May 21	♊	Gemini (twins)	November 22	♐	Sagittarius (archer)
June 21	♋	Cancer (crab)	December 22	♑	Capricorn (goat)
July 23	♌	Leo (lion)	January 20	♒	Aquarius (water bearer)
August 23	♍	Virgo (virgin)	February 19	♓	Pisces (fish)

In a horoscope, we plot these signs against the twelve houses of the Earth's daily rotation. The houses show what is possible in life, the structure and the limits of existence. They are universal; they refer strictly to the Earth and its fixed compass points. The zodiac shows individual character; it refers to the relationship between Earth and Sun and shows the eccentricities of that relationship, the tilt of Earth's orbit that causes the seasons.

Now let's look at the houses and the zodiac in more detail.

The Twelve Houses. A horoscope charts the houses as follows:

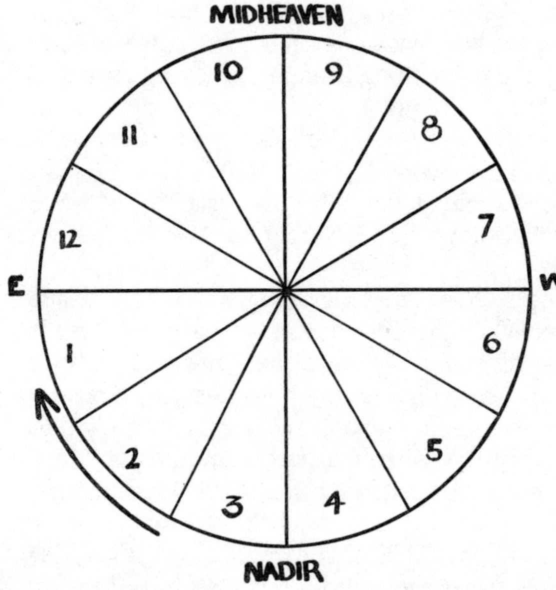

Arrow shows direction of rotation through the day.

The four most important houses, the *angular* houses, are 1, 4, 7, and 10. The Eastern, or ascendant, house, is 1; it represents activity. The Western, or descendant, house is 7; it represents passivity or potentiality. The Southern house, or the Midheaven, is 10; it represents objectivity and the conscious mind. The Northern house, or the Nadir, is 4; it represents subjectivity and the unconscious mind. We can also imagine a double movement among these houses. There's an East-to-West movement, which shows the self reaching out to others, and a North-to-South movement, which shows the subjective becoming objective. (This is according to the system of Marc Edmund Jones, one of the most high-minded writers on astrology.)

There are two other kinds of houses besides the angular. These are the *succedents* (which follow the angles and reveal the potential of the future) and the *cadents* (which precede the angles and represent past experience). The basic way of interpreting the system of houses is to match each angle with a cadent and a succedent. To do this, we take each angle in turn and draw an equilateral triangle with the angle as its apex. Thus, for the tenth house, we get:

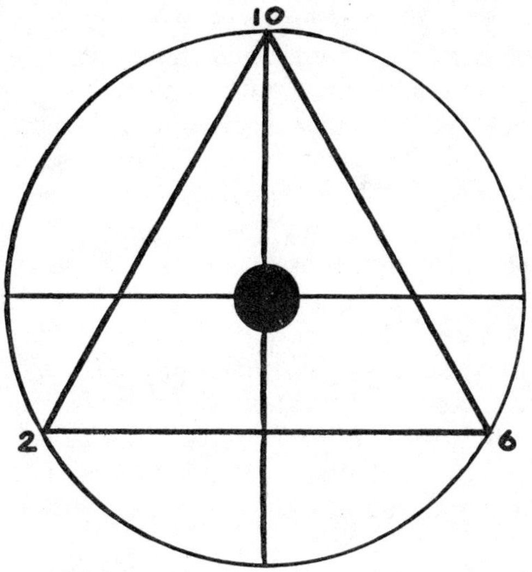

This is the Southern triad, composed of the tenth, second, and sixth houses. The second house shows the tenth house's influence on the Eastern nadir; the sixth house shows the tenth house's influence on the Western nadir.

Here is a breakdown of the triads:

Eastern triad (1, 9, 5): The triad of everyday life and of the self in its simplest sense. The first house rules your identity in the immediate, physical sense. The ninth house, as a cadent, is concerned with the past, specifically past experience, all that you as an individual have learned. The fifth house, a succedent, rules your instinctive, trial-and-error activity, plus all the projections of your image (including your children).

Western triad (7, 3, 11): The triad of everyday life as it involves others. The seventh house rules partnerships—your life in relation to other people. The third house, a cadent, rules your personal background—family, neighborhood, and old friends. The eleventh house, a succedent, rules the objectives of your social energies—friendships and social encounters.

Southern triad (10, 6, 2): The triad of impersonal social life, your experience as part of a political system. The tenth house rules your status in society. This is society in the immediate sense—your job, clubs, and circle of acquaintances. The sixth house, a cadent, rules the economic and political nature of your background; it also shows your past work and your social duties. The second house, a succedent, shows your potential status, money, and helpers.

Northern triad (4, 12, 8): The triad of spiritual depth. The fourth house rules the self in the sense of its being a spirit or soul. The twelfth house, a cadent, shows your spiritual experiences. It is the house of fantasies, the inner world, and your deeper resources. The eighth house rules your potential for spiritual and emotional regeneration. It is the house of death and immortality, and also, oddly enough, of money.

In addition to analysis by triads, you can look at the houses in sequence. Houses 1, 2, and 3, taken as a group, represent the basic, unself-conscious ego, its material wants, and the personal background it takes for granted. These three houses lead to 4, 5, and 6, which represent conscious effort: 4 shows the self that has become conscious of itself, 5 shows self-evaluation, and 6 shows the self's awareness of duties and of the relations between superiors and inferiors. This leads to the houses of personal relations: 7 shows one's awareness of others as equal beings, 8 shows one's awareness of death and immortality as the ultimate goal of life, and 9 shows one's awareness of the influence of other people. This leads to the houses of political awareness: 10 shows one's status in groups, 11 shows what one can achieve in the world, and 12 shows what social experiences went into one's makeup. That leads back to 1.

By now you may have noticed a third way of analyzing the houses: to take them as pairs of opposites. The houses balance each other across the horoscope in this way:

Awareness of self (1) balances awareness of others (7).
Material goals (2) balance spiritual goals (8).
Personal environment (3) balances intellectual background (9).
Self-awareness (4) balances awareness of social status (10).
Action that extends the self (5) balances action directed toward the world (11).
Order and duty (6) balance one's private, inner world (12).

As you can see, the houses are not a static system. Rather, they have their own dynamic. They push and pull against each other; their meaning arises out of their tension and movement. Indeed, movement—the Earth's daily rotation—is their essence. When you superimpose the zodiac on the houses, you get still more tension and movement.

The Zodiac. The houses reveal the structure present in anyone's life. The zodiac is more personal; it reveals character.

As with the houses, there are interrelationships within the zodiac. First, there is the system of triplicities. We organize the zodiac according to the classical elements of fire, water, air, and earth. Each element corresponds to three signs, or a triplicity.

Fire: Aries, Sagittarius, Leo. Fire is a symbol of self-sufficiency, individuality, and identity. People who are greatly influenced by fire signs are often unaware of the unique reality of other people.

Water: Cancer, Pisces, Scorpio. Water is a symbol of participation in life. People who are greatly influenced by water signs are expansive, nonjudgmental, and often try to assimilate other people (though in a naive, simple way).

Air: Libra, Gemini, Aquarius. Air is a symbol of one's reaching beyond oneself, of testing experience. People who are greatly influenced by air signs are often uncertain and indecisive; they have a need to participate in others' lives.

Earth: Capricorn, Virgo, Taurus. Earth is a symbol of self-realization. People who are greatly influenced by earth signs are often critical and practical, with great inner strength.

We can also analyze the zodiac according to quadruplicities. These are based on the solsticial and equinoctial signs—Cancer, Libra, Capricorn, and Aries—which are considered to be *cardinal* signs. They are similar to the angular houses in importance. In every horoscope, the cardinal signs give clues to the subject's most basic, unconditioned responses. People with strong cardinal-sign influences tend to enjoy independence and often like crises. They feel most at home in direct experience.

There are two other kinds of signs besides the cardinal—mutable and fixed. The mutable signs—Gemini, Virgo, Sagittarius, and Pisces—lie clockwise from the cardinal signs. People influenced by them tend to be contrary and perverse, attempting to be different from other people. At the same time, the mutable signs in every horoscope show your need or ability to get help from others, to bring other people into your life.

The fixed signs—Aquarius, Taurus, Leo, and Scorpio—lie counterclockwise from the cardinal signs. They show your potential for independence and your ability to rise above circumstances. They reveal the depth of your self-knowledge and your ability to see life as a whole.

There is one more refinement to the analysis of the signs—they can be broken down into *decanates*. Each sign contains three decanates, each of which is equal to ten degrees of the zodiacal circle. The first decanate is the same as the sign itself; the second and third decanates are the other two signs in the main sign's triplicity. For example, given the sign of Cancer, the first ten degrees of the sign would be Cancer pure and simple; the next ten degrees would be the decanate of Scorpio (that is, Cancer considered as having an influence from another water sign, Scorpio); and the last ten degrees would be the decanate of Pisces (Cancer with an influence from the water sign Pisces). In Leo, the three decanates are Leo, Sagittarius, and Aries; in Virgo, the decanates are Virgo, Capricorn, and Taurus; and so forth.

In summary, here are tables of the zodiac and the houses.

Table of the Zodiac

♈ Aries	Fire	Cardinal	Hope.	Rules head and brain. Relies on oneself.
♉ Taurus	Earth	Fixed	Peace and virility.	Rules neck and throat. Stable, eager for experience.
♊ Gemini	Air	Mutable	Liveliness and joy.	Rules shoulders, arms, and lungs. Wants to change the world.
♋ Cancer	Water	Cardinal	Expansion and patience.	Rules chest and stomach. Wants to control experience.
♌ Leo	Fire	Fixed	Assurance and glory.	Rules upper back, spine, and heart. Seeks active involvement.
♍ Virgo	Earth	Mutable	Assimilation and purity.	Rules intestines. Tries to make sense of experience.
♎ Libra	Air	Cardinal	Balance and beauty.	Rules lower back and kidneys. Wants to distill experience.
♏ Scorpio	Water	Fixed	Creativity and justice.	Rules pelvis and genitals. Desire to project oneself through experience.
♐ Sagittarius	Fire	Mutable	Administration and wisdom.	Rules thighs. Desire to embody oneself in the world.
♑ Capricorn	Earth	Cardinal	Discrimination and reverence.	Rules knees and skin. Desire to find oneself through experience.
♒ Aquarius	Air	Fixed	Loyalty and truth.	Rules calves, ankles, and blood. Desire to objectify oneself in experience.
♓ Pisces	Water	Mutable	Sympathy and love.	Rules feet, liver, and lymph glands. Desire to draw experience into oneself.

Table of the Houses

1—Angular. The unself-conscious ego; immediacy; appearance.
2—Succedent. Potential for status and possessions; material desires.
3—Cadent. Family background; old friends; short journeys.
4—Angular. The spiritual self; self-awareness.
5—Succedent. Self-expression; projection of one's image; love affairs; children.
6—Cadent. Economic and political background; duties; health.
7—Angular. Close partnerships; marriage.
8—Succedent. Spiritual regeneration; death and immortality; money and legacies.
9—Cadent. Past experience; knowledge; dreams; travel.
10—Angular. Social status; awareness of the world.
11—Succedent. Action within society; plans; ambitions; acquaintances.
12—Cadent. The inner world; spiritual resources; sickness; the influence of society; limitations.

How Does Astrology Work?

You now should have some abstract understanding of the houses and the zodiac, the individual experience in relation to the universal structure. What's missing is function—the individual's action within the structure. In astrology, eight planets together with the sun and the moon indicate function. When you coordinate the planets with the houses and the zodiac, you at last chart the horoscope.

Here, in summary, are the planets and their meanings.

Table of the Planets

☉	Sun	Self-assertion; identity; objective life.
☾	Moon	Emotion; participation; subjective life.
☿	Mercury	Intelligence; communication; personal experience becoming universal.
♀	Venus	Love and beauty; the attempt to subordinate matter to spirit.
♂	Mars	Energy; determination; the attempt to subordinate spirit to matter.
♃	Jupiter	Health; breadth of mind; love of life.
♄	Saturn	Suffering and failure.
♅	Uranus	Sudden change; revolution; inventiveness; reflection.
♆	Neptune	Inner power; the occult.
♇	Pluto	Change and transformation.

In casting a horoscope, you must interpret the meaning of each planet in relation both to the house and the sign of the zodiac in which you find it. The next two charts show, in summary, what the planets reveal according to houses and to signs.

The Planets in the Houses

Sun	Indicates subject's practical direction.
Moon	Indicates subject's area of deepest personal experiences.
Mercury	Indicates subject's focus of awareness.
Venus	Indicates what subject wants from life.
Mars	Indicates what things favor subject's activity.
Jupiter	Indicates subject's psychological predisposition.
Saturn	Indicates areas of special sensitivity.
Uranus	Indicates what encourages individuality.
Neptune	Indicates what subject demands of life.
Pluto	Indicates subject's social views.

The Planets in the Zodiac

Sun	Indicates how subject senses himself.
Moon	Indicates how subject reacts to experience.
Mercury	Indicates how subject tends to think.
Venus	Indicates how subject enjoys himself.
Mars	Indicates how subject acts.
Jupiter	Indicates how subject's awareness develops.
Saturn	Indicates how subject might fail.
Uranus	Indicates how subject defines himself.
Neptune	Indicates ways in which subject conforms.
Pluto	Indicates how subject views history.

As you will notice, when a planet is in a house it shows something objective about a person. When a planet is in a sign of the zodiac, it shows activity—*how* rather than *what*.

Most astrologers do what I have done in the above charts and give you a series of key words to characterize the houses, signs, and planets. They do so in order to condense information and give the new astrologer something that he or she can memorize. There's a danger in this, though, one that author Richard Cavendish pointed out very well: "Suppose you had Jupiter in Scorpio in the third house of your chart. This could be interpreted as: the *expansive* influence of Jupiter will show itself *passionately* (Scorpio) in *mental capacities* (third house). . . . [Your astrologer] might say that you have a strong desire to broaden your interests and mental outlook, or he might tell you your mind is obsessed by sex, or he might say any one of a hundred other things. And he could equally well have stated the same planetary position in entirely different key words as: the influence of Jupiter to *prosperity* will show itself *secretively* (Scorpio) in *short journeys* (third house), which perhaps might mean that you should be able to make money as a bookmaker."

Let that be a warning. All those wonderful tables mean nothing outside the context of a specific horoscope. You have to see each horoscope in its entirety and understand it as a *system in motion*. Please keep this in mind throughout the following explanation of the process of casting and interpreting horoscopes.

The Natal Chart. The most common type of horoscope shows the position of the heavens at the time of the subject's birth. This chart will define the subject's character and tell his or her life story. If an astrologer draws up a subsequent chart to answer a question for the subject or solve a problem (in the method called *horary astrology*), that second chart will have to be compared with the natal chart.

In a natal chart the houses must be synchronized with the zodiac. This means that you should find out which sign was rising on the horizon at the moment of birth. This is the *ascendant*; it's especially important since it will show where the first house begins, and the location of the other houses will follow from this calculation.

You will have to do some arithmetic to find the ascendant. Look at a table of houses (there are several, put out by various publishing companies), and you will find that the ascendants are given according to something called *Sidereal Time*. Sidereal Time is a division of the year into twenty-four hours; each day of the calendar year is equal to about three minutes, fifty-six seconds of Sidereal Time. The table of houses will show the ascendants only for Sidereal Time. The reason for this is that it would be impossible for a publisher to print figures on the houses and planets for each time zone and each place on the globe. Therefore, you will have to convert your subject's time of birth to Sidereal Time. That's not a difficult process, but it is too long and involved to describe here. The clearest guide to these calculations is Michael R. Meyer's *A Handbook for the Humanistic Astrologer* (New York: Anchor/Doubleday, 1974).

Let's assume that you have put your subject's time of birth into Sidereal Time and found the ascendant. We'll say for example that at the moment of birth, Cancer was 27° above the horizon. Therefore, the first house begins at 27° Cancer. Now you must locate the starting points (or *cusps*) of the other houses. The easiest method is the *equal house* system. In this method, you divide the 360° of the horoscope's circle into twelve equal slices; each house is exactly 30°. So in our example, the second house would begin at 27° Leo, the third house at 27° Virgo, and so forth.

Unfortunately, there's a problem with this method. In our example, the Midheaven should be 27° Aries. In fact, that's not always the case. The true Midheaven is much more likely to be some other reading—for example, 1° Aries. So if you don't want your horoscope to be askew, you'll have to use a more sophisticated system of house division.

There are several such systems of division. The oldest is the Porphyry system, dating from the third century A.D. It requires you to use the ascendant and Midheaven to find one quadrant of the horoscope, then divide that quadrant in three; you can then derive the remainder of the houses from those first three. The Campanus system (thirteenth century) and the Regiomontanus system (fifteenth century) relate the circles of the houses and the zodiac and then divide them spatially. The Placidus system (eighteenth century), until recently the one in most common use, divides the houses according to time rather than space. Again, these systems are too complicated to describe here. To learn how to work with them, see Margaret E. Hone's *The Modern Text-Book of Astrology*, 4th ed., (London: Fowler, 1968). The *Occidental Table of Houses*, put out by the Occidental Publishing Company, also gives details for systems of house division.

Let us assume that you've found the ascendant and Midheaven and have somehow divided the horoscope into houses. The next step is to fill in the position of the planets. To do this, you will consult an *ephemeris*. It will show the positions of the planets as calculated by Sidereal Time for Greenwich, England. Again, you will have to do some arithmetic to figure out the positions for your subject's time and place of birth.

Once you have completed this drudgery, the fun begins. You will begin by seeing in which house and sign each planet lies (and I hope you will be judicious about applying key words in interpreting these positions). The most important points to watch, of course, are the sun sign and the ascendant. Also notice which planet and house will rise on the horizon just before the sun; this will give you an important reading on the subject's practical direction in life. Finally, look at the system of *rulership*. Each planet exerts special power on one or two signs and houses. If you find a planet in the sign or house that it rules, it will be especially strong. There is usually a subsidiary sign that will give the planet a special boost; this is called the *exaltation*. The signs and houses that weaken a planet are called the *detriment*; the signs that oppose a planet less drastically are called the *fall*.

Planet	Rules	Detriment	Exaltation/Fall
Sun	Leo/5	Aquarius/11	Aries/Libra
Moon	Cancer/4	Capricorn/10	Taurus/Scorpio
Mercury	Gemini/3	Sagittarius/9	
	Virgo/6	Pisces/12	Virgo/Pisces
Venus	Taurus/2	Scorpio/8	
	Libra/7	Aries/1	Pisces/Virgo
Mars	Aries/1	Libra/7	Capricorn/Cancer
Jupiter	Sagittarius/9	Gemini/3	Cancer/Capricorn
Saturn	Capricorn/10	Cancer/4	Libra/Aries
Uranus	Aquarius/11	Leo/5	Scorpio/Taurus
Neptune	Pisces/12	Virgo/6	Cancer/Capricorn
Pluto	Scorpio/8	Taurus/2	

Now that you've considered the planets and their positions individually, you must start to look for patterns of relationships. Begin with the *aspects*, the angles that two planets form with one another. The most important aspects are:

Conjunction: 0°. These planets will intensify each other's influence. A conjunction represents the beginning of a new cycle.

Semisextile: 30°. The planets have a mild tendency to work together. A semisextile represents the emergence of something new in a cycle.

Semisquare: 45°. The planets oppose each other to a mild degree. A semisquare represents individual expression in a cycle.

Sextile: 60°. A stronger version of the semisextile. A sextile represents the development and productive use of skills.

Square: 90°. The planets are in a position of stress. The square represents a moment of crisis and the need to take action; it shows the manifestation of a relationship.

Trine: 120°. The planets are in their most harmonious relationship. A trine shows the expansion of knowledge and understanding and the harmony of the individual with the environment.

Quincunx: 150°. The planets are in slight tension with one another. A quincunx shows maturation and the bringing into focus of relationships.

Opposition: 180°. This is the aspect of maximum tension and conflict between planets. It shows the high point of a cycle, the moment of greatest objectivity and polarization.

Of course, you will hardly ever find these precise aspects in a horoscope. More often there will be an aspect that is close to standard, but is off by a few degrees. For example, Mars and Jupiter may be 123°12′ apart—almost a trine but not quite. In interpreting the horoscope, you would consider that aspect to be a trine, but you would also take into account the deviation, or the *orb*. In this case, we round off the deviation and say that there is an orb of 4°.

You can interpret the orbs on a numerological basis, according to the method of Marc Edmund Jones and others. The degree of the orb will show how the aspect will manifest itself in the chart's subject.

1°: The aspect will have an immediate and unconscious influence.
2°: The subject will be aware of the aspect's influence.
3°: The aspect will come out through harmony and understanding.
4°: The aspect will come out in a practical, concrete way.
5°: The aspect will come out through self-expression.
6°: The aspect will come out through the use of skills.
7°: The aspect will come out in partnerships and friendships.
8°: The aspect will come out in an individualistic, perhaps material way.
9°: The aspect will function through self-actualization.
10°: The aspect will function in a complete, encompassing way.

After noting the aspects in the horoscope, see if any of the aspects form larger patterns. These will show special emphasis in the chart. Here are some of the more important patterns you might find:

T-Square: Two planets in opposition with a third at their geometrical midpoint. The planet at the midpoint will act as an outlet for the tension of the planets in opposition. A T-Square reveals the subject's need to take action in a particular area.

Grand Trine: Three or more planets 120° apart from each other. If the planets involved have some affinity with each other, they will show an area of experience in which the subject has great sensitivity or talent. If there's no common factor among the planets, the subject will probably be a little scatterbrained and dreamy.

Grand Cross: Four or more planets 90° apart. This formation reveals a particular stress and purpose in the subject's life. It indicates a compulsion toward activity.

After the planetary formations, you can look for still larger groups in the chart, patterns that the young, hip astrologers are calling Gestalt formations.

Funnel, Wedge, or Basket: A close grouping of nine planets with the remaining planet opposite them, ideally at their center of gravity. The large group generates a lot of energy, which the lone planet focuses. The lone planet might show the potential for great achievement, or it might indicate a nagging source of trouble.

See-Saw: The planets fall into two main groups, separated by at least two houses. There should be at least one opposition between the groups. Obviously, this formation reveals great conflict, perhaps even a split within the individual. Richard Nixon has a see-saw pattern in his birth chart.

Tripod: The planets fall into three main groups, ideally in trine formation. This pattern reveals a potential for resolving conflicts.

Cluster or Bundle: All the planets lie within an area of 120°. A person with this formation will show a limited but highly charged nature.

Open-Angle: The planets all lie within an area of 240°, with 120° of the chart left open. This is often an indication of a mystical nature. This pattern reveals a subject's tendency to be in the world but not of it.

Star: Occasionally you will find a five- or six-pointed star in a chart. This shows an unusually well-balanced and integrated personality.

Finally, look for focal points within the chart. For instance, if you find four or more planets within a single house or sign, you have a *stellium*. This indicates that the area of life represented by that sign or house will be intense for the subject, perhaps overpowering. Look for preponderances in elements and modes. Does the subject have a lot of water signs, or cardinal signs, or cadent houses? That would be significant. What areas are missing from the chart? Is there special emphasis on any one of the quadrants?

Sometimes planets appear to have slipped backward in their orbits. This phenomenon is called *retrogradation*, and you should make a note of this, too. When five or more planets are in retrograde, the chart indicates that the subject will have a special awareness of his or her inner nature.

To conclude this section, let's look at the horoscopes of two famous people: the great Romantic poet and painter William Blake, and the psychologist Carl Jung.

William Blake (November 27, 1857; London). Blake's sun is in Sagittarius in the fifth house. The sun rules the fifth house and therefore has an especially strong influence here. The fifth house is a house of self-expression and self-projection; the sun is the planet of individuality; and Sagittarius, a mutable sign, indicates a person who tries to be different from other people. The overall indication is for flamboyance, eccentricity, and self-direction—qualities that certainly were evident in Blake.

Mercury and Jupiter are just in front of the sun in Blake's chart; they, too, are in the fifth house, though Mercury is in Scorpio rather than Sagittarius. The indication here is of a strong predisposition to mental effort and communication. Scorpio adds elements of creativity and sexuality to this predisposition. Again, the fifth house's influence indicates self-expression.

Here, in a small cluster of fifth-house planets, we see the William Blake who would identify creativity with sexuality, who would declare that he had to build his own system—of poetry, painting, and thought—or be enslaved by other men's. We also see the source of the self-reliance that enabled him to labor for eighty years while being ignored and maligned.

The ascendant reinforces this reading. Neptune, the planet of inner power, is in the first house, the house of selfhood. Neptune is also in Leo, a fire sign, which accords well with the sun in Sagittarius, another fire sign.

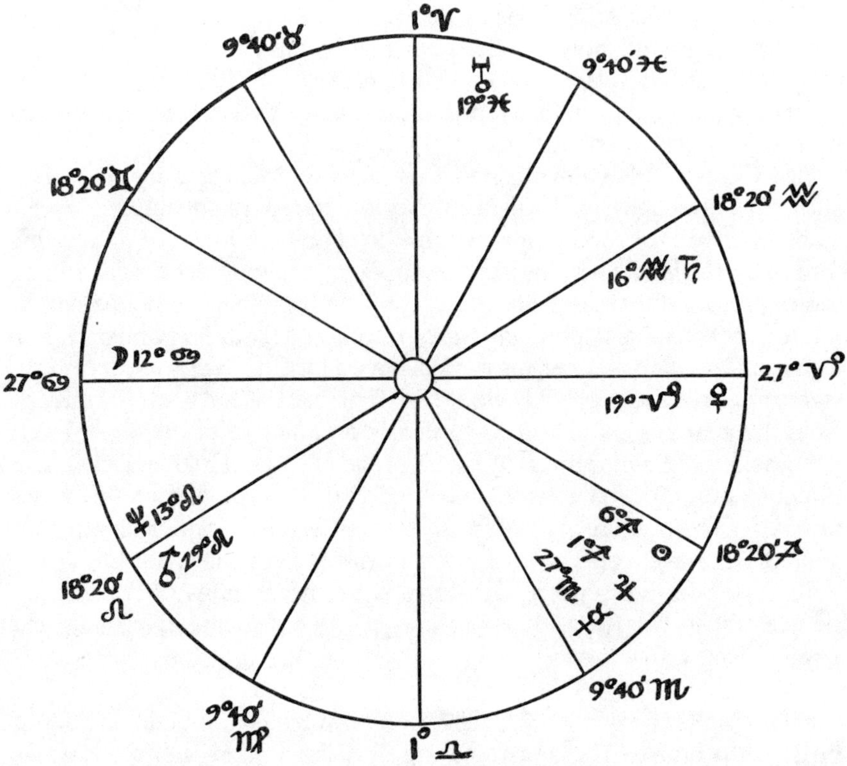

The rising sign, though, is Cancer, which leads us to an analysis of the tensions in Blake's chart.

Blake's moon is in Cancer; Blake's Venus is in Capricorn; together they form an opposition with an orb of 7°. The moon, indicator of Blake's emotional life, is in the twelfth house and in Cancer—a sign of dreaminess and the deep importance for Blake of his inner world. Venus is in the sixth house and in Capricorn—in an entirely practical, dutiful position. The orb of 7° shows that the conflict involved will come out in partnerships or marriage. This was exactly the case with Blake. His relations with his wife were often strained; they were aggravated as well by material concerns, since Blake was not a good provider. Whereas Blake had a strongly positive attitude toward sex, he had a negative view of love (he thought it always went together with jealousy and was on the whole a trap for the spirit). Witness as well his ambivalence in his poetry toward the soft, sensual, restful side of life, what he called "the moony realms."

Notice also that Saturn is in the seventh house, the house of marriage. Here is another indication of Blake's problems with family life. Saturn is also in opposition to Neptune in the first house. Here, though, the opposition has an orb of 3°, which shows that Blake could resolve the tension through creativity—as indeed he did.

Houses 4, 8, and 10 are empty on this chart. Blake, of course, had great trouble all his life with practical affairs, money, and social status; his life was in fact empty in these areas.

C.G. Jung (July 26, 1875; Kesswill, Switzerland; 7:20 P.M.). Jung's sun is in Leo in the seventh house. Since the sun rules Leo, this is a strong position. Leo is a fixed sign, one that reveals a depth of self-knowledge; it is also a sign that inspires people to seek involvement in experience. Here it's in the house of partnerships and awareness of others, which is, you have to admit, a good omen for a psychologist's horoscope.

There's a problem here, though. Jung has Saturn retrograde in Aquarius in his first house. This indicates both a certain inwardness in Jung's ego and a potential problem in the area ruled by Aquarius, namely the desire to objectify oneself in the world. Jung admitted that the most important experiences in his life were inner events and that the outward story of his life was of no interest to him (or, he supposed, to others). His energy indeed was directed to the inner and not the outer world.

However, there's a strong sympathy with other people here—notice Uranus in Leo in the seventh house, an indication that Jung can define himself and involve himself only with other people. Uranus here is in opposition to the first-house Saturn with an orb of 9°. This shows the conflict between Jung's inwardness and his need for participation in other people's lives. The degree of the orb shows that he could resolve the conflict through self-actualization. And of course he did, by reaching such depths in his own psyche that he encountered the collective unconscious, the level of the mind that literally belongs to everyone.

Jung's chart resembles Blake's in that he, too, has a conjunction of planets preceding his sun. Here he has Venus and Mercury in Cancer in the sixth house. Like Blake, Jung will have an intellectual direction in life, but his will be in close harmony with both love and duty. Perhaps the conjunction of Mercury and Venus tells us something as well about the importance women had in Jung's life and work. (Jung's first encounter with the collective unconscious involved a dialogue with the *anima*, the soul considered as an archetypal woman.)

Like Blake, Jung has a preponderance of planets in the bottom hemis-

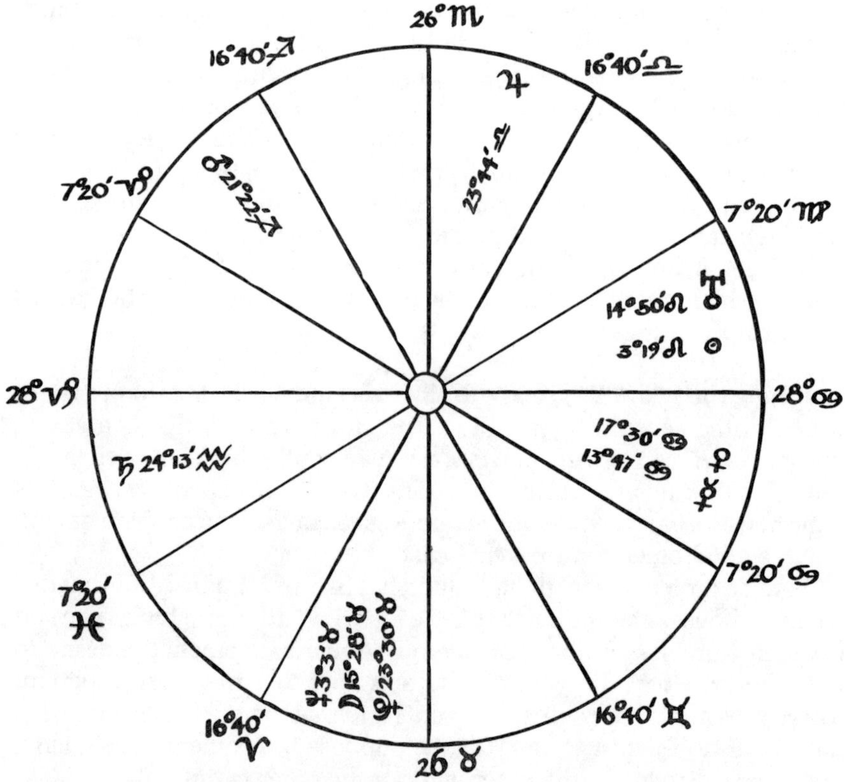

phere, indicating great concern with subjective matters. Even more telling, though, is the fact that Jung's moon in the third house is in conjunction with Pluto. This reveals the importance of change, transformation, and history in Jung's emotional and creative life. The fact that the moon is in Taurus emphasizes this aspect.

Perhaps the most arresting feature of Jung's horoscope, though, is its overall shape—it includes a five-pointed star, which you can see by connecting Jupiter, Mars, Saturn, Uranus, and the Moon-Pluto conjunction. The star reveals the high degree to which Jung's faculties were harmonized.

Now I will confess that in the interpretation of Blake's and Jung's horoscopes, I have cheated. Since I know their biographies, it is not difficult for me to see the facts of their lives in the stars. However, I have not brought in these charts to show off my skill as an astrologer. The purpose is to give you brief examples of horoscope readings and to show you as well one of the best practice methods for beginning astrologers. Get the birth information for some famous people, cast their charts, and then study their biographies as a way of checking your work. This is much more productive than casting charts for acquaintances and then playing guessing-games with them over the results.

Remember, astrology is a complex system, but anyone can work with it. All it takes is a bit of practice, intuition, and arithmetic.

For Further Reading

In this section I've relied heavily on the work of Marc Edmund Jones, particularly his *Astrology: How and Why It Works* (New York: Penguin, 1971); I've also referred often to *A Handbook for the Humanistic Astrologer*, by Michael R. Meyer (Doubleday, 1974). Another good introductory text is *The Astrologer's Handbook*, by Frances Sakoian and Louis S. Acker (New York: Harper and Row, 1973). For an authoritative survey of the subject, see *The Modern Text-Book of Astrology*, by Margaret E. Hone, 4th ed., (London: Fowler, 1968). Also see its companion volume, *Applied Astrology* (London: Fowler, 1953). I should also mention two of Dane Rudhyar's books: *The Astrology of Personality* (New York: Doubleday, 1970), and *The Practice of Astrology* (Baltimore: Penguin, 1970). For the history of the subject, see: *L'astrologie grecque*, by A. Bouche-Leclercq (Paris: E. Leroux, 1899); *Encyclopedia of Astrology* by N. DeVore (New York: Philosophical Library, 1947); and *Astrologumena*, by W. and H.G. Gundel (Wiesbaden: F. Steiner, 1966). The quotation in the article from Richard Cavendish comes from *The Black Arts* (New York: Capricorn, 1967).

Tarot

Of all the occultist's tools, the Tarot cards are the most symbolically powerful and mysterious. No one knows their origin. Antoine Court de Gébelin, the eighteenth-century scholar and Freemason, thought they came from Egypt, brought to Europe by the gypsies. Many occultists, including Eliphas Lévi and Aleister Crowley, went along with this explanation, though there is no evidence for it whatever. D.R.P. Boiteau d'Ambly and Romain Merlin believed the gypsies brought the cards from India or China, rather than from ancient Egypt. There's no evidence for this theory either. (We do know for a fact, though, that there were playing cards in Europe before the gypsies came.) A few writers suggest that the Tarot is of Roman origin, and that its name is an anagram of the Latin *rota*, meaning a wheel. Finally, there are occultists who believe that a group of Kabbalistic sages designed the cards early in the thirteenth century. This is the least likely theory of all. (I should add that most occultists who write about the Kabbalah have never read it; in fact, they do not know how to.)

The Tarot is a deck of 78 cards divided into two groups: highly symbolic picture cards (the 22 cards of the Major Arcana), and 56 cards that are much like those of a regular deck (the Minor Arcana). The first extant examples of the Major Arcana date from 1393 and belonged to Charles VI of France; the first whole pack we know of came from Bologna in the early fourteenth century.

The Tarot is most commonly used for fortune-telling. I will explain some standard methods of divination later in this section. But since the symbolism of the cards is so intricate (and plays such a great part in fortune-telling), I will begin with a description of the Major Arcana.

There are 21 numbered cards in the Major Arcana plus one unnumbered wild card, the Fool. There's some disagreement as to where one should place the Fool in the sequence of the cards. Some people place it at the beginning of the Major Arcana; others put it between numbers 20 and 21. I prefer to put the Fool at the beginning and the end of the series. Granted, this is an eccentric method, but it makes clear the natural groupings of the Major Arcana. The cards tend to come in groups of three: an opposition and its resolution. The 22 Major Arcana fall into seven such groups; in the central one, cards 12 and 13 function as a double card. Here is my arrangement:

0 The Fool: The hidden source of life; the primal void.
1 The Juggler (or Magician): The creative will; the erect penis.
2 The High Priestess: Divine thought; the vulva; the gateway to the Temple.

3 The Empress: The Earth impregnated with spirit; fecundity.
4 The Emperor: Male energy; the intellect; temporal authority.
5 The Pope (or Hierophant): Spiritual authority; knowledge.
6 The Lovers: Adam and Eve; innocence; free will and temptation.
7 The Chariot: Mastery of the physical world and of one's animal nature.
8 Strength: Mastery of the occult world; awareness of God within.
9 The Hermit: Self-knowledge; isolation; asceticism.
10 The Wheel of Fortune: The rhythms of life; karma.
11 Justice: The balancing of opposites; purgatory; the judgment of the dead.
12 The Hanged Man: Martyrdom; orgasm; death of the outer self; the unconscious.
13 Death: The beginning of a new life.
14 Temperance: The aspiration of humans to become divine.
15 The Devil: Lust, pride, and evil.
16 The Falling Tower: Expulsion from Paradise; ruin; the destruction of false doctrines; ejaculation.
17 The Star: Hope, youth, and inner truth.
18 The Moon: Dangers; illusions and fantasies; the child in the womb.
19 The Sun: Self-liberation; childhood.
20 The Day of Judgment: Sexual desire; death and resurrection.
21 The World: Both the world of our senses and the astral plane.
0 The Fool: The primal void behind 20 and 21.

As you see, this arrangement gives the cards a certain rough symmetry lacking in other methods. If you like it, use it.

Everyone feels some fascination with the Major Arcana. Each one is so highly charged with symbolism that one has to assume that they represent what Jung called archetypes, those forces present in the deepest level of everyone's unconscious, which are so strong and primal that they act like independent beings. We cannot understand them directly, but we can apprehend the self-representations that they throw into our consciousness from time to time. The Major Arcana are such representations.

Taken as a group, these cards serve as a map of the human mind. They touch virtually every area of our inner landscapes. They become an even more powerful tool when coordinated with astrology and certain Kabbalistic ideas.

As I said above, one should not take occultists' versions of the Kabbalah too seriously. However, there are some occult doctrines that may not be good Kabbalah but that are intriguing nonetheless. The coordination of the Tarot with the *sephirot* is one such doctrine, and it deserves a digression.

The Kabbalah offers a map of the universe based on ten attributes of God, or ten emanations of divine light. These ten *sephirot* correspond as well to ten orders of angels and the heavenly spheres. The *sephirot* are usually shown in a diagram called a tree, with the active, male *sephirot* on the right side and the potential, female *sephirot* on the left. The ones in the middle are nonsexual; they go beyond sexuality.

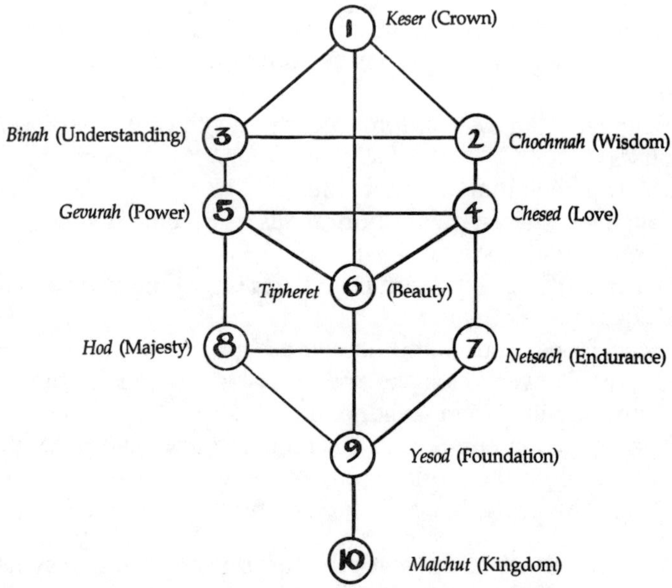

This diagram also represents the universe as seen as a single male body (called *Adam Kadmon*). The top triangle is the head, the middle triangle is the torso and arms, and the bottom triangle is the legs and genitals. (*Yesod* in particular represents the genitals.)

Some definitions are in order here. *Keser* (crown) is the emanation closest to God, the pure light that was the beginning of Creation. *Keser* is not the unreachable, uncreated God, but it's as close as you can get. The next two *sephirot* are the immediate aspects of *Keser: Chochmah* (wisdom as an active principle) and *Binah* (knowledge and pure consciousness). These three generate the other *sephirot* (the rest of the Creation). In the second triangle, *Chesed* is a protective love, the love of a shepherd for his flock or of a father for his children. *Gevurah* is the strength of Nature (and is thus imagined as a female strength). *Tipheret* (beauty) needs no explanation. Notice that this second triangle is a mirror image of the first.

In the third triangle, *Netsach* refers to God's eternity: His kingdom endures forever, and He is present in it always. *Hod* represents God's transcendence: He is always greater than and above the Creation. *Yesod*, the genitals of *Adam Kadmon*, is the link between God and our world (*Malchut*).

Thus, the first two triangles of the *sephirotic* tree represent God's self-creation: the first emanation of light, the accompanying aspects of light, and God's self-reflection as beauty. The third triangle represents the Creation as such: God's presence in it and transcendence of it, the link between God and our world, and finally our world itself.

Here are the traditional correspondences for the *sephirot*:

Hebrew	Planet	Angels	English
Keser	Primum Mobile	Living Creatures	Crown
Chochmah	Crystal Firmament	Ophanim	Wisdom
Binah	Saturn	Arelim	Understanding
Chesed	Jupiter	Chashmalim	Love
Gevurah	Mars	Seraphim	Power
Tipheret	Sun	Shinanim	Beauty
Netsach	Venus	Tarsishim	Endurance
Hod	Mercury	B'nai Elohim	Majesty
Yesod	Moon	Ishim	Foundation
Malchut	Earth	Cherubim	Kingdom

I bring up this subject because there are 22 paths through the *sephirot*, and these paths match the 22 cards of the Major Arcana. Furthermore, each path corresponds to a planet, an astrological sign, or an element. In other words, a knowledge of the 22 paths gives you a complete spiritual map. You can judge the importance of this for yourself.

Here is a chart of the paths, together with a table of their correspondences:

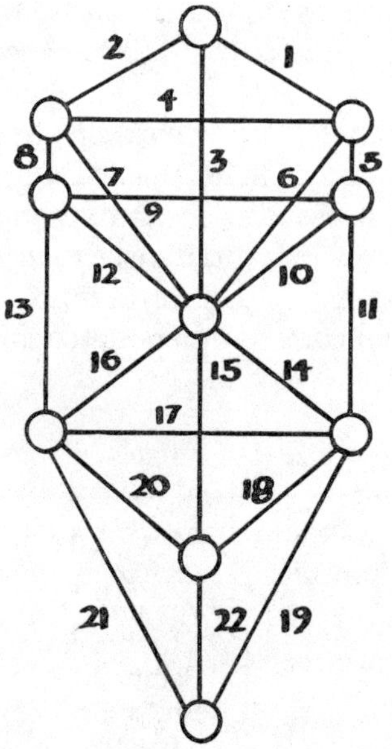

Path	Tarot Card	Astrological Symbol	Hebrew letter
1	Fool	Air	aleph
2	Juggler	Mercury	bet
3	Female Pope	Moon	gimel
4	Empress	Venus	daled
5	Emperor	Aries	he
6	Pope	Taurus	vav
7	Lovers	Gemini	zayin
8	Chariot	Cancer	chet
9	Strength	Leo	tet
10	Hermit	Virgo	yud
11	Wheel of Fortune	Jupiter	chof
12	Justice	Libra	lamed
13	Hanged Man	Water	mem
14	Death	Scorpio	nun
15	Temperance	Sagittarius	samech
16	Devil	Capricorn	ayin
17	Falling Tower	Mars	pe
18	Star	Aquarius	tsadik
19	Moon	Pisces	kuf
20	Sun	Sun	resh
21	Day of Judgment	Fire	shin
22	World	Saturn	tof

You can read these paths in either direction: as the emanation of spirit into Creation, or as the ascension of the human to the divine.

By now you should have an idea of the amount of meaning jammed into each Tarot card. There are still more systems and correspondences involving them. But no amount of systems-making will explain the cards in their entirety. There's always something tricky about them, something elusive. However entertaining it may be to see what relations you can find among the cards, finally it's more important to feel the resonance of each card with your spirit. The vital question is how much of yourself you can bring to the reading of the cards.

Divination by Tarot

After all this rarefied and technical discussion, the subject of fortune-telling seems to be something of a letdown. On the other hand, fortune-telling is the most common use people have for the Tarot, and it probably always has been so. Some occultists (among them Arthur Edward Waite) have been squeamish about this subject, but that is not something we have to worry about.

The meaning of the cards depends on whether in laying them out you find them right-side-up or upside-down (reversed). The following are the divinatory meanings of the Major Arcana:

Fool: Madness, extravagance (Reversed: apathy, carelessness)
Juggler: A choice or a gamble; skill (Reversed: a doctor; failure)
High Priestess: Secrets; wisdom (Reversed: illicit sex)
Empress: Creativity (Reversed: ill health; insanity)
Emperor: Success; protection (Reversed: sorrow, injury)
Pope: Inspiration and assistance (Reversed: danger, persecution)
Lovers: Love, marriage, and choices (Reversed: divorce, indecision)
Chariot: Fame, travel, success (Reversed: bad news; accidents)
Strength: Harmony; a test (Reversed: legal problems)
Hermit: Prudence; old age (Reversed: lies, secrecy, and fear)
Wheel of Fortune: Good luck (Reversed: bad luck)
Justice: Health and courage; a good woman's influence (Reversed: illness; a bad woman's influence)
Hanged Man: Sacrifice; early death; eccentricity (Reversed: selfishness; crime and punishment)
Death: Change; destruction (Reversed: birth; laziness)
Temperance: Good health (Reversed: poverty; drunkenness; arguments; priests and churches)
Devil: Sex; the arts (Reversed: evil fate; weakness)
Falling Tower: Disaster and ruin (Reversed: change for the better)
Star: Good prospects (Reversed: bad luck)

Moon: Concealed enemies; illicit sex (Reversed: blame and deception)
Sun: Happiness and prosperity; a good marriage (Reversed: trouble; divorce)
Day of Judgment: A fresh start; a reunion (Reversed: mistakes, suffering, and loss)
World: Success and travel (Reversed: stagnation and despair)

In addition, each of the cards of the Minor Arcana has a divinatory meaning. The Minor Arcana consist of four suits of fourteen cards each: ace through 10, page, knight, queen, and king. (In some packs the page is replaced by a princess.) The four suits of the Tarot correspond to the suits of an ordinary pack of cards: wands (clubs), cups (hearts), swords (spades), and pentacles (diamonds). (The pentacles are sometimes called coins or deniers.)

The wands correspond to the element of fire and generally indicate lightness and energy. Cups correspond to water and indicate dreaminess and romanticism. Swords correspond to air; they're the suit of loss and sorrow. Pentacles correspond to earth and represent the material world. Each of the court cards also corresponds to an element. The kings are fire; queens, water; knights, air; and pages, earth.

Here are the meanings for the 56 cards of the Minor Arcana:

WANDS

King: A prosperous, honest man; good news (Reversed: good advice)
Queen: An honorable woman; success in business (Reversed: deception)
Knight: An impetuous young man; a departure (Reversed: quarrels)
Page: A faithful lover (Reversed; bad news; indecision)
10: Burdens and difficulties (Reversed: difficulties)
9: Strength and endurance (Reversed: bad luck)
8: Falling in love; a journey (Reversed: jealousy)
7: Success (Reversed: anxiety)
6: Good news (Reversed: fear; betrayal)
5: A struggle (Reversed: disputes; legal problems)
4: Peace and quiet (Reversed: prosperity and happiness)
3: Help (Reversed: the end of troubles)
2: Wealth (Reversed: a surprise)
Ace: A birth (Reversed: a false start; disappointment)

CUPS

King: A helpful, influential man (Reversed: a dishonest man; injury and loss)
Queen: A good wife and mother (Reversed: a rich marriage)
Knight: A romantic young man; a visitor or a message (Reversed: a rogue; trickery)
Page: A handsome or pretty child; news (Reversed: seduction; deceit)
10: A happy marriage; friendship (Reversed: quarrels)
9: Contentment (Reversed: loyalty)
8: Modesty (Reversed: happiness)
7: Fantasies (Reversed: desire)

6: Happy memories (Reversed: an inheritance)
5: A disappointing inheritance (Reversed: a reunion)
4: Sadness (Reversed: a new relationship)
3: Abundance (Reversed: excess; an orgy)
2: Love and romance; friendship (Reversed: passion)
Ace: Love and joy (Reversed: change; instability)

SWORDS

King: A powerful man; a lawyer or doctor (Reversed: an enemy; cruelty)
Queen: A widow; sterility (Reversed: an evil woman; deceit)
Knight: A chivalrous young man (Reversed: rivalry; extravagance)
Page: A lively boy or tomboy; watchfulness (Reversed: surprising news; illness)
10: Pain; sorrow (Reversed: temporary success)
9: Death; failure (Reversed: fear; prison)
8: A crisis or scandal; illness (Reversed: problems and accidents)
7: Hope; a possibility of failure (Reversed: good advice)
6: A voyage (Reversed: a declaration of love; an announcement)
5: Pride and a fall (Reversed: a funeral)
4: A coffin; a will (Reversed: foresight and economy)
3: Antagonism; separation (Reversed: confusion; loss)
2: Deceit (Reversed: disloyalty)
Ace: A death (Reversed: a broken marriage)

PENTACLES

King: A successful man; courage (Reversed: an old, evil man; corruption)
Queen: A clever, sensuous woman; wealth (Reversed: suspicion; ill health)
Knight: A responsible, conventional young man (Reversed: stagnation)
Page: A scholar and dreamer; a messenger (Reversed: bad news)
10: Money; a house (Reversed: a robbery)
9: Foresight and success (Reversed: disappointments)
8: Profitable work (Reversed: greed)
7: Business; a loan (Reversed: impatience; money problems)
6: A gift (Reversed: jealousy; greed)
5: Poverty; deception (Reversed: waste; unhappy love)
4: A legacy (Reversed: delay)
3: Fame; skill (Reversed: obscurity)
2: A social occasion; messages (Reversed: letters; apparent harmony)
Ace: Riches and happiness; great good fortune (Reversed: wealth that corrupts)

The next question is, how are these cards used for divination? I will outline three methods: the Celtic Cross, the Oracles of Julia Orsini, and the method of the Order of the Golden Dawn as modified by Aleister Crowley.

If you are going to use any of these methods, certain precautions are in order. You will gain an affinity with the cards only by using them; in effect, a personal link develops between you and the pack. Therefore, do not let anyone else handle your Tarot deck. Keep them properly covered (most people prefer to wrap them in a silk scarf), and set them in a safe place. When you do a reading for someone, keep your mind blank as you shuffle the cards; let your hands tell you how to shuffle and when to stop. Try not to have an emotional involvement with the question or the questioner. For obvious reasons, you will have trouble doing a Tarot reading for yourself. When you have a question, let another fortune-teller read the cards for you.

A common element in all three methods of reading is the use of the Significator. This is a card that represents the querent. In general, you should use a king or queen to represent a mature man or woman and a knight or page to represent a younger man or woman. Wands and cups represent people with light complexions; swords and pentacles, those of darker complexion. Use your intuition, though. If a certain card seems to go with the querent, by all means use that card, even if the connection is not obvious.

The Celtic Cross. Put the Significator face up on the table. Shuffle the cards, turning some of them over so that you get a good mixture of upright and reversed cards. Cut the pack three times as you shuffle. Keep the cards face down.

Now lay out the following figure:

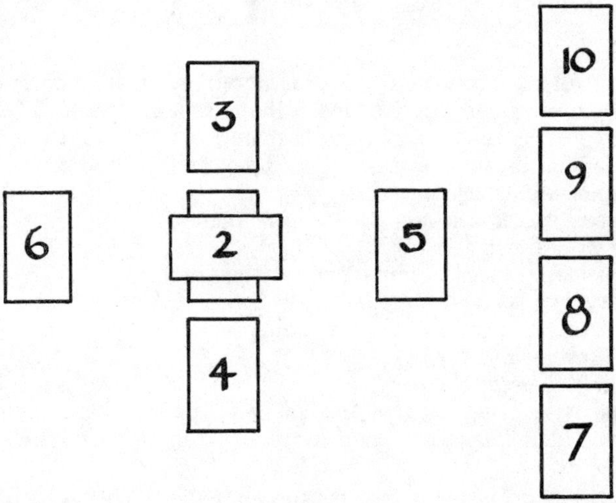

The first card goes directly over the Significator. This card covers the querent; in other words, it indicates the general influences on the subject and the atmosphere affecting the inquiry.

The second card goes crosswise over the first card and the Significator. This card crosses the querent; it indicates the obstacles and opposing forces in the matter at hand.

The third card, which goes above the Significator, crowns the querent; it shows the querent's goal and the best possible outcome of the matter.

The fourth card, which goes under the Significator, shows the basis of the matter, in particular the experiences that the querent is bringing to bear on it.

The fifth card goes behind the Significator, depending on where the figure on the card is looking. (In the diagram above, the Significator would be facing left.) This card shows what is behind the querent, the influence that is passing away.

The sixth card goes in the direction the Significator faces. It shows what is before the querent, the influence that is now coming into effect.

The last four cards go in a vertical row to the right of the cross. The seventh card represents the querent's position on the matter in question. The eighth card shows the querent's environment and its influences. The ninth card shows the querent's hopes or fears. The tenth card shows the outcome and therefore deserves special attention from the reader.

How are you to interpret the cards once you have laid them out? It's up to you. Look at them, think and use your imagination. You should of course have memorized the divinatory meanings of all the cards before you begin, and you should have an idea of their higher symbolism as well. But real reading of the cards doesn't start until you can forget all that information and pick up intuitions directly from the cards. Nobody can teach you how to do this, but most people can develop the faculty to some extent by practice.

Sometimes, using the Celtic method, the tenth card (or the outcome) seems inconclusive. In that case, take the tenth card as the Significator, reshuffle the deck, and do a second reading. This is especially useful when the tenth card is a court card. In that case, the card represents a person who has a decisive influence on the matter at hand. By doing a second reading for that person *in absentia*, you gain a lot more insight into the question.

The Oracles of Julia Orsini. This is an old French method that uses the Significator plus 42 cards.

Take the whole pack—leave the Significator in—and shuffle it. Let the querent cut the pack, using the left hand. (This is the exception to the rule about not letting other people handle your cards.) Now you will deal six packets face down onto the table. The first packet should have seven cards. To the left of it, deal a second packet of seven cards, and proceed to the left till you have all six packets.

Now you will do some reshuffling. Take the first packet, the one at the far right, and lay out the cards in it face down, from right to left. Put the cards from the second packet face down on top of the cards from the first, again right to left. Continue through the packets. Now you have seven packets of six cards each.

Now take the top card from each packet. Shuffle them and lay them on the table face up, from right to left. That's your first line. Take the next two cards from each packet, shuffle them, and lay them in two lines under the first. Then take the remaining cards, shuffle them, and lay them out in three bottom lines. Now you have six horizontal lines of cards, each line seven cards long.

The first thing to do is look for the Significator. In this method, the Significator for men is always the Juggler; the Significator for women is the Female Pope. If the Significator is in one of the rows you have laid out, set it aside and fill the gap with a card chosen at random from the pack. If the Significator is not in the rows, find it in the pack and put it to one side.

Now read the cards, beginning with the far right of the top line and ending with the far left of the bottom line. Again, you must rely on your imagination for the reading—with 42 cards you have a lot of material to interpret. Look for patterns in the layout; use what you know about numerology to give the reading a structure; above all, try to understand what the querent wants to know.

The Golden Dawn Method (Aleister Crowley). This is one of the most elaborate of the Tarot techniques. It is actually a series of five readings, each based on a different aspect of occult symbolism. The first is a reading according to the four elements (or of the Tetragrammaton, the four-lettered name of God). The next three readings are astrological, based on the signs of the zodiac, the houses, and the decanates. The fifth reading is based on the *sephirotic* tree.

These readings involve a counting method that takes some time to explain. I will outline the method here, and then as you read the descriptions of the techniques you can refer back to the outline.

For a king, queen, or knight of any suit, count 4.
For a page of any suit, count 7.
For 10 to 2 of any suit, count the number on the card.
For an ace of any suit, count 11.
For the Fool, the Hanged Man, and the Day of Judgment, count 3.
For each of these cards, which correspond to signs of the zodiac, count 12: Emperor, Pope, Lovers, Chariot, Strength, Hermit, Justice, Death, Temperance, Devil, Star, Moon.
For each of these cards, which represent planets, count 9: Juggler, Female Pope, Empress, Wheel of Fortune, Falling Tower, Sun, World

Now here are the five readings, as interpreted by Aleister Crowley.

I: Shuffle the cards. Have the querent cut them while thinking about the question. Hold the deck so that it is face down and cut it to the left. Cut each of the piles again to the left so that you have four piles. Taken from right to left, these represent:

1. Yud: Fire, work, and business.
2. Heh: Water, love and marriage, and pleasure.
3. Vav: Air, trouble, and loss.

4. Heh: Earth, money, and material concerns.

The querent has not told you the question. (This is in distinction from the Celtic cross method and the Oracles of Julia Orsini, in which the querent *should* tell you the question.) Look through the four piles and find the Significator. Explain to the querent the significance of the card's location and ask whether it appeared in the appropriate pile. If the querent says no, stop right there. Something has gone wrong, and you'll have to start again.

If the Significator did show up in the appropriate pile, set the other three to one side. Turn your pile face up and lay the cards in a circle. The Significator goes at the top of the circle. The cards that were above it go to the right in order; the cards that were below go to the left. (Some people tell you to lay the cards in a horseshoe shape; I think you might just as well go all the way and make a circle.)

Now the counting begins. Let's assume the Significator was the Queen of Wands. For a queen, you must count 4. Start at the queen and count around the circle in the direction she's facing. When you get to 4, stop. That is the first card you must interpret. If it is the 10 of Cups, when you are finished thinking about the card, count it as 1 and then count around the circle until you reach 10. That is the next card to interpret. Each card in turn becomes 1. Keep going around the circle until you land on a card a second time. Then you stop.

To finish this stage of the reading, interpret the cards as pairs. The Significator is at twelve o'clock on the circle. What is at six o'clock? What are the other oppositions?

II: Shuffle the deck. Have the querent cut it to the left. Replace the cut. Now deal twelve stacks of cards, representing the twelve houses of a horoscope. These should be face down.

Instead of wasting time looking through each stack for the Significator, decide the proper astrological house for the question (you should have some idea of it by now), and look through the appropriate stack. If the Significator isn't there, look through a related house. If you still have not found the Significator, stop. Something has gone wrong, and you will have to start again.

If the Significator is in the right stack, set the other eleven stacks to the side. Lay out the cards in a circle (as in the first reading). Interpret them by counting around the circle and pairing them up.

III: This is the same as the second reading, except that the twelve stacks now represent the signs of the zodiac. Interpret the cards accordingly when you lay them out.

IV: This is similar to the second and third readings. This time, though, deal the cards in 36 stacks, corresponding to the 36 decanates of the horoscope. (See the section on astrology in this chapter for an explanation of the distinctions among houses, signs, and decanates.)

V: Shuffle and cut the cards. Deal the entire deck into ten stacks, laid out as if on the *sephirotic* tree. (You can follow the diagrams earlier in this section.)

Decide in which stack you should find the Significator. If it is not there, go on anyhow. There's no turning back now. Just take the discrepancy into account.

Lay out the cards in a circle as in the other four readings. Interpret them by counting around the circle and by pairing.

For Further Reading

The best-known book on the Tarot is Arthur Edward Waite's *The Pictorial Key to the Tarot* (New York: Weiser, 1973). In this section I have relied heavily on Waite's book and on the work of Richard Cavendish, especially his *The Tarot* (New York: Harper and Row, 1975) and *Encyclopedia of the Unexplained* (London: Routledge and Kegan Paul, 1974). The divinatory meanings given here are substantially the same as those given in Cavendish's *Encyclopedia*. A useful, recent book is *Dictionary of the Tarot*, by Bill Butler (New York: Schocken, 1977). A book that serves as a sort of companion to Waite is *The Complete Guide to the Tarot*, by Eden Gray (New York: Crown, 1970). For an interesting historical text, see *The Tarot of the Bohemians*, by Papus (New York: Weiser, 1967). I also recommend a look into P.D. Ouspensky's *The Symbolism of the Tarot* (New York: Dover, 1976).

I Ching

When you cast a horoscope, or deal out the Tarot cards, or find the numerological meaning of someone's name, you are working on a certain assumption—that chance events can be meaningful. With the Tarot, for example, you ask a question, shuffle the cards, and deal; then you try to establish the significance of the fact that you had that particular sequence of cards out of all the possible sequences.

The kind of thinking entailed here is called *synchronicity*. Synchronicity is a way of looking at events not as part of an endless chain of cause and effect, but as simultaneous expressions of a given moment. To return to the example of the Tarot: The fact that you asked a certain question does not cause the cards to appear in a certain sequence. The connection between your question and the laying out of the cards is simply in their happening at the same time.

In *I Ching*, the *Book of Changes*, the Chinese developed a science of synchronicity. *I Ching* is based on a group of sixty-four, six-line drawings, or hexagrams. To consult *I Ching* for advice, you toss coins or play a counting game with yarrow stalks and thus come up by random with one of the hexagrams. The hexagram, when properly interpreted, will offer an answer to your question. According to C.G. Jung, this works because the hexagram is "an indicator of the essential situation prevailing in the moment of its origin." In other words, you could just as well interpret the shadows that were on the wall when you asked your question, or the noises that were in the street. The hexagrams of *I Ching* are, however, more convenient to interpret, so we use them.

Originally, the Chinese did not use hexagrams for divination. They would ask questions that could be answered yes or no and then go through a ritual process (such as counting yarrow stalks) to find the answer. They represented *yes* as an unbroken line — and *no* as a broken line – –. At an early date, though, the Chinese combined these lines in a system of eight trigrams. The trigrams, which symbolized a cycle of transformation, were as follows:

☰	Ch'ien	The creative	Strong	Heaven	Father
☷	K'un	The receptive	Yielding	Earth	Mother
☳	Chên	The arousing	Inciting motion	Thunder	First son
☵	K'an	The abysmal	Dangerous	Water	Second son

☶	Kên	Keeping still	Resting	Mountain	Third son
☴	Sun	The gentle	Penetrating	Wind, wood	First daughter
☲	Li	The clinging	Light-giving	Fire	Second daughter
☱	Tui	The joyous	Joyful	Lake	Third daughter

Eventually, perhaps as early as 2200 B.C., the Chinese combined these trigrams into the present system of hexagrams. In 1150 B.C., King Wen (the head of a western state) and his son, the Duke of Chou, added advice to each hexagram. In the fifth century B.C., Confucius added to the text. Gradually, *I Ching* became corrupted with a lot of divinatory gibberish, which the scholar Wang Pi cleared away in 226–249 A.D., establishing the text as we now know it.

How to Consult *I Ching*

The best method is to use fifty yarrow stalks. (Any thin sticks will do.) To begin, set one of the stalks aside. Then divide the remaining heap of forty-nine into two parts. Take one stalk from the right-hand pile and hold it between the little finger and ring finger of your left hand. Now pick up the left pile with your left hand. Take away stalks, four at a time, with your right hand until you have four or fewer left in the pile. Put these between the ring and middle fingers of your left hand. Now count off the right-hand pile in the same way. Put the remainder between your middle and index fingers. Now count how many stalks you are holding in your left hand. You will have either five or nine.

Here comes the confusing part. To find a line of a hexagram, you have to go through the above process three times. The first time, you must disregard the stalk you put between the little and ring fingers. So, even though you are holding five or nine stalks in your hand, you must regard them as four or eight. Mark down how many stalks you are holding, then put them aside. Now repeat the process, using the remaining pile. This time, *do* count the stalk between your little and ring fingers. The total should be four or eight. Set those aside and go through the process a third time. Again you should get four or eight.

Each time you get four stalks, count them as a 3. For eight stalks, count them as 2. (I don't know why—just do it.) Thus, for each of the three times you counted the stalks, you will get a 3 or a 2. Add these and you will get 9, 8, 7, or 6. The meanings are: 9—a moving yang line (—); 6—a moving yin line (--); 7—a yang line (—); 8—a yin line (--). (Do not worry about moving or unmoving—we'll get to that later.)

The line you have just reached is the bottom line of the hexagram. Now pile all the yarrow stalks together and go through the process five more times to get the full hexagram. It takes a long time, but it is important.

People in a hurry can use the coin method. The inscribed side (tails) is yin and has a value of 2. Heads, yang, counts as 3. Each toss of the three coins will give you one line of your hexagram.

The next question is, how to interpret the hexagram, after all this trouble? For an example, I will rely once again on Jung. He contributed a foreword to what is the standard English edition of *I Ching*, translated by Richard Wilhelm and rendered into English by Cary F. Baynes (New York: Bollingen/Pantheon, 1950). In preparing his foreword, Jung asked *I Ching* what its opinion was about its forthcoming appearance in the West. The answer he got was Hexagram 50: *Ting*, The Cauldron. ䷱

The upper trigram is Li, or fire; the lower trigram is Sun, or wood. The Judgment (the first part of the commentary) is: "The Cauldron. Supreme good fortune. Success." The Image (the second part of the commentary) is: "Fire over wood: The image of The Cauldron. Thus the superior man consolidates his faith by making his position correct." (The book's passages about "the superior man" reflect the fact that for centuries *I Ching* served as a manual of statecraft.)

Jung interpreted the hexagram as follows: The cauldron referred to here is a ritual vessel containing cooked food. The food in this case symbolizes spiritual nourishment, which *I Ching* has to offer.

There's more to interpret. When Jung cast the hexagram, the second line came out as a moving yang line, and the third was also moving yang. Therefore, Jung had to pay special attention to the commentaries on these lines. The commentary for the second line reads: "There is food in the *ting*. My comrades are envious, but they cannot harm me. Good fortune." In other words, spiritual nourishment is indeed present. The commentary for the third line reads: "The handle of the *ting* is altered. One is impeded in his way of life. The fat of the pheasant is not eaten. Once rain falls, remorse is spent. Good fortune comes in the end." Jung interpreted the handle as the concept one has of *I Ching*. People in the West are no longer able to grasp the book's meaning. But the hexagram indicates that the book is about to receive new recognition.

As to the nature of moving lines: They are in the process of changing into their opposite. Thus, a moving yang line is about to become yin. To complete a reading, one must change the moving lines into their opposites, thus arriving at a second hexagram, which also must be interpreted. In this case, lines two and three of the Cauldron are moving. So this hexagram changes into Hexagram 35, *Chin*, Progress. ䷱ becomes ䷢.

The Judgment for Progress is: "The powerful prince is honored with horses in large numbers. In a single day he is granted audience three times." The Image is: "The sun rises over the earth: the image of Progress. Thus the superior man himself brightens his bright value." Jung says of this that the book "anticipates general understanding, but is afraid of misuse." When you take this hexagram into consideration with the other, you get a complete answer to the question. Is it adequate? Jung, at least, was satisfied. The book, he said, "faces its future on the American book market calmly and expresses itself here just about as any reasonable person would. . . ."

䷀ 1. Ch'ien — The creative
The movement of heaven is full of power.

䷁ 2. K'un — The receptive
The earth's condition is receptive devotion.

䷂ 3. Chun — Difficulty at the beginning
Clouds and thunder

䷃ 4. Mêng — Youthful folly
A spring wells up at the foot of the mountain.

䷄ 5. Hsü — Waiting (Nourishment)
Clouds rise up to heaven.

䷅ 6. Sung — Conflict
Heaven and water go their opposite ways.

䷆ 7. Shih — The army
In the middle of the earth is water.

䷇ 8. Pi — Holding together (Union)
On the earth is water.

䷈ 9. Hsiao Ch'u — The taming power of the small
The wind drives across heaven.

䷉ 10. Lü — Treading (Conduct)
Heaven above, the lake below

䷊ 11. T'ai — Peace
Heaven and earth unite.

䷋ 12. P'i Standstill (Stagnation)
Heaven and earth do not unite.

䷌ 13. T'ung Jên Fellowship with Men
Heaven together with fire

䷍ 14. Ta Yu Possession in great measure
Fire in heaven above

䷎ 15. Ch'ien Modesty
Within the earth, a mountain

䷏ 16. Yü Enthusiasm
Thunder comes resounding out of the earth.

䷐ 17. Sui Following
Thunder in the middle of the lake

䷑ 18. Ku Work on what has been spoiled (Decay)
The wind blows low on the mountain.

䷒ 19. Lin Approach
The earth above the lake

䷓ 20. Kuan Contemplation
The wind blows over the earth.

䷔ 21. Shih Ho Biting Through
Thunder and lightning

䷕ 22. Pi Grace
Fire at the foot of the mountain

䷖ 23. Po Splitting apart
The mountain rests on the earth.

䷗ 24. Fu Return (The turning point)
Thunder within the earth

䷘ 25. Wu Wang Innocence (The unexpected)
Under heaven, thunder rolls.

䷙ 26. Ta Ch'u The taming power of the great
Heaven within the mountain

䷚ 27. I The corners of the mouth (Providing nourishment)
At the foot of the mountain, thunder

䷛ 28. Ta Kuo Preponderance of the great
The lake rises above the trees.

䷜ 29. K'an The abysmal (Water)
Water flows on uninterruptedly and reaches its goal.

䷝ 30. Li Clinging (Fire)
That which is bright rises twice.

Second Series

䷞ 31. Hsien Influence (Wooing)
A lake on the mountain

䷟ 32. Hêng Duration
Thunder and wind

䷠ 33. Tun Retreat
The mountain under heaven

䷡ 34. Ta Chung The power of the great
Thunder in heaven above

䷢ 35. Chin Progress
The sun rises over the earth.

䷣ 36. Ming I Darkening of the light
The light has sunk into the earth.

䷤ 37. Chia Jên Family
Wind comes forth from fire.

䷥ 38. K'uei Opposition
Above, fire; below, the lake.

䷦ 39. Chien Obstruction
Water on the mountain

䷧ 40. Hsieh Deliverance
Thunder and rain set in.

䷨ 41. Sun Decrease
At the foot of the mountain, the lake.

䷩ 42. I Increase
Wind and thunder

䷪ 43. Kuai Breakthrough (Resoluteness)
The lake has risen up to heaven.

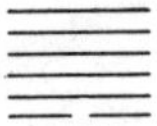
44. Kou Coming to meet
Under heaven, wind

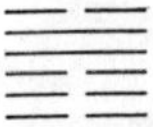
45. Ts'ui Gathering together (Massing)
Over the earth, the lake

46. Shêng Pushing upward
Within the earth, wood grows.

47. K'un Oppression (Exhaustion)
There is no water in the lake.

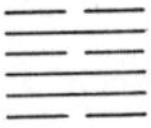
48. Ching The well
Water over wood

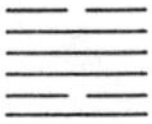
49. Ko Revolution (Molting)
Fire in the lake

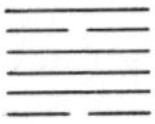
50. Ting The cauldron
Fire over wood

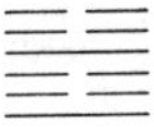
51. Chên The arousing (Shock; Thunder)
Thunder repeated

52. Kên Keeping still
Mountains standing close together

53. Chien Development (Gradual progress)
On the mountain, a tree

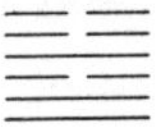
54. Kuei Mei The Marrying Maiden
Thunder over the lake

55. Fêng Abundance (Fullness)
Both thunder and lightning come.

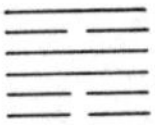
56. Lü The wanderer
Fire on the mountain

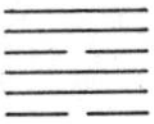
57. Sun The gentle (The penetrating; wind)
Winds following one upon the other

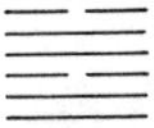
58. Tui The joyous (Lake)
Lakes resting one on the other

59. Huan Dispersion (Dissolution)
The wind drives over the water.

䷻ 60. Chieh — Limitation
Water over lake

䷼ 61. Chung Fu — Inner truth
Wind over lake

䷽ 62. Hsiao Kuo — Preponderance of the small
Thunder on the mountain

䷾ 63. Chi Chi — After completion
Water over fire

䷿ 64. Wei Chi — Before completion
Fire over water

Meditation

Numerology, astrology, Tarot, *I Ching*—all the occultist's symbolic systems—are useful but imperfect tools. They make a map of experience, which can be useful. But there is experience that cannot be mapped; there are moments we all live through that are beyond rationalization, beyond even language, the most subtle of all systems. As people learn more about the psychic realms, they usually come to feel that an inexpressible reality lies behind every moment of life. They feel they can describe everything except that reality—the essence always escapes them. As the Taoist classic, *Tao Te Ching*, says, "The Way that can be named is not the true Way."

Meditation is the technique that can take you into the inexpressible reality. Where the maps end, meditation begins. And so it has always been an essential part of religious practice all over the world, in Western and Oriental faiths alike.

The Buddhist Tradition

Perhaps the most complete text on meditation is a Buddhist manual titled *Visuddhimagga*, which was written down in the fifth century A.D. by a monk named Buddhagosa. An English translation by Nanamoli Thera is now available (Berkeley: Shambala, 1976). The *Visuddhimagga* divides meditative training into three parts: moral purification, meditative concentration, and insight. The student must practice all three more or less simultaneously.

For ordinary people, moral purification consists in the observance of five precepts: not to kill, steal, lie, use intoxicants, or have illicit sexual relations. (There are 227 precepts for those who intend to study meditation seriously or become monks.) These precepts should not be followed by the use of rigid self-control. Instead, you must attain a state of mindfulness, so that you remain aware of desires, without feeling compelled by them.

To reach such a state you must observe. For example, ask yourself who you really are. Are you your face? No—you can easily imagine yourself as the same person with a different face. Are you the other parts of your body? No, for the same reason. Are you the things you see and hear and touch? No again—your sensations change constantly, whereas you do not. Now ask yourself the trickiest question of all—are you your thoughts? On reflection, you will understand that thoughts are much like sensations. They pass through the mind independently of you. So you are not your body or your senses or your thoughts. Having understood this, you should be able to observe the moral precepts. If you should think about something horrid—molesting a six-year-old child, for example—you would be able to ignore the idea. It's only a thought—it passes in a second. The same is true of the emotion that goes with the thought. There is no need to feel attached to either one. In this way moral purification is practiced through the use of some meditation.

The *Visuddhimagga* also gives directions for the student's proper mode of life and habits. For example, a monk must not practice astrology or dream interpretation, since those occupations are great distractions. The student must also beware of ten categories of attachments, which might impede progress in meditation. These are: home, family, admirers, teaching, work, travel, friends, illness, study, and psychic abilities. (In other words, everything but meditation itself.)

At the same time, the disciple also practices meditative concentration. This involves training the mind to focus on a single object and ignore everything else. The *Visuddhimagga* recommends forty-two objects as suitable for meditation as outlined below:

1. Imaginary colored wheels, composed of earth, fire, air, water, light, pure space, dark blue, yellow, white, or red.
2. Ten stages of a corpse's decay, as disgusting as possible.
3. The four elements: earth, fire, air, water.
4. Infinite space, infinite consciousness, the primal Void, and the revolting nature of food.
5. The states of kindness, compassion, equanimity, and sympathy with others in their joy.
6. The thirty-two parts of the body, the act of breathing, and various abstract notions such as the inevitability of death and the Buddha's attributes.

These objects give different results in meditation. The disciple (usually aided by the guru) picks the one that best suits his or her temperament.

There are five basic stages in the practice of concentration meditation. At first the student can hardly concentrate at all. A noise in the street, a cramp in the leg, hunger pangs, sexual desire, memories, fantasies—all these will distract the student. Even when he or she learns to ignore outside influences and physical discomfort, the inner distractions continue. Most people have an unspoken running commentary going on in their minds; the main problem here is to learn to ignore the commentary. It's all right for you to chatter to yourself, as long as you do not get caught up in what is being said.

In stage two, the student achieves prolonged periods of concentration on the chosen object. This leads to stage three, in which the student must overcome new distractions—the energy and bliss released by meditation. Along with this comes stage four, in which the student has visions. Because these can be highly vivid, students may mistake them for reality, or grow too fond of them. In either case, they are a dangerous temptation.

At last comes stage five, which is full absorption in the object of meditation. This is called *jhana*. The mind seems to enter the object; consciousness of self ceases. The student in effect becomes the object, however briefly. This is an unstable state at first. The student must learn to stay in it.

Jhana is actually eight states, each deeper than the next. The first four are called material states; the last four are called formless states. Different objects of meditation will help you reach different levels of *jhana*. By meditating on corpses, for example, you can reach only the first level. The imaginary colored wheels can take you all the way to eight. No matter what the object, you must eventually give it up in order to attain the final levels.

The levels of *jhana* are:

1. Sudden absorption into the object of meditation; feelings of rapture and bliss; total loss of distractions; cessation of pain.
2. Rapture and bliss but without awareness of the object. (*Rapture* is an energetic, quasi-physical state; *bliss* is nonphysical and contemplative.)
3. Bliss without rapture; feeling of great concentration.
4. Loss of bliss and bodily pleasure. The dominant feeling now is of equanimity.
5. Awareness of infinite space.
6. Awareness of pure consciousness.
7. Awareness of the Void.
8. Loss of distinction between perception and nonperception.

All this may seem too elaborate and daunting, but it's only the preliminaries. According to the *Visuddhimagga*, the real discipline is the practice of insight, or *puñña*.

Puñña also involves five stages. The first one corresponds roughly to the stage you reach in concentration meditation just before *jhana*. This is called the state of mindfulness, or nonattachment. It is close to the state of moral purification described earlier. You observe without feeling compelled by anything you observe; you are aware but feel no emotional involvement. This leads to the second stage of insight where you realize that all thoughts, emotions, sensations, and perceptions are independent of the mind that observes them. They are meaningless in themselves, nothing more than a constant succession of events.

Stage three is called pseudonirvana. The student gradually becomes aware of each perception as it arises and passes. The clarity of mind this brings is overwhelming. But the joy and energy of pseudonirvana fade, and the student enters stage four. Now the student notices only the end of perceptions and with them the end of the mind that perceived them. Not only the objects, but the mind itself, vanish from moment to moment; this is an unendurable, apparently endless situation. Misery and disgust oppress the meditator, who wishes only for the mind itself to vanish permanently. The only way out of this state is to concentrate on each moment of suffering, including the physical pain that comes with stage four.

Finally comes stage five, which is *nirvana* (literally, a burnt-out state). The first entry into *nirvana* is very brief, but it brings about a great change. The meditator achieves permanent purity (unlike *jhana*, where the meditator's impurities merely recede to the background). The *Visuddhimagga* says that once one enters *nirvana*, one is sure of attaining final liberation within seven more incarnations. *Nirvana* first burns away selfishness and greed in the meditator; later, ill-will and the desire for sensory objects disappear. Finally, one becomes an *arahant*, an awakened being who acts only to help others or to preserve his or her own body.

Christian meditation

The Christian tradition of meditation corresponds roughly to what the *Visuddhimagga* calls meditative concentration. The difference lies not in the substitution of Jesus for Buddha but, first, in the fact that the Christians are much more simple and direct in their meditation and, second, in the Christian concern with salvation.

The early Christian ascetics lived in constant prayer, the most popular being what is generally called the Jesus Prayer: "Lord Jesus Christ, Son of God, have mercy on me, a sinner." The short form of this is the *Kyrie Eleison*, which Christian hermits used to recite silently with every breath. Hesychius of Jerusalem, who lived in the fifth century, the period when organized monastic life first took root, wrote that one can attain purity of heart only by stilling the mind. The goal of constant prayer is to fix the mind solely on Jesus so that one can live with God. Some monks went to extraordinary lengths to reach this goal. St. Simon Stylites lived on a pillar set in the middle of a desert. A more common approach in the sixth century was for the hermit to shut himself in a tiny room and remain there for years, living in his own filth.

In the *Philokalia*, such early Christians as St. Nilus gave instructions on how to attain oneness with Christ through meditation. You must live alone in a comfortless cell, eat as little as possible, observe all rituals, and pray constantly to Jesus for mercy. The practice of such meditation through prayer (usually called Hesychasm) has remained an important tradition in the Eastern church. Hesychasm gained popularity at Mt. Athos in the fourteenth century and is still practiced there.

Another important Christian tradition was developed by St. Ignatius. He taught his followers to visualize scenes from the life of Jesus and to participate emotionally in their visualizations. One had to set the scene, enter it imaginatively, and at the end draw some moral from the meditation. This tradition, too, is still with us, largely because of the poetry of John Donne. You can trace the steps of Ignatian meditation for yourself by reading Donne's "Holy Sonnets."

Mantras and other methods

The Hindu tradition is called *bhakti* meditation. The disciple concentrates on a favorite god or avatar, such as Krishna or Rama, using the god's name as a mantra, and repeating it constantly. The best-known example of this, of course, is the *Hare Krishna* chant. *Bhakti* meditation usually requires the help of a guru; there are some people, in fact, who maintain that the meditation is useless without devotion to the guru, and that the mantra gains meaning only when imparted directly by the guru.

The Sufis, who are Moslem mystics, meditate on what they call a *zikr*, or remembrance. The main one is *La ilaha illa 'llah*, "There is no God but Allah." The *zikr* is most effective when repeated silently. Ibn al-Najib (1097–1168) wrote the classic Sufi text on meditation, in which he advised the novice to seek a good teacher, rise above all desires, and follow the rules of the faith. By meditation and devotion to the teacher, the novice will break down the habits of mind that keep him from union with Allah.

The Nicherin Buddhists, followers of an old sect that gained new popularity after World War II, meditate on the mantra *Nam myoho renge kyo* and are quite overpowering in their conviction that theirs is the highest and most effective mantra. Students of Transcendental Meditation are equally confident about the power of their technique (which is a version of the meditation taught by the yogin Sankaracharya in the eighth century A.D.). (For more on TM, see the entry on Maharishi Mahesh Yogi in chapter five.)

There is at least one great modern teacher who is *not* convinced of the usefulness of mantras. Krishnamurti believes that concentration meditations of all kinds are worthless. This is totally consistent with his way of thought; Krishnamurti opposes all systems and authority. As he puts it, "By repeating Amen or *Om* or Coca-Cola indefinitely you obviously have a certain experience because by repetition the mind becomes quiet. . . . This is a most stupid, ugly thing, which any schoolboy can do because he is forced to." In Krishnamurti's view of meditation, "There is no how, no method." Just be aware. Start right now and keep it up. Be aware, and you will achieve understanding.

This is much the same thing that Zen masters say (or *would* say, if they felt inclined). Zen requires you to practice a form of meditation called *zazen*, in which you sit. That's all. You sit for several hours, and every once in a while the man who runs the meditation hall comes around and hits you with a stick if he does not like the way you look. Westerners say the purpose of *zazen* is to help the student attain enlightenment, or *satori*. That is not exactly correct. Zen masters often deny that there is such a thing as *satori*. They say that *satori* is your ordinary mind; therefore, you have nothing to attain. Ask a Zen master what all his students are doing in *zazen*, and he may well answer that they are sitting.

It seems that meditation, too, has its limits. Consider the state of *samadhi*, which the yogins consider to be the endpoint of meditation. Now consider what the Zen master D.T. Suzuki wrote: "That moment of coming out of *samadhi* and seeing it for what it is—that is *satori*."

For Further Reading

There is one outstanding recent book on meditation, Daniel Goleman's *The Varieties of the Meditative Experience* (New York: Dutton, 1977). Goleman gives a synthesis of a number of meditative traditions. In doing so, he sometimes underestimates the individuality of the systems he is describing, but the results are definitely worthwhile. The quotation from Krishnamurti given above is from *The Quiet Mind*, by J.E. Coleman (London: Rider, 1971).

Hypnosis

Many Westerners who lack the patience necessary to practice meditation are interested in hypnosis and autosuggestion as useful alternatives. However, there is considerable confusion as to what these states really are, and to what extent they overlap.

From Mesmer to Freud

People usually credit the modern rediscovery of hypnosis to Franz Anton Mesmer (1734–1815), a flamboyant Viennese doctor who had a way of making friends and enemies. Mesmer received his medical degree from the Faculty of Vienna in 1766. As a student, he showed great interest in the works of Paracelsus and the influence of the stars on people's health. Like many scientists of his time, he believed in the existence of a universal vital energy, and he thought ill health was the result of an imbalance of this energy within the body—an idea which, we have seen, manifests itself in a variety of forms. In 1774, these ideas came together for him when he met Father Hell, a Jesuit who settled in Vienna in that year to take up the post of professor of astronomy at the University. Father Hell was also interested in the influence of the stars on health and in the concept of universal energy. He had developed a system of medicine that involved placing steel plates on the patient's body, and by means of the plates, Father Hell claimed, he regulated the body magnetically. Mesmer was intrigued by the idea, and, working with Father Hell's methods, he devised his own system.

Mesmer had his patients swallow a preparation containing iron. Then he attached magnets to the patient's stomach and legs. The patient often reported feeling a flow of force through the body; the experience of the force was often accompanied by a brief fit, after which the patient would report relief from the symptoms of the disease. Mesmer soon gained quite a following by his use of this method. However, his colleagues were suspicious; they accused him of practicing magic, and in 1777 Mesmer left Vienna to try his luck in Paris.

In Paris, a provincial *curé* named Father Gassner had also been practicing a form of psychosomatic medicine that involved sending the patient into a cathartic fit. Father Gassner didn't bother with magnets and energetic flow and astral influences; he used the rite of exorcism. Father Gassner had gained a large following by his methods, and so in a sense had prepared the way for Mesmer. Within a few years of his arrival in Paris, Mesmer was giving group treatments with as many as twenty patients. His methods were similar to the sort of treatments now used at Esalen. He sat a number of well-to-do people in a big wooden tub, played music for them, and encouraged them to go into convulsions. People loved it.

Mesmer continued to do well until 1784, when the King of France appointed two commissions to study the theory of animal magnetism. The commissions included, among other prominent scientists, Lavoisier and Benjamin Franklin. The King wanted a report on the existence of a vital, magnetic force, rather than on its usefulness in medicine. The commissions reported that they found no evidence for such a force. This was a terrible blow for Mesmer, but it did not destroy his practice. The Revolution did that.

Mesmer's work was superseded when researchers concluded that the regulation of vital energy was of less interest than the sleepwalking that seemed to accompany the patients' convulsive fits. An English researcher, James Braid, said that the patient was more responsible than the mesmerist for the somnambulistic state. It was not a question of the mesmerist's will but of the subject's suggestibility. Braid was the man who coined the name *hypnosis* (from the Greek word for sleep). We now know, however, that hypnosis and sleep are very different states and that hypnotic visions differ physiologically from dreams.

Throughout the nineteenth century, hypnosis gained popularity with doctors. James Esdaile (1808–1859) performed some three hundred major surgeries using hypnosis to anesthetize his patients (this at a time when chemical anesthetics were virtually unknown). Other doctors used hypnosis to relieve the symptoms of various diseases. But hypnosis gained greatest acceptance among psychologists, who found that it gave them a way to probe their patients' minds. Jean Martin Charcot and Pierre Janet were especially interested in the psychological uses of the technique, which they identified closely with hysteria and states of dissociated consciousness. And of course there was Freud, who began his career working with hypnosis.

The Hypnotic State

No one knew then how hypnosis worked, and nobody really knows today. There are in fact a great many researchers who deny that a distinct hypnotic state exists. Theodore R. Sarbin believes that the subject willingly tries to act the role of a hypnotized person. (Sarbin uses the word *role* in a broad sense; he also interprets schizophrenia as a kind of role-playing.) Theodore X. Barber has similar views, though he places the emphasis on setting and procedures. Ernest R. Hilgard believes there *is* an altered state of awareness in hypnosis, but he's very cautious about defining that state.

The general reluctance to define the hypnotic state is only to be expected in view of all the variables associated with the most common hypnotic phenomena. First, there are the motor and sensory reactions. The hypnotist suggests that the subject's arm is so light that it will float upward, and the arm floats upward. But you can get an identical response from a cooperative person without hypnosis. To a large extent, the same can be said of the visions or hallucinations that go with hypnosis.

There is also the question of the degree to which the hypnotist controls the subject's will. In a series of experiments carried out by various researchers from 1939 to 1965, subjects who were deeply hypnotized carried out dangerous acts on command—they handled snakes and threw what appeared to be nitric acid into a lab assistant's face. The interesting thing about these experiments is that there was always a control group of people who were not hypnotized, and these people, too, handled snakes and threw acid on command.

Age-regression and posthypnotic suggestion are both frequently associated with hypnotism, and both provide only inconclusive evidence of it. Cooperative people can go through spontaneous age-regression, and obedience to posthypnotic suggestion tends to be uneven.

However, certain phenomena *do* point to a difference between the hypnotic state and the ordinary, waking state. People who are in hypnosis experience a kind of trance logic (dreamlike or childlike, if you will). They become willing to give up preconceived ideas. The fantasies suggested to them are extraordinarily clear. Some subjects experience synesthesia—they taste colors, smell sounds, and so on. Others undergo out-of-the-body experiences. And of course there can be changes in memory. Subjects will recall things they had long ago forgotten, and they will forget other things on command. Two researchers, Kenneth S. Bowers and Patricia Greig Bowers, believe a subject's creativity increases in hypnosis.

Hypnosis and Psi

For occultists, hypnosis is most interesting as an influence on psi abilities. Chapter two contains information about the work of Milan Ryzl, the Czechoslovakian doctor who has used hypnosis to develop psi powers in his subjects. Ryzl is not alone in this. Stanley Krippner and Charles Honorton of the Maimonides Center in New York have concluded that hypnosis increases ESP abilities. Their findings have been confirmed by Dr. Burton S. Glick of Elmhurst Medical Center, Queens, New York; until he checked the Maimonides results, Glick was a skeptic on the subject of ESP.

There is evidence, some of it quite old, that hypnosis and ESP are related phenomena. In 1823, A.F.J. Bertrand, a French hypnotist, discovered that his subjects had telepathic links with him. For example, if he ordered a subject to write down his first name, and if at the same time he thought about the subject's *last* name, the subject would become confused and show distress. As soon as Bertrand matched the thought and the command, the subject would relax again and carry out the order. The technique of mutual hypnosis offers even more intriguing evidence. In this method, the researcher hypnotizes a subject and takes him to a deep level of trance.

Then he commands that subject to hypnotize a second subject. The two subjects tend to develop a very strong telepathic link while in trance, and through the experience they may become very close emotionally.

When you consider hypnosis as a technique, you see at once that it bears a great resemblance to meditation. In fact, a useful, though oversimplified, definition of hypnosis might be meditation directed by another person.

First of all, the hypnotist establishes a rapport with the subject. Usually, the hypnotist will try to make the subject comfortable and chat for a while about what is going to take place. Then the hypnotist has the subject concentrate on something. This could be a swinging pendulum, a shiny object, a sequence of counting, a mental image—anything that will get the subject's attention away from the immediate surroundings, or as hypnotists now call them, the generalized reality orientation (GRO).

In general, any prolonged concentration will cause a fading in the GRO. There was a well-known experiment in which subjects were asked simply to stare at a blue vase for fifteen minutes. The subjects reported that as time wore on, the vase seemed to become more vivid, even luminous. The outline of the vase faded; the subjects' impressions of the third dimension collapsed. In short, the subjects experienced typical absorption responses as seen in Hindu and Buddhist concentration meditation (see above). In hypnotic induction, the subject goes through the same process, but with the hypnotist as a guide.

As the subject's GRO fades, the hypnotist encourages the subject to let the process of hypnosis happen. The usual instructions are to relax, to feel as if you are floating, to let your mind drift. This, too, is a lot like meditative techniques in which the thoughts must drift by unimpeded. Again, the difference is that the hypnotist gives the thoughts direction.

By now the subject should have lost the sense of the GRO and should show signs of being more suggestible. The hypnotist will now use a deepening technique. The hypnotist suggests that the patient's arm is growing lighter, that it is so light it will begin to float upward. The hypnotist says that the higher the arm floats, the deeper the trance will become. If the subject responds well to this suggestion, the hypnotist can assume that hypnosis has been accomplished.

It should be obvious by now that hypnosis involves a social interaction; therefore there is no such thing as self-hypnosis, strictly speaking. There is, however, such a thing as autosuggestion. This is concentration meditation with some psychological self-help added.

Autosuggestion is simple to practice, so simple that there are no specific instructions as to how to do it. Essentially, you just relax and use your imagination—the way you use your imagination is up to you.

For example, you could follow the suggestions given by Donald Gibbons in his book *Beyond Hypnosis: Explorations in Hyperempiria* (Power Publishing,

1973). Gibbons has developed suggestions that he believes will lead to an expansion of consciousness through hypnotic means. To adapt these suggestions for your own use, you would have to imagine yourself in front of a massive cathedral. You must visualize the cathedral as clearly as possible and then begin to count from one to ten. At one, the cathedral's outer doors open, and you step into the entry hall. At two, the inner doors open; you hear organ music and smell incense. At three, you let the music and incense enter into you; you step into the nave. From four to six, you proceed down the nave, all the while getting more relaxed and expanding your awareness. From seven to ten, you approach the altar. At the count of ten, you will be in a state of expanded consciousness. You will also be able to suggest ideas to yourself and have them plunge directly into your subconscious. This method will not work if you happen to be Jewish, or dislike cathedrals, or are allergic to incense.

To develop your own system of autosuggestion, there are a few general rules you should observe. Practice in a quiet, isolated place where you know you will not be disturbed, and only when you know you will not be interrupted. For example, don't practice when you know you have to leave for an appointment in half an hour. Sit in a comfortable position and close your eyes gently. If you squeeze them shut, it will be impossible to relax. Now concentrate on breathing deeply and evenly. Your breathing should become smooth, slow, and regular. When it does, you are ready to relax more. Concentrate on your feet. Tell yourself they're relaxed and that they feel heavy. Take your time; don't go on until you actually feel the heaviness in your feet. Then feel the heaviness spread up your legs. Relax your whole body in this way. Then enter a controlled fantasy, something that will let let your mind drift but that won't allow you to fall asleep. If you do not like cathedrals, think of walking down a spiral staircase, of descending in an elevator, or of lying on the beach and letting the tide lap higher and higher on your body. Your fantasy should include motion of some sort as a cue for you to go deeper and deeper into the meditative state.

When you feel yourself to be at a good depth, try giving yourself suggestions. These days, nine people out of ten tell themselves to stop smoking or to eat less; you needn't be that mundane. The state of autosuggestion is useful for practicing clairvoyance and astral projection, for example. A lot of ceremonial magicians rely on this state, too (see chapter four). Again, use your imagination. You're the one giving the suggestions.

Perhaps the most important point is to make the experience enjoyable. If you have to strain, you won't get very far. Relax, have a good time, and see what you can find out about yourself.

For Further Reading

For a good, scholarly introduction to the subject, see *Methodologies of Hypnosis: A Critical Appraisal of Contemporary Paradigms of Hypnosis*, by Peter W. Sheehan and Campbell W. Perry (New York: Wiley, 1976). Another good introduction is *Hypnosis: Trance as a Coping Mechanism*, by Fred H. Frankel (New York: Plenum, 1976). To get a little deeper into the subject, see *Hypnosis: Research Developments and Perspectives*, edited by Erika Fromm and Ronald E. Shor (Chicago: Aldine/Atherton, 1972). A defense of the theory of hypnosis as an altered state of consciousness is in Ernest R. Hilgard's *Hypnotic Susceptibility* (New York: Harcourt, Brace and World, 1965). For a discussion of hypnosis and psi, see Charles Panati's *Supersenses: Our Potential for Parasensory Experience* (London: Cape, 1975).

Drugs

In a Neolithic cave in Granada in the south of Spain, archeologists have found a group of twelve skeletons positioned in a circle around a thirteenth skeleton (who had been robed in leather). The cave floor was strewn with poppies. We do not know exactly what this Neolithic congregation did, but the general idea is clear enough. Drugs have served a sacramental purpose from the very earliest times, and they have continued to do so through history. In classical Greece and Rome, Dionysian sects used alcohol and magic mushrooms to achieve God-inspired frenzy. In rural Europe through medieval times, people used plants of the *Solanaceae* family—deadly nightshade, henbane, mandrake, and thorn apple—in order to see visions. Witches believed these plants gave them the power to fly. Indians in Central and South America had the same beliefs. Don Juan Matus, the informant for Carlos Castaneda's books, taught the use of Jimson weed for flying. (Jimson weed is of the same genus as thorn apple.) Mazatec Indians in Oaxaca, Mexico, eat psilocybin mushrooms in a nocturnal family ceremony so as to get in contact with the spirit world. Indians in Colombia and Peru do the same with the vine *Banisteriopsis caape*, which they variously call *yagé*, *ayahuasca*, and *caapi*. The Arabs had a hashish cult (from which we derive the word *assassin*), much like the modern *ganja* cult of the Rastafarians. Coleridge and Baudelaire took opium. Aleister Crowley was a junkie and proud of it.

But in the present-day marriage of drugs and spirituality, one particular drug has the place of honor. Dr. Albert Hofmann first synthesized it for the Sandoz laboratories in Basel, Switzerland, in 1938. He thought it might serve as an analgesic to relieve migraine. He did not discover its real nature until April 16, 1943, when he accidentally ingested some of the drug. Soon Dr. Hofmann felt restless and dizzy. He couldn't work. It was late in the day. He left his laboratory and, getting on his bicycle, began to pedal his way back home. It turned out to be an extraordinary bike ride. The drug Dr. Hofmann had synthesized was LSD.

If there has been a change in Westerners' ways of thinking in recent years, Dr. Hofmann surely must get a large measure of the credit or blame. Psychedelic drugs, particularly LSD, have encouraged an inwardness in people, an awareness of spirituality. Drugs have fostered creativity, occultism, music, sexual freedom, and much gibberish.

Styles in drug use may come and go, but LSD seems to have had a permanent effect. Think of how many times you've heard people, even people who have never used drugs, say *trip* when they mean *experience*, *spaced out* when they mean *vague* or *disconnected*, *bummer* when they mean *misfortune* or *unhappiness*. LSD has conditioned the way we all think.

Moreover, it's done so in a particular way, largely as prescribed by one particular man. Dr. Hofmann synthesized the drug, but it took Timothy Leary to make it what it is today.

Timothy Leary and LSD

Leary was born in Springfield, Massachusetts, on October 22, 1920. He was raised a Catholic, and his father was an Army dentist (one of his patients was Eisenhower). So from the start, Leary was concerned with authoritarian structures, because he grew up with two of the biggest. In his academic training, he showed a tendency to skip around—Holy Cross, West Point, the University of Alabama, Washington State University. He received his doctorate in clinical psychology from Berkeley in 1950, and for a time settled into a career.

Then the first great shake-up came: His wife, Marianne Busch, committed suicide on his thirty-fifth birthday. Leary struggled to keep going, relying on those two great anesthetics, work and alcohol. But finally he left his job as director of psychological research at Kaiser Foundation Hospital and took his children to Spain. There the second great shake-up happened: He fell ill with a disease he picked up from a whore. He lay in bed for days, delirious and covered with sores, and at the crisis point of the disease he received an overpowering feeling of enlightenment. He said it was his first trip.

His first drug trip took place in August 1960. At a rented villa in Cuernavaca, Leary ate twelve psilocybin mushrooms—six males and six females. Interestingly, the first known Westerners to participate in the Mazatec mushroom ceremony, Valentina and Gordon Wasson, did so in 1955, the year Marianne Leary killed herself. In that same year, Aldous Huxley's wife Maria died of cancer; the experience was the source of Huxley's interest in LSD therapy for the dying.

Leary and some others who had eaten mushrooms relaxed by the swimming pool and waited for the effects. A bearded student who had not eaten mushrooms sat with them and took notes. When the mushrooms hit, Leary's first reaction was to convulse in laughter at how Jewish, scholarly, and ugly the note-taker looked.

Consider his reaction. That one moment, that first reaction, was a miniature of his entire system of thought, the system that was so persuasive for so many people. In Leary's first psychedelic rush, he felt no compassion, or love, or enlightenment, or sexual desire. He felt contempt.

To be more precise, he laughed at the contemptible absurdity of three things:

1. The man was ugly. In Leary's mind, he should have been beautiful. The assumption here is that nature is beautiful, and therefore the man, since he was ugly, must have been cut off from nature.

2. The man was scholarly. That, too, seemed unnatural to Leary, who has a basic streak of anti-intellectualism. In his writings on drugs, Leary has consistently called the intellect a higher function than the emotions, but by *intellect* he merely seems to mean an absence of emotional involvement. Leary seems always to have felt that the reason is unreliable and twisted, while the emotions are sloppy.

3. The man was Jewish. Here Leary's feelings about authoritarian structures emerge. I don't think Leary was being anti-Semitic. I think he found it convenient to project his feelings about the Church and the Army onto this perfectly innocent young man who was patiently making a record for Leary's use while enduring stoned ridicule.

At that moment, Leary wasn't about to question his motives and prejudices—not when the psilocybin had made everything so clear. He merely knew, beyond doubt, that the drug was good, and that it was good because it could free people from emotional entanglements, remove the limits of reason, overturn authoritarian social conditioning, and return everyone to a state of nature. Surely that was the nature of the drug experience, Leary thought. Surely everyone would agree with him once they'd tried the drug.

Within a few years, Leary had evolved a complete system for interpreting the LSD experience. With the aid of his two closest associates, Richard Alpert and Ralph Metzner, Leary adapted the Tibetan *Book of the Dead* as a Bible for acid trips. (For more information about the *Book of the Dead*, see chapter two.) Following the *Book of the Dead*'s divisions, he stated that there are three main phases to a trip:

1. First Bardo: A state transcending words, space, time, and self, a state without visions or thoughts. What remains is spontaneous, egoless action and pure awareness.
2. Second Bardo: A period of visions (not only hallucinations, but also heightened awareness of external reality).
3. Third Bardo: Return from the trip.

There are identifiable periods within each of these phases:

1. (a) Clear Light. This is the state of perfect enlightenment. (b) A lesser experience of Clear Light, in which the tripper is aware of energy flow, both within the body and in external reality. (In the perfection of Clear Light, of course, one cannot even distinguish between energy and nonenergy, perception and nonperception.)
2. (a) The Source, or Creator, Vision. The tripper conceives of the Clear Light as God. (b) Internal Flow of Archetypal Processes. The tripper, with eyes closed, sees cellular and biological forms and various abstract designs. The tripper also hears a variety of sounds. To stay at this level, the tripper must avoid analyzing the visions intellectually. (c) Fire-Flow of Internal Unity. The tripper experiences intense emo-

tions and sees visions of the circulatory system. To stay on this level, one must be willing to melt into the cosmic ocean of emotion. (d) Wave-Vibration Structure of External Forms. The tripper becomes fascinated with the properties of light, sound, touch, and so forth. (e) Vibratory Waves of External Unity. The tripper feels an emotional participation in external reality. (f) The Retinal Circus (a term borrowed from Henri Michaux). The tripper free-associates rapidly, experiencing a kaleidoscopic review of life—his own, his family's, his friends', everybody's. (g) The Magic Theater (a term borrowed from Hesse). The tripper sees other people as gods, heroes, and demons. Finally, there is a great variety of Wrathful Visions, fantasies (principally paranoid ones) frightening enough to turn the tripper into a cowering, babbling idiot, or send him screaming through the streets.

3. (a) Feelings of extraordinary strength and perception. (b) Feelings of panic and persecution; hallucinations of torture. (c) Restlessness. (d) Feelings of stupidity and inadequacy. (e) A feeling of being dead or cut off from reality. (f) A feeling of being crushed. (g) A feeling that everything has turned grey. While in the Third Bardo, the tripper may also imagine he's being judged by others; or he may become very preoccupied with sex.

(For more details, see *The Psychedelic Experience*, by Leary, Metzner, and Alpert. [New Hyde Park: University Books, 1964.])

Not everybody who took LSD accepted this system. Most people weren't even aware of it, at least not in its details. But a surprising number of people did accept the underlying assumptions—that LSD could magically make one transcend the limits of language and society and that drugs put one back in touch with nature.

Leary had only one serious rival as proselytizer for LSD, and that was Ken Kesey. Kesey, of course, was chief of the Merry Pranksters, the group of Zen clowns and cowboys who spread LSD enlightenment through California. They achieved their greatest fame in Tom Wolfe's *The Electric Kool-Aid Acid Test*. Kesey was probably the person most responsible for the social and political forms that LSD use took. He did not invent those forms, of course, but he helped shape them. Kesey was not given to telling people what they should think about their LSD experience. That was Leary's strong point—interpreting the experience for people—and his great influence comes from the fact that most people have accepted his interpretation.

There was one person in Leary's circle who did *not* believe any of Leary's theories. He was Art Kleps, founder and chief Boo-Hoo of the Neo-American Church, and in the mid-1960s he was living at Leary's New York State retreat, Millbrook. Kleps objected strongly to Leary's attempts to systematize the psychedelic experience, saying that, since everything is an illusion and nothing really exists, including Leary and Kleps, it's a major waste of energy to be systematic.

Kleps was one of the more endearing people to come out of that period; certainly he was one of the wittiest and one of those least given to cant. For example, he used to recommend the use of television for divination. The images TV throws up, he explained, are much more appropriate for us than the images from the Tarot or *I Ching*. (You can use this method only if you watch television rarely and select the station at random.) Kleps also took a hard line on the use of LSD as a sacrament. When called upon to testify on drugs before a Senate committee, he resolutely maintained that laws regulating the use of LSD were a violation of the First Amendment guarantee of freedom of religion. Even Leary took a more moderate stand (for which Kleps blamed him). However, even Kleps adopted some of Leary's terminology.

One more notable aspect of Leary's system was his emphasis on sex. Leary believed that acid and sex went together like cookies and milk. (Again, this was part of the return-to-nature ideology.) Unfortunately, Leary believed natural sex to be heterosexual—while his chief associate, Alpert, was gay. There are reports (though of uncertain reliability) that Leary tried to "cure" Alpert by arranging stoned orgies. (For more lurid stories, see *Timothy Leary, the Madness of the Sixties and Me*, by Charles W. Slack. [New York: Wyden, 1974.] Slack knew Leary and writes from some experience. For more information on Alpert, see chapter five, under Baba Ram Dass.) Psychedelic drugs can heighten sexual pleasure, but that does not mean they always will. Paul Krassner, another friend of Leary's and editor of the much-lamented *The Realist*, once wrote about the problems of combining sex and acid. Krassner said the act seemed so silly to him that he kept collapsing with laughter, and after a few hours he gave up.

The Risks and Rewards

What good are psychedelic drugs? Are they of any use to occultists? The answer is yes.

First, however, you must recognize and understand the dangers. As Leary's experience showed, drugs will not help you transcend your basic beliefs. Indeed, they may trap you in them. As Leary himself wrote of an early trip, "I began to get a sinking feeling. Psychedelic drugs didn't solve any problems. They just magnified, mystified, clarified to jewel-like sharpness the basic problems of life and evolution," or what Leary *thought* were those basic problems.

Just as drugs magnify and mythify your prejudices, they intensify your personality traits. You may find your faults turning into major deformations. Moreover, psychedelics are habit-forming (though not addictive), and this, too, can aggravate your problems. One particular trap of LSD is that the nervous system becomes used to it when you take it often. After a while, normal dosages are not enough. The temptation then is to keep taking more and more, with less and less effect. This is the back-yourself-into-a-corner-and-kick-yourself method.

Some people go in for serial tripping. They set aside a week and do nothing but trip. On the first day, they take one dose. On the second day they take two; on the third day, three; and so forth. This is not to be recommended. Even mystics have to give their nervous systems a rest.

However, if you are careful, drugs can indeed be useful. They give you a new respect for the power of the mind, encourage new ways of thinking, and show you that the world you ordinarily experience is not necessarily the only world there is. Perhaps most important, they open you to emotion, and to such a degree that afterward you may suspect you've never truly felt anything before.

Occult Pharmacology

Psychedelic drugs affect the nervous system in the following way. There's a gap between the nerve cells, called a synapse. Therefore, impulses never run directly along the nervous system. At each synapse, a chemical called a transmitter closes the gap. There are three groups of transmitters. One of them consists of chemicals from the indole group, including serotonin. Most psychedelic drugs, including LSD and psilocybin, are indole derivatives. Mescaline has a structural similarity to the indoles; it also resembles chemicals in a second group of transmitters.

So psychedelic drugs tend to resemble transmitter chemicals. Obviously, these drugs can plug directly into the nervous system. However, we do not know how they function. Indeed we do not really understand how the nervous system functions under ordinary conditions. (For information about LSD, serotonin, and the Third Eye, see the section on astral projection in chapter two.) It seems likely that the drugs act principally as catalysts. They set off an effect in the nervous system, and within a short time pass out of the body with the urine. We also know that psychedelic drugs are nontoxic. There is no evidence that they cause chromosome damage. Nor are they addictive. They do affect the memory, but we don't know as yet to what degree. The dangers involved in their use are psychological, not physiological.

LSD. The drug's full name is N,N-diethyl-D-lysergamide, or D-lysergic acid diethylamide. Its chemical formula is $C_{20}H_{25}N_3O$. LSD is a derivative of lysergic acid, which in turn comes from grain (most often rye) infected with ergot fungus.

LSD is effective in very small amounts (150–250 micrograms). It is usually eaten and takes effect in an hour to one-and-a-half hours, depending on the user's metabolism and what else he or she has eaten. Purer, stronger doses take effect more quickly. LSD can also be ground into a powder and inhaled, in which case it takes effect still more quickly; or it can be injected with a syringe.

Users generally feel some tension before the drug takes effect. It's doubtful whether this is caused by the drug itself. Experiments show that people who are given placebos which they are told are LSD also feel muscular and nervous tension after about an hour. The user most often feels the drug take effect in a series of waves of nervous energy, or rushes. The waves gain in intensity and frequency for a period of fifteen to forty-five minutes, after which the trip has begun.

No one has written an adequate account of the LSD experience, and no one ever will. This is because LSD *has no content*. There are no events that are characteristic of the drug, no set of experiences one can expect. Each trip is personal and unique. Certainly you can catalog certain effects—hallucinations, awareness of patterns of light and dark, increased physical sensitivity, synesthesia—but within the context of the trip the primary factor is one's state of mind, and that, of course, is a purely individual matter.

At the most intense part of the trip, the peak, people often lose the ability to verbalize. They see objects and understand perfectly well what those objects are, but they will not automatically name them. If the name should occur to the person, it will probably seem a strange coincidence that the name should go with the thing. When the ability to verbalize goes, the sense of self usually goes with it. Some people panic at this point, especially if you ask them a question they feel they have to answer (for example, "Which way is the bathroom?"). They know where the bathroom is, and given enough time they might be able to stutter directions to it, but as they do so they tend to wonder just who is working the mouth and tongue. (This is still an *external* description of the experience, you will notice. The individual's understanding of the experience is still the important factor, and no generalizations can be drawn from that.)

The trip usually lasts for several hours (from four to eight in most cases), with aftereffects lasting for a day or two, till the nervous system can recover.

From an occult viewpoint, the important thing about LSD is its intimate relation with death. It's not coincidence that Timothy Leary used the Tibetan *Book of the Dead* to map the LSD experience, or that Aldous Huxley took LSD on his deathbed, or that Stanislav Grof gives LSD to dying cancer patients. It's not coincidence that Norman Mailer speaks of LSD as useful for people who need to die a little. One does not necessarily see coffins and graves and angels during a trip (though it's been known to happen). The death that occurs is the death of the self. When that happens, you can learn very quickly what mystics mean by a sense of nonattachment to the world. A lot of people who go through this experience start to take themselves and their Big Trip very seriously. Others want to nail down the feeling permanently, and so they rush into mystical sects. There are some people, though, who react by developing something that looks like a sense of humor but that is really something more. If you take LSD, I recommend that you try to follow their example.

Mescaline. The drug's chemical name is 3,4,5 trimethoxyphenethylamine. In its pure form it is an alkaline oil. More often it appears in sulfate and chloride salts as a white, crystalline powder. Mescaline is derived from the peyote cactus (*Lophophora williamsii*). Taken in its chemical form in a capsule or tablet, is is usually eaten. When the drug is taken directly from the plant, the user chews the peyote buttons thoroughly but does not swallow them. The buttons are bitter and usually cause vomiting. Several buttons must be chewed; for a strong experience, from seven to fourteen are required.

The effects of mescaline are substantially similar to those of LSD. The drug takes effect more gradually than does LSD. It often gives the user a sense of inner stillness, but it also can cause greater disorientation than LSD. In moderate doses it does not cause hallucinations as such; rather, it seems to reveal external reality with great clarity. Objects appear as perfect in themselves; the user's esthetic sense is heightened. The user will also tend to identify with objects, to feel a participation in their existence.

With larger doses, especially those taken in the form of peyote, the user may see visions. The sense of external reality may alter radically. Users also experince a strong identification with the peyote plant iself. According to Carlos Castaneda, one may even encounter a personification of the plant, a being called Mescalito. Castaneda believes that Mescalito is in reality an independent power and that peyote is merely his agent. In writing of his encounters with Mescalito, Castaneda writes that "whatever is contained in the cactus *Lophophora williamsii* had nothing to do with me in order to exist as an entity; it existed by itself out there, at large."

Mescaline tends to be less of a shock to the system than LSD. It is useful for people who want a smoother, more contemplative trip.

Psilocybin. The chemical name is O-phosphoryl-4-hydroxy-N, N-dimethyltryptamine. The drug is derived from the mushroom *Psilocybe mexicana*. Like LSD, psilocybin is an indole derivative. In its effects, it is a lot like LSD, but it tends to be subtler. The user may be unaware of its influence until some bizarre event reveals that the drug has indeed taken effect. On the other hand, a psilocybin derivative, DMT (dimethyltryptamine), is much more brutal than LSD. Users say that whereas LSD is like flying in a jet plane, DMT is like being shot out of a cannon.

Marijuana and hashish. These are both drived from the resin of the unripened hemp plant, *Cannabis sativa*. Their active ingredient is Δ^1-Tetrahydrocannabinol (or THC). Marijuana and hashish are usually smoked, but they can also be eaten if they are first baked. They taste awful, so most people bake them in something that will mask the taste and texture.

William S. Burroughs defines marijuana as an intensifier. It amplifies the emotions and the senses but reduces the ability to think critically. Marijuana is most useful as an aid to exploring one's fantasies; it also improves one's concentration (though you cannot guarantee you will concentrate on the right thing). Marijuana works as an aphrodisiac for most of the people most of the time.

There is no evidence that marijuana is addictive. Some people get to be too fond of marijuana, but then other people are too fond of oatmeal cookies. A test done a few years back seemed to show that marijuana reduces one's ability to drive a car safely. But the dosages used in the test were so high that it was a wonder the subjects could fasten their seat belts, let alone steer. More recently, a study showed that heavy use of marijuana may cause men's mammary glands to develop.

Marijuana not only intensifies your senses, it can also intensify your problems. Some people get in the habit of feeling miserable every time they smoke marijuana. Their shortcomings seem to attack them like angry demons; everything becomes a source of worry. If this happens to you, there's one sensible answer: Stop smoking marijuana.

Here's some information on popular nonpsychedelic drugs.

Cocaine. Cocaine is an alkaloid crystal that comes from the leaves of *Erythroxylum coca*, a bush found in Peru, Bolivia, and Colombia. The chemical formula is $C_{17}H_{21}NO_4$. Cocaine stimulates the cortex of the brain, sharpens the senses, and increases self-confidence and energy. With prolonged use, it can foster paranoia. Typical symptoms of overuse are sleeplessness, restlessness, hypersensitivity, and a burned-out nose. It's true that shamans in South America use cocaine, but they do so either by chewing coca leaves or brewing them into tea. The effects thus tend to be much milder. Cocaine, as we know it, is a lot of fun, but it's not very enlightening spiritually.

Opiates. These come from the fruits of poppies (*Papaver somniferum*). The direct product is opium, which can be either smoked or eaten. Opium is mildly addictive. It is a relaxant and encourages dreams and visions. For this reason it's enjoyed a long popularity with writers and artists. The principal alkaloid derivatives of opium are morphine and codeine; heroin is a derivative of morphine. All of these are addictive and are useful only for limited medical purposes.

The poppy, by the way, was unknown in China till the seventh century A.D. Originally the poppy grew only in Greece and Mesopotamia. As for opium smoking, it began sometime after Columbus's voyages—tobacco smoking came first. The use of opium first became a problem in China in the mid-seventeenth century. The Chinese government made repeated, unsuccessful attempts to stamp out its use. These attempts often failed because of foreign intervention. In the Opium Wars (1839–42 and 1856–60), Britain and France forced the Chinese to stay in the opium trade, which was proving disastrous for the health of the Chinese but highly profitable for the Europeans.

Barbiturates. (Valium, Quaalude, Tuinal, etc.) Of no use whatever. Wise up.

For Further Reading.

Modern interest in the spiritual potentialities of drugs began with Aldous Huxley. *The Doors of Perception* and *Heaven and Hell* (New York: Harper and Row, 1963) remain classics. For Timothy Leary's views and a partial autobiography, see his *High Priest* (New York: World, 1968). For a different clinical interpretation of LSD, see two books by Dr. Stanislav Grof: *Realms of the Human Unconscious: Observations from LSD Research* (New York: Dutton, 1976), and *The Human Encounter with Death* (New York: Dutton, 1977). Grof, who works at the Maryland Psychiatric Research Center, believes that psychotheraphy with LSD provides a quick way for leading the patient first into Freudian realms of the personal unconscious and then into the deeper, Jungian realms of the collective unconscious. I should also mention Andrew Weil's book, *The Natural Mind: A New Way of Looking at Drugs and the Higher Consciousness* (Boston: Houghton-Mifflin, 1972). It's a very foolish book, but it has had a wide influence. To learn about drugs on a more scientific level, you might begin with *Psychedelic Drugs*, edited by Richard E. Hicks and Paul Jay Fink (New York: Grune and Stratton, 1969).

Chapter Four

Magic

(The Attainment of Spiritual Mastery)

• Ceremonial Magic • Know Your Enemy—A Dossier on Demons • Witchcraft and Satanism • Voodoo

Ceremonial Magic

For those to whom occultism is a way of life, the practice of magic is the culmination of their spiritual science. Ceremonial magic encompasses all the other disciplines and is their destination. In order to practice magic, the adept must strengthen and develop the physical and etheric body, become expert in the techniques of astral travel and psi, master the symbols of the Universal Mind in all their forms. The earlier chapters of this book have given you an indication of how this should be accomplished, how the adept can rise through the planes of existence. This chapter will offer you instructions on the practice of ceremonial magic, including the evocation of spirits. You will learn the theory behind magic, the use of magical instruments, the correct procedures for magical evocation, and the nature of the spirits to be called.

This information is not for the immature. Unless you are a highly developed individual, you will only harm yourself by trying to practice magic. In the first place, you are likely to get weak results, or no results at all. In that case you will become frustrated and angry; you will tend to pour more and more energy into useless evocations, and so you will weaken yourself. In the second place, should you succeed, you will not be able to control the spirits you summon. In that case, you will not have used magic—magic will have used you. The outcome is best left to the imagination.

Therefore, you must read this article carefully and in its entirety before trying to practice magic. Pay special attention to the section on the initiation of the magician. It could save you a lot of wasted effort.

How Magic Works

Magicians make spirits appear and talk with them face to face. They materialize balls of fire, or watery globes, and set them to work. They penetrate other people's minds; they travel to the farthest parts of the world as quickly as thought. How can they do all this?

The answer is that magicians learn to use the universal energy called ether. Some call it *akasha*, a Sanskrit word meaning "bright, shining." Ether is not matter, but it is the origin, or substratum, of all matter. It infuses the entire universe: the universe is nothing but ether.

Ether emanates directly from the Deity. At its purest, at the point where it is closest to the Deity, it is pure light. As it emanates outward, it becomes more and more gross. The different levels of what we call the astral plane are levels of ether. What we call the material plane is the lowest, grossest form of ether.

Magicians use the Ptolemaic scheme of the universe as a map of the etheric levels. In this scheme, the universe is made up of ten astral spheres and four material spheres. In descending order, these are:

Higher astral plane	Primum mobile (first mover) Crystal firmament Fixed stars
Lower astral plane	Saturn Jupiter Mars Sun Venus Mercury Moon
Material plane	Fire Air Water Earth

As you can see, magicians, in describing the material plane, use the ancient division of four elements: earth, water, air, and fire. In this scheme, ether serves as the fifth element—or, in Latin, the *quinta essentia*, or quintessence.

Because ether (or akasha, or quintessence) has no bounds of time or space, anyone who learns to use it will be able to penetrate all levels of the universe thoroughly and instantly. The magician can thus work equally well on the mental, astral, and material planes.

Types of Magic

There are different ways of using the ether. The first distinction to be made is between true magic (or white magic) and the practice of sorcery and necromancy (the black arts). Sorcery is the unenlightened use of the outward forms of magic, either for material gain or to harm others. Necromancy is the evocation of the spirits of the dead, often through the medium of a corpse. Necromancers work almost exclusively to foretell the future, again for material gain.

A true magician understands the degradations and dangers of sorcery and necromancy and will not practice them. This section, therefore, is concerned with white magic, specifically Hermetic magic, which is the main tradition in the West. It will also mention Faustian magic (evocation of devils), the Enochian magic of John Dee, Rosicrucianism and the magic of Abramelin—all of them used in contemporary magical practice.

Hermetic Magic. What we know of Hermetic magic dates from the first century A.D. Of course magical knowledge goes back farther than that. But Hermetic magic is a mixture of traditions. It combines Egyptian knowledge with ideas of the Greeks and Jews who lived in Egypt, principally in Alexandria, at the time of Christ. (For more historical information on Hermetic magic see chapter seven.)

These three groups all claimed that the knowledge they held in common was divinely inspired. There are two different accounts of how the knowledge had been received.

The first account derives from the apocryphal *Book of Enoch* (which has nothing to do with Enochian religion). In a passage that amplifies Genesis vi, 1–5, Enoch tells how 200 angels descended from heaven to Mount Hermon and took wives from the "daughters of men." The angels taught their knowledge to these women and to the children they bore. For this presumption, the angels were thrown out of heaven.

Hermetic scholars recognize in this account a parallel to the myth of the Tree of Knowledge of Good and Evil. In the Gnostic interpretation of Adam and Eve's fall, Jehovah is not the Deity, but a powerful though lesser spirit who built the material world and rules over it. Because of his jealousy and pride, Jehovah forbade knowledge to Adam and Eve, hoping they would worship him as the Highest God. The serpent in this interpretation is not Satan but the spirit Ouroboros, sent by Wisdom (Sophia) to liberate the minds of men and women. Magical knowledge is thus a higher and more pious wisdom than obedience to Jehovah. The serpent Ouroboros, far from being humankind's enemy, is one of its greatest saviors. (For more on Gnosticism, see chapter seven.)

In a second account, magicial knowledge came from Hermes Trismegistus (Thrice-Great Hermes), who has given his name to the magical sciences. Hermes was a god of the Greek settlers in Egypt, also identified with the Egyptian God Thoth (see chapter seven). Through the agency of an ancient Egyptian king, this god gave humankind forty-two books of knowledge, of which fourteen short fragments in Greek survive. The most important of these is the *Emerald Tablet*.

From the Hermetic tradition we derive not only ceremonial magic but also alchemy. Magicians have usually practiced both sciences; and both are said to have been taught by the angels of the *Book of Enoch* and by Hermes Trismegistus. The difference between them is that, in alchemy, the magician tries to bring about a special physical manifestation of ether. This is the philosopher's stone, the *prima materia*. With it the alchemist can transmute base metals to gold, which is the highest material form. The ceremonial magician, on the other hand, manipulates ether to call upon spirits and to learn from them. Obviously these are two similar, though different, branches of one science. (For more on alchemy, see the entry on that subject in chapter seven.)

What we derive from Hermes above all is the doctrine of correspondence: "That which is above is like that which is below."

In other words, each man and each woman is a small model of the cosmos. Each mind is a model of the Divine Mind. The four material elements—earth, fire, air, water—are models of four universal principles. The Ptolemaic scheme of the solar system is a model of the system of astral spheres.

The doctrine of correspondence is essential to magic, and to all occult studies. (For more on the importance of correspondence, see The Occult Bible section.) In describing the practice of magical evocation, we will return to it again and again.

Faustian Magic. Faustian magic is the evocation of demons, and it began to develop well before the sixteenth century when Faust lived—as the books of magic reveal.

THE EMERALD TABLET OF HERMES TRISMEGISTUS

'Tis true, without falsehood, and most real: that which is above is like that which is below, to perpetrate the miracles of one thing. And as all things have been derived from one, by the thought of one, so all things are born from this thing, by adoption. The sun is its father, the moon is its mother. Wind has carried it in its belly, the earth is its nurse. Here is the father of every perfection in the world. His strength and power are absolute when changed into earth; thou wilt separate the earth from fire, the subtle from the gross, gently and with care. It ascends from earth to heaven, and descends again to earth to receive the power of the superior and inferior things. By this means, thou wilt have the glory of the world. And because of this, all obscurity will flee from thee. Within this is the power, most powerful of all powers. For it will overcome all subtle things, and penetrate every solid thing. Thus the world was created. From this will be, and will emerge, admirable adaptations of which the means are here. And for this reason, I am called Hermes Trismegistus, having the three parts of the philosophy of the world. What I have said of the sun's operations is accomplished.

The first great book of magic known to us is the *Testament of Solomon*, probably copied down in the second century A.D. This book purports to be Solomon's autobiographical memoir of the building of the Temple, which he accomplished with the slave labor of devils. With the help of a ring given him by the angel Raphael, Solomon bound the vampire devil Ornias and forced him to work on the Temple. From Ornias, Solomon learned the names of other devils and bound them as well. Among these were the

succubus Oneskelis; Asmodeus, who destroys marriages; Tephras, who destroys fields; Obizuth, who murders infants; and thirty-six spirits of the Zodiac, who cause various diseases. All these demons are inimical to humans. None will do good unless bound in slavery.

By the twelfth or thirteenth century, a list of fifty-one useful demons had crept into copies of the *Testament of Solomon*. These are demons who can be persuaded to bring material benefits to sorcerers.

The next great magic book, the *Key of Solomon*, appeared in the fourteenth century. It was concerned almost wholly with the practice of magic for personal gain. It contained no hierarchy of demons, but it did offer a system of magic based on the drawing of pentacles, five-pointed stars inscribed with charms. These were grouped according to astrological signs. The pentacles of Saturn, for instance, were useful for causing earthquakes, inciting demons to fall upon victims, and in general bringing about "ruin, destruction, and death."

The *Lemegeton*, or *Lesser Key of Solomon*, appeared not long after the *Key of Solomon*. It includes a complete hierarchy of seventy-two devils whom the sorcerer can evoke for his benefit.

Next came the *Constitution of Honorius*, first printed in 1629 and attributed to Pope Honorius III (1216–27). Its main contribution was to put a strongly Roman Catholic construction on magical evocation.

Manuscript copies—corrupt ones—of the *Constitution of Honorius* made their way into Germany well before 1629, and they were translated from French. Elements of the *Constitution* mingled with certain other available texts, and from these arose the strange mixture of practices that can properly be called Faustian magic.

We do not know how much Faustian magic the sixteenth-century wizard, Dr. Johann Faust, actually practiced. There are several copies extant of a book attributed to him, *Doctoris Iohannis Fausti magiae naturalis et innaturalis*, printed in Passau in 1505. The most significant of the magical practices advocated by these books is the use of a book of spirits, or *Liber Spirituum*.

The *Liber Spirituum* must be written on virgin paper. On the left-hand pages are pictures of demons; on the right-hand pages are oaths that the demons have taken to the sorcerer. Each oath is signed by the demon's mark. The book must be consecrated by a priest, who says three holy masses over it.

In Faustian magic, the sorcerer must go with his *Liber Spirituum* to a crossroads between midnight and one o'clock. There he draws a magic

circle, or rather three concentric magic circles. In the innermost, he writes texts from the Old and New Testaments; these can be any texts appropriate to the particular evocation. In the second, he writes the first chapter of St. John and the names of the seven archangels: Raphael, Michael, Uriel, Gabriel, Ithuriel, Zephon, Lucifer. In the outer circle, he writes the Schemhamphoras, the three great Hebrew names of God, each seventy-two-letters long. These names are taken from Genesis xiv, 19, 20, and 21. The three verses, each of seventy-two letters, are written one beneath the other, the first left to right, the second right to left, the third left to right.

Having drawn his magic circle, the sorcerer sprinkles it with holy water, lights and consecrates a fire, and steps into the circle. As he steps into the outer circle with his right foot, he says, "In the name of God the Father." As he steps into the middle circle with his left foot, he says, "In the name of God the Son."

Then he steps into the inner circle with both feet, saying, "In the name of God the Holy Ghost." He recites the first chapter of St. John and then lights five candles. He places four of them at the points of the compass and holds the fifth. He lights a censer of incense.

Then, facing east, he calls to the demons in a loud voice. He commands them to appear in the name of the ten Kabbalistic Sephirot: Keser, Chochma, Binah, Chesed, Gevurah, Tiferet, Nisah, Hod, Yesod, Malchut. He commands them in the name of the torments of hell. He calls them by Behemoth, Leviathan, the Furies, Cerberus, the infernal rivers of Styx, Acheron, Cocytus, and Phlegeton. Finally he calls them by the seventy-two names of Christ: the Schemhamphoras read, not as three horizontal lines, but as seventy-two vertical ones.

THE SEVENTY-TWO NAMES OF GOD, ACCORDING TO HONORIUS

Trinitas, Sother, Messias, Emmanuel, Sabahot, Adonay, Athanatos, Jesu, Pentagna, Agragon, Ischiros, Eleyson, Otheos, Tetragrammaton, Ely, Saday, Aquila, Magnus Homo, Visio, Flos, Origo, Salvator, Alpha and Omega, Primus, Novissimus, Principium et Finis, Primogenitus, Sapientia, Virtus, Paraclitus, Veritas, Via, Mediator, Medicus, Salus, Agnus, Ovis, Vitulus, Spes, Aries, Leo, Lux, Imago, Panis, Janua, Petra, Sponsa, Pastor, Propheta, Sacerdos, Sanctus, Immortalitas, Jesus, Christus, Pater, Filius Hominis, Sanctus, Pater Omnipotens, Deus, Agios, Resurrectio, Mischiros, Charitas, Aerternas, Creator, Redemptor, Unitas, Summum Bonum, Infinitas.

The demons appear, and the sorcerer forces them to sign his *Liber Spirituum*. Or, more probably, they force him to be their slave for eternity.

Enochian Magic. What we know of Enochian magic comes from a book called *A True and Faithful Relation of what Passed For many Years Between Doctor John Dee and Some Spirits*, edited by Meric Casaubon and published in 1659. The book is a memoir of the Welsh scholar, John Dee (1527–1608), concerning the experiments he conducted with the aid of the psychic Edward Kelley (c.1554–95).

Dee was a mathematician and astrologer at the court of Elizabeth I. Kelley was a psychic; he was also probably a sorcerer and necromancer. Dee learned that Kelley had a gift for contacting spirits by means of crystal-gazing, and from 1582 to 1587, he used Kelley in arduous attempts to learn the wisdom of the angels.

Kelley, for his part, was never sure he was communing with angels. He constantly tried to withdraw from the experiments, claiming that

> . . . our Teachers were deluders, and no good, or sufficient Teachers, who had not in two years space made us able to understand, or do somewhat; and that he could in two years have learned all the seven Liberal sciences, if he had first learned Logick, etc. wherefore he would have no more to do with them in any manner of way, . . . and said that . . . he took our Teachers to be deceivers, and wicked, and no good Creatures of God. . . .

However, Dee convinced Kelley to continue. Eventually, the spirits (chiefly a guide named Enoch) communicated, through Kelley, a spiritual language. This Enochian language had an alphabet of twenty-one letters. The spirits supplied nineteen invocations in this language, and they translated these for Dee. They also dictated magical diagrams, primarily squares, some of them containing as many as 2,401 letters, and instructions for their use.

Here is a sample of Enochian language, as given by Richard Deacon, a biographer of John Dee:

"Madariatza das perifa Lil cabisa micaolazoda saanire caosago of fifia balzodizodarasa iada. Nonuca gohulime: micama adoianu mada faods beliorebe, soba ooanoa cabisa luciftias yaripesol, das aberaasasa nonucafe jimicalazodoma larasada tofejilo marebe pereryo Idoigo od torezodulape."

In English, that means: "O you heavens which dwell in the first air, you are mighty in the parts of the earth, and execute the judgment of the highest. To you, it is said, Behold the face of your God, the beginning of comfort, whose eyes are the brightness of the heavens, which provided for you the government of the earth and her unspeakable variety."

Despite the wealth of knowledge it encompassed, Enochian magic fell into obscurity for many years. It was revived by the Order of the Golden Dawn (for more on this Order, and on John Dee and Edward Kelley, see chapter seven). Thus it exerted a powerful influence on twentieth-century magical practice. Indeed, Aleister Crowley claimed to be a reincarnation of Edward Kelley.

The Rose and Cross

Another major element of contemporary magical practice is Rosicrucianism, and this too was revived by the Golden Dawn.

The founder of Rosicrucianism, a German named Christian Rosencreutz (Rosycross), died in 1484 at the age of 102. Yet so secret was the order he founded that the public knew nothing of it until 1614. In that year, a German pamphlet named *The Reformation of the World* appeared. It was the translation of a satirical allegory by an Italian, Trajano Boccalini. Appended to the German translation was a brief manifesto, also in German, titled *Fama Fraternitatis, or a Discovery of the Fraternity of the Most Laudable Order of the Rosy Cross.*

The manifesto explained how Christian Rosencreutz had travelled to Arabia in search of knowledge. At Damcar, a group of wise men met him, "not as a stranger but as one whom they had long expected." Rosencreutz stayed at Damcar for three years, learning from these sages and translating into Latin a book of wisdom titled *M*. From Damcar, Rosencreutz went on to Fez. There he sought knowledge from "elementary inhabitants who revealed unto him many of their secrets."

Rosencreutz returned to Germany and established the Rosicrucian Brotherhood. At first there were only four members; later there were eight. They agreed to cure the sick without reward, to wear no special clothes, to meet every year in the House of the Sainted Spirit, and to keep the Fraternity secret for 100 years.

When Rosencreutz died in 1484, the Brothers buried him in secrecy. Thus the location of his tomb was lost. Some years later, however, when building work was being done in the Brotherhood's house, a workman discovered a large brass nail set in a wall. The Brothers pulled out the nail and exposed a hidden door inscribed with the words POST CXX ANNOS PATEBO—after 120 years I shall stand open.

The Brothers opened the door and revealed a seven-sided room. In the center stood a round altar covered with a brass plate. The Brothers lifted the plate, and there lay the body of Christian Rosencreutz, whole and uncorrupted, surrounded by his books of knowledge.

Abramelin Magic. *The Sacred Magic of Abramelin the Mage* is another puzzling text with no definite provenance. As far as we know, it began as an eighteenth-century French manuscript that was dated 1458 and that claimed to have been translated from Hebrew. MacGregor Mathers, the founder of the Order of the Golden Dawn, came across the text and translated it into English. Since then, it has had a strong influence on the practice of magic.

Abramelin sets forth a semi-Gnostic doctrine, that the world was created and is maintained by demons, who work under orders from angels. A magician, given the help of a guardian angel, can learn to control the demons. The adept depends heavily on word-magic in the process and especially on palindromic magic squares.

The following squares, given as samples, may be inscribed on parchment. They have various uses.

M	I	L	O	N	
I	R	A	G	O	Place this on top of your head.
L	A	M	A	L	The spirits will give you knowledge
O	G	A	R	I	of all things.
N	O	L	I	M	

R	O	L	O	R	
O	B	U	F	O	This will permit you to fly
L	U	A	U	L	through the air in the shape
O	F	U	B	O	of a crow.
R	O	L	O	R	

N	A	Q	I	D	
A	Q	O	R	I	This will win you the love
Q	O	R	O	Q	of a woman if she's presently
I	R	O	Q	A	in love with someone else.
D	I	Q	A	N	

S	A	T	O	R	
A	R	E	P	O	This very ancient square, which is almost
T	E	N	E	T	in Latin, will bring you material
O	P	E	R	A	possessions, drive away witches, and put out fires.
R	O	T	A	S	

On the subject of magical diagrams, we might also mention the Abracadabra triangle. This, the most famous word-spell of all, appears as far back as the works of Quintus Serenus Sammonicus, physician to the Emperor Severus early in the third century A.D.

The triangle should be written as follows:

A B R A C A D A B R A
A B R A C A D A B R
A B R A C A D A B
A B R A C A D A
A B R A C A D
A B R A C A
A B R A C
A B R A
A B R
A B
A

According to Sammonicus, you can write the triangle on a piece of paper and hang it around your neck for nine days in order to cure tertian fever (fever that recurs every third day). The fever will diminish, just as the word does. After nine days, you must throw the talisman backward over your shoulder into a stream. The charm can also cure asthma.

Eliphas Lévi commented that *abracadabra* is an eleven-letter word. Thus, it combines 1 (the divine number) with 10 (the number that represents the world).

Famous Magicians

Pythagoras of Samos (Sixth century B.C.). Much of what we know about numerical magic derives from Pythagoras (see chapter three). Some say Pythagoras received his knowledge in Babylon; according to Plutarch, Pythagoras was taught by Egyptian priests. Eliphas Lévi says Pythagoras learned Kabbalistic doctrines from Daniel and Ezekiel. Pythagoras taught the doctine of metempsychosis (the transmigration of souls), and he could remember his previous incarnations. These were: Aethalides, a son of Hermes; Euphorbus, son of Panthus, who died in the Trojan War; Hermotimus, a prophet from Clazomenae; and a poor fisherman. (For more about the life and work of Pythagoras, see chapter seven.)

Merlin (Fifth century A.D.) According to Geoffrey of Monmouth, Merlin built Stonehenge, transporting its stones magically from Ireland and erecting them on Salisbury plain. He was the subtle power behind King Arthur. At first he concealed Arthur's royal birth, placing the infant in a vassal family; then, when the time suited him, Merlin arranged for Arthur to be recognized and crowned. He predicted Arthur's death, but could not foresee his own fate—he was seduced by a sorceress and confined forever in a rock. Merlin is of central importance in occult theory; to judge by his present popularity, he's managed to escape his rock.

Theophrastus Paracelsus (1493–1541) Paracelsus was born in Einsiedeln, Switzerland. In 1526, he was appointed professor of medicine at the University of Basel. In that same year, he publicly burned the works of Galen and Avicenna. An alchemist as well as a physician, he outraged his colleagues by claiming that health arises from living in harmony with one's own nature and with the etheric influences that come to us from the stars. He also upset his fellow doctors by writing in German instead of Latin and by insisting on the practice of empirical medicine. He was one of the first doctors to treat syphilis with preparations of mercury. He died in poverty.

Gilles de Rais (1404–1440). Although he was a gallant Marshal of Brittany who fought with Joan of Arc against the British, Gilles is better known as Bluebeard. He inherited a great fortune and squandered it, whereupon he turned to sorcery in an attempt to get gold from Satan. His chief accomplice was an Italian priest named François Prelati. In 1440 Gilles was summoned to appear before the bishop of Nantes to be tried for sorcery. He confessed (probably under torture) that he had slaughtered dozens of infants as sacrifices for his black masses. He was condemned to death and buried alive.

Henry Cornelius Agrippa von Nettesheim (1486–1535). A Neo-Platonist and Kabbalist, Agrippa taught and lectured throughout Europe—at Cologne (where he was born), Turin, Pavia, Metz, and Geneva. He attended the courts of the Emperor Maximilien, François I, Henry VIII, and Margaret of Austria. He was imprisoned for ı Brussels for failure to pay his debts. Agrippa's *Three Books of Occult* *ıy* (1529) teach that magic is the highest of the sciences, since it encompasses ,, mathematics, and theology. Agrippa also taught methods of sympathetic magic—frogs' eyes to help cure a man's blindness, mules' urine to make women sterile. Later in life he renounced magic and declared that all the occult sciences were frauds. Pursued as a sorcerer, he was tortured and died in poverty.

Johann Faust (ca. 1480–ca. 1540). Faust was probably born in Swabia and was described by a contemporary as "a most filthy beast, the midden of numberless devils." He was as notorious for his homosexuality as he was for his reputed pact with Mephistopheles. When he died, there was "a great noise and shaking of the house that night. . . . In the morning he was found dead, with his necke rung behind him; the Divell whom he served having carried his soule into hell." Although he sold his soul for material gain, he seems to have died in poverty.

John Dee (1527–1608). Early in his career, when he was a fellow of Trinity College, Cambridge, Dee constructed a mechanical flying scarab for a stage production of Aristophanes's *Peace*. This invention alone was enough to give him a reputation as a wizard. He was court mathematician to Queen Elizabeth I, tutor to the Earl of Leicester, and cast horoscopes for Queen Mary of England and King Philip of Spain. His library was destroyed by a mob in 1583. He died in poverty. (See chapter seven for more information.)

The Apprenticeship

It should be clear by now that an aspiring magician cannot rely very heavily on books. As you have seen, magic books always appeared in print years after they were written. By that time, the texts had become corrupted, secrets had been suppressed, and whole new doctrines had been grafted onto the older teachings.

But this is no cause for despair. The practice of magic is a highly individual matter. A true adept devises his or her own methods of evocation. Magic is an inner discipline, and the mistakes you find in books are errors in external matters. The inner meaning cannot vary. In other words, the exact wording of an invocation makes little difference. What matters is the magician's state of mind, the psychic force invested in the invocation.

The same applies to the student's initiation into magic. Before one can practice magic, one must attain a high level of development on the mental, psychic, and physical planes. But the way in which one attains that level has to be left to the individual to a great extent.

We can offer suggestions. The following is a ten-stage program of initiation based on the contemporary German magician Franz Bardon's *Initiation into Hermetics*. As you will see, it allows a lot of flexibility for individual temperaments. You should expand on the program according to what suits you. In its intentions and goals, however, such a program should be followed assiduously by anyone who wants to practice magic.

The program is difficult but rewarding. It will teach you nothing less than the way to fully develop your psychic abilities. But you must be ready to spend a long time on the program—not months, but years.

Before you begin, prepare to *give up the idea that you own your thoughts*. Most people believe their thoughts are part of their minds, just as their hands are part of their bodies. This is not true. Your thoughts live freely in your mind, just as wild animals roam through a forest. Unsophisticated people dread this idea and resist it. However, it must be grasped if you are to understand and master the process of magical evocation.

The spirits you will evoke inhabit your mind just as independently as your thoughts. They live in your mind because it is part of the Universal Mind. Therefore, if you evoke a spirit associated with the sphere of Venus it will not arrive from outer space. The sphere of Venus exists in the Universal Mind, not on the material plane. If at first you don't understand this, think some more about the Hermetic doctrine of correspondence, as it was explained above.

The spirits do appear and work on the material plane, of course. They originate in the mind but they are quite real. The point is, you must look within yourself for the spirits. Look outward and you merely delude yourself.

Once you understand this idea fully, you can begin the ten stages of the initiation. They will prepare you mentally, psychically, and physically for the practice of magic.

Stage One. Mental: Now that you understand that your thoughts are like living beings, you must become more aware of them. You can do this through meditation. Any of the methods explained in chapter three will do. You might consider basic yoga as well. Learn to concentrate on a single thought for short periods (ten minutes or so). Exclude all other thoughts during that period. Focus sharply on the one thought and force it to hold still for you. Also, learn to empty your mind entirely for brief periods.

Psychic: To be a magician, you must understand your own character thoroughly. Therefore, analyze your good and bad qualities as completely as possible. It helps to keep diaries for this—one for the good, one for the bad.

Then, categorize these qualities according to the four basic elements. For example, jealousy and hatred pertain to the principle of fire; frivolity and gossip pertain to air; laziness and shyness pertain to water; melancholy and dullness pertain to earth. Of the good qualities, enthusiasm and courage pertain to fire; joy and kindness to air; modesty and compassion to water; endurance and responsibility to earth.

Physical: You should already be following a program of diet, exercise, and hygiene. In addition, learn to concentrate on proper breathing. Imagine that the air you breathe is suffused with desirable qualities, such as health, peace, and energy. Concentrate on absorbing these qualities with each breath. You should make a similar effort of concentration when you eat.

Stage Two. Mental: Choose any common object from your home and study it. Concentrate in turn on its sight, sound, smell, taste, and feel. Then, for short periods, close your eyes and imagine those aspects of the object as vividly as possible. Do this as well for animals and people.

Psychic: Using the diaries from stage one, find which elemental qualities predominate in you. Then begin to bring all four qualities into balance.

To eliminate bad qualities, use autosuggestion. When you meditate, or just before you go to sleep, imagine each deficiency as already having been corrected. For example, tell yourself, "I don't smoke," instead of "I shouldn't smoke." In this way, you not only correct bad qualities but learn to work on the psychic level.

Physical: Concentrate on breathing not only through the lungs but through the pores of your skin. Practice physical control by sitting or standing absolutely still for brief periods. Learn which positions are most helpful for your meditation, and learn to stay in those positions indefinitely.

Stage Three. Mental: Concentrate on two or three sensory aspects of an object simultaneously. For example, imagine both the sight and sound of a clock. Then, think of a place you have visited. See the place as clearly as possible. Then hear it, then feel it. Your imagination must be as vivid and detailed as possible. Also, try to imagine animals and people. Then try places and people you have never seen before.

Psychic: Concentrate on inhaling, and becoming one with, each of the four elements. This can be done through active use of the imagination. You can imagine the fire principle, feel its heat, see its color, and draw it into you with every breath. Be sure to practice with each of the elements. After absorbing an element in this fashion, be careful to let it pass outside of you again.

Physical: You have learned to breathe fully through your lungs and through the skin's pores. Now learn to breathe through various parts of the body individually.

Just as you are learning to breathe in the elements on the psychic level, learn to breathe in the air's vital force. Learn to retain vital force and expel it at will.

Stage Four. Mental: Concentrate on an object. Then transfer your consciousness into that object. Do not get discouraged if you fail at first; this is an extension of exercises you have already done. Practice as well with animals and people. Train yourself actively to take their points of view.

Psychic: Learn to draw individual elements into individual parts of the body. Make sure to practice with all four elements and all parts of the body.

Physical: Determine symbolic meanings for parts of your body. The symbolism must be personal and secret. For instance, you might make your thumb an energy locus for water; your forefinger, for fire; middle finger, ether; ring finger, earth; little finger, air. You must then learn to concentrate fire's energy by a ritual gesture of the forefinger. Again, you must determine the ritual by yourself. The important thing is to begin to use your body for ceremonial purposes.

Stage Five. Mental: Take an object, and concentrate on being in its very center. (It's useful to use symmetrical objects at first.) Then learn to concentrate wholly on your own etheric center, which is located at your solar plexus.

Psychic: Learn to project elements outward. Begin by concentrating an element at your center. Then imagine the element emanating from you in the shape of a ball. Practice until you can make the emanation vivid and detailed. Try other shapes as well. Then, try to form an emanation directly from the universe, without first concentrating an element in your body.

Physical: You must now learn to differentiate between your physical and etheric bodies.

Concentrate on raising one finger, not with muscle power, but with will power. When you succeed, learn to raise your hand, then your whole arm.

Next, lay one hand on a table and imagine your etheric hand projecting from it. Concentrate on the etheric hand. It's your real hand. The physical hand is a dream hand. Let your physical hand drop into your lap while your etheric hand stays in place on the table.

Once this exercise has been mastered, it should be easy for you to practice automatic writing. You must simply let a spirit guide your etheric hand, which in turn guides your physical hand.

Stage Six. Mental: Learn the elemental functions of your mind. These are:

will—fire
intellect—air
feeling—water
consciousness—earth

Also learn to be fully conscious of your activities, such as walking. For short periods, concentrate on the way your mind moves both your astral and material bodies when you walk. Next, concentrate on seeing with the mind through the physical and astral eyes. Do the same for the other senses.

Psychic: You have gained a balanced mastery of the four elements. Now concentrate on absorbing and focusing ether. Since the elements all come from ether, you thus learn to control all of them simultaneously and in balance on the astral and physical planes. Devise rituals of your own for the control of each element.

Physical: You should now be able to project elementals to work for you. Elementals are creatures without independent wills. They are composed of one element only and work on the mental plane. They usually serve to influence other people.

Project an element. Give it a shape, then a name, then project on it the image of the job you want done. Most important, set a time limit to the elemental's life, and dissolve it when that time is up.

Beware of larvae, which, unlike elementals, are mental beings that grow out of the magician's unconscious desires and fears. They acquire lives of their own and sap the magician's energy.

Stage Seven. Mental: Going on from stage six, learn which elements predominate in your mind. Then bring those elements, and their corresponding faculties, into balance.

Psychic: Going on from stage six, use your mastery of the elements to begin to develop clairvoyance. To develop your astral eyes, concentrate light (from the element of fire) in your eyes. (Some magicians develop only one astral eye, prefering to leave the other untouched.) A similar exercise helps you develop clairaudience.

Physical: You have created elementals. Now learn to create elementaries. These are creatures of two or more elements that can work on the material and astral levels. In fact, you can create them with entire astral and mental bodies. Just be sure to give them a shape and composition appropriate to the job you want done. Follow the same precautions as in creating elementals, and be sure to confine the elementaries when they are not working. You can form them freely in air (as you did with elementals), or project them onto an appropriate object, such as a wax doll.

Be very careful with all manufactured beings. Alexandra David Neel, a scientist and the author of *Magic and Mystery in Tibet*, once created a double of herself (a *tulpa*) in the form of a Tibetan monk. It took her five months of solitary labor to do the job. Then, to her dismay, the *tulpa* started to get out of her control. It followed her around when she didn't want it and looked very sly. She decided to get rid of it, a job that took her some three months to finish. The moral is, once you make something like that, you must know what to do with it.

Stage Eight. Mental: In this stage, you will learn to separate your mind from your body.

As a first exercise, look at your face in a mirror and project your mind into the reflection (as you did in stage four). Do this until you can look at your physical face from the viewpoint of your reflected face.

Then, assume your position for meditation. Concentrate on the action of your mind through your body, as in stage six. Your mind is seeing through your eyes; your mind is hearing through your ears. Your eyes and ears are empty shells for your mind. Lift your mind away from them.

At first, practice for brief periods only.

Psychic: You must now learn to control two specific qualities of the elements: the positive (or electric) force inherent in fire, and the negative (or magnetic) force inherent in water. Draw electric and magnetic force into your body from the universe, and extend these forces from your body. It helps to know that the head and chest are the body's locus of electricity; the stomach and legs are the locus of magnetism.

Next, learn to concentrate both forces simultaneously. Charge the upper body with electricity, the lower body with magnetism. Focus and extend the forces through your hands. If you are right-handed, extend electricity through your right hand, magnetism through your left.

These are the two forces that energize the universe. A little practice with them should prove to you that you can do what nonadepts would call the miraculous.

Physical: By this stage, the magician should need no more physical training. You can begin to prepare the ceremonial objects described in the next section.

Stage Nine. Mental: The magician is ready to project his mind far away from his physical body. Therefore, for his protection, he must rid himself of any remaining elemental imbalances caused by incorrect methods of training. These are imbalances in the elements of:

1. Fire, caused by clairvoyant experiements that involve staring at objects (e.g., crystal gazing)
2. Air, caused by experiments with vapors and gases
3. Water, caused by experiments with drugs
4. Earth, caused by practices involving physical distortion.

Psychic: At this point you can dissociate your astral body as well as your mind from the physical body.

Separate your mind from both bodies, as you learned to do in stage eight. Then let your mind observe both bodies. By an act of will, it must now draw the astral body out of the physical body. *Concentrate on breathing in the astral body*. That will help you center your mind there. At the same time as you breathe in the astral body, the physical body will stop breathing. It will go into a kind of coma.

As soon as you stop breathing in your astral body, you will feel your physical body pulling at it. The physical body will seem to suck the astral body away from your mind; the physical body will start to breathe again.

Practice carefully and for short periods at first.

Stage Ten. Mental: You are ready to begin exploring the spheres of your mind, the spheres that correspond to the fourteen levels of the Ptolemaic astronomical system. Through such exploration, you can learn about the spirits you will evoke in your ceremonies.

Psychic: If you have truly mastered the four elements, the two forces of electricity and magnetism, and ether, if you have strengthened your astral body till it can be free of the physical body, you have completed your initiation. You have realized your full potential as a human. Now you know that you are not merely a small model, a correspondence, of the universe. You are an image of the Deity itself.

Calling The Spirits

You can evoke and control spirits because you are an image of the Deity.

You have thoroughly mastered the four elements in yourself. Your body thus becomes a living image of the Tetragrammaton, the four-lettered name of God: YUD HE VAUV HE.

You are therefore a complete being. The spirits you evoke, on the other hand, are incomplete beings. Each is ruled by one of the elements. For that reason you have mastery over them.

Ritual Tools. For ceremonial evocation of spirits, you will need certain ritual tools. These are:

The Wand. The wand is a symbol of the magician's will. Through it, he or she exerts influence on the spheres. Most magicians have several wands, each suited to a different sphere. The wand can be made of wood or a variety of metals. Some wooden wands are fitted with metal rings corresponding to the spheres.

Saturn-----------------Lead
Jupiter-----------------Tin
Mars-------------------Iron
Sun--------------------Gold
Venus -----------------Copper
Mercury---------------Brass
Moon------------------Silver

The sword or dagger. All beneficent spirits will respond to the wand. Negative spirits, though, need to be reminded more graphically of the magician's power. For this, the magician uses a sword or dagger, symbolic of the sword with which the archangel Michael drove Lucifer from heaven. Some magicians use a trident instead.

The crown. As a symbol of the dignity of the intellect, the magician wears a crown. An embroidered cap or headband will serve the same purpose. The cap, crown, or headband must be made of the finest materials available. It should be inscribed or embroided with a symbol of the unity of the macrocosm and microcosm. The magician must choose and design this symbol by himself.

The Robe. The robe must be made of silk. It buttons from the neck to the toes; the sleeves must extend to the wrists. The robe may be made of one of three colors: violet (the color of ether), white (for evocation of positive spirits), or black (for evocation of negative spirits). Some magicians have a different robe for each astral sphere. The colors for these are:

Saturn-----------------dark violet
Jupiter-----------------blue
Mars-------------------purple
Sun--------------------yellow or gold
Venus -----------------green
Mercury---------------opal
Moon------------------silver

The belt. The belt must be of the same color and material as the robe. It should be embroidered with a symbol of the balance of the four elements.

To be effective, all of the above must be properly consecrated. The magician must regularly infuse his or her power imaginatively into the wand and sword, thus charging them with the will. The garments must be sanctified with a personal oath. All of these tools must be made of new materials, never before used for any common purpose. When not in ritual use, the tools must be put away carefully in a special repository. No one other than the magician may see or touch them.

The magician should also keep a book of spells. This cannot be merely a corrupt old grimoire. It must be a book written by the magician. It is a record of the magician's studies and experiences. Like all other ritual objects, it must be kept safely hidden and see no mundane use.

The Ceremony. When you are ready to perform the ceremony, prepare yourself by bathing. The water will purify you, taking away not only dirt, but all imperfections of mind and psyche.

Go to whatever room you have consecrated as your temple, and lay out your ritual tools on a fresh cloth. Then put on the ritual clothes. As you put on the robe, concentrate on the way it will insulate you from all mental and psychic influences, both good and evil. As you put on the belt, concentrate on your inner balance of the elements. As you put on the crown, concentrate on the unity of your mind with the Universal Mind. Let no mundane thoughts intrude.

Now light the magic lamp. This should be an oil-burning lamp hung in the middle of the temple. Its fuel is made of two parts methyl alcohol to one part camomile blossoms; the mixture is left to steep for nine days, then filtered. The lamp must be covered with glass or cellophane of a color appropriate to the spirit to be evoked.

The lamp's light creates an atmosphere favorable for the spirit's manifestation. But the lamp is not enough. You must intensify the atmosphere by projecting the element and color appropriate to the spirit. Concentrate until you have changed the temple's atmosphere into the atmosphere of the spirit's astral level.

Now draw the spirit's symbol. Again, this must be done with paper and ink of an appropriate color. The paper, ink, and pen must have been specially consecrated for the ritual.

It is now time to draw the magic circle. Most unsophisticated sources claim that the circle is drawn to protect the magician. Actually, the circle is drawn as a symbol of the universe. The circle becomes a microcosm, and the magician, standing in its middle, takes the place of the Deity.

Therefore, the magician must be at the highest level of consciousness when he or she draws the circle. The Deity itself must guide the magician's hand in the drawing. Otherwise, the construction will be an empty gesture.

If the ritual is being conducted outdoors, the magician draws the circle in the earth with the magic sword. If the ritual is inside, the magician may use chalk on the floor. Previously prepared circles can be used as well. These can be simple pencil drawings on paper, or elaborate embroideries on silk. One can even use a chain of magnetized iron. The magician is free to embellish the circle with symbols of his or her own choice. However, they must be symbols the meaning of which the magician fully understands.

If you are using a previously prepared circle, you must run either your wand or your right hand over its outline to ready it for the ceremony. Lay out the magic triangle in the same fashion, either drawing it fresh or running over the outline of a previously drawn triangle.

The triangle is the symbol of manifestation. It is here that the spirit will appear. A magician will do well to study the symbolism of the triangle and of the number three. Among other things, the triangle represents the Trinity, the triple nature of our world (mental, psychic, and physical), and the electromagnetic dynamism of the universe (the positive and negative principles united by neutrality).

Put the paper with the spirit's seal in the center of the triangle. If you like, light three small oil lamps, one for each corner of the triangle.

Light a censer and place it either in the middle of the triangle or between the triangle and the circle. The incense that you burn in the censer is an additional aid in creating the proper atmosphere for the spirit. The following incenses are recommended:

Sublunar spheres	sage powder and elder pith
Moon	aloe powder
Mercury	mastic
Venus	pulverized cinnamon
Sun	sandalwood powder
Mars	pulverized onion seed
Jupiter	pulverized saffron
Saturn	powdered black poppy seed

As an all-purpose incense, you can use church incense, myrrh, storax, benzoin, and aloe. Use small quantities of whatever incense you choose.

If you wish to summon a beneficent spirit, slip your sword through your belt on the left side, and take your wand in your hand. If you are summoning a negative spirit, hold the wand in your left hand and keep the sword in your right. Now step into the magic circle.

You must be prepared to act and feel like the God of the microcosm you've created. Your concentration on the ritual must be absolute. With your full power, project yourself to the sphere of whatever spirit you're summoning. Mentally call the name of the spirit; project the name through the entire sphere. At the same time you are calling the spirit, you are showing yourself to the spirit, manifesting your strength and your will.

As soon as you hear the spirit answering you, as soon as you see the spirit in your mind, return to your physical body. Now you must call the spirit aloud. Begin quietly, in a whisper, and let your voice gain strength. Call the spirit with whatever invocations you've found to be most powerful.

As the spirit begins to appear, you must concentrate to make sure it appears on all three planes: mental, psychic, and physical. To do this, you must fully retain consciousness of your own existence on those three levels.

It is impossible to describe communication with spirits. You should know, however, that spirits do not use spoken language. They communicate telepathically by images, and this is the method of expression you must use with them.

When you've finished communicating with the spirit, you must help it return to its sphere. Do so by projecting yourself to that sphere once more and concentrating on the spirit's return.

Once again, I recommend caution above all else. The aspiring magician will do well to remember the experience of Eliphas Lévi (ca. 1810–1875), who (to our knowledge) attempted only one evocation during his lifetime.

Lévi—the most famous magician of his period—barely survived.

Lévi, it seems, wanted to raise the spirit of the pagan philosopher Apollonius of Tyana. He prepared very carefully. He fasted for twenty-one days, used a highly elaborate altar and incantations, and was of course accustomed to thinking in the proper way about the evocation. At last, a ghostly figure appeared in the altar's smoke—and Lévi became frightened. He pointed at the spirit with his ritual sword and commanded it to obey him; but his arm became numb to the elbow, a wave of fatigue went through him and he fainted. It took him several days to recover.

Summoning Demons

No doubt there will be a few people who will be dissatisfied with the ceremony given above. For them, here is a method for invoking evil spirits taken from the *Lemegeton*, as edited by Arthur Waite in his *Book of Ceremonial Magic*.

When you step into the magic circle, say:

> I invoke and conjure thee, O Spirit ——, and, fortified with the power of the Supreme Majesty, I strongly command thee by Baralamensis, Baldachiensis, Paumachie, Apoloresedes and the most potent princes Genio, Liachide, Ministers of the Tartarean Seat, chief princes of the seat of Apologia in the ninth region; I exorcise and command thee, O Spirit ——, by Him Who spake and it was done, by the Most Holy and glorious Names Adonai, El, Elohim, Elohe, Zebaoth, Elion, Escherce, Jah, Tetragrammaton, Sadai: do thou forthwith appear and shew thyself without any deformity or horror; do thou come forthwith, from whatever part of the world, and make rational answers to my questions; come presently, come visibly, come affably, manifest that which I desire, being conjured by the Name of the Eternal, Living and True God, Heliorem; I conjure thee also by the particular and true Name of thy God to whom thou owest thine obedience; by the name of the King who rules over thee, do thou come without tarrying; come, fulfil my desires; persist unto the end, according to mine intentions. I conjure thee by Him to Whom all creatures are obedient, by this ineffable Name, Tetragrammaton Jehovah, by which the elements are overthrown, the air is shaken, the sea turns back, the fire is generated, the earth moves and all the hosts of things celestial, of things terrestrial, of things infernal, do tremble and are confounded together; speak unto me visibly and affably in a clear, intelligible voice, free from ambiguity. Come therefore in the name Adonai Zebaoth; come, why dost thou tarry? Adonai Saday, King of kings, commands thee.

Say this a few times. If it does not work, go on to the invocation below:

> I invoke, conjure and command thee, O Spirit ——, to appear and shew thyself visibly before this circle, in fair and comely shape, without deformity or guile, by the Name of On; by the Name Y and V, which Adam heard and spake; by the Name of Joth, which Jacob learned from the Angel on the night of his wrestling and was delivered from the hands of his brother Esau; by the Name of God Agla, which Lot heard and was saved with his family; by the Name Anehexeton, which Aaron spake and was made wise; by the Name Schemes Amathia, which Joshua invoked and the Sun stayed upon his course; by the Name Emmanuel, which the

three children, Shadrach, Meshach and Abednego, chanted in the midst of the fiery furnace, and they were delivered; by the Name Alpha and Omega, which Daniel uttered, and destroyed Bel and the Dragon; by the Name Zebaoth, which Moses named, and all the rivers and waters in the land of Egypt brought forth frogs, which ascended into the houses of the Egyptians, destroying all things; by the Name Escerchie Ariston, which also Moses named, and the rivers and waters in the land of Egypt were turned into blood; by the Name Elion, on which Moses called, and there fell a great hail, such as never was seen since the creation of the world; by the Name Adonai, which Moses named, and there came up locusts over all the land of Egypt and devoured what the hail had left; by the Name Hagios, by the Seal of Adonai, by those others, which are Jetros, Athenoros, Paracletus; by the three Holy and Secret Names, Agla, On, Tetragrammaton; by the dreadful Day of Judgment; by the changing Sea of Glass which is before the face of the Divine Majesty, mighty and powerful; by the four beasts before the Throne, having eyes before and behind; by the fire which is about the Throne, by the Holy Angels of Heaven, by the Mighty Wisdom of God; by the Seal of Basdathea, by this Name Primematum, which Moses named, and the earth opened and swallowed Corah, Dathan and Abiram; do thou make faithful answers unto all my demands, and perform all my desires, so far as thine office shall permit. Come therefore peaceably and affably; come visibly and without delay; manifest that which I desire; speak with a clear and intelligible voice, that I may understand thee.

If that does not work either, say:

> I conjure thee, O Spirit ____, by all the most glorious and efficacious Names of the Great and Incomparable Lord the God of Hosts, come quickly and without delay, from whatsoever part of the world thou art in; make rational answers to my demands; come visibly, speak affably, speak intelligibly to my understanding. I conjure and constrain thee, O Spirit ________, by all the aforesaid Names, as also by those seven other Names wherewith Solomon bound thee and thy fellows in the brazen vessel, to wit, Adonai, Prerai, Tetragrammaton, Anehexeton, Inessensatoal, Pathumaton and Itemon; do thou manifest before this circle, fulfill my will in all things that may seem good to me. Be disobedient, refuse to come, and by the power of the Supreme Being, the everlasting Lord, that God Who created thee and me, the whole world, with all contained therein, in the space of six days; by Eye, by Saray, by the virtue of the Name Primematum, which commands the whole host of Heaven; be disobedient, and behold I will curse and deprive thee of thine office, thy joy and thy place; I will bind thee in the depths of the bottomless pit, there to remain until the Day of the Last Judgment. I will chain thee in the Lake of Eternal Fire, in the Lake of Fire and Brimstone, unless thou come quickly, appearing before this circle, to do my will. Come, therefore, in the Holy Names Adonai, Zebaoth, Amioram; come, Adonai commands thee.

If you still have no results, invoke the aid of the King of the Demons.

O thou great and powerful King Amaymon, who rulest by the power of the Supreme God, El, over all Spirits, superior and inferior, but especially over the Infernal Order in the Dominion of the East, I invoke and command thee by the particular and true Name of God, by the God Whom thou dost worship, by the Seal of thy creation, by the most mighty and powerful Name of God, Jehovah, Tetragrammaton, Who cast thee out of Heaven with the rest of the Infernal

Spirits; by all the other potent and great Names of God, Creator of Heaven, Earth and Hell, of all contained therein; by their powers and virtues; by the Name Primematum, which commands the whole host of Heaven. Do thou force and compel the Spirit ______ here before this circle, in a fair and comely shape, without injury to myself or to any creature, that he may give me true and faithful answer, so that I may accomplish my desired end, whatsoever it be, provided that it is proper to his office, by the power of God, El, Who hath created and doth dispose of all things, celestial, aerial, terrestrial and infernal.

As a last resort, you can say:

O thou wicked and disobedient ______, because thou hast not obeyed or regarded the words which I have rehearsed, the glorious and incomprehensible Names of the true God, Maker of all things in the world, now I, by the power of these Names, which no creature can resist, do curse thee into the depths of the Bottomless Pit, to remain until the Day of Doom, in the Hell of unquenchable fire and brimstone, unless thou shalt forthwith appear in this triangle, before this circle, to do my will. Come, therefore, quickly and peaceably, by the Names Adonai, Zebaoth, Adonai, Amioram. Come, come, Adonai, King of Kings, commands thee.

That should do the trick. When you're finished with the demon, say:

O Spirit ______, because thou has diligently answered my demands, I do hereby license thee to depart, without injury to man or beast. Depart, I say, and be thou willing and ready to come, whensoever duly exorcised and conjured by the Sacred Rites of Magic. I conjure thee to withdraw peaceably and quietly, and may the peace of God continue for ever between me and thee. Amen.

For Further Reading.

The aspiring magician cannot find any better guides than two books by Franz Bardon: *Initiation Into Hermetics* and *The Practice of Magical Evocation* (Wuppertal: Dieter Ruggeberg, 1970 and 1971). The only problem with these two books is that they are available only in a grotesquely bad translation. Two books by Eliphas Lévi will give the student that adept's fascinating and individualistic viewpoint: *Transcendental Magic* and *The History of Magic* (New York: Samuel Weiser, 1973 and 1974). For the texts of the grimoires, go to Arthur Edward Waites's *The Book of Black Magic and of Pacts*, which has been reissued under the title *The Book of Ceremonial Magic: A Complete Grimoire* (Secaucus: Citadel, 1973). Kurt Seligmann gives a good general history of the subject in *Magic, Supernaturalism and Religion* (New York: Pantheon, 1948). For a more specialized history, see *Ritual Magic*, by E.M. Butler (Hollywood: Newcastle, 1971). It analyzes magical texts from the viewpoint of literary history.

Know Your Enemy: A Dossier on Demons

The following are the names of some of the demons known to be operating on Earth. Where possible, additional information is given. The reader should be warned that demons change their identities rather frequently. All of the following are to be considered armed and dangerous.

Abigor. A Grand Duke of Hell. Commands sixty legions of devils. Tall, handsome, swaggering. Customarily dresses in armor. Carries a lance or scepter. Can foretell the future and answer questions about war.

Abraxas. First appeared in early Egypt. Has the head of a king and two tails or serpents instead of feet. Sometimes carries a whip. According to some, has also appeared on earth impersonating Jesus Christ. He is the chief god of many Gnostic sects.

Acaos. One of the demons with which Urbain Grandier enslaved the nuns of the convent of Loudun in the 1630s.

Adramalech. A demon with many titles, including Keeper of the Wardrobe of the Demon King and President of the High Council of Devils. A dry old man who appears as a mule or as a peacock. Enjoys the sacrifices of children.

Agares. Another Grand Duke of Hell. Appears mounted on a crocodile, carrying a hawk on his wrist. Is in charge of titles and offices. Can teach any language. Gives courage to cowards and victory to weak generals. Commands thirty-one legions of Hell.

Agathodemon. One of the few demons who seem well-disposed toward the human race. Appeared in ancient Egypt as a serpent with a human head. Also has appeared as a dragon or flying serpent. Ancient peoples often worshipped him.

Ahazu-Demon, alias "The Seizer." Has appeared only in Semitic nations, where he causes a foul disease.

Ahrimanes. The leader of a group of rebel angels who were expelled from heaven for their sins and who came to earth among the ancient Persians. Ahrimanes and his followers now live in the space between the Earth and the fixed stars. Ahrimanes has a twin brother, Ormuzd, who is on the side of the Good.

Alastor. Cruelest of all the demons, called "The Executioner" by Zoroaster. He fulfills this post in the kingdom of Hell. He was known to the Greeks as Nemesis and to the early Christians as Appolyon, the Destroying Angel. He is mentioned in the Book of the Apocalypse.

Aldinach. A demon who first appeared in Egypt. Takes pleasure in sinking ships. Can command waves and wind. Takes the shape of a woman.

Alexh. One of the demons with which Urbain Grandier bewitched the nuns of Loudun.

Allat. Powerful female ruler over the Chaldean hell. She judges souls.

Alocer. Resembles the Cowardly Lion. Has ruddy complexion, burning eyes, and sorrowful expression. Often appears mounted on a huge horse. Knows astronomy and the liberal arts. Can grant family happiness. Commands thirty-six legions of Hell.

Alpiel. A Jewish demon who strikes at fruit trees.

Alu-Demon. One of the first bogey-men to haunt the Semitic peoples. He enjoys jumping out from dark corners to scare people, or pouncing suddenly into their beds. Stalks dark alleys at night. During the day, hides in caves or dark corners.

Amduscias. A Grand Duke of Hell who can command invisible orchestras upon request (a sound technician). Appears in human form, also in that of a unicorn. The trees can hear his music all the time; people hear it only rarely. One of the demons enslaved by Solomon, he helped in the building of Solomon's Temple.

Amon. A really dangerous enemy. Looks like a human but with an owl's eyes and sharp fangs. He knows both the past and the future. Forty legions are under his command. Sometimes appears as a wolf with a serpent's tail, breathing fire.

Amoymon. A proper, bureaucratic demon. Can only be reached from 9 to 12 A.M. and from 3 to 6 P.M. One of the Kings of Hell.

Amy. A slithery, disreputable character, known to be a double agent. Has told humans the whereabouts of demonic treasures. Known to be actively lobbying to be allowed to return to his place in heaven, where he once occupied the seventh throne. Sometimes appears in a flame.

Anarazel. Guard of the underground treasures of the demons. This is a lowly job that requires much physical labor. The treasure must be moved constantly to escape humans who seek it. The movement of the treasure causes earthquakes, rings mysterious bells, and tempts ghosts to rise out of their graves.

Andrealphus. One of the demons enslaved by Solomon to help in the building of the Temple.

Antichrist. The Big One. The universal enemy of mankind, he has appeared under various guises. Will appear for the last time at the end of the world. He is difficult to recognize. In a recent visit he appeared as a small man with a neat black moustache and a stiff arm. In an earlier life he appeared as the magician Aleister Crowley. In the Middle Ages and the Renaissance, he appeared as several different popes, and in modern times he has appeared as Charles Manson. He often visits lunatic asylums and takes over the bodies of the inhabitants.

Appolyon, alias "The Destroyer." See Alastor.

Ardat-Lile. Female demon who has appeared to the Semitic peoples. Enjoys marrying good human men and then making their lives miserable.

Arioch. No known description. Specializes in vengeance.

Ashtoreth. Appeared to the Benedictine monk Don Calmet. Also, through the agency of Grandier, to the nuns at Loudun. Was worshipped in ancient times in female form under the names Astarte, Astrith, and Aphrodite. In male form, looks like a bandit chief. Once very powerful on earth as the Great Mother Goddess.

Asmodeus. Demon of anger and lust. Has many heads, including one of a cow and one of a goat. Through Urbain Grandier, appeared to the nuns of Loudun. Provokes people to the deadly sin of lechery.

Axaphat. One of the demons used by Urbain Grandier to bewitch the nuns of Loudun.

Azaradel. A fallen angel mentioned in the Book of Enoch. He taught the secrets of the moon to selected humans.

Azazel. First appeared to the Jews during their wanderings in the wilderness. Was in charge of the scapegoat onto which the sins of the people were transferred. Often appears in goat form. Mark the Heretic used Azazel on several occasions. Seen by John Milton, who described him as the standard bearer for the infernal armies.

Baal. First King of Hell. Lives in the eastern section of Hell, commands sixty-six legions. One of the most powerful demons in human history. Was worshipped as the principal god on earth for thousands of years. Commonly appears in the form of a bull. In this form he successfully tempted the Children of Israel in the Wilderness. He suffered defeat at the hands of the Hebrew prophet Elijah and even more severe defeat at the hands of the Christians. Continues to have a strong human following. He is sometimes pictured as having three heads, one of a crab, one of a cat, and one of a man.

Baalberith. A secretary of Hell.

Babau. Ogre that scares naughty children. Eats them in salads.

Bad. Commands winds and tempests; appears in Persia.

Balan. Another King of Hell. Rides on a huge bear. His eyes burn like fire, and he has a serpent's tail. He has three heads, one of a bull, one of a man, and one of a ram. It is thought that Balan may simply be a powerful emanation from Baal, representing his fierce aspects. Appeared in the Old Testament.

Balberith. Entered the body of Sister Madeleine at Aix-en-Provence. At that time gave authorities list of other demons operating in the same body.

Baphomet. For centuries has had a curious and highly secret following among humans. Appears to humans as a goat-god. In this form has been worshipped by inner circles of several occult brotherhoods. Appeals to sadomasochistic tendencies of his followers by representing himself as the scapegoat for all forces of evil in the body. Probably also the mysterious "Bearded Demon."

Barguest. Goblin who sits on gates. Appears in the daytime.

Barkaial. According to the *Book of Enoch*, the fallen angel who taught the secrets of astrology to selected humans.

Baron. The signer of the pact with Gilles de Rais, or Bluebeard. Promised Bluebeard the secret of the Philosopher's Stone in return for the bodies of infants.

Barqu. Scholar and alchemist. Has discovered the secret of the Philosopher's Stone and guards its secrets.

Bathym. A steady, dependable country-doctor sort of demon. Knows the virtues of herbs. Is hearty and robust in appearance. Rides a grey horse.

Bayemon. A confidante of Pope Honorius.

Bearded Demon. A mysterious figure only rarely seen. Can teach the secret of the Philosopher's Stone. Has been variously identified with Hermes, Jesus Christ, or Baphomet. Has sleek, long, pointed beard, the greatest source of his pride.

Bechard. A sound-and-lights technician. Can control winds, tempests, hail, and thunder.

Beelzebub. Named by Jesus Christ. Seen by an Ursuline nun at Loudun. Some say he is a Prince of Hell. Others say he is a seraphi of the First Hierarchy. Has been spoken to by Gurdjieff. Can provoke humans to commit the deadly sin of gluttony.

Behemoth. Possessed a nun, Sister Jeanne des Anges. Under his influence she began to blaspheme. First appeared in Egypt in the form of a great beast, probably a hippo.

Belphegor. Handyman and inventor. Can find ingenious solutions to most practical problems. Can make you rich. Often appears as a young woman. In more grotesque form, he was worshipped by the Moabites. He is sometimes pictured as having a gaping mouth and a phallic tongue. Can tempt humans to the deadly sin of sloth.

Benemmerinnen. Earth-bound demons who live among the Hebrews. They appear as witches who steal newborn children.

Bensozia. A female devil, enchantingly beautiful, who has great power in human affairs. She has trained her followers to carry on guerrilla warfare against the male world. She was much worshipped and feared in ancient times, and until the advent of Christianity had armed followers among humans. She was known as Diana by the ancient Gauls, and was also called Nocticula, Herodias, or Luna. Her symbol is the moon. As Bensozia she was worshipped by witches in the Middle Ages.

Bes. Less than a foot tall, he has a penis of similar dimensions, so he looks rather like a sideways "T." A mischevious imp, he was once worshipped as a fertility god and as the consort of Diana of the Ephesians.

Biffant. A small-time operator. Once succeeded in inhabiting the body of a human girl, Denise de la Caille. He was exorcised but left his claw marks on her body.

Bifrons. The lamplighter. He lights the grave lights that are sometimes seen hovering over corpses. Has a Renaissance education in geometry, herbology, and astrology. Although really a monstrous-looking beast, he sometimes takes the form of an elegantly dressed man.

Bitru. Responsible for arousing human lust, he is at present enjoying great popularity. Takes the form of a leopard with the wings of a griffin. Commands seventy legions of demons. Is one of the Princes of Hell.

Bogey. General term applied to the rank-and-file demons. They are but pawns in the game. Their functions are reduced to frightening children into good behavior and haunting chimneys and country lanes at night. Can occasionally infiltrate television and the popular press.

Buer. A handsome young doctor. Appears in nature as a star. Knows philosophy and medicinal herbs. Has command of a modest force of fifteen legions. Was enslaved by Solomon to help in the building of the Temple of Jerusalem.

Bune. A Grand Duke. Preserves the awe of his followers by refusing to speak except in sign language. Appears frequently around cemeteries and corpses. In Central Asia the followers of Bune were once a dreaded armed force. In other guises, he has been worshipped in Africa and South America.

Cabiri. A secret group of demons about whom much has been written but very little is known. They have influenced the affairs of human secret societies since the beginning of the race. They made their first appearance as sea gods, perhaps indicating a pre-Atlantean origin. Some scholars believe the poems of Homer were written in their honor. The Cabiri are thought to be completely infiltrated throughout occultism.

Cacodaemons. Demons of the lowest caste, born with especially spiteful natures. One is assigned to each human. They report to Ahrimanes. Your personal cacodaemon is the devil who made you do it.

Cambions, or Campions. Half-breeds. Demons born of one human parent. They are usually quite docile and not very intelligent. They are said to weigh far more than humans. They occasionally show deformities that belie their demonic origin.

Catabolignes. A group of demons who amuse themselves by wandering around killing people, especially by crushing them or dropping them from great heights.

Cagrino. A demon who lives among the Gypsies. Its form is that of a hedgehog, and it has power over horses. It is from this demon that the Gypsies get their horse-trading and horse-thieving skills.

Cedon. One of the demons with which Urbain Grandier bewitched the nuns of Loudun.

Cham. Another demon personally acquainted with Grandier.

Chesme. A cat-lady. She lives near wells in Turkey and tempts young men to fall to their deaths.

Cimejes. A Spanish demon summoned by Solomon to help with the work of building the Temple.

Ciupipiltin. Vampire demons who sucked the blood of the ancient Mexicans.

Crocell. One of the demons commanded by Solomon.

Dagon. A god with a fish body and male head. Was much worshipped by the Phoenicians and other Mediterranean peoples. Was seen by John Milton.

Dantalion. One of the demons commanded by Solomon.

Daviers. Rank-and-file demons assigned to the Hindus. There are 300 million of them. They live in the air.

Decarabia. One of the demons commanded by Solomon.

Devil. The absolute ruler of darkness. The enemy of God. All other devils are but emanations of him. His origin is unknown, nor is it known whether he can finally be conquered. He is the creator of darkness and chaos. He has been given many names, but is most often known as Satan or Lucifer. His name is usually capitalized to distinguish the Devil from other devils who are merely acting on his orders.

Diakka. Not strictly speaking devils, but candidates for the demonic orders among recently dead human spirits. They are humans who have not adjusted to the idea of being dead. They often appear as ghosts. They are the ones who tap the tables at séances and perform other kinds of misleading mischief.

Divs. Rank-and-file demons of the Persian areas of the world. There are millions of them, and they are responsible for the day-to-day operations of the malevolent forces. There are both male and female divs. The females ruled the world until two thousand years after the creation of Adam. The divs appear to be the same beings that the Persians call *Daivers*. They appear on earth in many guises, including those of dragons, serpents, she-wolves, and other terrifying creatures.

Dragons. Among many demon groups, a popular form in which to appear to humans. Devils in dragon form have fought humans since prehistoric times. Bones of some dragons are exhibited in museums.

Du-Sith. Also known as "The Black Elf." A quiet little demon, but handy with a bow and arrow. He steps out of the forest and twangs an arrow into the back of your enemy's neck just as your enemy is about to let fly an arrow into yours.

Eblis, or *Haris*. A demon who appears in the form of fire. He was cast out of heaven for refusing to bow down to the first humans, and has been torturing humans ever since. His followers have included the Persian Magi and the European alchemists.

Elves. Among the smallest and least harmful of the bad spirits. They are more apt to do mischief than to cause serious harm. These devils have lived among humans so long that they have acquired human habits. Many of them are little more than human pets. They perform small household tasks and help merchandisers sell toys.

Essas. One of the demons with which Urbain Grandier bewitched the nuns of Loudun.

Familiars. Little demons who appear to help witches and sorcerers. They often appear as cats or other pets.

Fleuretty. A lieutenant general in hell. He brings hail. Usually works during the night.

Freya. The Scandinavian goddess of love and queen of the underworld. She is worshipped by witches on her special day, Friday.

Friar Rush. A bartender. Has a distinguished service record for his work among the monks of Germany. Usually drunk.

Frimost. Not very active. Can only be invoked between nine and ten o'clock on Tuesday evenings.

Furfur. A count of Hell. Appears as an angel. Sometimes also appears as a stag with a flaming tail. Commands twenty-six legions of demons.

Goblins. Hobo demons who camp out in abandoned houses. Not usually to be feared.

Guecubu. Rank-and-file demons of Chile.

Gusion. One of the demons commanded by Solomon.

Habondia. A demon queen. She presides over witches, fairies, furies, harpies, and ghosts of wicked women. She has been known to appear to lonely male writers living in remote country houses.

Haborym. Controls holocausts, so is kept busy these days. Has three heads, one of a cat, one of a man, one of a viper. Rides a viper. Commands twenty-six legions.

Hanon-Tramp. A truly terrible demon who appears to humans in nightmares and suffocates them while they sleep. Teach yourself to wake up.

Hecate. One of the aspects of the goddess Diana, the moon goddess. Can command all the natural powers of the earth. Has had various manifestations, as Luna, Herodias, etc. Often represented as a woman with writhing serpents for hair. Very powerful.

Ifrits. Rank-and-file demons who appear in various hideous guises to the Arabs. Ifrits congregate in isolated places and ruined villages, from which they sally forth in guerrilla-style to prey upon humans.

Incubus. A demon who is constantly seducing human women. Not to be trusted with affairs of importance, since all his energies are directed toward seduction. There are a great many incubi on earth.

Jinn. Rank-and-file demons among the Arabs. They include both good and evil forces. Some Jinn were servants of King Solomon.

Kabotermannekens. Fat, mischievous, little German demons who play tricks on women working in the fields.

Kamrusepa. A female demon, worshipped among the Hittites as Katah-zipuri. She was skilled in witchcraft.

Kelpie. A nature demon of Scotland. Kelpies appear as water spirits, haunting streams and lakes.

Keteb. The noonday devil of the Kabbalists. He is the personification of danger and evil.

Kostchchie. A disgusting old miser who lives in the mountains of Russia. He comes down occasionally to find women. He especially likes young girls. He pays them well, for he is immensely rich. His body is nothing but a skeleton and his head is that of Death. He carries an iron club.

Lamia. A type of female demon, who appear to men as the loveliest of creatures, but who are in reality vampires. They steal newborn infants in order to suck their blood. These demons are named for Lamia, a loathsome woman in Greek mythology.

Leviathan. One of the most terrifying, awesome gods of ancient times. Appears in the form of a sea monster. Was seen by Milton. Tempts people to the deadly sin of envy.

Lilith. Another powerful, beautiful demon woman. She was thought by the Jews to have been Adam's wife before Eve and to have been the mother of all demons. She was known to enjoy newborn infants as sacrifices. In later times she was worshipped as Herodias; in Greek times as Diana.

Lucifer. The demon most often recognized by humans. Appears as dazzling white light. He is a direct manifestation of the Devil himself. Lucifer rebelled against God and was cast out of heaven into hell, from which he sends forth his legions. He also walks to and fro upon the earth, seeking whom he may devour.

Lucifuges. A class of demons known to John Weir in the Middle Ages. They never appear in daylight, as they are able to take on human bodies only at night.

Malphas. A Grand President of the infernal regions. In the construction business. Responsible for building towers and ramparts. Can also help you destroy the powers of others. Appeared frequently in medieval battles. Sometimes appears as a crow. When he appears in human form, he can be recognized by his loud, croaking voice.

Mammon. Among the most important demons on earth today. Tempts people to the deadly sin of avarice. Controls the distribution of wealth and the flow of cash. Has shaggy black hair, fierce bandit eyes, and a mustache.

Mandragoras. Rank-and-file demons who have retired from active service. They are allowed to roam among humans and act as consultants to sorcerers. They are little old, beardless men.

Mastiphal. A demon prince. Very little is known about him.

Medea. An enchantress who seduced the Greek hero Jason and then murdered the princess whom he really loved. She murdered her own children by Jason as well. Although her appearances have been infrequent, she still exercises power over the human literary imagination.

Melusina. A strange half-breed female demon from France who turns into a serpent from the waist down on Saturdays. She wanders the earth as a ghost. She had an unpleasant life on earth because her husband didn't understand her predicament. Some say he shut her up in a dungeon.

Mephistopheles. The demon who bargained with Dr. Faustus for his soul. Has been variously portrayed as a thin, satyr-like, little man with a goat beard and as a tall, handsome courtier.

Merlin. A human enchanter who has been inhabited at times by demonic forces. On the whole he is on the side of the good, however.

Morgan le Fay. An English and Irish enchantress who often serves the demonic side. She is the sister of Merlin. Rumored to be a follower of Diana. Exerts hypnotic powers. Still a favorite companion of witches.

Naberus. A marquis. Sometimes appears as a crow. Gives instruction in speech and theater arts.

Nat. Rank-and-file demons assigned to Burma.

Nebiros. A Field Marshal. Can predict the future. Knows the essential properties of things.

Nick. An alias used by demons in England.

Obizuth. One of the demons bound by Solomon. He murders infants.

Old Scratch. A nickname for the Devil among the Teutonic tribes. Appeared as half man and half goat.

Ornias. A vampire-devil who was enslaved by Solomon and who assisted in the building of the Temple. Under duress he supplied the names of his fellow demons.

Orton. A demon who became the familar of one Lord of Corasse in medieval Europe.

Ouroboros. The name given by the Gnostics to the serpent in the Garden of Eden. The Gnostics do not consider this being a demon but a spirit sent by Wisdom to liberate the minds of humans. Since this idea as yet is unproven, it is best to regard subject as a double-agent.

Paigoels. Rank-and-file demons assigned to the Hindustani. Like their brethren everywhere, they can inhabit human bodies and work all sorts of evil against the human race. Some are also assigned to individuals.

Peor. One of the demons seen by John Milton.

Rabdos. Was once a human wise man. Inhabits the magic wands used by sorcerers and magicians. Also known as The Strangler.

Rahu. Known as The Tormenter. He appears among the Hindus, who worship him so that they may be guarded against evil spirits.

Rakshasa. A black demon with blonde hair. Wears a crown made of entrails. Appears among the people of India.

"Red Man." Nickname given to a demon who controls the tempests.

Satan. See *Devil*. Some worship Satan as a creature separate from the Devil. However, all his characteristics are those of the Demon King himself.

Seik Kassos. Rank-and-file demons in Burma. They inhabit trees.

Sargatanas. The demon to call when you've locked yourself out. Can open any lock. Has the power to confer invisibility. A brigadier general.

Succubus. Any demon who takes the shape of a woman in order to sleep with mortal men. These demons are generally beautiful and seductive. They do not always harm their male admirers, but must be treated carefully.

Thammuz. One of the demons seen by John Milton. Worshipped as a fertility god in ancient Mesopotamia.

Vampires. Not actually demons but humans who serve the demonic forces. They are people who by rights should be dead, but who remain on earth by sucking the blood of the living. They sleep in coffins during the day. At night, they emerge as tall, gaunt men, flittering bats, or patterns of moonlight.

Veltis. A rank-and-file demon who distinguished himself by escaping long imprisonment by Solomon. After years in a copper kettle, he escaped and attempted to assault St. Margaret. She overcame him, however. He admitted he had been assigned specifically to her, to turn her from righteousness.

Werewolves. Not devils, but humans who have turned into wolves.

Wild Women. Demons of the rank-and-file. They are little old ladies who live deep in the woods. They know the secrets of herbs and can cast spells. Some are humans who have made pacts with Satan; others are the children of Succubi or of women who have slept with Incubi.

Zaebos. A Grand Count of Hell. He appears mounted on a crocodile.

Zagam. Shares with Jesus Christ the ability to turn water into wine. Appears as a bull with the wings of a griffin. His name is often invoked in magical incantations.

Zazel. According to the *Book of Enoch*, one of the leaders of the rebellious angels.

Zepas. Appears in the form of a warrior. Casts human men into horrible passions.

Witchcraft and Satanism

In all parts of Europe, for as long as anyone can remember, people have worshipped the Goddess of the Moon and the God of the Hunt. They called the goddess Diana, Dana, Dianom, Luna, Isis, Hecate, Ishtar; they called the god Bacchus-Dionysus, Priapus, Balor, Sabasius, Pan, Cernunnos, Herne. Once a month the gods' followers would gather at night to worship. A priestess, representing the goddess, would lead the ceremony. A priest, wearing an animal's horns and skin, would represent the god. We have no idea how ancient such ceremonies are; but a Paleolithic drawing on the walls of the Caverne des Trois Frères at Ariege shows a man wearing the antlers and skin of a stag and dancing.

The Roman Church, once it had gained mastery in Europe, tried to stamp out these pagan ceremonies. To a very large degree it succeeded. True, fifth-century peasants carried in procession little dolls of linen and flour representing the old gods. In the eighth century, the Council of Leptines complained that pagan sacrifices were still being made in peasants' cottages. In the twelfth century Burchard of Worms admitted that no matter how much the Church threatened, the old ceremonies went on. But Pan and Diana, though they were still worshipped, had shrunk in stature, and so had their fellow gods. They had become little more than goblins, elves, and fairies.

Here is the great historian of witchcraft, Jules Michelet, describing the remnants of the pagan gods and the woman who worshipped them:

> She carries shut within her breast a fond remembrance of the poor ancient gods, now fallen to the estate of spirits, and a feeling of compassion for them. For do not for an instant suppose, because they are gods, they are exempt from pain and suffering. Lodged in rocks, in the trunks of oaks, they are very unhappy in winter. They greatly love heat, and prowl around the houses; they have been surprised in stables, warming themselves beside the cattle. Having no more incense, no more victims, poor things, they sometimes take some of the housewife's milk. She, good managing soul, does not stint her husband, but diminishes her own portion, and when evening comes, leaves a little cream behind in the bowl.
>
> These spirits, which no longer appear except by night, sadly regret their exile from the day, and are eager for lights. At nightfall the goodwife hardens her heart and sallies out fearfully, bearing a humble taper to the great oak where they dwell, or the mysterious pool whose surface will double the flame in its dark mirror to cheer the unhappy outlaws. . . . Whispering low, the anxious wife prefers to address her prayer to some old-world deity, adored as a rustic god of yore, and whom such-and-such a church has been good-natured enough to make into a saint.

People are used to thinking of the Dark Ages as a frightening time, a time of terrible superstitions. Yet, as you can see from the passage above, the pagan gods of the Dark Ages were mild and sympathetic.

Nor was the devil all that frightening. The Church at this time was inclined to define evil as the absence of good. The devil, therefore, was far from being a powerful agent of evil. St. Augustine wrote that "the devil is a chained dog; he can bark, but he cannot bite." According to St. Bernard, "if the devil had the power to do evil, he has at any rate not the will to do it." Such opinions were current as late as 1489, when Ulrich Molitor wrote, in *Von den Unholden odor Hexen*, that "the devil cannot, by himself or with the help of man, stir up the elements or harm man and beast. He cannot render man inept to generation, if he does not receive such power from the most merciful God."

But over the centuries the devil's power had grown and become more palpable. By the thirteenth century the devil had finally become Satan, Prince of Darkness—devious, strong, an omnipresent enemy. Some went so far as to call Satan the ruler of this world. And how could he not be, when Europe was a scene of almost unrelieved war, famine, and plague, when the Church itself was in chronic disorder?

Here was the great turning point for witchcraft. For the Church now identified the witches' horned god as Satan. And many of the witches accepted the Church's definition. As Michelet writes, Satanism could not take root until "Hell itself should appear a shelter, an asylum, a relief, as contrasted with the Hell of this world." Given the misery of their lives, why shouldn't the poor have turned to Satan?

From Witches' Sabbath to Black Mass

The earliest ceremonies were almost purely fertility rites, called Sabbaths after the goat god Sabasius. There were two main festivals: Samhain (Halloween), dedicated to the horned god, and Beltane (May Eve), dedicated to the goddess. There were lesser festivals at Candlemas (February 2) and at Lammas (June 21, Midsummer Night's Eve). The coven (usually consisting of thirteen members) would dance in a circle, pray to their gods, offer sacrifices, and share a meal. Possibly the witches used drugs to attain a state of trance, in which they would see themselves flying through the air; hence the legends of witches flying on broomsticks. It's more likely that the witches, holding broomsticks between their legs, leapt through the fields in an exercise of sympathetic magic. They were encouraging the crops to grow high; the broomstick between the legs seemed an appropriate instrument of encouragement.

By the fourteenth century, these practices had turned into the Black Mass.

The priestess, who had now become Satan's bride, set up a wooden statue of the goat god. She pronounced a diabolic parody of the *Introit* to the Mass. The celebrants then denied Jesus; the priestess embraced the statue.

Next the celebrants ate their meal and danced the Witches' Round; in pairs, the witches interlocked their arms and danced back to back.

The coven's priest interrupted the dance to pronounce the *Gloria* to Satan. He followed this with the coven's *Credo*, then celebrated the Eucharist, using the priestess's body as the altar. The hosts might be holy wafers, stolen from church, or small, crescent-shaped cakes made of meal, wine, salt, and honey. Sometimes the cake had been baked in a little oven that was set on the naked genitals of the priestess.

After the priest had consecrated (or desecrated) the host, the priestess rose from the altar and with her bare hands decapitated a live toad. The other congregants, responding, would also mangle and even eat toads.

An orgy followed. The orgies varied in their nature and intensity, but we can be sure that they gave some relief to the peasants' sexual tensions, which were enforced by poverty and the Church.

The most important point about the Black Mass is that it was a political act, a defiance of both the nobility and the Church. In fact, the mockery of the Eucharist probably arose from a custom of the peasant revolts, in which groups of fighting men drank each others' blood and ate earth as a symbol of their solidarity.

From these ceremonies arose most of the tales of the evil of witches. Witches mate with Satan and lesser devils. Witches destroy crops and cattle. Witches murder infants. Witches steal the penises of Godfearing men and collect them in boxes, where they writhe like worms. Witches trouble peoples' sleep, possess their minds, wrack their bodies so that they vomit toads and pins.

Then, in the seventeenth century, these evils began to die away. Had they been conquered by the centuries-long persecution of witches? No, argues Michelet; they were killed by Kepler, Galileo, Descartes, and New-

ton. It is as if the pagan nature-gods had won their war with the Church by advancing on a different front. "The Witches' Sabbath disappears; and why? The reason is, it is *everywhere* henceforth; it is a part of men's ordinary habits; its practices are those of everyday life." The spirits of nature had become the scientists' Law of Nature, and they had triumphed.

Perhaps it's best to let Michelet sum up:

> Foolishly men had said, "Great Pan is dead." Then presently, seeing he was alive still, they had made him into a god of evil; and in the gloom and chaos of those days the mistake was possible enough. But lo! he is alive now, and with a life in harmony and sweet accord with the sublime and immutable laws that guide the stars of heaven, and no less surely govern the deep mystery of human life.

(For more about the history and significance of witchcraft see chapter seven, in the section "The Age of the Church.")

Where the Witches Came From: An Italian Legend

Diana greatly loved her brother Lucifer, the god of the Sun and of the Moon, the god of Light, who was so proud of his beauty, and who for his pride was driven from Paradise.

Diana had by her brother a daughter, to whom they gave the name of Aradia.

> In those days there were on earth many rich and many poor.
> The rich made slaves of all the poor. . . .

Many slaves escaped. They fled to the country; thus they became thieves and evil folk. Instead of sleeping by night, they plotted escape and robbed their masters, and then slew them. So they dwelt in the mountains and forests as robbers and assassins, all to avoid slavery.

Diana said one day to her daughter Aradia:

> . . . Thou shalt be the first of witches known;
> And thou shalt be the first of all i' the world;
> And thou shalt teach the art of poisoning,
> Of poisoning those who are great lords of all;
> . . . And when a priest shall do you injury
> By his benedictions, ye shall do to him
> Double the harm, and do it in the name
> Of me, Diana, Queen of witches all!

And so Aradia learned the secrets of witchcraft and taught them to humans so that they might destroy their oppressors.

From *Aradia: Gospel of the Witches*, by Charles G. Leland.

The Witch of En-dor: A Biblical Legend

Now Samuel was dead, and all Israel had lamented him, and buried him in Ramah, even in his own city. And Saul had put away those that had familiar spirits, and the wizards, out of the land.

And the Philistines gathered themselves together, and came and pitched in Shunem: and Saul gathered all Israel together, and they pitched in Gilboa.

And when Saul saw the host of the Philistines, he was afraid, and his heart greatly trembled.

And when Saul inquired of the Lord, the Lord answered him not, neither by dreams, nor by Urim, nor by prophets.

Then said Saul unto his servants, Seek me a woman that hath a familiar spirit, that I may go to her, and inquire of her. And his servants said to him, Behold, there is a woman that hath a familiar spirit at En-dor.

And Saul disguised himself, and put on other raiment, and he went, and two men with him, and they came to the woman by night; and he said, I pray thee, divine unto me by the familiar spirit, and bring me him up, whom I shall name unto thee.

And the woman said unto him, Behold, thou knowest what Saul hath done, how he hath cut off those that have familiar spirits, and the wizards, out of the land: wherefore then layest thou a snare for my life, to cause me to die?

And Saul sware to her by the Lord, saying, As the Lord liveth, there shall no punishment happen to thee for this thing.

Then said the woman, Whom shall I bring up unto thee? And he said, Bring me up Samuel.

And when the woman saw Samuel, she cried with a loud voice: and the woman spake to Saul, saying, Why hast thou deceived me? for thou art Saul.

And the king said unto her, Be not afraid: for what sawest thou? And the woman said unto Saul, I saw gods ascending out of the earth.

And he said unto her, What form is he of? And she said, An old man cometh up; and he is covered with a mantle. And Saul perceived that it was Samuel, and he stopped with his face to the ground, and bowed himself.

From 1 Samuel XXVIII, 3–14.

What the Witches Had in Their Cauldrons

According to Pierre de Lancre, in his *Tableau de l'inconstance des mauvais anges et demons* (1612), the witches' brew is brackish green water containing the juices of a flayed cat, a toad, a lizard, and a viper. Sometimes witches lay the above ingredients on live coals until ashes form and turn into stinging worms. The concoction, whether liquid or powdered, can be used for poisoning crops. A drop on a man's clothes would kill him. A little of the oil on the door-latches of a house would kill all the inhabitants.

According to Thomas Middleton's play *The Witch*, the principal ingredient is an unbaptized infant. Then:

> The magickal herbs are down his throat;
> His mouth cramm'd full,
> His ears and nostrils stuff'd;
> I thrust in eleoselinum lately,
> Aconitum, frondes populeas, and soot.
> Then sium, acorum vulgare too,
> Pentaphyllon, the blood of a flitter-mouse,
> Solanum somnificum et oleum.

Eleoselinum is parsley; aconitum is a common herb used to treat neuralgia; frondes populeas are poplar leaves; sium is water parsnip; acorum vulgare is calamus; pentaphyllon is cinquefoil; a flitter-mouse is a bat; solanum somnificum is nightshade; oleum is oil.

According to the recipe given by the three witches in *Macbeth*, the brew begins with a toad that has sweated poison under a rock for thirty-one days and nights. Add to this the filet of a swamp snake. Then stir in:

> Eye of newt and toe of frog,
> Wool of bat, and tongue of dog,
> Adder's fork, and blindworm's sting,
> Lizard's leg, and howlet's wing . . .
> Scale of dragon, tooth of wolf,
> Witch's mummy, maw and gulf
> Of the ravined salt-sea shark,
> Root of hemlock digged i'th'dark,
> Liver of blaspheming Jew,
> Gall of goat, and slips of yew
> Slivered in the moon's eclipse,
> Nose of Turk, and Tartar's lips,
> Finger of birth-strangled babe
> Ditch-delivered by a drab
> Make the gruel thick and slab.
> Add thereto a tiger's chaudron
> For th'ingredience of our cauldron. . . .
> Cool it with a baboon's blood,
> Then the charm is firm and good.

Witches' Poisons

When the great Renaissance doctor Paracelsus publicly burned the works of Galen and other medical authorities, he declared that all he knew of medicine he had learned from good women (i.e., sorceresses), shepherds, and hangmen. Shepherds, of course, had to have much practical knowledge about the treatment of disease. Hangmen were among the few authorities on anatomy. And sorceresses were the common people's pharmacists.

Witches made extensive use of a family of herbs called *Solanaceae*. The plants of this family are common, numerous, and tricky to employ.

Among the least potent are such plants as the aubergine and the tomato. In the same category we may include the mulleins, which are calmatives.

Bittersweet, which many people thought was a poison, is potent and useful for deadening pain. The slight, prickling irritation it causes has made it a homeopathic cure for diseases of the skin. Black mullein, a somewhat stronger herb, serves a similar function.

More potent still, and truly dangerous, is henbane (*hyoscyamus*). Applied in a plaster, it works as a sedative, softens tissues, and relieves pain. Finally, there is belladonna, used by witches as an anesthetic. It was useful for difficult childbirths and as a cure for St. Vitus's dance.

Witches were bold indeed in daring to use these agents for healing. Michelet writes: "How came the great discovery? No doubt by simple application of the great satanic principle *that everything should be done backwards*. . . . The Church had a holy horror of all poisons; Satan utilizes them as curative agents."

How to Make Yourself Invisible

To make yourself invisible, you will need five black beans and the head of a dead man.

On Wednesday morning, before the sun rises, put one bean in the head's mouth, two in its eyes, and two in its ears. Then draw on the head the symbol of your familiar spirit. (The familiar is a guiding demon, who usually appears as a household pet.) Bury the head face up.

Every day before sunrise, for nine days, water the head with brandy. On the eighth day, you will find the familiar spirit standing by the head. He will ask, "What are you doing?" You must say, "I am watering my plant." He will say, "Give me that bottle. I will water it myself." You must refuse until he stretches out his hand and shows you there the same symbol that you drew on the head. Then you will know that you're talking with the right spirit. Give him the bottle of brandy. He will water the head and leave.

On the ninth morning, your beans will be ripe. Pop one into your mouth, and you will become invisible. Put the rest in a safe place.

How to Cure Sprains and Broken Bones

Tie seven knots at regular intervals along a piece of thread. Then tie the thread around the injured limb. Chant the following three times:

Baldur rade. The foal slade.
Set bone to bone,
Sinew to sinew,
Heal!—in Odin's name.

Or chant:

Phol and Woden fare to the wood.
There was Baldur's foal's foot sprained.
Then charmed Woden, as well he knew how
For bone sprain, blood sprain, for limb sprain.
Bone to bone, blood to blood, limb to limbs
As though they were glued.

What to Call Your Familiar

Achitophel
Ball
Cuffin
Dodge
Elemanzer
Fennil
Grizel Greediguts
Graymalkin
Hotkittel
Illiskin
Jumperthug
Kettel
Lemuel
Lumpkin
Malacaster
Nedad
Obelphuel
Paddock
Pyewacket
Quem
Rann
Sack and Sugar
Sathan
Tibb
Udderguts
Vinegar Tom
Watchbilly
Xander
Yddilmisk
Zeb

Familiar Spirits

Familiar spirits generally come to you. You cannot seek them out. One night your cat will turn around and look at you strangely; or a toad, lizard, hare, or fly will appear in the room even though all the doors and windows are shut. The animal will speak to you in a high, hollow voice and demand to be fed. You must then prick yourself with a pin and give it a drop of your blood. Every time the familiar does you a service, you must feed it. The marks made by the pin pricks will be permanent.

You, too, can appear in the form of an animal. One of the most popular forms for medieval witches was the hare. To change into a hare, say:

I shall go into a hare
With sorrow and sighing and mickle care,
And I shall go into the Devil's name
Till I come home again.

To change back into human form, say:

Hare, hare, God send thee care.
I am in a hare's likeness now
But I shall be in a woman's likeness even now.

Things to Do With Simple Household Items

Make a doll out of clay, wax, or wood, and give it the appearance of one of your enemies. Name it after the enemy; steal a piece of your enemy's clothes, a lock of his hair, or his fingernail parings, and put them on the doll. Now you can stick pins into the doll's limbs to give your enemy pains. A pin in the head causes madness; a pin in the heart causes instant death. For lingering deaths, let the doll melt before a slow fire. These were the methods two male witches tried to use in 1323 to kill the Prior of Coventry at the request of twenty-seven burghers of that town.

Instead of using a doll, you can drive pins into a live bird or toad. Candles can be used in the same way to cause lingering deaths.

To kill someone by means of stolen clothing, take the item (a glove is ideal), boil it in water mixed with blood, prick it, and bury it. Margaret and Philippa Flower were executed in 1619 in Lincoln for the successful use of this method against Lord Rosse, his brother, and his sister.

If you want to bring on a thunderstorm, throw a flintstone over your left shoulder toward the west. Or, simply throw a handful of sea sand into the air. Or dig a pit in the dirt, fill it with water, and stir it with your fingers. Or bury sage until it's rotten. Reginald Scot, in his *Discovery of Witchcraft* (1665), says that all these methods work.

Remedies for the Bewitched

Don't panic. Mix some of your blood with rosemary balm, marigolds, and ale; drink the mixture. Also, wear marigold flowers and balm in a bag around your neck.

It also helps to bottle some of your urine and simmer it over a fire. The only problem there is that the witch will probably make the bottle burst, whereupon the charm will lose effect. According to the transcript of a witch trial held in Leicester in 1717,

> When the patients urine was set to stew by the fire some one of the witches was allways observed to come into the room, sometimes in the shape of a cat and sometimes a dog, who would run in panting as if he was upon a hard chase, and these dogs and cats would come in tho: the doors and windows were shut and all passages except the keyholes and chimneys stopt, and could never be catched but would grin furiously, and approaching near the bewitch'd persons would give them great pain and so vanish.

Witches and Sex

Probably the best-known case of demonic possession combined with sexual frenzy is that of the devils of Loudun.

Early in the seventeenth century, a priest named Urbain Grandier arrived in Loudun. He was brilliant, handsome, and reckless. In 1618 he had written a polemic against Cardinal Richelieu, a bold and foolish thing to do. Not long after his arrival in Loudun, he seduced the daughter of the king's solicitor and flirted with the daughter of the king's councilor.

News of Grandier reached the mother superior of the convent of Loudun. The mother superior was known as Joan of the Angels. She had never met Urbain Grandier, but she began to dream of him. He appeared to her and spoke seductively. When she couldn't rid herself of these dreams, she asked some of the nuns to whip her. They did, and within a few days they, too, were dreaming about Urbain Grandier. Joan appealed for help to Canon Mignon, who sent an exorcist to the convent. The exorcist's ceremony sent Joan into convulsions, and all the other nuns present followed. They threw fits, shrieked gibberish, and called Grandier's name loudly.

Grandier was accused of having bewitched the nuns. In 1634 he was burned at the stake. Since his legs had been broken by torture, he had to be carried to the execution.

The exorcisms at the convent continued until 1637. The exorcists came away from the convent with one strange document, signed by the demon Asmodeus, promising to leave Joan of the Angels alone. The document is in the Bibliothèque Nationale in Paris.

How Do They Do It?

If we seek to learn from these Authorities how it is possible that the Demon, who has no body, yet can perform actual coitus with man or woman, they unanimously answer that the Demon assumes the corpse of another human being, male or female as the case may be, or that, from the mixture of other materials, he shapes for himself a body endowed with motion, by means of which body he copulates with the human being; and they add that when women are desirous of becoming pregnant by the Demon (which occurs only with the consent and at the express wish of the said women), the Demon is transformed into a Succubus, and during the act of coition with some man receives therefrom human semen; or else he procures pollution from a man during his sleep, and then he preserves the spilt semen at its natural heat, conserving it with the vital essence. This, when he has connexion with the woman, he introduces into her womb, whence follows impregnation.

From *De Daemonialitate* (seventeenth century), by Friar Ludovico Maria Sinistrari, translated by Montague Summers.

A Monk Describes the Witches' Sabbath

Fr. Maria Guaccius (Guazzo), a brother of the Milanesian Order of the

Ambrosiani, describes the sabbath in his *Compendium Maleficarum* (1608). According to him, there are eleven steps in the Sabbath.

1. The witches renounce the Christian faith by saying, "I deny the creator of heaven and earth. I deny my baptism. I deny the worship I formerly paid to God. I cleave to thee [Satan], and in thee I believe."
2. The devil marks their foreheads with his claw.
3. The devil baptizes them with filthy water and gives them new names.

4. They deny the sacramants and renounce their godparents.
5. They give the devil an article of their clothing. Sometimes they give him one of their children.
6. The devil draws a magic circle on the ground, and they step into it and swear allegiance to Satan.
7. The devil inscribes their names in the Book of Death.
8. They promise to strangle a child for Satan every two to four weeks. They also promise to make whatever mischief they can.
9. They give a gift to the devil (something black); otherwise he will beat them.
10. The devil places a secret brand on their bodies.

11. They promise to stay away from the cross, holy water, and all other consecrated things. They promise to fly to the sabbath whenever it is held, and to bring others to Satan.

The Devil's Prayer

You can't hold a Sabbath in the grand style without knowing the Lord's Prayer backwards. Here it is:

> Malo a nos libera sed: temptationem in nos inducas ne et; nostris debitoribus dimittimus nos et sicut, nostra debita nobis dimitte et, hodie nobis da supersubstantialem nostrum Panem. Terra in et caelo in sicut tua voluntas fiat; tuum regnum adveniat; tuum nomen sanctificetur, caelis in es qui noster Pater.

How Many Died?

With the aid of such guidebooks as Sprenger and Krämer's *Malleus Maleficarum* and King James I's *Daemonologie*, witch hunters tortured and killed people—the vast majority women—throughout Europe. The height of the persecution was the sixteenth century. Pennethorne Hughes, in *Witchcraft*, writes that "Six hundred were said to have been burned by a single bishop in Bamberg, where the special witch jail was kept fully packed. Nine hundred were destroyed in a single year in the bishopric of

Wurzburg, and in Nuremberg and the other great cities, there were one or two hundred burnings a year. So there were in France and in Switzerland. A thousand people were put to death in one year in the district of Como. Remigius, one of the Inquisitors, who was author of *Daemonolatvia*, and a judge at Nancy boasted of having personally caused the burning of nine hundred persons in the course of fifteen years. Delrio says that five hundred were executed in Geneva in three terrifying months in 1515. The Inquisition at Toulouse destroyed four hundred persons in a single execution, and there were fifty at Douai in a single year. In Paris, executions were continuous. In the Pyrenees, a wolf country, the popular form was that of the *loup-garou*, and De L'Ancre at Labout burned two hundred. . . . The number who died as witches is purely problematical. Someone has suggested nine million. It may be many more."

Gerald Gardner, King of the Witches

Probably the most important figure in contemporary witchcraft is Gerald Gardner (1884–1964). Born in Lancashire of wealthy parents, Gardner traveled widely in his youth, visiting the Canary Islands, North Africa, Ceylon, Malaya, Borneo, and Cyprus. He worked at various jobs and picked up various enthusiasms, including a liking for weapons. In 1936 he returned to England to retire.

In 1939 Gardner took up nudism for its therapeutic benefits. He also joined the Folk Lore Society. At his inauguration, he gave a lecture about a box of witches' relics that he said he owned and that had belonged to the seventeenth-century Witchfinder General, Matthew Hopkins.

In 1939 Gardner also joined a coven in Hampshire run by a woman called Old Dorothy. From Old Dorothy he got the information that witches are members of an ancient, secret society that had survived in England from pre-Christian times. The society is named *Wicca*, the Anglo-Saxon word from which the word *witch* is derived. Gardner said *wicca* meant "a wise one." The accepted etymology is that the word comes from an Indo-European base, *weiq*, meaning "violent strength."

Gardner did much to revive interest in witchcraft; many present-day covens use his rites, and his followers think him nothing short of saintly.

For Further Reading

The standard work on this subject is *Satanism and Witchcraft: A Study in Medieval Superstition*, by Jules Michelet (New York: Citadel Press, 1939, translated by A.R. Allison). A more recent work is *Witchcraft*, by Pennethorne Hughes (Baltimore: Penguin, 1965). Kurt Seligmann's *Magic, Supernaturalism and Religion* (New York: Pantheon, 1948) also has some valuable material. For a brief, popular history, including material on Gerald Gardner, see *Modern Witchcraft*, by Frank Smyth (New York: Harrow, 1973). For the pro-Gardner viewpoint, see *Witchcraft from the Inside*, by Raymond Buckland (St. Paul: Llewellyn, 1975). *Aradia: Gospel of the Witches*, by Charles G. Leland (New York: Samuel Weiser, 1974) is invaluable as a source. Much other good source material is in Christina Hole's *Witchcraft in England* (New York: Collier, 1966). The full text of Sinistrari's *Demoniality* can be found in *Eros and Evil: The Sexual Psychopathology of Witchcraft*, by R.E.L. Masters (Baltimore: Penguin, 1974).

Voodoo

Voodoo has a bad name among occultists and nonoccultists alike. People picture it as a primitive, even savage, religion, a bloodthirsty cult that victimizes the superstitious.

In reality, it is a make-do kind of magic. Granted, it has used the simplest materials because they were the only ones available. However, of all systems of magic, it is one of the most complex, and it has managed to assimilate a great many different influences without losing the purity of its original intent: to establish vital links between the material world and the world of spirit.

Origins

Voodoo was brought to Haiti and the Caribbean by African slaves, but the slave-trade drew on dozens of tribes, mostly from the Gulf of Benin, and each of these tribes had its own practices and beliefs. Some of the tribes were traditional enemies—the Western Yoruba and the Dahomeans, for example. Yet slavery had brought all these groups together, and so from the start, voodoo was a synthesis.

Dahomey exerted the greatest influence. Many of the voodoo gods—Legba, Damballah, Erzulie, Agwé, Ogoun—are still worshipped in Dahomey, Togo, and Nigeria. Many voodoo words came from Fon, a language of Dahomey and Togo, including the word *voodoo* itself, which derives from the Fon for "a god." As for the various nations (or *nanchons*) of the gods, the older of the two main groups, the Rada, derive their name from Arada, a town in Dahomey. Dahomey was a well-organized, monarchical society based on cooperative agriculture. The Rada gods fit this pattern of life. They were above all protective, unlike the second of the two main groups of gods, who were aggressive and more able to inspire a slave people to revolt.

The Petros are more difficult to trace than the Rada. According to one account, they were introduced in 1768 by a Spanish *houngan* named Don Pedro. (*Houngan* is a difficult word to translate. It means a priest, doctor, advisor, fortuneteller, community leader; it, too, derives from Fon, meaning literally "the master of a god.") Don Pedro supposedly introduced new rites to the Haitian slaves, including a dance that was wilder and more violent than the old Rada dances. He also introduced the practice of drinking a mixture of rum and finely crushed gunpowder. Therefore, the Petro cult and its gods are named after him, the divine messenger responsible for their worship.

A more likely explanation is that the Petro gods came from Indian cults. Slaves used to run away from their masters in great numbers; they would take to the hills, and there they would meet Indian tribesmen. (Running away was the safer of the slaves' two methods of protest. The other was open revolt, which despite its dangers was attempted frequently. Slave-trade to Haiti began in 1510; the first revolt came in 1522.) We know that the runaway slaves adopted some of the Indian gods, notably those that were tougher than the African gods, and so we can speculate that Petro is derived from the Spanish *petreo*, meaning "stony."

In addition to African cross-influences and Indian influences, voodoo assimilated one more notable strain. This was Roman Catholicism. Voodoo has made free use of the Trinity and the saints, thereby offending the Church and earning for itself a very bad press. But perhaps too much has been made of the Catholic influence, in scholarly as well as popular accounts. Voodoo hasn't travestied Church rites—it's reclaimed them. Remember that many of the saints started out as pagan deities.

The idea, the central feeling that holds together all these various elements, is that of the mutual dependence of the material and spiritual worlds.

Cosmology

Voodoo practitioners believe that one is born into the world simply as a body. Then, from the body is born a kind of double, or mirror image, called the *gros-bon-ange* (or great good angel). The gros-bon-ange is not so much a soul as a personality, the complex of energy and intelligence that makes each person individual. In addition, everyone has a *ti-bon-ange* (little good angel), which may be considered as the conscience; the ti-bon-ange is impersonal, and ultimately of less importance than the gros-bon-ange.

At death, the ti-bon-ange hovers over the body for nine days, and then goes to heaven, never to be heard of again. The gros-bon-ange goes to the world of the dead, *les Invisibles*. Its story has just begun.

In voodoo mythology, the dead live in *Zilet en bas de l'eau*, the Island Below the Sea. Voodoo locates *Guinée* (Africa) in this same sea, where the dead live in marine and insect forms. This sea lies below the surface of the earth, an idea that does not seem naive if you imagine Haiti to lie on the opposite side of the globe from the African Slave Coast. In that case, the fastest way for a gros-bon-ange to get back to Guinée would be to go straight down.

So on the other side of the earth, in a cold, wet, mirror world, the dead spirits remain for a year and a day. Then their families call them back in a ceremony named *retirer d'en bas de l'eau*, or bringing back from the bottom of the water.

Near the community's main sanctuary, the houngan sets up a tent, usually made from a white sheet. He places the tent by a pond or stream; if there's none nearby, he makes do with a trough of water. At the start of the ceremony, attendants proceed from the sanctuary to the white tent, each carrying a clay jar called a *govi*. The govis are to be the new homes of the recalled gros-bon-anges.

After his initial invocations, the houngan begins to call on gros-bon-anges by name. And they come. Their voices emerge clearly from whatever body of water he's used to represent the deep waters of les Invisibles. An account of such a ceremony, written by Maya Deren (in her book *Divine Horsemen*), goes into great detail about the speeches of the newly returned dead to their families and to the houngan. If the houngan is a ventriloquist, he's a very good one. If he's a hypnotist, he's one who can work in the midst of an active, joking, interrupting crowd.

After each gros-bon-ange has spoken, it goes into a govi, where it will remain near its family, ready to be of help when advice is needed. Born of the body, it returns to the material world after its death.

But this is not the end of the cycle for some gros-bon-anges. These become *loas*, in which case they can return to the body—anybody's body.

The Loas

Loa is the Congo word for "spirit." The loas are sometimes called gods, and at times they seem to have the strength of nature's forces; but probably they are strong, ancient gros-bon-anges, and they too were once born of the body. The ultimate purpose of voodoo is to let them return to living bodies, to mount them as a rider mounts a horse. (Loas, when possessing someone, seem to climb on the host's shoulders, pitching him forward.) In this way the living and the loas strengthen each other. The living draw on the knowledge and energy of the loas. In return, the living give the loas a way to manifest themselves, and—most important—they give the loas food. Without the service of the living and their offerings of food, the loas would weaken and finally vanish.

Who are the loas? In our language they would be called the Old Man, the Gangster, the Warrior, the Joker, the Mistress. They resemble figures from Tarot cards or characters from familiar fairy tales, and they're African gods too.

For purposes of voodoo ceremony the most important loa is *Legba*, the interpreter of the other loas, the gatekeeper, the old man at the crossroads.

He's pictured as an old peasant who's worked hard all his life, walking on a crutch down the road, a pipe in his mouth and a small sack on his back. When he possesses people, their limbs contort as if crippled, and their faces look ancient and weary. In his origins Legba was a Dahomean sun god, but now he's a setting sun. He's keeper of the gates because he's just this side of death.

He's the old man at the crossroads because in voodoo any cross has symbolic meaning. Remember that the quickest way to go to the spirit world of les Invisibles is to go straight down. For this reason the most important ceremonial object in voodoo is a stick plunged into the earth. Trees have a similar ritual symbolism—they, too, represent an intersection of the horizontal plane of the living with the vertical plane of the spirits.

Legba allows all the other loas to rise through the stake plunged into the ground, the *poteau-mitan*. He's keeper of the keys to the spirit world. Trees, dedicated to Legba, stand near every voodoo sanctuary. Every Rada ceremony begins with an invocation to him.

On the other side of death is *Ghede*, the loa of death, the loa invoked at the close of every Rada ceremony. Whereas Legba is the setting sun, Ghede is the rising sun. Legba dresses in peasant's tatters; Ghede dresses in clown's motley. Legba often carries a wooden crutch; Ghede likes to appear wearing a giant wooden phallus.

He's death itself, but he's a joker. He especially delights in embarrassing people sexually, with the large repertoire of dirty songs which he sings in a nasal voice, prolonging certain notes indefinitely. And, like the grave itself, he's insatiably hungry. All loas must be fed, but Ghede, when he appears, is particularly insistent. A man or woman possessed by him will eat prodigious amounts of the ritual food offered. Ghede likes to wear dark glasses and appear at ceremonies uninvited.

In his Petro versions, Ghede appears as Baron Samedi, Baron la Crois, Baron Cimetière. His symbol is a black cross on a tomb, the cross draped with a black coat and surmounted with a top hat. Baron Samedi is the loa most invoked in voodoo black magic. As a Rada loa, Ghede is better known to be a healer.

Ogoun, the warrior, is as various in his aspects as Ghede. He's an ironsmith, a politician, a gangster, a fire—a god who embodies power. Unlike the other loas, he is invoked with the ceremonial pouring of rum, which is then set on fire. When he appears, he usually demands a drink of rum by shouting, "Grains moin fret!" (my balls are cold). When he gets his rum, he often sprays it out through his teeth. His special methods of strengthening people are to slap them and lift them into the air. (Many people devoted to Ogoun are members of the Masonic order, and many small rituals devoted to Ogoun are Masonic in origin—another influence absorbed.)

Ogoun consorts with *Erzulie*, the principal female loa. She's a great lady, and a rich one. Her primary attribute is luxury. When she possesses someone, her first act is to wash herself in the ritual basin kept for her in the sanctuary, where she's provided with fresh soap, basil leaves (for purification), fresh towels, combs, perfume, and a silk handkerchief to tie around her hair. Her favorite drink is champagne, and her symbol is a pierced heart—also a symbol of the Virgin Mary. Unlike the Virgin, perhaps more like Mary Magdalene, she has a highly erotic character.

In a Petro form, she appears as Erzulie Gé-Rouge (Erzulie Red Eyes). All her muscles clench, her lightness and grace evaporate, and she sobs uncontrollably. She becomes a figure of despair, hopeless because no one can love her enough.

Ogoun is not her only lover. She is also married to *Agwé*, the royal loa of the sea. Celebrations for Agwé are complex. They involve, first, a large banquet at which not only Agwé but other major loas are fed. Erzulie is feasted as Agwé's royal consort; in these cases, she goes by the name La Sirène. Then the participants prepare, before the sanctuary's altar, a luxurious double bed, representing the nuptial bed of Agwè and Erzulie. The hougan (or more often the *mambo*, or priestess) keeps watch over the bed all night. Then, the next day, the participants go to the sea. They wade in with a special boat consecrated to Agwè and loaded with his offerings, and there they perform their service to him.

AT VOODOO CENTRAL, USA—1920

PaPa LaBas' Mumbo Jumbo Kathedral is located at 119 West 136th St. . . . PaPa LaBas climbs the steps of the Town house. He moves from room to room: the Dark Tower Room the Weary Blues Room the Groove Bang and Jive Around Room the Aswelay Room. In the Groove Bang and Jive Around Room people are rubberlegging for dear life; bending over backwards to admit their loa. In the Dark Tower Room, artists using cornmeal and water are drawing veves. Markings which were invitations to new loas for New Art. The room is decorated in black red and gold.

A piano recording plays Jelly Roll Morton's "Pearls," haunting, melancholy. In the Aswelay Room the drums sleep after they've been baptized. A guard attendant stands by so that they won't get up and walk all over the place. PaPa LaBas opens his hollow obeah stick and gives the drums a drink of bootlegged whiskey. . . . There is a room PaPa LaBas calls the Mango Room, so named to honor the great purifying plant. On a long maple table covered with splendid white linen cloth rest 21 trays filled with such delectable items as liqueurs, sweets, rum, baked chicken, and beef. The table is adorned with vases containing many types of roses. This room is the dining hall of the loas, and LaBas demands that the trays be refreshed after the Ka-food has been eaten. His assistants make sure that this is done. The room is illuminated by candles of many colors. On the tables sky-blue candles are burning. In the other main room attendants have been guided through exercises. Once in a while 1 is possessed by a loa. The loa is not a daimon in the Freudian sense, a hysteric; no, the loa is known by its signs and is fed, celebrated, drummed to until it deserts the horse and *govi* of its host and goes on about its business. . . . The last thing these attendants would think of doing to a loa's host is electrifying it lobotomizing it or removing its clitoris, which was a pre-Freudian technique for "curing" hysteria. No, they don't wish it ill, they welcome it. When a client is handled by an especially vigorous loa the others stand around this person and give it encouragement.

From Ishmael Reed's *Mumbo Jumbo*

Certain other couples are important in voodoo. These include Damballah, the Serpent of the Sky, and his consort Ayida, the rainbow; Loco and Ayizan, who were the first houngan and mambo (priestess); and the Marassa, the twins. The twins are especially mysterious. They are the parents of the human race and as such are the only loas created directly by God. However, they are thought of as children, and on the rare occasions when they mount someone at a ceremony, they inspire the person to act like a child. The Marassa seem like Adam and Eve, divine in strength but human in behavior.

The Ceremony

Voodoo has a bad reputation, which has come mostly from sensationalized accounts of its ceremonies. Two elements in particular disturb white writers and stimulate their imaginations: the use of animal sacrifice to feed the loas, and the fact that ceremonies are held at night. In reading the following description of a ceremony, therefore, you would do well to remember two things. First, Haitians are a rural people, and therefore used to slaughtering animals. Second, the ceremonies have to be at night, since the Haitians work during the day. It's cooler at night, too, so it's easier to dance. Haitians do not have much electricity in their villages, so they are as used to the dark as they are to animal blood.

Ceremonies take place within the *hounfor*, a clearing on which the people have erected sanctuaries. Usually there are at least two—one for the Rada loas and one for the Petro. At the entrance to the hounfor stand one or two trees dedicated to Legba. These are often the hounfor's only boundary markers.

The sanctuary itself is simply a hall with a thatched roof (or more often a roof of corrugated iron); it's called a peristyle. There are doorways in the center of three of its four walls. In the peristyle's center, in line with all three doorways, stands the poteau-mitan, the center pole dedicated to Legba through which the loas arise. Often it's carved in a spiral; it may resemble a snake creeping up a tree. One or more circular concrete steps at the base of the poteau-mitan serve as an altar. Drums hang from the peristyle's ceiling. The main wall is usually painted with the hounfor's colors and the name and symbols of its patron loa.

Along this main wall stand small rooms separated from the rest of the peristyle by doors or beaded curtains. These are loas' rooms, called caye-mystères, bagi, badji, or sobadji. At the back of each stands a small stone altar called a pè. The rooms are jammed with govis, pots, rattles, cards, clothes, candles, and pictures of saints. Here the houngan keeps objects associated with the loas: Legba's crutches, Baron Samedi's top hat, Ogoun's sword, a wooden phallus for Ghede, Erzulie's basin and toilet articles. All these objects, as well as the altar, the peristyle, and the hounfor itself, have been properly baptized to give them psychic strength. The loas have been invited to visit them and use them.

The congregation assembles—the regular congregants (*serviteurs*), the initiates (*hounsis*), the priestesses (*mambos*), the houngan, visiting mambos and houngans. Women usually wear long white dresses, with long sleeves and a high neck, and white handkerchiefs on their heads. Men wear white trousers and shirts. Everyone is barefoot.

To start the ceremony, the houngan lifts a jug of water to the four cardinal points of the compass. He calls on Legba, the Trinity, the loas, the dead, the Marassa. Then, going to the peristyle's front, he pours water three times at the entrance. He pours water in a thin line from the entrance to the poteau-mitan. He draws two similar lines of water from the other two entrances. Then he gives the jug to dignitaries who may be visiting so that they, too, may offer water at the entrance.

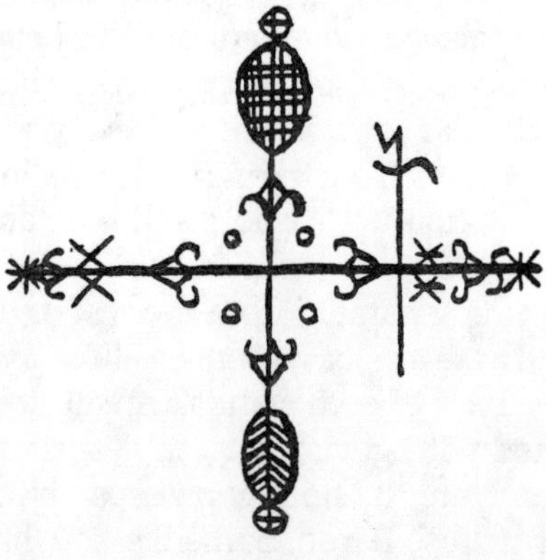

The houngan or his assistant, the *la-place*, next lights a candle and draws the *vèvès*. These are intricate, symbolic emblems of the various loas to be invoked. In some ways they resemble wrought-iron traceries and mandalas. They're drawn on the ground with flour or ashes; if many loas are to be invoked in the ceremony, the vèvès are usually drawn in advance.

When the vèvès are finished, the door of the patron loa's room opens. The la-place, carrying a sword, comes out with two hounsis, each carrying a flag. (Every hounfor has two flags.) The la-place and the hounsis come out backwards (as is appropriate, since they're calling the loas from a mirror world) and make an elaborate procession through the peristyle, saluting the entrances, the poteau-mitan, the drums, the houngan, and the visitors. The houngan and the visitors now salute each other as well. These greetings can take a very long time, since they're highly ritualized and must be done four times each, to each of the points of the compass.

Once everyone has been properly greeted, the congregation begins its prayers. These, too, can be very long. They include Catholic prayers—the Ave Maria and Pater Noster—and the *prière Guinée*, which is recited almost entirely in *langage*, an African-based speech no longer understood completely by anyone except the loas.

The drums begin the *battérie maconnique*, a beating on the doors of les Invisibles. (The drums, by the way, are considered to be sacred and are fed, just like the loas.) This is the time for the sacrifices to begin. Different loas may be fed at different ceremonies, but at every voodoo ritual the serviteurs perform the act of reinvigorating the loas.

The most common sacrifice is a chicken. The houngan holds out the chicken to the four points of the compass, then makes the rounds of the congregation, passing the chicken over the body of each serviteur. Next he swings the chicken through the air, then holds it down to a vèvè. The chicken eats some of the ritual food that's been placed on the vèvè—fruits, grains, vegetables. The houngan then kills the chicken, twisting its neck or slitting its throat. He gives the bird to a cook, who prepares it for the loa's altar. For more elaborate ceremonies, goats, or even a bull, may be sacrificed, affording the loas stronger food.

At last the houngan is ready to call the loas. He begins an invocation, again in langage; the drums beat an appropriate rhythm; the *ogan* (a loud, iron clapper) joins in; the serviteurs sing to the loa. Again, the people perform ritualistically and formally; the patterns are prescribed.

Nevertheless, the congregation feels anxious. They've waited a long time—hours—for the invocation to begin. And the drummers, though they don't improvise, are compelling. The smallest drum taps out a light staccato; the middle drum adds a rounder, rolling tone; the largest drum booms so deeply that it seems to shake the earth. All the serviteurs are up and dancing. Their feet pound the ground; their voices reverberate through the peristyle. The ceremony has become all sound and motion, one great, steadily rising vibration. And then, from the back of the hall, there rises a raucous, nasal laugh. Ghede has appeared.

The loas have begun to mount the serviteurs, some of whom lose their balance and pitch forward on one leg while the loa mounts. Others fall backward abruptly as if struck. Those standing by help to support the serviteur until the loa is well mounted.

The loas identify themselves by their actions. Ghede demands food; Damballah, the serpent loa, hisses; Ogoun struts like a tough soldier. The hounsis at once bring out whatever ceremonial objects they have for the loa (Legba's crutches, for example, or Ogoun's rum). The serviteurs sing a song of welcome; attendants fan him and wipe the sweat from his face. The serviteurs kiss the ground before him, and he in turn prostrates himself to the houngan or mambo, to the poteau-mitan, and to the drums. He shakes hands (usually the left hand) with everyone. It's truly the loa who does all this, because the host, while the loa is mounted, has ceased to exist.

Serviteurs may test the loa to make sure no trickster is at work. They ask Ghede to drink a concoction of rum and twenty-one hot spices; they spray the drink into his eyes. Only Ghede could stand this test. Sometimes a loa will test himself. Ogoun likes to plant his saber in the ground by the hilt, then balance himself on its point. He comes to rest horizontally, his full weight on the saber's point, which pierces his shirt but not his flesh.

When asked for advice or help, loas may perform the miraculous. A story recounted by Maya Deren (in her book *Divine Horsemen*) concerns a ceremony held to heal a dying girl. The serviteurs invoked Ghede, who took possession of one of the mambos at the rite. As part of his cure for the girl, Ghede reached between his legs—that is, the legs of the woman he's possessed—and drew forth a handful of semen, with which he washed the girl. The child lived.

Voodoo Black Magic

We have been discussing the public rituals of voodoo carried out by the houngan and serviteurs, but there are also private rituals carried out by a *bokor*, or sorcerer. One of the ironies of voodoo is that these private rituals owe as much to the black magicians of France as they do to Africa. This influence is not a pleasant one.

The bokor calls primarily on two loas: Carrefour (the Petro counterpart to Legba) and Baron Samedi (the Petro Ghede). Rada loas, incidentally, have little to do with black magic, except when they help to counter it. In sorcery, the Petro loas dominate, and a houngan who's known to be very devoted to the Petro often is accused of "working with both hands"—practicing black magic.

One of the bokor's principal techniques is the *expédition*—sending the dead to trouble or kill an enemy. The bokor first invokes Baron Samedi, who shows his willingness to help by mounting the bokor and giving him orders on how to proceed. Then the bokor goes to a cemetery at midnight and makes an offering of bananas and potatoes in front of the Baron's symbol, the top hat and black coat on a tomb's cross. The bokor takes a handful of cemetery earth for each of the dead he intends to send. He will spread this on a path that the victim frequently takes. To complete the ritual, the bokor recites an invocation to St. Expédit.

Another means of sending the dead is to drive two nails into the roof-beam of the house where someone has died. Then the spirit of the dead person cannot leave. Frustrated, it takes revenge by persecuting its own family.

Bokors also make zombies. Contrary to popular belif, zombies are not evil spirits; rather, they are empty bodies, bodies without gros-bon-anges, and the bokors use them as slave labor. Usually they are taken from people who seem to have died—who have lapsed into a deep coma, for example—and whose families have mistakenly performed the ceremony of separating the gros-bon-ange from the body. In order to avoid such a ghastly error, some Haitians mutilate corpses to make sure they're dead. They also make sure that all clippings from the corpse's hair and nails are buried safely. Bokors can use those, too.

Bokors make use of loas who are greedy enough to sell their services, and of *baka*—gros-bon-anges separated from zombies. Baka often manifest themselves as black cats, dogs, pigs, or cows. The bokor may sell one to a person who's desperate or ambitious. The baka is then called a *point chaud*. It will demand to be fed with the blood of the person's family and will almost certainly end by destroying the person himself.

Sometimes sorcerers who have taken points chaud will band together in a group called a *zobop*. The zobop gathers outside cities and villages for ceremonies at which they wear long red or white robes and hats made of tin horns or high straw cones topped with a lighted candle. They invoke Baron Samedi's aid to help them kill the "goat without horns." Then they find a victim and kill him, usually by waylaying somebody incautious enough to be walking around at night. Occasionally, they will give the victim a chance to join the zobop. To prove himself, he will have to murder a member of his family.

Houngans try to counter the bokors with amulets, talismans, and preparations. To cure illness and reconcile enemies, for example, they use the charm bath of Damballah, a mixture of jasmine flowers, orgeat syrup, powdered almonds, holy water, and champagne. (This preparation will also help one get a job.)

The practices discussed here are not true voodoo, but the kind of medicine-man trade that used to be (and still is) practiced in New Orleans.

MARIE LAVEAU, THE VOODOO QUEEN OF NEW ORLEANS

Marie Laveau held meetings at night in the backyard of her house on St. Ann Street. The following description is by Gerald July, who heard of the meetings through his grandfather's stories.

> They used to meet there every Friday night. . . . A white sheet was spread out on the ground, and lighted candles was stuck up all around the edge of it, and in the middle was about five empty bottles. All the dancers, men and women, was naked. The first thing they did was to dance around on the sheet with bottles of whiskey and rum in their hands, sprinkling the sheet with liquor and throwing it on each other. Then they would begin to do another kind of dance, crossing hands from one side to the other, and all the time singing them Creole songs. Marie Laveau used to stand in the middle, and she was the only one with clothes on. She always wore a long blue dress with a full skirt that reached to her ankles. Sometimes she had her hair loose and hanging down her back, and sometimes she wore a kerchief tied with seven knots and the points sticking straight up. It was what they used to call a *tignon*. She always wore gold hoop earrings and big gold bracelets on her arms.
>
> She would call the numbers—you know what I mean? She would tell the dancers what to do and holler all kinds of funny things. . . . My grandpa said that she would call her snake and make it crawl all over the dancers' legs. . . . She would wrap that snake around her shoulders and she'd shake and twist herself like she was a snake. Her feet would never move. She had another dance she did with a fish. She'd hold a big red fish behind her head and do her snake dance. My grandpa said that was something to see.

From *Voodoo in New Orleans*, by Robert Tallant.

New Orleans

Perhaps some New Orleans adepts practiced the Rada and Petro rites. For the most part, though, New Orleans voodoo was degenerate, reduced to the working of charms, usually through *gris-gris*.

Gris-gris is another term for the *paquett* that is prepared as a charm in Haiti. This is a padded wallet, shaped like an onion, prepared at the full moon and stuffed with various offerings to a loa. The paquett's top is decorated with a tuft of feathers, a mirror, or a cross of Ghede. It must be prepared over a vèvè, consecrated to a Petro loa.

In New Orleans, even the preparation of such paquetts was degraded. For example, the most popular gris-gris, John the Conqueror, wasn't prepared at all. It was simply a phallus-shaped root, used by men to help them get women. There were Love Powder, Sacred Sand, Dragon's Blood, Black Cat Oil, Controlling Oil, Devil's Shoes Strings, and, later, such products as St. Jude Aerosol Spray. A lot of these items can still be ordered from mail-order catalogs.

New Orleans voodoo did have a more serious aspect, but it had little to do with conjuring. Domestic slaves often knew a lot about the lives of their white masters—sometimes more than the masters wanted anybody to know. The slaves would give their information to a houngan or mambo, who thus got the kind of power even loas don't supply.

Dr. John was one such houngan. He was a free black in New Orleans in the first half of the nineteenth century; his most active period was in the 1840s. He said he was a Senegalese prince who had been taken into slavery by the Spanish and brought to Cuba. Eventually his master set him free, whereupon he made his way to New Orleans. There he gained a reputation as a fortune-teller and maker of gris-gris. He saved his money and built a house on the Bayou Road, then began buying slaves. This need not have been as reprehensible as it sounds, for the only safe way for a black to get another black out of slavery was to buy him. On the other hand, all the slaves that Dr. John bought were young and female.

One of Dr. John's informants was Marie Laveau, who for a while worked as a hairdresser, a job that helped her learn family secrets. By 1830 Marie was a voodoo queen. She had a special gift for promotion—she used to sell tickets to ceremonies she held at Lake Ponchartrain. Dozens of white guests paid their money and got their thrills.

Even here there were still elements of real voodoo. According to one witness, Marie would sometimes take a mouthful of whiskey at a ceremony and "blow it in someone's face." Maybe no one else at the ceremony remembered, but Marie did. It was the gesture of Ogoun.

For Further Reading

This article drew heavily on two excellent books: *Divine Horsemen: The Voodoo Gods of Haiti*, by Maya Deren (New York: Delta, 1972), and *Voodoo in Haiti*, by Alfred Métraux (New York: Oxford University Press, 1959). The approach of the first is mythological; of the second, anthropological. *Secrets of Voodoo*, by Milo Rigaud (New York: Pocket Books, 1971), gives a more popular, but rather less reliable, account of the ceremonies. For the story in North America, see Robert Tallant's *Voodoo in New Orleans* (New York: Collier, 1962)—racist and sensationalistic, but at times worthwhile. For more about voodoo's African origins, and for similar forms of ritual, a good place to begin reading is Harold Courlander's *A Treasury of Afro-American Folklore* (New York: Crown, 1976). Also see the very useful *Ecstatic Religion: An Anthropological Study of Spirit Possession and Shamanism*, by I. M. Lewis (Baltimore: Penguin, 1971).

Chapter Five

Gurus

GURU: From the Sanskrit *gur*, to raise or lift up. Any figure who takes personal responsibility for the spiritual lives of a group of disciples; a religious teacher; the head of any religious personality cult; a real or supposed embodiment of God.

"For there shall arise false Christs, and false prophets, and shall show great signs and wonders; insomuch that, if *it were* possible, they shall deceive the very elect."—Matthew 24:24

Babaji (Yogananda)

Somewhere in the Himalayas, probably near Badrinarayan, is an avatar—God in human form. The avatar's name is Babaji, and he's remained in the same body for centuries, perhaps millennia. Babaji casts no shadow; when he walks, he leaves no footprint. He taught Shankara, the great ninth-century philosopher of Vedanta, and Kabir, the medieval yogin saint.

Babaji usually keeps a small group of disciples with him. His closest associate is Jesus Christ, with whom he is in constant communication. Babaji, ultimately, *is* Jesus; the only difference between the two avatars is that Babaji has chosen to remain in his body, whereas Jesus remains in our world only as spirit. As for Babaji's body, it looks like that of a muscular, twenty-five-year-old man with dark eyes and long, copper-colored hair. Babaji requires no food, of course, but he will occasionally eat with a visitor out of courtesy. He prefers astral travel to walking, though he does both. He usually speaks Hindi. He also has a sister, who is called Mataji (or Holy Mother). She lives in an underground cave near Dasasamedh and is reported to be almost as holy as Babaji.

People occasionally go to the Himalayas in search of Babaji, but they rarely find him—he prefers to call disciples. There is a story that on one occasion a seeker did manage to find Babaji and his disciples, who were sitting together on a mountaintop. The seeker begged Babaji to accept him as a disciple. When Babaji refused, the seeker exclaimed, "If you will not accept me, I have nothing to live for. I will jump off this cliff."

"Then jump," Babaji said. "I cannot accept you in your present state of development."

The stranger then jumped off the cliff to his death. Babaji told his disciples to bring back the body. When they did, Babaji touched the stranger, who immediately came back to life. "You are now ready for discipleship," Babaji said, and from then on the man stayed with him.

Given that access to Babaji is so limited, how do we know about him? The information comes from Babaji's principal nineteenth-century disciple, Lahiri Mahasaya. Lahiri Mahasaya was the guru of Sri Yukteswar, who was the guru of Paramahansa Yogananda, who brought word of Babaji to the United States.

In the fall of 1861, Lahiri was working as a government accountant in Danapur. One day a telegram arrived at his office with orders for him: he was to transfer to Ranikhet, 500 miles away in the Almora District of the Himalayas. Lahiri made the trip by horse and buggy, accompanied by one servant. He settled into his duties and in his spare time went climbing in the mountains.

One afternoon, while he was hiking, Lahiri heard someone call his name. He climbed up Drongiri Mountain in search of the caller and came upon a young man who bore a striking resemblance to Lahiri himself. This was Babaji, but Lahiri did not recognize him. When the strange young man explained that it was he who had arranged for the transfer to Ranikhet, Lahiri reacted with disbelief. So Babaji struck Lahiri on the forehead and thus returned to him the memories of his past life, when he'd been one of Babaji's disciples. Lahiri joyously embraced his master and begged to stay with him. Then Babaji materialized a palace in the mountains, in which he initiated Lahiri into Kriya Yoga. This, it seems, is the ancient spiritual science that Krishna taught Arjuna. It teaches the purification of the body by *prānā* and the techniques of astral projection. After the initiation, Lahiri begged permission to give Kriya Yoga to all seekers, even those unprepared for a life of renunciation. Babaji agreed to this, saying, "Give Kriya freely to all who humbly ask for help."

Lahiri taught Kriya Yoga to Sri Yukteswar (1855–1936), who also had the privilege of meeting Babaji three times. Sri Yukteswar taught Kriya Yoga to Paramahansa Yogananda, whom he then sent to the West to teach in 1920. The story of this transmission of knowledge is in Yogananda's *Autobiography of a Yogi* (published by the Self-Realization Fellowship).

Yogananda was born Mukunda Lal Ghosh on January 5, 1893, in Gorakhpur. His father was a Bengali of the military and administrative caste, and both his parents were disciples of Lahiri. According to the *Autobiography*, the boy recovered miraculously from cholera at age eight by praying to Lahiri.

Yogananda's guru sent him to the United States so he could show the West the underlying unity of the Christian and Hindu scriptures. In a surprise visit, Babaji himself gave Yogananda authorization for this project. Babaji told him, "You are the one I have chosen to spread the message of Kriya Yoga in the West." To that end, Yogananda founded the Self-Realization Fellowship and the Yogoda Sat-Sanga Society, which are still active. He died on March 7, 1952.

Baba Ram Dass

Ram Dass was born in 1931 as Richard Alpert, the son of the president of the New Haven Railroad. He grew up in Boston; his religious education was Jewish, of the assimilationist variety. Upon completing his graduate studies, he took a job in the Harvard psychology department and settled down to what should have been a life of material comfort and professional success. Then he met Timothy Leary.

As Ram Dass tells it, he was ready for Leary. For some time he had been troubled by the thought that nobody at Harvard, nobody *anywhere*, had real answers to the important questions. This seemed especially true in Alpert's own field, psychology. People knew a little about behavior and the brain, but who really knew anything about consciousness itself? Who could say what the mind is?

Hoping for an answer, Alpert took a psilocybin trip one night in 1961 at Leary's home. He and Leary spent most of the trip worrying about Leary's dog. The dog had been out in the snow, and it looked chilled when it came in. It looked ill. Probably it was deathly ill. For what seemed like hours, Leary and Alpert tried to decide what to do about the dog. Then one of Leary's children called, and the dog bounded up and walked away, wagging its tail healthily. "Psilocybin," Alpert decided, "wasn't anything to write home about."

Thinking the trip had nothing more to offer, Alpert went alone to the darkened living room and sat down on the couch, his mind still racing from the drug. As he sat there, mulling over his experiences, he suddenly saw an image of himself. He tried to focus on it, but as soon as he did, it changed into a different image of him, a picture of Alpert living a different role. As soon as he understood which of his roles he was seeing, the image would change again. This *was* something to write home about. But a question started nagging him: Where was the real Richard Alpert among this series of images and roles? When this question became insistent, Alpert put his head down and looked at his own body—and saw it had disappeared. He was staring down at an empty couch—nobody was sitting there.

Then, an overwhelming feeling of joy and freedom came over Alpert. The experience was so powerful that he spent the next six years trying to regain it with drugs. During this period, he helped found the Castalia

Foundation, lived with Leary at Millbrook, and travelled widely as a proselytizer for LSD. But, he says he always felt a dreadful doubt. He knew as much about LSD and the psychedelic experience as anybody, perhaps as much as there *was* to know, and still he didn't know anything. The thought was terrifying.

In 1967, when the psychedelic movement was getting out of hand, Alpert left the United States for India. He felt he had to get away to clear his mind. He was also hoping to find someone who could tell him what LSD was, and to that end he carried with him a bottle of LSD tablets. He travelled alone for the most part, talking with holy men, disciples, and other travellers, always hoping to find some answers.

Then he met a young man who told him that he should see Neemkaroli Baba. The young man himself was one of the guru's disciples and was going back to see him; Alpert could follow.

The trek to the guru was long and dispiriting. His introduction to the man was even worse. Neemkaroli Baba was a little old man sitting on a blanket; one of the first things he asked Alpert was whether he would buy him a van of the sort that Alpert had. Baba was hardly a figure to inspire confidence. Still, Alpert had come a long way to see him, so he decided to stay for awhile.

Gradually, Alpert began to understand that Baba only *looked* like a little old man. There was actually a great deal more to him, as Alpert realized one day when Baba began to talk about Alpert's mother. Baba mentioned some thoughts Alpert had been having about his mother and her death, and that upset Alpert since he knew there was no way Baba could have known about those thoughts. At that moment, Alpert surrendered to Baba. Baba knew his thoughts, he realized, because Baba *was* Alpert, and Alpert's mother, and all his disciples, and everybody else. He was a universal consciousness embodied in an old man.

Baba also told Alpert something about LSD. One day Baba swallowed four of Alpert's tablets, enough to give anybody the heebie-jeebies. But Baba didn't seem to react at all. Alpert sat up with the guru all night. The only reaction Baba showed was an occasional giggle. Evidently, LSD had no effect on Baba because Baba *was* LSD.

Alpert returned to the United States in 1968, now as Baba Ram Dass. He lectured widely and effectively, telling his story and offering a fairly non-sectarian explanation of his experiences. He returned to India for more study in 1970, then came to the United States again, this time with Swami Muktananda Paramahansa. In 1971, Ram Dass went to Bodh Gaya (the place where Gautama Buddha attained enlightenment) and began serious meditation. This was at the insistence of Neemkaroli Baba, who had lectured him on the unity of all religions and then thrown him out of the ashram. Ram Dass then took up Theravadan Buddhist meditation as taught by Anagarika Munindra.

At present, Ram Dass is a highly successful lecturer and best-selling author. His most successful work is *Be Here Now* (published by the Lama Foundation). He remains unpretentious and nondogmatic, freely admitting that it's hard to remain an ascetic when money and fame follow him. "Well," he says, "that's show biz."

Bubba Free John

Bubba Free John was born Franklin Jones on November 3, 1939. According to his promotional literature, he "enjoyed the Enlightened or Radiant Condition of Divine Ignorance" from birth. But for thirty years he lived an obscure, ordinary life, willingly submitting to human experience as preparation for his teaching. In September 1970, while meditating in a temple at the Vedanta Society in Hollywood, he completed the first stage of his life by becoming an *avatar*, a manifestation of God.

Bubba said that after his apotheosis he "realized in meditation that I was no longer meditating this body. All its limitations were already obvious, not binding any longer. In meditation I experienced many, many, many people. And I could meditate them. I could be completely identical to them. . . . I could awaken the God-Realizing process in them because I did not have to presume the limited point of view that they were."

Bubba first revealed himself in his writings. He explained his spiritual transformation in his autobiography, *The Knee of Listening* (Los Angeles: The Dawn Horse Press, 1972). In 1972 he began to teach disciples directly. His followers put special emphasis on two periods of his early ministry. In the first half of 1974, he used yogic powers to give people visions, heal the sick, control the weather, and so forth. In the second half of 1976, he encouraged people to seek wealth, power, and physical immortality. Both these periods, his followers say, were intended as theater. Bubba was putting on a show to demonstrate the pitfalls of materialism and spiritualism. The disciples who understood what Bubba was doing came to understand that both material wealth and spiritual powers are ultimately false.

In late 1976, Bubba moved from his Northern California headquarters, Vision Mound Sanctuary, to a secluded house in Hawaii. This was evidently also a theatrical gesture, intended to free his followers from dependence on their surroundings at the sanctuary. He wanted to force them into relying solely on him. This accomplished, he moved back to California in the spring of 1977.

There are four stages to Bubba's teaching: the Way of Divine Communion, the Way of Relational Enquiry, the Way of Re-cognition, and the Way of Radical Intuition. All of these together make up the Way of Divine Ignorance.

A disciple must begin by realizing that the basic human condition is ignorance. You don't know what anything really is, not even your Self. You try to hide this condition from yourself by being self-absorbed, concerned with your self-image, memories, and fantasies. Once you are ready to forget all that and admit to your ignorance, you are ready to follow Bubba Free John. You must surrender yourself to him (the Way of Divine Communion), whereupon he will transform your life, both in its outward aspects (the Way of Relational Enquiry) and in its subtle, spiritual forms (the Way of Re-cognition). Having done so, he will return you to your original, divine condition of ignorance (the Way of Radical Intuition). Because you end up where you began, you must understand that Bubba's teaching is itself a deception of sorts. This is what Bubba calls "the paradox of instruction."

Nonetheless, Bubba claims that his intervention is necessary for true awakening. The disciple's attitude must not be merely devotional, but sacrificial. "Your attachment to me will become overwhelming," he says, "without any goal whatsoever, but a motive of happiness, an indetible simplicity. You will simply commune with me. The energy of your attention will rest with me day by day, hour by hour, moment by moment. And without your doing anything about it, I will meditate you. I will do everything."

Buddha

Buddha was born on the day of the full moon in May, 563 B.C. His father was Suddhodana, King of the Sakyan territory (on the border of modern Nepal and India). His mother, Queen Mahamaya, came from the neighboring Koliya kingdom. She was on the way back to her parents' home in Koliya when she went into labor, and so Buddha was born outside his father's capital of Kapilavastu in Lumbini Park. Mahamaya bore him under a blossoming sala tree. She named him Siddhartha, meaning *wish fulfilled*.

The infant Siddhartha had black hair, blue eyes, and a golden skin. He also had certain markings on his body that indicated to the court sages that he might become an enlightened teacher. King Suddhodana wanted none of that; as far as he was concerned, Siddhartha was to rule the kingdom when the time came. So Suddhodana took measures to guard against Siddhartha's ascetic tendencies. He saw to it that the boy never saw death or decay, and so Siddhartha grew up in uniformly pleasant surroundings. He married his cousin, Yasodhara, after which Suddhodana felt that the prince was safe from asceticism.

But when Siddhartha was twenty-nine, he went for a ride in the country with his charioteer, Channa, and saw an old man. He'd never before seen an old man, and he was appalled. On three subsequent rides, Siddhartha saw an ill man, a funeral procession, and an ascetic wanderer, all of which were new sights to him. In great distress, Siddhartha realized that the essence of life is suffering. Therefore, he abandoned his kingdom, his wife, and his infant son and crossed the river Anoma to the Magadha Kingdom, where he took up an ascetic life.

At this point Siddhartha gave up his given name and started calling himself by his clan name, Gautama. Five Brahmins—Kondanna, Bhaddiya, Vappa, Mahanama, and Assaji—joined him, and they all went to seek a guru. The first one they found was the yogin Ālāra Kālāma. Soon Gautama was Ālāra's equal in meditation. But Ālāra couldn't teach Gautama how to escape from illness, old age, and death, and so Gautama left. His second guru was Uddaka Rāmaputta, who also taught meditation. This time Gautama surpassed his teacher; but again, he was dissatisfied and left. Finally he and his followers settled at Uruvela, determined to find their own way.

Gautama became still more ascetic. His body shrank, and he suffered from pain and hunger. He ignored the weather and often meditated in the graveyard. After six months of this, he collapsed. A shepherd found him and nursed him back to health, after which Gautama rejoined his five followers. They were so upset to see that he'd given up asceticism that they left him. So he continued his spiritual search on his own.

On the night of his birthday, while he sat under a Bodhi tree in meditation, he finally achieved enlightenment. He saw worldly temptations and spiritual delights, his past lives, and the nature of suffering. Some say the meditation lasted for seven days. At the end of it he attained liberation from the cycle of rebirth.

Gautama immediately went to the deer park of Isipatana, near Benares, to find his five followers. He began his ministry by teaching them that the essence of life is suffering, and suffering is caused by desire. People want youth, health, love, sex, peace, pleasant surroundings, good food—but in the course of life all these desires are bound to be frustrated. Therefore, to eliminate suffering, one must eliminate desire, or attachment to the world. The way to eliminate desire is to follow the Noble Eightfold Path. This path is a middle way between asceticism and materialism. The eight parts of this path are ethical precepts that guide the seeker in correct thought and action.

Thus, at age thirty-five, Buddha began his ministry, which was to last for forty-five years.

Some time after he became famous as a teacher, Buddha returned to Kapilavastu at his father's request. There he won over his father to his teaching. He also acquired two important disciples—his son Rahula, whom he'd abandoned at birth, and his cousin Ananda, who became his personal attendant.

After a period of illness, Buddha died in a place called Kusinara (modern Kasia) on the river Hirannavati. He died on the anniversary of his birth. His attendant Ananda made a place for him to lie under two sala trees, and he gave his final instructions to his disciples. After his death his body was cremated.

There is a tradition that Buddha's final illness was caused by some mushrooms he ate. The composer John Cage, who is a student of both mushrooms and Buddhism, was once asked to comment on this tradition. Cage says he reflected for a while on the ecological function of mushrooms. He had read that mushrooms feed on decay, and that if there were no mushrooms, the floors of forests would be choked with decaying matter. His conclusion was that mushrooms exist to dispose of useless garbage, and therefore Buddha died a natural death.

Chögyam Trungpa

Trungpa is what the Tibetan Buddhists call a *tulku*, a being who is an incarnation of high spiritual energy. Such beings used to be fairly common in Tibet, which was the last truly theocratic society in the world until the Chinese conquered it in 1951. Tibet was, in effect, one large monastery governed by an extensive hierarchy of *tulkus*. The highest of the *tulkus*, the Dalai Lama, extended divine compassion and energy to the next highest order of *tulkus*, who in turn passed it on till it reached the lowest classes.

All this changed as the Chinese invaders began to destroy the Tibetan spiritual hierarchy in 1951. According to one of Trungpa's teachers, this meant that "a new era has begun in which the pure doctrine of the Lord Buddha lies in the hands of individuals. . . . We can no longer rely on groups and communities. . . ." Trungpa was twenty years old and a member of the Kagyi school. Since he had received such extensive spiritual education and had become a *tulku*, he had the responsibility to preserve the teaching, and so his teachers ordered him to escape. He fled through the Himalayas with a group of followers and went to India. Later he made his way to Scotland, where he attracted a great many disciples. In the mid-1970s, he moved to the United States and established the Naropa Institute in Colorado, which is now affiliated with the University of Colorado in Boulder.

(Trungpa is not the only *tulku* active in the United States; he is merely the most prominent. Tarthang Tulku is active in the San Francisco area, where he has established the Nyingmapa Meditation Center and the Nyingmapa Institute.)

At the center of Trungpa's teaching is the concept of the *Bodhisattva*, the person who is enlightened but who stays in the world for the purpose of helping others. The *Bodhisattva* is characterized by *Karuna*, meaning *compassionate heart*. "He does not act on 'religious' or 'charitable' grounds at all," Trungpa says. "He just acts according to the true, present moment, through which he develops a kind of warmth. . . . His actions are not limited by anything and all sorts of creative impulses just arise in him and are somehow exactly right for that particular moment."

Don Juan Matus

Matus, who is usually known simply as don Juan, is a Yaqui Indian who was born in Sonora, Mexico, in 1891. In 1900, the Mexican government exiled don Juan and other Yaquis to central Mexico; he lived there (and in the south) until 1940. At that time, apparently, don Juan went to live in Arizona, where he met Carlos Castaneda, a graduate student in anthropology, in the summer of 1960.

Castaneda has recounted his first meeting with don Juan a number of times. The meeting took place in a bus depot, where don Juan was waiting; a friend of Castaneda pointed out the old Indian as a possible informant on the Indian use of plants. Castaneda saw a dark, old man of medium height; his face was lined and he had white hair, but his body seemed light, and his eyes shone. The meeting was uneventful except that Castaneda rambled a lot about peyote (of which he knew little). Then the old Indian got on a bus and left. That would have been the end of it, except that something in the man had intrigued Castaneda, who sought him out at his home a few months later. The two became friendly, and in the summer of 1961, don Juan explained that he did indeed have special knowledge of plants, which he was willing to teach Castaneda. Don Juan, in fact, was a *brujo*, or sorcerer, and Castaneda was to be his apprentice.

The apprenticeship lasted until 1965. During that period, don Juan instructed Castaneda in the use of peyote, Jimson weed, and a smoking mixture that probably contained ground psilocybin mushrooms. Don Juan claimed that the use of these plants would teach Castaneda to become a "man of knowledge" and to gain "power" (an ambiguous but important word in Castaneda's writings). The culmination of this apprenticeship came when Castaneda, during a ritual peyote session, saw the embodiment of peyote, a spiritual personality called Mescalito. Shortly thereafter, Castaneda ended his apprenticeship, claiming he was afraid to go on.

Castaneda's first book on don Juan, *The Teachings of Don Juan: A Yaqui Way of Knowledge*, came out in 1968. Castaneda brought a proof copy to show don Juan and so began his second apprenticeship, which he wrote about in *A Separate Reality*. During that period, don Juan tried to teach Castaneda about seeing (or, as he has it, *seeing*). When one *sees*, the world appears fresh, new, unpredictable, incredible. Living beings appear luminous, and landscapes cease to be solid. Most important, one *sees* that a man of knowledge is not bound by ordinary reality. He can, for example, travel ten miles in an instant, as Castaneda himself saw. Such tricks are used mostly for instructional purposes, to free the student from being "chained to reason."

A Separate Realty supplies three more bits of information about don Juan. He had a son named Eulalio, who died in a rockslide while doing construction work on the Pan-American Highway. He also has a grandson named Lucio, who was born in 1938 and who likes to drink and dress well. Lucio, it seems, will never be a man of knowledge. Finally, don Juan has a friend named Vicente Medrano, who is also a *brujo*. Vicente and don Juan used to sell medicinal concoctions in the market in Oaxaca.

There is no more to know about don Juan. As he explains early in Castaneda's third book, *Journey to Ixtlan*, a man of knowledge must "erase personal history." When Castaneda asked don Juan the names of his mother and father, the *brujo* replied, "Don't waste your time with that crap.

. . . One day I found out that personal history was no longer necessary for me, and, like drinking, I dropped it."

Castaneda seems to have followed don Juan's example. There are no known photographs of Castaneda. There is one pencil drawing of him, which he erased in part. He keeps his whereabouts secret and has revealed little of himself in his writings, only that he comes from South America, that his mother left him when he was six, and that he was raised by a series of aunts. We also know that the anthropology department of UCLA gave him a doctorate in 1973 for *Journey to Ixtlan*.

Beginning with that book, a noticeable change comes into Castaneda's writings. Don Juan sounds less naturalistic and more high-flown. He drops the use of drugs (which he had used only as a preliminary teaching method, to shock Castaneda out of ordinary reality). The conversation becomes more and more concerned with other-worldly topics. This trend continues in *Tales of Power*, in which don Juan and his fellow *brujo*, don Genaro, teach Castaneda about the *tonal* and the *nagual*—the sum of existence and the great Void that lies all around it. At the end of the book, Castaneda plunges off a cliff into the *nagual*. He says that in the jump his perception "went through seventeen elastic bounces between the tonal and the nagual. In my moves into the nagual I perceived my body disintegrating. I could not think or feel in the coherent, unifying sense that I ordinarily do, but I somehow thought and felt." The jump was his farewell to don Juan and don Genaro; he was to see them no more.

But in his most recent book, *The Second Ring of Power* (1978), Castaneda meets a sorceress named doña Soledad who has been sent by don Juan to frighten him into higher knowledge and power. Doña Soledad is assisted by four other dangerous women, all of whom try to steal Castaneda's luminosity.

Nobody knows, of course, how much of this is true. I believe that the first book is substantially factual, that Castaneda did meet don Juan Matus and have the experiences he recounts. Don Juan comes across as a credible figure; the don Juan of that book is the original source of Castaneda's popularity. He is the don Juan who became a guru in the late 1960s, a spiritual guide who helped millions of people make sense out of the psychedelic experience.

As for the other books, they seem to become more and more fictional. Richard de Mille, who wrote a study of Castaneda, shows that Castaneda has borrowed liberally from such authors as Gordon Wasson, Mircea Eliade, Michael Harner, George Foster, and Weston LaBarre. (LaBarre, who is perhaps the most knowledgeable student of peyote, says flat out that Castaneda is a fraud.)

More troubling still is Castaneda's attitude toward women. In his very first book he narrated an encounter with a murderous sorceress named la

Catalina. By the fifth book, we have doña Soledad and her grisly crew. In a review of that book, the poet and mystic Robert Bly wrote that Castaneda had regressed to the level of infantile fantasy and that doña Soledad was a blown-up version of his kindergarten teacher.

Is this a reason to reject don Juan as well as Castaneda (supposing for a moment that one can separate them)? Perhaps Bly had the answer when in the same review he commented on the roots of Castaneda's popularity: "Castaneda good-naturedly gives the capitalist college students what they want—fantasies of gaining power without becoming more compassionate or more honest."

Werner Erhard

Werner Erhard entered this world on September 5, 1935, as John Paul Rosenberg, the son of a Jewish convert to the Episcopal church. He grew up in Philadelphia and married shortly after graduating from high school. Young Rosenberg worked in a variety of places—a construction company, an auto dealership, a meat-packing plant—and seemed to do best as a salesman. He and his wife Pat had four children.

In 1959 he abandoned his family "to avoid the responsibilities I had." He took off for St. Louis with a woman named Ellen (whom he later married); on the way he changed his name to Werner Hans Erhard, which he liked when he saw it in a magazine. He needed a new name in case his wife tried to have him traced. Werner Hans Erhard, he decided, was "as far from John Paul Rosenberg" as he could get. (Erhard now admits freely that he was wrong to abandon his family. He doesn't express regret at having done it, but he says it was wrong.)

Erhard sold used cars in St. Louis for a while and then moved to Spokane, where he sold Encyclopedia Britannica's *Great Books* sets. From 1963 to 1969, he worked for *Parents' Magazine* and was so successful with them that he became a vice-president. Then he took a job as manager for the Grolier Society, which sold encyclopedias door-to-door.

All this time, Erhard says, he was studying various disciplines that might help him in business. These included Zen, hypnosis, and scientology. He took the scientology communication course and completed the first four grades of scientology training. He admits, again quite freely, that he borrowed scientology techniques and doctrines when he developed his own training program, est.

In developing est, he made use of one more training program, Mind Dynamics. This was a course developed by Alexander Everett, based on the teachings of the Christian Unity Church and methods of hypnotism. Erhard became a Mind Dynamics teacher and for a period was the organization's national sales director.

In 1971 Erhard had an experience of enlightenment while driving down a

California highway. Suddenly, Erhard says, the quality of his experience was transformed. That transformation was to be the key to his est training. So he left Mind Dynamics and founded est.

A few words about the est training: It is done in large groups (often several hundred) over a period of four days, each of which lasts from six to ten hours. Usually, the first two days are a weekend; there's a midweek evaluation session, and then the last two days are the following weekend. There's also a post-training meeting.

During the four days of training, the subjects must stay in their seats without talking. They are not allowed to leave the room, even to go to the bathroom. They must not smoke, eat, wear wristwatches, or sit next to anyone they know. Anyone who breaks these rules is thrown out of the training.

Much of the training consists of lectures about cause and effect, the nature of reality, and the phenomenon of time. The trainer relieves the boredom by browbeating his audience and calling them assholes. Every once in a while, the trainer leads the subjects in relaxation exercises and "affirmations" (the subjects repeat, "We are all feeling good. We can be great. We are great," and so forth). There are visualization exercises as well. The subjects are asked to picture a "psychic workshop," complete with electronic equipment, file cabinets, and assistants.

The est organization is careful to point out that est is not a method of psychotherapy. The est president, Don Cox, also says that "No claims, guarantees or promises of results are made for the est training." He does claim that est can "transform . . . one's experience of experiencing, one's experience of knowing, one's experience of self." Critics of est often point out that such statements are gibberish. Followers of est agree and then ask why that should matter.

Erhard is now a guru in two senses. The people in est revere him as a teacher and leader, and he qualifies on that count alone. But more important, he qualifies as a salesman. Even the most enthusiastic est followers admit that est is a patchwork of other mind-control methods. Erhard has packaged those methods. He is the spiritual salesman for our times, and it's made him a rich man.

Wallace D. Fard

Wallace Fard was a door-to-door peddler who appeared in the black community of Detroit in 1930. He sold raincoats and silk. As part of his sales pitch, he would talk about the "home country"—not just his home, he emphasized, but the home of all black people. In a short time, by means of his vivid stories about a vague homeland, he attracted a following. He began to hold meetings in people's homes, advising them about diet and health and interpreting the Bible for them. He explained that the Bible was a distorted text, a code of sorts, whose true version was the Koran, a book, unfortunately, little known to his followers.

When the house meetings became large enough, Fard rented a building, established the Temple of Islam, and began to proclaim his message more boldly. He had come from Mecca, he said, to announce that the Battle of Armageddon would take place soon in North America and that it would be fought between blacks and whites. Islam was the natural religion of the black man (Fard refused the term *Negro*); Christianity was a hoax invented by the white race. Fard (or Wali Farad, Professor Ford, W.D. Farad Muhammad, F. Mohammad Ali, depending on the occasion) had the authority to reveal these truths because he was himself the Supreme Ruler of the Universe.

The Detroit police, having gotten word of Fard's teachings, began to harass him. They jailed him in 1932 and ordered him out of Detroit in May 1933. He went to Chicago to proselytize and was jailed again. Meanwhile, his following grew. He set up a University of Islam, a Muslim Girls' Training Class, and a quasimilitary organization, the Fruit of Islam. Then, gradually, he withdrew from leadership of the Nation of Islam. He disappeared in June 1934.

Fard was neither the only black avatar of the period nor the only black man preaching religious nationalism. In the same year that Fard appeared in Detroit, a preacher from South Carolina, George Baker, declared himself reborn as Father Divine. His home church, in Sayville, Long Island, became known as Heaven; his Peace Missions (combination communes, soup kitchens, and employment agencies) spread crosscountry. At the peak of his popularity, in the mid-1930s, he had hundreds of thousands of followers who believed he was God. Somewhat earlier in the century, Timothy Drew (also known as Noble Drew Ali) founded the Moorish Science Temple of Newark. Like Fard, he emphasized the Eastern origin of American blacks, taught that Islam was superior to Christianity, and predicted the destruction of the white race. Fard was in many ways more mysterious than other preachers of his time, but he was not unique.

Why, then, did Fard's Nation of Islam—or Black Muslims—survive where other sects failed? The answer lies in the abilities of the man Fard picked as his Minister of Islam, Elijah Muhammad.

Muhammad was born in Georgia in 1897 as Elijah Poole. He came to Detroit in the 1920s and became one of Fard's earliest converts. After Fard's disappearance, when power struggles broke out in the Temple of Islam, Muhammad moved to Chicago and set up his headquarters at Temple Number 2, which remains to this day the center of the Nation of Islam. Muhammad revealed that Fard had been Allah; Muhammad himself became the Messenger of Allah.

Muhammad's teachings are in all likelihood taken faithfully from Fard.

According to these beliefs, one of the greatest falsehoods of the white race is "that God is a spirit (spook) and not a man. . . . Well, we all know that there was a God in the beginning that created all these things and do know that He does not exist today. But we know again that from that God the person of God continued until today in His people" (i.e., in the black race, which is divine).

According to the Muslim cosmology, God, who was "one of our scientists," tried to destroy the world some sixty trillion years ago because he couldn't get all the people to speak the same language. Therefore, he engineered a great explosion, which tore the planet in two. The smaller part became the Moon and the larger, the Earth. The tribe of Shabazz, which was left on Earth, explored their new planet and made their capital in Mecca. Those black people in exile in America are the lost tribes of Shabazz.

The troubles of Shabazz began when an apostate scientist named Yakub created the white race by means of a grafting experiment, which took him 600 years. Allah decreed that the whites would rule the world for 6,000 years, a period that ended in 1914. Now we are in a seventy-year grace period in which Allah will gather the lost Muslims of the West.

Elijah Muhammad died in 1975. His son, Wallace Muhammad, became head of the Nation of Islam, and under his leadership the group has modified its beliefs and policies. It no longer teaches that whites are devils, and it admits white members. The group has not changed its social policies: It emphasies black pride, self-help, self-defense, and the rescue of convicts, addicts, and bums. These social policies have made a lasting contribution to black Americans. Perhaps a more fitting theology is evolving.

Guru Maharaj Ji

Guru Maharaj Ji, the world's youngest Perfect Master, was born in Hardwar, India, on December 10, 1957. He was the youngest of the three sons of Yogi Raj Param Sant Satgurudev Sri Hans Ji Maharaj, a man from a wealthy family who had devoted his life to preaching to the poor. When Sri Hans Ji died in 1966, he passed on his status as Perfect Master to Maharaj Ji, who was nine at the time. The young *satguru* also inherited leadership of the Divine Light Mission, which his father had founded in 1960.

The Guru first came to the United States in 1971 and attracted scant notice. He came back in 1972 and attended a festival held in his honor in Colorado. By then he had a sizable following. In 1973 he had enough followers to rent the Houston Astrodome for a three-day festival. By 1974, a publicist for the Divine Light Mission claimed that sixty thousand Americans had become followers of the Guru.

What did he have to offer? Guru Maharaj Ji claims to transmit Divine Knowledge personally and directly. This technique is called *gurukripa* and is practiced by others as well. (See the section on Swami Muktananda in this chapter.) The Guru, or a teacher empowered by him to transmit Knowledge, offers four inner essences for the initiate to meditate on. The essences are inner light, inner sound, inner taste (or nectar), and a *mantra* that attunes the devotee to cosmic energy.

The Guru's detractors claim that all this is trickery. The initiate sees an inner light because the *mahatma* jams his fists against the disciple's closed eyes. For the inner music, the *mahatma* cups his hands over the initiate's ears (the roar-in-a-seashell effect). For the nectar, the *mahatma* tips back the disciple's head, whereupon the disciple swallows a trickle of mucous. These tricks work because the disciple has been kept in a small room and harangued for two hours or so, after which he or she is impressionable.

Still, the Guru's followers are content with what they've received, and no scandal would have attached itself to the Divine Light Mission if it hadn't been for Pat Halley. On August 7, 1973, in Detroit, Halley threw a shaving-cream pie in the Guru's face. News cameras caught the incident. Halley told reporters he'd done it because "I always wanted to throw a pie in God's face." Not long thereafter, two men, a young American and a middle-aged Indian, contacted Halley, saying they had become disaffected with the Divine Light Mission and wanted to reveal its secrets to him. With Halley's consent, they came to his apartment and told him they would show him how the Guru transmitted Divine Knowledge. Then they beat in Halley's skull with a bludgeon. He lived, but only just, and he now wears a plastic plate in his skull.

The alleged attackers were Richard Fletcher (one of the Guru's first American converts) and Mahatma Fakiranand (who is authorized by the Guru himself to give Knowledge). There was little or no effort by the police to arrest these men or by the Guru to discipline them.

On May 19, 1974, Guru Maharaj Ji married his twenty-four-year-old secretary, Marilyn Lois Johnson. His mother, Sri Mata Ji, reacted angrily, announcing that he was no better than a playboy. She appointed his oldest brother, Bal Bhagwan Ji, to be the new head of the Divine Light Mission and to be Perfect Master. A lawsuit followed, and in May 1975, an Indian judge refused to rule on the case (though he did lecture both Bal Bhagwan Ji and Maharaj Ji on the evils of "deceiving others in the name of God").

Following the end of the suit, Guru Maharaj Ji returned to his home in Denver, leaving his mother in effective control of the Divine Light Mission.

Haile Selassie

Unlike the other gurus in this chapter, Haile Selassie claimed neither divinity nor enlightenment. He had divinity thrust upon him by a Jamaican sect, the Rastafarians, who have become famous in recent years through the influence of reggae music and marijuana. There are no reliable figures on the sect's membership, but there are probably about seventy thousand Rastafarians, almost all of whom live in Jamaica. There is an expatriate group in the United States. And, of course, there are many sympathizers who know the Rastafarians principally through Bob Marley and the Wailers.

The movement began in 1930, soon after the coronation of Haile Selassie as Emperor of Ethiopia. Until his coronation, he was known as Ras Tafari (or Prince Tafari); hence the name of the cult. Like the other emperors of Ethiopia, Haile Selassie claimed to be the only true descendant of King David. This claim attracted the notice of several Jamaicans, notably Leonard Howell and Joseph Hibbert. Both men were widely travelled and in the habit of reading the Bible for hidden meanings. Working independently, both came to the conclusion that Haile Selassie was God.

The key Biblical passage in their argument was Jeremiah 8:21: "For the hurt of the daughters of my people am I hurt; I am black; astonishment hath taken hold of me." This is proof that God is black. The God of the white people is actually the Devil. The true God had appeared before as Moses, Elijah, and Jesus; His final incarnation is Haile Selassie, who will lead his people, the true Israelites, out of their exile in Jamaica (or Babylon).

One of the early tenets of the Rastafarians was that the Jamaican government had £23 million in its treasury for the repatriation of black people to Ethiopia. The money had been untouched since the emancipation of 1834. With the ascension of Haile Selassie to the throne, the use of the money was imminent. This belief becomes more understandable in the context of the time. Marcus Garvey's back-to-Africa movement had recently failed, destroying the hopes of many Jamaicans. Messianic movements were becoming more common in black communities. (See the entry on Wallace D. Fard in this chapter.)

The Rastafarians, as black nationalists, met immediately with police harassment. Howell responded by setting up a commune (or shantytown) called Pinnacle, with ganja as a cash crop. The harassment continued, and by the early 1950s, security was a preoccupation at Pinnacle. The Rastafarians acquired fierce guard dogs and adopted the custom of letting their hair and beards grow freely, giving them an appearance that the police found threatening. The hairstyle became known as *dreadlocks*, appropriately enough. There was a Biblical justification for it as well, in Leviticus 21:5: "They shall not make baldness upon their head, neither shall they shave off the corner of their beard, nor make any cuttings in their flesh."

In 1954 the Jamaican government broke up Pinnacle. As an attempt at destroying the Rastafarians, this was a complete failure. The Rastas returned to Kingston, where they were highly visible and obstreperous. They had major clashes with the police in 1958 and again in 1959, after the failure of a repatriation scheme. The long, slow decline of the Jamaican economy has added to their number.

Curiously, the death of Haile Selassie seems to have had little effect on the cult. Rastafarians maintain that there can be no death for the true believer. Thus, Haile Selassie lives for them, even though his body has been dispersed to the elements.

L. Ron Hubbard

Hubbard, the founder of the Church of Scientology, was born in Nebraska in 1911. For most of his early life he was a writer of pulp science fiction (see the article on him in chapter eight). His career as a religious leader began in 1950 with the publication of his book *Dianetics: The Modern Science of Mental Health.*

Dianetics, in Hubbard's own words, is "a milestone for Man comparable to his discovery of fire and superior to his inventions of the wheel and the arch." Hubbard claimed to have used rigorous scientific methods to prove that the human mind is composed of two parts: the analytical mind and the reactive mind. The analytical mind (what we usually call the conscious mind) is fully rational and works much like a computer. The reactive mind is irrational and can override the functioning of the analytical mind. All of our problems can be traced to the tyranny of the reactive mind.

The problem, Hubbard claimed, is that the reactive mind is always at work, recording everything that happens. That's fine, so long as we are awake and well. But when we are asleep, or when the analytical mind is clouded by illness, the reactive mind has nothing to check it. At such times, the reactive mind is liable to record painful experiences, which later block the functioning of the analytical mind. These blocks are called engrams. Not only do engrams prevent us from thinking clearly, but they also block out our very knowledge of the reactive mind. Moreover, engrams can be formed prenatally, and they can be carried over from one incarnation to the next. Thus, our problems often are based on experiences we didn't even know we had, and the mechanism that maintains those problems is in our own bodies. The reactive mind is located in the body's cells.

Despite Hubbard's claims of having established dianetics scientifically, he has never produced any experimental evidence acceptable to the scientific community for his theories, much less obtained independent verification. Indeed, it's hard to imagine anyone's attempting to verify theories that are so foreign to everything known about physiology.

But if dianetics is unsupported from a scientific viewpoint, what are we to think of its outgrowth, scientology? According to Hubbard, his greatest discovery, the keystone of scientology, was made in July 1951 in Phoenix, Arizona. As he explained in *Scientology: The Fundamentals of Thought*, "I established along scientific rather than religious or humanitarian lines that the thing which is the person, the personality, is separable from the body and mind at will without causing bodily death or derangement."

In other words, Hubbard had become interested in the soul and astral travel. He named his "scientifically verified" soul a *Thetan*. In order to enlighten the Thetans of this world, he incorporated the Founding Church of Scientology in Washington, D.C., in 1955.

The basic technique of scientology is called auditing; the basic equipment is called an E-meter. An E-meter is a device that measures the electrical resistance of the body. The "patient" holds two cans, which are attached to a battery and a meter; an emotional disturbance in the patient will register on the meter. In other words, an E-meter is a junior-high-school version of a lie detector. It is used in auditing to detect the patient's engrams. The counselor (or "auditor") chats with the patient and notes which subjects tend to disturb the meter's needle. Then the auditor works with the patient until there's no longer a measurable reaction to those subjects. The engram is then declared to be dissolved. When most of one's engram's are dissolved, one becomes a "release," free from neurosis and psychosomatic illness. When all the engrams are dissolved, one becomes a "clear." Hubbard says that clears are to ordinary humans as ordinary humans are to the hopelessly insane.

Having become a clear, one may then go on to become an Operating Thetan, free of all the bad influences that have built up over the past thirty-five billion years. An Operating Thetan not only can leave the body at will, but can create matter, energy, space, and time.

In the course of becoming an Operating Thetan, the scientologist attempts to project his problems onto other people (this is called "R2-46 type processes") and to recognize enemies, in particular enemies of scientology. This leads us to the question of the politics of scientology.

Formerly, the scientologists had a category of enemies called FAIR GAME. Hubbard described this category in a now-famous bulletin: "A person relegated to Condition of Enemy is considered FAIR GAME: may be deprived of property or injured by any means by any Scientologist, without any discipline of the Scientologist. May be tricked, sued, or lied to, or destroyed."* In October 1968, Hubbard rescinded this bulletin.

More recently, the church has been involved in a federal court case. In July 1977, the F.B.I. raided the church's headquarters in Los Angeles and Washington, D.C., and seized some 48,000 church documents. In 1978, federal prosecutors used the documents to issue an indictment of the church for conspiracy to infiltrate government agencies, burglarize government offices, and bug federal property. Church officials replied by saying the indictment was part of a twenty-year government program of harassment. They accused the government of violating the First and Fourth

---

*Quoted in *Mindstyles/Lifestyles*, by Nathaniel Lande (Los Angeles: Price/Stern/Sloan, 1976).

Amendments and initiated a successful suit to get documents that the National Security Agency had compiled about the church.

Meanwhile, Hubbard remains above the fray. He is in semiretirement on a yacht that cruises in the Atlantic and the Mediterranean (the yacht is part of a fleet called the Sea Org). Hubbard can well afford his expensive home. The standard estimate of his personal wealth is $7 million.

Jesus of Nazareth

There are too many interpretations of the life of Jesus, too many occult variations on the story of his life to summarize here. The basic historical information is as follows.

He was born in a time of rebellion. In the year he was born (probably 6 B.C.), the Romans crucified some two thousand Jewish rebels, hanging their bodies around the walls of Jerusalem. (Crucifixion was reserved for political criminals.) In Nazareth, the village in Galilee where Jesus grew up, rebel sentiments were especially high, so much so that the words *Galileean* and *Zealot* meant almost the same thing.

The Israelites had lost their independence in 586 B.C. with the Babylonian exile and regained it for a brief period under the Maccabees (168–165 B.C.). During Jesus' life, however, Palestine was ruled by the Romans, who had taken control in 63 B.C. Some of the Jews had accommodated themselves to Roman rule. The Sadducees, the Jewish priestly class, kept up close relations with the Romans. The Pharisees, a large sect that had arisen in the second century B.C., thought it best to go about their business and avoid conflict with the Romans. They observed the law strictly and had little political influence. But at least two sects, the Essenes and the Zealots, were actively opposed to the Romans, and Jesus had close ties with both.

The Zealots, among whom Jesus lived in Galilee, were violent and directly political. The Essenes, who had a monastic center in the desert at Qumrān, were more ritualistic and mystical. The two sects shared an apocalyptic belief that was both religious and political. They believed God was about to send a Redeemer, who would lead Israel in battle against the Romans and with the aid of the armies of Heaven establish the Kingdom of God.

So when people called Jesus the Messiah, the word had a political and national meaning as well as a religious one. The same was true of the term *Son of David*. Only the term *Son of man* had an essentially religious meaning; but it too had nationalistic overtones. None of these terms implied divinity. The Messiah was to be heaven-sent, but human.

This is the background, the context of Jesus' life. As for the facts, he was born in Bethlehem (as prophesied in the Old Testament) to a carpenter named Joseph and a woman named Miriam (Mary). They gave him the name Joshua, meaning *God helps*. According to Matthew, Bethlehem was

Joseph's home. According to Luke, Joseph and Mary were in Bethlehem because that was Joseph's ancestral town, to which they had to go for purposes of an imperial census and tax collection. Whatever the case, Jesus grew up in Nazareth. He had four brothers: Jacob (James), Joseph, Judas, and Simon—and a famous cousin, John the Baptist.

John was an ascetic who lived in the desert and prophesied the coming of the last days. He called on people to purify themselves and repent in preparation. John's cult wes popular, and Jesus evidently belonged to it for a while, as evidenced by his baptism. (The gospels, especially that of John, have passages addressed to the members of John's cult, trying to demonstrate that John was not the Messiah but the reincarnation of the prophet Elijah, who was to foretell the coming of the Messiah.)

After his baptism, Jesus went into the desert to pray and meditate. Perhaps he was in contact with the Essenes at this point. Then he began his ministry in Galilee, mostly around the northwest bank of Lake Gennesaret. This part of the ministry lasted for about a year. The details are familiar to everyone—the gathering of the disciples, the Sermon on the Mount, the miracles, the Transfiguration, the prophecies of his death and Resurrection. Then Jesus went to Jerusalem. He challenged the authorities almost at once by driving the moneychangers out of the Temple. He was arrested by the Romans and taken before the Sanhedrin, the Jewish council of elders, for examination. They gave him a show trial (the Sanhedrin did not have the authority to issue the death penalty, and the gospels' accounts of Jesus' trial by them are historically suspect). Then the Roman governor of Judea, Pontius Pilate, ordered Jesus' execution. He was crucified, probably on the day before Passover, along with two other rebels. (The word the Greek text uses for the two men means both *robber* and *rebel*.)

Then, according to the gospels, Jesus rose from the grave, showed himself to his disciples and others, and ascended to Heaven.

In the years following Jesus' ministry, Christianity remained a Jewish sect, whose adherents continued to interpret the idea of the Messiah in the Jewish manner. They did not see Jesus as divine. But after the Church split (see Acts 15), the disciples began to preach to non-Jews. From then on, the concept of the Messiah had more than a nationalistic meaning (though it still probably had anti-imperial connotations). Jesus was the Redeemer of *all* the nations; he was not only the Son of David but also the Son of God.

In what sense was Jesus the Son of God? The followers of the bishop Athanasius believed Jesus was of the same substance as the Father. The followers of the bishop Arius believed Jesus was of a *similar* substance to that of the Father—thus, Jesus was the highest being of Creation but was still less than God. In 325, the Church adopted Athanasius's belief at the Council of Nicea and declared Jesus to be "very God of very God, begotten not made." Still, that wasn't the end of the matter. The question of Jesus' divinity was settled by politics and force of arms, not church councils.

The history of mainstream Christianity is of course well known. For the esoteric side of church history and its influence on the occult, see chapter seven.

For more on the life of Jesus, see *The Problem of the Historical Jesus*, by Joachim Jeremias (Philadelphia: Fortress Press, 1964); *Jesus: A New Biography*, by S.J. Case (New York: Greenwood Press, 1968); *Jesus*, by David Flusser (New York: Herder and Herder, 1969); *A New Quest of the Historical Jesus* by James M. Robinson (Naperville, Ill.: A.R. Allenson, 1959); and *The Historical Jesus and the Kerygmatic Christ*, edited by Carl E. Braaten and Roy A. Harrisville (New York: Abingdon, 1964). For a good popular summary, see *The Wilderness Revolt*, by Diane Kennedy Pike (Garden City: Doubleday, 1972).

Strange Beliefs and Practices of the Christians

Few occult groups can rival the cult of Jesus Christ for religious extremism. Christianity has brought us desert hermits who slept in their own filth and lusted after demons; bands of self-flagellants who roamed medieval Europe rejoicing in the plague; snake-handlers; sects that practiced herbalism, speaking in tongues, frenzied dancing, and even free love and nudism.

The first Christian churches had little in common except a reverence for Jesus. Some Christians were pious Jews who observed every scruple of the Mosaic law; others were Greek gnostics who knew nothing about Moses. Some Christians withdrew from the world, fasted, and awaited the apocalypse. Others organized armies of illiterate monks who destroyed pagan and heretic temples.

The principal Christian rite, communion, is, in its most basic form, an attempted act of cannibalism. The early church was split as to whether the rite should be sexual as well. Some Christian "love feasts" were orgies of the Dionysian sort. Other churches restricted communion to celibates. The Eastern Orthodox Church disapproved of sex to such an extent that the monks of Mount Athos barred all females, including donkeys and chickens, from their community. Origen, the first great church philosopher, went still further. He castrated himself in devotion to God.

After the Church became established in the third century, it began a long and unsuccessful campaign against heresy. In A.D. 373, the Church destroyed most of antique literature by burning the Empire's libraries as part of a campaign against heterodoxy. Despite such measures, the Church never defined or eliminated heresy to everyone's satisfaction. Gnostic cults remained in most medieval cities, and new heretics continued to arise—Cathars, Albigensians, Anabaptists. The orthodox accused each group in turn of sexual license, homosexuality, and traffic with demons. (These were the same charges that reformers and heretics, from St. John Chrysostom through Savonarola, levelled at the established Church.)

The Reformation didn't improve matters. Each of the four hundred Protestant sects went through its own special form of extremism as it arose.

In the sixteenth century, Martin Luther railed against not only the Roman Church but also the Jews and the poor. In an act that set something of a precedent in Germany, he invoked God's approval for the slaughter of 100,000 peasants in the revolt of 1524.

In the seventeenth century, George Fox encouraged his Quaker followers to disrupt public meetings and church services by walking naked through the crowds, crying "Repent!" His contemporaries attributed much of Fox's success to his charm with women.

In the eighteenth century, John Wesley, the founder of Methodism, was as popular with women as Fox had been, sending them into ecstatic convulsions with his preaching. Wesley also predicted that Halley's comet would incinerate the Earth on its next approach, thus making him the first religious leader to combine Christianity with science fiction.

In the nineteenth century, Protestant zeal took its most striking forms in America. Members of the Church of Jesus Christ of Latter-day Saints (Mormons) believe that their founder, Joseph Smith, found and translated a holy book written in the fourth century A.D. by a native American prophet. Members of the Church of Christ, Scientist, agree with yogins and Buddhists that the material world is an illusion, a projection of mind. (This did not stop the sect's founder, Mary Baker Eddy, from having a telephone installed in her crypt in Mount Auburn Cemetery, Cambridge.) Members of the Jehovah's Witnesses hold many beliefs in common with the Arian heretics. (See above article on Jesus Christ.) They also maintain, contrary to considerable evidence, that the Kingdom of God began in 1914.

Centuries of theological squabbles have not clarified even the most important points of faith and practice. So Christianity remains a remarkably diverse faith. It has produced not only its Anselms and Abelards but also its A.A. Allens. (Allen, an evangelist who worked out of Miracle Valley, Arizona, was famous for the slogan, "Let God be your dentist.") Christian brothers practice ancient tribal religious feasts in Africa and marry homosexual couples in America. Christian sisters take lifelong vows of silence in convents or, like Aimee Semple McPherson, hold forth from the pulpit.

New Christian cults are being formed all the time. There are now some American Christians who believe that Jesus is living on Venus and will return in a spaceship. The Mormons await the establishment of the Kingdom of Heaven in Independence, Missouri. Billy Graham has pontificated on God's plan of salvation for extraterrestrial visitors, should any such lost souls appear. Some groups of Jesus people take drugs as part of their communion. All indications are that Christianity will continue to diversify, welcoming even more generations of religious lunatics to their natural spiritual home.

Jim Jones

Jim Jones, the founder and god of the Peoples Temple, invented something genuinely new in religion—voluntary mass martyrdom. Granted, there is already a long history of religious suicide: Groups of early Christians actively sought persecution, thousands of Jews accepted death rather than abandon their faith, devotees of the Hindu god Jagannath celebrated his processions by throwing themselves under the huge cart that bore his idol. But with the suicide of Jones and some nine hundred followers in Guyana, we have something radically modern. Jones thought his followers had sinned by living in a racist, capitalist society. For this collective sin, there had to be a collective crucifixion. This notion, however crazy, is a consistent synthesis of the teachings of Jesus and Lenin—the two gods Jim

Jones claimed to embody.

James Warren Jones was born in 1931 in Lynn, Indiana, a farm town. His mother supported the family by working in a factory and doing odd jobs. His father, an invalid, mostly stayed inside, except when he had a Ku Klux Klan meeting to go to. As a schoolboy, Jones rebelled against his parents in two ways: He declared himself to be against racism, and he became attracted to the more emotional fundamentalist sects, such as the Church of the Nazarene and the Pentecostal Church.

In 1950, Jones moved to Indianapolis, where he became a pastor in a church, spoke out for civil rights, and began taking classes part-time at Butler University. (He received his bachelor's degree in 1960 and was ordained as a minister in 1965.) He opened the Peoples Temple in 1956 as a church committed to social action, where blacks and whites would be equally welcome. His reputation was good enough that in 1960 he received an appointment as director of the Indianapolis Human Rights Commission.

Within his church, though, he already was showing signs of erratic behavior. He set up an interrogation committee to discipline church members who differed with him. He took up faith-healing. In 1963, he had a vision of a coming nuclear war and decided he had to move his church out of the way of the bombs.

The spot he chose was Ukiah, California. In the summer of 1965, about 150 emigrated to the new Peoples Temple there. Jones set about making friends with local officials and organizing a travelling revival show to spread his good news. During this period he acquired an armed bodyguard and began claiming to have resurrected people.

In September 1972, Jones bought a building in San Francisco and moved the Peoples Temple there. Again, he made friends with local groups, politicians, and the press. Membership expanded. He degenerated.

He began to direct the sex lives of his followers, using the principle that he was the only one allowed to have any. He forced couples apart and used the Temple members, male and female, as his harem. He became addicted to pills. He used beatings to discipline his followers; for unruly children, he used electric shocks. He pressed his followers to contribute the bulk of their salaries to the Temple. Many of the members were on Social Security and turned their checks over to Jones. (The Temple's financial secretary, Deborah Layton, said the Temple cashed $65,000 in Social Security checks each month.) By 1977, the Temple had assets of $10 to $15 million. Membership in the Temple was three-quarters black; the ruling clique was two-thirds white.

Some of these details began to come out in the press in 1977 (particularly in *New West* magazine). Jones decided it was time to leave the country. In 1974, he had leased 27,000 acres of land from Guyana and begun to build

Jonestown in the jungle. Within a few months in 1977, he moved some four hundred followers there.

There was a loudspeaker system in Jonestown, and Jones used it for about six hours a day. During his sermons, or harangues, he revealed that he was the reincarnation of Jesus and Lenin. He also began to talk about mass suicide in the cause of socialism. Once a week, he would organize a White Night, a suicide drill in which Temple members would drink Kool-Aid that was supposedly poisoned.

These newest details reached not the press, but the government. The families of some Temple members appealed to California Congressman Leo Ryan to help get their relatives back. Ryan took the stories he heard seriously, and on November 14, 1978, he left for Guyana with a crew of newsmen and fourteen relatives of Temple members. After difficult negotiations, Ryan and some of his party got to tour Jonestown. Despite the efforts of Jones and his lieutenants to keep everybody in line, twenty people approached Ryan and asked to be taken away.

On the afternoon of November 18, Ryan's party and some of the Temple fugitives left Jonestown for the Port Kaituma airstrip, where two planes were waiting to take them away. While Ryan's people were making their way to the planes, three or four of Jones's lieutenants drove up in a tractor and began shooting. Another of Jones's lieutenants had entered a plane with a group of fugitives; he, too, began to shoot. There were several Guyanese soldiers on the scene, but they were afraid to open fire on the attackers—they couldn't get a clear shot. By the time the attack ended, five people were dead, Leo Ryan among them.

That same afternoon, Jones ordered his lieutenants to mix vats of Kool-Aid and cyanide. Over the camp loudspeakers, he ordered his followers to accept their doom—children first—because "We're going to meet in another place." Those who would not willingly drink the poison were forced at gunpoint.

An afternote: A study commissioned by Secretary of State Cyrus Vance, released in May 1979, charged the State Department with "errors and lapses" in its handling of the Peoples Temple. The report said that the State Department had received warnings and petitions about the church beginning in May 1978, but that the warnings had been ignored.

Krishna (Kṛṣṇa)

Krishna was the eighth *avatar*, or incarnation, of the god Vishnu (Visnu). His name means *black* or *dark as a cloud;* artists often portray him with blue skin. (The historical Krishna was probably a man named Vāsudeva-Kṛṣṇa, a prince who had attained the status of a god by the fifth century B.C.)

Krishna's mother Devakī was the sister of a wicked king named Kaṃsa who ruled a place in Uttar Pradesh. Kaṃsa had heard a prophecy that his sister's child would slay him. Therefore, he tried to have all of Devakī's children slaughtered. But Krishna's parents smuggled the infant across the River Yamuna to Gokula, where a cowherd named Nanda took charge of him.

Krishna thus grew up as a cowherd. While still a child he performed many miracles, such as silencing the thunder god, Indra. When he played the flute, the wives and daughters of the cowherds would follow him, enchanted, to dance with him in the forest. His favorite lover was Rādhā.

Upon growing to manhood, Krishna went home with his brother Balarāma and killed King Kaṃsa. Then he led his clan west and set up a court at Dvārakā, in Gujarāt. His chief wife there was Rukmiṇī.

When two related clans, the Pāṇḍavas and the Kauravas, went to war with each other, Krishna refused to take sides. Instead, he offered to loan his army to one side and to fight on his own for the other. The Pāṇḍavas chose to have him personally on their side. Thus, Krishna became charioteer for the great warrior Arjuna. The two armies gathered for battle at Kurukshetra. But on the eve of battle, Arjuna fell into doubt. Rather than kill his kinsmen, he decided, he would retire from the battle and let the enemy kill him. Krishna then taught him that he had to do his duty, act correctly, and leave the consequences to God. Krishna's teachings to Arjuna are in the *Bhagavadgītā*, Book Six of the Indian epic *Māhābhārātā*.

Krishna's death followed closely on those of his brother and son, who were killed during a fight among clan chiefs. Krishna went to the forest to mourn for them. A hunter, mistaking Krishna for a deer, shot him in his one vulnerable spot, his heel, whereupon Krishna died.

The most visible followers of Krishna in the West are the members of the International Society for Krishna Consciousness, an organization headed by His Divine Grace A.C. Bhaktivedanta Swami Prabhupada. Prabhupada came to the United States in 1965, when he was seventy years old, with seven dollars, a suitcase full of scriptures, and a letter of introduction to a family that might help him. Prabhupada has succeeded brilliantly in building up his movement within the United States. The organization now has centers in most major cities, a large school near Dallas, and an incense business. Prabhupada, however, is not the movement's guru, although he is influential and revered. The guru is Krishna, and members of the organization must devote themselves to Krishna by adopting the monastic rules and chanting the *Hare Krishna* mantra.

Krishnamurti

Krishnamurti is an outstanding spiritual teacher precisely because he is *not* a guru. At one point he was a guru, but his teaching began at the point when he gave up that privilege.

Krishnamurti was born to a Brahmin family in India in 1895. His father, who was very poor, had connections with the Theosophical Society, and he brought his family to the Theosophists' headquarters in Adyar. There they lived simply and obscurely until Krishnamurti (or Jiddu, as he was then called) was thirteen. At that time he caught the attention of the two leaders of the Theosophical Society, Annie Besant and C.W. Leadbeater. Leadbeater in particular was intrigued with Jiddu. He spent hours with the boy, teaching him occult subjects and examining his past lives. Eventually Leadbeater (and Besant as well) became convinced that Jiddu was to be the incarnation of Lord Maitreya, the World Teacher for whom the Theosophical Society had been waiting.

The elevation of Jiddu to Lord Maitreya caused problems. Jiddu's father became upset at the way Leadbeater had "adopted" the boy, and at one point he accused Leadbeater of kidnapping. Many Theosophists (such as Rudolf Steiner) became disgusted at the hoopla Leadbeater was making over Jiddu. There was a split in the Society, and many members left. Leadbeater and Besant, meanwhile, were becoming more and more committed to Krishnamurti—or to the Krishnamurti they were trying to create. They founded a new society, the Order of the Star in the East, dedicated to Krishnamurti's glorification.

For a brief period it looked as if Krishnamurti would take on the role of Lord Maitreya and be the Messiah of the Theosophists. Then, at a mass meeting of the Order in 1929, he declared that he was leaving. The message was succinct: You have no need of the Order of the Star, the Theosophists, any of the occult theories, or me. You can attain awareness now, on your own, without any help. Go to it.

That was the end of the Order of the Star (and to some extent of the Theosophists). It was the real beginning for Krishnamurti. Over the years he has travelled widely, talking to thousands of people and encouraging them to pay attention. He has established a school called the Educational Centre at Brockwood Park, near London, and he gives a regular series of talks each summer at Saanen, Switzerland.

Krishnamurti refuses to let his listeners take refuge in jargon and formulas. He will ask them a question about their own mental processes, for example, and then firmly reject any easy answer the listeners come up with. "You're all so eager to answer," he'll say. "Go into it. Go slowly." He will not be satisfied until he sees that the listeners—some of them, anyway—have actually looked at themselves and their way of thinking.

Jacob Needleman, a student of Eastern religions transplanted in the West, has this to say of Krishnamurti: "We shall find in his thought no God, no religion, no ethical norms, no life beyond the grave, no new theories or explanations. Nor can we comfortably side with him when he rejects society so totally: because he quickly makes it very clear that we, you and I, *are* society, and that society is brutal, barbaric and chaotic because we, you and I, are brutal, barbaric and chaotic within."

Krishnamurti has turned out to be the World Teacher, exactly as announced. His teaching is quite different from what was expected. But that, he would point out, is not his fault.

Maharishi Mahesh Yogi

We have very little biographical information about Maharishi, the guru of the Transcendental Meditation movement. He studied physics at Allahabad University in India, then went through a thirteen-year apprenticeship with his guru, Swami Brahmananda Saraswati, the spiritual leader of the North Indian followers of Shankara.

After Brahmananda's death in 1953, Maharishi went by himself to a cave in the Himalayas in a place called Uttar Kashi. For two years he lived there as a hermit; then he decided to return to the world, and so he went to South India, where he began to lecture and teach. In December 1958, at a gathering in Madras to celebrate Brahmananda's eighty-ninth birthday, he founded the Spiritual Regeneration Movement. Shortly thereafter, Maharishi began to travel to spread the work of his new movement. He first came to the United States in 1959. In 1965 he formed the Students International Meditation Society (SIMS) to bring the work of SRM to young people. Since then he also has founded the International Meditation Society, the American Foundation for the Science of Creative Intelligence, and Maharishi International University.

Although Maharishi is of great importance to practitioners of Transcendental Meditation, he does not take personal responsibility for them and so in a sense is more a teacher in the Western tradition than a guru. This is in keeping with his claim that TM is a practical, nonreligious technique.

The novice receives a mantra—a special sound—which he must keep secret. During meditation (which lasts for twenty minutes, twice each day), one must simply repeat the mantra mentally while ignoring all other thoughts. Regular meditation is supposed to let the mind descend to the deepest level of consciousness. The meditator experiences full relaxation, renewed energy and creativity, and a sense of well-being. There's a political side to TM as well. The more people meditate, says Maharishi, the better society will become.

But in all fairness to the Maharishi, TM *is* a religious system. The use of mantras comes directly from the Hindu yoga tradition (see chapter one for details), and the "deepest level of consciousness" of which Maharishi speaks seems to be identical with the ground of being, i.e., Brahman. For these reasons, Maharishi can be considered a guru. Those followers who discount his religious role are misguided at best.

Charles Manson

Charles Manson, the Christ of California, first entered the land of his ministry in 1955. He was driving a stolen Mercury and had with him his wife, Rosalie, who was seventeen and pregnant. Manson, who had been born in 1934 in West Virginia, had stolen cars and other things before. He had been in and out of reform schools and prisons since the age of thirteen. As a result of his first appearance in California, complicated by some stupid parole bungling, he got a three-year sentence at Terminal Island Penitentiary in San Pedro. After his release in the fall of 1958, he worked in Los Angeles as a small-time pimp; he also stole credit cards and tried to pass bad checks. He was again arrested on federal charges, and on June 23, 1960, he was sentenced to ten years at McNeil Island Penitentiary in Washington.

There he began his studies. According to Ed Sanders, on whose account I am relying (see below), Manson studied "magic, warlockry, hypnotism, astral projection, Masonic lore, scientology, ego games, subliminal motivation, music, and perhaps Rosicrucianism." (For seven or the above ten, see the appropriate entries in this book.) He also was taken with Robert Heinlein's *Stranger in a Strange Land*, a popular neofascist fantasy novel about a Messiah from Mars who has a stable of women and kills his enemies with a clear conscience. In the summer of 1966, Manson was transferred back to Terminal Island. There he continued his studies, especially his musical ones. He was greatly impressed with the Beatles' success and wanted to be a star like them.

On March 21, 1967, Manson left prison. He was thirty-two-years old. At first he went to the Bay area. He hung around in Berkeley and the Haight, where he picked up his first two disciples, Mary Brunner and Lynn (Squeaky) Fromme. He also took LSD for the first time, an experience that convinced him that he was Christ. Satisfied with that knowledge, he packed his women into a microbus and took off down the coast. He and the Family lived in Santa Barbara and Topanga Canyon, where they supported themselves by theft (especially of credit cards) and drug dealing. Manson spent some time at Universal studios, making a demo tape of his songs and acting as script consultant for a movie. He became friendly with Terry Melcher (Doris Day's son) and with Dennis Wilson, one of the Beach Boys. He so impressed Wilson that Wilson gave the Family the run of his mansion. The Beach Boys even recorded a song by Manson. The title he gave it was "Cease to Exist."

Manson also made contact with various Satanist groups in Los Angeles. These "sleazo inputs," as Ed Sanders calls them, were: The Process Church of the Final Judgment; the Solar Lodge of the Ordo Templi Orientalis, "a loony-tune magical cult specializing in blood-drinking, sado-sodo sex magic and hatred of blacks"; and an underground occult group that Sanders calls the Kirké Order of Dog Blood.

In 1968, the Family moved out of town to the Spahn Ranch, a former set for Western movies. There Manson, in his wisdom, banned books, eyeglasses, and Jimi Hendrix records ("black slave music," he called them). The Family held an outdoor LSD session-cum-crucifixion with Manson as the star and followed it with an orgy.

On the subject of orgies, Manson's disciples claim he had sex seven times a day without fail, and he himself said, "I am the god of fuck." Moreover, he looked upon birth control devices as an abomination. Even so, Manson fathered only one child during his time with the Family.

From the Spahn Ranch, the Family moved on to Death Valley late in 1968. There Manson worked miracles, say his disciples, such as reuniting the parts of his severed penis after a woman passionately bit it in two. He found a large hole in the desert, the entrance to a cave and subterranean river; he was sure the hole had significance. And he began to interpret the inner meaning of the songs of the Beatles' *White Album.*

He suddenly realized that the song "Helter Skelter" was a warning: the blacks were arming themselves for a revolution. They would destroy the cities and take over the country. But after about fifty years, the blacks would realize they were unfit to govern and would turn over the country to Manson. Meanwhile, Manson and the Family would have to hide in the hole he had found in the desert. Manson worked parts of the Book of Revelations into this teaching. He was to be "the angel of the bottomless pit." But for the sake of consistency, he took this to mean that he would be the fifth Beatle. Whenever he listened to the *White Album*, he would hear the Beatles calling him to join them.

It seems probable that the Family had been entertaining itself with murder all through this period. The police think that Family members may have murdered the following people, among others: two women outside Ukiah, California, on October 13, 1968; a young girl in Hollywood Hills, December 29, 1968; a thirteen-year-old girl from Claremont, June 24, 1969; a sixteen-year-old boy, July 20, 1969; and an unknown young girl, also sometime in 1969. On July 1, 1969, Manson shot a black dope dealer named Bernard Crowe and left him for dead (Crowe recovered). And on July 26, 1969, Manson's associate, Robert Beausoleil, murdered Gary Hinman. Beausoleil was an Aleister Crowley enthusiast. Hinman was a sociology student and Beausoleil's music teacher. Hinman was also a scientologist and a member of the Nicherin Shusho Academy.

The murder of Sharon Tate and her friends came on August 9, 1969. Through his Hollywood contacts, Manson had long been aware of Tate and her husband, Roman Polanski. On the night of August 9, Manson sent four of his disciples—Linda Kasabian, Susan Atkins, Katie Krenwinkel, and Tex Watson—to kill the inhabitants of the Polanski home. They murdered

Sharon Tate, Jay Sebring, Steve Parent, Voityck Frykowski, and Abigail Folger.

One day later, the Family murdered Leno LaBianca and his wife Rosemary at their home.

The police captured Manson on October 12, 1969. They captured the rest of his Family, twenty-seven in all, in Death Valley on October 15. The ensuing trial was chaotic and sensational—with Susan Atkins testifying to how good it felt when the knife went into Sharon Tate, and Manson flashing Masonic hand signals to the judge. Satanist groups took up Manson as a cause. Bernadette Dohrn of the Weather Underground commended him for having "put the knife into the Pig's belly." Researchers at the University of Southern California Neuropsychiatric Institute found that Tex Watson's I.Q. had dropped thirty points during his time with the Family.

Manson was sentenced to perpetual imprisonment. The State of California has not sought to impose the death penalty, no doubt fearing that Manson would then become a martyr. By law, the state had to set a parole hearing for December 1978, but there's no question that Manson will remain in close confinement until he dies. Meanwhile, his cult continues to grow.

One of Sanders's conclusions: "A scientific, scholarly study . . . is needed on techniques of psychedelic brainwashing and criminal behavior under complex hypnotic suggestion-patterns. Young people need to know the techniques a guru or so-called leader might use to entrap them in a web of submission so that they can keep a constant vigil against it."

For those with any remaining doubts as to how great an evil Manson represents, I recommend Ed Sanders's *The Family: The Story of Charles Manson's Dune Buggy Attack Battalion* (New York: Dutton, 1971). Sanders was himself something of a cult figure in the 1960s as a Yippie shaman and leader of a vanguard rock band, the Fugs. His book on Manson is a work that took both extraordinary research and personal courage (Manson cultists and others threatened Sanders's life).

Mary

In the popular mind, the cult of the Virgin Mary has rivaled and often outstripped the cult of Jesus, despite the fact that there are only a few references to Mary in the scriptures, and those are sketchy.

According to Matthew and Luke, Mary became pregnant while engaged to Joseph, "before they came together." In Luke, the angel Gabriel comes to her and announces that the Holy Ghost will be the agent of conception. (Luke is the only scriptural authority for the virgin birth. The passages in Matthew are ambiguous, and there is no mention of a virgin birth in Mark or John.)

We read of Mary again in the accounts of the flight to Egypt, the Passover visit to Jerusalem, the marriage at Cana (where she is not mentioned by name), and an episode in which she tries to see Jesus while he's teaching. At the crucifixion, Jesus entrusts her to the disciple John. There is one more reference to her, in Acts 1:14, as being among those who gathered for prayer after Jesus' Ascension.

The first church built to Mary was erected in Ephesus, an interesting coincidence, since Ephesus was the center of the pagan cult of Diana. Probably the Ephesians were inclined to worship the mother more than the son when they converted to Christianity. Indeed, every pagan cult that worshipped a god who died and was resurrected also worshipped a mother goddess. Isis had Osiris; Diana had Adonis-Tammuz. It was to be expected that Mary would eventually equal Jesus in importance.

All the fathers of the church believed in the virgin birth, and by the fifth century Mary had been decreed a "perpetual virgin" despite the fact that the gospels mention the four brothers of Jesus.

The next important attribute she acquired was that of "mother of God," or *Theotokos*. This term became popular in Alexandria in the third and fourth centuries, and became general after the Council of Nicea decreed that Jesus was indeed God. Nestorius, the patriarch of Constantinople, objected to the term on the grounds that it blurred the distinction between Jesus' humanity and divinity. He preferred the term *Christotokos*, mother of Christ. But the Church voted him down in 431 (at Ephesus, incidentally), and Mary officially became the mother of God.

A further step in Mary's deification was represented by the doctrine of the immaculate conception. Medieval theologians (Aquinas, for example) believed that Mary was essentially sinless—she had never committed a sin, and by special grace God had suppressed original sin in Mary before her birth. In the thirteenth century, Duns Scotus put forth the doctrine that Mary's conception itself had been sinless. Pope Pius IX made this dogma in 1854. He declared that "at the first instant of her conception [she] was preserved immaculate from all stain of original sin."

The final step in her deification came in 1950. For centuries people had believed in Mary's assumption, that she was taken up physically into Heaven. After all, there were no relics of Mary and no official tomb. (Traditionally, she was said to have "fallen asleep"—rather than died—in Ephesus.) In 1950, Pope Pius XII made it dogma that Mary had been "assumed in body and soul to heavenly glory."

Mary thus officially acquired the prestige she had always enjoyed. She remains in the true sense a guru, a personality through whose intercession the devotee can win divine grace.

Meher Baba

Meher Baba, also known as the Avatar of the Age, was born on February 25, 1894, in Poona, India. His parents, who were Persians, educated the boy in the Sufi traditions of Moslem mysticism. They named him Merwan Sheriar Irani.

Baba attended a Christian high school and then went to the Deccan College in Poona. There, at age nineteen, he met a woman named Hazrat Babajan, who was a Moslem saint and one of the age's five Perfect Masters. (According to Baba, there are five Perfect Masters alive in the world at any given time.) Babajan kissed him on his forehead between the eyebrows, thus ripping away "the veil which separated him from his consciousness as the avatar of the present era." (The phrase comes from one of Baba's official biographies, *Meher Baba's Universal Message*.)

According to Baba, God had incarnated in previous ages as Zoroaster, Krishna, Rama, Buddha, Jesus, and Muhammad. God's final avatar in our cycle of time was Baba. This meant that, following Hazrat Babajan's kiss, Baba had the consciousness of God while still being in human form, still present in the world of illusion. This caused him such suffering and frustration that at times he would bang his head against walls and windows. It took Baba nine months to come down from the God-consciousness Babajan had imparted. During this time he neither slept nor ate, nor was he aware of his surroundings.

When he regained consciousness of the ordinary world, he went to consult a second Perfect Master, Sai Baba of Shirdi. (For more on Sai Baba, see the section in this chapter on Satya Sai Baba.) Sai Baba directed the young avatar to a third Perfect Master, Upasni Maharaj of Sakori. Upasni was a Hindu saint of the rough sort; he lived in a temple, where he sat naked in the midst of filth. When Meher Baba approached him for the first time, Upasni greeted him by throwing a rock, which struck him on the forehead in the same spot that Babajan had kissed. Thus began the process of integrating Baba's God-consciousness with consciousness of the world of illusion. This task took seven years, during which time Baba stayed with Upasni.

In 1921, Baba gathered his first disciples and established an ashram near Bombay. It was at this time that his followers gave him the name Meher Baba, which means *Compassionate Father*. He later started a colony at Meherazad, seventy miles northeast of Poona, and this remains the headquarters for his followers. The disciples do much social work: they care for the poor, build schools, and establish hospitals. Baba himself worked with lepers and the insane, both the psychotic and the God-intoxicated.

In 1925, Baba stopped speaking. He maintained his silence for the rest of his life. For most of that period he used an alphabet board to answer people and to compose his works (including his *Discourses*, dictated from 1938 to

1943, and his later work, *God Speaks*). In 1956 he gave up the board, too, and from then on communicated by hand gestures only.

Why the Silence? As Baba explained, "I have come not to teach but to awaken. Understand therefore that I lay down no precepts. . . . Because man has been deaf to the principles and precepts laid down by God in the past, in this present avataric form, I observe Silence. You have asked for and been given enough words—it is now time to live them." So he remained a living lesson, a physical manifestation of God, but a silent one. For years, rumor had it that Baba would break the silence just before he died, thereby shaking the world's foundations. But when he did die (or "drop the body") on January 31, 1969, he evidently maintained the silence. However, some Baba-lovers claim that he *did* speak, but we do not know about it yet. Stories continue to circulate about his last moments. According to one report, at the very end he offered three final hand gestures, which signified "Going, going, gone."

Baba's organization, Sufism Reoriented, continues to be very active. Its followers devote their lives to the love of Baba, in return for which, they claim, he extends his grace to them and removes all their cares. His best-known message to them, and to the world, is "Don't worry. Be happy."

Muhammad

Muhammad is the prophet and highest spiritual authority for some 600 million Moslems. In his success in forging a religious and political union—a success he achieved in his own lifetime—he was a Messiah in the precise, ancient sense of the word. From that viewpoint, Muhammad had reason to claim that he was a greater prophet than Jesus. He did not insist on it, however, preferring to compare himself favorably with Moses. There too he had some justification.

Muhammad was born in Mecca, around 570 A.D., into the Hāshim clan of the Quraysh tribe. The Hāshim were one of the lesser clans, and Muhammad's status was lowered still further by his family's poverty. His father had died two months before Muhammad's birth; his mother died when the boy was six. Then his grandfather cared for him for two years, until he too died. For the rest of his childhood, Muhammad was cared for by a benevolent uncle.

Muhammad worked as a camel driver for a wealthy woman named Khadijah. When he was twenty-five, she proposed marriage to him, and he accepted. She was forty at the time and had already been married twice, but the marriage was a happy one that lasted twenty-five years, until Khadija's death. During that time, Muhammad took no other wives. After her death, though, he did take other wives; the number usually given is eleven.

Muhammad was illiterate (as might be expected of a poor camel driver from a minor clan). But he did have access to information and new ideas. At the time of his birth, Mecca was the main stop on the caravan route between Abyssinia and India. It was also the capital city of the Arabian peninsula, which was effectively under Bedouin control. Mecca was an isolated spot of civilization in the midst of the nomads, and so it was alive with news and stories from the Christian empires of Abyssinia and Byzantium.

Muhammad had visionary tendencies, which were perhaps increased by epilepsy. He would go into trances and break into a sweat. At age forty, quite suddenly, he received the call of God (or Allah), and from then on he knew that he was a prophet, like Adam, Noah, Moses, and Jesus, only greater.

He began his ministry by preaching against idolatry. At that time, the people of Mecca, like the Bedouins, worshiped nature gods and idols. Muhammad declared that there was only one God, Allah, and that his day of judgment was coming. On the last day, the dead would be raised and judged. Idolators would be punished in hell. Muhammad's teaching attracted followers (mostly from his own class), but he was distressed and angered to see that most Meccans ignored him. This led him to formulate a theory of predestination not unlike that of John Calvin—Allah willed some people to be believers and others to be infidels. Muhammad also came to believe that his mission was to found the *ummah*, or community of believers, which would, in time, become a nation of believers.

In 622, Muhammad left Mecca and went to Medina, a small town (little more than an oasis) about 275 miles to the north. This so-called flight from Mecca was the *Hijra* that marks the beginning of the Muslim era. Actually, Muhammad was not chased out of Mecca. Indeed, he was invited to Medina to help settle a territorial dispute between two tribes. Henceforth, Muhammad combined his religious and political careers. He began to spread the faith not only through discourses and revelation, but by force of arms, including brigandage. In 624, Muhammad and his followers made a particularly successful raid on a Meccan caravan. Meanwhile, they blockaded Mecca and increased the wealth of Medina. Thus, Muhammad's power grew.

Muhammad continued to teach, of course. During his years in Medina he was still receiving the revelations that are collected in the *Qur'ān*, or *Koran*. He taught that Allah had created and ordered the universe and that humans were the highest beings in Creation. (There is also a species parallel to the humans. These are the *jinn*, creatures made of fire.) Humans are frail and sinful, and therefore they must submit to the will of Allah. (*Islam* means "surrender.") If they do, Allah will always forgive their sins.

Muhammad also instituted the five pillars of the faith:

1. The profession of faith: There is no God but Allah and Muhammad is his prophet.

2. Prayer five times a day, with accompanying ablutions.
3. Charity.
4. Fasting.
5. The *hajj*, or pilgrimage to Mecca, an old custom he reinstituted when the Jews of Medina refused to accept him as their prophet. Until then he had directed his prayers to Jerusalem.

By the time Muhammad died in 632, he had conquered the entire Arabian peninsula. His followers carried on the holy war (*jihād*) that he had begun. Abu Bakr, the Muslim leader from 632 to 634, finished the conquest of the Bedouins and extended his power into Iraq and Syria. 'Umar completed the conquest of Syria and also took Egypt and the Persian plateau (634–644). By 714, Arab armies were in possession of Spain, Kashgar in Central Asia, and parts of India.

Swami Muktananda Paramahansa

Muktananda is the leading practitioner in the United States of Siddha Yoga, a method of transmitting enlightenment directly from guru to disciple. This form of yoga is also known as *gurukripa* (guru's grace) and *shaktipat* (transference of creative energy). In this method, the guru transmits the enlightening energy by a word, look, or touch. The disciple then experiences the awakening of *kuṇḍālinī*, effortlessly. The disciple may then spontaneously perform yoga *asanas*, see colored lights, or compose poems—all this without prolonged concentration or training.

Muktanada received his power of *gurukripa* from his own guru. Since Muktanada has written a biography of that guru, Bhagawan Nityananda, we have a rare opportunity for studying the transmission of a teaching from one generation to the next.

We know little about Nityananda's birth and background. He was probably ordained in the Nandapadma Order as a young man and he lived in the Himalayas for about six years. He first revealed himself, while still quite young, in the South Kanara District, near Kanhangad. There he lived in a cave in the midst of a mountainous wilderness. Since there was no water in the vicinity, Muktananda says, Nityananda miraculously created a spring, which is still flowing. About four miles from his cave, Nityananda built an ashram.

Nityananda used to travel widely on foot, healing the ill and offering comfort to the troubled. He never had problems with money because he had the power to make objects materialize. Thus, when he needed money, he would just reach into his loincloth and pull some out, or pick up a rock and find some lying on the ground. Nityananda's powers also extended to the animal kingdom. He once ordered all the snakes out of a jungle so workmen could build his ashram in peace. On one occasion, when the people of Bantwal insulted him, the Netravati River rose up of its own volition and flooded the village, killing hundreds. When the survivors prayed to Nityananda, he appeared to them and performed the wonderful miracle of making the waters recede.

Muktananda emphasizes that Nityananda did not consciously perform any of these miracles. As a perfect master, he was one with Brahman and therefore never did *anything* willfully. The miracles simply happened around him.

After several years in and around Kanhangad, Nityananda eventually settled at Ganeshpuri, a mile-and-a-half from a famous temple to the Great Mother, and there built the Shree Gurudev Ashram. He remained there for the rest of his life, absorbed in concentration on his inner powers. According to Muktananda, the guru perpetually contemplated the inner light in his heart, the inner sound that resonated in his consciousness, the inner taste of the ambrosia that flowed from the *sahasrara chakra*, the inner fragrance that arose from his *ajna chakra*, and the inner sensation of his own *prānā*. Given that he was thus absorbed, Nityananda spoke little. When necessary, he would communicate by small gestures and with his eyes.

To take up Muktananda's own story: He was born in Bangalore in 1908 and was the only son in his family. Thus, when he left home at age fifteen, his mother was heartbroken. Muktananda still regrets having hurt her. Muktananda travelled for years till he came to Shree Gurudev Ashram and decided that Nityananda was to be his guru. He would sit in the back of the ashram and meditate for hours on Nityananda, overwhelmed with love for the guru's grace and admiration for his physical beauty.

On August 15, 1947, Nityananda let Muktananda approach him. The guru touched Muktananda with his body, stared into the disciple's eyes, and gave the disciple his sandals to worship. This was the beginning of Muktananda's spiritual awakening. For a while, he was in a state of great confusion, especially since the awakening of *kuṇḍālinī* had plagued him with visions of irresistible women. Gradually, though, he mastered the power of *śakti* and entered deep meditative states. While in these states, he travelled to such spiritual locales as Tandraloka (the World of Higher Consciousness), Siddhaloka (the Realm of Perfected Souls), Pitraloka (the World of the Ancestors), and Indraloka (or Heaven, a great city where the gods speak Sanskrit).

From 1956 to 1961, Muktananda and Nityananda were inseparable. Then, on August 8, 1961, Nityananda died. At the last moment, the guru's *ajna chakra* throbbed in his forehead, and the room resounded with the sound of "OM." Then Nityananda left the body, while Muktananda clutched his hands in reverence.

From then on, Swami Muktananda was the guru of Shree Gurudev Ashram. In 1970 he came to the United States with Baba Ram Dass, and he has had a popular following here ever since.

Swami Satchidananda

Satchidananda is a refreshing guru. He admits to having had a human childhood (he was even in the Cub Scouts and Boy Scouts). He went to an art college and an agricultural school, drank too much coffee and smoked too many cigarettes, and worked at a variety of jobs. He helped run his uncle's auto dealership, distributed movies for a studio, and supervised a welding workshop and a plant that made electrical motors. He was married for five years (another novelty for a guru) and had two sons.

Satchidananda was born on December 22, 1914, in the village of Chettipalayam, outside Coimbatore, South India. His father was Sri Kalyanasunderam, the village headman, chief landowner, and justice of the peace. His mother, Sri Velammai, cooked and cleaned. Satchidananda was her second child, and she named him Ramaswamy.

From an early age, Ramaswamy showed unusual intelligence and sympathy for other people. But he had no pretensions to the miraculous. He was deeply religious, but he did not devote himself entirely to religion until he was twenty-eight, the year his wife died. He returned to his father's house and took up a tife of meditation and study. To stay healthy, he also practiced hatha yoga. Ramaswamy was especially devoted to the goddess Parvati, and during this period he began to see visions of her presence during meditation. The visions encouraged him, and he took up the life of a *sadhu*, an ascetic who has renounced the world.

His first guru was Sri Sadhu Swamigal, who taught tantric yoga. Later, Ramaswamy became a devotee of Swami Ranga Nath, who was known for his miracles, especially his ability to make things materialize. But Ramaswamy became dissatisfied with Ranga Nath, and one day he challenged the guru. Ranga Nath had asked Ramaswamy to run an errand that would require cash; Ramaswamy had none, so the guru made some money appear. Ramaswamy, cautiously taking the money, asked, "Is this money real?"

Ranga Nath was outraged. "Of course it's real," he said.

In that case, Ramaswamy explained, he had a serious problem. Either the money had been transported magically from a bank or from someone's pocket—in which case it was theft—or the guru had manufactured the money—in which case it was forgery. The guru had worked a miracle, Ramaswamy said, but it was still a crime. Ranga Nath asked him to leave the ashram.

Ramaswamy wandered as a beggar for four months. Then he entered the Ramakrishna Mission at Timpurraiturai and became an initiate, taking the name Sri Sambasiva Chaitanya. In 1947 he left South India and started on his way to Rishikesh, where Swami Sivananda's ashram was. Sivananda, he had decided, was to be his final guru.

Sivananda was born in 1887 in Pathamadar, near Tinnaveli, in South

India. As a young man he practiced medicine and was devoted to the idea of healing people. At one time he established a practice in Malaya, since he felt that was where he was needed the most. Then he gave up medicine and became a *sadhu*. In 1924 he settled in Rishikesh and began to attract followers. In 1932 he founded his ashram there, and in 1936 he established the Divine Life Society, through which he intended to spread knowledge of yoga and Vedanta.

Ramaswamy arrived at Sivananda's ashram in 1949. He found that Sivananda was a huge man—nearly seven feet tall and weighing 250 pounds. Sivananda at once ordered coffee for his new follower. Ramaswamy was astonished—*sadhus* are not supposed to drink coffee. But Sivananda's attitude was that if Ramaswamy liked coffee, he might as well drink it.

This was typical of Sivananda's nondogmatic attitudes, which Ramaswamy soon picked up. His teaching methods, too, were original. Once Sivananda tricked Ramaswamy into swallowing a hot pepper. When Ramaswamy yelped with pain, Sivananda laughed and asked what had become of the equanimity he was supposed to practice.

Sivananda gave Ramaswamy the name Satchidananda. He sent Satchidananda on a tour of India in 1951. In 1953, he sent him to Ceylon to teach. Satchidananda settled there and became famous. He was unknown in the West, though, until the filmmaker Conrad Rooks met him and brought him to Paris in 1965. Rooks introduced Satchidananda to illustrator Peter Max, who then brought Satchidananda to New York.

Satchidananda now has a large following in the United States through his Integral Yoga Institute. Integral Yoga, he explains, "integrates the various branches of Yoga in order to bring about a complete and harmonious development of the individual." His teaching, like that of Sivananda, is nondogmatic and practical. "A spirit of detachment," he says, "doesn't mean that you run away from the world and become no good for it. On the other hand, you are the best person to do something in the world because you have the proper understanding."

Satya Sai Baba

Sai Baba, one of modern India's most popular saints, was born in the mid-1800s in the village of Patri, part of the Nizam of Hyderabad's state. We know little about his parents except that they were probably Brahmins. While a youth, Sai Baba had two gurus. The first was a Sufi adept, with whom he studied for five years. The second was a government official named Gopal Rao, with whom Sai Baba lived in Selu. Rao, who was a deeply religious man, recognized Sai Baba as the reincarnation of the yogin saint, Kabir. Understandably excited, Rao devoted himself to giving Sai Baba a thorough spiritual education. Before Rao died (reportedly of his own will), he told Baba to go to the village of Shirdi in Bombay. Baba followed his guru's orders and took up permanent residence there in 1872, in an abandoned mosque, where he carried out constant devotions to his favorite gods.

Word of Baba's arrival spread. A few people came to see him, mostly out of curiosity. Soon, though, when Baba began to perform miracles, people came flocking to him. He healed the sick, gave people visions, appeared to disciples when they needed him (even at great distances), made the childless become fertile, and cast out demons. By 1910 he was surrounded by pilgrims, who would cover him with jewelry and lead him through the streets in processions, riding on a silver chariot. Baba's biographers claim he disliked this treatment but allowed it because he saw it was what the people wanted of him. He died in Shirdi in 1918.

That is not the end of Sai Baba's story, for thousands of people believe he has been reincarnated as Satya Sai Baba of Puttaparti.

Satya Sai Baba was born Satyanarayana Raju in Puttaparti on November 23, 1926. (November 23, by the way, is a day sacred to Śiva. Satya Sai Baba was born exactly at sunrise.) His paternal grandfather, a learned religious man, gave the boy religious instruction.

As a schoolboy, Baba was very popular, since he used to give the other children presents of candies, fruits, and small toys, all of which he would pull out of an empty brown paper bag. Baba had discovered a gift for making things appear. Evidently, nobody else knew about his gift until a crisis occurred in 1940. On March 8, a scorpion stung Baba. He lay unconscious for a period; upon recovering, he began to quote long passages from the Vedas, sing sacred songs, and discourse on ethics. Then for periods he would become cataleptic. His parents, who were frantic, took him to exorcists, but without success.

On the morning of May 23, Baba called together all the members of his family and began to make candy and flowers materialize for them. Soon the neighbors were crowding the house and receiving presents as well. Baba's father, who was at work, heard reports of the miracles and ran back home, convinced that his son was performing black magic. Rushing into the house and pushing through the crowd, Baba's father asked, "What are you?" The boy calmly replied, "I am Sai Baba."

It took a while for people to accept this claim. Certain demonstrations helped. The Rani of Chincholi, who had been a devotee of Sai Baba of Shirdi, invited Satya to her palace. Upon arriving, Satya immediately commented on changes that had taken place there since 1918. Satya has given people visions of Sai Baba of Shirdi—glowing, three-dimensional ones—and at times he will hold up his palms and reveal there small pictures of his former face and his present one.

At present, Satya Sai Baba is one of the most popular gurus in India. His ashram is called Prasanti Nilayam—Abode of Great Peace. Some seven hundred people live there permanently, and there are always streams of visitors. The residents claim two benefits from being at the ashram—they enjoy Baba's presence, and they receive instruction in the chanting of the Vedic literature. Vedic chanting is a dying art that Baba is trying to revive. A proper course of instruction takes thirty years. Baba takes no money for the instruction. In fact, he takes no money at all.

When people come to see Baba, they find a genial-looking little man with a huge halo of black hair. His first gesture to the newcomer is usually to offer a present. He will wave his right hand in the air, the palm open and held downward. Then, when he turns his hand over, it will be holding the present. If he knows his observer is a skeptic, he plays a game—he pulls his sleeve up to the elbow before producing the object. When he really wants to prove a point, he will produce an object with his palm held upward a few inches from the viewer's face.

The object he produces most often is a holy ash called *vibhuti*. It has healing properties, and it also seems to serve a symbolic purpose. The original Sai Baba always kept a flame burning in his mosque so as to have a supply of holy ash ready for healing. When Satya Sai Baba produces *his* ash, it seems as if he has taken it from an invisible dimension where the first Sai Baba's flame is still burning.

Each year, at the Mahasivarati Festival, Baba performs two public miracles to honor Śiva. Usually one of these is the materialization of a Śiva *lingam*—an ellipsoidal stone that represents Śiva's erect penis and the god's union with Śakti. Baba has materialized as many as nine of these at a time. He pulls them out of his mouth. Sometimes the *lingams* are so large that they tear the sides of his mouth. Most of the *lingams* dematerialize after a while.

Among his other miracles, Satya Sai Baba has cured tuberculosis, paralysis, and cancer. In 1953 he raised a follower named Radhakrishna from the dead (Radhakrishna had been lying in the ashram for three days and had begun to stink). Baba performed a second resurrection in 1972, this time on an elderly man from California named Walter Cowan.

Sun Myung Moon

Moon was born in 1920 in Pyungyang Province, Korea. He was raised as a Presbyterian and studied electrical engineering in Japan. He seems to have been a deeply religious man from the first.

On Easter morning in 1936, while he was praying on a mountainside, Jesus appeared to him and told him of a mission that Moon had to accomplish. Jesus also began to reveal to him the hidden meaning of the Bible. Moon spent nine years meditating on these revelations and eventually developed a system of Divine Principles, by which he claims to make plain the nature of spiritual and temporal history.

According to Moon, God intended for Adam and Eve to give birth to a perfect family. But "under the false fatherhood of Satan, Adam and Eve united as a couple unlawfully, without God's blessing or permission." The result was disaster. Therefore, God in his mercy sent his son, Jesus, to be the second Adam. Jesus was to choose a bride to reign as queen in the Kingdom of Heaven, which he was to have established on earth in his own time. Jesus and his queen would then start a perfect family, which would unite the peoples of the world as children of God. He was to have been aided in this by the three Magi and John the Baptist, who were supposed to be his disciples. But his intended disciples did not recognize Jesus and neither did Israel, and so he died on the cross, a failure. Traditional Christians find it hard to believe that Jesus was not supposed to die, but Moon says it's so. "If God had wanted His son to be crucified," Moon explains, "He did not need 4,000 years to prepare the chosen people. He could have sent Jesus to a tribe of barbarians, where he could have been killed even faster."

Moon says we are to have one more chance. Jesus is to come again, and this time he will succeed in founding a new universal family. The world will be united as one nation and one faith, and the forces of Satan (which are most obvious as the Communist nations) will be vanquished. Indeed, this Second Coming is already upon us. Moon says that Jesus has already been reborn as a Korean. And although Moon's followers won't say so in public, it's obvious that they think this Korean is Moon.

Moon unquestionably has great faith, both in his ideas and in himself. Shortly after the partition of Korea, he was arrested by the North Korean authorities and beaten. Later he was arrested again and sent to a forced-labor camp at Hung-nam. He managed to survive there for almost three years; reportedly, most prisoners lasted six months. On October 14, 1950, United Nations forces freed the camp. Moon made his way to Seoul on foot. There he continued his preaching, though again he was unpopular with the authorities. In 1954, he founded the Holy Spirit Association for the Unification of World Christianity, better known as the Unification Church. The church now has branches in forty countries and maintains centers in some 120 U.S. cities.

The Unification Church also owns businesses, of which Moon is the president. Some of these, such as a titanium plant in South Korea, are quite lucrative, especially since the workers are church members who accept minimal wages. The church has bought some $5 million worth of property in and around Tarrytown, New York, where Moon maintains one of his homes.

We also know that Moon had good ties with the government of South Korea. He got along well with President Park Chung Hee, and his chief aide is Colonel Bo Hi Pak, formerly a Korean military attache in Washington. In June 1978, the international relations subcommittee of the House of Representatives released an intelligence summary that alleged Moon had accepted money from the Korean Central Intelligence Agency. The KCIA in return got the use of Unification Church members for political demonstrations in the U.S. The Unification Church has strongly denied this allegation, which remains unproved.

Two recent books have offered first-person accounts of life within the church: *Crazy for God*, by Chris Edwards (Prentice-Hall, 1979) and *Moonstruck*, by Alan Tate Wood (Morrow, 1979). The Edwards book gives more information on prosetylization and the life of rank-and-file members. The Wood book is the work of a man who was fairly high up in the church before he left it. He estimates that in 1978 the church took in between $109 and $210 million through street solicitation. The church has disputed this claim, saying the figure was more like $20 million.

Part Two

The Occult Bible

Chapter Six

The Occult Bible

• *The Book of Systems* • *The Book of Lesser Lost Lands*
• *The Chronicle of Atlantis* • *The Book of Cataclysms*
• *The Book of Visitations* • *The Book of Miracles and Mysteries*

The Book of Systems

In the beginning God created the heaven and the earth.
And the earth was without form, and void; and darkness was upon the face of the deep. And the Spirit of God moved upon the face of the waters.
And God said, Let there be light: and there was light.

Thus begins the account of Creation in the sacred writings of the Hebrews. In this story we read one of the great truths common to all philosophies: that the Cosmos was created through the Divine Word, or Spirit, and that the first creative principle was light.

Other creation stories have come down to us also, which elucidate the Genesis story. For these other accounts tell not only of the light of Creation, but of the darkness of the period that preceded it.

Adepts of spiritual science understand what took place during the time when "the earth was without form and void," for the true adept understands the principles both of darkness and of light, and comprehends that both are manifestations of the One. Some of the adepts are Hidden Masters, who are also called Mahatmas or the Great White Brotherhood. They preserve the spiritual mysteries throughout all time and eternity.

Now, in these last days, these spiritual authorities have deemed it proper and fitting that some of the esoteric truths be made public. For only now have humans become technologically capable of communicating with and understanding the Forces of the Spirit.

This, then, is the record of the thought systems that have been revealed to us by the Hidden Masters in our time, systems that were known by the ancient sages of China, Egypt, and even South America. These were the revelations given to Pythagoras, and Hermes Trismegistus, and even Jesus Christ. And Zoroaster, too, in his time received the revelation and communicated it to his followers.

To all of these it was revealed that there is but one One, one Unity outside of which, there is nothing. The One has no point of origin and no sense of time. It pervades all things and encompasses all things, and yet is distinct from all things.

Knowledge of the One can be achieved only by uniting with it. The state of union with the One is characterized by pure white light. This state has been achieved by mystics from many different religious systems, in many different ways, but is true for all of them.

The aim of all secret, or *occult*, knowledge, is to arrive at clear perception of, and mystic union with, the One. For when one unites with the One, one may control the forces of the One. But such knowledge is given only to the elect.

The elect are souls that have cleansed themselves of all but their pure spiritual impulses. This process of purification takes many lifetimes.

The upward progress of a human soul toward union with the One is not an inevitable process but is controlled by the individual consciousness. For you are possessed of the same consciousness that you have held through many lifetimes.

The good work that is done by you in this life will continue to augment good in the next. And the evil that you do in this life will impede the progress of your soul in the next. That is the meaning of the ancient saying that the sins of the fathers will be visited on the children.

Pay heed to the doctrines that follow. Some will seem simple, even simpleminded. But the simple must be mastered before the complex. The babe must learn to digest milk before he can learn to digest vegetables.

Cosmic Shapes and Cosmic Numbers

The human eye perceives the world in terms of simple numbers and shapes. This faculty is given to us so that we may better understand the Cosmic Order.

The Shapes. The circle is a shape without beginning or end. It signifies God or eternity. It also signifies the Cosmos. The Gnostics pictured the Cosmos as a serpent swallowing its own tail. This represented to them the eternal process of death, regeneration, and life.

The vertical line represents both God and Man. It represents God because it is the numeral 1. It also shows Man on his feet, stretching toward the heavens.

The horizontal line represents the Earth, or the earthly sphere of existence. The horizontal line moves on a single plane. Thus, it also represents the time dimension.

The circle divided by a vertical line stands for the first division of the Cosmos into Darkness and Light.

The cross is composed of a vertical line intersecting a horizontal line. Thus, it stands for the interaction of Man with the Earth and also of God with the Earth. The Gnostics and ancient Egyptians used the form of the cross called the *tau*, which is like our letter T.

The Egyptians also used a looped Tau Cross called the *ankh*—the Key of Life or the Key to the Nile. Some say that this symbol represented the Nile River swollen behind a dam. But it also represented the storing-up of Cosmic knowledge that took place after union with the Divine.

The cross surrounded by a circle is the symbol of Creation. Man has united with the Divine; God has come down to Earth and created a Form. This symbol was used in remote times past to symbolize the Sun, the creative force.

The Egyptian Hermetics, Gnostics, and Neo-Platonists, and the later alchemists, interpreted the symbols in this way:

The circle represents the "egg of the world." The vertical line in the circle represents the male element; the horizontal line, the female element. Thus the Sun contains both male and female elements—all that is needed for creation.

The triangle represents the holy mountains upon which God reaches It also represents Man in his striving toward the Divine. For just as the base of a triangle is grounded on Earth (the horizontal line), so the point of the triangle always directs the eye upwards to the Divine.

The triangle also represents the female, for she is always firmly based upon the Earth.

The inverted triangle represents the male principle. The male is by nature connected to the heavens and must be brought constantly into the reality of the earthly sphere.

Thus you see that the most ancient symbols teach that males are by nature divine, partaking of the Divine Light, while women are by nature earthbound, partaking of the Dark Forces of Earthly life.

The imposition of a triangle upon an inverted triangle results in a six-pointed star, the ancient symbol of magic known as Solomon's Seal. This name is also given to the five-pointed star.

The five-pointed star, or pentagram, is the most commonly used symbol in magical rites. Its points stand for the five senses and the five points of the human body—the head and the four extremities. Among the Druids, this star was the symbol of the Divine. The churchmen of the Middle Ages called it the Goblin's Cross.

The square stands for order, Nature, and the world. Like the circle, it is an enclosed figure, in which the eye tends to travel toward the center. This represents the limited view of those who act only upon the material plane.

There are many other signs and symbols, which for the occult student are guideposts toward wisdom. The meanings of these symbols, their provenance, and the proper uses of them are recounted elsewhere in this book.

The simple numbers must also be examined if we are to gain proper understanding of the Cosmic Order.

The Numbers. *One* stands for the Divine, the indivisible, the One. One is a number that cannot be multiplied. Just as there is One God in the universe, so there is one being, Man, capable of communicating with God. There is one sun for our solar system, one Philosopher's Stone by which we can gain wisdom, and one Earth, which encompasses all other Earths. Thus spoke William Blake: "One thought fills immensity."

Two is the number of division and is therefore evil. It contains both male and female. It contains all the opposing tensions of the unresolved universe: good/bad; light/dark; one/many. That this number is unclean was known to Noah, who put all unclean beasts of the field into the Ark by two's.

Three is the number of the triune God; and also of history, which has a past, present, and future. So also is Man able to communicate in earthly, intellectual, and psychical spheres. Three occurs when Two unites with One The trident of Neptune the pyramids of Egypt and the Three Fates are all manifestations of the number three in history. Three has elements both of the material and spiritual, both of the human and the divine.

Four is the number of strength, foundation, and judgment. The ancient Hebrews recorded many instances of judgments in four's. The Flood of Noah lasted forty days and forty nights; the Tabernacle and the Ark of the Covenant both had four sides; the Children of Israel were captives in Egypt for four hundred years: they wandered in the desert for forty years.

The Christians, too, made use of this number. Jesus was tempted in the desert for forty days and nights. Christ chose four Evangelists to establish the Church in the world.

There are four directions, four elements, and four seasons.

Five is the number of justice, for it evenly divides Ten, which is the sum of all numbers. There are five senses, five fingers on each hand, five toes on each foot, and five wounds on the body of Christ.

Six is a perfect number, "because it alone by the addition of its half, its third, and its sixth reforms itself." The world was created in six days. The number six also represents labor, for it is written, "Six days shalt thou labor."

Seven is the number of miracles. For it is composed of one and six, the numbers of Unity and Perfection. And it is also composed of three, the number of the Soul, and four, the number of the Body. The seventh day of the week is the Sabbath, the day on which God rested from his labors of creation. All the ancient religions taught that the universe had seven spheres.

Eight represents justice.

Nine is the number of the spheres, the modern planets, the orders of angels, and the orders of demons. Nine is three times three.

Ten is completeness. For one cannot count beyond ten without using other numbers. So it is written that there were ten kings of Atlantis, and ten kings of Ancient Rome. There are ten emanations of God in the Kabbalah. There were ten days of initiation in the ancient Hermetic mysteries. Ten is the sun, plus the nine planets. Ten is the number of the Commandments. Ten is also the number of fingers on both hands.

Eleven is unity and completeness.

Twelve is the number of the apostles, the signs of the zodiac, the knights of King Arthur's Round Table, the months of the year, the tribes of Israel. It is composed of one plus two. Thus twelve, like three, could be symbolized by the pyramid.

There are many other numbers, and each has a meaning. The meanings of the numbers and the applications of them for life-guidance can be found in another section of this book.

But these shapes and numbers must be learned for they are necessary in understanding the Cosmic Systems. Do not think that you know these numbers merely because you can count them on your fingers. This is not knowledge. True knowledge of numbers and shapes comes from meditating upon them and their inner significance. For shapes and numbers are given to us not only as useful servants, but also as indications of higher things.

The Doctrine of Correspondences

Another truth must be grasped before Cosmic Systems can be understood. This is the Law of Correspondences, which states that everything in the material world corresponds with the spiritual world. Thus, the outward objects are given to us as signs of spiritual truth. All the sages have taught this.

Microcosm and Macrocosm. The human being is a model of the universe. Various aspects of the microcosm (Man) correspond to aspects of the macrocosm (the Cosmos).

The parts of the physical body correspond to the signs of the zodiac and to the planets. These, in turn, correspond to colors, plants, animals, and metals. Everything in the Cosmos is interconnected in web of correspondences.

The Ram, Aries, governs the head, face, eyes, and ears of a human. This sign is dry, fiery, and masculine. The head is hot-tempered and bold. The colors of Aries are red and white.

The neck and shoulders of a human correspond to Taurus, the Bull. It is a melancholy, cold, earthly sign.

The arms of a human correspond to Gemini, the Twins. Some say also that Gemini rules the upper chest and lungs. Gemini's colors are also red and white.

Cancer, the Crab, rules the upper abdomen of humans. It is a watery, moist, phlegmatic sign, and female in its character. The colors of Cancer are green and russet.

Leo is the sign of the Lion, and of the heart of humans. The heart rules the human, just as the lion rules the forest and the sun rules the sky. The colors of Leo are red and green.

Virgo, or the Virgin, rules the belly and lower abdomen of the human. Its colors are black and blue.

Libra, the Balance, rules the intestines and governs colors that are red or tawny.

The sexual organs are ruled by Scorpio, the Scorpion, which is a phlegmatic, feminine, nocturnal sign. Its color is brown.

The thighs of the human correspond to Sagittarius, the Archer, whose colors are green and red

The knees of a human correspond to the Goat, or Capricorn. Its colors are black and brown.

The lower legs correspond to Aquarius, the Water Carrier. The colors of Aquarius are grey and blue.

The feet of a man correspond to the Fish, Pisces. Its color is white.

There are many other correspondences. Each sign of the zodiac rules certain countries or cities. The planets also govern and correspond to humans, especially the seven planets known to the ancients. The planets that have been discovered more recently are not known to influence human behavior greatly.

Saturn influences the teeth, the spleen, the bladder, and the right ear, and corresponds to all these parts of the human body. Saturn is a malefic planet, and can foretell accidents, deaths, and disasters. Saturn corresponds to the metal lead and to the color black.

Jupiter dominates the liver, the lungs, the semen, the ribs, and the pulse. Jupiter is full of honor and concerned with physical beauty. Its color is blue and its metal is tin.

Mars governs the left ear, the kidneys, the sexual organs, and the gallbladder. Its color is red and its metal is iron.

Venus governs the womb, the loins, the testicles, and the breasts. Her color is green, and her metal is copper.

Mercury corresponds to the tongue and the right hand. He is the planet of communication and commerce. Mercury's metal is quicksilver and its color is grey.

The Moon, which was considered a planet by the ancients, corresponds to the brain and digestion. Her metal is silver and her color is white.

The Sun rules the head and heart. Its color is yellow, and its metal is gold.

The ancient sages used their knowledge of correspondences to heal and regulate the flow of bodily substances. The healers of old could look upon the lines of the forehead of the suffering person and tell which disease was afflicting him.

For the human forehead is marked with lines, each of which corresponds to the planets, signs, and elements. The line of the Moon is right above the eyebrows. Next come the lines of Mercury, Venus, Uranus, the Sun, Mars, Jupiter, and Saturn. In like manner, the hands of humans are marked unmistakably with zodiacal and planetary lines.

The lines of the human body correspond also to the energy channels that cover the earth. It is the principle of correspondence that is recognized by yogins, acupuncturists, and other healers of the East.

The Temple and the City. The ancients also taught that human edifices corresponded to larger structures in the Cosmos. The ancient temples were models of both the internal temple of the human soul and the celestial temple of which the human soul is but a pale reflection.

Likewise, the temples corresponded both to the physical world and the celestial world. The ancients deliberately built according to their perceptions of Cosmic Order.

The Algonquin and Sioux Indians built their sacred lodges around central poles. The roof of a lodge corresponded to the dome of the sky; and the four walls corresponded to the four directions, or cardinal points (north, south, east, and west).

Even today there are peoples among whom these truths have not been lost. The Mongolian nomad pitches his tent around a central pole, which he regards as the Axis of the World. And the opening above the central pole he calls the Window to Heaven.

All the ancient peoples knew that the world revolves on an axis, and they used this principle to bring themselves into harmony with the Divine. The axis corresponds to a man standing upright, and the point where the figure of the standing man intersects the horizon corresponds to the center of the Cosmos. Thus the symbol of the Cross also stands for the center of the Cosmos.

This same principle governed the construction of ancient cities such as Baalbek. The city was seen as a cross within a circle, the symbol of creation. For was not the city the creation of man? And was it not also a scale model of the Cosmos?

The center of the ancient city was called the *navel,* and it was the place where the city's two principal streets intersected. The temple was built at this point of intersection. The four directions of the city streets corresponded to the outstretched limbs of the human. The human head, seat of understanding and wisdom, corresponded to the temple.

The pyramids of the ancient Egyptians were built with four sides, which corresponded to the four directions. The four grounded corners corresponded to the four extremities of man, and the fifth—elevated—point corresponded to the head. The ancient Peruvians and Mexicans also built four-sided mountains, or pyramids. As in Egypt, Atlantis, Babylonia, and Israel, the point of the pyramid, or the top of the mountain, corresponded to the human head. It was the point of meeting place with the Divine.

The ancient Hebrews built their temples and cities according to Cosmic Correspondences. The Jews believed that the Holy Land was the center of the world. Jerusalem, at the center of Israel, contained at its center the temple of Solomon. The foundation stone of Solomon's temple corresponded with the foundation of the world.

The Christians, too, followed the ancient doctrine of correspondences, teaching that everything in the Old Testament, as well as everything in Nature, corresponds to the Truth of Christ. The Tabernacle and the Temple of Solomon were types, or correspondences, of the Divine Man, Jesus. St. Paul called Jesus "Christ, our Tabernacle," and Jesus himself, when he threw the moneychangers out of the temple, said, "In this place is one greater than the temple."

But in this Jesus was following Hermetic teachings. For it is written that Christ journeyed to Egypt as a young man and there was taught by Hermetic priests. (And others write that Christ learned the ancient secrets on Atlantis; and still others say that Christ was taught by priests on Venus.) They, too, taught that the temple corresponded to the states of enlightenment. The outer court of the temple corresponded to the exterior life of man; the inner sanctum corresponded to the spiritual life of man. The innermost sanctum—what the Hebrews called the Holy of Holies— corresponded to man in the state of enlightenment.

This is what St. Paul meant when he wrote to the Corinthians, "Know ye not that ye are the temple of God, and the Spirit of God dwells in you?"

The Christians look for the coming of the New Jerusalem, to which the old Jerusalem corresponds:

> And he carried me away in the spirit to a great and high mountain, and shewed me that great city, the holy Jerusalem, descending out of heaven from God.
>
> Having the glory of God: and her light was like unto a stone most precious, even like a jasper stone, clear as crystal:
>
> And had a wall great and high, and had twelve gates, and at the gates twelve angels, and names written thereon, which are the names of the twelve tribes of the Children of Israel:
>
> On the east three gates; on the north three gates; on the south three gates; on the west three gates.
>
> And the wall of the city had twelve foundations, and in them the names of the twelve apostles of the Lamb.
>
> And he that talked with me had a golden reed to measure the city, and the gates thereof and the wall thereof.
>
> And the city lieth foursquare, and the length is as large as the breadth: and he measured the city with the reed, twelve thousand furlongs. The length and the breadth and the height of it are equal.
>
> And he measured the wall thereof, an hundred and forty and four cubits, according to the measure of a man, that is, of the angel.
>
> And the building of the wall of it was of jasper: and the city was pure gold, like unto clear glass.
>
> And the foundations of the wall of the city were garnished with all manner of precious stones. The first foundation was jasper; the second, sapphire; the third, a chalcedony; the fourth, an emerald;
>
> The fifth, sardonyx; the sixth, sardius; the seventh, chrysolyte; the eighth, beryl; the ninth, a topaz; the tenth, a chrysoprasus; the eleventh, a jacinth; the twelfth, an amethyst.
>
> And the twelve gates were twelve pearls; every several gate was of one pearl: and the street of the city was of pure gold, as it were transparent glass.

> And I saw no temple therein: for the Lord God Almighty and the Lamb are the temple of it.
>
> —Revelations 21:10–22

Thus we see that the temple and the city, two structures built by human hands, are but models corresponding to the larger Cosmos, which was fashioned by Divine hands.

It is this doctrine, this Law of Correspondences, upon which magicians, sorcerers, and priests all rely. For the magician changes the smaller object in order that he might also affect the Cosmic object. In like manner does a priest approach God in a temple. His actions correspond to the approach of the human soul to the Divine soul.

Nothing in the Cosmos is accidental. Everything is connected; everything is part of the system. And there are systems within the systems, wheels within the wheels, and these too are all interconnected.

Cosmic Spirals

The circle, though it is the symbol of completeness, is itself incomplete, for it encompasses only space, not time. Time can be expressed only through motion.

The symbol for motion through time and space is the spiral, or coil. The coil begins at a central point and circles out to infinity. It simultaneously moves inward, toward the center.

The coil or spiral is one of the oldest symbols for the spiritual progress of the human soul. The labyrinths of the ancient temples represented man's journey into himself, back into the womb, into the regions of death, and back out to life.

The journey into the center and back out is a double spiral. The ancients saw the life of a human as just such a double coil. It spirals out toward maturity, and then back to death. It falls through the center, which is a void, and reenters the spiral of life in reincarnation. Each reincarnation is a repetition of this double-spiral pattern. These ancient secret truths have been vindicated in our own time by the discovery that the DNA molecule, which transmits the genetic code, has the form of a double spiral.

Modern science has also discovered that the planetary orbits are not fixed concentric circles, but elliptical spirals around a sun that is itself moving. The sun draws the planets spiralling after it.

Carl Sagan, a well-known astronomer, has described our entire galaxy as "a vast, ponderously rotating pinwheel of about 250 billion suns." And Sagan also points out that "our galaxy is one of at least billions, and perhaps hundreds of billions, of galaxies. Our particular sun and its companion planets constitute no more than one example of a phenomenon that must surely be repeated innumerable times in the vastness of space and time."

From the smallest particles within the atom to the vast galactic systems, the universe is ordered in circling spirals. The "spheres" seen by Pythagoras, Zoroaster, and the Egyptian Hermetic priests in visions have been proven by modern science to be literally existent.

And in recent times it has been revealed that both space and time are curving rather than linear. The cosmologist J.A. Wheeler speaks of the new science of *geometrodynamics*, "the dynamics of curved empty space." We are thus returning to the outlook of Pythagoras, who was a patriarch both of geometry and of occult thought. Pythagoras taught the mathematical harmony of the spheres and said that the spheres of the universe corresponded to the states of the soul.

This is perhaps the greatest mystery: that the human consciousness itself spirals, out from the subconscious to the state of separation of mind and object, and then back in again to the realization that subject and object are one. As the poet and mystic Gertrude Stein might have said, "There is no out there out there."

How is it that the ancients, who lacked our technological sophistication, understood the spiralling nature of life? Were they in direct contact with the Divine? Or could visitors from outer space have come down to teach them? We do not as yet know, though many have spoken on these subjects. The writings of these Speakers and Seekers are recorded in these pages.

The ancients, though not technologically advanced, were quite as able as we to observe Nature and make deductions from their observations. In the temples of Egypt, Mesopotamia, Peru, Mexico, and China, they watched the stars in their courses and noted changes in their relationships to the earth.

They kept their astronomical records for long periods, even thousands of years, and thus they noted patterns in the Cosmos. They saw that the cycles of the Cosmos were predictable: The same planets and stars appeared at the same time of the year. They also saw that each year was different, for the constellations seemed to move through space and time.

These mysteries of the stars were known only to a few priests, who jealously guarded the secrets for themselves, that in their knowledge they might gain more power. Now, in these last days, the astronomical mysteries are open to all who care to study them. This is yet another sign that the end of our present cycle is at hand.

The ancients observed the spiralling shells of snails and other creatures, the vortex of water in a whirlpool, the spiralling traces of some insects on the leaves they consume, and the spiralling outward of the plant's shoot from the seed.

The ancient priests sacrificed animals and looked into their entrails and brains. Thus, they discovered that animals and humans had upper and lower cavities in their bodies, the upper cavities being filled with the spiralling matter of the brain, the lower being filled with the coils of the intestines.

They associated the coils with the coils of the serpent and with the coiling tunnels that wound down into the Earth.

They also associated the coiling serpent with the moon, for they conceived of the waxing and waning of the moon as a spiralling process. The moon's cycles corresponded to those of Woman, from whom every person begins the cycle of life.

The Spirals of Life. The human begins life as a microscopic egg, formed by the union of male and female. This egg is at first attached to the wall of the womb. It gradually evolves an umbilical cord, through which it receives its nourishment.

The ancients of India taught that the universe was a Golden Egg, within which was contained a serpent coiled and floating on a Cosmic ocean. The god Vishnu reclined upon the serpent and dreamed Creation.

Vishnu preserved the Cosmic order by coiling the serpent around the Axis of the World. The forces of Good and Evil pull the serpent in opposite directions, thereby churning the waters of life. Thus the processes of life are continued in the action of a moving double coil.

The Hermetic, Kabbalistic, Tantric, and Gnostic traditions all spoke of the "serpents of wisdom," whose windings around the spine circulate energy through the body. The yogins call this energy *kuṇḍālinī*. It is the goal of yoga and other spiritual exercises to regulate the flow of energies through the body.

The ancients believed that healing came about through the regulation of spiralling energies around the spine. And even today the symbol of the doctor remains the coiled serpent.

The Gnostic and Hermetic priests visualized the Axis of the World as a *Tau* cross around which serpents were coiled.

This knowledge entered the secret traditions of Judaism through Moses. For Moses was educated as an Egyptian prince, and therefore was an initiate into the Egyptian mysteries. He also married Zipporah, the daughter of the priest of Midian.

The first miracle performed by Moses after his call by Yahweh was the transformation of a rod into a serpent and back again. Precisely such a manifestation would have been necessary to convince the Israelites and Egyptians that Moses spoke by Divine authority.

The Israelites acknowledged the Hermetic truths even after the Law of God was revealed to Moses on Mount Sinai. The Hebrew scriptures make it clear that the Hermetic wisdom came from God.

> And the people spake against God, and against Moses, Wherefore have ye brought us up out of Egypt to die in the wilderness? for there is no bread, neither

is there any water, and our soul loatheth this light bread.

And the Lord sent fiery serpents among the people, and they bit the people; and much people of Israel died.

Therefore the people came unto Moses, and said, We have sinned, for we have spoken against the Lord, and against thee; pray unto the Lord, that he take away the serpents from us. And Moses prayed for the people.

And the Lord said unto Moses, Make thee a fiery serpent, and set it upon a pole: and it shall come to pass, that everyone that is bitten, when he looketh upon it, shall live.

And Moses made a serpent of brass, and put it upon a pole, and it came to pass that if a serpent had bitten any man, when he beheld the serpent of brass, he lived.

—Numbers 21:5–9

The cross, or pole, around which the serpent was coiled, was the axis of the world, the human spine, the direct line of communication with God.

This is the mystic meaning of the crucifixion of Jesus Christ. For Christ Himself explained it thus:

And as Moses lifted up the serpent in the wilderness, even so must the Son of man be lifted up;

That whosoever believeth in him should not perish but have eternal life.

—John 3:14–15

The Mystic Spiral. The spirals of energy within the body correspond to the spirals of the soul toward God. This, too, was part of the ancient secret doctrines.

Like Pythagoras, the Hermetic priests taught that the soul ascended through the heavenly spheres to reach the Divine. There were seven of these spheres, each of which corresponded to one of the seven planets.

The initiate among the Egyptians was likened to a scarab. This beetle moves in a spiral path, pushing its egg along before it. Each stage of enlightenment corresponded to a new birth of the scarab beetle.

In all the ancient mysteries, the passing from one cycle of reincarnation to the next was regarded as rebirth. Enlightenment also is considered a new birth.

This is the meaning of the teachings of Jesus:

> Verily, verily, I say unto thee, Except a man be born again, he cannot see the kingdom of God.
>
> Nicodemus said unto him, How can a man be born when he is old? Can he enter a second time into his mother's womb, and be born?
>
> Jesus answered, Verily, verily, I say unto thee, Except a man be born of water and of the spirit, he cannot enter into the kingdom of God.
>
> That which is born of the flesh is flesh, and that which is born of the spirit is spirit.
>
> Marvel not that I say unto thee, Ye must be born again.
>
> The wind bloweth where it listeth, and thou hearest the sound thereof, but canst not tell whence it cometh or whither it goeth. So is everyone that is born of the Spirit.
>
> Nicodemus answered and said unto him, How can these things be?
>
> Jesus answered and said unto him. Art thou a master of Israel, and knoweth not these things?
>
> —John 3:3–10

The final question of Jesus to the scholar was delivered in a voice not of mockery but of puzzlement. For already, in that time, the Jewish Kabbalistic tradition was old.

The Kabbalists pictured the upward progress of the soul and the downward progress of Divine truth as a Tree of Life. The Tree's central trunk was the direct route from Malchut (Earth) to Keser (Crown). There were twenty-two paths that circled upward around the central trunk. These paths were traced through ten *Sephirot*, or Manifestations of the Divine.

Kabbalists still teach that each of the *Sephirot* corresponds to a planet. The tenth planet is the Sun. The other nine planets are those of our solar system.

The Moslems, too, teach that the soul ascends to God and Divinity descends to Man in spiral patterns. This is the meaning of the whirling dances performed by the Sufi mystics, the dervishes. The Moslems believe the soul goes through seven upward spirals. This path is enacted by the pilgrim upon visiting Mecca when he walks seven times around the *Kaaba*, the sacred stone. The seven paths of Islam correspond to the seven days of creation and the seven planets.

The spiralling movement of the soul was spoken of also by the alchemists. Nicholas Flamel wrote:

> These are the two serpents which are fixed around the Caduceus, or Staff of Mercury, and by means of which Mercury wields his great power. . . . So long as Nature remains untamed, the opposition of the two forces is manifest in destructive and poisonous mode.

Each phase of the alchemist's Great Work corresponded to one of the signs of the zodiac. Indeed, without acknowledging the zodiac, the alchemist could not achieve the Stone. The Philosopher's Stone, like the Kaaba of the Moslems, the Axis of the Hindus, and the Tree of the Kabbalists, is a central point around which the serpent of Wisdom winds. (And the Great Work of the alchemists also corresponded to the seven planets, and to the seven metals, and to the colors of these planets and metals.)

Many are the instances of mystic spirals, in all religions, in all times and places, and many are the maps that have been drawn of them. For the Mandalas of the East are nothing but maps of the soul or consciousness, and the prayer wheels of the East are models of the soul's ascending spirals.

Truly, to attain Divine Wisdom, to understand the Secrets of the Universe, one must, like the prophet Ezekiel, see Visions of Wheels within Wheels.

The Ages of the World

Just as the human being corresponds to the Cosmos, so does the Cosmos correspond to its own history. Written in the Book of Nature is the whole key to what has gone before, what now is, and what will be.

The ages of the world have been revealed to seers in visions. These privileged ones have been able to read the Akashic Record, the record of all events of the soul since the beginning of time. This record exists on the astral plane and can be read only by spiritual means.

The ages of the world have been many, and we have records of only a few of them. The events of past eons are told here in the Book of Cataclysms. The events of more recent ages are told in the Chronicles of Lemuria, Mu, and Atlantis, and in the Book of Visitations.

The Biblical Ages. Many difficult passages in the Hebrew and Christian Bible make sense only when understood as images of occult truths. Like any other sacred book, the Bible has two levels of meaning: the outer meaning, which is apparent to the casual reader, and the inner, or esoteric, meaning, which is revealed only to the diligent Seeker.

The prophet Daniel was called before Nebuchadnezzar, King of Babylon, and ordered both to recall and to interpret one of the king's dreams. This is what Daniel said to the king:

> Thou, O king, sawest, and behold a great image. This great image, whose brightness was excellent, stood before thee; and the form thereof was terrible.

This image's head was of fine gold his breasts and his arms of silver, his belly and his thighs brass

His legs of iron, his feet part of iron and part of clay.

Thou sawest till that a stone was cut out without hands, which smote the image upon his feet that were of iron and clay, and brake them to pieces.

Then was the iron, the clay, the brass, the silver, and the gold, broken to pieces together, and became like the chaff of the summer threshing floors; and the wind carried them away, that no place was found for them: and the stone that smote the image became a great mountain, and filled the whole earth.

This is the dream; and we will tell the interpretation thereof before the king.

Thou, O king, art a king of kings: for the God of heaven hath given thee a kingdom, power, and strength, and glory.

And wheresoever the children of men dwell, the beasts of the field and the fowl of the heaven hath he given into thine hand, and hath made thee ruler over them all. Thou art this head of gold.

And after thee shall rise another kingdom inferior to thee, and another third kingdom of brass, which shall bear rule over all the earth.

And the fourth kingdom shall be strong as iron: forasmuch as iron breaketh in pieces and subdueth all things: and as iron that breaketh all these, shall it break in pieces and bruise.

And whereas thou sawest the feet and toes, part of potters' clay, and part of iron, the kingdom shall be divided; but there shall be in it of the strength of the iron, forasmuch as thou sawest the iron mixed with miry clay.

And as the toes of the feet were part of iron, and part of clay, so the kingdom shall be partly strong, and partly broken.

And whereas thou sawest iron mixed with miry clay, they shall mingle themselves with the seed of men: but they shall not cleave one to another, even as iron is not mixed with clay.

And in the days of these kings shall the God of heaven set up a kingdom, which shall never be destroyed: and the kingdom shall not be left to other people, but it shall break in pieces and consume all these kingdoms, and it shall stand forever.

—Daniel 2: 31–44

This passage has exercised the ingenuity of biblical scholars for generations. In general, the scholars agree on this interpretation, that the four kingdoms mentioned by Daniel were those of the Babylonians, the Medes and Persians, the Greeks, and the Romans. The Babylonians were the head of gold, the Medes and Persians the breast and arms of silver, the Greeks the belly of brass, and the Romans the legs of iron. The feet, then, represent to most scholars the Roman Empire after its East/West split ("Part iron and part clay").

Some Christians teach that the stone, which rolls down, destroys the image, and then swells into a mountain, represents the Church of Christ.

But the follower of occult truths can see the real meaning of this passage. The feet of iron and clay represent the Christian Church, for it contains both Roman (iron) and pagan (clay) elements.

The Stone is the Philosopher's Stone. It is "cut out without hands"—that is, formed inside the athanor of the alchemists. The stone will indeed swell to the size of a mountain and fill the whole earth.

The mountain—or pyramid—is the symbol of occult communication with the Divine. The initiate who has achieved direct communication has achieved eternity, nirvana, a state outside the ordinary bounds of time and space. This is a kingdom that will stand forever.

The Creation and History. Some Christian scholars teach that the seven days of Creation correspond to seven periods of human history. Each of the six creative days corresponds to one of the seven "dispensations" of Divine Grace on earth.

During the first dispensation, the only notion men had of God was the light of their own consciences. The first day was the day on which God created Light. The first dispensation ended with the Flood.

The Flood marks the beginning of the second dispensation, and corresponds to the second day of Creation, on which God divided the waters from the heavens. During this period, people knew God through direct, divine government.

On the third day of Creation, the Earth appeared above the waters. The third dispensation lasted from the time of Abraham to the coming of Christ. During this period, God talked only to his *earthly* chosen people, the Jews. The third dispensation lasted for 1,960 years and was divided into four cycles of 490 years each.

The fourth day of creation was when the sun, moon, and stars were set to reign in the heavens. The fourth dispensation begins with a star—the Star of Bethlehem. Jesus is the Star of the Morning, the Sun of the Christian heaven. Just as the church reflects the glory of God in the world, so does the moon reflect the sun.

The fourth dispensation, the Age of the Church, is divided into seven periods, each of which corresponds to one of the seven churches listed in the Book of Revelations. The prophet John saw these seven churches as *seven stars*.

The names of the seven churches are Ephesus, Smyrna, Pergamum, Thyatira, Sardis, Philadelphia, and Laodicea. We are now living in the Age of Laodicea, of which the prophet wrote:

> And unto the angel of the church of the Laodiceans write; These things saith the Amen, the faithful and true witness, the beginning of the creation of God;
>
> I know thy works, that thou art neither cold nor hot: I would thou wert cold or hot.
>
> So then because thou art lukewarm, I will spue thee out of my mouth.
>
> Because thou sayest, I am rich, and increased with goods, and have need of nothing; and knowest not that thou art wretched, and miserable, and poor, and blind, and naked:
>
> I counsel thee to buy of me gold tried in the fire, that thou mayest be rich; and white raiment, that thou mayest be clothed, and that the shame of thy nakedness do not appear; and anoint thine eyes with eyesalve, that thou mayest see.
>
> As many as I love, I rebuke and chasten: be zealous therefore, and repent.
>
> —Revelations 3: 14–19

The lukewarm civilization of our present time will end, as it was revealed to John, and be followed by the Second Coming of Christ. There is much disagreement as to what form this Second Coming will take

John saw a vision of a Great White Throne set in heaven. The throne was surrounded by the seats of twenty-four elders, all of whom had golden crowns. Here is John's description of the occupant of the throne:

> And he that sat was to look upon like a jasper and a sardine stone: and there was a rainbow round about the throne, in sight like unto an emerald.
>
> —Revelations 4: 3

The occult interpretation of the seven churches differs somewhat from that held by the majority of Christian scholars. For the occultists believe that our lukewarm civilization will be followed by a general period of illumination and spiritual vision. This could be the meaning of the Second Coming.

All agree, however, that the present age will end soon, and will be Cosmic in its dimensions of expansion.

The fifth dispensation corresponds to the fifth day of Creation, during which the waters of the earth brought forth life.

It will begin with the Rapture of the Saints, in which all those who believe in Christ will be caught up to meet him in the air. There are some who say that this meeting will take place by means of spaceship transportation, and that Christ is even now on Venus, preparing his spacecraft for this divine event.

The sixth day of Creation was that in which God created Man in his own image. The sixth dispensation will be that of the millenium, a time of peace on earth and in heaven.

On the seventh day of Creation, God rested. The seventh dispensation is eternity.

The Christian and Hebrew systems speak only of historical time—the period between the birth and death of the human race. There are other systems that outline the whole history of the Cosmos, even before humans appeared in it.

The Astrological Ages. The ages of the Earth can be divided into Great Years, each of which contains about 26,000 years of our time. Each great year is divided into twelve zodiacal years, each about 2,166 years long.

The stars are the most fixed and permanent record of Nature. Every 2,166 years, the Earth enters into another zodiacal phase. Thus, the affairs of Earth come under the influence of a different constellation.

From about the year 10,000 B.C. to about the year 8,000 B.C., the Earth was under the rule of Leo. During this period the people worshipped the Sun, Leo's planet. Also in this period, kings began to govern humans. The subjects of these god-kings used the Sun and the Lion as symbols for their rulers. Thus were built the great temples to the Sun and the great half-human half-lion figures such as the Sphinx

Around 8,000 B.C., the Age of Cancer began, and people began worshipping in Moon Cults. It was during this era that the worship of the Great Mother was spread around the known world.

The age of Gemini, which began around 6,000 B.C., was marked by the influence of the planet Mercury. It was, indeed, during that era when writing and commerce were first developed on this planet.

Around 4,000 B.C., the Age of Taurus, the Bull, began. Cattle were domesticated, and the Bull Cult spread around the Mediterranean world. Then followed the Age of Aries, when the worship of sheep predominated. The ancient Hebrews left Egypt around the beginning of the Age of Aries, and they received the instructions for their religious practices, which included the sacrifice of lambs.

The Age of Pisces began with the coming of Christ, whose symbol was the fish. (The Greek letters of the name Christ also spell "fish.") The Age of Pisces corresponds to the fourth day of Creation in the Christian system, which is also the Age of the Church. This present age will end around 2,000 A.D.—the same time that the Christians look for the coming of Christ again to Earth.

The next age will be that of Aquarius, an age of peace and harmony, when occult knowledge, extraterrestrial communication, and thought transference will be common among the Earth's inhabitants.

There is only apparent contradiction between the systems that have been revealed at various times and places. The systems can vary in detail, as indeed they must since those who record them are human. But in general outline, the truths are the same.

The Akashic Ages. For how long has the Earth been whirling in the heavens? When did the cycles of history begin? These things are great mysteries that no person on Earth may solve without occult assistance.

All the sages of the ages have proclaimed that history moves in cycles, and that at periodic intervals the Earth's age ends in conflagration, inundation, and cataclysm. This is the most ancient tradition of the human race.

The sacred Hindu books spoke of four ages of the world and claimed that the fifth age was that of the present. The Hindus called these world-ages *Kalpas* or *Yugas*.

And in the *Zend-Avesta*, the book of the revelations of Zoroaster, it is recorded that the prophet saw seven world-ages, each age ending with signs and wonders on the Earth.

The American Indians also preserved traditions of world-ages. Their high priests taught that the sky changed with each shift into a new cycle. In their sacred writings they called each age a Sun.

The records of the ages are preserved in the Astral Plane, that they might be revealed in special times and places to enlightened humans. And so it was that the knowledge of the ages came to Madame Blavatsky. The Brotherhood of Mahatmas, who reside eternally in the mountains of Tibet, appeared to Blavatsky and showed her a book; and the name of the book was the *Book of Dyzan*.

Blavatsky looked, and she saw the book was written in a language she did not know. The name of that language was called Senzar, and the origin of the language was Atlantis.

At the same time, Spirit Guides appeared also to Annie Besant, and Henry Steele Olcott, and Rudolf Steiner, and many others who sought enlightenment.

To all these the Guides revealed that there was written in the astral plane an Akashic Record of all that had gone before. Many of the enlightened ones were taken up into the heavens and given a glimpse of the Akashic Record, in which the plan of the ages is revealed, from eternity to eternity.

The Record states: That since the foundation of our Earth there have been five Root Races, and there will be seven Root Races before the world perishes. But each Root Race ends in cataclysm. This is the plan of the ages.

The First Root Race was called the Polarean, and the second was called the Hyperborean.

The Third Root Race was the Lemurian; the Fourth Root Race was the Atlantean; and the Fifth Root race, even now, is the Aryan.

The Sixth Root Race shall begin with the rising of the continents, and mankind will live once again upon Lemuria.

And the Seventh Root Race, which shall be the last, will be in regular contact with beings from other planets. And in the last days of the Earth some humans will leave the Earth. They will travel to Mercury, in order to begin human life anew.

This is the record of those called Theosophists. Other revelations, too, have been received.

To Alice A. Bailey and her followers there appeared a committee of Spirit Guides, and they spoke of the ages of the Earth.

The Guides said: There are seven superuniverses, which are arranged around a central universe. And the name of the central universe is Havona. At the center of Havona lies the island of Paradise, "where God dwells at the geographic center of infinity."

That which we call the planet Earth is in reality the planet Urantia. And Urantia is part of a small universe called Nebadon, which lies within the superuniverse of Orvonton.

The capital of Orvonton is called Uversa. The Guides resided in Uversa.

Then a different revelation came to Rudolf Steiner. He saw that the Earth had been three other planets, and was still to be three other planets, so that the total of the planets of the Earth was to be seven.

These are the planets of the Earth: Saturn, Sun, Moon, Earth, Jupiter, Venus, and Vulcan. Each was a planet different from the Earth, and each contained the Earth. For each planet grew out of the preceding one.

They were not separate planets but separate stages of one planet spirit. Yet, in each stage, the planet was entirely transformed so that it became an altogether different planet. This is one of the ancient mysteries of occult science.

During the first, or Saturn Stage, human consciousness developed into its dullest first stage. At that time people existed in a deep trance-consciousness. Saturn was divided into seven cycles, or rounds, which correspond to the names of higher spirits. In each round, another type of higher spirit revealed itself.

In the first round, the Spirits of Will, which were called Thrones by the ancient Hebrews; in the second round, the Spirits of Wisdom, which were called Dominions by the Hebrews; in the third round, the Spirits of Motion, which were known as Principalities; in the fourth round, the Spirits of Form, which were known as Powers; in the fifth round, the Spirits of Personality, or Primal Beginnings; in the sixth round, the Spirits of the Sons of Fire, or Archangels; and in the seventh round, the Spirits of the Sons of Twilight, the Angels.

And in the seventh cycle of the first planet there developed a predisposition to Atma, or spirit, which began the life of the spiritual Man.

Thus the cycle of the planet Saturn was completed. Then followed the cycles of the Planet Sun.

During the Sun-cycles the human body became like a plant, because an ether body was incorporated into it. And the cycles of Sun were like the cycles of Saturn.

In the first round of Sun the ether body was poured out by the Spirits of Wisdom. In the second round the Spirits of Motion began working on the ether body. In the third round the work upon the ether body by the Spirits of Form began. In the fourth round of the Sun the ether body was given selfhood by the Spirits of Personality. In the fifth round came the Spirits of Fire; in the sixth round, the Sons of Twilight. Each spirit acted upon the ether body, and in the seventh round Man himself acted upon the ether body. And at the end of the seventh round of the Sun, there came into being an activated monad, the combination of the germ of Atma (Spirit-Man) and the Life Spirit (Buddhi).

Then came the seven rounds of the Planet Moon, during which man developed the knowledge and use of symbolic images.

The first round of the Moon repeated the rounds of Saturn; the second round of the Moon repeated the rounds of the Sun. In the third round of the Moon there took place a great outpouring of the Spirits of Motion, and thus was created the Astral Body. Then the Moon split off and revolved around the Sun. In the fourth round of the Moon the Spirits of Twilight inhabited human bodies. Then the Spirits of Personality inhabited astral bodies. In the fifth round of the Moon the spirit-self joined with the activated monad, which was formed at the end of the Planet Sun. During the sixth and seventh rounds, the Moon began to revolve closer and closer to the Sun. At the end of the Moon Cycle, the Sun united with the Moon. Thus, the whole formed was united in a deep sleep. And the Cosmos did not again awaken until the Age of the Planet Earth.

In the Saturn Age mankind developed consciousness. In the Sun Age the ether body was developed; in the Moon Age the Astral Body; in the Earth Age the physical body.

Thus we can see that the spiritual evolution of mankind is upward. In time we shall develop facility in communicating with the Thrones, Powers, Dominions, Archangels, Angels, and other spirits.

Systems Within Systems

Nothing in the Cosmos is accidental. Everything is connected. Everything corresponds. Everything has meaning.

The seven ages of the world, which have been known since ancient times, correspond to the stages of man's spiritual consciousness. And this correspondence is true for the history of the human race as well as for the soul of the individual man.

In every age there are adepts who understand the system. And in every age there are apprentices to the adepts. The apprentices of each age form the seed of the age that is to come. So has it always been in the history of the Cosmos, and so shall it be.

The Cosmic Systems have been understood by all the Wise Ones in human history. The priests of Hermes taught these truths, as did the Hebrew prophets and the Savior, Jesus. So also taught Zoroaster and Muhammad and Buddha. And so have taught the prophets that have appeared in modern times.

And the prophets have also taught that the human body and spirit contain systems, which correspond to the wider systems of the universe. Systems demonstrate the order of the Cosmos.

The Cosmos is ordered according to Divine Plan. Nothing is accidental. Everything is Truth.

The Book of Lesser Lost Lands

The earth in ages past has seen many civilizations and races without number. Each of these arose, and each one fell. Such are the cycles of eternity.

Knowledge of the past has been preserved for us in the Akashic Record. Some histories, such as that of Atlantis, have been made known in full detail. Other civilizations were far older than Atlantis and thus have receded farther from our memories. Only fragments of them remain. These civilizations are known as the Lesser Lost Lands.

They were not lesser in power, or strength, or occult significance. For each age of the world has its own value in the Cosmic Mind. But they are lesser in terms of our knowledge of them. Our human memory is sadly limited.

The Chronicle of Mu

This is the record of the civilization of Mu, a continent that once filled what is now the Pacific Ocean and which perished in a volcanic explosion many thousands of years before written history.

The inhabitants of Mu were a noble and happy people, and their civilization was in many ways superior to ours. The details of life on Mu have come to us through the teachings of Brasseur, James Churchward, Le Plongeon, and their disciples.

Brasseur, Le Plongeon, and Churchward were scholars and men of renown. They ventured into the most dangerous lands of Earth in search of the knowledge of Mu.

Brasseur was a priest who lived in France, and he travelled to Spain, in order to seek wisdom from the libraries of that land.

In the Historical Academy of Madrid, Brasseur discovered an ancient manuscript. And the name of the ancient book was *Account of the Affairs of Yucatan*. The name of the writer was Bishop Diego de Landa, who served as a priest of the Church of the Christians in Mexico. And he lived among the Mayans, an ancient and pagan people.

Now de Landa had been exceedingly angry with the priests of the Mayans because they would not convert to the Christian God. So he ordered all the sacred books of the Mayans to be collected and burned. And only three books were saved from the flames.

Then the bishop repented of what he had done, and he began to study the knowledge that he had previously tried to eradicate. De Landa studied the old books and learned the Mayan alphabet from them. It was this alphabet that Brasseur discovered in Madrid.

Then Brasseur began to read from the old books of the Mayans and to translate them according to the alphabet of de Landa. And these truths were found by Brasseur in the Mayan writings: that the Mayans held a tradition that their race had been founded by white men, who came from a vast continent that had been sunk by a volcanic explosion. And the Mayans called this continent Mu. Brasseur believed that Mu was the Mayan name for Atlantis.

Augustus Le Plongeon, a Digger of great repute, believed this also. He journeyed to the land of Yucatan and found there the ruins of great cities. He lived among the descendants of the Mayans and learned from the tribal elders. And he gazed also at the walls of the ruined Mayan cities, where he read inscriptions of immense antiquity.

Thus it was revealed to him that thousands of years before, in the Land of Mu, there had lived a woman named Moo, Queen of Mu. And Queen Moo of Mu was fair to look upon.

Now in those days it was the custom on Mu for the members of the royal family to marry only their own siblings. Thus they kept the ruling house pure.

Now Queen Moo had two brothers, Prince Coh and Prince Aac. Each loved Moo better than life itself. The brothers each tried to win her heart. But Moo herself favored Coh and gave herself to him in marriage. Then Aac rose up in jealousy and killed his brother Coh. And there was great sorrow throughout the land of Mu, especially in the court of the Queen.

Then the high priests of Mu came to Queen Moo and cried, "O Queen, live forever." And they bowed low before her.

"Know, O Queen, that this favored land is soon to perish beneath the waters of the ocean, for a great fire shall come from heaven and destroy this land. So have the oracles spoken."

Queen Moo was sickened at their words. But she had been full of sorrow since the death of her brother and lover, and Mu had lost all its joys for her. So the Queen prepared great ships and loaded her treasures into the ships, along with her books and the sacred objects of the temples of Mu. And she sailed east from Mu, leaving behind forever the land of her birth. Many other Muvians went with her also. Others heeded the warnings of the priests and departed for distant lands. And some went north to America; and some went south to Peru; and some went west to China; and some went east to Central America and Africa.

Then were heard rumblings in the deep, and fire spurted up out of the ocean, and the land of Mu upheaved. The continent was torn asunder and scattered, and the waves covered the place where the land had stood. Thus were the prophecies of the priests fulfilled.

Meanwhile, Queen Moo and her ships crossed the isthmus of Central America (stopping only to found the Indian civilizations) and journeyed across the Atlantic Ocean to Egypt. When the Egyptians saw the ships on the horizon, they wondered greatly. When Queen Moo came to the land, she spoke to the Egyptians with great majesty and authority. And they bowed down to her as if she were a goddess, and they called her Isis.

Then Queen Moo appointed priests to serve her, to guard the sacred objects of Moo and to instruct initiates in Muvian wisdom. The Wisdom of Mu has come down to us through the priests of Isis.

But the greatest revelation concerning Mu was written down by Churchward, who studied the culture and language of Mu for many years. He journeyed to Tibet and India in search of Muvian Wisdom.

In India, he came upon a remote temple. As he entered the temple, he was consumed by a strange excitement. His excitement grew when he saw mysterious markings on the temple walls. The priest of the temple revealed to Churchward that the temple was inhabited by the Naacals, the Holy Ones of Mu. And the priest who spoke was the only Naacal left on Earth. He had two students, and only among those three could the sacred language of Mu be spoken.

So Churchward, too, learned the language of Mu, so that he might preserve the knowledge of Muvian history. This is the method by which Churchward learned it: he entered the temple and stared at the walls for many hours. The symbols became impressed upon his brain, and united with symbols already therein. So Churchward reached an understanding through the Eye of the Mind.

To Churchward it was revealed that Mu was not identical with Atlantis, but that it had been far more ancient than Atlantis and had existed in the Pacific Ocean. Mu was a paradise of tropical splendor, with gently rolling hills, lush vegetation, and fresh meandering streams. The land was rich in meadow grasses, fruits, and flowers. And all manner of plants, birds, and beasts thrived in the land.

And Mu contained 64 million souls. These people were mostly of white skin. There were some of yellow, brown, and black skin, but they remained under the subjugation of the people of white skin.

The Muvians were rich and noble. They dressed in gorgeous attire, covered with jewels and embroidery. They built ships, roads, schools, and temples. And Mu was the mightiest land on Earth.

But the earthquakes and volcanoes came, and fire rained from heaven, and the land shook and the seas roared. The destruction of Mu took place over many generations. At times the people of Mu tried to rebuild, but they were unable to circumvent the Divine plan. So most perished.

But the inheritance of Mu is to this day among us. For the fleeing Muvians took their culture to all parts of the globe. All the knowledge of Chaldea, Egypt, Greece, and India originated in Mu.

The Chronicle of Pan

In the eighth decade of the nineteenth century of Pisces, there lived in the city of New York a man named Dr. John Ballou Newbrough. He was a dentist by profession, but he was also a medium, and in contact with the Spirit Guides.

An angel appeared to Dr. Newbrough, and took hold of his hand, and guided him in his writing. And this is what the angel wrote.

In the beginning there were no humans, but certain ocean creatures had high intelligence. These creatures were like seals in form. The angels mated with these creatures and produced offspring, half-fish and half-human. These were mermaids and mermen, and they were the first human gods.

This mating took place on the continent of Pan, which was once located in the northern Pacific. The islands of the Bering Straits are all that survive today of Panic Land.

The angel also revealed to Dr. Newbrough the Panic Language, which the doctor wrote down automatically. Thus was preserved for us the story of a land otherwise lost to the human imagination.

The Chronicle of Lumania

All the lost civilizations of the past have reached levels of achievement like our own. Then they have either pressed on to higher ground or been destroyed by the Cosmic Forces.

Each civilization functions as a unit of reincarnation. When the people of a civilization destroy themselves, they learn from their previous error, mend their wicked ways, and reach a higher level in the next reincarnation.

There are civilizations that reached such high planes of enlightenment that they left the Earth altogether and went to live on other planets. The great civilization of Lumania developed from the remainders of such a civilization.

The goal of the Lumanians was to develop a nonviolent, unaggressive strain of human being. They achieved this by genetic engineering, and they created biological safeguards against violence.

The Lumanians developed the use of the waves which today we know as ultrahigh-frequency vibrations. They applied these waves to the sick, and in that manner all diseases were healed.

The Lumanians also used magnetic force-fields for their own defense. They built vast cities underground, and they closed off these cities with force-fields. Their outpost cities were spread as far as the Pyrenees.

The entrances to their cities were located in caves. The Lumanians marked the cave entrances with drawings and other art.

So it was that, many generations later, the people of the Stone Age found the Lumanian cave drawings and copied them. The Cro-Magnons also imitated the Lumanian art.

The Lumanians were not destroyed by a cataclysm but merely faded away. The biological safeguards they had created blocked their physical energy. They survived only in the mental plane. And the few that survived in the physical plane knew that their civilization had utterly failed.

Then the remaining Lumanians left their great cities and went into the wildnerness to live among primitive tribes. They taught the tribes' people their religion, which included a belief in a powerful male god. In time the God of the Lumanians became known to human generations as Jehovah.

Also from the Lumanian civilization there survived Speakers, whose oral teachings comprise the most ancient body of religious knowledge in the world. The Speakers passed on the mysteries which we know as the occult. From Lumania, the Speakers spread the Word to Africa and Australia.

And the central teaching of the Lumanian speakers was this: That thought creates Matter, and that no matter exists apart from Mind.

These teachings of the Lumanians have been preserved in our times through the speech of Seth, who has spoken to the medium Jane Roberts. Seth has also revealed that the Speakers are still operating in our world. They enter the dreams of humans and impart their spiritual knowledge to the sleeper.

The knowledge of the Lumanian speakers was passed down through the priests of Egypt and through the Druids, and finally through Christ.

The Chronicle of Lemuria

In the days of Queen Victoria, there went out scientists, explorers, and other men of wisdom, travelling to all countries. They travelled from Britain, from Germany, France, and the United States. And they journeyed to India, China, and Africa. And when they returned, they spoke and wrote among themselves, saying:

"How comes it that in India, which lies far to the east, there can be found the same plants and animals as in South Africa, which lies to the west and south?"

The scientists puzzled especially over an animal called the lemur. This animal resembled an ape, but also a man. The lemur lived in India and on the island of Madagascar. And the wise men said, "By what means could the lemur have travelled so many thousands of miles?" They were puzzled, because vast expanses of ocean surrounded the two kingdoms.

Then some factions arose among them, scientists who said, "Clearly, what is now ocean was once land. Then, when the land sank, the previous parts were isolated from each other in their present manner."

Some scientists mocked this theory, saying, "How could a whole land mass have disappeared thus without a trace?" But others believed the theory, and they searched for evidence of lost lands. And they named the lost land for which they searched Lemuria, in honor of the lemur.

Among those who believed was a German called Ernst Haeckel. He was a naturalist of renown, who made expeditions to Ceylon and drew the likenesses of plants and insects. Haeckel believed that Lemuria must have been the primeval home of Man.

Another supporter of the theory was Alfred Russel Wallace. He speculated that Lemuria had once stretched "from West Africa to Burmah, South China, and the Clebes."

The views of Wallace, Haeckel, and the other scientists were reported in the press, and printed in journals. And the fame of Lemuria spread to America.

Meanwhile, there arose Mahatmas, or Manus, in Tibet, and they travelled around the world seeking people whom they might enlighten. The Mahatmas appeared only to those who wished to see them, for they travelled on the astral plane.

The Mahatmas appeared to Helen Petrovna Blavatsky, a Seeker from Russia, who had ventured to England in search of truth. They dictated to Madame Blavatsky the entire history of the world, including the story of Lemuria. They showed her an ancient text called the *Book of Dyzan*. This book had been written in Atlantis, in the language called Senzar. The Mahatmas taught Madame Blavatsky to read and write in the Senzar tongue, they spoke also to her disciples.

Thus came Madame Blavatsky by the secret knowledge which she revealed to the world, as was her mission. The Mahatmas spoke also to Blavatsky's disciples, Annie Besant, W. Scott-Elliot, and Rudolf Steiner. This is the message of these prophets:

The continent of Lemuria once covered nearly all the area in the southern hemisphere that is now ocean. Lemuria rose out of the ocean at the time when the Second Root Race neared the end of its allotted time on the planet.

Then the Manus, who were then, as now, directing the spiritual evolution of the human race, chose Lemuria as the next place for experimenting with various life forms.

The first Lemurians were creatures of jelly. But under the direction of the Mahatmas they evolved the ability to stand and walk. The early Lemurians were hermaphrodites. They gave birth by laying eggs.

These creatures had ideas, but no memory. Therefore, they had no language but communicated by grunts, cries, and other natural sounds. And yet the Lemurians had no need of language, for they derived their thoughts from Divine energy and communicated without words. They understood the inner lives of animals and plants.

They also possessed incredible control over their own bodies. If a Lemurian wished to lift a huge boulder or tree trunk, and the strength of his arm failed, he had only to think to the arm, and the arm would receive the message, and the arm's strength would be increased.

In appearance the Lemurians were like monsters—twelve-to fifteen-feet tall. Their faces were flat. Their eyes were set wide apart, enabling them to see sideways. They also had eyes in the backs of their heads, so they could see behind them. Each Lemurian, therefore, had three eyes. The third eye survives in the present human body as the pineal gland. The Lemurians did not have noses and mouths as we know them, but large muzzles like those of the other mammals.

The Lemurians walked upright, but their arms and knees were permanently bent. Their feet and hands were huge. The heels of their feet protruded in such a manner as to allow them to walk backward as well as forward.

Daily Life in Lemuria. The Lemurians did not build houses, but lived in caves and other dwellings provided them by nature. They directed their building skills toward the construction of sacred areas—arrangements of stones at places of Divine power.

The Lemurians kept great reptiles and beasts of burden as pets. They also used the reptiles as companions in the hunt. But other giant reptiles also lived in the land, and the Lemurians feared these. In the last periods of Lemurian civilization, the giant beasts so overran the continent, that the Lemurians were nearly extinguished.

In all eras of its history Lemuria was a harsh, rugged land. So the people educated their children to endure much pain and hardship. Those children who could not bear tortures or undergo dangers were left to perish. For the Lemurians believed that a child should be killed in its youth rather than grow to be an adult whose weakness might endanger others. The male Lemurians, especially, were educated in this harsh manner. The female Lemurians possessed strong powers of the imagination, and their education was planned so that these powers would increase.

The Lemurians worshipped at sacred places where they could feel the flow of energy to be the strongest. They communicated with the One by means of thought waves.

The Lemurians were also guided in their evolution by supernatural beings whom they thought to be Lhas. These were the same beings whom today we call Mahatmas. They are also called Manus.

The Sexual Division. Until the middle of the Lemurian Root Race, which is to say the Third Root Race, human beings were hermaphroditic. That is, they were of both sexes in one body.

The form of the human being before the division was soft, malleable and warm-blooded. The creature's sense organs had not yet developed, but only the organs of will and motion.

There was as yet no separation between physical and soul activities, for the soul felt directly the life-energies of the Cosmos.

There were among these hermaphrodites certain superhuman individuals who were able to perceive directly the astral world. They directed the affairs of the other Lemurians, for they were in direct contact with the spirits Whereas the ordinary Lemurians acted only according to energy and will, the superhumans acted also according to love.

The Beings of Love transferred the thought of love into the minds of the developing humans. Thus began sensual love, and thus began the development of the sensual organs. Then the Lemurians, delighted with their new senses, began touching and exploring the bodies of the animals on the Earth. They also experienced the pleasures of eating and drinking, and the comforting warmth of the Sun.

They neglected their spiritual energies as they developed their physical energies. Then some of the Lemurians began to look with lust upon the reptiles, birds, and other animals, and they lay with them, and copulated with them, and bore children by them. The children were ugly mutants, half-human and half-animal.

Then the Lhas, the Beings of Love, looked upon the human race in horror and repented of their plan to create sensual love. The Beings of Love said, "We will not work any longer at the task we were appointed to do. For we cannot be responsible for directing the spiritual evolution of such a perverse and stubborn people."

Now at that time, there was on the planet Venus a mighty and advanced civilization, which had monitored the Earth for some time by means of thoughts, and the Venutians "heard" the complaints of the Lhas.

The Venutians visited the Earth and communicated with the Lhas. And the Lhas called these Venutians the Lords of the Flame, because they arrived in the form of fire.

The Venutians said to the Lhas, "Behold, the people sleep with animals because they have none of their own kind with whom to sleep. For no person can copulate with a person that is like himself, but every person must copulate with its own kind.

"Therefore, you should make two kinds of humans, one male and one female. And each shall desire the other, and they shall copulate only with their own kind."

The Lhas did what the Venutians told them, and male and female divided. This division, which took place over many generations, was a biologically controlled experiment by the Lhas with Venutian technical advice. (There are some who say that the sexual division is still going on among us, that there are some who are male in body but female in spirit, and female in body but male in spirit.)

The Lemurians copulated in their temples and sacred places, which were also their schools of learning. Copulation to them was a sacred duty. It was done in accordance with the skies and the seasons.

The Development of Thought. After the Lhas and their Venutian advisors perfected the biological division of the sexes, they began working on the development of intelligence. The Lhas copulated in order to improve the genetic pool This is the meaning of the ancient enigmatic legend of the Hebrews:

> There were giants in the earth in those days, and also after that, when the Sons of God came in unto the daughters of men, and they bare children to them, the same became mighty men which were of old, men of renown.
>
> —Genesis 6: 4

After infusing humanity with their own seed, the Lhas began to implant the desire for wisdom in the human soul. Just as humans had been taught to love bodies other than their own, so now they were taught to love minds other than their own.

This was the beginning of the mysteries. For with the desire for wisdom began the idea of the Divine. That is why all the ancient religious rituals were sexual, because humans recognized that the same faculties that enabled them to love sexually also enabled them to love spiritually.

The Rise of Memory and Language. Then the Lhas chose the most advanced of the humans—among them many of their own offspring—and took them to sacred places.

And they initiated them into the sciences of universal laws and taught them to control and know the forces of nature. They instructed them also in the clairvoyant use of the imagination. Women especially were made adepts. For the Lhas had decreed that the female nature should be soulful and imaginative, and that the male nature should be willfull and adventurous. Certain Lemurian women achieved such a state of contemplation that they could retain images in their heads. Thus began human memory.

The wise women would make certain noises as they focused their thoughts. Certain sounds were spoken to recall certain objects. Thus began language. Thus also began the mysteries of the power of the Word. For without the Word we cannot remember the Object. Memory is language, and language is memory.

Good and Evil. The priestesses also brought about the ideas of good and evil. For they remembered, along with name and object, their feelings and intuitions about the objects. Thus, certain words became charged with negative power and others with positive power. In time, people forgot the object-word distinction. They then thought of Good and Evil as entities separate from their objects.

The Epochs of Lemuria. Just as seven races divide the history of the world, so seven subraces divide each race, and so seven subraces divided Lemuria. And these were the subraces of the Lemurians:

In the first subrace, the Lemurians were in jelly form. In the second, they became firmer and more dense. In the third subrace, the Lemurians divided into sexes. In the fourth, they began to desire knowledge. In the fifth subrace, the Lemurians began to reproduce just as we, making possible the eventual physical perfection of the human species, which has not as yet been accomplished. They also learned to achieve reincarnation. In the sixth subrace, the Lemurian continent began to sink. Some of the Lemurians were transported to other parts of the world by the Lhas. The great beasts began to multiply in the land.

In the seventh subrace, the Lemurians took on something resembling present human form. They also mastered the basic arts of civilization. They began to build dwellings, expanding their caves by adding fences and huts in the manner of Robinson Crusoe.

The Last Days of Lemuria. During the time of the sixth subrace, portions of Lemuria began to tremble and sink. It was a time of cataclysms throughout the whole Earth.

One peninsula of Lemuria separated itself from the rest of the continent and became the continent of Atlantis. In this same manner is one civilization always born from the one before it.

The Lhas established colonies on Atlantis, and they sent the finest minds of Lemuria to those colonies, to develop a purer mental strain.

Then began the great movements of beasts throughout the earth. The beasts were gigantic, winged reptiles and cold-blooded mammals, which towered over the humans, even over the Lhas.

The Lemurians were kept virtual prisoners in their caves by the rampaging, ravaging, and roaring of the great beasts, saying, "Why did you develop our mental powers at the expense of our physical ones? For if we had been left alone we would have evolved the strength to defend ourselves."

Then once again the Venutians and other beings from outer space came and communicated with the Lhas. They especially communicated with the Atlanteans, who had evolved far more technological skill.

Then beings came from Sirius and Venus and Mars and Saturn. And they instructed the Atlanteans in the use of destructive weapons against the beasts.

Then the Atlanteans came to Lemuria, and took away some of the Lemurians in their airships; and the Lemurian, Atlantean, and other delegates consulted on how best to wage war against the reptile monsters.

Meanwhile, the Earth began to rumble more day by day. And the Lhas and the beings from other planets warned the people of Lemuria of a coming cataclysm. Some of the Lemurians heeded their warnings and volunteered to leave and form Lemurian colonies elsewhere. The people of China have Lemurian blood, as do the peoples of the Pacific, Peru, and Africa.

The final sinking of Lemuria took place in about 50,000 B.C. in the Great Cataclysm, during which much of the world was covered in ice. The ice also destroyed the great beasts.

Thus rose and sank Lemuria. For it is written, that as surely as every continent rose up out of the water, so also will every continent sink back into the water. Those are the ways of the Cosmos.

The Chronicle of Atlantis

It has been handed down to us from ancient ages that there once existed, in the part of the globe now under the Atlantic Ocean, a vast continent called Atlantis, in which humans first rose from barbarism to civilization. And from Atlantis went forth colonizers to Egypt and the Mediterranean in the East and to Mexico and Peru in the West.

Atlantis was created a paradise, and for much of its history it was inhabited by technologically superior creatures who had high spiritual powers and were in contact with aliens from outer space. But in time, the Atlantean powers became corrupted; the civilization decayed; and Atlantis perished in a terrible convulsion of Nature.

Atlantis was the true Antediluvian world: Valhalla, the Elysian Fields, the Gardens of the Hesperides, the Garden of Eden. All humans alive on Earth today retain memories of this great primeval land, where humans once lived together in peace and happiness.

Atlantis was the seat of the Aryan, Semitic, and Turanian races of humans. It was the source of all the great civilizations of the Gulf of Mexico, Peru, the Amazon, the Mediterranean, northern Africa, and western Europe. To the Atlanteans we owe all that we know of writing, domesticating animals, weaving, and all the other civilized arts down to radio and television broadcasting.

And it is to the Atlanteans that we owe our spiritual heritage, a heritage that seeks meaning in direct contact with the All-Illuminating Rays of the Divine One.

The First Age

Beginnings. In the Book of Cataclysms it is recorded that five races of humans sprang up simultaneously in five regions of the world. These humans were of the White, Red, Yellow, Brown, and Black races. Lemuria was the home of the Yellow race. Atlantis was the home of the Red race.

Some chroniclers record that the Atlanteans were the fourth Root Race of the world, and that they were divided into seven subraces. These were: (1) the Rmoahal, black people up to ten feet tall, (2) the Tlavatli, (3) the Toltec, who were as tall as twenty seven feet, (4) the Turanians, (5) the Semites, ancestors of the Aryans, the Jews, and the Arabs, (6) the Akkadians, the earliest settlers of Mesopotamia, and (7) the Mongolians.

These various chroniclers are only apparently in contradiction with each other. As we shall see, Atlantis existed for hundreds of thousands of years and underwent several evolutions of culture and race. But the original Atlanteans were Reds.

For the first several hundred thousand years, the Atlanteans existed only in spirit form, as did Amelius, the first human soul on Earth. These first people communicated without words, solely by thought or spirit waves. Therefore, they had no need of material bodies, and without these encumbrances they could travel anywhere they wished. They communicated directly with the animals, plants, stones, trees, and even with the aliens from outer space who occasionally visited Atlantis.

At this time Atlantis was as perfect a Paradise as any on Earth. Its climate was perfection itself: soft, balmy breezes, daily rain and sunshine, a moderate temperature.

The spirits began amusing themselves by taking on material bodies, so that they could feel the sensual pleasures of their rich land. These first bodies were merely thought projections. But the more the spirit beings experienced physical sensations, the less easily they were able to return to the spiritual plane.

And so, in time, the material impulses overcame the spiritual ones. The spirits, in their assumed material forms, began mating with animals. This gross offense has come down to us as the Original Sin.

The offspring of these first matings were grotesque forms, half-human and half-horse, bird, or fish. According to the Greeks, they were semidivine creatures—centaurs, satyrs, and mermaids. But to the Atlanteans, still strong in their spirit powers, these grossly embodied creatures were not human. In fact, the Atlanteans called these creatures Things. And they set the Things to work, forcing them to do all forms of manual or menial labor.

Then the Divine One saw that His offspring were not content with being divine, timeless imitations of the One Light, but wished to reproduce their own kind as did the other creatures on earth. They were, in other words, more enamored of the Divine creation than of the Eye and Mind that created it.

The first human bodies were androgynous—that is, they contained within them both male and female forms. In this form Amelius appeared in his material body. In this form also did Christ appear when he descended to Atlantis. This was the purest bodily form, a reflection of the Divine One.

But humans still desired the pleasure of sexual intercourse with creatures other than themselves. So the Divine One created two beings, male and female, whom he named Adam and Eve.

In each of the five regions of the world there was created a different Adam and a different Eve, one Adam and Eve for each different race. But these first parents did not, like the first five human spirits, spring up simultaneously. They were created first on Lemuria and then on Atlantis.

Many believe that the process of creating Man is still in progress, directed by reincarnating Atlanteans who still live secretly among us. Others teach that the Atlantean creation of Man culminated with the creation of Jesus Christ, the Perfect Man. The answers are known only to the elect.

The first rulers of Atlantis were called Atlas and Heputh by the Greeks. The Greeks called Amelius by the name of Poseidon. The Greeks regarded Amelius and the other spirit beings, who were in actuality the first humans on earth, as gods.

Thus Plato wrote about the beginnings of Atlantis:

> The gods distributed the whole earth into portions differing in extent, and made themselves temples and sacrifices. And Poseidon, receiving for his lot the island of Atlantis, begat children by a mortal woman, and settled them in a part of the island which I will proceed to describe. On the side toward the sea, and in the center of the whole island, there was a plain which is said to have been the fairest of all plains, and very fertile. Near the plain again, and also in the center of the island, at a distance of about fifty stadia, there was a mountain, not very high on any side. In this mountain there dwelt one of the earth-born primeval men of that country, whose name was Evenor, and he had a wife named Leucippe, and they had an only daughter, whose name was Cleito. The maiden was growing up to womanhood when her father and mother died; Posiedon fell in love with her, and had intercourse with her; and, breaking the ground, enclosed the hill in which she dwelt all round, making alternate zones of sea and land, larger and smaller, encircling one another; there were two of land and three of water, which he turned as with a lathe out of the center of the island, equidistant every way, so that no man could get to the island, for ships and voyages were not yet heard of. He himself, as he was a god, found no difficulty in making special arrangement for the center island, bringing two streams of water under the earth, which he caused to ascend as springs, one of warm water and the other of cold, and making every variety of food to spring up abundantly in the earth. He also begat and brought up five pairs of male children, dividing the island of Atlantis into ten portions: he gave to the first born of the eldest pair his mother's dwelling and the surrounding allotment, which was the largest and best, and made him king over the rest; and the others he made princes, and gave them rule over many men and large territory. And he named them all: the eldest, who was king, he named Atlas, and from him the whole island and the ocean received the name of Atlantic.

Atlas and his descendants were priests as well as rulers of their people. For they remained spiritual beings, able to discard their physical bodies and travel by astral projection.

The first Atlanteans knew how to use the energy force that came from the Divine One. No special tools or equipment were necessary other than their own minds, which were images of the Divine Mind.

But Atlantis was a divided land, even from the beginning. For on the one hand, there were the kings, priests, rulers, and nobles (the godlike Atlanteans). And inhabiting the same land were the bestial Things, whom the Atlanteans regarded as subhuman.

The Atlanteans lived in a state of harmony for a hundred thousand years. But over the centuries two factions began to grow up among them. The two factions were the Sons of the One Law and the Sons of Belial.

The Sons of the One Law believed that the human soul was a projection of the Divine Soul, and they therefore sought to keep their race pure by constant spiritual exercise.

But the Sons of Belial believed that the human soul originated all things. They had no moral standards save of self. They were no longer able to communicate directly with the Divine Mind, although they retained their powers of mind-communication with each other.

Disagreements between the Sons of Belial and the Sons of the One Law were destined to continue until the continent's final destruction.

The Golden Age of Atlantis. The Atlanteans were blessed with a rich and fertile land, and they lived as well as any peoples that ever inhabited this earthly sphere. Plato's description of their civilization, though written from a later perspective, would apply equally well to most of Atlantis's history.

> . . . they had such an amount of wealth as was never before possessed by kings and potentates . . . and they were furnished with everything which they could have, in both city and country. For, because of the greatness of their empire, many things were brought to them from foreign countries, and the island itself provided much of what was required by them for the uses of life. In the first place, they dug out of the earth whatever was to be found there, minerals as well as metal, and that which is now only a name, and was then something more than a name—orichalcum—was dug out of the earth in many parts of the island, and, with the exception of gold, was esteemed the most precious of metals among men of those days. There was an abundance of wood for carpenters' work, and sufficient maintenance for tame and wild animals. Moreover, there were a great number of elephants in the island, and there was provision for animals of every kind, both for those which live in lakes and marshes and rivers, and also for those which live in mountains and on plains, and therefore for the animal which is the largest and most voracious of them. Also, whatever fragrant things there are in the earth, whether roots, or herbage, or woods, grew and thrived in that land; and again, the cultivated fruit of the earth, both the dry edible fruit and other species of food, which we call by the general name of legumes, and the fruits having a hard rind, affording drinks, and meats, and ointments, and good store of chestnuts and the like, which may be used to play with, and are fruits which spoil with keeping—and the pleasant kinds of dessert which console us after dinner, when we are full and tired of eating—all these that sacred island lying beneath the sun brought forth fair and wondrous in infinite abundance.

It is not surprising that people inhabiting such a paradise should become accustomed to luxury. The people lived in large villas, which they later introduced all over the Mediterranean. They lived as much outdoors as in, in flowerfilled atria and gardens with fountains and singing birds. Some say that they wove shelters of branches for themselves.

The people of Atlantis were red-complexioned. They had protruding noses, sleek black hair, and black eyes. They enhanced their natural coloring with the juices of berries, and in some eras they painted their toenails and fingernails with gold. The Atlanteans dressed in togas and sandals, much like the ancient Romans.

The religion of the Atlanteans was the worship of the Divine One, especially through His earthly representative, the Sun. The name of the Divine One was seldom mentioned, as it was held in such great reverence.

Worship on Atlantis centered on the holy mountain. Plato described their temple complex in this manner:

> The entire circuit of the wall which went round the outermost building they covered with a coating of brass, and the circuit of the next wall they coated with tin, and the third, which encompassed the citadel, flashed with the red light of orichalcum. The palaces in the interior of the citadel were constructed in this wise: In the center was a holy temple dedicated to Cleito and Poseidon, which remained inaccessible, and was surrounded by an enclosure of gold; this was the spot in which they originally begat the race of ten princes, and thither they annually brought the fruits of the earth in their season from all the ten portions, and performed sacrifices to each of them. Here, too, was Poseidon's own temple, of a stadium in length and half a stadium in width, and of a proportionate height, having a sort of barbaric splendor. All the outside of the temple, with the exception of the pinnacles, they covered with silver, and the pinnacles with gold. In the interior of the temple the roof was of ivory adorned everywhere with silver and gold and orichalcum; all the other parts of the walls and pillars they lined with orichalcum.

The early Atlanteans achieved a high standard of morality. As Plato tells us,

> For many generations, as long as the divine nature lasted in them, they were obedient to the laws, and well-affectioned toward the gods, who were their kinsmen; for they possessed true and in every way great spirits, practicing gentleness and wisdom in the various chances of life, and in their intercourse with one another. They despised everything but virtue, not caring for the r present state of life, and thinking lightly on the possession of gold and other property, which seemed only a burden to them: neither were they intoxicated by luxury; nor did wealth deprive them of their self-control; but they were sober, and saw clearly that all these goods were increased by virtuous friendship with one another, and that by excessive zeal for them, and honor of them, the good of them is lost, and friendship perishes with them.

But although the early Atlanteans were highly moral, they did not follow our present conventions in regard to marriage and sex. Homosexuality was not regarded as indecent among them. Neither was it regarded as indecent for people to have sex without marriage, so long as the act was done with care to keep the Atlantean race pure.

For it must be remembered that Atlanteans lived for many hundreds of years in the Golden Age. It would be most unreasonable to expect that they would maintain stable domestic arrangements over such long periods.

The Atlanteans' belief in reincarnation influenced their sexual habits. For they believed that all souls had been both male and female in previous lives and that each soul was constantly in search of its missing half. Therefore it was natural that some men should mate with other men, and women with women.

They believed that children were but spirits who had chosen to dwell for a while on the Earth in material form. Therefore, children were instructed as if they were newcomers from another country, not as if they were inferior to adults. The priests instructed them in language, arts, and sciences.

An Atlantean citizen kept close connections with the temples for all of his or her life. It was common for adults to go into long periods of retreat, during which they lived in the temples and dedicated themselves to God.

Among the temples were some whose purpose was to secure the spiritual happiness of the Things by removing the vestiges of their bestiality and reeducating them. These temples were built by the Sons of the One Law.

And there were yet other temples, in the domain of the Sons of Belial, and their priests practiced black magic and all manner of forbidden arts.

But though the Atlanteans had spiritual voices among them, they were not given the gifts of philosophy and religion as had been given to the Lemurians.

Instead, the Atlanteans were given the gift of technology. The priests of Atlantis were also scientists, and the powers they harnessed were the spiritual and physical forces of the Earth.

Atlantean Science. With the help of beings from outer space, the Atlanteans learned to use crystals to harness the energy of the sun. These crystals were used to power laborsaving machines, allowing the Atlanteans to live in idleness and luxury.

And they called the crystals *firestones*, and they kept the firestones in their temples. The prophet Cayce spoke of the manner in which the firestones were kept

> . . . in the center of a building which today would be said to be lined with nonconductive stone—something akin to asbestos. . . . The building above the stone was oval; or a dome wherein there could be . . . a portion for rolling back, so that the activity of the stars—the concentration of energies that emanate from bodies that are on fire themselves, along with elements that are found and not found in the earth's atmosphere. . . . The building was constructed so that when the dome was rolled back there might be little or no hindrance in the direct application of power to various crafts that were to be impelled through space—whether within the radius of vision or whether directed under water or under other elements, or through other elements.

The Atlanteans had the power to go through solid walls and other heavy substances, so great was their power.

The firestones were also used to cure bodily infirmities. Rays from the stones were applied to the afflicted parts, burning the disease away. Thus many of the Sons of the One Law applied firestones to the Things, removing their mutations and purifying their spirits.

The early priests had used the firestones to direct their own energies toward union with the Divine One. Thus, the firestones became the symbols of Illumination, or union with the Divine. For others, the firestones were but symbols of the mental accomplishments of man.

At the height of the Golden Age, the priests and scientists began to dream of owning a Great Crystal, a firestone so pure and strong that it would allow them to power ships even to outer space. Beings from outer space materialized and helped the scientists of Atlantis in this great effort. They guided the Atlanteans in finding a large crystal, or piece of quartz. They cut thousands of facets into the surface of the quartz, so that the crystal would reflect all the sun's and moon's rays at once.

Then they built huge vats of copper. In these vats they stored the solar energy not needed for each day's use. The work of making the crystal took many years, and many more years were taken up in building the temple in which to house the crystal.

The temple was in the form of a pyramid, in imitation of the holy mountain that stood in the center of the island. And they placed the pyramid in the western part of their land.

The energy from the Great Crystal was concentrated near the top of the pyramid, and it was here that the airships landed and repowered themselves. But under the Crystal, within the pyramid itself, was also a place of great power. Indeed, those who spent time within the pyramid were renewed in body and spirit.

Once charged by the Great Crystal, Atlantean airships and submarines moved along the paths of the Earth's magnetic flow. The Atlanteans constructed giant earthworks to guide the ships from the air. The remains of these navigation-aides, which mark the paths of the Earth's currents, can still be seen in the mysterious lines of Nazca in Peru, as well as in the "ley lines" that traverse the British Isles.

The Atlanteans understood the magnetic currents of the sun, moon, and stars as well as of the Earth. They translated this knowledge into mathematics and music, two arts at which they excelled.

They also possessed knowledge of the movements of the stars and planets and kept elaborate calendars on which were recorded the spiritual symbols of mankind. These calendars survive in simple form in the calendars of the Mayans, Incas, and Egyptians.

The Atlanteans travelled all over the globe, and perhaps even to other planets. At this period they were not bent on world conquest, so the spread of their civilization was beneficial to all. And many came to Atlantis to live, people who were not of the Red race. Some Lemurians, people of the Brown race, came, as did colonies of Whites.

Daily Life in the Golden Age. The Atlanteans lived in both city and countryside. Their main city was called Poseidia and was located in the northeastern section of the continent. But there were other cities and towns as well.

Wealthy Atlanteans lived on large estates, where there were orchards and vineyards. These estates were surrounded by high walls as protection against the great beasts. The estates were guarded by Things, who were also responsible for the menial labor on the farms.

The Atlanteans kept sheep on their estates, and they considered the sheep to be their friends and companions. Children played with them in much the same manner as people today play with dogs.

Even in the country, the Atlanteans lived in great palaces which were open to the air. These palaces were decorated in the most luxurious manner.

The Atlanteans used carrier pigeons to send messages to each other. The rulers and nobles spent their days in merriment and leisure, attending large parties at each other's estates. They travelled in basketlike conveyances that were powered by crystals.

But this life was not ideal. The lot of the Things was a sad one. Many Atlanteans did not regard them as human and therefore made no attempt to alleviate their suffering. Also, there was the invasion of the great beasts.

The War Against the Beasts. In the days of old, when Lemuria was still young and humans existed only in spirit form, great beasts began to walk upon the Earth. And the names of these beasts were Dinosaurs and Mammoths, and their legions were called Tyrannosaurus, Stegosaurus, and Brontosaurus.

In the Chronicle of Lemuria it is related how these animals became so gigantic and menacing that they threatened to extinguish the Lemurian race. These same giant beasts also overran Atlantis and the whole known world.

But in Atlantis they did not hold complete sway, for the Atlanteans were technologically advanced. They were able to build walled towns to protect themselves. The necessity of living together in towns further strengthened the social and scientific tendencies of the Atlantean races.

In the Chronicle of Lemuria it is told how the Atlanteans arrived in their airships to aid the Lemurians in fighting the monsters. In this manner the Atlanteans traveled to all lands, inviting the people to a great war conference.

Thus were assembled on Atlantis all the great scientific minds of that day. And they spoke among themselves to decide the best manner of eradicating the beasts. The prophet Cayce records that this conference took place in 50,722 B.C.

Some say that it was the War Against the Beasts that first tempted the

Sons of Belial to assume powers for themselves that rightly belonged only to the Divine One. For in this war the scientists of the Earth, led by the Atlanteans, developed new instruments of destruction.

The Atlanteans' early airships were merely balloons, which resembled the Graf Zeppelin. During the War Against the Beasts, the scientists developed more sophisticated flying machines, powered by the Great Crystal.

The Atlanteans also perfected a kind of "death ray," rather like what is known today as the Laser Beam. This ray could be directed against the brain of an adult dinosaur, causing its immediate disintegration.

Intoxicated by this evidence of their own powers, the scientists began a campaign against the very breeding grounds of the Great Beasts.

The younger scientists and Sons of Belial began to dream grandiose dreams of world conquest. And the priests of the Sons of Belial encouraged them in this perverse thinking. So progressed the War Against the Beasts, until the hand of the Divine One was once more seen on the Earth, and the Earth erupted in the Great Cataclysm.

The Great Cataclysm. In the Book of Cataclysms it is recorded that the Earth has been rocked on diverse occasions by violent catastrophes. The first of these catastrophes in human memory is called the Great Cataclysm, though it was undoubtedly not the greatest to occur in all time. Such things are known only to the Elect.

The Great Cataclysm took place around 50,000 B.C. It was this disaster that sank the continent of Lemuria. As has been recorded, many Lemurians believed the forewarnings of disaster and fled to other lands.

The Atlanteans, too, received warnings of the Great Cataclysm. Beings from outer space had seen unusual formations of clouds and global energy currents, thus foreseeing the cataclysm. And some Atlanteans migrated from their island land, to Africa, Egypt, and South America, where they established colonies and built themselves temples in the shape of pyramids.

The immediate cause of the Great Cataclysm was the shifting of the polar axis of the Earth. The evil was even worse than had been prophesied. Volcanoes erupted. Whole continents rose and sank. The Earth was covered with howling winds and raging waters. The upheavals were said to have taken place in the twinkling of an eye.

There were great changes in the geography of the Earth. Only the highest peaks of Lemuria remained above the waters. In northern India great sections of flatland were suddenly thrust upward to the heavens. Thus, the Lemurian colonies on the shore became hidden in remote, high mountain valleys, in the land now known as Tibet.

In Mexico and Peru as well, great cities that had been built at the level of the sea were suddenly located on the tops of high peaks.

The middle of North America, which had formerly been under the ocean, now became dry land. This new landmass became attached to the eastern coast of Lemuria, another section of that continent that did not sink. This is the land now known as California.

Throughout the upheaval the civilization of Atlantis endured, though many lives were lost to the furor of the winds and waves. Some of the western lands of Atlantis were engulfed by the ocean waters, and the land of Atlantis became a smaller island in the eastern part of what is now the Atlantic Ocean. The Western peaks of the former continent remained above water.

The weather, also, changed dramatically during these cataclysms of the Earth. In the north, there were sudden freezings, creating the Ice Ages. The dinosaurs and other Great Beasts died by the hundreds-of-thousands, thus ending forever their domination of Earth.

The climate on Atlantis was no longer balmy and perfect, but became more torrid.

The Second Age.

The second period of civilization on Atlantis lasted from the sinking of Lemuria, around 50,000 B.C., until around 28,000 B.C., when another portion of Atlantis sank. During this long era, Atlantis ruled the globe.

But though the Atlantean power was now unchallenged, the Atlanteans were greatly weakened in their spiritual and psychic powers.

The cause of this weakening was the sinking of Lemuria, which the Atlanteans had perceived as the mother of civilization, the source of all spiritual energy. Many Atlanteans grew bitter and questioned the purposes of the Divine One. For had not the Lemurians been spiritual leaders and religious teachers? Yet their faith had not saved them.

The nonspiritual factions on Atlantis grew in strength, as the leaders became obsessed with power and military control. They began to send out the airships and to direct the death rays toward other lands in pursuit of earthly glory and conquest.

But there was still a minority that pursued the ancient truths. This minority became the priestly class. After the Great Cataclysm, many surviving Lemurians were welcomed into Atlantean temples. And so the rays of Divinity were kept alight.

Factions arose among the priests as they did among the people. As the memory of the Great Cataclysm receded, the temples became centers of political and scientific intrigue.

Now, in this second period, the lives of Atlanteans were no longer as long as they had been in the Golden Age, so the memory of Divine events was more difficult to preserve. So some of the priests invented writing, in order to keep more perfect records. Some say that writing was taught to the priests by visitors from other planets. Others say that aliens did not again visit Atlantis after the Great Cataclysm.

The writings were kept in pyramids, each pyramid topped by a crystal. Some of the writings of this Atlantean period are still intact, buried under the pyramids of Egypt and America. However, these writings have not yet been found.

And the Atlanteans began trading among the nations of the Earth, and thus their wealth and power grew ever greater. They traded metals and precious gems, salt, sugar, and Black slaves.

The Atlanteans of the second period were universally hated and feared. Their scientists directed the Great Crystal toward lands to the East and West, threatening with extinction those nations that did not submit.

Religion in the Second Age. After the Great Cataclysm, when even the priests began questioning the Divine Will, the religious system of Atlantis acquired ritual and dogma, to the detriment of direct belief. Fewer and fewer inhabitants were able to communicate directly with the Divine by means of telepathy. Instead, they relied on priests as intermediaries. Thus was formed the great religious system of Atlantis, which survives in human memory in the religious records of the Incas, Mayans, and Egyptians.

Like the old religion, the decadent religion was based on worship of the Sun. But in ancient times the Sun had been but a symbol of the Divinity. In the age of decadence, the Atlanteans forgot the Divinity and worshipped only the symbol.

Only a few priests and people retained the old ways, and as time went on they were forced underground, to avoid persecution for their views. Thus began the Secret Tradition, which is still preserved among us.

And the Atlanteans worshipped the Sun both in its rising and setting, and their temples were constructed so as to focus the sun's rays at these key points during the day.

The temples were pyramids, for the most part, though some were also domed. At the top of the pyramid was a flat place where they constructed the altar. Sometimes the altar was inside the pyramid and the structure came to a point on the outside. Both kinds of pyramid-temples survived into recorded historical times.

The priests in their temples studied the stars and planets in search of omens, and their rituals included the reading of these omens both for individuals and nations.

And they began the barbarous custom of human sacrifice. They used Things for their victims, and offered the sacrifice of blood to water the fields of the Sun God.

At the beginning of spring plowing they sacrificed a Thing, and again at the time of planting, and again at the time of the first fruits, and again when the harvest was done. They also sacrificed for the summer and winter solstices.

As the centuries progressed, the Atlantean priests became more and more depraved, seeking any excuse for human sacrifice, and choosing as their victims all who objected to the power of the scientists and rulers.

In this period of decadence, the kings ruled by brute force rather than moral virtue. The priests and scientists, acting as puppets of the rulers, made virtual slaves of the Atlantean people. Even those who were nobles could not remove from their station in life, and they married only on command. No longer could an Atlantean live and produce children without marriage. All the functions of daily life were controlled by the state.

The priests, lackeys of the imperial powers, took over the task of directing waves from the Great Crystal into the brains of the Atlanteans, the better to keep them in subjection. In time, the memory of the old ways almost faded.

There were priestesses, as well as priests, on Atlantis during this time. But the priestesses in the Second Age were not allowed to marry and were required to take vows of perpetual celibacy. They lived in large convents within the temples, as virtual prisoners of the priests and scientists to whose needs they attended.

Some of the evil ones took advantage of the helpless state of these women, and used them as if they were prostitutes, even convincing many of the women that their acquiescence was required by religious duty.

And so the Atlanteans continued their wickedness, until once again their civilization was hit by disaster.

The Crystal Explodes. The scientists of Atlantis began directing their forces toward China, a civilization on the other side of the world.

China had been the home of the Yellow race from the time of the creation of humans. The civilization of China was further strengthened by the influx of Lemurians fleeing the Great Cataclysm. Thus China was the only civilization on Earth as advanced as the Atlanteans. In fact, although the Chinese lacked the technological skills of the Atlanteans, they were far more advanced spiritually, because of the Lemurian influence.

The Atlanteans began to charge and supercharge the Great Crystal, hoping to power it all the way around the globe and attack the mainland of China. Some scientists conceived the idea of directing the Crystal's rays directly through the center of the Earth.

It was thus that the second great disaster in Atlantean history occurred. The Crystal exploded and sank, sending up huge walls of flame and causing enormous floods around the world. These floods have come down to us in world records of the Deluge.

The Crystal itself was not deactivated, but sank many leagues under the sea, in the area of the world now known as the Bermuda Triangle. In this area the Great Crystal still sends forth its rays, which, though they are greatly weakened by the water, are powerful enough to sink ships and planes.

The explosion of the Crystal caused great storms and floods throughout the world. The entire western section of Atlantis sank, and the river that separated Poseidia from the rest of the continent was widened further. All that remained of the former mighty continent were two small islands. These were located in what had been the northeastern section of Atlantis, directly in front of the Pillars of Hercules.

It was this Atlantis that was described by Plato. It was a land much diminished in power and influence.

Atlantis after the Deluge. With the loss of the Crystal, Atlantis underwent a major spiritual and physical revolution. No longer could Atlanteans fly through the air or direct their death rays at their enemies. They still had smaller crystals, but these could only be used to power small machines and transport people in baskets for short distances. For longer trips, the Atlanteans were forced to use ships with sails and to fight in conventional combat.

The land itself was a source of sorrow. Desolation reigned in the countryside, and there was not sufficient food for the populace. The Atlanteans struggled for survival.

But there was a revival in things spiritual, for the Wise Ones, who had maintained the True Religion during the long centuries of decay and corruption, now went about in the streets proclaiming the truth and preaching repentence. And many heeded them.

For people could see that their land, once mighty and glorious, was now greatly reduced due only to Man's pride and lust for power.

Most of the Atlanteans paid no heed to the preaching of the Wise Ones and continued their wicked ways. And the priests of the Sons of Belial now turned even more to black magic, hoping thus to regain some of their former power over their fellows.

They increased the number of sacrifices made of the Things, and treated them even more cruelly. And they mated some of the Things with Blacks, whom they had captured and enslaved in Africa. These creatures, half-blacks and half-Things, still appear in the arts of the South American Indians. And pictures of the creatures from many centuries back are preserved on Central American ruins.

The Wise Ones began to preach that, unless the scientists stopped their experiments and unless the priests stopped practicing black magic, the remainder of Atlantis would sink as well. And those that heeded the Wise Ones began to talk of migrating to other lands.

The Atlantean Colony in Egypt. Egypt was one of the earliest Atlantean colonies, having first been settled when the Atlanteans went in their airships to collect people for the war conference against the Great Beasts.

It was from this Egyptian colony that there arose a great prophet after the Deluge. And his name was Throm.

Throm appeared suddenly. There is no record of either his birth or his death. Some say that he was none other than the god Hermes (or Thoth), the Emanation of Divine Wisdom, who had appeared in Atlantis during the Golden Age as Mercury and Jesus Christ.

Throm communicated with some of the Wise Ones and invited them to strengthen further the colony in Egypt with their presence. Some of them heeded the invitation and went to Egypt, where they built temples and established schools.

In time huge numbers of Atlanteans poured into Egypt, for they had been warned that the final destruction of their land was near. The Atlanteans came to outnumber the native Egyptians, who were of the Brown and Black races.

By this time the Atlanteans were no longer entirely Red, having long since intermarried with the Yellow, White, and Brown races. Only a few Atlanteans maintained the pure bloodlines.

In about 11,000 B.C. there arrived in Egypt an invasion of White people from the north, from the Carpathian region. And these people conquered Egypt and became the ruling class. And there was great tension between these rulers and the ruled.

There was a priest among the Carpathian tribes by the name of Ra-Ta, and he was mighty and learned. Ra-Ta became caught up in the political intrigues of the land, seeking to help the native Egyptians obtain power with the new rulers. And for this subversive activity he was banished into Abyssinia.

Meanwhile, the Atlanteans were still arriving, in greater and greater numbers, bringing with them advanced scientific knowledge, which even in its decayed state was still far ahead of the thinking of the Carpathians or Egyptians. The Carpathian rulers began to realize that the Atlanteans constituted a real threat to their power, and they began looking for a leader under whom all the factions in Egypt could unite.

Finally they recalled Ra-Ta from his exile, and he became the prime minister of Egypt during this troubled time. Ra-Ta established two great temples, the Temple of Sacrifice and the Temple of Beauty. Both temples were places of healing as well as places of worship.

In the Temple of Sacrifice the people could undergo surgery to remove unwanted physical deformities. And to this temple repaired the Things who had come out of Atlantis, for the final removal of their wings, scales, and beaks. The Temple of Sacrifice was dedicated to the purification of the body.

The Temple of Beauty, on the other hand, was dedicated to the purification of the mind.

Ra-Ta made these two temples into centers of learning, engineering, and science as well, thus restoring some of the technological advances that had been lost at the time of the Great Crystal's explosion.

And in the two temples there were certain initiates. These, through the rituals of the temples, were altered radically in their personal appearance, so that their heads became large and elongated in shape. And these altered individuals became the parents of a master race who were to keep the ancient truths of Atlantis alive.

And the temples were centers for instruction in agriculture, mathematics, and music. And grain from all over Egypt was stored in the temples, and was recorded and dispersed by the temple priests.

There were priestesses, too, in the temples, and these administered to the needs of the ladies, both of the Atlantean and Egyptian races.

The temples were also the schools, where they taught not only the revelations of the Golden Age of Atlantis, but also the wisdom of the Gobi land and the land of Said, which is today called India. For these two places were the home of the Aryan race at that time.

Thus, under the guidance of Ra-Ta a colony of learning and wisdom flourished in Egypt by 10,000 B.C.

During this millenium, Jesus Christ visited Egypt and spoke with Ra-Ta. (As usual, Jesus also bore the name Hermes.)

The doings of Ra-Ta and the state of Egypt during his period of rule are known to us, for Ra-Ta has appeared in America in our own time. He took on the name of Edgar Cayce and lived among us in Virginia Beach, Virginia.

So detailed was Ra-Ta's memory that he told even how the priests of Egypt were dressed.

> The robes of the priest would be blue-gray with the hooded portion back from the head, while about the waist would be a cord of gold color with a purple tassel.

During Ra-Ta's sojourn in Egypt, the Atlanteans built the Great Pyramid at Giza, which still stands. Some say that the pyramid was built under the direction of the great Hermes himself. This tradition persists among the Arabs, who are themselves descendants of Semitic peoples fleeing Atlantis.

Thus, the wisdom of Atlantis has come down to us through the priests and temples of Egypt. For thousands of years later, at the beginning of our recorded history, the Egyptians still worshipped in the Atlantean manner, calling the Sun their god. And the secret tradition of the Egyptians has also continued to this day.

The Atlantean Colonies in Britain and Europe. It is well known that about 28,000 to 25,000 B.C. Europe was invaded by a race of people from the West, who are known to us as the Cro-Magnons. These people were the first colonizers from Atlantis, who left that land after the sinking of the Great Crystal.

The Cro-Magnons were tall and strong, possessing broad shoulders and wide foreheads. They were also artists of high ability. When the first pioneers arrived from Atlantis, they settled in caves. And they decorated the caves with pictures of mammoths and other beasts from Atlantean legends. Their paintings can still be seen today.

Spain was among the first of the lands of Europe to be settled by the Atlanteans. From Spain the Atlanteans moved inland and north to the British Isles.

The Atlanteans were the ancestors of the people known today as Basques. The Basque language resembles that spoken on the lost continent.

Ireland was also settled early, by colonizers from Atlantis whom the people called Formorians. The Formorians arrived in Atlantis before the Deluge and set up great temples to the Sun. Many of the temples were built on ley lines, those markings of the Earth's magnetic flow that had been previously used by Atlantean airships. The temples in Ireland took the common form of great circles of stone.

The Atlantean priests of Ireland were called Druids, and they were followers of the Law of One. This is known because the Druids of Ireland did not practice human sacrifice, but instead offered up fruits and flowers, as had been the custom in the Golden Age.

The chief ceremony of the Irish Druids was the lighting of the ceremonial fires at the solstices. This custom came directly from the Wise Ones of Atlantis.

Atlanteans also settled in Britain, but not all of these pioneers were followers of the Law of One. For the Druids of Britain and Gaul practiced human sacrifice and performed acts of black magic, as did the decadent priests of Atlantis.

But in Britain there was one site where the true worship of the Atlantean Golden Age was maintained. That site was Glastonbury.

Some say that Joseph of Arimathea brought the Holy Grail to Glastonbury. And at Glastonbury there appeared that Divine Being who had also appeared in Atlantis and Egypt, under the names of Thoth, Hermes, and Mercury. In Britain he was called by the name of Merlin.

Merlin caused a great stone circle to be moved from Ireland to Britain, in order that Sun worship might be properly established in Britain. This great

stone circle, Stonehenge, still stands.

And Merlin instructed the priests of the Sun in the secret mysteries of the old Atlantean religion, and taught them the arts of meditation and achievement of knowledge through mystical union with the Divine Mind.

And the Druids of Stonehenge accomplished many great miracles. Stonehenge and Glastonbury are still centers of Atlantean power. At these sites has been preserved the secret Western mystery tradition.

Some say that the great King Arthur was introduced to the Western mysteries by the priests of Atlantis. For even after the continent had been drowned in the final cataclysm, the souls of Atlanteans were reincarnated on the Earth. It is said that Arthur himself was a reincarnated Atlantean, and that it was to that land he returned when he sailed, dying, off into the

West.

These things have been revealed to many in modern times, especially to the priestess Dion Fortune, herself a reincarnated Atlantean.

The Atlantean Colonies in Central and South America. The Atlanteans had journeyed to Central and South America long before their final settlements there. Indeed, the traditions of South American peoples speak at length about white, bearded settlers from an eastern land. These White people were probably colonizers from Atlantis, the Atlanteans having long since ceased to be exclusively red, as we have seen.

The immense civilizations of the New World resembled those of Atlantis in many respects. The Indians of Peru and Mexico built great pyramids and worshipped the Sun. They had calendars like those of the Atlanteans, and similar systems of writing, record-keeping, irrigation, and communication.

The first Atlanteans in Central America were followers of the old ways. They were led by a priest whose name survives in Central American legend as Quetzalcoatl. He condemned all sacrifices except those of fruits and flowers.

The priests who finally settled Peru, Mexico, and Guatemala, however, were for the most part later practitioners, for they introduced human sacrifice as part of the Sun worship. However, there remained a secret tradition among the Incas and others.

The Atlanteans first settled in what is now Brazil. There they built a great empire which flourished for many thousands of years, in land now overgrown by jungles. From this flat land the civilization spread West to Peru, where it met with previous civilizations founded by the Lemurians. Thus, the high civilizations of the New World contained both Atlantean and Lemurian elements.

The priests in Central and South America, like those in Egypt, lived and worked in the great temples, which also served as solar and astronomical observatories and as hospitals.

There were priestesses in South and Central America as well. In Peru these were called the Virgins of the Sun. They lived in their own temple and were dedicated to the worship of the One God. The priestesses of the Sun were from the noblest families in the land, and they were selected for their beauty and accomplishments.

Other Atlantean Civilizations. Those who believed in the coming disaster and fled the islands of Atlantis spread throughout the lands bordering the doomed continent. They travelled up the Mississippi Valley and formed the great Mound Cultures of North America. They colonized Africa as well. Traces of Red races are to be found all along the African coast. Pictures of these Red Africans are found in many of the paintings of ancient Egypt.

The Final Catastrophe. Around the year 10,000 B.C., a series of violent earthquakes shook the remaining Atlantean lands, and the continent sank beneath the waves forever.

Only a few mountain peaks remained above the water. These peaks form what are now the Canary Islands, the Azores, and, in the West, the Antilles.

There are many accounts of this final sinking, and all agree that it was an awful and cataclysmic event. Some, indeed, say that it was the final sinking of Atlantis, not the second catastrophe, that is recounted in the Deluge legends of the world.

It is recounted by Plato that the final deluge occurred during a period when Atlantis was at war with Athens. His account shows that, even in its final, degraded state, Atlantis was still a magnificent power.

> The vast power thus gathered into one, endeavored to subdue at one blow our country and yours, and the whole of the land which was within the straits; and then, Solon, your country [Athens] shone forth, in the excellence of her virtue and strength, among all mankind; for she was the first in courage and military skill, and was the leader of the Hellenes. And when the rest fell off from her, being compelled to stand alone, after having undergone the very extremity of danger, she defeated and triumphed over the invaders, and preserved from slavery those who were not yet subjected, and freely liberated all the others who dwelt within the limits of Heracles.
>
> But afterward there occurred violent earthquakes and floods, and in a single day and night of rain all your warlike men in a body sunk into the earth, and the island of Atlantis in like manner disappeared, and was sunk beneath the sea. And that is the reason why the sea in those parts is impassable and impenetrable.

The Lessons of Atlantis. Thus perished the greatest kingdom the world has yet known, the result of human pride and lust for power. And so it will always be when nations forget the Divinity to whom they owe their origins, and overreach themselves in vaulting ambition.

For the forces of the Earth are given to us to be harnessed for good, not for destruction. Those that harness them for destruction are the evil ones who, like the evil scientists of Atlantis, will certainly bring destruction on their own lands.

But the prophet Cayce has written that Atlantis will rise again, that it is even now rising again. The first evidence of the lost land has already been found in Bimini, in the Bahamas. The rising of Atlantis will be accompanied by violent changes in the geography of the earth. Once more the poles will shift, as they did at the time of the Great Cataclysm. And portions of the East Coast of America will disappear forever. The great and wicked city of New York especially will be destroyed.

The waters of the Great Lakes will pour down into the Gulf of Mexico. And California will be split down the spine of its mountains and will also sink.

At that time the Divine One will reappear in the sky; perhaps He will come in a spaceship, for in each age he appears in a manner befitting that age.

Then Thoth will be on Earth once again and mankind will learn the wisdom of Hermes. And perhaps once more there will be a Golden Age, in which humans can communicate with the gods, and in which people will live for centuries, enjoying the peace, prosperity and spiritual richness of Atlantis.

The Book of Cataclysms

The secrets of the universe have been revealed to us in the sacred writings of Earth's various kingdoms. All the sacred writings tell of the violent cataclysms which have periodically shaken this planet.

With the cataclysms have come raging floods, howling winds, and tempests. Ancient oaks have been uprooted as if they were young saplings, and the very tops of the mountains have been blasted into the air, and the molten centers of the Earth have oozed forth The Earth was born in a cataclysm and will perish in a cataclysm.

Few know the exact age of the Earth, for such knowledge belongs only to those who have read and comprehended the Akashic Record. Some scholars say that the Earth was recently formed, and that the cataclysms caused signs to be engraved upon the Earth, signs we have heretofore misinterpreted as signs of the Earth's age. For example, the layers of deposits of sand, at their present rate of erosion, would have taken hundreds of thousands of years to form, had time moved at its present rate. But it is the traditions of the ancients that these apparent signs of age were actually created by a great upthrusting of energy from within the surface of the Earth. This violent explosion was itself triggered by the celestial wars raging in the heavens immediately above the Earth.

The land masses were like playing cards shuffled together. And in this way the present layers were formed. Therefore, the mountains, rocks, and trees, which bear every outward sign of antiquity, are actually of quite recent creation.

Such an explanation would bring the geological sciences into harmony with the accounts of the learned priests and priestesses of the past, and with the accounts preserved in the Hebrew Bible.

Other scholars say that the cataclysms of the Old Testament are only apparently recent, that the Biblical stories are based upon older racial memories of Atlantis, Mu, Lemuria, and other lost lands.

In the Book of Systems it is written that the Earth had many cycles of evolution, and many races and types of intelligences have lived upon it. At the end of every cycle the Earth is cataclysmically destroyed. In some generations the destruction has been by fire; in some by ice; in some by earthquake; in some by flood.

The Holy Ones of Mu, who were called Naacals, explained the cataclysms this way: the Earth's surface was not solid but porous. The underlayers of the land were honeycombed with chambers by which the gas of the interior was conducted through the stones of the Earth. The Earth was formed by the cooling and solidification of gas, and the center of the Earth is made of gas.

> Gases have been the active agents responsible for all changes in the earth's surface. Gases are responsible for our mountains and mountain ranges; gases are responsible for the depths of our seas and oceans; and gases are today responsible for our earthquakes and volcanoes. *Had the gases Remained Inactive from the Beginning, Not an Inch of Land Would Ever Have Appeared Above the Surface of the Waters.*

So the prophet James Churchward wrote in *The Cosmic Forces of Mu*. The Naacals understood that an upset in the Earth's magnetic fields would cause catastrophes of weather and other natural forces.

The oldest surviving written records of the human race tell of the cata clysm of a great Deluge, which covered the whole face of the Earth. This is the same Deluge that was recounted in the most sacred tales of the Chaldeans.

In the old kingdoms of China, that vast and mighty offshoot of the Lemurian race, there was also a Deluge tradition. During the reign of Yahou, of remote and magnificent memory, a cosmic catastrophe overwhelmed China and the sun did not set for ten days.

This miracle is remarkably like that recorded in the Old Testament:

> Then spake Joshua to the Lord in the day when the Lord delivered up the Amorites before the children of Israel, and he said in the sight of Israel, Sun, stand thou still upon Gibeon; and thou, Moon, in the valley of Ajalon.
>
> And the sun stood still, and the moon stayed, until the people had avenged themselves upon their enemies. Is not this written in the book of Jasher? So the sun stood still in the midst of heaven, and hasted not to go down about a whole day.
>
> —Joshua 10: 12–13

Tibet also was once under water, though subsequent cataclysms have thrust its temples and palaces of wisdom far up against the roof of the world.

The Hebrew Bible records the story of Noah, whom God preserved from the Deluge, and the same Deluge story was revealed to the prophet Zoroaster.

The Greek legends also spoke of the Flood. In the Chronicle of Atlantis it is written how Plato and his students knew of the previous civilization of Atlantis and of its tragic and cataclysmic end in an upheaval of the Earth.

So in Egypt, Mesopotamia, Atlantis, Lemuria, and South America, even in Tibet and China, legends of the Deluge remain. And not only of the Deluge, but of the age before it.

What caused the Deluge? Was it an explosion from outer space, or the welling up of dark forces from within the Earth?

Cosmic Comets

Some scholars have taught that great comets have crossed the path of the Earth, caused disturbances in the magnetic field of the Earth, and even reversed the direction of the Earth's spin in its orbit.

This was the teaching described by Jonathan Swift, that learned churchman and Irish patriot, in his vision of the intellectual attainments of the scientists of Laputa. The Wise Ones of Laputa believed:

> . . . that the Earth by the continual Approaches of the Sun towards it, must in Course of Time be absorbed or swallowed up. That the Face of the Sun will by Degrees be encrusted with its own Effluvia, and give no more Light to the World. That the Earth very narrowly escaped a Brush from the Tail of the last Comet, which would have infallibly reduced it to Ashes; and that the next, which they have calculated for One and Thirty Years hence, will probably destroy us. For if in its Perihelion it should approach within a certain Degree of the Sun, (as by their Calculations they have reason to dread) it will conceive a Degree of Heat ten Thousand Times more intense than that of red hot glowing Iron; and in its Absence from the Sun, carrying a blazing Tail Ten Hundred Thousand and Fourteen Miles long; through which if the Earth should pass at the Distance of one Hundred Thousand Miles from the *Nucleus*, or main Body of the Comet, it must in its Passage be set on Fire, and reduced to Ashes. That the Sun daily spending its Rays without any Nutriment to supply them, will at last be wholly consumed and annihilated; which must be attended with the Destruction of this Earth, and all the Planets that receive their light from it.

In modern times this revelation came also to Ignatius Donnelly, who wrote of Atlantis. Donnelly wrote down his visions in a book, and he called the book *Ragnorak, the Age of Fire and Gravel*. Thus, Donnelly fulfilled the prophecies of the scholar Swift.

Velikovsky's Cataclysm Theories have written of comets and of the destructions they cause upon the globe. In recent days the comet message has been spread by Immanuel Velikovsky, the reviled, denounced, and now vindicated scholar who dared to defy the narrowminded bigotry of modern science and propose that the theories known to the ancients be seriously reconsidered in light of modern astronomical discoveries.

This is what Velikovsky has written about the cataclysms of the world: That cataclysmic events, collisions of stars and comets within our solar system, have taken place within relatively recent human history; indeed, that there can be no better explanation for some of the events in the Hebrew Scriptures than the arrival in the Earth's orbit of a planet or comet from elsewhere in space.

Velikovsky showed that a global catastrophe hit the Earth around 1500 B.C.—the same time that the Children of Israel left Egypt for the Promised Land. Thus he explains the mysteries of the dreadful Plagues of Egypt, which were performed by Moses in the presence of the Egyptian Pharaoh.

These were the ten plagues:

1. Waters turned to blood (Exodus 7:14–25)
2. Frogs (Exodus 8:1–7)
3. Dust turns to lice (Exodus 8:16–19)

4. Flies (Exodus 8:20–32)
5. Death of cattle (Exodus 9:1–7)
6. Boils (Exodus 9:8–12)
7. Hail (Exodus 9:18–35)
8. Locusts (Exodus 10:1–20)
9. Darkness (Exodus 10:21–29)
10. Slaying of the firstborn (Exodus 11 and 12)

Velikovsky searched patiently among the works of the past and among sundry legends and found strikingly similar physical effects in the histories of several widely divergent peoples. His discoveries seemed to indicate that all of the Plagues of Egypt were effects of the near-collision of the planet Earth with a comet that later became the planet Venus.

The approach of Venus near the Earth's orbit was viewed by all the wise ones on Earth with a growing sense of horror. Like the ancient Egyptians, the ancient Mayans told of a great cataclysm in which the rivers flowed red like blood. The comet was accompanied by showers of meteorites. These were the "hailstones" that fell from the sky during the seventh plague. That fact has been part also of Midrashic and Talmudic secret tradition for centuries.

The descent of the comet and its accompanying debris was responsible for the subsequent establishment in world religion of the cults of fire. For the cataclysms caused crude oil to be rained down on Arabia and the Middle East. This oil was worshipped by the priests of Zoroaster.

The merciless battle between celestial elements rained down fire and brimstone, and caused the people's skin to break out in pestilences not unlike those caused by the nuclear weapons of today.

The magnetic pull of the approaching comet also accounts for the story of the parting of the Red Sea, which up until now, people have found difficult to reconcile with either the claims of science or of faith. Many nations have legends of the seas being torn asunder in violence by wind and waves—the comet was probably responsible for these too.

A great many other "miracles" of the Old Testament are more readily understood when the presence of a comet is postulated. For the Bible tells us that the entire journey from Egypt to Israel was accompanied by unusual phenomena: a pillar of fire by night and of cloud by day, dark thunderings in the mountains, and, above all, the mysterious dew that provided moisture and the manna that came with it.

Velikovsky proclaims that the cataclysm of Exodus is the same cataclysm as that which sank Atlantis. But on this point he is much disputed by others of the Elect.

Velikovsky is of the mind that Plato erred in his computation of the dates of the Atlantis Chronicle. And others have shown that such errors need not be admitted because Plato's account can be verified as absolutely historically accurate.

The comet, which later became Venus, was originally ejected from the planet Jupiter. Jupiter itself was involved in a planetary collision, discharging the comet as a result of the jolt. Then the comet flew in a wide arc toward the Earth.

The Earth avoided total destruction because it did not collide directly with the comet, but passed instead through the comet's tail.

Then, fifty-two years later, just as the Israelites were entering the Promised Land at last, the comet approached again. This time its approach arrested the very spin of the Earth, which wound to a stop like a giant top. Then the force of the unwinding caused it to spin out again, in an opposite direction. Everything that once was east is now west, and all that was once west is now east.

This is the explanation of the miracle of the sun standing still, which is recorded in the Book of Joshua. The miracles of the parting of the River Jordan, and the fall of the city of Jericho, make sense when one understands how great were the cosmic forces raging in the sky at that time.

The comet may also explain the sky dragon legends that abound all over the Earth. In the Icelandic Eddas, in the Norse sagas, in the Babylonian *Epic of Gilgamesh*, the story is the same. "Vala's Prophecy," from the Scandinavian *Edda of Soemund*, relates.

> The shadows groan on the ways of Hel [the goddess of death], until the fire of Surt has consumed the tree. Hyrm steers from the east, the waters rise, the mundane snake is coiled in jotun-rage. The worm beats the water and the eagle screams; the pale of beak tears carcasses; [the ship] Nagflar is loosed. Surt from the south comes with flickering flame; shines from his sword the Valgod's sun. The stony hills are dashed together, the giantesses totter; men tread the path of Hel, and heaven is cloven. The sun darkens, earth in ocean sinks, fall from heaven the bright stars, fire's breath assails the all-nourishing, towering fire plays against heaven itself.

The approach and near-miss of the comet explains the proliferation, all over the world, of cults of the planet Venus, the Morning Star. The ancient Mexicans recorded the birth of the planet Venus—that is, its transformation from a comet to a planet—in their legends of Quetzalcoatl, for they associated that star with that god. They pictured the god Quetzalcoatl as a plumed serpent, who appeared in flames of fire. The old texts confirm that the star was worshipped because of the intensity of the catastrophe out of the midst of which it had appeared.

This catastrophe was the same catastrophe that accompanied the Exodus from Egypt. The Mexicans have a legend of a fifty-two-year interval between two world catastrophes, just as the ancient Hebrews do.

After the comet passed the Earth the second time, it continued in its orbit, leaving behind great destruction as the direction of the Earth's spin was reversed. The comet then collided with the planet Mars, and with its satellites. The planet Mars was sent out of its orbit, and came very near to colliding with the Earth. (These cataclysmic events took place in the eighth and seventh centuries before the Age of Pisces.) The near-disaster with Mars again caused fire to rain down from the heavens, thus explaining the destruction of the armies of Sennacherib, another puzzling text in the Hebrew scriptures.

The Martian encounter was received by the priests of Mesopotamia as a revelation, and it is from this that the fire-worship of the Zoroastrians comes. For Zoroaster saw the fire from heaven with his own eyes.

Talmudic sources agree that the camp of Sennacherib was destroyed in a consuming blast of fire. It was in exactly those terms that Zoroaster described the celestial wars of good versus evil.

After colliding with Mars, Venus settled into her present fixed orbit. And the trembling astronomers who had watched her progress through the heavens offered her sacrifices that she might remain in her place and not further upheave the Earth. Thus arose the worship of the Great Mother, who is the Morning Star, Venus. The Greek goddess Pallas Athena was Venus; the Egyptian Isis was Venus; the Cappodicean Ishtar and the Syrian Astarte were Venus; the goddess Kybele was Venus. With all these bright goddesses there was connected a flaming serpent with a tail.

Cataclysms in Recent Times. The cataclysms of the Earth, which some say have taken place in quite recent times, have left their record in the geology of the Earth. In geology more than any other field, the scientists have confirmed the accuracy of the ancient records. For the near-collisons with the planet Venus and the planet Mars caused thundering earthquakes, and the rocks were torn asunder, and fire belched out of the deep.

In recorded times there are many instances of such cataclysms. In the New Testament we read of an intense darkness that covered the land during the time of Christ's crucifixion. The Romans recorded a day of darkness during the reign of Julius Caesar. The great classical city of Pompeii was devastated and completely buried by the eruption of the volcano Vesuvius.

And for many years Pompeii was buried, until all memory of it had left the earth. There were many who scoffed and said Pompeii had never existed. But then the ruins of Pompeii were found and the scoffers were objects of scorn. So it shall be with all those who do not believe in the cataclysms.

In the year 1973 a great volcanic eruption struck the island of Heimaey, near Iceland, and a mountain burst forth from the sea. Thus it can be seen that it is perfectly possible for mountains to grow up overnight.

In 1822 there was a great earthquake on the island of Java, near the mountain of Gulang Gung. The earthquake was described by the geologist

Lyell and reported by the prophet Donnelly:

> A loud explosion was heard, the earth shook, and immense columns of hot water and boiling mud, mixed with burning brimstone, ashes, and lapilli, of the size of nuts, were projected from the mountain like a water-spout, with such prodigious violence that large quantities fell beyond the river Tandoi, which is forty miles distant. . . . The first eruption lasted nearly five hours; and on the following days the rain fell in torrents, and the rivers, densely charged with mud, deluged the country far and wide. At the end of four days (October 12th), a second eruption occurred, more violent than the first, in which hot water and mud were again vomited.

The catastrophes that caused the parting of the Red Sea and the destruction of Sennacherib were far more violent than that described above. They laid waste the entire world, not just a small section of it. Only by a miracle did human life survive on the planet.

Nuclear Power in Past Ages. Not all scholars attribute the Earth's cataclysms to the effects of comets. There are others who say that the civilizations of the past developed nuclear weapons, even as we have today, and destroyed themselves with the destructions thus unleashed.

However, not enough is known about the generations before the Deluge, for what remains is no more than would remain if our own society were suddenly to be consumed in a nuclear conflagration.

The Hebrew scriptures have been supported by the testimony of visionaries and seers, who have asserted that many of the past cultures were technologically advanced. On Atlantis, for example, the scientists were able, with the help of beings from outer space, to build the Great Crystal, with which they powered their airships. The crystal worked by absorbing energies from the Earth, energies which were then magnified by the rays of the sun. This is an accurate description of the way nuclear power works.

There are fragments of evidence in support of a technologically advanced civilization in ancient Mesopotamia also, although those fragments have been frequently overlooked by scientific investigators.

A number of different traditions assert that before the Flood people lived a lot longer than they do now. The Hebrew scriptures claim that Methuselah, Enoch, and the other early patriarchs survived for a great many years. Clearly, they had learned the secret of prolonging life through harnessing the Earth's energies.

Cosmic Ice. Another scholar, Hans Horbiger, who was an inventor and engineer and thus a man of some mechanical and scientific accomplishments, said that the catastrophes of Atlantis, and all the other disasters that have ravaged the globe, were caused by collisions in outer space between cosmic ice and molten metal. The sudden juxtaposition of hot and cold caused the elements to explode in raging fires.

At that moment of explosion, the impact was so great that uncountable particles of cosmic material were thrown into space, and they were captured by the magnetic fields of some suns and stars.

The cosmic particles spiralled inward to our Sun, and as they crossed the orbits of the planets, the temperatures on the planets changed and they became encased in ice.

One of the cosmic particles was captured by the Earth's magnetic field and became our moon. Atlantis perished at the time a new moon was formed in the heavens.

The Coming Cataclysms. All the great mystics of all religions agree that the global age will end in a cataclysm. The *Book of Mormon*, for example, gives this vision of the last days:

> And they that kill the prophets and the saints, the depths of the earth shall swallow them up, saith the Lord of Hosts; and mountains shall cover them, and whirlwinds shall carry them away, and buildings shall fall upon them, and crush them to pieces and grind them to powder.
>
> And they shall be visited with thunderings, and lightnings, and earthquakes, and all manner of destruction, for the fire of the anger of the Lord shall be kindled against them.

So also the Christian Bible, in the Revelation of St. John, contains these words describing the cataclysms at the end:

> And there were voices, and thunders, and lightnings; and there was a great earthquake, such as was not since men were upon the earth, so mighty an earthquake, and so great.
>
> And the great city was divided into three parts, and the cities of the nations fell; and great Babylon came in remembrance before God, to give unto her the cup of the wine of the fierceness of his wrath.
>
> And every island fled away, and the mountains were not found.
>
> And there fell upon men a great hail out of heaven, every stone about the weight of a talent.
>
> —Revelations 16:18–21

When will the end of our age come? The prophet Edgar Cayce predicted that in the eighth decade of the twentieth century of the Age of Pisces, the continent of Atlantis would once more begin to rise up out of the sea. This rising will be accompanied by increased earthquake and tidal-wave activity along the east and west coasts of America.

Some say that the sinking of New York and California will take place because of the rising of Alantis; others assert that there will not be a sinking of the land so much as a rising of the waters, as we enter an age of excessive rainfall and precipitation. And others say that we are entering another Ice Age.

And there are other prophets who warn that the final cataclysm may come because of our abuse of nuclear power. For there are ominous signs that the scientists and powermongers of today are committing the same errors committed by great civilizations of the past—trying to take over the functions of the Cosmos. It is the sin of overreaching, and it may end in the most devastating conflagration of them all.

The Book of Visitations

This is the record of the visitations by Beings from outer space to the inhabitants of Earth. These Beings have descended at sundry times and places to humans of special intelligence, who have afterward been known as Prophets, Priests, and Kings.

And some were taken up by the Space Gods into their flaming vehicles, which they described in the language of their times as chariots. Thus it was written of the Hebrew prophet Elijah:

> Behold, there appeared a chariot of fire, and horses of fire, and parted them both asunder; and Elijah went up by a whirlwind into heaven.
>
> —2 Kings 2:11

All the great advances of human civilization are due to the careful, intelligent monitoring of the Space Gods, who discovered the first signs of intelligent life on Earth several hundred million years ago.

The Gods are in possession of technologically advanced recording devices, and they are able to record the brain waves of every intelligent species. At certain times in history they have decided to appear personally to the beings on Earth.

The Space Gods have been controlling our progress, through a series of experiments in genetic engineering. In this manner they developed Man, a creature capable of perceiving forms higher than itself. The human creature then evolved the means to communicate with the Space Gods.

The Space Gods, seeing that humans were desirous of communicating with them, and taking pity on their fallen condition, made arrangements to meet with certain humans and take them up into their spacecraft, instructing them on the Laws of Life and the Cosmic Secrets.

Thus is explained the mysterious vision of Jacob, which has been recorded of old:

> And he dreamed, and behold a ladder set up on the earth, and the top of it reached to heaven: and behold the angels of God ascending and descending on it.
>
> —Genesis 28:12

And the Space Gods hovered in one of their craft over Mount Sinai, and Moses went up to meet them, and received from them the Ten Commandments, as it is written:

> And it came to pass on the third day in the morning, that there were thunders and lightnings, and a thick cloud upon the mount, and the voice of the trumpet exceeding loud; so that all the people that was in the camp trembled.
>
> And Moses brought forth the people out of the camp to meet with God; and they stood at the nether part of the mount.
>
> And Mount Sinai was altogether on a smoke, because the Lord descended on it in fire: and the smoke thereof ascended as the smoke of a furnace, and the whole mount quaked greatly.
>
> —Exodus 19:16–18

And the Space Gods gave Moses directions for constructing a wooden box, an energy accumulator and transmitter, with which to communicate with the spacecraft hovering above. The Hebrews called this box the Ark of the Covenant, and they revered it as the seat of their God.

This also explains the mysterious messages left to us by the ancient Egyptians, who identified the sign of a seat or throne with the symbols of Isis and Osiris. These were two of the original Space Gods who appeared in Egypt from the star system of Sirius.

The Space Gods appeared also to the ancient Mesopotamians and to the tribes along the West Coast of Africa who drew pictures of their Gods that they might worship them. The people of West Africa pictured their Space Gods as having the torsos and heads of humans but the tails of great fish.

The Mesopotamians also drew pictures of great winged gods who wore helmets and drove in chariots. And in some cases they pictured these Gods as having the tails of fish!

To some humans the Space Gods were creatures of great repulsion, and they have survived in legends as dragons, or fiery serpents. To other humans the Space Gods appeared as enticing and compelling. Their appearances are the origins of the tales of mermaids and mermen. (Indeed, there are some who say that the legends of Atlantis arose through local misunderstandings of the arrival of these fish-creatures on land. For many were confused and, unable to comprehend that the creatures came from outer space, decided instead that they had come from a mysterious land across the sea. Others say that the mermaids and mermen were Atlanteans, that the Atlanteans were themselves giants and descendants of the Beings from outer space. But such things are known only to the Elect.)

Why did the great cultures of the past draw pictures of Gods that were winged? Why did they picture their kings and rulers as being able to fly? Why are there so many ancient traditions of messengers from the heavens? Is a spaceship the most logical explanation of the Vision of the Prophet Ezekiel?

> And I looked, and, behold, a whirlwind came out of the north, a great cloud, and a fire enfolding itself, and a brightness was about it, and out of the midst thereof as the color of amber, out of the midst of the fire.
>
> Also out of the midst thereof came the likeness of four living creatures. And this was their appearance; they had the likeness of a man.
>
> And every one had four faces, and every one had four wings.
>
> And their feet were straight feet; and the sole of their feet was like the sole of a calf's foot: and they sparkled like the color of burnished brass.
>
> And they had the hands of a man under their wings on the four sides; and they four had their faces and their wings.
>
> Their wings were joined one to another; they turned not when they went; they went every one straight forward.

As for the likeness of their faces, they four had the face of a man, and the face of a lion, on the right side: and they four had the face of an ox on the left side; they four also had the face of an eagle.

Thus were their faces; and their wings were stretched upward; two wings of every one were joined one to another, and two covered their bodies.

And they went every one straight forward: whither the spirit was to go, they went; and they turned not when they went.

As for the likeness of the living creatures, their appearance was like burning coals of fire, and like the appearance of lamps: it went up and down among the living creatures; and the fire was bright, and out of the fire went forth lightning.

And the living creatures an and returned as the appearance of a flash of lightning

Now as I beheld the living creatures, behold one wheel upon the earth by the living creatures, with his four faces.

The appearance of the wheels and their work was like unto the color of a beryl: and they four had one likeness: and their appearance and their work was as it were a wheel in the middle of a wheel.

When they went, they went upon their four sides: and they turned not when they went.

As for their rings, they were so high that they were dreadful; and their rings were full of eyes round about them four.

And when the living creatures went, the wheels went by them: and when the living creatures were lifted up from the earth, the wheels were lifted up.

Whithersoever the spirit was to go, they went, thither was their spirit to go; and the wheels were lifted up over against them: for the spirit of the living creature was in the wheels.

When those went, these went; and when those stood, these stood; and when those were lifted up from the earth, the wheels were lifted up over against them: for the spirit of the living creature was in the wheels.

And the likeness of the firmament upon the heads of the living creature was as the color of the terrible crystal, stretched forth over their heads above.

And under the firmament were their wings straight, the one toward the other: every one had two, which covered on this side, and every one had two, which covered on that side, their bodies.

And when they went, I heard the noise of their wings, like the noise of great waters, as the voice of the Almighty, the voice of speed, as the noise of an host: when they stood, they let down their wings.

And there was a voice from the firmament that was over their heads, when they stood, and had let down their wings.

And above the firmament that was over their heads was the likeness of a throne, as the appearance of a sapphire stone: and upon the likeness of the throne was the appearance of a man above it.

And I saw as the color of amber, as the appearance of a fire round about within it, from the appearance of his loins even upward, and from the appearance of his loins even downward, I saw as it were the appearance of fire, and it had brightness round about.

As the appearance of the bow that is in the cloud in the day of rain, so was the appearance of the brightness round about. This was the appearance of the likeness of the glory of the Lord. And when I saw it, I fell upon my face, and I heard a voice of one that spake.

—Ezekial 1:4–28

A Brief Commentary on the Ezekiel Passage

Few passages in the Bible give such a detailed picture of the vision of God. Is it not astonishing that the description should coincide so carefully with descriptions of modern aircraft?

We can now fly in machines. We are at last beginning to approach the technological expertise of our Space God ancestors. And now we are just able to interpret this passage, which has been troubling Biblical scholars for centuries.

For isn't Ezekiel's vision a precise step-by-step, almost journalistic account of the landing of a helicopterlike space vehicle, the blasting of its jets, the roaring of its flames, its tremendous voltage as it lowers itself onto Earth, causing the whole Earth to shake and tremble, the whole apparatus moving about on wheels, and having folding wings, and flashing with lights the color of amber?

And is it not possible that the wheels within the wheels were giant gears? Could the eyes that Ezekiel saw around the rim of the vehicle have been portholes in a spacecraft? And what was the terrible crystal on top of the Space God's head, if not the transmitting helmet device that connected it to the mother ship?

Ezekiel was one of many prophets who tried to record their encounters with the Astronaut Gods. Fortunately, in the last few decades modern anthropologists and archeologists have uncovered hard new evidence that astronaut contact did exist in ancient times.

The Nazca Lines

In the southern region of Peru, on the desert that lies along the coastal plain, there is a large flat region. And on the flat surface of the plain there appear enormous straight lines, running to the horizon. These straight lines *can be seen only from the air*!

Next to the lines, near the same place in the plain, there appear the likenesses of winged creatures and great coils. These were, without question, the early attempts of the Peruvians to communicate with their astronaut visitors. And would not the natural response of the Space Gods be to come down and build the long, straight lines as runways for themselves?

In the literature of ancient Peruvian Indian tribes we find the story of the Space Gods' first descent. Their craft landed on a high plain near Lake Titicaca. This remote lake, one of the great mysteries of nature, was chosen as the place for the Space Gods to land.

For has it not been written that the Space Gods had the form of fish? Would that not seem to indicate that they were amphibious creatures? If so, would they not look for the largest available body of water on which to land?

This, then, is how the Inca civilization preserved the memory of its Space God founders:

In the ancient days, humans were in a barbarous state, little better than animals. And they killed each other and feasted upon each other's bodies. But the Sun, the parent of the human race, had pity on people. He decided to send down two of his children to communicate with the natives on earth and teach them the arts of civilization.

The spacecraft of the descending Sun Children landed on the plains near Lake Titicaca, at a site on which later was to be built the magnificent Temple of the Sun. (The mathematical precision and intricate technological markings on the art and architecture of Tihuanaco and other Bolivian ruins are mute testimonies to the grandeur and power of civilization as established on Earth by the Space Gods.) The Incas called these first Space Gods Manco Capac and Mama Occlo. The two astronauts left Lake Titicaca and made their way down the valley, carrying a golden wedge.

Their orders were to carry the golden wedge until they reached a spot where the wedge would suddenly sink into the ground. They travelled to Cuzco. There the wedge disappeared into the Earth. Thus the Incas called Cuzco "the navel of the world."

Does it not seem likely that the golden wedge of the Incas was actually some kind of metallic homing device for keeping in touch with extraterrestrial vehicles? Is it an accident that the same type of golden wedge probably also crowned the ancient Egyptian pyramids? Is it not likely that this venerated Inca Wedge was the same object that was used by the Atlanteans and—according to their traditions—powered their spacecrafts?

For it has come down to us that the Atlanteans were helped in their technological advances by Beings from outer space. What could those be but the Space Gods?

Space Gods of the Arabs

All the great religious traditions teach the advent of the Space Gods. In the 57th Sura of the Koran, for example, there appears an astonishing description of what could only be a contact with Space Gods. (In those days, the Space Gods appeared to the Jews and Arabs as angels.)

> Elif. Lam. Ra. These are the signs of the Book, and of a lucid recital.
>
> Many a time will the infidels wish that they had been Muslims.
>
> Let them feast and enjoy themselves, and let hope beguile them; but they shall know the truth at last.
>
> We never destroyed a city whose term was not prefixed.
>
> No people can forestall or retard its destiny.
>
> They say: "O thou to whom warning hath been sent down, thou art surely possessed by a djinn:
>
> Wouldst thou not have come to us with the angels, if thou wert of those who

assert the truth?"

—We will not send down the angels without due cause. The Infidels would not in that case have been respited.

Verily, we have sent down the warning and verily, We will be its guardian;

And already We have sent Apostles, before thee, among the sects of the ancients;

But never came Apostles to them whom they did not deride.

In like manner will We put it into the hearts of the sinners of Mecca to do the same:

They will not believe on him though the example of those of old hath gone before.

Even were We to open above them a gate in Heaven, yet all the while they were mounting up to it,

They would surely say: It is only that our eyes are drunken: nay, we are a people enchanted.

We have set the signs of the zodiac in the Heavens, and adorned and decked them forth for the beholders,

And we guard them from every stoned Satan,

Save such as steal a hearing, and him doth a visible flame pursue.

A Brief Commentary on the Koran Passage

The Koran is a difficult book to interpret without some years of study and discipline. Observe, however, the direct—the unmistakeable—reference to some secret that has been passed down "among the sects of the ancients." And observe that the speakers, who call themselves We, specifically refer to a gate that must be mounted up to Heaven. Could that not be an entry ramp for one of the extraterrestrials' spaceships?

Is it not true that the sects of the ancients knew how to control the energy force fields of the universe? Did they not use pyramids to concentrate the energy force fields in some way unknown to our present "advanced" technology?

How could the ancient Arabs have learned such advanced astronomy and mathematics, save from these outer-space instructors?

Can it be an accident that two great series of civilizations—the Middle Eastern and the South American—independently developed exactly the same belief patterns, architecture, clothing styles, forms of transportation, systems of government, and religious rituals?

Did not the heroes and gods of both the ancient Egyptians and the ancient Incas wear helmets? Did not the gods of both civilizations have wings? Did not both cultures build pyramids?

What about the small boxes, which are shown in the statuary of both the Egyptians and the New World Indians? These small boxes look like small transistor radios. Would it not make sense to assume that the boxes were devices for communicating with the extraterrestrials? Does such an explanation involve anything that is "miraculous" to us? Doesn't the Space God arrival make sense in terms of the discoveries of modern science?

It is established, then, that gods arrived a long time ago from outer space—perhaps from the planet Venus, perhaps from Sirius—and are overseeing human development on Earth. How do the Space Gods operate among humans? Is there any evidence of their influence in recorded human history?

The Order of the Illuminati

Thousands of years ago, when human life was beginning to take its present form, in the days of Lemuria, the flame of intelligence such as we know it now was set burning in the human brain. The Space Gods planned this experiment carefully. They implanted the flame only in the minds of those who had been biologically—genetically—programmed to receive it properly.

They thus developed a separate race, as it were, within the human race. These Superhumans were able to communicate readily with the Space Gods and receive their instructions.

Compared to the ordinary run of humanity, the Superhumans were gods and heroes. And so they are remembered today. The ancient Greeks preserved tales of heroes who had wings, or who mounted on winged steeds to fly off over the highest mountains. These myths developed because of the human inability to comprehend what was happening when large, flaming machines descended from the sky.

The Superhumans of Lemuria were the founders of the Order of the Illuminati. It was recognized by the Space Gods that day-to-day monitoring of the activities on Earth could best be done on the planet itself. They therefore set up "monitoring" stations, at which their officials—the priests and kings—could regularly report to them and receive instructions.

This, incidentally, was how the custom of crowning the kings and queens originated. The first human rulers wore elaborate headsets through which they received their instructions from above.

This also was the origin of the custom of having an inner chamber within the temples, into which only the High Priest could enter. It was inside the "Holy of Holies" that the transmitting and receiving equipment must have been kept.

Moses was in communication with the Space Gods, as his forefather Abraham had been. Jesus, too, was in communication with them, having contacted them in the wilderness and been taken to Egypt among the Hermetic priests.

The Hermetic priests of Egypt were long the guardians of the sacred truths and relics of the Order of the Illuminati. They understood the mysteries of the pyramids, and of the stars in the heavens. Those in the inner circles of initiation were regularly received up in the spaceships, and flown to other planets and space stations, and given some acquaintance with the physical realities of the wider Cosmos.

The Order of the Illuminati has continued through history as a secret order that exists within the ranks of other secret orders.

The medieval order of the Knights Templar, for example, contained many Illuminati members, but not all Templars belonged to the higher, more esoteric order. Even among the Templars who belonged to the Illuminati, there were many who did not know the true secrets of the sect. Those secrets are known only to a few.

Among the Dervishes of Turkey there are Illuminati, and among the African secret societies there are Illuminati, and among the Masons there are Illuminati.

Not all Masons are Illuminati. Not even all 33rd-degree Masons are Illuminati. But all Illuminati are 33rd-degree Masons.

In modern history, the Illuminati conspired to cause both the American and the French Revolutions. George Washington and Thomas Jefferson were 33rd-degree Masons, and much of their correspondence suggests they were also Illuminati. The folk philosopher, printer, and statesman Benjamin Franklin was certainly a member of the Illuminati Order.

But the names of the Inner Order of the Illuminati will always be kept secret, until long after the age in which the members lived.

There are some who say that the true Illuminati are very ancient, that they are composed of spirit only and not of body, for they exist on the astral plane. Therefore, the Illuminati can inhabit certain humans at will, and they select certain human forms in which to manifest themselves. Thus, the Illuminati chose the bodies of Benjamin Franklin, George Washington, and Thomas Jefferson, and used them only occasionally, as they saw fit. The truth is known only to the Elect.

The Order of the Illuminati perpetuates the knowledge of the star system of Sirius, knowledge that has long been a part of occult tradition.

Sirius is the chief star in a constellation that was known to the ancient Egyptians as "The Phoenix." Aleister Crowley, the twentieth-century magician and prophet, took "Phoenix" as his secret name when he joined the Ordo Templi Orientis. His manuscript, "The Book of the Law," was dictated to him by a messenger from the spaceships of Sirius.

The Order of the Golden Dawn contained within it some Illuminati, though many more fools who knew not what they did. And Madame Blavatsky also had connections with Sirius, as did Gurdjieff. The latter was initiated into a secret society by Beings from Sirius.

The mission of Blavatsky, Gurdjieff, and Crowley was to prepare their fellow humans for future contacts with the Space Gods, who manifest themselves to more people all the time. For the Illuminati have also been preparing the human race scientifically for the next stage of its development. The Illuminati are behind the current space missions, which are sending human communications to Venus. Can Sirius be far behind? Is it any accident that the man trusted with the mission of being first on the moon was a 33rd-degree Mason?

Dr. Timothy Leary, who has been much persecuted for his valiant defense of the enlightened point of view, has recently revealed that he has been in contact with extraterrestrials from Sirius. The text of their communication with him is contained within the writings of Robert Anton Wilson.

Who are the Illuminati? We do not know. What is their purpose with us? We do not know. And what should be our attitude toward them? Alas, even that we do not know. For there are some who say that in recent times there have arisen factions even within the Order of the Illuminati. Only those in the trusted inner circle know what direction the Order is taking.

Some say that the Illuminati have become power-hungry, that they have forsaken the principles of the past and that, in their greed, they are working through the capitalist system to bring about the subjugation of the human race. So there also have arisen anti-Illuminati organizations, which are perhaps run by the *real* Illuminati, directly from Sirius.

One thing is certain. The presence of the Illuminati among us cannot remain hidden forever. Already it influences the day-to-day running of the world. Beings from Sirius and other planets will be contacting more humans in the years to come.

The return of the Space Gods has been predicted in the apocalyptic literature of all the great religions. Some scholars—Dr. Leary, for instance—are making attempts to get in contact with them first. These pioneers are talking of space missions, made up of carefully selected groups of colonists. These colonists would carry human civilization into outer space.

Could it be that the fate which befell Atlantis and Lemuria is also about to befall us? If the warnings of the prophets of coming doom are true, as they were true in the ancient cases, then perhaps we should consider leaving the Earth on spaceships to start life elsewhere.

The civilization of Lemuria was preserved by those who fled before the cataclysms. And the civilization of Atlantis also was preserved only by those who left before the Deluge and went to Egypt. Might not our civilization be preserved only by those who have left before the final Inferno?

k of Miracles and Mysteries

of Light

Praise to the Cosmic Force, which has caused to appear among humans certain attuned individuals to act as messengers between this world and other worlds.

These messengers are called Speakers, or Beings of Love, or Tibetan Mahatmas, or the Great White Brotherhood, or the Priests of Hermes, or the Illuminati.

Their aim is to seek knowledge and power, and to grant these to qualified individuals in the human race.

The Spirits of Light are always among us. But we cannot know the names of the spirits who live among us, only the names of those who lived in the past.

These are the names of the known Spirits of Light:

Lucifer, Prince of Light, who was cast out of heaven for leading a rebellion against God and who was confined to the lower regions of the earth. He is called the devil by some. But others worship him as Wisdom.

Space Gods from the star Sirius, from the planet Venus, and from an unknown planet that has since disappeared from our solar system have appeared on Earth at various times and have been called Spirits of Light. For the Space Gods were far more technologically advanced than the civilizations among which they appeared.

Amelius, who taught among the Atlanteans; Ra-Ta, who was a priest among the Atlanteans in Egypt; King Solomon the sorcerer and commander of legions of demons.

Michael, Raphael, and Gabriel, angels who appeared in Bible times; Abraham, Moses and Jesus, who received messages from the angels;

Pythagoras of Greece; Hermes of Egypt; Zoroaster of Persia; Buddha of India; Ezekiel and Daniel of the nation of Israel;

Plotinus the scholar; Plato the philosopher; Paracelsus the physician;

Joseph of Arimathea, who brought the Holy Grail to England; Merlin, who appeared to King Arthur and his court;

The prophet Muhammad, to whom Allah appeared in the desert; Quetzalcoatl, who appeared among the ancient Mexicans; Mamma Occle and Manco Capac, who appeared among the Peruvians;

Emmanuel Swedenborg, who saw visions of planets and angels; William Blake, who conversed with devils as well;

Mesmer, who rediscovered healing by magnetism; Benjamin Franklin, who experimented with forms of electricity;

Comte de Saint-Germain, who knew the alchemical secrets, could enlarge jewels, and was perhaps a vampire;

Joseph Smith, to whom the angel Moroni appeared with golden tablets;

Helen Petrovna Blavatsky, who received communications from the Mahatmas of Tibet, especially one Koot Hoomi;

Aleister Crowley, who was visited from Sirius and who performed many awesome and violent rituals of magic;

Rudolf Steiner, who built hospitals and schools, established farms, and wrote books to spread truth;

Gurdjieff, who also worked to establish harmony among humans and was in contact with Spirits of Light from Sirius;

Edgar Cayce, who was known as the sleeping prophet, saw in his dreams the people of Atlantis, and remembered one of his own incarnations in Egypt at the time of the sinking of Atlantis. And his name in those days was Ra-Ta.

The Spirits of Light are still among us, spreading the Seed of Light. But they appear to no one save those who are ready to receive them.

Omens in the Skies

The forces of the Cosmos are great; at their command are the vagaries of the weather and the caprices of the wind; the formations of the clouds and the composition of the rain.

Strange celestial events, recorded since the start of human history, have borne witness to the power of Cosmic energies.

Many days have been reported when darkness encompassed the Earth, without eclipse or any other scientific explanation. In the *Visuddhimagga* of the Buddhists are recorded catastrophes of darkness, fire, and flood. The sun stood still for Joshua when the Israelites were entering into the Promised Land. The Mexicans spoke of a time in the past when the Earth had no moon or sun. The Finns tell of a period of darkness in the *Kalevala*. Darkness was one of the plagues of Egypt. The sky was dark when Moses ascended Mt. Sinai, and when Jesus was crucified. Even in modern times, there have been days of unaccountable darkness. In 1780, the sky darkened over the northeastern United States for fifteen hours.

Flaming stones have fallen out of the skies. The Israelites witnessed their enemies, the Egyptians, being plagued by fiery hail. Aristotle recorded the fall of a meteorite at Aegospotami. Meteorites showered on southern France in 1790. A single meteorite, which fell in Siberia in 1908, filled the sky with debris for two years. The Indians spoke of red-hot stones being hurled down from the heavens. Oil rained down on Arabia. The Portuguese say that it rained blood in Lisbon in 1551. And meteorites have been found with inscriptions on them, proving the existence of intelligent life elsewhere in the universe.

Manna, a mysterious food from heaven, fed the Israelites in the wilderness. Sand and grit have rained down on many occasions. Rouen, France, was hit by a flying iceberg in 1880. In the Middle Ages, flaming crosses fell several times. Stone hatchets were showered on Sumatra. Flaming planks blasted down on Touraine. Fish fell without warning from the sky in many places, most notably in Singapore in 1861. In the late nineteenth century, a huge load of hay flew through the air in Wales.

Also in the skies luminous visions have appeared. To the children of Israel there appeared a pillar of fire by night and a cloud by day. Constantine saw a lighted cross appear in the sky. Visionaries through the ages have spoken with angels and have been whirled up into the clouds. Winged beings appeared in Palermo, Italy, in 1880. Winged beings also appeared over the battlefield of Mons in 1914. They appeared to the English soldiers below as English bowmen, and they were led by St. George.

What is the meaning of these extraordinary events? Many explanations are put forth. And there are many possible meanings for these explanations. The truth is known only to the Elect.

But this should be known: that there are many things that cannot be explained through rational science, for there are more things on heaven and earth than are dreamed of in our philosophies.

Mysteries of Architecture

The Spirits of Light taught the people of Earth the arts of architecture, the principles of construction of temples and palaces.

The ancients especially learned the secret of centering cosmic forces by means of building. They built in accordance with the ley lines of the Earth, thus making easier the transmittal of cosmic energy.

These are among the Earth's architectural mysteries:

The pyramids of Egypt, and the Sphinx, which gaze wisely across the desert sands, preserving the secrets of the ancients. The pyramids are astronomical laboratories, tombs, sacred temples, prophetic records, and places of mystic initiation. The Sphinx is a storehouse of ancient treasures, even from Atlantean times.

The stone megaliths at Stonehenge, Malta, and other places, which resemble nothing so much as landing fields or centering devices for cosmic forces. In the center of each megalith is an altar, a point of communication with the Spirits of Light. Each megalith is carefully arranged so as best to attract cosmic energy.

The ruins of the Temple of the Sun at Tihuanaco, far older than any other city in South America, a culture that appeared mysteriously perhaps as long ago as the sinking of Atlantis, and disappeared equally mysteriously. It is known of the Tihuanaco people that they worshipped the Spirits of Light. And the Tihuanaco people are said to be the founders of the mighty Inca empire. To the Incas they appeared as Spirits of Light.

The huge lines transcribed on the plains of Nazca in Peru, which can be seen only from the air, and which are landing messages for spacecraft above.

The immense statues of Easter Island, a remote spot in the Pacific. The natives do not know from where these giant heads came with their huge red helmets.

Today many places of mysterious spirit force lie buried under landslide or overgrown by jungles. Once they were thriving centers of spiritual science, but they have not yet been discovered by modern science. The location of the mysterious cities is known to the Elect. Some say there is such a settlement on Mount Shasta in California. Other say that Machu Picchu, in Peru, is such a place of power.

In recent times, people have been returning in greater numbers to the ancient places of power, to absorb the cosmic energies and thus better understand the secrets of the universe.

Mysteries of Nature

The heavens declare the glory of God, and the firmament shows his handiwork.

Thus the Hebrew Psalms speak of a truth that has been known since the earliest times, that Nature herself is the best laboratory for learning cosmic secrets.

For until we can explain the mysteries of nature, the events that happen outside the jurisdiction of our so-called "scientific" laws, we cannot understand the final cosmic Truth.

Here are some of Nature's unexplained mysteries:

The Bermuda Triangle, a three-sided area in the western Atlantic into which numerous planes and ships have disappeared. Some say that the triangle marks the spot where once stood the Great Crystal of Atlantis.

The Loch Ness Monster, which has been seen by thousands and yet is intelligent enough to escape capture, even though many of the scientists in the world have tried to catch it.

The Big-Footed Beasts, which inhabit the snowy regions of Tibet and the American Northwest, and who are variously declared to be bears, or monstrous survivals of some ancient species.

The eerie lights of Mount Shasta, which have been seen on numerous occasions from passing trains and planes.

The "Devil's Sea," a section of the ocean near Japan, where ships and planes disappear as mysteriously as they do in the Bermuda Triangle.

The Earth is an unknown place, in spite of all the advances of our technology. We still cannot explain why dowsing works. We do not know why energy increases within a circle of stones.

Nor can we explain how the alchemist can create within the athanor the spiritual model of the Cosmos.

Nor can we explain why the Moon is steadily falling toward the Earth. Nor why a new moon is provided by Nature for each epoch in world history.

Nor can we explain the eternal conflict in nature between Ice and Fire.

We have no idea why there was a tremendous explosion in the air above Siberia in 1908. A column of fire arose on the horizon, and the forest was burned all about. The force of the blast was felt in London, Moscow, and Paris.

Could the explosion have been a nuclear blast? Could an interstellar craft have exploded in our atmosphere? Or was the explosion the result of some immense natural force we have not yet discovered?

Why is it that the evidence shows the world is hollow?

What about the great Ice Ages that periodically cover the Earth? What possible explanation could there be for them? Have any of the modern so-called scientists succeeded in giving an adequate explanation?

How could the mammoths in Siberia have been frozen so fast that their meat did not even rot for thousands of years? What overnight changes in the weather could have quick-frozen that magnificent species?

We do not understand nuclear physics, or astronomy, or advanced mathematics, or the new computer technologies. How then are we fully to understand the wisdom of the ancients, who were far more advanced than we?

Occult Relics

It has been observed with awe over the centuries that certain objects in themselves transmit occult powers. These objects are venerated as sacred and treated with due reverence and pomp.

The Holy Grail, the dish in which Joseph of Arimathea was served the holy meal, has appeared to many on Earth in various times and places. There are many who claim to have possessed this vessel. But its exact location is not known.

The Spear of Longinus, which pierced the side of Christ, conveys vast power to those who possess it. It was owned by Bismark and also by Hitler. Today the spear is in a museum in Austria.

The Holy Shroud of Turin, on which there appears, unmistakably, the face of Jesus. The blood of San Gennaro, which congeals and uncongeals in Naples.

The Philosopher's Stone, so ardently sought by the alchemists. It is also called the Powder of Mercury and the Elixir of Life.

From time to time there are idols, which make their way from the tropic regions into civilized countries, and cast their curse on all who possess them.

And we must not forget the artifacts left behind for us by vis other planets. The Coso artifact, with its core of bright metal an material—could this be proof of advanced civilizations in the pa

The figurines of Acambaro, Mexico, which show dinosaurs and other prehistoric animals thought to be extinct for millions of years. How could the Mexicans have known about these beasts, if they were not instructed by technologically superior beings?

The Tulli Papyrus, found by Prince Boris de Racheiviltz, in the secret papers of a director of the Egyptian Vatican Museum. The payrus reports that a circle of fire was seen coming from the sky.

The relics are but minute traces of a mighty day gone by, when the Earth was first contacted by other beings in the solar system. That we are finding them now adds weight to the claims of the visionaries, that we are entering a new era of interstellar communication.

Unidentified Flying Objects

In recent times the Space Gods, who represent the Beings of Light, have been increasing the number of their attempts to contact humans. So more and more people have seen the strange objects flying in the sky. No one knows the meaning of these objects, and they are called UFOs.

The nature of the UFOs is this: Some are long and thin, and some are round and flat, shaped like saucers. They have often been seen hovering over Loch Ness, wherein dwells the long-sought Monster.

Enoch, Moses, Ezekiel, Daniel—all had visions of objects in the sky. They described the objects as "Chariots of Fire."

In 1947 nine flying disks from outer space were sighted by a pilot flying near Mount Rainier, in the state of Washington.

Three glowing discs were sighted by an entire crowd at an air show in Longview, Washington.

There were over seventy sightings of UFOs within a two-and-a-half-month period in one small district of England.

In testimony before a House Committee, six leading scientists urged further investigation of UFOs.

In 1955, the pilot and copilot of a DC-3, when they were flying above Ithaca, New York, spotted a 150-foot-wide object cruising five hundred feet above their plane. This object was seen by other pilots also.

An egg-shaped craft landed near a farm in Libya. There were six men in yellow coveralls inside. Many people have been burned or suffered electrical shocks from touching the spacecraft. Some have been knocked unconscious and some have been left with weak hearts.

In Venezuela a boy discovered six dwarves loading stones into their spacecraft. They shot at him, and their weapons paralyzed him.

In Ely, Nevada, two truck drivers on a lonely night road were buzzed by highly illuminated globes the size of volleyballs.

The UFO sightings have recently increased in number, but there have been reports of them for centuries.

On January 18, 1644, residents of Boston saw lights the size of moons along the waterfront.

In Putney Hills, New Hampshire, there were many sightings of glowing balls between 1750 and 1800.

Betty and Barney Hill were actually taken up into a spacecraft. To aid the cause of science, the Hills have allowed themselves to be hypnotized and questioned about their experiences. Even under hypnosis, they have stuck to their story.

Can all these facts be mere coincidences? Contact with beings from outer space could mean the difference between the life and death of our planet. Is it not time that we did something about it?

Bibliography—Occult Bible

Bailey, Alice. *A Treatise on Cosmic Fire*. Lucis Co., 1930.
Barrett, Francis. *The Magus: or Celestial Intelligencer*. Dover, 1971.
Baxter, John and Thomas Atkins. *The Fire Came By*. Doubleday, 1976.
Bergier, Jacques. *Extraterrestrial Intervention: The Evidence*. Regnery, 1974.
Berlitz, Charles. *The Bermuda Triangle*. Doubleday, 1974.
Besant, Annie. *The Ancient Wisdom: an Outline of Theosophical Teaching*. Theosophical Society, 1910.
Blavatsky, Helen Petrovna. *The Secret Doctrine*. Theosophical Society, 1947.
———. *Isis Unveiled*. Theosophical Society, 1947.
Campbell, Elizabeth Montgomery and David Solomon. *The Search for Morag*. Walker & Company, 1974.
Campbell, James M. *UFOlogy*. Celestial Arts, 1976.
Cayce, Edgar. *Cayce on Atlantis*. Association for Research and Enlightenment, n.d.
Churchward, James. *The Lost Continent of Mu*. Crown, 1961.
———. *The Second Book of the Cosmic Forces of Mu*. Paperback Library, 1968.
Crowley, Aleister. *Magick in Theory and Practice*. Peter Smith, n.d.
———. *The Book of Lies*. Weiser, 1970.
Donnelly, Ignatius. *Atlantis: The Antediluvian World*. Dover, 1976.
Eddy, Mary Baker. *Science and Health with Key to the Scriptures*. First Church, n.d.
Edgar, Morton. *The Great Pyramid: Its Symbolism, Science, and Prophecy*. Bone & Hulley, 1924.
Fortune, Dion. *The Mystical Qabbalah*. Beem, 1970.
Fuller, John G. *Aliens in the Skies: The New UFO Battle of the Scientists*. Putnam, 1969.
Hall, Manly Palmer. *Secret Teachings of All Ages: An Encyclopedic Outline of Masonic, Hermetic, Qabbalistic, and Rosicrucian Philosophy*. Philos Res, n.d.
Holzer, Hans. *The UFOnauts*. Fawcett, 1976.
Hynek, J. Allen. *The UFO Experience: A Scientific Inquiry*. Regnery, 1972.
King James Bible.
Koran.
Lemurian Fellowship. *Lemuria, the Incomparable, the Answer*, 1939.
Michell, John. *The View over Atlantis*. Ballantine Books, 1969.
Montgomery, Ruth. *The World Before*. Fawcett, 1977.
Napier, John. *Bigfoot: The Yeti in Myth and Reality*. Dutton, 1973.
Noorbergen, René. *Secrets of the Lost Race*. Bobbs-Merrill, 1977.
Pauwels, Louis and Jacques Bergier. *The Morning of the Magicians*. Avon Books, 1972.
Peerman, Maximal. *The Macrocosmic Mystery*, 1931.
Phylos the Tibetan. (Oliver, Frederick S.) *A Dweller on Two Planets*. Steinerbooks, 1974.
Sacred Order of the Blue Flame. *A Key to Blue-Flame Science*, 1925.
Sitchin, Zechariah. *The Twelfth Planet*. Stein and Day, 1976.
Smith, Joseph. *The Book of Mormon*. Church of Jesus Christ of Latter Day Saints, 1966.
Steiner, Brad. *Mysteries of Time and Space*. Prentice-Hall, 1973.
Steiner, Rudolf. *Cosmic Memory: Atlantis and Lemuria*. Rudolf Steiner Publications, 1969.
———. *An Outline of Occult Science*. Anthroposophic Society, 1972.
———. *The Mystical Basis of Christianity*. Anthroposophic Society, 1972.
Stenman, Roy. *Atlantis and the Lost Lands*. Doubleday, 1977.

Swift, Jonathan. *Gulliver's Travels*.
Temple, Robert K.G. *The Sirius Mystery*. St. Martin's, 1976.
Velikovsky, Immanuel. *Worlds in Collision*. Pocket Books, 1977.
———. *Earth in Upheaval*. Pocket Books, 1977.
von Däniken, Erich. *Chariots of the Gods?* Putnam, 1970.
———. *Gods from Outer Space: My Pictorial Evidence for the Impossible*. Bantam, 1972.
Wilson, Colin. *Enigmas and Mysteries*. Doubleday, 1977.
Wilson, Robert Anton. *Cosmic Trigger: The Final Secret of the Illuminati*. And-or Press, 1977.
Woodman, Jim. *Nazca: Journey to the Sun*. Pocket Books, 1977.

Part Three

The Dissenting Viewpoint

Chapter Seven

A History of the Occult

In this chapter I will attempt to explain how Western civilization got entangled in the occult. My approach will be that of the orthodox historian. That is, I will assume that events happen according to cause and effect. I assume, therefore, that fourteenth- and nineteenty-century occultism were different, because people of the two centuries differed in their political expectations, their economic status, and their religious outlook.

Some occultists may be disappointed by this approach, for occultism has its own view of history. This view is that occultism is not merely a part of history but the guilding spirit behind it. There are hidden masters, it is believed, who have been working behind the scenes controlling the destiny of the human race. What we perceive as history, then, is illusion. The "real truth" has falsely been labelled "myth."

Unfortunately, few of the myths have any documentary base. Most of the information about them comes from trances, spirit messages, and other sources that historians regard with some suspicion. These sources are not likely to convince those who insist on factual evidence, nor will factual evidence change the minds of those who believe the myths.

That is why there are two history chapters in this book. This chapter is based on material that was recorded by ordinary mortals and exists in concrete form—letters, manuscripts, artifacts, etc. In the section called "The Occult Bible," I have presented the evidence transmitted by spirit guides, angels, Tibetan masters, and aliens from outer space. You may judge for yourselves which web is illusion and which is reality.

Occult Roots

Occult ideas are among the oldest, most deeply embedded notions in the human memory. Early occult beliefs grew out of observations of nature coupled with a belief in sympathetic magic—the idea that like controls like. The most common example of sympathetic magic is the small wax or wood doll representing an enemy. By harming the doll, one can also cause one's enemy to suffer. Sympathetic magic of this sort has been reported all over the world in all ages. Small wooden dolls apparently used for this purpose have been found as far back as the cave settlements of Cro-Magnon Man (before 10,000 B.C.).

Paleolithic religion was probably like that of hunting and gathering societies today. Paleolithic people seem to have venerated the animals that they hunted. They observed the sun in its regular changes and connected it with the annual cycle of the seasons. They also connected the setting of the sun with death and cold, and the rising of the sun with life, which in turn was linked to fire and warmth.

Shamanism. Like modern occultists, primitive peoples believe in a reservoir of supernatural force that pervades all things and that can be tapped by humans. In Melanesia, the force is called *mana*; in Mexico and Central America it is called *nagual*; in Peru it is called *huaca*; among the North American Indians it is called *orenda*. Some African tribes call the force *ngai*, and some Australian tribes call it *boolya*. Although each group attaches its own nuances of meaning, each of these words can roughly be translated as "spirit-force."

The *shaman* was an individual who, because of greater intelligence, psychic sensitivity, or force of personality, had more control over the spirit forces. Shamans were often people whom today we would call mentally deranged.

As primitive society settled down to agriculture, the shamans evolved into priests, the possessors of secret knowledge that allowed them to communicate with the divine. Their earliest rituals for communication with the spirits involved divination, prayers, and sacrifices.

The Worship of the Great Mother. One of the oldest forms of religious belief appears to have been the worship of the Great Mother, a personification of the procreative powers of nature. Small statuettes of female figures with grossly exaggerated thighs, breasts, and hips have been found in Cro-Magnon caves.

Primitive peoples often do not understand the connection between the sexual act and childbirth. Thus, women, with their childbearing ability, and with the correspondence between their twenty-eight day menstrual cycle and the cycle of the moon, inspired awe and dread.

Women were keepers of the cave and the hearth, and so from very early times they were associated with fire and with snakes (who emerge from holes, just as children emerge from their mothers' bodies). The snake, the coils of the umbilical cord, and the coiled passages of the cave were all linked by sympathetic magic. The tides were associated with menstrual flow; the disappearance of the moon was connected with death. The sites at which the Great Mother was worshipped were all dread places—burial sites.

In Palestine there were burials in caves dedicated to the Great Mother, and among the symbols that appear in these caves are the serpent and the coil, two of the most powerful occult signs. Cowrie shells also have been found at many burial sites—their physical resemblance to female genitals appears to have imbued them with magical power. Significantly, many early burials were in the crouching position—the position of a woman giving birth. The burials were accompanied by some kind of fire ritual, with an altar taking the place of the hearth. There is evidence that infant sacrifice was practiced.

Cults of Bulls, Sheep, and Goats. When people began to domesticate animals, they were at last able to observe male participation in childbearing. Their new knowledge was reflected in their rituals. The worship of animals, especially the sheep, goat, and bull, began. These cults were associated with the worship of the Great Mother.

At sites in Egypt, Syria, Anatolia, and Mesopotamia, the shepherd's crook appears as a symbol of human authority. The coil, the snake, and the horn are symbols of the spirit world. The double coil, an ancient spiral pattern, stood for the eyes of the Great Mother. The star and the cross, used by herding nomads for guidance, became symbols of the religious quest.

By 2500 B.C. the Minoan culture was flourishing in Crete, one of the most elaborate of the early urban civilizations. Although we do not know the exact nature of Minoan religion, it seems obvious that the people there were primarily followers of a bull cult, perhaps brought to the island by earlier seafaring people. (There were bull cults in Turkey, also.) Wall frescoes in temples on Crete show a curious ritual called bullleaping, in which skilled acrobats seized bulls by the horns and then did flips, landing on the bull's back.

The Minoans were seafarers and traders. Their ships took Minoan culture to all parts of the Mediterranean world. There is evidence of Minoan influence at many sites in Greece, Egypt, and Turkey, including Troy.

The Megaliths. The megaliths (large stones) that were constructed by early peoples have been found in Britain, France, Spain, Portugal, Sweden, the Balkans, Northern Africa, Syria, Persia, Korea, Japan, the Pacific Islands, and Alaska. Stonehenge is the best known example.

Some megaliths may have been burial sites, perhaps of priests, chiefs, and other important persons. Others, such as Stonehenge, seem to have been sites for worship of the sun, stars, and trees.

The enormous complex of temples and megaliths on the island of Malta has afforded many insights into the nature of Great Mother worship. Malta was apparently a very holy place from early times. Perhaps it was one of the original "islands of the dead"—a common theme in world mythology. There are over thirty temples and innumerable caverns on Malta and on the nearby smaller island of Gozo.

The temples are built near complex labyrinths that lead to burial chambers deep within the earth. Coils, spirals, and other symbols abound. At one site, Hal Tarxien, the feet and legs of a large Mother Goddess statue were found guarding the entrance to an inner chamber. Many small figures huddle under the robe of the goddess. A wall frieze shows a ram being sacrificed.

The Oracles. The early Greeks placed a great deal of importance on the various oracles that were scattered throughout the country, usually in caves or groves.

The priests and prophets of the various oracles were the only important religious figures of the early Greeks, and the oracles were the sites of the first Greek temples. The most well-known oracles were at Delphi, Eleusis, Dodona, and Epidaurus, but there were many others as well. Each spoke in a different way. At Delphi, the oracle spoke through a priestess called the Pythia, named after the sacred snake, the python.

The Pythia would sit above cracks in the ground, from which vapours arose from underground hot springs. She was usually intoxicated. She spoke in a state of psychic frenzy, as if in a trance. The oracle might well have been a remnant of an earlier religion of the Great Mother, who was also associated with snakes and caves.

Ancient Mesopotamia

Over four thousand years before Christ, a settled society had already developed near the deltas of the Tigris and Euphrates Rivers, in what is now Iraq. From the first, Mesopotamia's importance was due to trade.

We can't say with certainty just where the religious and magical practices of the Mesopotamians originated. Archeologists have found the names of over one thousand deities. Temples to the gods were among the first buildings in the region.

Divination and Magic. Everyone in Mesopotamian society seems to have believed in the active participation of the spirits in everyday life. The priests held many beliefs that became central to occultism. One of these was the idea that learning the real name of an entity meant gaining control over that entity. The use of drugs to contact the spirits was well established, as was the use of wax dolls to harm one's enemies. The priests drew magic circles to call up spirits. They also used incense, holy water, and amulets.

The priests and priestesses were especially skilled in the arts of divination, or foretelling the future. Incubation—sleeping in the deity's chamber—was one widely used method. Another was the reading of the entrails of sacrificed animals. (A clay model of a sheep's liver, dated from 2000 B.C., has been found near Ur. The model is marked off in squares and inscribed with directions for reading the different sections of the liver.) The priests also interpreted dreams.

The divination method most important to later occultism was the practice of reading the stars. There are continuous records of astronomical observations in Mesopotamia dating from 2230 B.C. The practice of telling the future from the stars must have been far older. The early Mesopotamians had a calendar. They identified and named the twelve signs of the zodiac. From their astronomical observations, they also discovered some principles of mathematics, such as division of the circle into 360 degrees.

Witchcraft. The Mesopotamians distinguished between white and black magic at a very early date. Hammurabi's law (1800 B.C.) states that black magicians—or witches—would be punished by death. In fact, the main function of the temple magicians seems to have been to counteract the spells and charms of the witches. The temples did a booming business in amulets to protect the ordinary mortal from demonic intervention.

Temple Rituals. Rituals in the temples of Mesopotamia were based on the idea that the temple was thought to be the home of the god or goddess to whom it was dedicated. The deity was represented by a statue, usually of wood covered with gold. The Mesopotamians believed that whatever was done to the statue also happened to the deity itself. Therefore, each day the deity was washed, sometimes dressed, bathed, and fed. At night it was put to bed in a special bedchamber.

The temple was staffed with cooks, bathers, waiters, weavers, and musicians, all trained to attend to the needs of the deity, the priests, and the temple officials.

At certain times of the year sacred festivals were held. These usually coincided with events in the agricultural year. Each city or city-state celebrated annual rituals for hitching and unhitching plows, sowing, and harvesting. The main festival was in the spring and was celebrated by fertility rituals.

The high point of the fertility ritual was the sacred marriage between the king and the high priestess of the temple. Their copulation was carried out with great solemnity, according to strict form. It may have been accompanied by orgies involving all the celebrants. It is likely that the "convents" of the early Mesopotamians were actually sacred brothels, and that the main function of all the priestesses was to ensure fertility of the land through copulation.

Sacred prostitution was practiced by ordinary women as well. In Babylonian times (ca. 1830–1530 B.C.), it was the custom of every woman to prostitute herself in the temple of Ishtar for one night each year.

As Sir James Frazer details in his monumental work *The Golden Bough*, Ishtar was another form of the Great Mother goddess, whose worship survived from Paleolithic times. Ishtar and her son Tammuz, who later came to be called Marduk, were the central figures in the spring fertility drama.

Ancient Egypt

Settled society in ancient Egypt arose at about the same time as in ancient Mesopotamia, and the two cultures were similar in many ways. There were, however, some important differences. The Pharaoh was the center of the Egyptian universe, not merely a representative of the gods but a god himself. Like the Mesopotamian rulers, the Egyptian Pharaoh delegated his authority to a class of priests, who administered vast temple lands. But Egypt's greater military and political stability meant that the priests were more under the direct control of the ruler than they were in Mesopotamia. All land in Egypt belonged to the Pharaoh, and every Egyptian worked directly for the temple and the ruling house.

Divination and Magic. The Egyptian conception of the gods approximated the most primitive belief in a spirit-force that pervades all things. In daily life, the symbols for the gods were invested not only with spiritual meaning but with direct magical powers. They were instruments of sympathetic magic, able to promote health and provide protection.

Egyptian religion was firmly based on magic. Magicians were among the priests employed by the temples. The Egyptians believed in the power of dreams, and some priests were skilled interpreters. They also practiced divination by reading the entrails of animals and by reading the stars.

Like the ancient Mesopotamians and early peoples everywhere, the Egyptians believed in the "power of the name"—the idea that one could gain power over an entity by learning its correct name. The "right word" or "word of power" was the link between the human and the divine.

"Black" magic was practiced in Egypt and counteracted by the temple magicians. Ordinary people seemed to have relied heavily on amulets to ward off evil spirits and counteract magic spells.

The Pyramids. The Egyptian pyramids were the most visible symbols of the power of the Pharaohs, and pyramids have been invested with spiritual force ever since. The first pyramidlike structure was the "step" pyramid near Abydos (ca. 2800 B.C.), the traditional birthplace of the Egyptian dynasties. The step pyramid resembled the Great Ziggurat at Ur in style. However, it was not a temple but a tomb.

The Pharaoh for whom the step pyramid was prepared was Djoser, a ruler of the Third Dynasty. The architect, Imhotep, was the Pharaoh's principal official. He was also a seer, an occultist, and a healer.

The first "true" pyramid, with smooth sides, was built in 2613 B.C. by Snefru, a Pharoah of the Fourth Dynasty. The Great Pyramid at Giza was built by his descendant Khufu, and the smaller pyramid at Giza was built by Khafre, his son, who also built the Sphinx to guard the royal necropolis.

Pyramids were, first of all, burial chambers for the Pharoahs. Their labyrinthine passages resembled those of the caves, which, in ancient Egypt as elsewhere, were the first burial places. The shape was probably meant to suggest a mountain. But the design was clearly intended to center divine power in some way. Each exit was carefully planned for the observation of certain heavenly bodies. Paintings on the walls of the inner chambers had mystic significance.

Not all the Egyptian rulers were buried in pyramids. Many of them, like Tutankhamun, were interred in caves located in sacred mountain valleys.

It was once thought that the pyramids were built by slave labor, maybe by the Hebrew tribes during their period of captivity in Egypt. Now, however, archeologists believe that the popular picture of the cruel Egyptian overseer whipping thousands of slaves as they struggled to drag the stones on crude sleds is misleading They think that the pyramids were built by the peasant population, during the period when the waters flooded the land. The great stones could be moved more easily over water than over land. The labor was probably performed as a religious duty, since all Egyptians believed that the Pharoah was divine and that the welfare of the land was dependent on the welfare of the ruler.

The Cult of the Dead. Egyptians believed in life after death and in the existence of the soul. Each Egyptian had three "souls," or inner spirit forces. The *ka* was a vital force that was created at the person's birth and survived after the death of the body. The *ba* was a bird-shaped spirit that inhabited each person and was set free at death. Perhaps the *ba* represented spiritual longing. The *akh*-soul was what we would think of as the person's aura or ghost. All these concepts are embodied in our modern conception of the human soul.

Mummification was an essential element of the belief in life after death. At first all Egyptians appear to have been mummified. Later the custom was reserved for the Pharaohs, their viziers, and other important personages. In the early dynasties, the survival of the individual after death was less important than the survival of the society, as embodied in the Pharaoh. Later Egyptians were more personally concerned with the question of salvation.

Isis and Osiris. Belief in life after death found expression in the myth of Isis and Osiris. These beliefs did not reach their full expression in ritual until the time of the Eighteenth Dynasty, around 1500 B.C. But the beliefs themselves were far older, containing elements of the earliest fertility myths.

Both Isis and Osiris were children of the sky goddess Nut and her lover, the earth god Seb. There were five children born of this illicit union: Osiris, Isis, Horus, Set, and Nephthys. Isis and Osiris were married to each other, as were Set and Nephthys. Horus, the falcon-headed god, was embodied

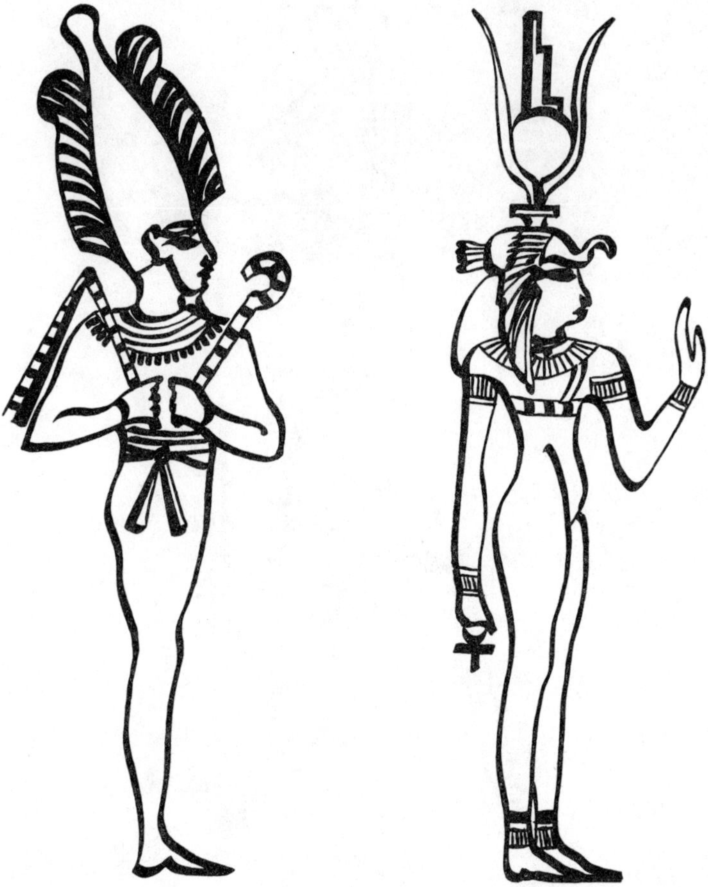

in the ruling Pharaoh.

Osiris and his wife Isis were given the land of Egypt to rule. Osiris gave laws to the people and taught them to worship the gods. Isis, having discovered wild grain and barley growing, talked Osiris into introducing agriculture. This was so successful that the land flourished, enabling Osiris to set off on a long journey to take the gospel of agriculture, religion, and law to other lands. Isis was left behind to govern Egypt.

While Osiris was gone, his brother (and brother-in-law) Set stirred up resentment against the rule of Isis and conspired to take over the kingdom. When Osiris returned, Set tricked him into climbing into a coffin. Set nailed down the lid and threw Osiris into the river. This betrayal took place in Osiris's twenty-eighth year.

Heartbroken, Isis went to look for Osiris in the marshes. While there, Isis bore a child named Horus. She had conceived Horus by taking the form of a falcon and hovering over the corpse of Osiris.

But Isis did not find Osiris in the marshes. The coffin with his body had floated out to sea and come to rest at Byblus, in Syria. There it had lodged in a bank, and a tree had grown up around it, enclosing the coffin in its trunk. Isis rescued the coffin, leaving the tree behind to be worshipped.

Isis brought the corpse of Osiris back to Egypt. This time the enemies of Osiris cut him into fourteen pieces. The sorrowing Isis buried each part of the body in a different place. At each burial site, she told the priest that the whole body was being buried and enjoined him to keep the burial a secret. Each priest was to worship Osiris in the form of some local animal. In return for this service, the priest in each place was given one-third of the land.

Isis and her sister Nephthys then went out into the marshes to mourn for their brother. Ra heard their cries and took mercy on their tears. He sent Anubis, the jackal-headed god of the dead, Thoth, the god of wisdom, and Horus (the older) down to comfort the weeping women. They all helped gather the scattered parts of Osiris and put him back together again. Then

Isis fanned the body with her wings and it came to life.

Osiris then became the Lord of the Underworld, the judge of the dead, and the Lord of Eternity. He was believed to rule the souls of all who died, and with forty-two judges (perhaps the three souls of each of the fourteen priests who worshipped him), Osiris weighed the soul of each dead Egyptian.

The Isis/Osiris myth bears remarkable resemblance to the Ishtar/Tammuz myth of the Mesopotamians, and was celebrated with very similar rites. Osiris was said to be killed with each harvest. During the dry months, the people mourned for the dead god, who had disappeared altogether from the land.

The sowing of the seed each November was a reenactment of the burial of Osiris. These rites of mourning climaxed with the carrying out of an image of Osiris. At the end of the feast, the people carried out a casket and filled it with the waters of the river, to symbolize the hope of Osiris's resurrection.

The rising of the river waters was said to be caused by the tears of Isis for her husband and brother. The growing crops were Osiris being raised from the dead.

The Hebrews

The early Hebrews were the first people to worship a universal supreme God and insist that He could be experienced by ordinary people. Their belief constituted a major religious and philosophical revolution in the ancient world.

Our account of the Hebrews' origins comes from the first five books of the Old Testament, which make up the Jewish Torah. The Torah tells the history of the Hebrews from the creation of the world to the time of their entrance into and settlement of Palestine. In other words, the Torah—the biblical books of Genesis, Exodus, Leviticus, Numbers, and Deuteronomy—tells the history of the Hebrews during the period in which they were a prosperous nomadic people, travellers and traders.

For some time the Hebrews regarded Mesopotamia as their homeland. Abraham sent a servant back to Mesopotamia, for example, to find a wife for his son Isaac (Genesis 24). But most of their nomadic wanderings took place in Palestine. The burial cave at Hebron was their most sacred place.

The Hebrews in Egypt. During the time of Abraham's grandson Israel, the Hebrews migrated to the land of Goshen, a district of ancient Egypt, just east of the Nile delta. There the Hebrews, or Israelites, remained for four hundred years. At first they were welcome guests of the Egyptian Pharoah, largely because of Joseph, one of Israel's sons, who was a high official under the Pharoah. Both Israel and Joseph were mummified according to Egyptian custom (Genesis 50).

Some time after the death of Joseph, the Egyptian Pharoahs, afraid of the growing power and numbers of the Israelites, enslaved them and put them to work building cities. "And they built for the Pharoah treasure cities, Pithom and Rameses."

One Israelite, Moses, was adopted by an Egyptian princess and given the education of an Egyptian prince (ca. 1300 B.C.). It was Moses who became the founder of the Jewish religion. The story of how Moses led his people out of slavery and into the promised land of Canaan is one of the most familiar Bible stories.

It was to Moses that God appeared on Mount Sinai and to whom God made the revelation on which the whole of Jewish law was founded:

> I am the Lord thy God, which have brought you out of the land of Egypt, out of the house of bondage. Thou shalt have no other gods before me.

The religion founded by Moses had many things in common with the religion of Egypt. The structure of the Tabernacle, the portable temple of the Israelites, was similar to the temples of the Egyptians, as were the rituals of washing and blood sacrifice and the robes of the priests. But in the Hebrew religion there was one startling difference. In the Holy of Holies, the inner sanctum of the Tabernacle, there was no idol.

Thou shalt not make unto thee any graven image, or any likeness of anything that is in heaven above or that is in the earth beneath, or that is in the water under the earth; Thou shalt not bow down thyself to them, nor serve them.

There is plenty of evidence in the Bible that the Israelites did not always follow this command. In fact, even while Moses was on Mount Sinai receiving the Ten Commandments, the Israelites, led by Moses's brother, the high priest Aaron, were building an idol to the Egyptian bull god, the Golden Calf (Genesis 32).

The Palestinian Kingdom. When the Israelites arrived in the Promised Land, they were constantly tempted to give up the worship of the One God and worship idols. In the books of Joshua and Judges, which tell the story of their conquests, we read time and again that "they forsook the Lord and worshipped Baal and Ashtaroth." Ashtaroth was yet another name for Astarte, or Ishtar, the Great Mother goddess.

The kingdom reached the height of its power under David and Solomon (ca. 1000 B.C.), as the books of Samuel, Kings, and Chronicles reveal. These books are full of the names of Egyptian, Syrian, Hittite, and Mesopotamian kings with whom the Israelites had dealings. The central position of their lands made them a constant prey to attack by the great powers to the south and west.

The Babylonian Captivity. In 721 B.C.., Sargon I, an Assyrian king, captured the northern section of the kingdom and carried the Israelite nobility into captivity. In 597 B.C. Jerusalem was taken and three thousand more nobles were carried off to Babylon. The Israelite kingdom had ended.

The exile of the Jews to Babylon was an important event in occult history. Some of the exiled Jews continued their careers as traders; many rose to prominence in Babylonian life. Jewish scholars learned much from the scribes of Mesopotamia, and the Jewish conception of God made an impact on Babylonian thought.

The Age of the Occult Prophets (ca. 650 B.C.– ca. 300 B.C.)

In the sixth century before Christ, there arose in Mesopotamia one of the greatest empires the world has ever known. It was founded by a Persian named Cyrus the Great (600–529 B.C.) and expanded under his successors

Cambyses, who reigned from 529 to 522, Darius (522–486), and Xerxes (486–465). Under Xerxes, the kingdom stretched "from India unto Ethiopia, over a hundred and twenty and seven provinces" (Esther 1:1). The Persian empire remained the most powerful in the ancient world until it was conquered by Alexander the Great in 331 B.C.

The power of the empire was based on its armies and on its bureaucracy of loyal civil servants, many of them Jews. To strengthen it further, Cyrus and his immediate successors built an efficient road sytem to all parts of their lands. The roads could bring the avenging Persian armies down on any rebelling provinces. They also carried the king's messengers and increased Persian trade.

To the east, the empire encompassed parts of India. Persian armies brought many changes to Indian life, including the widespread use of writing. At that period of history, India was in the midst of a religious and philosophical revolution. Two great religious teachers arose, Jina (599–527 B.C.), the founder of Jainism, and the Buddha, who lived from 563–483 B.C.

During the time of the Persian Empire, the civilization of ancient Greece reached its Golden Age. The Greek city-states had strong armies and even stronger navies. They alone of the peoples of the eastern Mediterranean were able to withstand the Persians; the rest was under Persian control. There was much peaceful contact between Persian and Greek traders, seafarers, and scholars.

Egypt was in a period of decadence and decline. As early as 671 B.C., the armies of the Assyrian Eserhaddon had captured the Egyptian capital, Memphis; although the Pharoahs and the priests still ruled in name, Egypt was actually a Persian province.

It was an age of increased communication and political unification. Ideas that had previously trickled through in the caravans of traders now flowed freely throughout the civilized world. The Greeks came into contact with the magical practices of the Mesopotamians and Egyptians; the Egyptians began to be influenced by the philosophy and spiritualism of the Greeks and Jews. The ancient sacred books of India, the Vedas and the Upanishads, came to the attention of people in the West. It was this exciting era that produced three great prophets of the occult: Zarathustra, Pythagoras, and Hermes Trismegistus.

Zarathustra and the Magi. Zarathustra was born in Medea (northern Iran) in about 628 B.C. He came from a modestly wealthy family and was trained as a priest. He was brought up in a tradition of polytheism. In his region, there were still many tribes of nomads, who practiced magic and shamanism.

Early in his priestly career, Zarathustra had a vision that set him at odds with his fellow priests and led to the founding of a new religion.

Zarathustra perceived that all creation was the work of one supreme creative principle, which he called Ahura Mazda, or "Wise Lord."

Nevertheless, Zarathustra was not a monotheist. In his cosmic system there were "two primeval spirits, revealed in a dream as twins." The two spirits were good and evil. Each person had a choice, to follow either the Truth or the Lie. At the end of life, people who chose evil would be punished by everlasting hellfire and damnation; those who chose good would live in eternal bliss.

This concept revolutionized religious belief. Although the Egyptians, Mesopotamians, and Greeks had all believed in life after death, and even in judgment after death, they had never seen any other end for human souls except in the underworld, which was viewed as a dark, rather frightening place but not as a place of torment. It was Zarathustra who introduced what we might call the "paranoia of personal salvation." Right action in life—and correct belief—acquired immense importance in the face of eternal punishment or reward.

Without Zarathustra, the Christian and Islamic systems of belief would not have been possible. Occultism would have become simply another form of religion. After Zarathustra, an initiate who wished to know *all*—evil as well as good—risked the eternal flames. Zarathustra was responsible for the fact that many occult beliefs—in fact, any occult beliefs that ran contrary to the current prevailing notion of "truth"—came to be associated with worship of the devil, even among occultists themselves.

After Zarathustra's death, his priests, the magi, set about the task of consolidating the sometimes ambiguous statements of the master into a religious sytem. They made the principles of good and evil into gods called Ohrmazd and Ahriman. The old Mesopotamian demons became devils, the followers of evil. Zarathustra had described seven "Beneficent Immortals," whom he thought of as attributes of Ahura Mazda. These became the angels.

Before long, the devils and angels acquired some of the names and attributes of the old gods. Ahura Mazda, for example, was identified with Marduk, the old god of Babylon. Through Zarathustra, and other Persians, belief in devils, angels, heaven, and hell entered Judaism. Not all the Jews accepted these doctrines. Disputes about them still divided the Pharisees and Saducees five hundred years later, at the time of Christ.

The organization of the Magi contributed much to later occult groups. There were three major grades through which an initiate had to pass: apprenticeship, mastership, and perfect mastership. The Magi's rites centered around fire worship, and as part of their rites they drank a hallucinogenic drug called *haoma*, claiming it allowed them to unite with the divine.

The Magi were the main religious authority during the reigns of Cyrus,

Cambyses, and Darius. Unquestionably, Darius was a Zarathustrian, since he was portrayed in his funerary statue with the symbol of Ahura Mazda over his head.

In the later Persian empire, the Magi were driven from power—probably because the ruler was afraid of their political influence. Most of them went to Cappadocia (modern Turkey), one of the most flourishing areas of the Greco-Roman world. From there their ideas spread to Greece and Egypt.

Hermes Trismegistus: The Wisdom of Egypt. Hermes Trismegistus was not a historical person. The name is Greek for "Thrice-Great Hermes"; Hermes was the Greek name for Thoth, the god of wisdom of the ancient Egyptians. Thoth was the inspirer of a large body of sacred writings that were written down by many different priests and scholars. But the priests believed that what they were writing constituted a continuous body of inspired knowledge. Possibly they chose to use the one name, Thoth, to avoid confusion and to focus attention upon a central truth.

Hermetic writings—those attributed to Hermes—were not written down until quite late in Egyptian history. The earliest of them were set down in about the third century B.C.; the latest in the third century century A.D.

The Hermetic writings seem to have been the product of an age when Egyptians had extensive contacts with the Mesopotamians and Greeks. For this reason, I have placed them chronologically with the Persian era. Many Hermetic teachings—such as magic spells, medical formulae, hymns to the gods, and astrological instructions—go back to an earlier age, and had been handed down orally. Other Hermetic books have many elements of the Greek neo-Platonists, indicating that they were written down at a late period.

Only a small part of these writings are still extant. Traditionally, there were forty-two books divided into six subject areas: priestly education, temple ritual, geography, astrology, hymns to the gods, and medical knowledge. In addition, the name Hermes Trismegistus was used on later theosophical writings that are largely Greek in content.

The Hermetic writings have been the subject of much debate and misunderstanding. For a long time they were viewed as an attempt to pervert the Christian faith, because of the similarity of many doctrines. But the occultists have always maintained that the Hermetic teachings were much older than Christianity, and modern scholarship has borne out this view. The influence undoubtedly worked in the other direction, for Hermetic writings throw much light on puzzling passages in the New Testament. There are even some scholars who posit that Moses drew his conception of the One God from the ancient worship of Thoth. Many occult groups claim the Hermetic writings among their sacred books.

The Worship of Thoth. Thoth was one of the Egyptian gods, but he was different from all the other gods. From earliest times, Thoth represented the unifying principle of the universe. The worship of Thoth was theosophical (from the Greek *theos*—god—and *sophia*, or wisdom). The rites, especially the secret ones, were directed toward knowing God. Thoth was called the Divine Word, the Scribe of the Gods, the Breath of the Gods, the Mind of God. His symbol was the ibis, a sacred bird.

There are many parallels between the worship of Thoth and the eastern religions. The Egyptians thought that Thoth taught adepts certain "words of power," which, when repeated continually, established links between the human mind and the mind of God. The concept of "words of power" is very similar to the eastern concept of *mantras*.

The Hermetic concept of salvation also resembled very closely the Buddhist concept of Enlightenment. One did not achieve personal salvation by surviving bodily after death, but in achieving an eternal state of illumination.

The Egyptian adept of Thoth passed through three states. The *Mortal* was a novice, a student or disciple, who had learned about the sacred writings but had not experienced the sacred vision. An *Intelligence* was a student who had experienced direct contact with God. A *Being of Light* was a person who had reached a state of cosmic consciousness—what the Buddhists call *nirvana*.

Thoth was also considered the Measurer or Limiter of the Universe, the source of all direct knowledge. It is no wonder, then, that the Hermetic teachers placed great emphasis on the inner meanings of all visible phenomena. They divided Egypt itself into three regions, and believed these three regions were only images of a heavenly place, which was watered by a Celestial Nile. The three regions were the Place of Inititation, the Place of Illumination, and the Place of Union with the Unseen Father.

The temple, too, was a model of the Celestial Kingdom. The outer courtyard, inner temple, and Holy of Holies corresponded to the stages in a soul's union with God.

Though the worship of Thoth was strongly mystical for the initiated few, it was corrupted in the popular mind. The "words of power" became, in the minds of the uninitiated, magical spells. As with every other body of mystical teachings, including those of Christianity, Islam, and Buddhism, the Truth was often obscured by symbols.

Much of what we call "occult science" concentrates on symbols. The followers of the Hermetic tradition would concentrate on the "inner meanings" of numbers, metals, and figures until those symbols themselves became magical rather than mystical in nature. The sections in this book on numerology, the Kabbalah, astrology, the Tarot, and alchemy show some of the ways in which Hermetic doctrines have filtered down over the centuries.

In all these "occult sciences," there have been a small number of adepts who used the symbols as keys to higher wisdom. But there have been far larger numbers of people who have read the symbols quite literally and can understand them only on that level. This same pattern can be traced in the history of the third occult prophet of the age, the Greek philosopher Pythagoras.

Pythagoras and the Pythagoreans. The historical person Pythagoras has been lost to us, although he certainly existed. His teachings were not written down until some time after his death, and by that time a great many fabulous tales had sprung up about him. The main elements of his story are as follows. He was born on the island of Samos, which had long been a center of magic and learning. He was probably from an aristocratic family, since his teachings were antidemocratic in character. He was said to have studied under the Magi in Persia and then under the priests of Thoth in Egypt. In 525 B.C.—the same year that the Persians captured Egypt—Pythagoras settled in Croton, a Southern Italian town on the Mediterranean. There he founded a school of philosophy.

Pythagoras had one of the most brilliant minds of ancient times. He was the first to discover many principles of mathematics, physics, and music, on which modern science is based. He was the first to assign ratios to the musical tones. We all encountered the Pythagorean theorem in geometry class. But Pythagoras believed himself to be an enlightened teacher, not a scientist in our sense. His main determination was to achieve union with the divine through the study of cosmic order.

Pythagoras believed that, at its deepest level, reality was mathematical in nature. He also believed that there were vibrations connecting all things to each other and to the divine. These ideas seem less and less esoteric since the discovery of the atomic structure of the universe and the modern theory of physics that light consists of particles. But Pythagoras was a mere child compared to today's high-school student in his mastery of physical science and math. He understood the universe primarily in mystical and philosophical terms.

Pythagoras organized his disciples into a brotherhood and imposed strict rules on them. There was a long period of initiation, during which the student was forced to be isolated from others, to fast and be celibate, and to maintain strict silence. Like the Egyptian priests of Thoth, the Pythagoreans were not allowed to reveal the inner secrets of their sect.

Pythagoras is chiefly remembered for his detailed doctrine of numbers, which is the basis for numerology (see the article in chapter three). But his teachings had many other aspects as well, for example, his theory of opposites. (The Egyptian priests of Thoth held similar beliefs.) Pythagoras thought that the universe was held together by tensions, created by universal opposites. He derived his list of opposites from studies of mathematics and physics, as well as from theosophy. The ten oppositions he recognized were: limited/unlimited; odd/even; one/many; right/left; male/female; rest/motion; straight/curved; light/dark; good/evil; and square/oblong. It is certainly possible that he derived this study of opposites from his masters, the followers of Zarathustra

Pythagoras held many beliefs that probably originated in the East, such as a doctrine of the transmigration of souls. He could remember all of his previous incarnations. In the popular mind, he was a magician and sorcerer, and people claimed he had magical powers of healing.

The Pythagorean Brotherhood was also political in character. When Pythagoras lived in Croton, the Roman Republic was beginning, and the ideals of democracy were being expounded throughout Italy. Pythagoras abhorred democracy, since he thought the rule of the many destroyed the cosmic order of the One.

The Brotherhood's political activities infuriated the local populace. Democratic mobs drove the Brotherhood from Croton in about 500 B.C. Pythagoras died in exile at Metapontum.

His Brotherhood split-up soon after his death. One group, the *mathematikoi*, were rationalists who concentrated on the scientific discoveries of the master. The other group were the *akousmatikoi*. They concentrated on Pythagoras's esoteric teachings. The akousmatikoi, in time, became a sect of wandering beggars—they are among the many unlikely candidates for the first Gypsies.

The Age of the Mysteries (ca. 300 B.C.—ca. 300 A.D.)

During the period between, roughly, 300 B.C. and 300 A.D., the predominant religions were occult faiths. These were the mystery cults, which stressed personal knowledge of, and control over, spiritual forces.

The age began with the astounding career of Alexander the Great. Alexander conquered most of the Middle East and marched his armies as far as India. He destroyed the last Egyptian dynasty and established a new Egyptian capital at Alexandria. The empire that Alexander conquered did not last long after his death. But his conquests spread Greek culture throughout the Near and Middle East. Just as important, Alexander's soldiers brought back Indian, Persian, and Jewish ideas to their homelands.

Even as Alexander marched, a new empire was forming in the West. By 256 B.C., the city of Rome controlled the Italian peninsula and began to extend its conquests abroad. The Punic Wars against Carthage, the capital of a rich North African kingdom, extended Roman power even farther. By a series of wars, treaties, and other maneuvers, Rome got control of Greece by 160 B.C. The Roman armies expanded into Turkey and down into Palestine.

Rome began as a republic, but in the first century B.C. it became an empire with the rise to power of Julius Caesar. His successor, Octavius, took the title Augustus.

The famous *Pax Romana* (Roman Peace) of Augustus lasted for two hundred years. It was a time of trade and economic growth, a time when the standard of living improved for many people, when political systems were perfected, and when learning became more widely available. But this peace was achieved through the iron rule of the Roman armies. Especially on the outskirts of the empire, in Judea and Gaul, for example, Roman rule was harsh. Peace was maintained only through repressive military occupation.

There were great disparities in wealth throughout the Empire. The slave population was very large. In the cities, starving mobs sometimes roamed the streets.

For the average person, the Pax Romana was a time of social unrest and political uncertainty. As national boundaries broke down, the old religions of the various Roman provinces received the influences of new ones imported from other areas. The new forms of religious belief that resulted stressed mystical experience over correct ritual, personal satisfaction over perpetuation of the state, and promises of eternal rather than temporal reward.

Magic, Divination, and Astrology. Because the Romans were the originators of many of our laws and customs, we tend to think of them as "modern" in a way that the ancient Egyptians and Mesopotamians were not. But Roman accomplishments in military strategy and government far exceeded their accomplishments in science or philosophy. The Romans were among the most credulous, superstitious people of their time, and their contemporaries in Greece, Carthage, and Egypt frequently derided them for their slavish and superstitious attachment to magic, signs, omens, and witchcraft.

Because the Roman armies had conquered such a vast territory, the Romans picked up superstitions from all over the known world. They were quite ready to believe in any gods or spirits. They were convinced that natural phenomena were portents of future victories or disasters. They set great store by such events as unexpected thunderstorms, eclipses, and unusual cloud formations.

Astrology assumed its modern form early in Roman times. As we have seen, people had practiced divination from the stars and heavenly bodies for thousands of years, and had even identified the twelve signs of the zodiac. But it was Greek and Egyptian scholars who, in the third century

B.C., systematized astrology and made it a matter of mathematical calculation. Where previously divination by the heavenly bodies had been primarily for public ritual use, in Roman times, the practice of casting personal horoscopes became widespread. Rich people had astrologers among their household staffs. More than one Roman emperor refused to make decisions without first consulting the stars.

The Romans seem to have been terrified of their own dreams and to have believed, again like many primitive peoples today, that in sleep a person's spirit left its body and wandered the Earth. Interpreters of dreams found easy employment, as did the makers of amulets to ward off evil spirits, potions to arouse sexual interest, and charms to bring rain or promote fertility.

The Mystery Cults. During the Roman Empire, a variety of sects arose that had in common the celebration of a mystery, revealed only to initiates in secret ceremonies. These cults were primarily Greek in origin, but they soon incorporated elements from Egypt and Persia. The cults rose in protest against the official Roman religion but were eventually brought under Imperial protection.

The cults principally celebrated fertility gods, such as the Roman Ceres, Liber, and Liberia. As Roman conquests spread, it became obvious that other people, too, had similar fertility gods. In Greece, the people worshipped the corn goddess Demeter; in Cappadocia they worshipped Cybele, the Great Mother, and her son Attis; in Syria they worshipped Astarte (Aphrodite) and her son Adonis; in Egypt they worshipped Isis and her son Osiris; in Persia they worshipped Ishtar and her son Marduk. Other fertility religions included the worship of the Cabiri, gods from Samothracia who helped seafarers, and the rites of Dionysius (the Greek Bacchus), the god of the grapes.

These religions did not grow up independently, but borrowed from each other as they developed. In Egypt, for example, the rites of Isis and Osiris developed a distinctly Greek caste, with more and more emphasis on the mysteries, which stressed mystical knowledge, and lessening emphasis on assuring the harvests.

The Roman soldiers were among the chief carriers of the new faiths. They brought the cult of Mithra, the sun god of the later Zarathustran priests, from the Middle East. The Mithraic rites were grafted onto those of Sol, the Syrian sun god.

Like all occult beliefs, the mystery religions were associated with the forbidden. Their appeal was primarily to the lower and middle classes, people who were denied Roman citizenship and thus the full benefits of Roman power. Some cults, like that of Dionysius, became politically powerful because their leading priests were wealthy burgesses, in just the way

that Freemasonry did at a much later date. Slaves were admitted to all the religions, which may have accounted for much of their popularity because all slaves were considered free during the major religious festivals.

The public rites of the cults varied from place to place. Many of the celebrations were drunken orgies of sex and violence, excuses for revelry and not much more. They were a publicly accepted way for repressed people to let off steam. In Rome, for example, the priests of the Great Mother, the Galli, were self-castrated eunuchs. They wore vulgar female dress, doused themselves with paint and perfume, and danced insanely in the streets. The Galli were given to working themselves up into hysterical frenzies and cutting themselves with knives, especially around their sexual organs. The word *bacchanalian* survives in our language as a reminder of those times.

Unfortunately, a certain number of occult sects have chosen to perpetuate this decadent and bloody tradition and they have given all occultists a bad name. But "mainstream" occultism claims a quite different heritage, in the private rather than public rites of the mystery sects.

In all the fertility cults, there were secret rites, or mysteries, which could be experienced only by initiates who had undergone certain tests. In all cases, the initiates were sworn to secrecy about the actual content of the rites, so the information we have about them is far from complete. Enough ancient texts have survived, however, to give us a fair idea of what went on.

Most of the secret rites focused on the idea of personal resurrection after death. The rites often were in the form of a sacred drama—a private version of the older Greek and Persian fertility dramas. Mime, song, and dance also played important roles.

Although each ritual was slightly different, most of the mysteries contained the following elements: (1) a confession of the initiate's sins to the group; (2) the swearing of secrecy on pain of death and eternal damnation; (3) the ritual drama; (4) baptism, either by water or fire; (5) the touching or handling of sacred objects; (6) the eating of a ritual meal, usually food that had been sacrificed to the gods; and sometimes (7) ritual copulation.

Like the rituals of the Magi and the Egyptian Hermetic priests, the mystery cults recognized different grades of aspirants. The highest plane of knowledge—that of complete union with god—was available only to a few, and then after long apprenticeship.

There is plenty of evidence that the mysteries were accompanied by a lot of fakery. In one manuscript, a manual for Dionysian priests, scholars have found instructions for making an eerie glow appear around the priest's head by means of a kind of alcohol burner concealed in a turban. By rubbing powder between his fingers, a priest could make a strange smoke rise. In a temple at Pergamum (modern Bergama, Turkey), archeologists found a network of secret passages leading through the temple walls, with holes strategically placed for the proper echoing effects. One passage led up into the hollow statue of the god, allowing the god to "speak."

Nevertheless, the evidence of fakery does not detract from the hold the mysteries had on their participants. Like many later occultists, the priests of the mysteries undoubtedly would have claimed—if they were caught—that the fakery was necessary to strengthen the faith of the worshippers.

The Druids. As the Roman armies pushed into Europe, they came into contact with the tribes that inhabited the northern forests. Among these peoples were the Celts. It is mostly to the writings of Julius Caesar that we owe our knowledge of the Celtic priests called Druids.

The Druids had existed in Ireland, Britain, and Gaul for a long time before the Romans arrived. The exact function of the Druids in Celtic society is not clear. The Romans thought they were magicians and medicine men; they were also said to be philosophers and judges. They shared their power with a caste of warriors; they did not bear arms. It is not even certain that the Druids were priests, in the sense of presiding over religious rituals. They were, however, present at sacrifices (some of them human) and major religious rites.

The Druids were members of the Celtic nobility and were chiefly responsible for the education of noble youth. They were the keepers of the secret wisdom of the Celtic tribes. Much of this wisdom was mathematical and philosophical in nature, having to do with such matters as the movements of the moon and stars. The Druids also kept a history of Gaul. The Druids used writing to record trade and political transactions. But their philosophical teachings were transmitted orally.

The philosophers of Alexandria and other Roman centers of learning were astonished to find that the Druids taught many of the same principles as the Greek philosophers. Both taught the theory of reincarnation through various spheres of existence. Both relied on number systems such as those formulated by Pythagoras.

In fact, the Druids may have been Pythagoreans or have had some early contacts with members of that Brotherhood. Marseilles in France was a Greek colony as early as 600 B.C., and trading between the coast and the interior was well established. One tradition has it that Zalmoxis of Thrace, Pythagoras's slave, was given his freedom and returned with his master's doctrines to his homeland. The Celts inhabited Thrace before they began to move into western Europe around the third century B.C.

Whatever the origins of the Druids' teachings, they seem to have been primarily mystical and occult in nature. According to the Romans, the Druids worshipped in sacred groves or forest enclosures. They may have been driven into the forests by the Romans themselves. Some Roman writers believed that the Druids were tree-worshippers but there is no clear evidence for this. There is much more reason to believe that the Druids were, like the Persian Magi, prophets and readers of omens.

Some of the Druids were women, although there seem to have been more Druid priests than priestesses. Two Druids that the Romans actually met were Divitiacus, a chief of the Aedui tribe and the older brother of the ruling king who met Julius Caesar, and an unnamed Druidess who prophesied to the emperor Diocletian.

The Druids were the targets of some persecution by the Romans, possibly because they were involved in anti-Roman political activity. We do not know whether the Romans actually killed them as they did the religious leaders of the Jews. But a series of Roman laws, the first of them issued in 1 B.C., closed the Druidical schools and substituted schools of Roman learning. The Druids retreated into the forests. In Wales, Ireland, and in small pockets throughout Europe, the Druids kept the old traditions alive. In Gaul and Britain, they were suppressed by 50 A.D.

Jewish Sects. The Jews suffered a great deal under Roman rule—perhaps more than any other imperial subjects. Unlike most of the other subject peoples, they refused to worship the emperor and the pantheon of Roman gods. Furthermore, the Jews thought of themselves not only as a religious body but as a nation, owing no allegiance to alien empires. The Jews were in a continual state of religious and political uprising against the Romans. And the Jews were the favorite scapegoats for the wrath of many Roman rulers.

In response to Roman harshness and to their loss of political independence, the Jews formed many different sects during this period. Some sects, such as the Essenes, believed that the only thing to do was to retire to the wilderness, observe the Law as strictly as possible, and await the coming of the Messiah, the religious and political liberator who, according to the Prophets, would appear in the last days. These sects became strongly apocalyptic (dependent on revelations).

Other sects were more mystical in their teachings. The Jews in Alexandria, like the other scholars in that city, leaned heavily toward the interpretation of symbols, numbers, and words.

It was during the Roman era that Jewish scholars began to formulate the body of teachings called the Kabbalah, which later became important to occultism. The Kabbalistic writings were only one manifestation of the Jewish absorption in questions of spiritual truth. Another manifestation is the apocryphal Book of Enoch, which was written down about a century before Christ. The Book of Enoch tells the story of the fall of the angels from heaven and of their introduction of magic on earth. The document also relates the Jewish tradition of Sheol, the place of the wicked, and its demonic inhabitants. The Book of Enoch was undoubtedly known to the early Jewish Christians, much of whose early teaching about angels and demons was derived from the Jewish tradition.

Some of the Jewish sects were actively political and anti-Roman. The Zealots were among the most important of these. Like the Essenes, the Zealots were awaiting the coming of a Messiah, a religious and political liberator, but they engaged directly in political violence and insurrection. The Zealots were especially active in Galilee, where Jesus grew up.

The Jews who were in power during this period had accommodated themselves to the Roman rule. Among these were the Jewish priestly class, the Sadducees. The Sadducees were hated by many of their fellow Jews because of this collaboration with the Romans. The Pharisees belonged to a large sect that taught strict adherence to the Jewish law. The Pharisees had little political power, but they believed it best not to interfere with Roman rule.

The Gnostics. The word *Gnostic* comes from a Greek word meaning "to know." The Gnostics were occultists in that they sought to achieve knowledge—and power—through magical means. Gnostic sects varied a great deal in their beliefs. Like the mystery sects, Gnostic cults incorporated beliefs from Egypt, Babylon, India, and Greece, and many of them also celebrated mystery rites. But the main distinction between the two types of sects was that the mystery religions concentrated on personal resurrection and fertility-based rituals, while the Gnostics sought knowledge, particularly in philosophy, mathematics, astrology, symbolism, and magic. They were the spiritual heirs of the Pythagoreans and the Egyptian priests of Hermes.

The importance of secret, magical, or divine words to the Gnostics cannot be exaggerated. This element was mostly Egyptian. The Gnostics also repeated meaningless sounds to achieve a state of ecstasy or harmony with the universe. Like the Pythagoreans, they believed in the power of numbers.

It is frequently hard to distinguish between the Gnostic sects and the contemporary schools of philosophy, such as Neoplatonism. In fact, there was much overlap in beliefs and teaching. The Gnostic sects, however, were actually organized as religions, with specific rites, magical spells, or whatever. Alexandria, the Greek capital of Egypt, was the center of their learning.

Many of the Gnostic doctrinal writings have been destroyed, because the Gnostics were much persecuted, both by the Roman emperors and, later, by the Christian Church. (Christian Gnostic sects had arisen.)

Although space does not permit a listing of all the known Gnostic groups and leaders, I will describe a few of them, to give the reader an idea of the variety of beliefs encompassed by the general term *Gnostic*.

Simon Magus. Simon Magus was a Gnostic magician and the leader of one of the largest occult groups in Roman times. He claimed to be a god and ordinary people worshipped him. Simon was the disciple of another occultist, Dositheus, who had also claimed to be the Messiah. Simon was baptized by the Apostle Peter, but fell into sorcery when he tried to usurp divine power for his own ends. In Acts Chapter 8, there is the story of an encounter between the Apostle Paul and Simon. Whether or not this meeting actually took place, it is clear that the early Christians considered Simon a serious rival, over whom the supremacy of Christianity had to be established.

An early Christian writer, Anastasius of Niceae, claimed that Simon had remarkable occult powers. Among other things, he could walk in fire without being burned, change himself into a serpent, levitate, make statues come to life, and turn stones into bread. (This last feat is especially interesting in view of the story of the Temptation of Christ in Matthew 21.)

Simon went to Rome, where he rose to a high position. The emperor Claudius had a statse erected to him. Simon's cult continued long after his death, and was revived during the nineteenth century in France. There are still occult groups today that claim Simon Magus as their spiritual founder.

In "The Act of Peter and Paul," an early Christian apocryphal book, we are told an amusing account of the end of Simon's life. It seems Simon had been made the official sorcerer at the court of Nero, for whom he performed all sorts of amazing feats. Nero, hearing of the equally amazing accomplishments of the Christian Apostles, sent for Peter and Paul and arranged a magical contest for his own amusement. Simon, gloating, lifted himself into the air and flew out the window. Then Peter said a prayer, at which point Simon crashed to the ground, breaking his legs and finally dying of his injuries. (At another point in his life, Simon was said to have been beheaded by Nero, but he was able to restore his own head by magical means.)

Apollonius of Tyana. Apollonius of Tyana was the greatest contemporary rival of Simon Magus. He was educated at Tarsus, where he undoubtedly studied with his contemporary, the Apostle Paul. Like Paul, Apollonius travelled widely. In his youth he visited Babylon and perhaps India. Many of his teachings had much in common with the Indian Brahmins, although he himself claimed to be a disciple of Pythagoras. Apollonius appears to have been more like a modern eastern guru than was Simon Magus. He emphasized inner enlightenment and knowledge rather than magic, although many miracles are attributed to him. He was remarkably clairvoyant.

No one knows how or where Apollonius died. He is said to have lived to be one hundred years old. Some of his disciples claimed he did not die at all but was taken into heaven.

The Ophites. This sect is mentioned frequently by early Christian writers, though very little is known about their beliefs. They placed heavy emphasis on symbols, especially those for spirit, fire, and life, and they claimed to be of Egyptian origin. They had an especially elaborate system of initiation. The serpent was at the center of Ophite worship.

The Carpocratians. This sect was founded in Alexandria by a teacher named Carpocrites, and it was Christian in its slant. The followers believed that Jesus had studied at the temple of Isis in Egypt, learned the Hermetic mysteries, and then transmitted them to his disciples. The sect lasted for several centuries. Some of its elements—especially the secret handshake—have been transmitted to modern occult groups.

The Basilideans. The founder of this sect, Basilides of Alexandria, claimed to have been instructed by Glaucus, who was in turn taught by the Apostle Peter. Like other Gnostic sects, the Basilideans placed great importance on the mystical significance of numbers, the grades of the mysteries, and the ability to ascend to higher spheres. They seem to have claimed, as did many other sects, that the divinity was hermaphroditic—that is, both male and female. Hermaphroditism became an important tenet of many later occult groups.

The Rise of Christianity (ca. 50 A.D.–313 A.D.)

Christianity became the official religion of the Roman Empire toward the end of its power, during the reign of Constantine. Constantine converted in the year 313, and that date marks the end of the Age of the Mysteries.

During the preceding three hundred years, however, Christianity had been by no means the predominant faith. When Constantine converted, he gave official status to what had before been a minority religion. Pagans still heavily outnumbered the Christians; many of them still regarded Christianity as a Jewish sect.

Jesus of Nazareth. Jesus was said to have been born in Bethlehem, as had been prophesied in the Old Testament. But he grew up in Nazareth in

Galilee, a center of anti-Roman activity. Like his father, Joseph, Jesus was a carpenter. When he was a young man, Jesus went to the wilderness, where he fasted, prayed, and studied. His masters were probably his cousin John the Baptist and the Essene hermits.

Jesus was not the first candidate for Messianic office. Judas Maccabeus, who led a temporarily successful revolt against the Romans in 168–65 B.C., was considered a Messiah in his time. The Jews continued to look for the Messiah until the Romans finally suppressed them and sacked Jerusalem in 70 A.D.

The history of Christianity can be seen as an attempt by the followers of Jesus to deal with his failure as a political Messiah. The first claim the disciples made was that Jesus had risen again from the dead after three days. It should be noted that resurrection after three days was also claimed for Simon Magus, John the Baptist, and other political and religious figures of the time. There is no question that the early disciples firmly believed that they had seen the resurrected Christ. There is no other way to explain their subsequent zeal in proclaiming the Christian faith.

Jesus was probably crucified in the year 27 A.D. In the period between that date and the fall of Jerusalem in 70, Christianity was primarily a Jewish sect. These first Christians were daily expecting the triumphal return of Jesus as the Messiah in the Jewish sense. They believed he would return from the sky and overcome the Romans, establishing once again the Jewish kingdom. The whole New Testament is imbued with this sense of expectancy. (For more about Jesus, see chapter five.)

Paul of Tarsus. Paul has been called the true founder of the Christian faith. Certainly, if it were not for Paul, the new faith would not have survived the end of Jewish political hopes. For it was Paul who gave Christianity a solid philosophical base and connected it with the other religions of his time. The epistles (letters) of Paul to the various groups of Christians are the earliest writings in the New Testament; they precede the gospels by as much as fifty years. Some of them were written before the fall of Jerusalem.

The Book of Acts gives us a clear account of the life and work of Paul. Unlike Jesus, who was from a poor background, Paul was a highly educated Jew of the upper classes, a Pharisee who spoke not only Hebrew and Aramaic (the language of Jesus) but also Greek. Paul's high class is proved by the fact that he was a Roman citizen. The privilege of Roman citizenship was granted at that time only to the leading families of the provinces. Paul was, therefore, much less apt to urge the overthrow of the Romans than Jesus was.

After Paul's conversion, which took place when he had a vision of the risen Christ, he went into the Arabian desert for three years to study. Why would he need to study more, when he was already highly educated in both the Greek and the rabbinical traditions? Because the desert was the center for *forbidden* Jewish learning. The teachings of the Essenes and other apocalyptic sects were precisely those Paul would have avoided as a member of the upper class.

We have no way of knowing who Paul studied under in the desert. But it is interesting to note that the Arabian desert was at the time the abode of many Hermetic philosophers from Egypt, as well as of Jewish mystical sects. Paul's initiation in the desert certainly included mystic experiences. Consider, for example, this passage from his second letter to the Corinthians.

> I knew a man in Christ above fourteen years ago (whether in the body, I cannot tell: God knoweth;) such a one caught up to the third heaven. And I knew such a man (whether in the body, or out of the body, I cannot tell: God knoweth;) How that he was caught up into paradise, and heard unspeakable words, which it is not lawful for a man to utter.
>
> (12:2–4)

But Paul's message was not of secret mysteries—quite the opposite. What was startling about Paul's teachings about the new Christian faith was that its mysteries were declared to be open to all. Throughout his epistles, Paul plays upon his readers' experience with the mystery religions. He begins "Behold, I show you a mystery . . ." or speaks of "the mystery of our faith." But he always tells the readers what the mystery is.

Paul was zealous in establishing the new faith as morally and philosophically superior to those of his time. For example, he disputed with the pagan scholars of Athens (Acts 16). This zeal of Paul's explains what to modern readers seems an overly fastidious view of sex, especially fornication. After all, Paul lived in an age of severe political repression, when dissenters were tortured and crucified, when people as an amusement watched beasts tear people apart, when slaves outnumbered free people. To us it seems petty—if not a bit perverted—for Paul to fasten on fornication as the chief sin, especially when he seems to condone slavery. But fornication was part of the central mystery of most of the rival pagan faiths. It is significant that Paul always mentions fornication in conjunction with eating meat offered to idols—another part of pagan mystery ritual.

Paul's main contribution to Christianity, however, was in making it an international rather than a specifically Jewish faith.

The Early Church. Through Paul and other zealous missionaries, the Christian church spread rapidly throughout the Roman Empire. Contrary to popular belief, the Christians were not always persecuted—certainly not as much as the Jews. The first Christian persecution, under Nero, was very short and was due to the emperor's whim. At various other times, Nero's wrath fell on Jews, on the followers of John the Baptist, on various Gnostic sects, and even on the followers of Simon Magus.

The new faith appealed strongly to the lower classes, especially slaves. Even though Paul urged slaves not to leave their masters, the message of Christianity was essentially democratic.

By the end of the first century the church had followers among all the classes of Roman society. Paul wrote his epistles in Greek, expecting to be read by educated people. The churches at Corinth, Antioch, and especially Rome, were prosperous ones. Among the Christians mentioned in the New Testament are members of the Roman army, merchants, lawyers, doctors, and slave-owners (the book of Philemon is addressed to one).

The more the church grew, the more threatening it became, not only to the Roman authorities, but also to the established systems of philosophy. The first two centuries of the Christian era were rife with attacks and counterattacks, not only between Pagans and Christians but between various Christian groups.

During this period there arose an immense body of tales, myths, and legends about the saints. Many of these tales simply incorporated elements of pagan religions: Dionysius became St. Denis, the Virgin Mary replaced Isis, and so on. Early Christian worship had many of the trappings of mystery religions. The worshippers confessed their sins to each other, ate a solemn sacrificial meal together, and centered their ritual around the resurrection of the dead.

There has been a great deal of argument about which elements in Christianity were borrowed from paganism and which were not. These discussions are only possible from a modern perspective. To the Christian in the first or second century, the new religion could only be seen in the context of the contemporary world. In the Roman world, religion was about mysteries, devils, demons, angels, miracles, magic, mystic knowledge, numbers, signs, symbols, and sacrifice. So Christianity was about all those things, too.

It is, therefore, possible to say that many early Christians were occultists. They believed in the active presence of spirits, both good and bad, and in the need to control those agents in some way. Magic was quite real to Roman Christians, and it was necessary for them to explain magic in terms of their new faith.

When the educated classes began to accept Christianity, they also understood it in their own terms, and interpreted it as they chose. Many of the early Christian scholars belonged to Gnostic sects, for example, and saw no contradiction in this. It was only later, when the church councils began to legalize church doctrine, that the persecution of heretics arose.

There was furious argument on many theological points. Probably the most ferocious debate was over the nature of Christ. The Arians argued that Jesus was begotten of God but was distinct from God, and was not therefore actually God. The Athanasians argued that Jesus was identical to God. These controversies seem a little irrelevant to us today, but to the scholars of the period, schooled in the mystic traditions, the questions were crucial.

In the second century of Christianity, the religion grew threatening enough to the Romans that persecutions of the Christians were stepped up. The Christians, like the Jews, refused to worship the emperor and the Roman gods, although they prayed for the emperor as part of their ceremonies. It was easy for enemies of the faith to accuse them of treason. The persecutions reached their height under the emperor Diocletian, who published an edict against the Christians in 303. But by then they were on the eve of their triumph.

Neoplatonism. The term *Neoplatonism* refers to an extensive system of philosophy and mystical thought that emerged in the Roman world in the third century after Christ. The center of Neoplatonism was Alexandria, Egypt. Neoplatonism formed an important part of the thought of the medieval era, especially in regard to magic, mysticism, and other aspects of the occult.

The founder of Neoplatonism was Plotinus of Alexandria. Plotinus, a pagan scholar, claimed to derive his ideas from Plato. He undoubtedly was also influenced by oriental teachings current in Alexandria, as well as by the writings of the Pythagorean Numenius.

The Neoplatonists were ascetics and their goal was to achieve mystic union with God through contemplation and philosophy, to fuse the soul with the infinite and thus lose perception of the distinctions between thought and object. Thus his conception of truth was similar to the oriental idea of enlightenment (see articles on yoga and meditation in chapters one and three).

In a letter to one of his disciples, Plotinus gave this advice on how to achieve illumination:

> Purify your soul from all undue hope and fear about earthly things, mortify the body, deny self,—affections as well as appetites, and the inner eye will begin to exercise its clear and solemn vision.

Like all mystics, Plotinus taught that the Infinite is only to be found within oneself, in contemplation of one's own divine essence.

> The wise man recognizes the idea of the Good within him. This he develops by withdrawing into the Holy Place of his own soul. He who does not understand how the soul contains the Beautiful within itself, seeks to realize beauty without, by laborious production. His aim should rather be to concentrate and simplify, and so to expand his being.

Plotinus believed that reason was given to people to aid them in their quest for Truth; the moment of illumination was achieved not through reason but in a state of ecstasy.

However, one of Plotinus' disciples, Porphyry, maintained that one never lost consciousness of self, even at the moment of ecstasy. He described ecstasy as a kind of dream state. Porphyry also introduced the idea of demons or evil spirits into Neoplatonist thought.

Iamblichus, the disciple of Porphyry, took the conception of demons even further and postulated whole hierarchies of evil spirits and angels. Iamblichus also placed much reliance on divination, magic, and other occult practices. Proclus, the last great Neoplatonist, was widely known as a magician. He corresponded with the major scholars of his day, both Christian and pagan. Like Iamblichus, Proclus was intent upon codifying systems of spirits and symbols by means of which the truth could be reached.

The influence of the Neoplatonists upon Christian thought was very strong. Like the Neoplatonists, the church fathers and medieval scholastics attempted to combine religion and philosophy. All were firm in their belief that everything in the universe must have an essential unity, a Supreme One that could be experienced by humans. This Supreme One would encompass everything, both good and evil. Thus the good spirits and the bad spirits must be subordinate to the same organizing principles. It was the task of the human mind, through reason, to discover those organizing principles.

The Kabbalists and alchemists of the Middle Ages were also Neoplatonist in spirit. The alchemist saw the chemicals in his laboratories as small models of the universe and sought to discover within them the universal truth.

The Age of the Church (313–1300)

The Age of the Church began with the gradual conversion of Europe to Christianity and reached its zenith with the advanced Christian civilization of the Middle Ages. It coincided with the decline and fall of the western half of the Roman Empire, which was in ruins by the middle of the fifth century. The eastern half of the Empire, with its capital at Constantinople, lingered into the fifteenth century.

In the seventh century, a major threat to Christian power arose in Arabia. Islam, the new religion, combined elements of shamanism, Judaism, and Christianity with militant fervor. By 714, Arab armies had conquered Spain, Northern Africa, all of Palestine and Egypt, Arabia, Central Asia, and parts of India.

By the tenth century the Western world was divided between two great religious empires, the Moslem and the Catholic. The first massive military confrontations between them were the Crusades, great outpourings of

religious and military feeling. Their purpose was to free Palestine from Moslem rule and restore the holy places to Christian worship.

The Crusades helped reopen a world that had been closed for centuries. Trade increased. European cities began to grow in size and political importance. The middle class of merchants, doctors, lawyers, and traders swelled in size. Magnificent cathedrals were built in the major cities of Europe. However, an objective observer of the Middle Ages would have seen that the church and the landed aristocracy were gradually losing power, and that the feudal system, supposedly at the height of its glory, was actually in its decline.

For the ordinary person daily life was wretched. The majority of people were serfs, at the mercy of their lords, their miserable living conditions, and the church. They were completely tied to the soil, and they had no more legal rights than animals. On many estates the horses and dogs of the overlord lived in splendor compared to his serfs.

Diseases and plagues were rampant. Many of these diseases were the result of malnutrition. Insanity caused by extreme hunger was another widespread ailment. The Black Plague, which swept Europe during the fourteenth century, killed almost a third of the population.

The medieval church had long since ceased to follow the teachings of Christ and his mercy toward the poor. Peasants were told that the sufferings of the present body were merely a trial to prepare them for the world to come. The church brought the world to come much closer by torturing people for what we would call minor offenses today.

The church's punishing arm was the Inquisition, which was to reach its most ghastly heights after the Protestant Reformation. But all through the Middle Ages the Inquisition was at work, persecuting first heretics and then witches. It began formally in 1215, when Pope Innocent III decreed that Catholics who took up the sword against heretics would enjoy the same favor as Crusaders who went to fight in the Holy Land. The bloodshed began in earnest when Gregory IX became pope in 1227. In the name of Christ, people were whipped, hammered, filled with water and then stomped upon, stretched on the rack, toasted on grills over hot coals, or hanged by their thumbs. Special torture machines were invented. The justification for these monstrosities was that the Devil—the enemy—was himself monstrous.

During the Age of the Church, witchcraft and magic flourished in Europe, helped greatly by their archenemy, the Christian church. Oriental magic, Hermetic philosophy, and Neoplatonist writings remained in the possession of the Greek-speaking Byzantines, as well as in the hands of Jewish and Arab scholars.

The occult ideas that developed and spread during the Middle Ages presented an increasing threat to the power of the church. The Age of the Church ended with a huge religious bloodbath. Witches and heretics were exterminated with the zeal formerly reserved for Moslem infidels. It was the church's last desperate grab for power. By the middle of the sixteenth century, the high Catholic civilization had been replaced by secular kingdoms. Unquestionably, occultism was an important factor in this transition.

The Old European Religions. The religions of most of the tribes to which the Christians sent missionaries were semipantheistic. The people had developed little theology or doctrine. They had not yet personified many of their gods. Instead they thought of their gods as spirits or forces.

The Teutonic tribes had no priesthood, but some tribal members, especially women, were sorcerers or magicians. The sorcerers, often the only literate people in their tribes, possessed the ability to read *runes,* the letters carved on stone monuments, weapons, and other mystical objects. The Teutonic people were heavily dependent on black magic, and they frequently employed witchcraft.

The Celts had an organized priesthood, the Druids. The Druids had a complex system of learning and a secret brotherhood that passed on this teaching from generation to generation. The Romans had described the Druids as having mathematical and philosophical knowledge, which they taught in their schools (see above). But in Britain in the fourth and fifth centuries, the Druids seem to have been primarily practitioners of magic. Among the feats attributed to them were rain-making, curing diseases, driving out spirits, and casting spells. Thus the Druids were more an organized class of magicians than a hierarchical priestly order.

Supporting the popular dependence on magic and witchcraft was a large body of folk beliefs, legends, and myths. In all the countries of Europe, people believed in the existence of fairies, gremlins, goblins, and other invisible wee folk with whom it was necessary for humans to come to terms.

Among many of the European peoples, there was a long tradition that gave women a special place among practitioners of the magic arts. Most "sorcery" practiced by the women was really only harmless folk medicine. But the church regarded their activities as immoral—in fact, as proof of the existence of demonic influences. The women had no choice but to escape to the forests.

The dense forests that covered most of Europe during the Dark Ages provided the perfect ambience for the occult arts. The forests were inhabited by various human castoffs, misfits, and runaways. The "wild women" were among the most popular of these, and they were believed to have considerable powers.

The peasants went to the women in the forests for simple remedies, love-charms, birth preventatives, fertility charms, amulets against the evil eye, and other spiritual necessities. The wild women were, of course, the forerunners of the witches against whom the medieval church was to campaign so cruelly.

The Christian Mind. It could be said that during the Age of the Church everyone in Europe was an occultist, in any sense that we define that term today. People believed in demonic forces as literally as we now believe in the forces of gravity or of nuclear power. They lived in the kind of world that today belongs only to the insane—although it can be visited with the help of hallucinogenic drugs. The European Christian in the fourth through fifteenth centuries could see demons and angels supercharging the air, battling for the souls of mankind.

A great many people believed they were living at the end of the world. The practices of Christian ascetics became ever more bizarre. St. Simon Stylites, the most famous example, spent forty-five years in the desert living on top of a pillar, standing for most of the time. People made pilgrimages to see him and hear his sermons.

Egypt, the Sinai Peninsula, Palestine, and Cappadocia were pockmarked with the caves of the hermits, who practiced severe bodily chastisement, sexual abstinence, uncleanliness, and fasting because they expected the end of the world. Not surprisingly, the hermits experienced apocalyptic visions, sexual fantasies of monstrous proportions, and perpetual concourse with other planes of existence.

Other preachers travelled the roads. Like their brethren in the caves, the wandering hermits prided themselves on their degree of filth and on their holy stench. They spoke of learning to love the lice on their bodies. (Lice spread typhus, and so the circle of misery was complete.)

Angels and demons had not been central to the teachings of either Jesus Christ or Paul. By the close of the fourth century, however, these heavenly forces had captured the imaginations of the Christians.

The church provided the material for their hallucinations. The church writers believed in the existence of the Devil and his attendants. The church fathers wrestled with dark spirits almost daily. St. Anthony was not the only one to whom horrible monsters and ugly devils made regular appearances. Christian scholars such as Isidore of Seville set out laboriously to describe the enemy and his works. Clement of Alexandria, at the beginning of the third century, subscribed to the Jewish view that the fallen angels had mated with earthly women, teaching them black magic and other demonic arts.

The Christian missionaries preached that the gods of the barbarian tribes were devils. Thus the ordinary barbarian found to his surprise that he was a devil worshipper. His confusion was further heightened when the church began incorporating elements of folk beliefs and practice into church ritual, by way of easing the spiritual transition. The peasant would dance round the hill fire at the autumn fire festival and then hear Mass the next morning on All Saint's Day. The fire festival gradually became All Hallow's Eve, or Halloween.

Occult Chivalry: The Knights Templars. Occult brotherhoods of the sixteenth, seventeenth, and eighteenth centuries claimed to have descended from a militant medieval order of chivalry, the Knights Templars. Although we still do not really know whether the Templars ever had anything to do with occultism, we must examine the details that led to the claims.

Founding of the Templar Order. The Order of the Temple was established in Jerusalem under Baldwin II, the second king of that Crusader's kingdom. The order was formally recognized by the church in 1128. The purposes of the new order were to rebuild the Temple of Jerusalem and to protect pilgrims making holy journeys to Palestine.

The Order of the Temple was, from the first, a secret brotherhood of knights. The first Grand Master of the Order was Hughes de Payens, who lived from 1070 to 1136. Nine other knights helped draw up the Order's rituals and laws. St. Bernard of Clairvaux, the Cistercian monk who was one of the most important figures in the medieval church, also may have helped to draw up the Templar rules.

Like the Cistercians and other monks, the Templars took vows of poverty, chastity, and obedience. The members of the order wore white mantles upon which were red eight-pointed crosses. They also built churches with eight sides. There were three types of members. Some were priests. Others were knights. The lowest order of Templars were the brethren, who waited on the knights.

Although the Templars had taken vows of poverty, their order soon grew rich. The source of wealth was not plunder from battles, but trade. In fact, the Templars seem to have had a remarkably peaceful sojourn in Palestine, with very little fighting against the Moslems. Their early peaceful coexistence was a powerful argument in the charges that were later brought against the Templars.

The Templars on Cyprus. In 1291 the city of Acre was recaptured by the Saracens, and the Templars were driven out of Palestine. They made their new headquarters on Cyprus, continued their trading activities, and grew even richer. The order owned lands and castles all over Europe.

With their increasing wealth and influence, the Templars encountered increasing resentment from outsiders. By order of Pope Eugenius III in 1172, the Templars were made independent of outside clergy. They had their own bishops, who reported directly to the Pope. The Templars were also under the protection of many European kings, beginning with the Emperor Frederick Barbarossa. By 1220, the Templars had more than fifteen thousand members, many of them nobles who commanded large armies.

The power of the Templars was exaggerated in the public mind by the secrecy with which the order conducted its business. Meetings of the Order were held in secret, and members were admitted into progressively more mysterious degrees within the Templars' discipline. Wild stories began to circulate about the nature of these secret rites.

The Templars seem to have been among the more arrogant members of the local aristocracy. As members of the order, they were not under local church jurisdiction. In fact, the Templars had the idea that they could do pretty well what they pleased. Were they not, after all, Christian knights and the embodiments of the chivalric ideal?

It is easy to see why the Templars held themselves above their contemporaries. They were much more widely travelled than the nobles who had not been in on the adventure of the Crusades. Because of their trading network they were in contact with the learning of the East. They knew much more about the Moslem and Jewish faiths and thus did not regard them with superstitious fear. They had experienced the luxury of oriental living, compared to which the castles of Europe seemed rude stone fortifications.

The church gave the Templars even more power by exempting them from many taxes. This angered the other nobles and churchmen even more. The Templars had many enemies, all waiting for some excuse to strike at the Order.

The Templars' Downfall. The excuse for attack came in 1306. There was a man from Languedoc, a region where many Templars lived, who was arrested by the church for heresy. In return for immunity from the church, the man informed on the Order of the Temple. The quality of the information overjoyed the Templars' main enemy, Philip IV of France. The Templars, their accuser alleged, took part in blasphemous occult secret rites. They worshipped an idol in the form of a goat called Baphomet. They took part in perverted sexual practices, especially sodomy. As part of their ritual they spat on the Christian cross and denied Christ.

Philip IV moved secretly and efficiently. He invited the unsuspecting Grand Master of the Templars, Jacques de Molay, to Paris. When de Molay arrived he was given a grand welcome with every outward show of respect. But once he was inside the King's palace, de Molay and all his followers were arrested. Meanwhile, Philip had sent secret orders to many parts of France to arrest the Templars. The rulers of Spain, Italy, and England all had received letters from Philip as well. So late in 1306, a mass arrest of the Templars and their associates took place. Some fifteen thousand persons were seized.

In France the Templars were cruelly tortured and punished. De Molay was burned at the stake in 1313. Many others underwent horrible tortures and imprisonment. Their lands and wealth were confiscated.

Some of them escaped to Portugal, whose ruler had found them innocent. Others were able to hide their connections with the Order and regroup under the names of other orders, such as the Order of Montesa in Spain. In England the Templars' wealth was confiscated, but the knights themselves were not tortured. Eventually the church declared the order to be disbanded.

Were the Templars Occultists? The medieval church had extremely efficient instruments of torture, and they had no trouble getting the confessions they wanted out of the knights. Very few of the "confessions" of the Templars would be admissable in a court of law today. But the various stories that emerged under persuasion did have certain elements in common, enough elements so that we can form some conclusions about the connections of the Templars with the occult arts.

It seems likely that the Templars had come into contact with Gnostic teachings during their time in Palestine and had incorporated these ideas into their rituals. Gnosticism had remained part of the teachings of many sects of the Eastern Church. Some of these sects were considered heretical by the Byzantine Empire, but they were allowed to practice in Moslem territories. Gnosticism had elements of Greek Neoplatonism, Egyptian Hermetic, and Jewish mystic thought. To good Catholics in Europe, these beliefs were nothing if not heresy, or, worse yet, outright idolatry.

The Templar churches in Austria and other countries were decorated with such Gnostic symbols as the flaming star, the triangle, the Seal of Solomon, and the tau, the Greek letter T. It is possible that the Templars took a mystical approach to the idea of rebuilding the Temple of Jerusalem. They would have consulted Jewish scholars about the proper plan for the rebuilding. The square and the level, two symbols of the architect's art, also appear in Templar buildings.

Gnosticism had retained many earlier Persian ideas about good and evil, male and female, claiming that all opposites were reconciled in the nature of the Divine. Gnostic dualism was perhaps the explanation for spitting on the cross and denying Christ in the Templar rituals.

The idol Baphomet is not so easy to explain. Not all the Templars confessed to having seen it. Many said that they had heard of such an idol but had not yet progressed to a degree that allowed looking upon it. At least two people confessed they had seen an idol with a demonic head and the body of a goat. But in the Middle Ages most people visualized the Devil as a goat. When accused of Devil worship under the thumbscrews, a certain number of people would be bound to tell the "confessors" what they wanted to hear.

The confessions made it clear, however, that there were degrees among the Templars, just as there had been in the secret occult societies of the East and as there were later to be in such groups as the Rosicrucians and Masons. The members who had not been admitted to the higher degrees had no direct knowledge of the inner rites, and those in the inner circle were those most likely to die before revealing the secrets. So we probably will never know whether the Templars worshipped the goat-god in their final mysteries.

But it is clear that the Templars were not orthodox Western Catholics, which was enough to condemn them in the eyes of the church. Reports that the men had to strip and be kissed lewdly by the other men on various parts of their bodies only heightened the conviction that the Templars were evil. Such a rite could have come from the Gnostic sects, many of whom regarded Jesus—and even God—as bisexual. There is no evidence that the

Templars practiced sodomy.

In the medieval mind, all forbidden things were connected with each other. Devil worship, Islam, sorcery, homosexuality, Judaism, magic, and secret doctrines were all condemned by the church. Any one of these charges brought against the Templars would most likely have been accompanied by the others. In addition, there was a strong church rule against usury, lending money for interest. Christians could not practice it; it was reserved for Jews and other outcasts. But the Templars could hardly have built up a trading empire without committing this sin, or without considerable contact with the Jewish sinners.

As Lewis Spence, the occult encyclopedist, put it, the Templars were "the victims of their own arrogance, their commercial success, and the superstitious ignorance of their contemporaries."

The Quest for the Holy Grail. Of all the stories of Arthur and his knights, the tales of the Holy Grail are those with the most occult significance. There is some evidence that they may have been brought from the East by the Knights Templars, and rewritten by Cistercian monks, who gave them a Christian mystic slant. It is also possible that the Grail stories were written as occult parables. The stories are different from the other Arthurian material in that their end is moral and spiritual. The great adventure in the Grail legends is the achievement of mystic union with God. The legends became popular early in the 1200s, at the same time that the doctrine of transubstantiation became dogma.

The Holy Grail was the vessel in which Christ's blood was caught while the Savior hung dying on the cross. Joseph of Arimathea was the owner of this dish, which was also one of the dishes used at the Last Supper.

The Grail stories tell how Joseph of Arimathea took the Grail and wandered to England, where he built a monastery at Glastonbury to house the sacred vessel. Alain, a younger relative of Joseph of Arimathea, was appointed guardian of the Grail, and he placed the Grail in a castle. The various Arthurian knights came to the castle, hoping to achieve a sight of the Holy Vessel. Only the purest knight, it was said, would attain this vision.

The Quest for the Grail was always attended by perils, and elements of former occult or magic stories were worked into the legend. In many of the stories, for example, Alain is a Fisher King, or Rich Fisher, who sits by a stream near the castle of the Grail. The knight must be questioned by the Fisher King before he can enter the castle. In some stories, the Fisher King has a wound that is healed when the knight achieves the Grail.

The wound of the Fisher King is sometimes connected with the barrenness of the land about the Grail castle. When the Grail is achieved, or sometimes, when the Fisher King is speared by the Grail Knight, the land is restored to fertility.

Inside the Grail castle, the hero had to answer riddles and pass various other tests before the Grail would appear. When the vessel did appear, it was often accompanied by sweet music or by a white dove. Other sacred objects, such as the lance with which Christ was speared, sometimes appeared in procession with it.

The descriptions of the Grail itself varied from story to story. Sometimes it was a large flat dish, a platter such as one would use to serve fish, and the platter might bear a severed head. In a hermit's cave in Turkey, there is a picture of a sacred meal in which Christ and his disciples are feeding from just such a dish. A large fish is on the platter. The Turkish painting dates from the ninth or tenth century. Obviously, at least some of the elements of the Grail legends existed in Eastern Christianity long before they appeared in the West.

The Grail is also sometimes pictured as a chalice, a large goblet like those used in the Catholic Mass. Whatever its shape, the Grail was endowed with magical properties. Among these was the ability to feed the hungry. When the Grail appeared, "every knight had such meats and drinks as he best loved in the world." Most probably, the sustenance referred to was spiritual rather than physical food. The Grail could also heal sickness and prolong life.

In some stories, the Grail is also a stone. Many writers have connected this with the Philosopher's stone of the alchemists, which like the Grail was used to prolong life. But the stone referred to might also be one of the Gnostic gems, stones that among the Eastern heretical sects were endowed with mysterious and occult powers. The connection of the Grail stories with the Gnostic sects is tenuous. But the appearance of the severed head on the platter and of the sword with which John the Baptist was decapitated are very suggestive. The nineteenth-century occultist Eliphas Lévi claimed that the Templars worshipped John the Baptist.

Regardless of the original intentions of the writers, the Grail stories have long been adopted by occultists as tales of great spiritual merit. Occult traditions have grown up around the Spear of Longinus, the lance used to pierce the side of Christ, as well as around the Grail itself.

King Arthur's Round Table, from which the knights set forth in quest of the Grail, has also been used symbolically by occultists. In some traditions, there were twelve knights of the Round Table, just as Jesus had twelve disciples. In other traditions, the knights of the Round Table were divided into twelve groups, each of which corresponded to a sign of the zodiac. The Round Table itself is, to some writers, another "magic circle" device. Merlin, the enchanter at King Arthur's court, figures in the cosmologies of many British occult groups. I have dealt with some of the versions of the Merlin story in the section called "The Occult Bible."

Devil Worship. Although almost every person in medieval Europe was required to be a Christian in practice, a great many people were not Christians in belief. Thousands followed a belief that was in direct opposition to the Church: the worship of Satan. The majority of Devil-worshippers were women, and the religion was especially strong among the peasants. But rich people, too, joined in. Even Catholic priests were guilty of taking part in the secret faith. Sorcery and black magic were attributed to kings, queens, and popes. Henry III of France and his mother, Catherine de Medici, were both sorcerers, and so was Pope Silvester II in the eleventh century.

It must be remembered that the church preached the literal existence of demons. The great cathedrals were covered with demonic decorations, as a way of exorting and terrifying the faithful. Medieval art is full of fantastic apparitions of evil spirits, devils, demons, and other Satanic monsters.

The church in the Middle Ages made a great deal of noise about the torments of hell. Most people were suffering enough on Earth to believe in such tortures in the hereafter. The never-ending suffering of the damned was a favorite theme in medieval art and literature. The miracle and mystery plays performed on saints' days and other church holidays dramatized the eternal struggle between good and evil and promised the torments of hell to those who did not repent.

Why, when the eternal risk was so great, did so many people take part in Devil worship? Most likely it was because they could see very little benefit in following Christ. The worship of the Devil offered everything that the church did not: the promise of power in the present world; the chance to enjoy sexual freedom; the chance for women to officiate at religious ceremonies; the opportunity for large numbers of peasants to gather in secret; and, most of all, the chance to come into direct contact with the spirit world.

Witchcraft. Witchcraft existed long before the Christian era—we have seen how it was condemned by Hammurabi in 1800 B.C. Unquestionably there also were witches in Egyptian, Greek, and Roman times.

With the Christian era, witchcraft acquired new dimensions. The Christian fathers made no distinction between the pagan religions and devil worship. The taint of witchcraft fell upon many people who had little to do with the black arts. In Europe, many peasants followed the old religions in secret, just as the peasants in Catholic South America do today. In the eyes of the church, these people were witches.

Jules Michelet's classic study, *Satanism and Witchcraft*, traces the development of the witch in popular culture. Michelet demonstrates that witchcraft was a social movement with political and economic, as well as religious, dimensions. It was a way to counteract the forces of authority, the forces which, in the eyes of the serfs, were most responsible for the misery of everyday existence.

Most witches were women, although there were also male witches called warlocks. The witch was often a folk healer, as was discussed earlier in this section. She knew the art of using herbs to cause abortions, prevent miscarriage, stop bleeding, heal ulcers, and abate fevers. Since people in the Middle Ages attributed disease to demonic influence, it followed that those who could cure diseases must be in communication with the Devil.

So the average citizen of the Middle Ages, even the noble, relied on the peasant witch for medical attention. And the witches healed more than physical ills. They also provided herbs that acted as love potions, herbs to get rid of enemies without suspicion, and even ointments that could cause visions. So witches possessed a certain degree of power. Women would never again enjoy such spiritual authority.

The witches themselves often believed their power came from the underworld. That was, after all, what they were told every Sunday at Mass. Although she may have felt in her heart that there was nothing wrong with what she was doing, the medieval witch was a citizen of her times. She performed her evil acts deliberately, knowing the church condemned her for doing so. The religion of Satan, then, was a religion of defiance.

Another factor in the rise of witchcraft was the sexual repression preached by the church. Hatred of the physical body was an important tenet of Christian monasticism. Hermits, priests, knights, and monks all took vows of chastity. Woman was the temptress, the embodiment of all that was evil.

This was the doctrine that the medieval woman heard from the day she was born. She was a cursed creature, and she had proof of that curse in the mysterious flow of blood from her body each month. People in the Middle Ages—even educated people—had very vague ideas about human reproduction. Knowledge of medicine in general was primitive; knowledge of the physiology of woman was nonexistent.

The Sabbat. The major gatherings of witches—the Sabbats—were celebrations of promiscuity and everything else that was forbidden. The Sabbats were not unlike the Bacchanalian festivals of Roman times, which may have survived in secret all through the fall of the Roman Empire and the Dark Ages. Gradually the festivals came to be associated with Devil worship.

The Sabbat had a lot more to offer in the way of entertainment than all the holidays of the church put together. Large meals, dancing, hallucinogenic drugs, and sex were all part of the ritual.

The typical Sabbat was held deep in the forest. The Black Forest in northern Germany and Sherwood Forest in England were two well-known gathering places. The witch prepared by undressing and smearing herself with an ointment that caused hallucinations.

The witch was supposed to fly to the Sabbat on her broom. Sometimes on the way there she would be transformed into a beast, usually a goat or a wolf. Toads, ravens, and black cats were also common transformations. A witch sometimes kept such an animal as a familiar spirit.

Some of the Sabbat gatherings were very large. Over twelve thousand people attended one Sabbat in the Basque country of Spain. Naturally the church would look askance at any such large gathering of peasants. It is possible that such secret gatherings preceded the great peasant revolts of the twelfth century.

Other gatherings of witches were smaller. Thirteen was the number for the local witch group, the coven. The head of the coven, usually a man, was considered the incarnation of the Devil. He had twelve witches to attend him. Like many other elements of witchcraft ritual, the coven was a parody of the church, in this case of Christ and his twelve disciples.

Some of the meetings of witches took place at the sites of megaliths or other ancient monuments. In England, Ireland, and Wales, it is probable that the Sabbats were also celebrations of the ancient druidic religions, which survived all through medieval times. But on the Continent, the witches were expressly dedicated to the worship of the Christian Devil.

The Sabbat was always held at night. As Michelet pointed out, the medieval peasant was a nocturnal animal, for it was only at night that he could escape his masters. A large bonfire marked the meeting place. Near the bonfire was the altar and a seat for the leader of the Sabbat, who was dressed as the Devil, all in black. Sometimes the leader wore an animal mask. Assisting the Devil was a priestess, who was called the Aged. Many of the priestesses were, however, quite young.

A Sabbat began with a roll call. All those present had to deny Christ and kiss the backside of the Devil. There was usually a second mask under the Devil's tail. The witches called each other by secret names, having renounced the names they were given at Christian baptism.

Next followed a period of general drinking, drug-taking, dancing, and celebration. Not all these gatherings were orgiastic. Michelet mentions some Sabbats to which families and children came. But there was a great deal of sexual license. At some gatherings, the people arrived in couples. No one was admitted without a partner.

The crowd took part in a huge round dance, known as the "Witches' Round." The effect of the dance was to work the crowd into a frenzy and prepare them for the consecration and Black Mass.

This last section of the Sabbat took place around the altar. It is possible that not everyone at the Sabbat took part in the final rites. The priestess lay on the altar, and the Black Mass was celebrated on her naked body. Toward the end of the Middle Ages, the Black Mass became a more exact parody of the Christian ritual. The Sabbat Mass was especially effective if it could be celebrated with a consecrated host that had been stolen from a church.

The Sabbat ended with the Devil having sex with the witches present. As there were a great many witches, it is probable that the Devil used an artificial phallus. This would explain the testimony of many witches under torture, who said that the Devil's penis was cold and metallic.

The major festivals for witches were May 1, June 21 (Midsummer's Eve), October 31 (Halloween), and February 2 (Candlemas). Other celebrations were held in conjunction with church holidays. Christmas, which occurred near the winter solstice, was observed diabolically as well as piously.

The church punished witches severely, although the mass persecution of witches did not take place until rather late in the Middle Ages. I will describe the witch trials in the Occult Reformation later in the book since they were indulged in by Protestants as well as Catholics.

Sorcery. Not everyone in the Middle Ages had to steal into the forest late at night to meet the Devil. The Devil lived in towns, too, and visited some people regularly in their rooms. Magic, divination, and casting of spells were studied by people of learning. Sorcery was, for the educated minority, what witchcraft was for the peasant masses—a way to gain power denied by the church.

Medieval sorcery was dualistic. It recognized the existence of both good and evil forces. Sorcerers often evoked demons in the name of Jesus Christ or Mary, and they inevitably dismissed them with the aid of the Christian divinities.

Books of Magic. Books of magic spells, like all books in the Middle Ages, were expensive and rare. Each book had to be copied by hand. The copying work of the church was done by monks with official approval. The copying work for books of magic and other occult subjects had to be done in secret.

A Black Book was part of many Satanic rites in the Middle Ages. Old woodcuts of witches at the Sabbat show the witches using demonic books as sacred objects. In the church, the Bible was also invested with immense power. One very early method of discovering whether a person was a witch was to weigh her or him against the church Bible. If the Bible weighed more, the suspect was in trouble.

The most important book of magic available in the Middle Ages was called *Clavicule de Solomon*, or *Key of Solomon*. This was a book of spells and formulae supposedly composed by Solomon, to whom were attributed special occult powers. The book entered Europe through the Moslem countries, especially Spain. More copies of it entered Europe with the Crusaders. It is certainly possible that the Knights Templars were among those responsible for bringing copies from Byzantine scholars to Europe.

Another important magic book was the *Grimoire of Pope Honorius*, which contained much of the same material. Honorius III became Pope in 1216 and was considered to be a sorcerer.

Only a handful of scholars knew about these books of magic. Roger Bacon, the English scientist and philosopher, who died in 1294, was one. The books contained not only printed spells and formulae, but drawings of symbols with mystical, demonic, and occult significance. Learning to draw those symbols was an important way of learning control over the spirit world.

The Magic Circle. The medieval grimoires showed how to draw the magic circle, a necessary step in evoking demons, summoning up the dead, and other magical practices. Several different formulae were described, but all the formulae had common elements.

The magic circle was a means of directing cosmic force into a small space, in the center of which the sorcerer stood. The circle was a map of cosmic order. The smallest circle, in the center, was for the sorcerer. He was surrounded by larger shapes—usually pentacles, squares, or triangles—

which represented other cosmic patterns. The whole was then circumscribed with another circle or circles, which represented the outer reaches of the Cosmos.

The circle was often inscribed with letters in Hebrew or Greek. One magic circle in *Key of Solomon* is inscribed with the seventy-two Hebrew names for God from Kabbalistic writings. It is unlikely that the sorcerers who used the names in this way really understood the Kabbalah or even knew of its existence. The names were mysterious magic symbols from a foreign place.

Careful instructions were used for drawing the magic circle and using it to contact the spirit world. Each writer had a slightly different ritual. It was important that each detail of the ritual be followed exactly in order to guarantee the result.

As to whether the magic circles work—you can try that for yourself. You will find detailed directions in chapter four of this book.

Casting Spells. Most medieval sorcerers earned their living by casting spells, as sorcerers in all periods of history have done. Spells could be cast for the most mundane reasons. They could be used to recover lost items, to curdle milk, to bring lovers together, to make married people quarrel—in fact, to bring about nearly any change one wanted in the universe. There were spells to help people become invisible and spells to make other people sick.

Even more impressive were the spells that controlled the weather and other natural forces. Sorcerers wrecked ships with their storms, burned towns with exploding volcanoes, caused earthquakes, and spread plagues over the land.

Evocation of Demons. Sorcerers got their powers by calling up demons and forcing them to obey. A really practiced sorcerer would summon the demons by name. Most sorcery was done in secret, underground, as it were. It is surprising how many of the names of devils have survived the book burnings of the centuries. A few of them are listed on pages 223–30.

Once a demon had been summoned, the sorcerer set about to make the demon do his bidding. Very few of the sorcerers ever got as good at this as Solomon, who summoned the jinn to build the Temple for him. But demons were very useful for a variety of household tasks. A thirteenth-century astrologer, Michael Scot, used demons to wait tables at dinner parties. Demons also cleaned up after the feast.

Pacts with Demons. The problem with evoking demons is that you can get easily carried away. You get used to the idea that demons can spare you the work of fixing meals and doing the dishes, and before you know it, you start thinking about other things the demons could do for you. Why couldn't the demons make you rich? Or kill your enemies? *The Sorcerer's Apprentice* is a relevant folktale that relates a great occult truth: Don't dabble in forces you don't understand without proper preparation. A little learning is a dangerous thing.

The medieval sorcerer could not always retain control over the spirit forces. The Devil and his dominions were powerful. And the demonic forces were fully in charge of a whole body of spiritual secrets. These could be obtained only by promising the demons something in return. What the demon wanted was the sorcerer's soul. However, the sorcerers, like the witches, so desired occult power that they were willing to risk the worst to obtain it. The sorcerers made their bargains with the Devil official by putting them in writing. Frequently the ink would be the sorcerer's own blood.

Once he had made the pact, the sorcerer entered a new world of the sensory and material delights of his own choosing. In time, the Devil would come to collect. The sorcerer was aware of his fate and struggled to escape it. The church made provisions to help people wiggle out of pacts signed with Satan. But few escaped damnation.

Necromancy, or the art of evoking the spirits of the dead, was one of the arts revealed to sorcerers after they had signed the Devil's Pact. Necromancy required greater psychic power than casting spells or even evoking demons, since it involved contacting the very forces of life and death.

To some extent, necromancy was a scientific endeavor. In Spain, necromancers dug up dead bodies and opened them for study. They examined the human interior for reasons of divination and magic. But they also made accurate observations of what they saw. From these first forbidden experiments arose much of our later knowledge of human anatomy. Necromancy is an instance of the connection between the occult arts and the medical sciences. Many other examples of this connection are found throughout this book.

But in most of Europe in the Middle Ages, necromancy did not involve digging up dead bodies but summoning up dead spirits. People would consult a necromancer to ask dead ancestors for advice, to talk to famous historical figures of the past, and to give and receive messages from the life beyond.

Medieval Astrology. Astrology was one occult art not forbidden in the Middle Ages. The church said astrology was proof of the Divine Universal Order. Nature operated according to Divine laws.

But what about human nature? Here the church had a problem. If astrology controlled human nature, then humans no longer had free will and thus were not really responsible for their sins. Theologians resolved the problem by saying that human bodies were ruled by the stars but that the human will was not. "The wise man rules the stars," was a medieval proverb. Casting horoscope fortunes was against church law.

Still, astrology flourished in France as early as the time of Charlemagne, who was crowned Holy Roman Emperor in 800. It was more than a fashion. People believed in it, and consulted the stars before planting, fighting, courting, or travelling.

Astrological Texts. People in Western Europe inherited astrology from the Roman Empire. They knew the writings of Ptolemy, the second-century Egyptian who codified astrology. Ptolemy's astrology was based on the idea that the Earth was the center of the universe. This theory was held by nearly everyone until the sixteenth century.

The other writers on whom medieval European astrologers relied were Firmicius (fourth century), Macrobius (fifth century), and Chalcidius (sixth century). Some of the early church fathers, such as Isidore of Seville and the Venerable Bede, also wrote about the stars.

The Venerable Bede's approach is curious to us today but well illustrates the early medieval mind. Bede wanted to make the zodiac into a Christian pageant, with the names of the twelve apostles replacing those of the signs. Bede saw no deceit in this approach. He felt that it was significant that God should foreshadow the coming of Christ by placing the identical number of signs in the sky as Christ had disciples and as Israel had tribes.

After the Crusades, astrology from the Moslem world began to spread across Europe. The Arabic system was far more mathematically precise than the European. It was based on continuing observation of the stars—studies that eventually led people to change their minds about the position of the humble Earth in the cosmic system.

Alphonso X of Castile gathered astrologers from all over the known world at his court. They helped him produce the *Alphonsine Tables*, a kind of encyclopedia of astrology. The best astrologers of the time—those that were employees of the noble houses—kept up with the latest Arabic developments in their science. Ibn Ezra, a Jewish writer from Toledo, Spain, was also widely known as an expert.

Astrology had been a branch of learning reserved for the upper classes of society. As towns grew, it began to spread into the middle classes as well. Astrology was placed on the curriculum of the University of Bologna, Italy, in 1125.

Medieval Astrologers. People in medieval times studied nature not for its own sake, but to establish the fact of universal order. Astronomy did not exist. The medieval astrologers are the forerunners of modern astronomers as well as of modern occultists.

I have already mentioned Pope Sylvester II as a practitioner of witchcraft.

Whatever his dealings with evil spirits, he was also a scientist. He owned astronomical instruments and made notes of his observations.

Michael Scot (1175–1234) was a priest who was also considered a magician. He was the official astrologer to the Emperor Frederick II. Scot knew Arabic, was an expert on Aristotle, and studied physiognomy as well as astronomy. Such advanced knowledge naturally made him a candidate for sorcery. People said he could raise the dead.

Guido Bonatti was a colleague of Scot's. They both served in Frederick's court. We know about Bonatti and Scot mostly through the writings of Dante, who placed them both in his *Inferno*.

Especially in Italy, the church maintained official contact with astrologers. The universities of Padua and Milan taught astrology to generations of friars who took the belief all over Europe. Pope Alexander IV and Pope John XXI were two thirteenth-century popes who supported astrological sciences.

Albertus Magnus and St. Thomas Aquinas both believed in astrology. So did Roger Bacon (1214–1294) the English scholar who knew about magic, and Duns Scotus (1265–1308) the radical theologian.

The Occult Renaissance (1300–1500)

The Renaissance was an era of great expansion of European consciousness. It was during this period that America was discovered, that the printing press spread Eastern thought among European universities, and that the Protestant Reformation took place. The period was marked politically by the rise to power of strong European monarchies, and economically by an increase in available capital and the rise of a strong middle class.

Scholarship and letters flourished. People began talking in secular rather than merely religious terms. Thomas More, Erasmus, and Francis Bacon were only a few of the many people who wrote about political *utopias*, or ideal societies.

The occult arts flourished as well. In fact, the great advances in learning made during the Renaissance were almost all connected directly to occult thought. Astrology had been given new depth by the infusion of Arabian mathematical knowledge into Europe. The modern science of astronomy was the result. Alchemy was practiced by many forerunners of modern chemistry. Various other "sciences"—cheiromancy (palm reading), metoposcopy (reading the lines of the face), and physiognomy (reading facial expressions)—gained widespread acceptance. These divinatory arts were the forerunners of modern medical diagnosis.

Europe grew out of its attachment to Mother Church by a long and painful process. Protestantism had smoldered throughout the Middle Ages. There was, however, no uniform Protestant theology until Luther, Calvin, and their peers formulated it. The Protestants in the Middle Ages had some Gnostic and other heretical tendencies, some of which they had acquired by contact with the Greek church of the East. The Cathari, Albigensies, and other Protestant sects, were strong among the middle and artisan classes in medieval towns. All these sects were persecuted by the Catholic Church.

After the Reformation, it turned out that a great many Protestant sects had either reformed themselves too far or not far enough to suit the majority opinion among theologians. Our much-invoked pilgrim fathers, you will recall, were fleeing from religious persecution by other Protestants, not by Catholics.

Here we get into the dark side of the Renaissance and Reformation. The period of rebirth was one of the bloodiest periods of European history. Warfare was perfected along with all the other human arts. It was now possible for a relatively small number of Spanish soldiers to wipe out whole populations of Indians. The musket was superior to the spear.

The wars against the Indians in the New World reflected the turbulence of Europe. From 1455 until 1800, there was no twenty-five-year period without a major war in Europe. At first, wars were fought ostensibly on religious grounds—between Catholics and Protestants. Religious wars continued through the sixteenth and into the seventeenth centuries. Then wars began to be fought over the question of succession to the various royal houses.

The bloodiest wars of all were those fought by both the Catholics and Protestants against witches, sorcerers, occultists, Jews, and other heretics.

But once the spirit of dissent had been let loose, there was no containing it. Networks of communication were established among scientists and other scholars. Their views spread especially rapidly through the middle classes. People believed that they were entering into a new social order.

Occult societies and other secret brotherhoods grew up in cities all over Europe. Even some monarchs (such as Rudolph II of Bohemia) cultivated occult ideas and tried to set up their governments from alchemical models. Unquestionably, many of the secret societies were political as well as occult in nature. The societies became an important factor in organizing the middle classes against the monarchies during the seventeenth and eighteenth centuries.

The Arabs: Astrology, Medicine and Mysticism. The occult renaissance began in the East. Throughout the Middle Ages, the imperial court at Constantinople attracted astrologers, mystics, and others who carried on Egyptian and Greek occult traditions. Astrology was first codified by Egyptian Greek scholars living in Alexandria. When the Moslems conquered Egypt in the seventh century, they inherited a body of astrological teaching, which agreed in many respects with the teaching of the Arab scholars from Persia. It is not surprising, therefore, to find that it was Arab scholars who perfected the science of astrology.

Among the names of Arabian astrologers that have come down to us are Aben-Ragel, who lived in Cordoba in the fifth century, Abou-Rhyan (Mohammed-ben-Ahmed), Albumazar, who lived in Korassan in the ninth century, and Alchabitius, who lived in the tenth century.

The study of medicine also made great advances under the Arabs of the early Moslem empire. Schools were established in Spain, Egypt, and throughout the Near East. In the city of Baghdad alone, there were more than 850 physicians who were licensed to practice. Arab physicians attended many of the noble families of Europe.

One such physician, Avicenna (980–1037), was a founder of modern medicine. At the age of ten, he could recite the entire Koran by memory and had mastered contemporary mathematics. He published a philosophical treatise at the age of twenty-one. While still a young man, he was appointed Grand Vizier under the Sultan Magdal Douleth. A revolution overthrew the dynasty, and Avicenna had to flee for his life. At a later date he was made personal physician to the Persian king. He lost that job because of reports of his debauched living. Indeed, Avicenna seems to have indulged in nearly every known form of excess.

He spent most of his life in retirement, reading and writing. He was the author of almost one hundred books on medicine and alchemy. In his interest in the latter subject, he was typical of his culture.

Islam was founded in an apocalyptic age, and its prophet, Muhammad, claimed to receive visions from God. So from the beginning, mysticism was part of the Moslem tradition. The Moslems placed great importance on education. Their schools and universities inherited the knowledge of the Egyptian Hermetic priests, the Greek Neoplatonists, and the Persian Magi.

The legends that grew up in the Arab world around the Hebrew King Solomon are a good example of the way the Moslem religion borrowed from Judaism. According to the legends, King Solomon, who prayed to God that he might be given wisdom, was a master of the occult arts. He understood the healing arts, and he learned how to make spirits work for him.

Folktales and legends about Solomon, including his knowledge of healing, were prevalent among Jews as early as the first and second centuries. After their conquests, the Arabs heard these tales and combined them with tales of Suleiman, the legendary ruler of a prehistoric race. Among the Arabs, then, Solomon was a wonder-figure, who could tame the winds and who knew the secrets of magic. Arab legend has it that Solomon's throne was carried every day throughout the whole Earth on a huge, green flying carpet. Also riding the carpet was Solomon's army, half-human and half-spirit forces. (Green in Islam is a holy color, and green carpets are not woven except for use in mystic contemplation.)

The Wisdom of Solomon was a title given to many different occult writings. All these writings claimed to be part of the mystic and occult wisdom that was given to King Solomon. At least two grimoires—books of magic spells—also have been ascribed to Solomon. Some of the magic spells attributed to Solomon are found in chapter four. Groups with occult affiliations—such as the Knights of Malta, the Rosicrucians, and the Freemasons—claim that their teachings were handed down through Solomon. Solomon has been identified with Thoth, or Hermes Trismegistus.

The Dervishes. Certain sects of Moslem priests seem to have incorporated rituals and teachings from the Persian magi into their Moslem faith. These priests were called dervishes. They formed themselves into secret brotherhoods, lived ascetically, and concentrated on spiritual exercises intended to induce mystic trance. The dervishes, like the mystic priests of Egypt and Mesopotamia, recognized several grades of initiates. They placed great importance on configurations of symbols, numbers, and words.

The most widely known sect of dervishes were the whirling dervishes, who still exist in Turkey and Iran. These priests achieve mystic trance by whirling round and round in a dance. The movements of the dance originally may have had some astrological or symbolical meaning—indeed, may still have to the inner circles of the sect.

Jewish Mysticism: The Kabbalah. Few systems of thought have been so important to occultism as the body of Jewish thought known as the Kabbalah. On the surface, the Kabbalah appears to be nothing but an elaborate magical system. But it is actually a tool for achieving mystic union with God.

The Kabbalah was not known even to most Jews but was reserved for an inner few. The teachings were passed on orally to each generation of scholars. Kabbalism, just like Moslem mysticism, owed a great deal to Greek Neoplatonists and Egyptian Hermetic thought.

Early Kabbalistic Writers. The *Sepher Yezirah*, or Book of Creation, was the first body of Kabbalistic thought to be committed to paper. It was written down sometime before the ninth century. This was followed by the *Bahir*, a word that means "brilliant." The *Zohar*, or "Splendor," was written down in the thirteenth century. A Jewish scholar from Spain, Moses de Léon, circulated the *Zohar* and was probably the author. De Léon claimed, of course, that the manuscript had actually been written much earlier, in the first century, by Rabbi Akiba ben Joseph. But at least some of the sections of the *Zohar* could not have been written that early, since they mention the fall of Jerusalem to the Crusaders. The Kabbalah, does, however, contain some very old material.

In the Moslem countries, where Jews had a considerable degree of freedom, Jewish universities were established. The Jewish scholars of Jerusalem and Alexandria continued their correspondence through the centuries. Spain too was a center of Jewish learning. One university, at

Gerona, was devoted to study of the Kabbalah. Its founder, Isaac the Blind, was widely known for his learning. (Isaac the Blind helped make reincarnation part of Kabbalistic doctrine.) There were other schools of Kabbalistic studies at Guadalajara and Segovia.

The Sephirot. The central part of Kabbalistic doctrine was meditation upon the ten emanations of God, or the *sephirot*. God's emanations were like rays shining forth from the Divine presence. The ten *sephirot* were Crown, Wisdom, Intelligence, Love, Justice, Beauty, Firmness, Splendor, Foundation, and Kingdom.

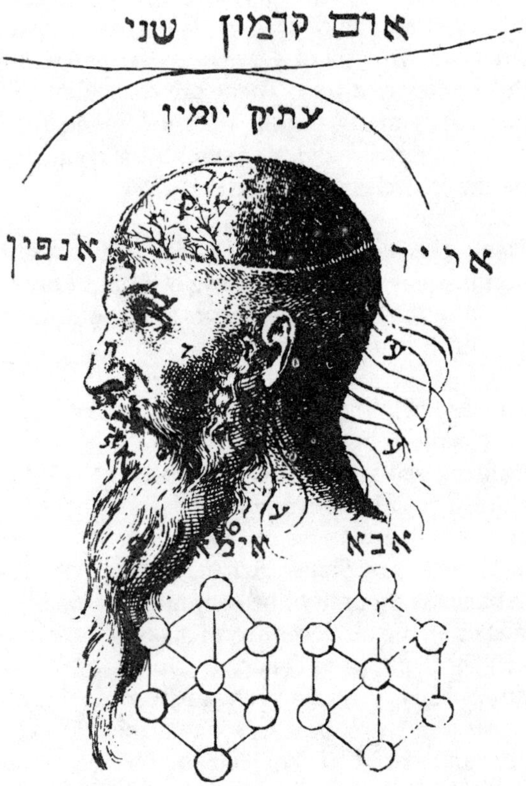

The Kabbalists drew diagrams illustrating the relationship of these ten emanations to each other. The most common diagram was the *sephirotic* Tree, or the Tree of Life, which showed how each emanation proceeded from the one before it. Some emanations proceed from unions of other pairs of emanations. For example, Wisdom and Intelligence unite to produce Mercy. Then Mercy and Justice unite to produce Beauty. (For a further discussion of the *sephirot,* see the section on Tarot in chapter three.)

Numbers, Letters, and Symbols. The Kabbalists devoted themselves to careful study of the Hebrew Scriptures, but from a special perspective. They believed that there was a hidden meaning in the Scriptures that was not recognizable by the ordinary reader. In order to understand the hidden meaning, the student had to meditate carefully on each word and letter of the holy writings. Further insights could be achieved by rearranging numbers, symbols, and letters.

One method of rearranging was to place words over each other and to read the letters vertically. Another method was to assign a number to each letter. Each word, then, was given a numerical value. By replacing words with others of the same value, the "true" meanings of the first set of words could be arrived at. This number-cipher system was called *gematria*. Another system required dividing the Hebrew alphabet in half and placing one half above the other. Each letter was then substituted for its pair.

Such a method of contemplation tends to distract the student's attention, so that the letters and numbers are invested with power in themselves. That is exactly what happened with the teachings of the Kabbalah. When knowledge of the Kabbalah spread outside the Jewish community, during the Renaissance, many Christian magicians used Kabbalistic words merely as magical spells (see chapter four).

The Names of God. In the Kabbalistic system, God had seventy-two names by which He made Himself known to man. Meditation upon these names was a path of contemplation. When Christians began to study the Kabbalah, they seized upon these names as the key to many of their own unsolved mysteries. Many of the names had the additional virtue of being totally unpronounceable by the European tongue. Thus they acquired even more mystery. The names of God came to be applied to alchemy, magic, and other occult systems.

Correspondences. Like the Neoplatonists and Pythagoreans before them, the Kabbalists believed that everything on earth was but a shadow or image of the Divine forms. Thus, earthly Man was only a shadow of the heavenly Man. The ten *sephirot* were not only the emanations of God. They also represented the various parts of the heavenly Man, who was created in God's image. The Kabbalists divided the *sephirot* into triads. Each triad represented part of the human body. Wisdom, Intelligence, and Crown were the head; Love, Justice, and Beauty were the arms; Firmness, Splendor, and Foundation were the legs. The tenth *sephira*, Kingdom, represented the whole Man. (For more about the importance of correspondence in all occult thought, see "The Occult Bible.")

Cosmology. Kabbalists viewed the universe as containing four planes of being. Each plane was a system of emanations. The first, or highest, sphere was that of the immediate emanations of God. Each descending sphere was less refined. The fourth sphere was the active world in which we all live.

Each human soul was created in the heavenly sphere, from which it descended into the earthly sphere. The task of each soul was to achieve reunion with the divine, to reenter the heavenly sphere. Some souls had to reenter the Earth three times in order to be fully purified.

Kabbalists also held a system of beliefs about the end of the world. They believed that when all the souls on Earth had returned to the heavenly sphere, a period of Jubilee would begin. At this time Satan would return to his angelic nature and peace would reign everywhere in the universe.

The Kabbalah and Folk Myth. Before about the fifteenth century, very few non-Jews knew anything at all about the Kabbalah. Among the Jews themselves the Kabbalists were sometimes considered wonder-workers or magicians. Among the Christians they were considered sorcerers or magicians. It was an age of mass ignorance and illiteracy. People regarded the written word with awe and some suspicion. Anything one did not understand was credited to supernatural agencies.

There were probably always rumors about some sort of inner sect in Judaism that claimed to know the mysteries, but these rumors would serve only to heighten the superstitious fear of most people to all that was alien to them. And, you must remember, people were taught by the church to hate Jews.

Popular conceptions of the Kabbalah have grown out of this continuing distrust and distortion on the part of the public The Kabbalah doctrine has never been part of mainstream Judaism. People have attributed to the Kabbalah any number of systems although few know what the system really was, or is. But the Kabbalah—or people's conception of it—continues to influence occult thought today.

Alchemy. Alchemy, a discipline that originated around the eighth century and flourished in the 1300s through 1500s, was an occult art in which scholars tried to transmute base metals into gold or silver. The alchemists carried out simple chemical experiments and made important discoveries about the nature of various elements. But where chemistry is based on observation and deduction, alchemy was based on ritual and meditation. It was more a spiritual discipline than a science. The stated aim of the alchemists—to turn base metals into gold—has led to much misunderstanding of alchemical study.

The gold of which the alchemists spoke was not the valuable metal after which all humans lust, but a rarified version of it, both symbolic and actual. Gold is an incorruptible metal. To the alchemists it symbolized the Divine Essence. Gold stood for the sun, which in turn stood for God.

Alchemical doctrine reflected a concern with order. It depended entirely on the doctrine of correspondences. The alchemist attempted to create a living model of the cosmos within his athanor, or egg-shaped oven. The climax of this recreation of the cosmos would be the formation of a golden substance, the Elixir of Life, or Philosopher's Stone.

There are many parallels between alchemical thought and the religious thought of the Far East. Those parallels are not a coincidence. The origins of alchemy may be sought in Mesopotamia, among the fire-worshipers of Zoroaster. This learning also travelled to the priests of Hermes in Egypt. Both in Mesopotamia and Egypt, there was early contact with Indian and Chinese thought.

The alchemists read the works of Hermes Trismegistus of Egypt and followed the thinking of the Pythagoreans and the Neoplatonists. They based their work on the significance of numbers. An alchemist consulted the stars before beginning his work—in fact, he performed each step of the work at the appropriate astrological time.

The Early Alchemists. Geber, whose full name was Abou Moussah Djafar al Sofi, was the first known practicing alchemist. A Moslem who wrote in Arabic, he lived in the second half of the eighth century, in Spain or Mesopotamia. Geber is assured a place in scientific history by his discoveries of nitric acid and red oxide of mercury.

Geber's most important work, *The Sum of Perfection*, was an important handbook for medieval alchemists. It remains a standard alchemical text. Geber also made important contributions to astrology and medicine. In medieval times, several writers used his name on occult treatises. There is, therefore, much more occult work attributed to Geber than he actually produced. From the large amount of writing on the occult published under Geber's name, we get the word *gibberish*.

Rhasis. Rhasis was a physician, scientist, philosopher, and alchemist who was born in Persia in the middle of the ninth century. He had a highly successful career. He traveled in Spain and Egypt and is said to have written 226 different works on the sciences of metals.

When Rhasis was a very old man, a curious incident occurred which made him blind. Rhasis had set up a laboratory, paid for by the Emir Almansour, Prince of Khorassan. The Prince invited himself to watch Rhasis perform some chemical experiments. Unfortunately, the experiments failed, the Emir was displeased, and ordered Rhasis to be beaten with one of his own books.

The Philosopher's Stone. Because many of the writings of alchemists are written in allegorical terms, we cannot be sure just what the Philosopher's Stone was. Some writers seem to have considered it an actual piece of rock. Other writings ascribe to it some of the properties of mercury. The Philosopher's Stone was also called the Powder of Projection.

The color of the Stone was sometimes black, sometimes red, sometimes green, sometimes white, depending on the writer. Whatever the Stone looked like, or whether it was in solid or liquid form, it had miraculous powers. Not only could it transmute base metals into gold, but it could also heal disease and give the student ultimate knowledge. For these reasons, it was called the Elixir of Life.

Alchemical writings made it clear that the achievement of the Philosopher's Stone, like all successes in alchemy, was a stage in spiritual development. The Stone was given only to those who had proved themselves worthy by years of meditation and proper action.

The Great Work. The Great Work of the alchemist—the creation of the Philosopher's Stone—took years of proper training and meditation. The creation itself had to be done according to the strict rules. The instructions are repeated in several alchemical texts and read almost like a recipe. However, if you attempt to reproduce the recipe with the help of your junior chemistry set, you will not learn the secret of Cosmic Order. The amateur chemist is the "puffer" who does not understand the significance of the art. The alchemists called those who took their instructions too literally "puffers" because of their heavy use of the bellows to keep the alchemical fires burning.

The Great Work was a protracted chemical experiment that took place inside a round, closed, casserolelike urn. At the same time, corresponding changes were taking place in the soul of the alchemist. Both the psychic and physical changes had to occur or the Great Work would fail.

The Great Work was divided into three stages. At the beginning of the first stage, the alchemist had to find the stone that would eventually be purified into the Philosopher's Stone. This substance was probably a form of mercury—although it was not the pure element we know by that name.

In order to secure this raw material, the alchemist had to journey to a mine and take the substance out of the earth himself, at the proper astrological time. Aries was an especially good time in which to begin the Great Work, since Aries corresponds to the nature of raw material in being primal and unstable. Taurus and Gemini may also be suitable.

After the alchemist found the raw material, he purified it by mixing it with a secret fire and with dew. The secret fire was most likely a salt, carefully prepared to be "a fire burning without flames." The alchemist pulverized the raw material, added the fire and dew, and then placed it into the Philosophic Egg, a hermetically sealed vessel. The egg was then placed inside an athanor.

Nicholas Flamel, a fourteenth-century French alchemist, described what went on inside the egg like this:

> These two [the mercury and salt] I say, being put together in the vessel of the sepulcher, doe bite one another cruelly, and by their great poyson, and furious rage, they never leave one another from the moment they have seized on one another (if the cold hinder them not) till both of them by their slavering venom, and mortal hurts, be all of a goarebloud, over all parts of their bodies; and finally killing one another, be stewed in their proper venom, which after their death, changeth them into living and permanent water; before which time, they loose in their corruption and putrification, their natural formes, to take afterwards one onely new, more noble, and better forme.

The first sign that the alchemist was on the right track was the creation of this period, when the opposites dissolved into each other. "No generation without corruption" was an alchemical saying.

After the period of so-called black gestation described above, there would suddenly appear a volatile humid substance. This "starry aspect," as Flamel called it marked the end of the first stage of the Great Work.

At the beginning of the second stage, the alchemist added more heat in the outer furnace and athanor. Inside the egg, the mercury flew around, as if "in the belly of the wind." A rainbow of colors appeared, including green, the symbol of regeneration. This stage of the operation was known as the Peacock's Tail. The second stage ended when a whitish substance, rather like the albumen of an egg, appeared.

In the third stage, the alchemist repeated the process of uniting mercury with salt. This time, however, the mercury was purified. The red sulphur combined with the white mercury to produce the Philosopher's Stone.

Alchemical Imagery. Alchemists often illustrated and described the alchemical operation in terms of allegory. The fusion of the two opposites—mercury and salt—was described in sexual terms. The male (mercury) and the female (salt) were dissolved into one, to reemerge as purified mercury and sulphur. In alchemical art, the male and female are often pictured as having crowns during the third stage of the process. The Philosopher's Stone is pictured as a hermaphrodite. The connections between these symbols and Tantric and Gnostic thought are obvious.

The elements of mercury and sulphur were also referred to as the White Rose and the Red Rose. Green appeared during the period of Peacock's Tail (during the second stage). It was the symbol of regeneration out of the blackness.

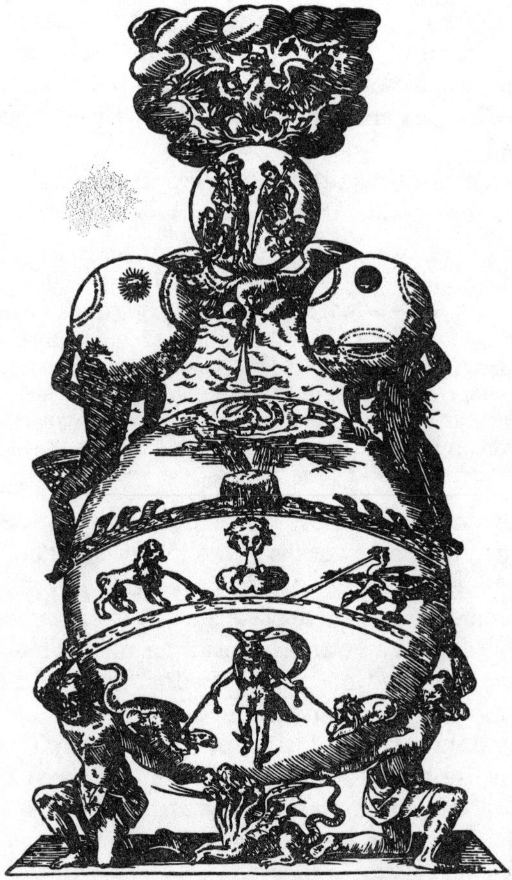

Animals figured heavily in alchemical symbolism. The black stage was represented by a fierce black dog or monster. The green serpent and red serpent represented the forming sulphur and salt. The serpent swallowing its own tail, the most common alchemical representation, stands for the eternal cycle of the universe. This is a very old symbol. Sometimes the serpent is a double one, both red and green. The green symbolizes the beginning of the Great Work and the red symbolizes the end.

The Philosopher's Stone was gold, of course, and was represented by suns and lions. The bull is often pictured, symbolic of the patience and determination with which the student must approach the work.

Medieval Alchemists. Some of the first Westerners to write on alchemy were students of Arabic cultures. Robert of Chester, who lived in the eleventh century, translated the Koran into Latin. He took part in the Crusades, on one of which he witnessed an alchemical operation in the East.

Artephus was a Hermetic philosopher who claimed to have discovered the Elixir and to be 1,025 years old. He died in the twelfth century. Some people said he was Apollonius of Tyana. He wrote about astrology as well as alchemy and published a work on the language of birds.

Michael Scot, who was primarily known as an astrologer, was also an alchemist. He apparently combined alchemy with some magical practices, which was common practice throughout the Middle Ages.

The best-known medieval alchemist, however, was Nicholas Flamel, whose instructions for the Great Work are quoted above. Flamel lived from 1330 to 1417; he was born in France and did most of his work in Paris. He claimed to have discovered an old book written by Abraham the Jew, in which the alchemical secrets were expounded. To help him understand the old book, Flamel journeyed to Spain to consult the Jewish Kabbalists.

In Spain he learned the secret of transmuting base metals into gold and then making the Elixir of Life. Many say that he is still alive somewhere. He was last reported seen at the Paris Opera in 1761.

All through the Middle Ages and for several centuries thereafter, some alchemists would claim to have discovered how to make gold. These were almost all charlatans, or self-deluded at least. There were a great many failed experiments, so many that Chaucer scorned the art:

> This cursed craft whoso wil exercise,
> He shal no gold have that may him suffise,
> For al the gold he spendeth thereaboute
> He lose shal, thereof, I have no doute.

The Occult Reformation (1500–1700)

Traditional history teaches that in the sixteenth and seventeenth centuries Europe gradually divided into Protestant and Catholic camps. But there was a third major religious group that also gained strength during this period. The third religion called for the abolition of religious sectarianism, for the advancement of science, and for the search for Divine truth through the mystic experience. Its proponents were Hermetic philosophers and alchemists. Its followers, persecuted by both Protestants and Catholics, met in secret and circulated their subversive ideas underground.

Subversive Utopianism. The "Occult Reformation" was a major influence, not only on modern occultism, but on modern science and politics. Many of the pioneers of modern thought—Kepler, Newton, Copernicus, and Descartes, for example—were involved with Hermetic philosophy during their careers.

Giordano Bruno. Bruno was an Italian philosopher, alchemist, and founder of a new "Hermetic Egyptian" religion. He traveled throughout Europe in the second half of the sixteenth century, preaching the need for religious and social reform. He believed that reform would come through contemplation of the Egyptian Hermetic mysteries and the reinstitution of good magic. He formed a secret Lutheran sect called the "Giordanisti," which attempted to combine Hermetic and Kabbalistic ideas with Lutheranism.

Bruno was always controversial and was often persecuted. He was a political agitator as well, vocal in his opposition to the growing power of the Hapsburg dynasty (who supported Catholic orthodoxy). He visited Elizabethan England and influenced the chivalric cults of Elizabeth that were formed by such young men as Sir Philip Sydney.

Bruno advocated the heliocentric theory of the universe at a time when Copernicus was still controversial, and taught that close observation of Nature was the key to knowledge. He was burned at the stake by the Inquisition in the year 1600.

John Dee and Edward Kelley. John Dee was the semiofficial astrologer at the court of Elizabeth I of England. He was also a mathematician, philosopher, and student of the Kabbalah. In the early years of his career, he enjoyed royal favor and travelled throughout Europe, lecturing on the stars and other subjects. He owed his influence at court to his pupils, especially to Philip Sydney.

But John Dee was not content with astronomical learning. Lewis Spence describes the mental state which was later to give Dee so much trouble.

> Living in comparative solitude—practicing astrology for bread, but studying alchemy for pleasure—brooding over Talmudic mysteries . . . immersed in contemplation of wonders which he longed to penetrate—and dazzled by visions of the Elixir of Life and the Philosopher's Stone, Dee soon attained to such a condition of mystic exaltation that his visions became to him as realities, and he persuaded himself that he was favored of the Invisible.

Dee's persuasions were strengthened by the appearance in his life of Edward Kelley, who was probably psychic, but was almost certainly one of the great con artists of all times. Kelley soon had Dee conferring daily with the spirits, who kept promising, but never delivering, the secret of the Philosopher's Stone. Kelley enmeshed Dee in systems of magic. (Some of their revelations are detailed in chapter four.)

In 1583, Dee, Kelley, and their families crossed to the Continent, where they began a protracted tour through some of the great houses of Europe. Various noblemen funded their searches for the gold-making substances. At least one noble, the Polish Count Laski, wasted his fortune in this manner. By 1588 the pair was established in Prague. There Dee came into contact with many other occult and Hermetic thinkers.

Dee and Kelley eventually split over the issue of sharing their wives (it was Kelley's idea). Dee returned to England, where he was given a minor post. He died in relative poverty and obscurity in 1604.

Robert Fludd. Fludd was one of the greatest exponents of Hermetic philosophy in Elizabethan and Jacobean England. He was born in 1574. Fludd studied with John Dee as well as in centers of learning throughout the Continent. After returning to England, Fludd published a great many writings on Hermeticism, alchemy, magnetism, and other subjects.

Michael Maier was a German alchemist who was a personal friend of both John Dee and Robert Fludd. He was the personal physician of Rudolph II, emperor of Bohemia.

The Rosicrucian Connection. Prague in the late sixteenth century was a center of occult learning. The official policy of the emperor, Rudolph II, was toleration toward Protestants, Jews, alchemists, and other heretics. The emperor outfitted his palace at Prague with alchemical furnaces, astronomical observatories, and other occult and scientific paraphernalia.

Prague was also a center for Protestant conspiracy. Many of Rudolph's nobles were members of the Protestant Bohemian Church. One of these nobles, a count named Rosenberg, played host to Dee and Kelley for a while.

Rudolph II died in 1612. He had been a Hapsburg, a member of the most powerful dynasty in Europe. The Hapsburgs were strong Catholics, and with the death of Rudolph, the toleration in Prague ended. The crown was given to Rudolph's brother Matthias, who was an old man. The Protestants could see that the next emperor was likely to be Archduke Ferdinand of Styria, a fanatical Catholic. The Protestants, therefore, were determined to place a Protestant on the Bohemian throne. Their candidate was Frederick V, the Elector of the Palatinate, a German Calvinist state. Frederick's position was apparently strengthened in 1613 by his marriage to Elizabeth, daughter of James I of England. Most Europeans interpreted this marriage as an expression of sympathy by James for the Protestant cause.

This was the political atmosphere in which the "Rosicrucian Manifestos" first appeared. The manifestos were two short pamphlets, published at Cassel in 1614 and 1615.

The first pamphlet was called *The Fama of the Fraternity of the Meritorious Order of the Rosy Cross Addressed to the Learned in General and the Governors of Europe*. It claimed to be a message from a secret brotherhood of adepts who were concerned for the moral future of mankind. Its hero was a knightly personage named Christian Rosencreutz, or C.R.C. C.R.C. was a magician of the highest rank, who had travelled in the Holy Land. The *Fama* called for the establishment of an order of illuminated men of science who would

help bring about religious reform and promote scientific progress.

The second pamphlet was called *Confessions of the Rosicrucian Fratern* and also was addressed to the learned men of Europe. The *Confesio* w more blatantly Protestant. It referred, for example, to the "asinine brayin of the Pope.

A third Rosicrucian document was an alchemical romance called *The Chemical Wedding of Christian Rosencreutz*. This work was written by Johann Valentin Andreae, who was the grandson of a famous Lutheran theologian and a writer on religious and political reform. Andreae might very well have been the author of the *Fama* and *Confesio* as well.

The *Fama* and the *Confesio* made frequent mention of a "secret doctrine" that was to be transmitted to the members of the Rosicrucian Brotherhood. Upon examination, the "secret doctrine" turns out to be a rewriting of the *Monas hieroglyphica*, the major alchemical work of John Dee.

We do not know whether Dee intended this political and reformist interpretation of his work. It is certainly within the realm of possibility that Dee and Kelley actually founded a secret Protestant society during their stay in Prague in the 1580s. During their Prague visit, Dee and Kelley were trying to make money by any means available; and Kelley would not have been blind to the possibilities in a chivalric order.

However, it is much more likely that the Rosicrucian Brotherhood was a myth. The *Fama* and *Confesio* read like allegorical romances rather than factual accounts. Andreae himself described the "*ludibrium* of the fictitious Rosicrucian fraternity." The word *ludibrium* is Latin for "a joke," or "a farce."

Whether or not the Rosicrucian Brotherhood existed, a great many people wanted it to exist. The response, both pro and con, was amazing. Attacks on the Rosicrucians were led by the chemist Libavius. The Rosicrucians were then defended by Michael Maier and Robert Fludd.

A great many scholars tried to get in touch with the Rosicrucians, mostly by publishing favorable articles about them. But none of them was contacted by an adept or initiated into the Brotherhood. So Fludd solved the problem by starting an English branch of the Rosicrucian Brotherhood on his own.

Frances A. Yates, in her book *The Rosicrucian Enlightenment*, demonstrated that "Rosicrucianism" was an actual movement of people committed to religious and political reform of the world. Its followers combined evangelical Christianity with alchemical symbols and Utopian ideals. Rosicrucianism was a bridge between the Hermetic and magical ideas of the Renaissance and the scientific discoveries of the seventeenth and eighteenth centuries.

The "Rosicrucian Manifestos" appeared during the time when attempts to place Frederick V on the throne were gathering strength among the Protestant nobles of Bohemia. The hopes of these conspirators were dashed in 1620, when Frederick lost the Battle of White Mountain. Frederick and his Queen, Elizabeth of England, went into exile at The Hague. Their court in exile continued to be a center of Protestant and reformist thought.

While it is extremely unlikely that there was ever a Rosicrucian society, Rosicrucianism had a direct influence on other secret brotherhoods, most notably the Freemasons.

Comenius. Johann Amos Komensky (Comenius) was born in 1592 in Bohemia. He was a Protestant pastor, a member of the Bohemian Brethren, a mystical branch of the Hussite Protestants. He was a student of Robert Fludd and Michael Maier and was one of the many young scholars who responded with enthusiasm to the news of the Rosicrucian Brotherhood.

Comenius developed a system of "pansophia," or universal wisdom, based on Hermetic, alchemical, and mystic ideas. His thought relied heavily on the doctrine of correspondences. He began thinking about macro-microcosmic theory under the influence of his friend Johann Valentin Andreae. Like Andreae, Komensky supported the movement to place Frederick on the Bohemian throne.

Even after the defeat of Frederick, Comenius continued to hope for universal reform. His book *The Labyrinth of the World* is one of the great classics of Utopian literature.

Jakob Boehme (1575–1624), the great German mystic, was not an occultist, but his ideas had a great influence on later occult movements. He used alchemical symbols to explain the nature of the Cosmos and to relate the Cosmos to the spiritual state of Man. His system of thought was based on the Christian scriptures, but he did not adhere to orthodox doctrine. He was a Lutheran, and was frequently denounced from Lutheran pulpits.

The Freemasons. Most of us know the Freemasons as men in funny hats who, like overgrown Boy Scouts, get their fun from marching in parades and exchanging secret handshakes, and in the process do valuable charitable fundraising work. Being a Freemason nowadays is no more subversive than belonging to the Rotary Club.

It was not so in the early days of the Masonic movement. During the fifteenth, sixteenth, and seventeenth centuries, Masons had to remain secret for fear of their lives. The witch craze was at its height. Monarchies were all-powerful. Meetings of prominent citizens for the purpose of talking about universal reform were naturally suspect. All over Europe, especially in Germany, the persecutions of witches can be directly linked to the strength of secret societies in the region.

We are not sure when the Freemasons began. The Masonic tradition states that a secret organization of builders and architects had existed since the early Egyptian dynasties. These societies guarded geometry and other professional secrets of architecture and passed them down through generations of adepts.

According to the Masons, temples were models of cosmic order, embodiments of Divine Wisdom. This idea, we have seen, was taught by the priests of Hermes in Egypt around the time of Christ. Masonic history teaches that Solomon's Temple was the culmination of the builder's art. Solomon, you will recall, was supposed to have had great occult and magical powers.

The societies of Masons continued throughout the Middle Ages, being responsible for the building of the great medieval cathedrals. They had many connections with the Templars, who were also obsessed with the plan of Solomon's Temple.

All these societies were made up of practical Masons—that is, people who actually were employed as stonemasons, builders, or architects. There is no evidence to suggest that they were substantially different from the other medieval guilds of weavers, goldsmiths, etc. The medieval masonic guilds were religious in character, but then, so was society as a whole.

Modern Freemasonry is speculative rather than practical. Few of its members are connected to the building trades. It is distinguished by its emphasis on orders and degrees, its chivalric ideals, its promise of secret knowledge, and its mystical symbolism.

The history of speculative Masonry begins in the "Rosicrucian" period—the end of the sixteenth and beginning of the seventeenth centuries. The earliest record of a Masonic initiation is on May 20, 1641. On that

date, Robert Moray joined a lodge in Edinburgh, Scotland. Another early initiate was Elias Ashmole, who was admitted into a lodge in Lancashire on October 16, 1646.

Both Ashmole and Moray were supporters of the Rosicrucian movement and founding members of the Royal Society, the first society exclusively devoted to the advancement of learning and science. Their respective lodges had clearly been in existence before they joined, but theirs are the earliest proven admissions. Probably such lodges went back only as far as Elizabethan England. Frances Yates says that these early secret societies were associated with cults of Queen Elizabeth and with the revival of chivalric ideals by such courtiers as Sir Philip Sydney. John Dee was an important influence.

Masonic lodges in various cities kept in contact with each other as their members travelled around Europe. In 1717, the Grand Lodge of England was formed. This was the first central governing body of the Masonic fraternity. Ireland formed a Grand Lodge in 1725. Scotland formed one in 1736. The movement spread rapidly in France.

During the eighteenth century, the Freemasons gained strong political influence. Although technically members of all religions could belong, the lodges tended to be anti-Catholic. Some members were Protestants. Even more seem to have been followers of magical, Hermetic, and Kabbalistic traditions. The anti-Catholic stance of early Masonry was often a result of the strong anti-Masonic stance taken by the Roman Catholic Church, especially the Jesuits.

The Catholic Church did much to propagate rumors that the inner circles of the Masons were devil-worshipers, occultists, or sorcerers. Since Masons are not allowed to publicize the secrets of their group, the rumors still continue to spread. It is impossible to establish the truth. Some of the more paranoid versions of the modern Masonic myth are presented in the "Occult Bible" section of this book. But it is safe to say that the majority of Masons have nothing whatever to do with the occult, except in their use of occult symbols in their rituals. Most of them regard their society merely as a philanthropic and social organization.

The Family of Love. This secret society was active in the Netherlands in the late sixteenth century. Its members maintained outward loyalty either to Protestantism or Catholicism but were secretly loyal only to the Family. The doctrines of the sect were Hermetic, alchemical, and mystical. The Family of Love is of great importance to the history of occult secret societies because many of its prominent members were printers. The DeBry firm of printers, for example, were Familists. They were also the publishers of the occultists Fludd and Maier. Christopher Plantin, a printer from Antwerp, was also a member of the family. Printers were, of course, extremely important in spreading Hermetic and reformist ideas throughout Europe.

The Witchcraft Trials. In the mass trials of witches, the Catholic Church and its Protestant rivals set out to demonstrate that they still held life and death power over a substantial portion of the human race.

No one knows how many witches were exterminated. Pennethorne Hughes estimates that over nine million people were killed in the course of three centuries. In Geneva, a bishop burned five hundred witches in three months. That was in 1515, just a few years before the Reformation. The bishop was following the instructions of Pope Innocent VIII, who had issued a papal bull against witchcraft in 1484.

Innocent's bull specifically recommended a book called *Malleus Maleficarum* (Hammer Against Sorcery), an official manual on witchcraft and demons. The *Malleus* listed many known demons and gave blow-by-blow accounts of how to extract confessions from witches. It was the textbook of the Inquisition. The *Malleus* officially identified any act of dissension with the church as heresy that must be stamped out immediately in the name of truth.

The *Malleus* arrived conveniently at a time when much of Catholic Europe needed a strong punishing arm. Sedition was breaking out everywhere. There were peasant revolts in the Rhine country. The German princes showed signs of discontent. The heretics had not been stamped out in France or Holland. And witchcraft, the religion of masses of peasants, was stronger than ever.

The church's new militancy changed the nature of witchcraft. It became more openly defiant of the church. Parodies of the Mass were expanded—the Black Mass reached its most polished form.

Not all the witches confessed under torture. Some admitted their practices in the clerical courts. The public hangings and burnings of witches were popular spectacles attended by mobs. The burnings were often preceded by whippings, water tortures, and other methods of giving the witch a taste of things to come.

Jane Shore (1445–1527), the mistress of Edward IV of England, was accused of witchcraft for political reasons. Lord Hastings, her co-conspirator, was beheaded. Jane Shore got off with severe penance, including having to parade through the streets of London in a white shift, the sort reserved by the Inquisition for heretics on their way to the stake.

The great occultist Cornelius Agrippa was popularly supposed to be a sorcerer. He defended a woman accused of witchcraft in 1518. Agrippa was never brought to trial, but he made many enemies among priests and had frequent brushes with the Inquisition.

The witch-hunters of Spain were the most zealous. The first *auto-da-fé* (act of faith), a ritualized killing of witches, took place in 1527, when thirty women were burned. Several more were burned in 1527 at Navarre.

In Italy, charges of witchcraft were brought against certain groups in Lombardy. In 1523 the church began to exterminate these witches, who were probably political activists. Northern Italy was a center for antichurch propaganda at that time.

In France the nobility kept the Inquisition out until after the middle of the sixteenth century. But in 1564, four persons were executed at Poitiers. More witches were burned for being wolves, or changing themselves into wolves, or attending the Sabbath riding on wolves. France was having a serious wolf problem in all its rural areas that bordered on forest land.

From May to August of 1609, the Inquisition set up court in the Basque provinces of Spain and France and tried over six hundred people. Of these, sixty to eighty were burned at the stake. Eight priests also were condemned, but five of them escaped and only three were roasted. The Basque trials are especially noteworthy for their strong sexual connotations. The judge who officiated, de Lancre, kept lascivious detailed accounts of the witches' confessions.

The Catholic Church concentrated the efforts of the Inquisition in Germany, a hotbed of Protestant heresy. In Würzburg, Prince-Bishop George II burned more than six hundred people as witches between 1625 and 1630. Würzburg was a place where Lutheranism was gaining power, and it was no coincidence that among those accused of witchcraft at Würzburg were prominent citizens of the middle and upper classes.

The Protestants were no better than the Catholics. John Calvin burned witches in Geneva. The Puritan Commonwealth leaders of England employed a witchfinder named Matthew Hopkins to help them rout out seeds of sedition and evil.

Both Protestants and Catholics genuinely believed in the existence of evil demons and felt that they had the right to torture people on Earth as God would someday torture them in Hell. It was a very convenient belief.

The public roastings stirred up many of the perversities that had been lurking in the church throughout the Middle Ages. The case of the nuns of Loudon (see chapter four) and their extraordinary "possession" by the priest Urbain Grandier is a vile little tale that well illustrates the mentality of the time. Grandier had spoken libels against Cardinal Richelieu—or at least the cardinal said he had. Grandier was executed in 1634.

The Salem Witchcraft Trials. Those sturdy Pilgrim forefathers who appear on school bulletin boards at Thanksgiving were mostly members of Protestant sects unacceptable to Protestants in Europe. The Pilgrims were noted for their rigidity. Their stern morals were complemented by a larger vision of the state as a commonwealth of citizens run for the glory of God.

The original voyagers on the *Mayflower* were supplemented by further migrations of English Protestants, who came to escape Cromwell's regime. After the Restoration, more Puritans migrated, so that they could live in a state where their church was the official one.

The New England witch hysteria did not get underway until late in the seventeenth century, and it was orchestrated by two ministers, Increase Mather and his son Cotton.

As Lewis Spence put it, "The fanaticism and diabolical cruelty of these two men has probably never been equalled in the history of human persecution." Spence wrote those words before Hitler and Stalin, but he was right in his general assessment.

The Mathers were people of power. Increase was the president of Harvard College. Cotton taught there and preached on Sundays in Boston. Both of them believed the Bible must be loyally, literally, unquestionably obeyed. They were Soldiers of the Cross. The Bible said, "Thou shalt not suffer a witch to live," which they thought left no room for argument.

The first outbreaks of witchcraft caused only small ripples. In 1688, an Irish washerwoman was hanged for somehow contaminating the children of a prominent citizen. In Salem, some black servants who were probably practicing voodoo were charged with sorcery.

After the Salem arrests, people began to get hysterical. They appealed to the governor, who called in the Mathers as scholars and resident demon experts. Cotton consulted his Bible and started lighting the fires. Hundreds of people were to be tortured or killed before the fires went out.

Cotton Mather circulated a book called *Late Memorable Providences Relating to Witchcraft and Possession*. The hysteria grew. A minister named George Burroughs was killed for stating he did not believe in witches. Several dogs and cats were burned as well, accused of being demonic familiars.

It did not take long for people to begin to realize that without its witches the population would be decimated. But by this time Cotton and Increase were in full stride. *Wonders of the Invisible World* and *A Further Account of the Trials of the New England Witches* appeared in their due course.

In the town of Andover, the Mathers ordered so many people arrested for witchcraft that the justice of the peace refused to arrest any more. He was himself arrested. The Mathers made a mistake, however, in trying to accuse the governor's wife. By then the governor had had enough.

People who had made witchcraft accusations withdrew them. Many signed confessions saying they had been deluded by the Mathers. An anti-Mather tract, *More Wonders of the Invisible World*, was circulated. Cotton Mather ordered the book publicly burned. But he lost political power soon after, and by 1700 the persecution was over. Both the Mathers lived to ripe old ages and never regretted any of their war service in the armies of the Lord.

The Occult Enlightenment (1700–1800)

The eighteenth was an optimistic century. Ideas that had been simmering in secret since the Renaissance began to circulate openly. Secular ideas triumphed over religious ones. The Industrial Revolution began and seemed to promise a golden age. People believed they were living in the Age of Reason, when the light of knowledge would finally triumph over the darkness of popery and superstition, and when technology would usher in a glorious work-free future for the human race.

The most optimistic ideas of all were those of the republican agitators who campaigned in cities all over Europe and America. Occultists were in the forefront of this political activity. Occult brotherhoods existed everywhere. These societies had large middle-class memberships and were hotbeds of revolutionary discussion.

The century ended with two great political revolutions, one in America and one in France. Both of these revolutions had occult dimensions. Occultism and free thought were very closely linked in an era when the old order was represented by authoritarianism and conservative religion.

Mystics and Charlatans. Occultism was a craze during the eighteenth century. It still had all the appeal of the wicked and forbidden, but the church had lost much of its power to burn at the stake, so that the forbidden ideas could be played with at less risk. Fewer people than ever believed in a literal hell, or in any of the literal doctrines of established religion.

In this atmosphere of intellectual freedom, new religious ideas developed, ideas that attempted to reconcile beliefs about the soul with new scientific discoveries. The major tenet of the new beliefs was that Man was divine by nature. This theory directly contradicted the official doctrine of original sin, that Man was by nature evil. The new view of Man helped the spread of democratic ideas and directly influenced the Romantic movement in literature.

Emmanuel Swedenborg. Swedenborg was one of the foremost scientists and inventors of his day and also one of the greatest mystic thinkers in Western history. He was born in Stockholm, Sweden, on January 29, 1688, and was educated as a mathematician and engineer.

Up until the age of fifty-five, Swedenborg devoted his life to scientific and technical work. His accomplishments were amazing. He drew an early plan for a flying machine. He formulated theories about atoms, geology, and physics.

Even when he was immersed in science, however, Swedenborg was interested in philosophical questions. In 1734, for example, he published a work on the relationship between the body and soul. He believed the secret would be found in the close study of anatomy. Some of his theories about the function of the brain anticipated the views of modern psychologists. He was fascinated with dreams. His *Journal of Dreams*, which he published in 1743, shocked many people by its blatant eroticism.

On April 7, 1744, Swedenborg had his first mystic vision of Christ. After that he gave up his scientific studies, retired from his royal patronage job on half-pay, and devoted himself to mystic contemplation. He published over thirty volumes of mystic writings.

Swedenborg spent most of this later stage of his life in states of mystic trance, wrestling with evil spirits or talking with angels. Many people simply write off his last thirty years as an unfortunate case of a great mind going senile. Others—such as the poet William Blake—considered Swedenborg a mighty prophet and seer.

In his mystic trances, Swedenborg visited both heaven and hell. He conversed with angels who taught him the doctrines of his New Church. The New Church was not to be a new organized religion but a spiritual brotherhood. He called his philosophy Illuminism because it emphasized the need for Inner Light.

Swedenborg taught a doctrine of correspondences—that everything in the tangible world was but a symbol of intangible (spiritual) reality. Swedenborg derived this doctrine largely from his reading of Jakob Boehme.

Swedenborg believed that humans at the beginning of the world were directly in touch with the divine, possessing both Divine Love and Divine Wisdom. But the flow of these virtues to the physical man had been impeded by sin. The flow of divine energy could be reestablished through the imagination.

Swedenborg believed himself to be in constant communication with the spiritual plane. He often visited other planets during his trances, describing their inhabitants, flora, and fauna. His scientific training had taught him habits of close observation, so he described many of his visions in great detail.

Societies of Swedenborgians were being formed even before the great mystic's death in 1772. His works were translated into English from 1778. Swedenborgian churches are still in existence, both in Europe and the United States.

Louis Claude de St. Martin. St. Martin was a French mystic and writer. He was born in 1743 into a noble family and was given a first-class education. He joined the army and, shortly thereafter, was initiated into a Masonic lodge, which had adopted a Kabbalistic rite. St. Martin also studied the writings of Swedenborg. In 1771, he resigned his army post to devote himself to philosophical writings.

St. Martin's teachings owe much to Swedenborg and Boehme, whose works he translated into French. He taught that Man contained within him the divine light, of which he is usually unconscious. This divine spark could be fanned into the flame of inner light through mystic contemplation and rejection of materialism.

St. Martin founded a sect called the Martinists, which had great influence within the eighteenth-century Masonic lodges. He was also famous for being able to fascinate women and for being scandalously involved with several noblewomen.

In 1789, St. Martin was arrested during the Reign of Terror because of his aristocratic background. But his Freemason connection saved his life. He died in 1803, after publishing several more philosophical and mystical works.

Comte de Saint Germain. This mysterious character showed up in Paris in the eighteenth century, claiming to have found the Elixir of Life and to be hundreds of years old. Many people believed him, and he moved among the best circles in Paris. He also had extensive contacts among the Freemasons, who initiated him into their highest degrees.

His birth and background were unknown. Some said he was a Portuguese Jew who had grown wealthy through trade. Others said he was the son of Prince Ragoczy of Transylvania. Whoever he was, he was immensely wealthy and gifted. He composed music, compounded medicines, and knew the secrets of enlarging jewels. (A skeptic might speculate that his wealth came from jewel smuggling. Saint Germain often did his noble patrons the favor of exchanging their paltry emeralds, rubies, and diamonds for larger, more brilliant gems.)

Saint Germain claimed to have travelled widely. From 1737 to 1742, he was at the court of the Shah of Persia. From there he went to England and to Vienna. In 1755 he went to India.

Saint Germain's political activities are also mysterious. In 1743 he was arrested in England as a Jacobite spy. By 1757 he had worked his way into

Louis XV's graces and travelled around Europe on the king's behalf. Louis XV sent him on various diplomatic missions. He was said to have helped the conspiracy to place Catherine II on the Russian throne. These facts would seem to make him a staunch Royalist.

Saint Germain was also a high-degree Mason, though modern Masons discredit this. His name appears in the lists of several occult brotherhoods. He was said to be a Rosicrucian, a member of the "Knights of Light" (a templar order), the founder of the Order of St. Joachim in Bohemia, and a follower of the Rite of the Philalethes. This latter group was charged by the Jesuits with immorality, republicanism, and anarchy.

The most startling claim about Saint Germain was that he was an adept who was immortal, one of the Great White Brotherhood who was really directing the future of the world. He did his best to keep such rumors afloat. He established a splendid temple, in which initiates were given a mystic vision of himself as a deity. He supposedly could heal people by touch. Although Saint Germain's death was recorded at Schleswig in 1784, he appeared several times after that. His most notable posthumous appearance was to Marie Antoinette, warning her to flee from the French Revolution. Many occultists claim he is still alive today, somewhere, still presumably pulling the strings.

Cagliostro. Cagliostro claimed to have been initiated into the mysteries of the universe by Saint Germain himself. Perhaps he merely learned from Saint Germain how easy it was to swindle the credulous.

Cagliostro did all he could to keep his own background mysterious. But it seems likely that he was the son of a Peter Balsamo of Palermo. His youth was spent in and out of trouble with the police. He also learned the apothecary trade in a Benedictine convent. This was the beginning of his interest in alchemy. He persuaded a goldsmith named Marano to pay sixty ounces of gold in exchange for the secret of the Philosopher's Stone. With this money he escaped to Messina, where he began calling himself a count.

At Messina he met a mysterious oriental named Althotas. In Althotas's company he visited Egypt, where he was supposedly initiated into the Hermetic mysteries in a vault under one of the pyramids. After that he journeyed with Althotas around Asia and Africa, studying with various adepts. (One of the most curious features of Cagliostro's history is that it is the same as that of Christian Rosencreutz, the hero of the "Rosicrucian Manifestos.")

After returning to Italy, Cagliostro married a beautiful woman named Lorenza Feliciani. They travelled throughout Europe, including two visits to London, where Cagliostro was initiated into a Masonic Lodge.

Also in London, Cagliostro found an old manuscript in an obscure bookstore. The manuscript supposedly outlined the Rite of Egyptian

Masonry. This Masonic rite included women as well as men. He and Lorenza had a great deal of success with this rite in Masonic lodges around Europe. They collected high initiation fees, in return for which they staged their mystic show.

After leaving England, Cagliostro and Lorenza claimed to have been initiated by the Comte de Saint Germain. Like Saint Germain, Cagliostro was widely believed to be a miracle-healer and to possess the Elixir of Life. Another similarity was that both men gave gold and free medical help to the poor.

Cagliostro and Lorenza moved to Paris, where they lived in mystery and luxury, performing their Egyptian Rite and transmuting gold for the rich. He was implicated in the infamous Affair of the Diamond Necklace. He also uttered several prophecies, predicting the fall of the Bastille and the French Revolution. In the 1780s in Paris, both were fairly safe bets, especially from someone who moved widely Masonic circles

Cagliostro and Lorenza moved on to Rome, where they made the mistake of trying to establish a Masonic lodge. They were arrested by the Inquisition, and both died in prison.

Mesmer (1734–1815) was the discoverer of animal magnetism, or *mesmerism*. He moved in the same circles as Saint Germain and Cagliostro. A detailed account of his life and work is found in chapter three.

Occult Brotherhoods. The craze for joining secret societies, which had begun with seventeenth-century Rosicrucianism, reached its height in the eighteenth century. It was very common for one person to belong to several different groups. Some were mystical or magical in purpose. Many more were political. All the secret societies made great use of rituals, degrees, and chivalric symbolism. The rising middle classes romanticized and then imitated aristocratic ideals of the past.

The societies maintained such theatrical secrecy that details about them are very hard to prove. Many of the groups claimed to have "unknown heads"—ageless adepts who were guiding the spiritual evolution of mankind. Among the groups that have been lost in historical muddle are the Canons of the Holy Sepulcher, the Knights of Providence, the Mopses, the African Brothers, the Knights of Light, the Beneficent Knights of the Holy City, the Canons of the Holy City of Jerusalem, the Clergy of Nicona in the Island of Cyprus, the Knights of St. John the Evangelist, and the Clergy of Auvergne.

Several attempts were made to revive the Templars, with those responsible claiming to be direct or spiritual descendants of De Molay, the Templar Grand Master who was discredited and stripped of power in the thirteenth century. Templar orders appeared in France, Germany, Sweden, Denmark, and Poland through the eighteenth and nineteenth centuries.

The Scottish Rite. The Scottish Rite is an order that is Masonic in character, having several degrees for its initiates and promising mystical knowledge to its inner believers. The rite was established among Masons in France in 1754. It spread quickly, especially to Germany and America. It is still in existence and has lodges in most countries.

The Illuminati. From the beginning of the Renaissance, various small groups of occultists called themselves Illuminati, a name that simply means "the enlightened ones." Like the other secret societies, these groups gradually evolved from being primarily magical and Kabbalistic in their teachings to being political or social.

The best-known Illuminati sect was founded in 1776 by Adam Weishaupt, a young professor of law at Igolstadt, Germany. There is much controversy about Weishaupt's purpose in founding the group. He said he wanted to combine philanthropy with mysticism. Others claim he was simply after power and was able to control his followers' minds by proper use of secret handshakes and by promises of secret occult knowledge. He used many of the rituals and passwords of Freemasonry.

Whatever Weishaupt's intentions, the sect was strongly revolutionary in character. Weishaupt attracted many young men from wealthy families into the group. Soon the influence of the group spread through the courts of the German princes. In 1780, a Baron von Knigge, an occultist and revolutionary, joined Weishaupt, and the group's influence spread further.

In 1782, von Knigge and Weishaupt made an attempt to take over the whole Freemason organization. This attempt failed, and the Masonic leaders reported their revolutionary tendencies to the Bavarian government. An edict was issued against them in 1785, and Weishaupt fled for his life.

That is, as far as recorded history goes, the end of the Illuminati. But not according to many occultists. Their interpretations, which involve George Washington and Thomas Jefferson as well as Aleister Crowley and Timothy Leary, are best reserved for the "Occult Bible" section.

Occultism in the Industrial Age (1800–1900)

During the nineteenth century the middle classes achieved economic and political power. Middle-class power was based on the Industrial Revolution. New technology made mass production possible. Trade of mass-produced goods was worldwide. Most middle-class people glorified the technology that made their new affluence possible. The nineteenth century was heralded as the Age of Progress.

During the two preceding centuries, occult thought had been radical compared to the prevailing beliefs of society. Occultism had been associated with middle-class political movements in the eighteenth century, but now it became a respectable middle-class faith, though a minority one. By the end of the nineteenth century it had become relatively conservative. Advances in comparative religion, archeology, anthropology, biology, and psychology made prevailing occult beliefs seem simplistic and naive.

The new conservatism of occultists was reflected in their obsession with occult history, their need to trace their beliefs to remote antiquity and thus to make occultism an established faith. Nineteenth-century occultists concentrated on establishing proper ritual, dogma, and tradition. There were revivals of the Druids and the Rosicrucians as well as of sorcery and witchcraft. Nineteenth-century occult "historians" were responsible for many of the myths—such as that of Atlantis—that form the canon of modern occult belief.

Occult Romanticism. Romanticism was a literary and artistic movement that swept over Europe in the late eighteenth and early nineteenth centuries. The tenets of the movement were an idealization of human nature, an emphasis on mystic communion with natural forces, and a nostalgia for the pre-Industrial past, especially for the Middle Ages.

The Romantic movement was accompanied by a revival of interest in the occult. In a sense, all the Romantics were mystics. But a great many of them worked with specifically occult material. The "Occult Fiction" chapter of this book contains summaries of their work.

The New Druids. The myth of the "noble savage" was an important element of Romantic thought. According to this myth, humans in their "uncivilized" state are in more direct communion with divine forces than are people who are trammeled by laws and religion.

Among the English Romantics, the belief grew that the Druids had been the "noble savages" of the British Isles. Stonehenge and other megaliths, where the Druids were said to have worshipped, were supposed to be evidence of a Golden Age, when "natural religion" had prevailed. (Modern archeologists have exploded this view, dating the megaliths to several centuries before the Druids.)

Among the first books to expound the new theories of Druidism was William Cooke's *An Enquiry into the Druidical and Patriarchal Religion*, which was published in 1754. The new Druids were officially organized in 1781; their founder, Henry Hurle, was a Freemason.

But the real mania began in 1784, when Edward Jones, a Welsh scholar, published *Musical and Poetical Relics of the Welsh Bards*. Jones's book included translations of a sixth-century Welsh poet named Taliesen. Jones admitted he found the meaning of much of Taliesen's work to be obscure.

Occultists, however, delight in the obscure. Another writer, Rowland Jones, already had suggested a Kabbalistic interpretation of the old Welsh writings. This idea was taken up by another Welshman, Edward Williams, who called himself Iolo Morganwg. According to him, the work of Taliesen contained a complete mystical system, an "inner doctrine" that had been handed down from Pythagoras through Merlin.

Iolo invaded an assembly of genuine Welsh folk poets called the Eisteddfod. The Eisteddfod had existed all through the Middle Ages, but had not enacted Stonehenge or any other religious rituals. Iolo Morganwg changed all that. He invented a long list of "Druid" rituals. In 1792 he built a stone circle on Primrose Hill in London and enacted the "ancient" drama. The celebrants danced around a stone altar and invoked the sun, moon, and stars.

The so-called "traditional" costume of the Druids first appeared in *Costumes of the Original Inhabitants of the British Isles*, published in 1815. The "archdruid's breastplate" and other regalia bear a rather suspicious resemblance to the robes of various Masonic orders.

A great many figures of the English Romantic movement were caught up in the craze for Druids. Among these were William Owen Pugh and the engraver William Sharp, both friends of William Blake.

Druidic organizations continued to be founded. One group, the British Circle of the Universal Bond, claims to have been organized in 1717 in Wales. This group has also claimed that Blake was one of its chieftains. In 1833, the Ancient Order of Druids split. One half abandoned its religious pretensions and became a charitable organization. The other group continued its mystic pursuits. One twentieth-century member of this second group was Winston Churchill, who was initiated in 1908.

Druidism reached its most absurd extremes in Victorian times. One Druid, Dr. William Price, was fond of appearing in an eccentric costume consisting of a white tunic, a red vest, and green trousers, wearing fox skins on his head in turbanlike fashion. Another Druid, Owen Morgan, attempted to reconcile Druidism and Methodism. He claimed that Taliesen was really Jesus Christ. Morgan also prayed to the Hindu goddess Kali.

The "revived" Druidism in England was responsible for some of the most inconsistent myths in modern occultism. Over the nineteenth century, the Druidic legend became jumbled with the Isis/Osiris story, the Atlantis legend, the Arthurian romances, and Hermetic philosophy. Taliesen has been identified as Merlin, Mercury, Hermes Trismegistus, Pythagoras, and extraterrestrial visitors. Since few of these beliefs have any proven historical basis, I have discussed them in the "Occult Bible" section of this book.

William Blake. A visionary and mystic, Blake was one of the finest artists and poets in history. It would be unfair to call him an occultist, for he subscribed to no belief system except his own. His system amplified the teachings of Paracelsus and Swedenborg and anticipated the findings of modern psychology, physics, and psychic research. His work has had an ever-increasing influence on modern occult thought.

Blake was born in London in 1757 into a family of artisans. His father was a hosier. Blake began his career as an artist at the age of ten. As a teenager he was apprenticed to William Basire, an engraver, and he supported himself as an engraver for the rest of his life.

When he was young, Blake was exposed to many occult and republican influences. He read the work of Swedenborg soon after it appeared in English translation. He also read Paracelsus and Jacob Boehme. Blake was active in antiwar activities in support of the American Revolution. He took part in the Newgate Prison riots of 1781. He also expressed his opposition to the slave trade and to child labor, and other evils of the Industrial Revolution.

In 1782 Blake married Catharine Boucher. The Blakes continued their mystic interests, becoming associated with a Swedenborgian society in 1789. But though Blake had connections with several groups and movements, he never joined any of them. He had beeen having visions since he was fourteen, and as he grew older, his inner world grew more real to him. Indeed, Blake considered his personal visionary world the real one, of which the material world was but an image or shadow.

Except for a three-year stay in the village of Felpham, Blake lived in London all his life. He had few admirers and lived in poverty. He died in London in 1827.

Blake's first published poems, *Poetical Sketches*, appeared in 1783. Soon he began printing his own work, on plates he illustrated himself. These "illuminated books" include *There is No Natural Religion* (1788), *All Religions Are One* (1788), *Songs of Innocence* (1789), *The Book of Thel* (1789), *The Marriage of Heaven and Hell* (1790–93), *Visions of the Daughers of Albion* (1793), *America: A Prophecy* (1793), *Songs of Experience* (1794), *Europe: A Prophecy* (1794), *The First Book of Urizen* (1794), *The Song of Los* (1795), *Milton* (1804–5), *Jerusalem* (1804–20), and several other works.

Blake's poems are difficult to understand, and so they have contributed to his reputation as an eccentric and misfit. The poems contain dozens of names (such as Enitharmon, Los, Urizen, and Rintrah) that are personifications of attributes or states of being, and other names, such as Golgonooza, which are both visionary places and spiritual states. Nevertheless, in the twentieth century, the view that Blake was an extraordinary genius has come to prevail. His poems are no less difficult to read, but the student is rewarded by glimpses of Blake's enlightened vision.

This vision consisted, first of all, of a new view of the human soul.

> Man has no Body distinct from the Soul; for that called Body is a portion of Soul discerned by the five Senses, the chief inlets of Soul in this Age.
>
> Energy is the only life and is from the Body, and Reason is the bound or outward circumference of Energy.
>
> Energy is eternal delight.

Blake's vision also included a new view of human redemption. By redemption, Blake meant the recognition that matter was spiritual in origin. Blake saw that the outward form of things was dependent on our perception of them, and that "if the doors of perception were cleansed, everything would appear to man as it is, infinite."

"The nature of my work is Visionary or Imaginative," said Blake. "It is an endeavor to restore what the Ancients called the Golden Age." In his last major poem, *Jerusalem*, Blake described the Golden Age.

> And they conversed together in Visionary forms dramatic which bright
> Redounded from their Tongues in thunderous majesty, in Visions
> In new Expanses, creating exemplars of Memory and of Intellect,
> Creating Space, Creating Time, according to the wonders Divine
> Of Human Imagination throughout all the Three Regions immense
> Of Childhood, Manhood, and Old Age; & the all tremendous unfathomable Non Ens
> Of Death was seen in regenerations terrific or complacent, varying
> According to the subject of discourse; & every Word & every Character
> Was Human according to the Expansion or Contraction, the Translucence or
> Opakeness of Nervous fibres; such was the variation of Time & Space
> Which vary according as the Organs of Perception vary; & they walked
> To & fro in Eternity as One Man, reflecting each in each & clearly seen
> And seeing, according to fitness and order.

The Revival of Magic. Ritual magic fell out of favor during the eighteenth century. There was no room for it in the dogmas of science. Since demons could not be discovered by scientific observation, they were held not to exist at all. But with the Romantic movement came a new wave of interest in magical practices. The new magic was a revolt against a strictly materialistic interpretation of the world.

The revival began in England in 1801, with the publication of *The Magus, or Celestial Intelligencer*, by Frances Barrett. *The Magus* is, to put it bluntly, a very dull book. Perhaps for this reason, it never achieved wide popularity.

The magic revival needed a writer with more flair and imagination. That writer was a Frenchman named Alphonse Louis Constant, who wrote under the pen name of Eliphas Lévi. His *Dogma and Ritual of High Magic*, which appeared in 1856, is the source of most modern magic rites. Lévi borrowed heavily from *The Magus* in writing this work. He also published a *History of Magic* (1860), *The Key to the Grand Mysteries* (1861), and several other books. His books were widely read, not only in France but in England, the United States, and Germany. The books were translated into English by A.E. Waite in the 1890s.

Constant began his career as a priest, but he was defrocked for preaching "doctrines contrary to the church." As a young man, he came under the influence of a prophet named Ganneau, who believed he was a reincarnation of Louis XVII and whose wife believed she was Marie Antoinette. Constant also read Balzac. He was especially influenced by Balzac's novel *Louis Lambert*, the story of a young mystic.

As Eliphas Lévi, Constant let his imagination run wild. He claimed to know the "secret doctrine," which had been handed down by adepts through the centuries. These adepts had revealed the magic rituals to him. He also said they had told him about Astral Light, a sort of force or ether that pervades all things. The purpose of his magic rituals was to direct the flow of this Astral Light. Lévi also claimed knowledge of the Kabbalah, although he did not know Hebrew.

Lévi died in 1875, having gathered a circle of disciples. His name was so revered in nineteenth-century magic circles that later groups, such as the Order of the Golden Dawn, felt it necessary to establish descent from him. His most influential English disciple was Edward Bulwer-Lytton, the author of, among other things, *The Last Days of Pompeii* (see chapter eight).

Occult Sects

We have seen how a variety of groups with occult affiliations arose in the seventeenth and eighteenth centuries. These groups evolved in several different directions. Many of the Protestant mystic sects connected with the Rosicrucian Movement in the seventeenth century emigrated to America. Other Rosicrucian brotherhoods pursued scientific or political aims. By the nineteenth century most of these brotherhoods, like the Freemasons, had shed most of their occult dimensions and become the social and philanthropic organizations they are today.

But the yearning for secret societies remained. Several secret societies were formed within the Masonic organization. Others arose in response to the Romantic revival of magic and medieval study.

The New Rosicrucians. By the mid-1800s, the rose-and-cross symbol had become part of any number of cults—Masonic, esthetic, Catholic—and Rosicrucianism had lost any specific meaning. In 1865, some British Masons founded the Societas Rosicruciana in Anglia (a group with branches in Scotland and the U.S.). In 1888, the Marquis Stanislaus de Gaita founded an occult college in Paris, the Kabbalistic Order of the Rose-Croix. In 1890, the novelist and painter Sar Peladan broke away from de Gaita's group and formed his own. At present, the best-known Rosicrucian society is the

Ancient Mystical Order Rosae Crucis, founded in 1915 in San Jose, California, by H. Spencer Lewis. AMORC maintains a headquarters that is a classic example of 1920s Hollywood Egyptian; much of their teaching is done through correspondence courses.

All this sounds harmless enough, and it probably is. But not all such cults have been so innocent. The group known as the Work of Mercy is a case in point.

Shortly after the French Revolution, a sect was formed in France that had as its purpose the restoration of Louis XVII to the throne. The boy prince had been imprisoned with Marie Antoinette and was said to have died in prison. No one saw the body, and so, inevitably, rumors abounded that he had escaped.

In 1832 a man named Karl Naunsdorf arrived in Paris, claiming he was the missing Louis. He gathered many supporters who remained loyal to him even after it was revealed that he was a German forger. Naunsdorf was expelled from France in 1836. The group's next leader was Martin de Gullardon, who had visions of angels.

When Gullardon died in 1839, the group's leadership passed to a man named Eugene Vintras (1807–1875). Vintras, the manager of a cardboard-box factory, received a visit from an old man whom Vintras later claimed was the archangel Michael. The archangel left him a letter, which predicted that France was about to enter a horrible period, from which it would emerge with Louis XVII on the throne. Then a Golden Age would begin. It is not known whether the letter was from Naunsdorf and, if so, why he chose Vintras to receive it.

Vintras began having visions shortly after the letter arrived. He set up a chapel in his factory. There, several miracles occurred, such as the appearance of bleeding Hosts. Vintras also had nightmares in which the Virgin Mary told him he was damned.

Word of the miracles spread. In 1842 Vintras was arrested on charges of fraud. The pope officially condemned the sect in 1843. During Vintras's five-year prison term, pamphlets appeared that charged him with homosexual practices, performing Black Masses, and masturbating on the Host. None of these charges was proved.

Upon his release from prison, Vintras went to England. There he declared himself to be the prophet Elijah. He began calling his group "Carmel," or the "Work of Mercy." He returned to France in 1863 and consecrated several priests into the Church of Carmel. By this time the sect had lost its passion for restoring Louis XVII. (Naunsdorf had died in Holland in 1845.)

Vintras's successor was a defrocked priest named J.A. Boullan. In 1859 Boullan had founded a religious community from members of the original group. The community taught that sex was the road to salvation. The members enacted a rite called Union with Life, which included hallucinations of sex with Jesus and Mary. Actual intercourse with Boullan was also part of the ritual.

Boullan frequently complained that the Rosicrucians were directing psychic forces against him. They went further than that. In 1886 the Work of Mercy was infiltrated by Stanislaus de Gaita, Sar Peladan, and another Rosicrucian adept. De Gaita threatened to expose Boullan's practices, and Boullan counterattacked with spells. The two groups kept up their psychic warfare for years. Boullan died in 1893 of a heart attack, which his follower, the novelist Huysmans, attributed to the Rosicrucians. De Gaita died in 1898, from drug abuse.

This fantastic tale is a fine illustration of the way the occult worked on the nineteenth-century imagination. The "wicked, forbidden thrill" of the sexual mass was obviously much stronger with French Catholics than it is now with us, for whom the whole story seems absurd. To understand how deeply the forbidden emotions were felt, and to grasp the degree of romantic self-indulgence of these occultists, read Huysmans's occult novel, *Là-bas*. This novel, as well as Huysmans's subsequent work, draws on the characters in the Rosicrucian vs. Work of Mercy war. Huysmans is instructive reading for those who think hysterical, drug-crazed occultism originated in the 1960s.

The Order of the Golden Dawn. The Golden Dawn is the best-known magical order in history because several famous people belonged to it and because it produced the magician Aleister Crowley. The history of the Golden Dawn is riddled with as much fraud and self-delusion as the history of the Work of Mercy. However, the element of sexual hysteria is missing. All the evidence shows that the rituals of the Order were conducted with suitable British decorum.

The Golden Dawn was begun by a Dr. William Wynn Westcott, a London coroner. Dr. Westcott was a Freemason, a student of the occult, and a member of the Societas Rosicruciana in Anglia. In 1887, he found an old manuscript written in cipher. He asked his friend and fellow Rosicrucian, Samuel Liddell MacGregor Mathers, to expand the material in the manuscript into a rite that could be performed.

Meanwhile, Dr. Westcott supposedly wrote to a German woman named Fraulein Sprengle, whose name and address he found with the cipher manuscript. Fraulein Sprengle turned out, conveniently, to be an adept and sorer (a performer of the "female" part of the alchemical process). Fraulein Sprengle held a high rank in a secret German occult order, and she authorized Westcott to begin an English branch of that order. The order was to have three chiefs. So, in 1888, Westcott, another Rosicrucian named W.R. Woodman, and Mathers opened the Isis-Urania Temple of the Hermetic Order of the Golden Dawn.

This official Golden Dawn history is almost certainly fraudulent. For one thing, the Fraulein Sprengle letters were not written by a German. They contain unmistakable English grammatical constructions and Anglicized spellings. Another problem was the alleged antiquity of the cipher. The rituals contained references to supposed correspondences between the Kabbalah and the Tarot deck. This element of magic ritual was almost certainly invented by Eliphas Lévi; at least, no earlier source is known. Furthermore, not one of the many people who tried was ever able to trace Fraulein Sprengle.

But this deception was not uncovered until the 1890s. In 1888, the new order began immediately to attract members. Unlike the Freemasons and the Rosicrucians, the Golden Dawn admitted women on an equal basis with men. Among the early members were Nina Bergson (later Nina Mathers), an artist and the sister of philosopher Henri Bergson; Constance Mary Wilde, wife of Oscar Wilde; William Crookes, a scientist; Annie Horniman, the daughter of a wealthy tea importer and later an actress and theater patron; Florence Farr, a popular actress who was then the mistress of George Bernard Shaw; William Butler Yeats, the great Irish poet; and Maude Gonne, the actress and Irish revolutionary. The order also included fourteen doctors and several second-rate novelists. Each member was known by a Latin motto. Later members included occult writer A.E. Waite, novelist Allan Bennett, and Aleister Crowley.

In other words, the Golden Dawn was frequented by some of the most intelligent, creative people in England. What made them fall for it? All of them began, of course, with a belief in the occult and a desire to learn to control psychic forces. But these motives could have led them to any number of occult groups. Theosophy was all the rage in London of the 1880s. There was even an Esoteric Section of the Theosophical Society that contained most of the same Hermetic, Kabbalistic, and Rosicrucian elements as the Golden Dawn. Several people were members of both groups.

What the Golden Dawn offered, first of all, was the charismatic personality of MacGregor Mathers, who by 1892 had completely edged out Westcott as chief of the Order. Mathers was tall, slim, and dashing. He had penetrating eyes, an air of mystic profundity, enormous energy, and a way with the ladies. He may have been slightly insane; he was, at least, self-deluded.

Mathers invented a noble lineage for himself, claiming that his ancestor, Ian MacGregor, had been a Jacobite who fled to France and was created Comte de Glenstrae by Louis XV. Mathers often used this title. He was also given to wearing kilts in the MacGregor tartan. Mathers was obsessed with the military. He had himself photographed in the uniform of a first lieutenant, even though the records list no such officer.

Years later, Yeats described Mathers as "a figure of romance," a person who "carried further than anyone else a claim implicit in the Romantic movement from the time of Shelley and Goethe," and, most significantly, "a figure in a play of our composition."

Love of theatrics seemed to be the real force behind the Golden Dawn. The costumes, settings, and rituals were all dramatically executed. After 1892, Florence Farr and Annie Horniman were responsible for these performances. The members were attired in gorgeous robes. The Chief Adept wore a white cassock, a red cloak, an Egyptian headdress, yellow shoes, and a yellow collar from which hung a Rosy Cross symbol. The settings included an elaborately painted vault, a reconstruction of the tomb of Christian Rosencreutz. Among the many rites of the Order were "The Ritual of the Cross and the Four Elements" and "The Rite of the Pentagram and the Five Paths." Each member possessed a lotus wand, which he or she had to make by hand and which was then consecrated in a special ceremony.

The Golden Dawn ceremonies, by the way, are now available in paperback. (Dr. Israel Regardie, *The Golden Dawn: An Account of the Teaching, Rites, and Ceremonies.* Llewellyn Publications, 1969.)

The Golden Dawn began to dissolve in the early 1890s. There were many personality conflicts, which were heightened by the fact that Mathers was directing operations from Paris while being supported by Annie Horniman. When she began to balk at his increasing money demands, he had her removed from membership. This incensed many of the other members. There was also a certain amount of scandal when Dr. Westcott's connection with the Order became known, as many outsiders felt a public coroner should not be a magician. But the real blow came in 1900, when Mathers, in an attempt to oust Westcott altogether, wrote Florence Farr that Westcott had "either himself forged or caused to be forged" the original documents on which the Order had been based.

Open revolt followed. Farr and some of the other members locked the vault, but it was recaptured by Crowley in the name of Mathers. Few of the others could stomach Crowley. Some members broke off and founded new orders. Those of Aleister Crowley and Dion Fortune were the most successful. Nina Bergson Mathers and Dion Fortune waged their own psychic war for a while, but neither seems to have been harmed by the evil magic of the other. Mathers died in 1918. Yeats claimed he had been killed by Crowley's magic.

Several modern magical groups call themselves the Order of the Golden Dawn, but the original group had disintegrated by the beginning of World War I.

American Mystic Faiths. America in the nineteenth century was pushing west. It was expanding on religious frontiers as well. The century began with the Great Western Revival. The revival took place on the frontier, which was then in western New York, Ohio, and Kentucky. The instrument of revival was the camp meeting. Worshippers at camp meetings exhibited every known form of religious hysteria, going into trances, speaking in strange spirit languages, dancing, barking, shouting, and "getting the jerks." These phenomena are recounted at length in *The Autobiography of Peter Cartwright*, a firsthand account by a Methodist circuit-riding preacher.

The outbreaks on the frontier were not surprising in view of the religious history of the United States. Dozens of heretical Protestant groups had emigrated to America in the seventeenth and eighteenth centuries. The Shakers, for example, were French medieval heretics who became Huguenots in the sixteenth century. They were expelled from France in 1688 and, after a stay in England, emigrated to America. The Quakers left England for America in the seventeenth century, as did numerous other sects of Quietists, Pietists, and Mennonites. The Moravian Brethren were a Bohemian Hussite sect that settled in North Carolina and Pennsylvania. Few of these groups were as physical as the Shakers. Many of them emphasized mystic and other "out of the body" experiences. All of them believed in the "Inner Light." They followed the teachings of such mystics as Swedenborg, Huss, and Boehme.

In the nineteenth century, mystic and utopian groups formed hundreds of communities in the United States. The most famous one, the Oneida community in western New York, combined socialism with ideas of free love. At the opposite extreme were the Shakers and the Pietists of New Harmony, Pennsylvania, who opposed sex altogether and thus assured their own extinction. The Hopedale Community, founded in 1842 by the Rev. Adin Ballou, taught a form of spiritualism. The Mountain Cove Community of Fayette County, Virginia, were also spiritualists. Another semioccult community, the Wisconsin Phalanx, combined socialism with the doctrines of Mesmer. The longest-lasting utopian community, the Mormons, moved several times before finally establishing the Kingdom of

God in Salt Lake City, Utah.

Some American groups were apocalyptic rather than utopian. They daily expected the end of the world. The most prominent of these sects was the Millerites. In the 1840s, Millerites sold all their worldly goods, dressed in white robes, and stood on the tops of hills waiting for Jesus to return. When he did not, the group went through severe changes. The Mormons, the Jehovah's Witnesses, the Seventh-Day Adventists, and the Christian Scientists are just a few of the present-day groups whose early histories are connected with the Millerite movement.

It is impossible to understand twentieth-century American occultism without remembering these groups. Writers on the occult tend to lose themselves in pages of documentation on Egyptian Hermetic mysteries, medieval witchcraft, and so on. But in spite of the veneers of "oriental thought" or "scientific principles," most American occult groups are probably following the noble American tradition of religious eccentricity.

Spiritualism. Spiritualism was the most important occult movement of the nineteenth century, and the one that seems destined to have the most far-reaching effects. Spiritualists claimed that they could communicate with the dead, travel outside their own bodies, cause events to happen by astral projection, and even foretell the future. These phenomena could be experienced through *mediums*, persons whose psychic powers tuned them in to spiritual forces in the universe. Biographies of many mediums are found in chapter two.

The Spiritualist Movement began in western New York State in March 1848. The first signs from the spirits (or whatever they were) took place in the presence of Kate and Margaret Fox, who were seven and ten years old respectively. The method the spirits chose was rapping. The Foxes began to ask questions of the spirits. Eventually, the spirits told Leah, the older sister of Kate and Margaret, to spread the Spiritualist word. The first meeting of Spiritualists took place on November 14, 1849, in Rochester. (For further information about the early spiritualists, see chapter two, under "Psychical Research.")

Why the Spirits Spoke. Spirits had spoken to humans before, of course, but always to isolated individuals, such as Swedenborg and Blake. The Spiritualist communications took place in front of thousands of people, many of whom had no particular mystic tendencies, and most of whom were certainly lacking in mental discipline. So why did the spirits choose that particular time and place to begin communicating after so many centuries of silence?

The section above gives part of the explanation. In the 1820s, 30s, and 40s, western New York State was the scene of thousands of religio-psychic phenomena. There were so many visions, trances, cases of speaking in tongues, and divine revelations that the area became known to historians as "the burned-over district." If the Fox sisters had not heard the rappings, someone else in the area would have. For people in the district were *expecting* something to happen.

Why did the manifestations spread so quickly all over America and Europe? The answer, I think, lies in the nature of the phenomena themselves. Table turnings, raps, knocks, smashing furniture, levitation, apparitions—all were manifestations that could be verified by the senses.

The idea that a thing must be proven by the evidence of the senses is what characterizes our scientific age. In the eighteenth century, that idea had been held by the educated minority. But by the nineteenth century, scientific materialism had percolated down even to people who couldn't read. This was especially true in the United States, which was without long centuries of religious orthodoxy. The American pioneer placed great importance on simple common sense.

But in conflict with common sense, there is always an uncommon sense—the recognition that there is a reality outside our sense perceptions. Since the materialist has no means of perceiving nonmaterial realities, those realities manifest themselves sensually. The rise of Pentecostal and other religions that depended on outward evidence paralleled the rise of the materialist, industrial age.

This helps to explain why the spirits never seemed to communicate anything very profound. The Spiritualist finds proof in the manifestations, and proof is all he's looking for.

These comments come from a twentieth-century viewpoint, of course. We believe in the subconscious mind, and we know (through drugs, among other things) that perception alters "reality." It is no longer particularly revolutionary to believe that psychological projection can cause events to happen. More than 250 years after William Blake, we are at last coming round to his point of view. When Blake asked the prophet Isaiah, "Does a firm persuasion that a thing is so, make it so?" Isaiah replied: "All poets believe that it does, and in ages of imagination this firm persuasion removed mountains."

The Spread of Spiritualism. The spectacular phenomena produced by early séances soon came to the attention of the press. Before long newspapers appeared that were specifically Spiritualist. In America, the phenomena were usually attributed to spirits or ghosts. Spiritualism also was connected to socialism, since it seemed to herald a new Golden Age when human progress could be directed by the great minds of the past. Benjamin Franklin was frequently summoned and asked for advice.

In Europe, the Spiritualist phenomena were more frequently connected with the theories of Mesmer and other magnetists. Most scientists assumed the mediums were fraudulent.

Among the first converts to Spiritualism in England was Robert Owen, a pioneer socialist. He published a periodical called *The New Existence of Man Upon Earth*, which promised a socialist utopia under spirit guidance.

The leader of French Spiritualism was Allan Kardec, a magnetist, whose teachings were known as "Spiritism." Kardec combined Spiritualism with doctrines of reincarnation. He was among the first to develop a religious and philosophical system based on the Spiritualist phenomena. (Among his present-day followers are many of the psychic surgeons.)

What Spiritualists Believe. Spiritualism has no official dogma, though some offshoots of Spiritualism, such as Theosophy, did develop very complex belief systems. Mary Baker Eddy's *Science and Health with Key to the Scriptures*, the bible of Christian Science, also owes much to Spiritualism.

Most spiritualists seem to hold these general beliefs:

1. Humans have both material bodies and spirit bodies. The spirit body is separated from the soul at death. (This belief was introduced into Spiritualism by way of the British Museum, which contained many objects found by Napoleon's troops in Egypt and which started a craze for all things Egyptian. A surprising number of the early spirit contacts were Egyptians. They were later superceded by Atlanteans, Lemurians, and, recently, people from Venus and Alpha Centauri.)
2. Just as one's physical actions leave their mark on the physical body, so one's moral actions leave their mark on the spirit body. (This is, of course, the same as the Hindu and Buddhist doctrine of *karma*.)
3. The individual is responsible for all his or her thoughts and actions. What happens in this life affects what happens to the spirit body after death. Most Spiritualists don't believe in heaven or hell except as mental states. But if you intend to come back in your spirit body to impart your wisdom to the human race, start getting your spirit body into shape now.
4. After death, the spirit body must purify itself. The soul progresses ever upward, toward a state of spiritual perfection. In the twentieth century, this belief is usually combined with belief number 5 below.
5. The spirit body must reincarnate into many different physical bodies in order to achieve purification.

Psychic Research. While Spiritualism led some people to form what is essentially a new religion, it led others to insist on objective investigation of the phenomena. The procedures and findings of psychic research organizations are detailed in chapter two.

Theosophy. The year 1875 was an important one in occult history. In that year Eliphas Lévi, Bulwer-Lytton, and Eugene Vintras died, and Aleister Crowley and Jung were born. And on September 7, 1875, Madame Helena Petrovna Blavatsky founded the Theosophical Society. Theosophy embraces Christianity, Spiritualism, Buddhism, Taoism, the Hermetic Mysteries, the Atlantis and Lemuria myths, and "secret doctrine." In short, it has something for every occultist. Today the Theosophical Society has relatively few members. But most occultists hold Madame Blavatsky's system of beliefs.

Blavatsky and Olcott. Helena Hahn was born in Russia in 1831. She was the daughter of a Russian colonel and the cousin of Sergei Witte, a count who later became prime minister. In later years she was to make much of her noble background, but in her youth she rebelled against it quite flagrantly. She was married at sixteen to a General Blavatsky, who was forty. She refused to consummate the marriage. Instead, she left him to begin a crazy career as a circus horseback-rider, a factory manager, a medium's assistant (her boss was Daniel Dunglas Home), and world traveller. She visited Mexico, Texas, Canada, and Tibet, as well as most of the countries in Europe.

In 1873, she arrived in America. Here her strange appearance and excessive habits, such as swearing and smoking marijuana, immediately gained the attention of the press. Her personality especially fascinated Henry Steele Olcott, who became her supporter and partner. Olcott was a newspaper writer by trade and a Spiritualist by inclination. His rank of colonel ws honorary.

Olcott was not Blavatsky's lover, though at the time there was much scandal attached to their liaison. Blavatsky had an intensely negative attitude toward sex, calling it "a beastly appetite that must be starved into submission." Blavatsky claimed that an accident in the circus had left her unable to have sex. "I am lacking something," she once admitted with typical directness, "and the place is filled up with some crooked cucumber."

Under Olcott's sponsorship, Blavatsky made a fairly good living as a medium, and in 1875 the two of them founded the Theosophical Society. But it was Blavatsky's first Theosophical book, *Isis Unveiled*, that brought her to prominence. She wrote most of it under the influence of marijuana. The book appeared in 1877. The book sold amazingly well, and the membership of the Theosophical Society swelled.

In 1878, Blavatsky and Olcott went to India. They had been in correspondence with a new Hindu teacher, Swami Dayananda Sarasvati, with whose movement they planned to merge. Theosophy did very well in India, in spite of the Swami's contempt for their naivete. Olcott, for example, couldn't seem to grasp that Hinduism and Buddhism were two different religions, and when he converted to Buddhism, the Swami refused further affiliation with the Theosophical Society.

While in India, Blavatsky received many further communications from the "Mahatmas," her Tibetan spirit guides. (Like many other occultists, Blavatsky had discovered that people would believe revelations from spirits that would be ridiculous coming from mere humans.) One spirit guide, a master named Koot Hoomi Lal Singh, even wrote letters to one of Blavatsky's followers.

In 1884, HPB (as her followers called her) returned to Europe. Her departure from India was hastened by increasing conflicts with Olcott, who was now claiming mediumistic powers of his own. She spent some time establishing the Theosophical Society in England, where the way had been prepared by A.P. Sinnet, with whom Koot Hoomi had corresponded. While Blavatsky was gone from India, her housekeeper revealed to a Christian missionary that Blavatsky was a fraud. The housekeeper showed the missionary some secret panels, dummies, and other paraphernalia for faking mediumistic effects. There is some evidence that the tricks could have been planted by the resentful housekeeper herself. That is, of course, what the Theosophists claimed. But the news of the supposed fraud got back to England. As a result, the influential Society for Psychical Research issued an unfavorable report on Blavatsky's powers.

The report tarnished HPB's reputation, but her magnetic personality overcame much of the criticism. In 1887 she settled permanently in England, and in 1888 she brought out her second major work, *The Secret Doctrine*. The book contained some of the Kabbalistic ideas of MacGregor Mathers, whom Blavatsky met in 1887, and who moved in the same circles.

Blavatsky remained a central figure in occult London until her death in 1891. She knew several of the members of the Order of the Golden Dawn, including Yeats—in fact, she seems to have founded the Esoteric Section of the Theosophical Society in 1888 primarily in response to the Golden Dawn's early success. There was considerable cross-pollination between the organizations.

Toward the end of her life, Blavatsky became something of an embarrassment to some of her London followers, who found her too flamboyant and coarse, though all declared their loyalty to her. Blavatsky continued to receive revelations from Koot Hoomi and others right up until her death in 1891.

Olcott vs. Judge. While Blavatsky and Olcott were in India, the American branch of the Theosophical Society almost died out. Then, in the 1880s, a man named William Q. Judge became a leader of the movement. After Blavatsky's death, Judge tried to take over the leadership of the international society. Under his direction, the American Theosophists were once again thriving.

Olcott had different ideas. He returned to America to engage Judge in battle. The result was a split in the ranks. Some members remained loyal to Olcott and the international society; others followed Judge. When Judge died in 1896, his movement was taken over by Catharine Tingley, who moved the headquarters to Point Loma, California. This organization, called the Universal Brotherhood, is still in existence.

The regular branch of the American Theosophical Society now has its headquarters in Wheaton, Illinois. It has an estimated five thousand members.

Annie Besant, C.W. Leadbeater, and Krishnamurti. In the years immediately after HPB's death, the Theosophical Society faltered because of disputes over leadership. Annie Besant and C.W. Leadbeater were the strongest contenders, and they shared the leadership for some time. Mrs. Besant published several new works explaining Theosophy and reedited some of Blavatsky's writings to take out some of the most patently absurd passages. After the death of Olcott in 1907, Mrs. Besant became president of the English society which by then had become independent. She soon became the most widely known Theosophical figure.

In 1911 an event occurred that caused further splits within the society's ranks. This was the discovery, by Leadbeater, of a thirteen-year-old "perfect master" named Jiddu, or Krishnamurti. The boy was from a poor family that lived at the Theosophical Society headquarters in Adyar, India, and Leadbeater was convinced that Jiddu was the incarnation of Lord Maitreya, the World Teacher for whom the Theosophists had been waiting. Mrs. Besant went to India, met Jiddu, and became equally infatuated with him. She founded a society called the Order of the Star in the East, dedicated to the advancement of Krishnamurti's thought. She even adopted him.

In 1929, Krishnamurti put a stop to their adulation by publicly renouncing Annie Besant, the Order of the Star, and Theosophy. He has, ironically, turned out to be a World Teacher after all, one of the most balanced and sane of the gurus who have now invaded the West. (Chapter five has more about Krishnamurti and his message.)

The Theosophists lost many followers as a result of the Krishnamurti affair. The society's membership has steadily dwindled over the years. In the meantime, however, its teachings have spread into the general culture. The Theosophists are the source of several of the myths in the "Occult Bible" chapter of this book.

Rudolf Steiner and Anthroposophy. Dr. Rudolf Steiner (1861–1925) was a brilliant Goethe scholar from Vienna who became a Theosophist in 1902. He soon rose to leadership in the German section of the society. Steiner's intellectual training got him into trouble with Besant, Leadbeater, and others, for he was contemptuous of the pseudoscholarship that pervaded Theosophy, which claimed to base its teachings on authentic Sanskrit texts. The society was never exactly replete with Sanskrit scholars. Steiner preferred to emphasize the German philosophical tradition.

Steiner did not break with the Theosophists until the elevation of Krishnamurti. He then (in 1912) formed his own movement, the Anthroposophical Society, and provided the movement with a whole new body of literature on subjects ranging from the lost continent of Lemuria to farming. He reintroduced many ancient Christian heresies into Theosophical teaching.

Steiner possessed a remarkable vision of the future of the world as it should be run. He wrote treatises on education, politics, and industry and established several institutions to carry out his ideas. The controversial Rudolf Steiner School in New York City has gained fame because of its emphasis on fostering creativity among its students. Steiner also formulated a method of body movement called *eurythmy*, which is based on the connections among mental, emotional, and physical states.

Because of the practical applications of his teachings and his work on mind/body coordination, Steiner was much more modern than Blavatsky or Besant. He is more widely read now than ever.

Alice A. Bailey. Bailey, the founder of the still-influential Arcane School, was born in Manchester, England, in 1880. Her family was middle class and devoted to strict, evangelical Christianity. As a young woman, Bailey did missionary work with the British Army in India, and there she met her first husband, Walter Evans. She and Evans emigrated to the United States, where he took orders in the Episcopal Church. After several years, the marriage ended in divorce.

Bailey became interested in occultism through the Theosophical Society, of which she was an active member. Eventually, she split with the Theosophists, and for the rest of her life she was highly critical of their factionalism. But her Theosophical training, as well as her evangelical upbringing, are evident in her later thought.

She came to believe that Koot Hoomi had guided her since age fifteen. This was the same master who had appeared to Madame Blavatsky, Colonel Olcott, and others. To Bailey, he revealed himself as a tall man in European dress. He explained to her that a spiritual hierarchy dwells within each human. Christ is the hierarchy's head; Koot Hoomi is one of its teachers. The hierarchy has evolved a Great Universal Plan, the details of which a Tibetan master began to dictate through Bailey.

In 1920, Alice Evans remarried, this time to a Theosophist named Foster Bailey. The two founded the Arcane School, put forth the books dictated to Alice Bailey, and gathered disciples. Bailey died in 1949.

As for Koot Hoomi, he is still active. He has appeared in a hidden cathedral at Mount Shasta, California, to Robert and Earlyne Chaney. In 1951, the Chaneys established the Astara Foundation to help spread the Mount Shasta revelations.

Mystics, Mentors, and Madmen

Madame Blavatsky was responsible for a great many fads in occultism, particularly the search for World Teachers, modern prophets who will be able to straighten out the universal mess. There had been a long tradition of Messianic movements among fundamentalists in the United States. Blavatsky added the international element: the idea that the World Teacher would come from the East and reunite East and West in religious harmony. As chapter five demonstrates, there have been several candidates for the post. In this section I will deal with several contenders who, intentionally or otherwise, have become modern prophets.

Some of them—Frazer and Jung, for example—would be appalled at the way their work is quoted to support occultists' claims. Others—such as Aleister Crowley—would be delighted. All the people mentioned here have had their beliefs or philosophies distorted by modern electronic media. These days there are more possibilities than ever for myths to develop, and for everyone to hear about them instantly. And there are more opportunities than ever for people with a little learning and the gift of the gab to turn a buck.

Rasputin. Rasputin was the son of a peasant. He made his living as a carter. In the early 1890s, when he was in his twenties, he made a pilgrimage to Mount Athos in Greece. When he returned home, he began holding prayer services and preaching to his neighbors. His reputation as a saint and healer grew. Today, occultists still attribute to him great powers, both saintly and demonic. Although biographers have attributed all sorts of excesses to him, most of the stories are untrue. Rasputin got drunk and fought a lot, qualities not unusual in people of his class and time. But he was not a magician, a charlatan, or a practitioner of quack medicines. His roots were in the monastic mysticism of the Russian Orthodox Church, and he had established a reputation as a holy man and healer among the Russian peasants long before anyone in the aristocracy had ever heard of him.

Rasputin arrived in St. Petersburg, the Russian capital, in 1905. At that time the aristocracy of Russia was enjoying the same craze for occultism that had swept through Paris and London ten and twenty years before. We know that Rasputin had an air of intense power and direct peasant speech. He was also very sexually attractive. And so he started getting invitations to the drawing rooms of the nobles.

He made many enemies among the nobility. They accused him of drunkenness and debauchery, a rather ironic charge in view of the habits of the aristocracy at that period. The major cause of alarm was his supposed influence over the Tsarina Alexandra, wife of the Tsar. Alexandra was Queen Victoria's granddaughter, and she herself was very unpopular among the Russian nobles.

Rasputin's influence over Alexandra arose because he alone seemed able to heal her son, the Tsarevitch Alexey. Alexey suffered from hemophilia, which had been passed through the female descendants of Queen Victoria to nearly all the royal houses of Europe. Alexandra suffered guilt at knowing herself to be the carrier of the disease that caused her son so much pain. Through Rasputin's healing touch, Alexey's life was saved on several occasions.

There is very little evidence that Rasputin used his influence to place his friends in high positions, as his detractors claimed. The complaints about his influence undoubtedly owed more to aristocratic paranoia than to reality. He did predict the coming of the Russian Revolution, a fact that impresses Colin Wilson (among others) as evidence of remarkable prophetic powers. However, Wilson's awe typifies the myopia of occultists with regard to considerations of class and politics. Not just Rasputin but every peasant in St. Petersburg knew the Revolution was imminent.

Rasputin's enemies finally murdered him on December 29, 1916. The story of how he refused to die is legendary. Whether or not it is true, it illustrates Rasputin's power over the imagination. He was supposedly poisoned with cyanide, which had no effect. Then he was shot several times, stabbed, beaten with an iron bar, and dropped into a river. He died by drowning.

Aleister Crowley. Aleister Crowley, who tried hard to be the worst person who ever lived, succeeded in being one of the most pathetic. He was the ultimate example of the "preacher's kid" who turns out bad. His father had made a fortune from brewing before he became a minister in the Plymouth Brethren Church. Aleister had a comfortable, though strict, childhood and he seems to have been nasty from the day he was born. He absorbed enough religion to equate sin with sex and to decide that he was the Great Beast prophesied in the Book of Revelations. He later claimed he got that idea from his mother.

At Malvern and then at Oxford, he devoted himself to enjoying the good life and writing bad poetry. His career in magic began when he moved to London and joined the Order of the Golden Dawn. The Golden Dawn disappointed him because there was no sex. Crowley never stopped being obsessed with sex. The only things he liked better were violence and drugs.

Crowley also was an accomplished sportsman, his specialty being mountaineering. He travelled all over the world to climb. But he did not exactly endear himself to his fellow sportsmen. On one expedition he was so sadistically cruel to the porters that the other climbers refused to follow him. They started to return to camp. A sudden avalanche buried them. Crowley ignored all pleas for help, and four men died.

In the early 1900s, Crowley married Rose Kelly, the first of several women whom he was to torture or drive insane. They honeymooned in Cairo and Ceylon. In Cairo, on the return trip, Crowley was finally able to contact his guardian angel, which he had been trying to do for years. The angel's name turned out to be Aiwass. Aiwass dictated *The Book of the Law*, Crowley's answer to the Bible. Its central point, "Do what thou wilt shall be the whole of the law," is still the favorite quotation of Crowley enthusiasts, who claim, quite falsely, that he got it from William Blake.

Crowley's own life is the best possible argument against this philosophy. Crowley got his kicks from beating up women, defecating on carpets, and watching the people around him go insane from his manipulations. He filed his front teeth into fangs so that he could bite women on the wrists and neck when he met them. He overused heroin, cocaine, hashish, mescaline, and opium. He turned several of his disciples into nervous wrecks.

For some years, he lived in a farmhouse on Sicily with his third wife, Leah, and his mistress Ninette Shumway, who also worked as the nurse for his children. Crowley involved both women—and any others who happened to visit—in his rites of sex magic. The narrative of life at the "Abbey of Theleme" ranges from the sordid to the sleazy. Sometimes animals were sacrificed, and the participants were made to drink the blood. The rituals included eating "sacred bread" baked with menstrual blood and feces.

So many accounts of Crowley's excesses have been published that it seems pointless to add any more of them here. Crowley's followers and admirers (Charles Manson is one) claim that he had great occult powers and knew the secrets of the universe. Given that he spent his whole life torturing other people and destroying himself, I suspect that whatever secrets he knew were not worth knowing. Crowley ended his life as a drug addict and alcholic. He died on December 5, 1947.

Gurdjieff. George Ivanovitch Gurdjieff was born in 1873 in the Transcaucasus. His family was probably Armenian or Greek. Gurdjieff's interest in the occult began in his youth.

In later years, Gurdjieff liked to talk of his years as a "seeker," during which he wandered through the monasteries of Tibet, Turkestan, Persia, and Egypt in search of Truth. The Truth was, as usual, more prosaic. He did travel widely, but he was a carpet dealer, a profession which made him rich. At least one biographer, Rom Landau, states that Gurdjieff was also an agent of the Russian secret police.

Shortly before World War I, Gurdjieff met his most famous disciple, P.D. Ouspensky (1878–1947). Ouspensky and Gurdjieff developed the ability to communicate with each other telepathically. They also began lecturing on occult subjects.

Gurdjieff was expelled from Russian soil after the Revolution. He went to the United States and then to England. With Ouspensky's help, he bought some buildings at Fontainebleau, near Paris. There he set up a teaching center called the Institute for the Harmonious Development of Man. The Institute was to provide him with a comfortable living and a forum for his ideas. It soon became fashionable, especially among British occultists.

Gurdjieff's personality inspired hero worship. He had an enormous amount of energy and, at the same time, an air of inner serenity. He wore a long, handlebar moustache and smoked expensive cigarettes. He had rather vulgar manners. He was a swearer, drinker, and womanizer. But he was also a brilliant leader, with charisma and a high sense of humor.

Gurdjieff taught that most people go through life asleep. The regimen at the Institute was designed to awaken his pupils to a state of higher consciousness. Hard physical labor was an important part of the routine, as were vegetarian meals, yoga, and breathing exercises.

Gurdjieff anticipated many later occult movements in his stress on physical and mental balance. He taught his disciples techniques of body control and dance, with amazing results. Gurdjieff said he had collected the dances on his travels, from such sources as the Whirling Dervishes. In 1924, Gurdjieff astounded New Yorkers with performances by a dance troupe from the Institute. The dancers executed incredible feats of gymnastics in a trancelike state.

A great many accounts have been published concerning life at the Institute. To his admirers, Gurdjieff was a sort of Western Buddha or Taoist saint. He often gave his disciples difficult or demeaning jobs to do, which in the end enlightened them. The harsh regimen at the Institute cleared the mind, improved health, and released psychic and occult abilities. Enthusiasts spoke of new energy and self-confidence.

His detractors, however, accuse him of brainwashing his followers, especially the women. He slept with several of his women students and fathered several illegitimate children. He caused more than one nervous breakdown by playing-off one student against another. The English novelist Katharine Mansfield died at the Institute. Gurdjieff had prescribed a rigorous fast for her and made her sleep on a gallery above the cattle stables. According to him, the cows' breath would carry health to her diseased lungs. (She had tuberculosis.) D.H. Lawrence, Mansfield's friend, called the Institute "a rotten, false, self-conscious place of people playing a sickly stunt."

Gurdjieff liked to say that the human body was a machine, and that to understand oneself, one must understand the machine. He placed great importance on "true will," a high degree of self-control that made humans masters of their bodily functions. But the phenomenon most often noted by outside observers was the total control Gurdjieff seemed to exercise over his followers. A person who was present at the 1924 New York dance debut remarked on the "incredible docility and robotlike obedience of the disciples. . . . They were like a group of perfectly trained zombies."

Gurdjieff died in 1949, at the age of seventy-six.

Frazer. Sir James George Frazer was a folklorist, classical scholar, and pioneer anthropologist. His major work, *The Golden Bough*, which was first published in 1890, is still regarded as an encyclopedia of comparative religion. *The Golden Bough* is also among the books most misquoted by modern occultists, especially by "good witches."

Frazer's life was outwardly unexciting. He was born in Glasgow on January 1, 1854. He entered Trinity College, Cambridge, in 1874 and became a Fellow in 1879. Except for one term in Liverpool, he remained at Cambridge for the rest of his life. In 1914, he was knighted for his contributions to anthropology and literature. He died at Cambridge on May 7, 1941.

Although Frazer's life was uneventful, his work made him one of the most influential people of our century. *The Golden Bough* traces the history of human belief in magic, religion, and then science, showing how certain rituals and customs have survived over the centuries. His objective was to explain the ritual that took place in the sacred grove of Diana near the lake of Nemi in Italy. The priest of Diana, known as the King of the Wood, had to guard a sacred tree in the grove. A man who aspired to this priestly office first had to kill the titleholder in single combat.

In explaining this ritual, Frazer drew on customs from many cultures, especially primitive tribes. He corresponded with the missionaries and explorers who in Victorian times had invaded the world's remote regions. *The Golden Bough* has thirteen volumes of data. (An abridged version is now available.)

Frazer's distinction between magic and religion is one of his most valuable contributions to anthropology. He defined magic as the attempt to control natural forces by technical acts based on faulty reasoning. Religion, on the other hand, assumed that natural forces were under the control of supernatural beings who must be appealed to. Frazer had other insights which have been extremely valuable to historians—for example, his identification of the dual functions of priest/kings in primitive societies.

Frazer's work is certainly not free of faults. He believed the Victorian myth of progress; he thought science superior to religion and religion superior to magic for the purpose of solving human problems. He wrote before scholars had generally accepted the existence or importance of the subconscious mind in human affairs, and so he ignored psychology, although Freud's theories of sexual repression and Jung's theories of archetypes and complexes can be supported by hundreds of examples in *The Golden Bough*.

But for all its shortcomings, *The Golden Bough* remains a masterpiece. Frazer and his fellow pioneers in anthropology were among the first to apply the scientific method of observation to nonrational areas of human behavior He collected hundreds of examples of how such themes as death, regeneration, and resurrection are expressed in human life.

Unfortunately, many of his readers assume that, because he recorded so many primitive rituals, he approved of them and believed they worked. Frazer's data have been quoted to "prove" that spirit forces exist, that witchcraft is a suppressed "true" religion, that shamans had supernatural powers, and that magic incantations actually produce rain. These ideas cannot be found anywhere in Frazer's writings. He wrote in the scientific spirit. He collected and analyzed data and then tried to formulate theories that explained those data. He *opposed* belief in magic, calling it "a spurious system of natural law as well as a fallacious guide of conduct; it is a false science as well as an abortive art."

Jung. Carl Gustave Jung was born in Switzerland in 1875. His father was a minister, as were many of the men in his family. But Jung broke with family tradition and became a doctor and psychiatrist. His work, like Frazer's, has been misrepresented and misunderstood.

In 1907, Jung began a five-year collaboration with Freud. Freud's theories were still highly controversial. Jung and Freud travelled to the United States to present those theories to American scholars and met with much success. In 1912, Jung broke with Freud over the issue of whether all neuroses had a sexual basis. Jung insisted that the sexual interpretation, though sometimes valid, was too narrow. He also considered Freud too materialistic because of his unwillingness to accept the reality of occult and spiritual phenomena.

Jung had had irrational and "mystic" experiences since his youth. He began taking notes on these experiences in 1912, soon after the break with Freud. His dreams and premonitions, as well as similar experiences by his patients, led him to develop his theory of archetypes. He developed the theory to explain the remarkable similarities of motifs in widely separated myths, fairy tales, and "in the fantasies, dreams, deliria, and delusions of individuals living today."

An archetype, Jung said, is "an irrepresentable unconscious, preexistent form that seems to be part of the inherited structure of the psyche and can therefore manifest itself spontaneously at any time."

Another influential idea of Jung's was his concept of complexes, which he defined as

> . . . psychic fragments which have split off owing to traumatic influences or certain incompatible tendencies. As the association experiments prove, complexes interfere with the intentions of the will and disturb conscious performance; they produce disturbances of memory and blockages in the flow of association; they appear and disappear according to their own laws; they can temporarily obsess consciousness, or influence speech and action in a conscious way. In a word, complexes behave like independent beings, a fact especially evident in abnormal states of mind. In the voices heard by the insane they even take on a personal ego-character like that of the spirits who manifest themselves through automatic writing and similar techniques.
>
> (*The Structure and Dynamics of the Psyche*)

This passage perfectly illustrates Jung's attitude toward the occult. Occultists delight in the fact that Jung wrote so much about occultism, without apparently noticing that Jung was interested in the *phenomena*, just as a biological scientist is interested in the phenomena he or she observes under the microscope. Jung was not a believer in the occult. He was, in fact, a Christian. But even about his own belief, he admitted, "We cannot tell whether God and the unconscious are two different entities."

Most of Jung's work was highly technical and scientific in nature and was addressed to his fellow psychiatrists. However, in his popular works, such as *Modern Man in Search of a Soul* (1933), *Essays on Contemporary Events* (1947), and *Answer to Job* (1947), he tried to relate his theories of the subconscious to modern religious movements such as occultism. In a 1959 essay, "Flying Saucers: A Modern Myth of Things Seen in the Sky," he pointed out the similarities between the projections of UFOlogists and primitive beliefs in gods and heroes. He was among the first to note that modern technology was forming its own religions in this manner.

Toward the end of his life, Jung dictated his autobiography on the condition that it be published only after his death. No doubt he anticipated the misuse into which it would fall. *Memories, Dreams, Reflections* is one of the great religious books of the twentieth century. In it Jung details his mystic experiences and dreams and expresses his personal beliefs about life after death and the existence of God. The book is a statement of faith as well as an attempt to deal directly with the problem of spiritual meaning in the modern world.

Unfortunately, *Memories, Dreams, Reflections* has become the most misquoted of all Jung's misunderstood writings. Occultists are among the worst offenders. Colin Wilson, for example, in his book *The Occult: A History*, misrepresents Jung's theories again and again. He also quotes story after story from *Memories, Dreams, Reflections*, each time using the story to "prove" some point of his own. In so doing, Wilson has chosen to ignore the many disclaimers that Jung placed in his autobiography, beginning on the very first page.

> Thus it is that I have now undertaken, in my eighty-third year, to tell my personal myth. I can only make direct statements, only "tell stories." Whether or not the stories are "true" is not the problem. The only question is whether what I tell is *my* fable, *my* truth.

Jung should certainly be read by anyone interested in the occult. But Jung himself would object strongly to his being made into an occultists' guru.

Aldous Huxley. Aldous Huxley was born in 1894 into what has been called the "literary aristocracy" of England His great-grandfather was Dr. Arnold of Rugby, a famous educator; his grand-uncle was the poet Mathew Arnold; his grandfather was the scientific philosopher Thomas Henry Huxley; his aunt was the novelist Mrs. Humphrey Ward. He knew nearly everyone in literary London, including Virginia Woolf and the other members of the Bloomsbury Group, D.H. Lawrence, the Sitwells, and, of course, Julian Huxley, his older brother.

Aldous Huxley's literary output was remarkable. His best-known books include *Crome Yellow* (1921); *Antic Hay* (1923); *Point Counter Point* (1928); *Brave New World* (1932); *Eyeless in Gaza* (1936); *Ends and Means* (1937); *The Art of Seeing* (1942); *Ape and Essence* (1948); and *The Doors of Perception* (1954). *The Doors of Perception* earns Huxley a place in this book, for in it Huxley recounts his experiences with mescaline and advocates the use of mind-expanding drugs in the modern search for religious meaning.

The search for meaning occupied him all his life. He was a close friend of the Buddhist writer Gerald Heard and of Krishnamurti. He was interested in yoga, meditation, and the Alexander technique. What most characterized his later writings was a spiritual vision of the world as it could be if people wanted to change it.

Huxley is often blamed for the misuse of LSD and other drugs among young people in the sixties. He had spoken of "the need for frequent chemical vacations from intolerable selfhood and repulsive surroundings." He was enthusiastic about mescaline—and later about LSD—because he believed that these drugs brought humans back into contact with spiritual realities that had been wrongly suppressed by strict rationalists (like his grandfather).

But Huxley never advocated the "turn on/drop out" philosophy that characterized the drug culture. He was always passionately concerned with larger social, economic, and political questions. He was a pacifist before and during World War II, when it was most unpopular and difficult to be one. He explored psychoanalysis, the problems of overpopulation, and, above all, the future of our technological society.

Huxley died at five o'clock in the afternoon on the same day John F. Kennedy was shot. Before he died, he requested that he be given LSD. His last moments were peaceful.

Occultism Now: Some Conclusions and Predictions

Occult beliefs are more widespread now than they ever have been. Twentieth-century occultism has many features in common with occultism of the past, but many new features as well. Eastern religion has been grafted onto Western esoteric thought and technological jargon to form all sorts of strange hybrids. These new breeds of occultism are detailed in the other sections of this book.

In this chapter I have discussed occultism in relation to the larger historical picture. At this point, I should like to distinguish some patterns in the way occultism and the general society seem to interrelate. These are only my perceptions and only time will show how accurate they are.

First: The nature of occultism changes according to what is forbidden at any given time. In the Middle Ages in Europe, occultism was associated with worship of demonic forces. When the church persecuted the first modern scientists, occultists were alchemists and believers in the heliocentric theory. During the era of strong European monarchies, occult secret societies aligned themselves with republicanism.

The twentieth century is a cerebral age, one that makes a religion of science and learning (without necessarily understanding either), one in which manual labor is disdained. Modern occultism, however, places great importance on the body and its control. It is no coincidence that in the 1970s, when feminist ideas gained such widespread acceptance, there has been a resurgence of "earth mother" cults and an increasing interest in Tantric yoga and alchemy. All these occult disciplines view woman in a very traditional manner and emphasize her difference from man.

The examples multiply. The "masses" are intruding on our lives more than ever. Not only are we more aware of the Third World, but we ourselves are losing our individual identities in our age of mass consumption, mass transportation, and mass communication. So occultism concerns itself more and more with developing the psychic powers of the individual.

Second: Modern occultism is well on its way to becoming an organized religion, not just a belief system.

The present situation among occultists is analogous to the situation at the beginning of the Christian era. There were a great many sects then, all of them with similar rites, mysteries, and world views. One sect—Christianity—eventually triumphed, but not before it had incorporated many of the themes and rituals of its rivals. Which of today's occult sects will predominate is anybody's guess. (My own guess is that it will be an amalgam of scientology, TM, and Crowleyian magic.) So far, a Messiah is lacking, although if neither Crowley nor L. Ron Hubbard gets elected, it won't be for lack of trying. There will be a Messiah, though—so many occult groups are expecting one.

Maybe some twentieth- or twenty-first-century Constantine will declare occultism the official faith. Then we will see Aquarian cathedrals (probably geodesic domes) erected in our major cities; we will witness absurd theological squabbles, with the Cybernetic bishops excommunicating the Crowleyian bishops and vice versa (probably over the issue of whether ritual magic affects machines). Then will come the august councils, to establish the canon of scripture. A certain percentage of the material in this book will be elevated to sacred status. The rest will be republished as apocrypha and lives of the saints. (I doubt that the sacred matter will be in book form. Most likely it will be on video tape or its technological successors. Baptism will consist of implanting a receiver into the believer's head, and all the recording and broadcasting equipment will be owned by the church.)

This science-fiction scenario is not a funny one, because some occult beliefs are socially dangerous. They are dangerous in that they encourage the proliferation of old prejudices that have already caused quite enough suffering in human history. If we are to have a new religion, let us at least take care that it is not merely the old one in a new disguise.

Occultism, Class, and Race. Two years ago in Cuzco, Peru, I came across a hotel desk clerk reading a Spanish translation of *Chariots of the Gods?*, and I asked him what he thought of von Däniken's theories. He enthusiastically agreed with them because, "Anyone can see that the Indians are far too stupid to have built the Inca civilization themselves."

The more occult literature one reads, the less astonishing this remark becomes. Phrases such as "the secret Aryan tradition," "Anglo-Saxon witchcraft," "the Western Mystery tradition," and "the teachings of the Great White Brotherhood" are standard. They reveal the racism underlying many occult assumptions.

Let's take the myth of Atlantis, for example. Ignatius Donnelly, who first wrote down the modern version of the myth, never stopped reminding us that we were dealing with *Aryan* history. Atlantis was "the original seat of the Aryan or Indo-European family of nations, as well as of the Semitic peoples and possibly also of the Turanian races."

The Atlanteans and their descendants are clearly superior beings.

> Civilization is not communicable to all; many savage tribes are incapable of it. There are two great divisions of mankind, the civilized and the savage; and, as we shall show, every civilized race in the world has had something of civilization from the earliest ages; and as "all roads lead to Rome," so all the converging lines of civilization lead to Atlantis. The abyss between the civilized man and the savage is simply incalculable; it rehresents not alone a difference in arts and methods of life, but in the mental constitution, the instincts, and the predispositions of the soul. . . . This abyss between savagery and civilization has never been passed by any nation through its own original force, and without external influence, during the Historic Period; those who were savages at the dawn of history are savages still. . . . We will seek in vain for any example of a savage people developing civilization of and among themselves.

The archeologists of Donnelly's time had already unearthed plenty of evidence that Indians and blacks had built great civilizations. But Donnelly could not accept their evidence at face value, because to do so he would have had to admit that they were not inferior to whites.

Closely allied to the story of Atlantis is the occult idea of the "Secret Tradition"—that there are esoteric mysteries that have been handed down (from Atlantis, Lemuria, Sirius, or wherever) to certain adepts who have ever since controlled the future of mankind. Madame Blavatsky expounded at length on this idea. It is by no means dead. Timothy Leary, for example, thinks he has been chosen by people from Sirius to spread the message of chemical enlightenment.

Now, why do these mysterious messengers—Tibetan Mahatmas, visitors from outer space, Atlanteans, etc.—usually choose to manifest themselves to white, middle-class people living in industrialized countries? Could it be that we are the Elect? That we are the Chosen Race? And what if space-gods do arrive? Isn't it assumed that they will communicate with us, those of us from "advanced" civilizations?

Adolf Hitler best illustrates the way in which the occult feeds racism. He was a firm believer in occultism, particularly in the "occult Aryan tradition." Hitler went so far as to replace "Jewish science" with "Nordic science." (Among the "Atlantean" scientists was Hans Horbiger, propagator of the Cosmic Ice theory.) Hitler was also a fanatic for astrology. A Nazi magazine proclaimed in 1933 that "awareness of one's national heritage and blood ties with the Aryan race are indivisibly bound up with astrological science."

Hitler was a member of the Thule Group, whose leader, Dietrich Eckart, was another one of the founding members of the Nazi Party. The founder of the Thule Group, Rudolf Glauer, got most of *his* ideas from Madame Blavatsky's *The Secret Doctrine*. The Thule Group members were Satanists and admirers of Aleister Crowley.

Another Nazi occult society was the Association of Invisible Aryans. (The similarity to the Invisible Empire of the Ku Klux Klan is apparent.) The Association's leader was Siegfrid Adolf Klummer, the author of a book published in 1932 called *The Holy Power of Runes*. Klummer believed that the ancient German runes had magical properties. They could cure disease, and meditation on them would inspire occult power. Through his group, Klummer promoted the worship of these relics, not the least of whose powers was the preservation of the pure Aryan race.

The association of Aryanism with occultism did not, alas, end with Hitler. Quite recently, a western group of Crowley admirers called the Solar Lodge of the Ordo Templi Orientalis held meetings to "radiate hate-vibrations into the Watts ghettos in order to start riots." Charles Manson is another occultist who hates blacks. His Family had hoped to blame their murders on blacks and start a race war.

Obviously, not all occultists are conscious racists. But I would suggest that few occultists have questioned the race and class assumptions that underlie their beliefs. I don't think it's accidental that a great upsurge of occultism has come in the 1970s. The events of the 1960s began to make Americans aware of the political effects of our technology and industry on the Third World. Now many Americans are in retreat from that horrifying knowledge.

Occultism is essentially a faith of the middle classes and lower-middle classes in industrialized countries. It has all the advantages of Christianity with the additional advantage that it requires no morality on the part of its believers. "Do what thou wilt shall be the whole of the law" is a convenient principle for those already on top of the heap, or for those who think they have a chance of getting there under the present political conditions. Are we obsessed with controlling psychic forces because we fear we are losing control?

Occultism and Science. In the twentieth century an ambivalent relationship has grown up between occultism and science. Occultists have been very loud in denouncing the limitations of science—to accuse it of stifling the human spirit, ignoring mystic reality, etc. On the other hand, occultists are fond of claiming "scientific" proof for their beliefs. The gusto with which occultists quote Pierre Teilhard de Chardin, Buckminster Fuller, and other "eminent scientists" is a tacit admission that vague ideas ought to be supported by some kind of measurable evidence. (Neither Teilhard de

Chardin nor Fuller is, however, particularly "eminent" in the scientific community.)

Science is so mysterious to most people that simply to say "According to modern scientific discoveries . . . "is to invest what follows with authority. This makes possible the presentation of outright lies as truth. Consider, for example, this statement from that sacred occult book by Louis Pauwells and Jacques Bergier, *The Morning of the Magicians*:

> Real, objective knowledge in the field of technology, which sooner or later englobes the domain of sociology, teaches us that the history of mankind follows a definite path, accompanied by an increase in man's powers, a rise in the general level of intelligence, and a compulsive force which acts on the masses transforming them into active thinkers and giving them access to a civilization where life will be as much superior to ours as ours is now to that of the animals.

Needless to say, the authors cite none of the research on which this "real, objective knowledge" is based. It doesn't exist. (Incidentally, I could just as easily have put this statement in the previous section on occultism, race, and class. The statement is *loaded* with such implications as "Technology causes a rise in the general intelligence," and "The masses are not active thinkers.")

Here's another example of misuse of science, from the same book:

> It has taken humanity 2,200 years, from Aristarchus of Samos to the year 1900, to calculate with sufficient accuracy the distance from the Earth to the Sun: 149,400,000 kilometers. To arrive at the same result it was only necessary to multiply by a thousand million the height of the Pyramid of Cheops, built in 1900 B.C.

Before you start marvelling at the Wisdom of the Ancients, look up the orbit of the Earth in any good encyclopedia. You will discover that the Earth has an elliptical, not a round, orbit, and that it is therefore impossible to calculate *any* fixed distance from the Earth to the Sun. Unless the height of the Great Pyramid expands and contracts with the Earth's orbit, the above statement—and the succeeding calculations based on it—are meaningless.

The book's authors are counting on the probability that their readers will never check their "facts," but will simply accept them in the name of "science." Here are a few more examples of pseudoscience from the book. You might try checking any one of them in the *Encyclopedia Britannica*.

> The farther we go back into the origins of the world, and the more closely we study primitive peoples, the more often we discover that their traditional secrets coincide with the present state of scientific research.

> Scientists generally agree that our universe was created by an explosion some three or four thousand million years ago.

> It is certain, then, that the Moon will end by falling on the earth.

> Nothing is known positively about nuclear forces. [Try this one on the people of Hiroshima.]
>
> Psychology is still based on a vision of a "finished" man, whose mental functions have been catalogued and classified in hierarchies once and for all.

These statements come from just one book, but the same kinds of errors dot the works of Velikovsky, von Däniken, L. Ron Hubbard, and the UFOlogists. Their theories may or may not be true, but if their reasoning is as reliable as their research, I would hate to bet on any of them.

Twentieth-century occultism is based on a logical contradiction, the pretence of using science in the service of religion. Here again, we may quote the authors of *The Morning of the Magicians*:

> All we are seeking is illumination of a kind that would enable us to see the whole human adventure in the context of eternity, and we are ready to use any means that will help us to achieve this end.

The scientific attitude is in direct contradiction to this one. The believer formulates a theory and then looks for facts to support it; the scientist observes and records data and *then* tries to formulate a theory that will explain the facts. Jung broke with Freud, you will recall, because Freud's theories did not, in his opinion, explain all the facts. Scientists are the first to admit that they have barely begun to observe the universe; scientific theory changes frequently as new observations are made. The recent missions to Mars and Jupiter, for example, have caused scientists to revise some of their theories about the origins of the solar system. But believers seldom revise their theories, no matter how many facts seem to contradict them. Wilbur Glen Voliva flew around the world several times lecturing on his "Flat Earth Theory." John Sladek's excellent book *The New Apocrypha* (Stein and Day, 1974) contains many more examples of such absurdities.

Jung was one of the many observers to note that science is entering our religious systems. One of the underlying assumptions of the new occult religion is that, through science, mankind will eventually achieve perfection. We will conquer death, disease, and social disorders; we will free ourselves from psychological imperfections; we will be able to communicate telepathically with people from other planets.

Scientists are the adepts of the new faith, the guardians of the Mysteries. Their esoteric knowledge is delivered in a language understood only by Initiates. (As in past religions, most of the adepts don't even know they *are* adepts, being too absorbed in their own lofty affairs.)

Rumors abound that scientists already have learned to freeze-dry bodies and thus prolong life indefinitely, that they can create human life, that they can improve human intelligence through genetic engineering—even that they are already communicating with UFOs and are not telling us for their own devious reasons. All of these rumors have some basis in current scientific research. But on the whole, the popular imagination, fed by science fiction, has leapt far beyond what research has verified.

The new cults of science have their sacred relics: the alpha-wave machine, the Scientologists' E-meters, the pocket biorhythym calculator, the computerized horoscope. All these objects "work"—but then so do rosary beads.

The discoveries of science inspire as much awe and fear as the acts of the gods did in past generations. This fear is not irrational. It is not paranoia to worry because someone at this moment may be making a decision that will blow us all off the globe in all-out nuclear war. It is not crazy to worry about the moral and social consequences of genetic engineering, computer technology, and behavioral psychology.

But we are controlled by what we fear. That much, at least, ought to be evident from this history of the occult. The new religion of science can serve only to widen the gap between us "mere humans" and the technological specialists, who are no more divine than we are. Already large numbers of people are so in awe of science that they believe human problems can be solved only by the advent of scientifically more advanced beings from outer space. It is always easier to believe than to doubt, for in believing one abdicates one's human responsibilities and places all decision-making in the hands of the gods.

As William Blake said:

> The ancient Poets animated all sensible objects with Gods or Geniuses, calling them by the names and adorning them with the properties of woods, rivers, mountains, lakes, cities, nations, and whatever their enlarged and numerous senses could perceive.
>
> And particularly they studied the genius of each city and country, placing it under its mental deity;
>
> Till a system was formed, which some took advantage of and enslaved the vulgar by attempting to realize or abstract the mental deities from their objects; thus began Priesthood.
>
> Choosing forms of worship from poetic tales.
>
> And at length they pronounced that the Gods had order'd such things.
>
> Thus men forget that All deities reside in the human breast.

Bibliography

Alleau, René. *History of Occult Sciences*. Geneva: Edito Services Ltd., 1966.
Bessy, Maurice. *A Pictorial History of Magic and the Supernatural*. Spring Books, 1964.
Blake, William. *Poems and Prophecies*. Dutton (Everyman's), 1927.
Cartwright, Peter. *Autobiography*. Abingdon Press, 1966.
Cavendish, Richard. *The Black Arts*. Routledge & Kegan Paul, 1967.
Chadwick, Nora K. *The Druids*. University of Wales Press, 1966.
Cles-Reden, Sibylle von. *The Realm of the Great Goddess*. Prentice-Hall, 1962.
Cooper-Oakley, Isabel. *The Count of Saint-Germain*. Rudolf Steiner Publications, 1970.

Crow, W.B. *A History of Magic, Witchcraft, and Occultism*. Aquarian Press, 1968.
de Givry, Grillot. *Witchcraft, Magic, and Alchemy*. Tr. by J. Courtenay Locke. Dover, 1971.
De Rola, Stanislas. *The Secret Art of Alchemy*. Avon, 1973.
Eliade, Mircea. *Myths, Dreams, and Mysteries*. Harvill Press, 1960.
Eliade, Mircea. *Occultism, Witchcraft, and Cultural Fashions*. University of Chicago Press, 1976.
Encyclopedia Brittanica, Eighteenth Edition.
Frazer, Sir James. *The Golden Bough: A Study in Magic and Religion* (abridged edition). Macmillan, 1922.
Frazer, Sir James George. *The Magical Origin of Kings*. Dawsons, 1968.
Gibbon, Edward. *The Decline and Fall of the Roman Empire*. A.L. Burt, 1907.
Graves, Robert. *The White Goddess*. Faber & Faber, 1959.
Howe, Ellic. *The Magicians of the Golden Dawn*. Samuel Weiser, Inc., 1978.
Hughes, Pennethorne. *Witchcraft*. Pelican Books, 1967.
Huizinga, J. *The Waning of the Middle Ages*. Anchor Books, 1954.
Johnson, Paul. *A History of Christianity*. Atheneum, 1976.
Keen, Maurice. *The Pelican History of Medieval Europe*. Penguin Books, 1968.
King, Francis. *Ritual Magic in England*. Spearman, 1970.
Lea, Charles (ed. Arthur C. Howland). *Materials Toward a History of Witchcraft*. Thomas Yoseloff, 1957.
Lévi, Eliphas. *History of Magic*. Rider, 1957.
Lot, Ferdinand. *The End of the Roman Empire and the Beginning of the Middle Ages*. Harper Torchbooks, 1961.
Mead, G.R.S. *Thrice-Great Hermes: Studies in Hellenistic Theosophy and Gnosis* (3 vols.). Theosophical Society, 1906.
Michelet, Jules. *Satanism and Witchcraft: A Study in Medieval Superstition*. Citadel Press, 1939.
Piggott, Stuart. *The Druids*. Thames & Hudson, 1968.
Scholem, Gershom. *Kabbalah*. Quadrangle, 1974.
Seligmann, K. *The History of Magic*. Pantheon Books, 1948.
Spence, Lewis. *An Encyclopedia of Occultism*. University Books, 1960.
Weston, Jessie L. *From Ritual to Romance*. Anchor Books, 1957.
White, Andrew Dickson. *A History of the Warfare of Science with Theology* (2 vols.). Dover, 1960.
Wilson, Colin. *The Occult: A History*. Random House, 1971.
Woods, William. *A History of the Devil*. Putnam's, 1973.
Yates, Frances A. *The Rosicrucian Enlightenment*. Shambhala Press, 1978.

Chapter Eight

Occult Fiction

(From Romance to Ritual)

"Choosing forms of worship from poetic tales . . ."

—William Blake

The occult fascinates writers, perhaps because writers are temperamentally attuned to the dark, creative urges, the forbidden forces of the universe.

That sentence would not have been written before the late eighteenth century and the beginning of the Romantic era. Romantic writers created the image of the writer as persecuted prophet and visionary. Romantic writers also created the most powerful occult heroes, who were themselves visionary outcasts—mad, mystical monks shamans alchemists sadistic Inquisitors Druids, monsters, and vampires.

Since then, romantic stereotypes of occultism have been reinforced by film, mass-market paperbacks, and television. Occult leaders have not hesitated to use mass media to spread their message. Several writers of occult fiction have become religious leaders, and many fictional systems have become occult dogma. The history of occult fiction is a classic case of the word becoming flesh and dwelling among us.

Most occult fiction is *formula writing*. Formula writing is a descriptive rather than critical term. Formula fiction projects the reader into an already existing world of illusion, one that has been created by the formula writers of the past. Dozens of these illusory worlds are known to most of us. For example, most people today think of Victorian London in terms of images created by Dickens and multiplied on film and television. This imaginary Victorian world is "real" to us.

Formula fiction is a mass-produced form of the folktale. Like folktales, formulas can be catalogued according to motifs and themes. In occult fiction, "the mysterious disappearing narrator" is a common formula. Coleridge's poem "The Rime of the Ancient Mariner" is the best-known example. Another common formula is "fantasy woman drives writer insane," which is a sexier version of "writer begins to believe his own fictions and goes insane." Other occult formulas include "ghost horse or carriage comes for soul," "trees come alive and call human to alien world," "supernatural force inhabits human body," "man meets moon goddess in oriental temple," "man turns to beast," and "man ravishes goddess."

Gothic Novels

Occult fiction formulas were established at the beginning of the Industrial Revolution, specifically with the Gothic novel. Gothic novels were the first bestsellers, the first books to be mass-produced on the new, efficient, power-driven presses. Those early Gothic novels were the ancestors of modern "supermarket Gothics," the paperback novels that are illustrated with women fleeing from sinister buildings. Gothics were also the forerunners of historical romances and adventure stories.

Gothics earned their name from their pseudomedieval settings. The stories usually took place in ruined abbeys or castles set in craggy, wild landscapes and furnished with old carved furniture, dungeons, confessionals, ghosts, and Inquisition torture chambers. Gothic writers sought to instill in their readers a dual sense of Beauty and Terror.

The first important Gothic novel was Horace Walpole's *The Castle of Otranto*, which was published in 1764. The Gothic form was further developed by Ann Radcliffe, whose best-known books were *The Mysteries of Udolpho* (1794) and *The Italian* (1797), and by Matthew Gregory ("Monk") Lewis, who published *The Monk* in 1797. A swarm of imitators soon descended and Gothic literary formulas were quickly established

Radcliffe introduced the Romantic Devil, who has been the hero of occult fiction ever since. The Romantic Devil is a solitary, silent, guilt-ridden outcast who arouses both our pity and disgust. He is usually slim, dark, handsome, and sensuous. Sometimes he is also sadistic and slightly insane. The Devil's victim is usually an innocent, fair, slender female who loves him to her own destruction. The Romantic Devil/Innocent Beauty story is a later development of *Beauty and the Beast*, which contains one of the oldest folktale themes.

Another popular Romantic novelist—Sir Walter Scott—added the dimension of historical detail to formula fiction. The Gothics were an expression of revival of interest in the Middle Ages. But the authors of Gothics were more interested in creating an atmosphere of Beauty and Terror than in recreating a specific period. Scott did his best to be historically accurate, thus helping invent the historical romance.

Coleridge, Byron, Shelley, and Keats all read Gothic novels in their youth, and all contributed to Romantic occult formulas through their work. Byron refined the image of the Romantic Hero, both in his writing and in his life. Shelley's writing career began with a "Rosicrucian novel," published in his university days. His second wife, Mary Godwin Shelley, wrote *Frankenstein*, which has probably produced more occult formulas than any other single work.

In the first part of the nineteenth century a new form of printed entertainment—the magazine—became popular. Magazines were an important new outlet for writers of fiction. Until television and paperbacks replaced the "pulps" as major mass-fiction forms, most occult writers depended on magazines for their living.

In America, Nathaniel Hawthorne began his career by contributing stories to *Atlantic Monthly* and *The New England Magazine*; and Edgar Allen Poe edited and wrote for *The Southern Literary Messenger*. In England, Wilkie Collins made his reputation by contributing to Dickens's magazine *Household Words*.

The occult story has changed gradually over the years. One important change has been in the nature of the ghosts or supernatural characters. During the Romantic era (which ended with the death of Sir Walter Scott in

1832), the ghost was not so much a personality as a part of the scenery. Ghosts tended to be described as "pale wraiths." They were dressed in white and were ethereal in substance. Early ghosts seldom touched their victims; if they did, the touch was cold and clammy.

Gradually ghosts assumed individual traits. They became active predators who inflicted physical harm on people—biting them, strangling them, or sucking their blood.

The Expansion of Formula Fiction

Several different types of formula fiction developed simultaneously during the nineteenth century. Detective stories, horror stories, adventure tales, historical romance, fantasy tales, and science-fiction tales all borrowed from each other during the course of their development.

When the first Gothic novels appeared, respectable parents, educators, and churchmen preached against them as fervently as people today preach against television. Social observers worried that the reading of too much fiction would ruin public morals and lead to a state in which people were no longer able to distinguish between fantasy and reality. Perhaps they had reason for alarm.

The mass distribution of formula fiction radically changed the thought patterns of Western civilization. It is difficult for us, after 200 years of a steady fictional diet, to grasp how great this change was. The Victorian "penny press," accompanied by a rapid rise in literacy, brought millions of people into the writer's market. Print was no longer the medium of only the educated classes. By the late nineteenth century, every child of school age and most adults in the Western world had been exposed to a steady diet of adventure, horror, mystery, detection, romance, and fantasy tales. We are still consuming fiction at an amazing rate, and it is inextricably woven together with reality in our minds.

Our impressions of African jungles, for example, were created by H. Rider Haggard, Edgar Rice Burroughs, and other adventure-thriller writers: Haggard and Burroughs both wrote fantasies of finding lost white races in the middle of the blackest jungle. These white people lived in immense treasure cities and worshipped the ancient solar gods. That image of "lost white priest races" is now regarded as gospel truth among occultists. Similarly, the present occult preoccupation with the pyramids can be traced to the rash of "Oriental temple" fantasies that infected the nineteenth-century reading public. Orientalism became big publishing business after Napoleon's expeditions to Egypt at the end of the eighteenth century. Another occult myth based on fiction is the idea that the solar god is a "white" god. Many occultists also believe—wrongly—that Egypt, Peru, and other sun-worshipping civilizations were monotheistic.

When spiritualism became fashionable in the middle of the nineteenth century, writers rushed to insert table-rapping, spirit manifestations, automatic writing, and other spiritualist trappings into their books. It is very difficult to judge how many of the spiritualist manifestations of the time were projections of group expectations. Most Europeans had read such bestselling spiritualist tales as Bulwer Lytton's "*Zanoni*" (1842) before they witnessed psychic demonstrations.

Ideas such as the "astral body," "the etheric plane," "the wisdom of the Arabs," "the secret society of Masons and Illuminati" had circulated through fiction twenty-five years before Madame Blavatsky and her contemporaries turned them into dogma.

We can discern two broad types of occult fiction developing over the nineteenth century. These are the "theological occult" story and the "psychological occult" story. The first type of story was written as much to convince the reader of the truth of occult and psychic reality as to entertain. The psychological occult story depended heavily on the device of the narrator's insanity, leaving the reader uncertain as to the difference between reality and illusion.

The fathers of the theological occult story were Nathaniel Hawthorne, Bulwer Lytton, and Wilkie Collins. They were followed by dozens of writers of tales ranging from sentimental domestic séance stories to adventure stories of trips by astral projection. Among occult novelists popular in the nineteenth century were Marie Corelli, Arthur Conan Doyle, Mrs. Margaret Oliphant, Mrs. J.H. Riddle, Vernon Lee, Charles W. Beale, and Amelia B. Edwards.

The fathers of the psychological occult story were Edgar Allen Poe and the Irish writer Sheridan LeFanu. Both writers used narrators whose drug habits made them prey to hallucinations and temporary insanity. Both writers were obsessed with questions of psychology and nervous illness.

Many writers wrote both kinds of stories. As the century progressed, occult writers were able to borrow elements from science fiction and "sword and sorcery" fantasies as well. H. Rider Haggard is best remembered for *She, King Solomon's Mines*, and other such adventure tales. But he also generated interest in the occult, especially by helping establish the occult fiction formula, "pagan idol pursues its Western owner."

There are many more parellels between occult fiction and occult belief. More of them will become apparent if you read this chapter in conjunction with "The Occult Bible."

Several occult leaders in the nineteenth century were also writers of formula occult fiction. Madame Blavatsky tried fiction before doctrine as a way to earn a living. Dion Fortune, at the beginning of the twentieth century, wrote sentimental spiritualist theological novels which are scarcely distinguishable from her doctrinal dissertations. Gurdjieff used

Beelzebub's Tales to his Grandson to make theological points. Annie Besant wrote spiritualist fiction. Aleister Crowley wrote an oriental temple fantasy, which contains much of the same theology as his *Book of Lies*. Both were inspired by the appearance of Crowley's guardian angel in a museum in Cairo.

In the twentieth century, the web of fiction has been immeasurably strengthened by reinforcements from film and television. The formula stories of H. Rider Haggard, Conan Doyle, and Robert Chambers were among the first to be made into films. Television has produced such classics of occultism as "Way Out," "The Outer Limits," "Night Gallery," and "The Twilight Zone." These series drew heavily on the hundreds of plot variations worked out by formula writers of the past. The immense success of *The Exorcist* in resurrecting the popular belief in demonic possession is worth noting here. That novel, like so many modern mass-market paperbacks, was published as part of a multimedia campaign.

Film and television also have been responsible for the modern wedding of the occult story with the science-fiction tale, most notably illustrated by the work of H.P. Lovecraft. Science-fiction heroes now possess occult abilities—they can levitate, travel on the astral plane, and read minds. The modern sci-fi hero is often a scientist/priest who rather resembles a priest in an oriental temple fantasy.

Since sci-fi has assumed many theological dimensions, it is hardly surprising to find occult beliefs incorporating myths from sci-fi. When Olaf Stapledon wrote *Odd John:Sirius* in the 1930s, he probably did not expect that within fifty years people would actually believe extraterrestrials from Sirius had visited the Earth. The Sirius legend had appeared before, of course—Madame Blavatsky, among others, helped create it. But Stapledon's *Sirius*, and Lovecraft's association of the dog star with the "Cthulhu mythos," are what gave the myth its authority.

The "sword and sorcery" or "magical fantasy" tale is so heavily laced with occult elements that separating the stories into "occult" and "nonoccult" is impossible. Magical fantasy stories, such as those written in the nineteenth century by William Morris and William Hope Hodgson, and in the twentieth century by C.S. Lewis and Tolkien, have done a great deal to build up the Arthurian myths. Arthur Machen wrote extensively on the Grail legends as well as turning out occult and horror stories. Through these means, and through the Romantic image of the druid, modern occultists have received the erroneous idea that the court of King Arthur was ruled by occult forces. Dion Fortune's "western mystery tradition" gives central importance to Merlin, whom, she claimed, was really Hermes Trismegistus.

Occult fiction writers have also been heavily influenced by their reading in such sciences as anthropology and geology, both new disciplines at the end of the nineteenth century. Occult writers were among the first to mass-distribute the ideas of Frazer. Fictional versions of Frazer's *Golden Bough* have been primarily responsible for the resurrection of "white witchcraft" in this century, though Robert Graves's book *The White Goddess* must share some of the blame, along with the writings of Margaret Murray, the lecturer on Egyptology at University College, London, who in the 1920s first put forth the theory that modern witchcraft is a survival of an ancient nature-religion.

Today, more than ever, we are seeing the fulfillment in reality of one of the oldest occult formulas: "writer believes own fictions." Unfortunately, in our multimedia world, the formula does not end with that. It ends, "writer founds religion." L. Ron Hubbard, one-time sci-fi writer and founder of Scientology, is the prime example but not the only one.

What has happened to occult belief because of fiction ought to make us rethink the role of the writer in an industrialized society. The Romantic image of the writer as the solitary outcast no longer makes sense when the writer who invents a fictional formula can become nothing less than a god, the maker of myths by which people live and worship.

In the section that follows I've tried to list those writers whose work has most contributed to present-day occult beliefs. In some cases, as in those of Arthur Conan Doyle and L. Ron Hubbard, the writer's influence has extended far beyond his writing. Other writers, such as Mary Shelley, created characters that were later given greater occult dimensions by others.

Postscript

In its broadest sense, the term "occult fiction" would have to include most sci-fi stories as well as fairy tales, folktales, classical myths, epic poetry, and magical fantasy stories. However, I have tried to limit this chapter by concentrating on stories that contain mostly occult formulas, by selecting those writers whose work has had the widest influence on occult thought and practice.

What is mere formula in the hands of a bad writer is inspiration in the genius. In this chapter there are some great literary names as well as the names of well-known hacks. I have tried to place each occult writer within the larger context of occult belief and to give you an idea of the reasons for each writer's popularity. I hope these brief notes will be a helpful introduction to new readers of occult fiction as well as a useful synthesis for people already familiar with this weird fictional world.

Abdullah Achmed

Abdullah Achmed was a pseudonym used by a writer of fantastic oriental tales, whose real name is not known. The titles of his books give the flavor of the writing: *The Mating of the Blaes; Mysteries of Asia; Steel and Jade; Swinging Caravan; The Thief of Bagdad;* and *Wings: Tales of the Psychic.*

The author's biography resembles his fictions. He was born in 1891 in Yalta, on the Crimean Peninsula. His father was Russian Orthodox; his mother was Moslem; he was educated by the Jesuits. He also was sent to Eton and Oxford, so presumably his parents were people of some means. He served in the British Army in India, Tibet, and Egypt.

During the 1930s Achmed moved to New York. There, reported the magazines, he lived in "oriental splendor." It is difficult to check the accuracy of the many stories he told of his narrow escapes, of palace intrigues, and his other adventures.

Achmed's books are adventure stories as well as psychic stories, in spite of their emphasis on oriental mysticism, the Wisdom of the Ancient Arabs, and so forth. The supernatural appearances in his stories resemble those in *The Arabian Nights*. The books were very popular in the 1910s and 1920s, at the height of the craze for things Egyptian and decadently oriental.

Achmed wrote about thirty books as well as short stories and plays. *Alien Souls, Swinging Caravan*, and *Honourable Gentlemen and Others* have been reissued in the Arno Reprint Series. They are available at public libraries.

Michael Arlen

Michael Arlen was famous not only through his popular writing but also through his appearances on the society pages of the newspapers. His marriage in 1928 to the Countess Atalanta Mercati was just the opportunity for success he needed. He was slim, beautifully tailored, fond of displaying his wealth, arrogant, and vain. He was also charming.

Arlen was born Dikran Euyumjian in 1895 in Bulgaria. His parents were Armenians. He was sent to England to school. His first book, *The Green Hat* (1924), was made into a hit play. Arlen's occult tales include *Ghost Stories; Hell, Said the Duchess: A Bedtime Story* (1934); *Man's Mortality* (1933); and *May Fair* (1925).

Arlen's stories have fairly standard, Poe-derived plots, full of drug hallucinations and melancholy apprehensions. Although they are rather too opium-hazy to retain the interest of the modern reader, the stories do have flashes of wit, especially when Arlen portrays eccentric society characters.

Most of Arlen's books are out of print, but they are readily available at public libraries.

Ambrose Bierce

Ambrose Bierce was born in a log cabin on the American frontier in 1842.

His parents were farmers and very poor. Ambrose hated his whole family except for his brother Albert. However, he was saved from his family by the Civil War. He entered the Union Army as a drummer boy and emerged as a lieutenant major. After the war, he settled with his brother in San Francisco, where he became a leading newspaper writer.

From 1876 to 1886, Bierce was the author of the weekly "Prattler" column in the *Argonaut*. In 1887, the column was picked up nationwide by Hearst, owner of the *Examiner*. He then began to have a national audience.

Bierce was a very popular columnist. He associated with such Western writers as Mark Twain, Bret Harte, and Joaquin Miller and helped popularize their work. During this productive period in San Francisco, he married and had two children. He also began writing fiction.

Among his well-known books, most of which are collections of short stories, are *Can Such Things Be?*, *Fantastic Fables*, *In the Midst of Life*, and *The Devil's Dictionary*. His fiction is in the direct tradition of Poe, though Bierce lacks Poe's florid style.

Bierce drew much on occult and psychic experiences connected with the Civil War. He used folk legends that circulated among the soldiers as his plots. For example, in "A Horseman in the Sky," a young Union soldier must decide whether to fire at an "apparition" of his father, a scout from the Confederate Army. The story also illustrates many of the values in Bierce's work, placing high value on duty, patriotism, and honor in quite a snobbish way. It is significant that the father in the story is a high officer. Bierce's work often betrays his own unease about his social origins.

Bierce also enjoyed using the device of phony horror. In "The Man and the Snake," for example, the victim is scared to death by his own imagination and too much reading of horror fiction. In "A Watcher by the Dead," two young doctors plant a "corpse" in a room and induce a man to spend a night with it. In both stories, the victim's cruel end is a result of his own susceptibility.

Ambrose Bierce is best known today for his *Devil's Dictionary*, a sardonic collection of definitions from the Devil's point of view. The book shows off his wit to great advantage. That was the quality that made him a popular columnist.

Bierce was apparently cruel, even sadistic, at times, especially in his later years. A series of personal tragedies—a divorce, the death of his son in an adolescent duel—embittered him. However, he continued to write through the turn of the century. From 1896 to 1909 he lived and worked in Washington, D.C. He was the Washington correspondent for the New York *American*.

In 1914, Bierce made a trip into Mexico, from which he never returned. The mystery of his disappearance has not yet been solved.

Thanks to Dover Books, Ambrose Bierce's writings are now readily available. Dover published *Ghost and Horror Stories of Ambrose Bierce* (1964); *Fantastic Fables* (1970); and *The Devil's Dictionary* (1970). New American Library (Signet Classics) publishes a paperback of *In the Midst of Life and Other Stories*. There is a hardbound Citadel Press edition of the *Collected Writings of Ambrose Bierce* (1960). Dover also published *The Sardonic Humor of Ambrose Bierce*, which concentrates on nonoccult pieces.

Algernon Blackwood

Blackwood was a very popular, very prolific writer of ghost and psychic stories and novels. His work appeared regularly in magazines of the 1910s, 1920s, and 1930s, and throughout World War II.

Blackwood was born in 1869 in Kent. He was raised in a conservative and prosperous evangelical home. His father was Sir Arthur Blackwood, KCB; his mother was the widow of the Fifth Duke of Manchester. He described his childhood and youth as having been full of conversions. He was educated at Wellington, Edinburgh University, and a Moravian college in the Black Forest.

He left home at the age of twenty and moved to Canada. His first job there was as a children's writer for the *Canadian Methodist Magazine*. He left the job after a few months to try his hand at farming and various small business ventures, all of which failed.

He drifted to New York, where he worked at various odd jobs, none of which paid well. His financial problems were solved when, through family connections, he got a job as the private secretary to a millionaire and was able to turn his full attention to cultivating his knowledge of the occult.

Blackwood's writing career began when a friend mailed off some of his private scribblings without telling him. The publishers loved the work; Blackwood had at last found a career at which he could be a success.

Blackwood read a great deal. His stories were among the first mass-market fiction to use themes from anthropology, which was then quite a new science.

Blackwood believed that there was a special force in Nature, consisting of energy and underlying all things, and that this force was worshipped in pre-Christian ("pagan") times. His titles reflect this belief: "The Man whom the Trees Loved"; "The Touch of Pan"; *The Human Chord; The Centaur*.

It is obvious from Blackwood's work that he believed in the occult ideas about which he wrote. He was known to be a mystic.

In style, Blackwood owed more to Hawthorne than to Poe. His dreams were not frightening nightmares but states of mystic trance. Blackwood seems more interested in convincing or converting the reader than in scaring him. For example, "The Trod" and "The Man whom the Trees Loved" are both stories of the futile struggle to resist the force of Nature, which calls humans toward the spirit world. The psychic struggle between man and the forces of "the other side" is one of Blackwood's favorite themes. Nature in both these storiee is wild and magical, but not overwhelmingly evil or frightening.

Blackwood's work reflects his reading of fairy tales, which in the nineteenth century were just beginning to be collected. He used such folktale plots as "mysterious carriage comes for victim" and "ice princess lures skater to frozen death" ("The Glamour of the Snow"). He had obviously read Washington Irving. He also owed a great deal to Arthur Machen. He created a seeker/sage figure, John Silence, who was much inspired by LeFanu's Dr. Hesselius and by Arthur Machen's Dr. Reymond.

Some of Blackwood's books included *Ancient Sorceries and Other Tales; The Bright Messenger; By Underground; The Centaur; The Doll and One Other; The Education of Uncle Paul; The Human Chord; The Extra Day; Full Circle; The Garden of Survival; The Italian Conjurer;* and *Pan's Garden*. They still circulate through public libraries, though most of them are now out of print. Dover Books has begun to remedy this misfortune with *Best Short Stories of Algernon Blackwood* (1973).

Helen Blavatsky

Madame Helena Petrovna Blavatsky, the founder of Theosophy, was one of the most important figures in the establishment of the modern occult movement. Her biography appears in the chapter "Occult History."

She deserves mention here because of *Nightmare Tales*, an attempt (in the early 1870s) to make a living as a popular writer. The *Tales* are standard gushy spiritualism. They were only moderately successful. She abandoned fiction in favor of doctrine.

Nightmare Tales is no longer in print.

Taylor Caldwell

Since her first successful novel, *Dynasty of Death*, was published in 1938, Taylor Caldwell has been one of America's most popular novelists, author of *Dear and Glorious Physician* (the story of Luke), *Captains and the Kings, Glory and the Lightning*, and many more. Caldwell is also the author of a number of books on occult subjects.

Caldwell is one of those rare and fortunate individuals who not only know their experiences in this life but can also remember the experiences of past lives. *The Search for a Soul: Taylor Caldwell's Psychic Lives* (Doubleday, 1973) lists some of her experiences in previous incarnations. She was a scullery maid to the novelist George Eliot; she was a physician in ancient Greece in 1000 B.C.; she was a courtesan named Melina in an Atlantean world; she was a follower of Fra Savonarola; she was a Spanish Jew; she was a maid in an elegant English household.

In the present life, Caldwell was born in Manchester, England, in 1900. Her family emigrated to the United States when she was six. She was a precocious child, and at the age of twelve she wrote a novel called *The Romance of Atlantis*. This book has recently appeared, presented as a possibly genuine psychic revelation of Atlantis. For how could a twelve-year-old child have written a romance that is better than most of today's bestsellers? (The question is more a comment on the quality of today's bestsellers than it is on Taylor Caldwell's "psychic memories" of Atlantis.)

For one who remembers so many other cultures and systems, Caldwell strays remarkably little from the hard line of the conservatives of the 1950s. In *Dialogues with the Devil*, an imaginary conversation between Lucifer and the archangel Michael, Lucifer reveals some of his trade secrets. His most effective tools: Big government, the welfare system, liberal politics, and feminism.

Caldwell is also fond of secret societies. The immense popularity of her books cannot be unrelated to the fact that the mysterious secret society plays a greater role than ever in the mythology of the occultist. An international secret society figures prominently in the plots of *Captains and the Kings, The Testimony of Two Men*, and *Ceremony of the Innocent*. Her recent novel, *Bright Flows the River*, pictures the world in the deadly grip of a "Fascistic Communist" conspiracy. The population, stupider than ever because of indiscriminate breeding, is unable to resist the gradual destruction of the middle classes by excessive income taxes.

In short, Taylor Caldwell's work exhibits all the worst racial and sexual prejudices of present-day American occultism. She seems to advocate "vigilante" organizations to keep "order" in the streets (and, presumably, protect the middle class). I should also mention her contributions, in *The Testimony of Two Men* and *Captains and the Kings*, to the myths growing up around political assassinations.

Her books are available at most public libraries. Pyramid Press and Fawcett World publish her work in paperback.

John Dickson Carr

John Dickson Carr is one of the best and most prolific mystery-story writers working today. His work is noted for its "occult" quality—that is, its sense of eeriness and mystery. He is fascinated by the macabre and the supernatural. In most of his stories, occultism is not central to the plot, but his characters are often occult believers.

In *The Burning Court*, one of Carr's best books, a young publisher reads a manuscript about witchcraft, which leads to contact with what he supposes is the supernatural. A murder is committed, apparently by supernatural means. The beauty of the plot lies in the fact that the murder is explained "rationally," but the rational explanation fails to convince the reader in the same way that the supernatural explanation does.

The Devil in Velvet, a pact-with-the-Devil story, is part occult thriller and part historical novel. It takes place in the court of Charles II of England, amid many political intrigues. The adventure and history elements of the plot are, however, more important than the pact with the Devil, so the book cannot be called an occult novel.

Both these books are good examples of the way Carr uses occultism to add interest and fear to his plots.

Carr was born in Pennsylvania in 1906. He lived in England for most of the 1930s and 1940s. In 1948 he returned to the United States Most of his books are available in paperback from Bantam Books. Some of his other books with occult elements include *It Walks by Night, Castle Skull, The Arabian Nights Murders, The Demoniacs*, and *To Wake the Dead*.

Arthur C. Clarke

Clarke was born in England in 1917. Although he gained a considerable following among sci-fi fans in the 1950s, he did not reach the status of a prophet until after the 1968 release of Stanley Kubrick's movie, *2001: A Space Odyssey*. *2001* was based on Clarke's 1950 story, "The Sentinel."

Clarke's work has contributed a great deal to the idea that the evolution of humankind is controlled by beings from outer space. Clarke is explicit about the religious implications of his ideas. About *2001* he said, "M-G-M doesn't know it yet, but they've footed the bill for the first $10,500,000.00 religious film."

The religious themes of *2001* appear throughout Clarke's sci-fi writing. In his first major novel, *Childhood's End*, he posited that humankind was gradually evolving into an overmind, which was itself under the supervision of extraterrestrials.

Clarke is a strong advocate for technology, envisioning a future world where mankind will be free of work. Only about 100,000 people will inhabit the Earth; the rest of the human race, presumably, will have been dispersed among other planets. Clarke has also been a strong advocate of space colonization as a way to solve the problems of the Earth.

Clarke's stories connect the science of the West with the ancient secrets of the East. For many years, he has made his home on Sri Lanka. A widely held belief among occultists is that Tibetan monks are in special communication with the cosmic forces. Clarke uses this idea in his most often reprinted short story, "The Nine Billion Names of God."

Clarke made international television news on tours promoting *2001*. He made a great many gurulike statements to the press, such as, "There are only civilized men and uncivilized men. Civilized men can do whatever they set their minds to." Here are some more of his epigrams: "All the problems in the universe—pollution, population, weather, and so on—can only be solved by going into space." "It is highly probably that Earth has been visited many times in the past and will be visited many times in the future." "Any sufficiently advanced technology is indistinguishable from magic." "Some of us have a chance of seeing the end of the Dark Ages."

Clarke's ideas have been picked up by von Däniken—who, in fact, quotes Clarke as a scientific authority. Admittedly, Clarke does have training in both physics and math (King's College, London) and does know more than the average person does about aeronautics (he was an RAF pilot in World War II). He makes his living as a writer of science fiction, however, which is not the same as being a scientist. Not yet.

Wilkie Collins

The name of Wilkie Collins is often associated with that of his friend Charles Dickens, with whom he worked on the magazine *Household Words*. In their time, Collins was the more popular writer. In fact, his stories often kept *Household Words* afloat and allowed Dickens to go on writing.

Collins was born in London in 1824, the son of a successful painter. Wilkie Collins's first novel, *Antonina, or The Fall of Rome*, subtitled *A Romance of the Fifth Century*, was published in 1850. His friendship with Dickens began shortly thereafter. Their friendship and literary collaborations lasted all their lives. Collins died in 1889.

Wilkie Collins's most popular novel, *The Woman in White*, appeared in the November 26, 1859, issue of *Household Words*. It was printed serially. The story was an immense success. The markets were flooded with Woman in White perfumes, Woman in White bonnets, Woman in White corsets. There was even a dance called "The Woman in White." *The Moonstone*, Collins's second major success, is one of the most entertaining popular novels ever written.

None of Wilkie Collins's major novels are really ghost stories, although Collins certainly wants the reader to think of the characters as ghostlike at times. The Woman in White is actually an escapee from a lunatic asylum who is killed in place of the heroine. In *The Moonstone*, the mysterious oriental figures skulking about are members of a secret religious order. The curse on the moonstone and the magical means of getting it back are occult elements in the story, but *The Moonstone*'s success is really due to its characterization and to its adventure-tale elements.

However, Collins belongs in this book because of the steady stream of horror and ghost stories that poured from his pen throughout his writing career. His was an important influence on the development of horror writing.

Among Collins's horror writings are *After Dark and Other Stories; The*

Haunted Hotel: A Mystery of Modern Venice; and *The Ghost's Touch and Other Stories*.

Occult themes appeared in his earliest work. "Basil" and "Hide and Seek," two of his earliest stories, have sinister magician characters in them. In "The Dream Woman," first published in *Household Words* in 1855, a man's ex-wife appears to him in a dream and tries to kill him.

In style, Collins was more "elevated" than Poe. Collins's supernaturalism had a more ethereal, less psychological quality. There is little of Poe's despair or madness. Wilkie Collins's characters are English types: brusque, good-humored squires, eccentric spinsters. His hero is usually the young middle-class professional man—a cheerful, good sort of fellow. Collins did wonderfully entertaining things with his plots, especially in *The Moonstone*. He could be very funny.

These books were the precursors of the spiritualist novels that abounded in the 1880s and 1890s, in which the characters were wafted on astral beams into loftier, more romantic planes of existence. Collins cannot be blamed for all those sentimental atrocities, but he did introduce a strain of sentimentality into the genre.

Critical opinion has remained remarkably uniform on Wilkie Collins. His contemporaries agreed that he was a master storyteller but not a great writer, and today's literary academics share that view, considering him to be a secondary figure. Like Arthur Conan Doyle, he is much read in secret by people of sophisticated literary tastes.

The Moonstone's plot is well known, since it was made into a popular PBS television series. The story is available in paperback from Penguin Books, as is *The Woman in White*. *After Dark and Other Stories* is available in some libraries through the Arno Reprint Series. Dover Books publishes *Tales of Terror and the Supernatural* (1972).

Aleister Crowley

Crowley is the official First Bad Man of the occult movement, a now-legendary devil-worshipper, magician, and theologian. He has a wide following among occultists. For his biography, consult the chapter "Occult History."

Like Madame Blavatsky, Crowley also entered the lists of occult fiction. His candidate was *Moonchild*, an exotic-oriental-temple story that purports to be about spiritual mysteries but is actually about Crowley's tastes in women. (He liked them nubile, wasted, shivering, naked, bleeding, and screaming.)

Crowley always promised more than he delivered in the way of wickedness. There is a British schoolboy element of naughtiness in *Moonchild*, as well as an occasional and generous dose of the decorous middle-class ritual for which Crowley savagely attacked the other members of the Order of the

Golden Dawn.

As for exotica (naked Nubian slave maidens, etc.), the novel is but a pale copy of Flaubert's *Salammbo* and other oriental fantasies of the nineteenth century.

Moonchild is available in paperback from Avon (1971). A library (hardcover) edition has been published by Krishna Press.

Ignatius Donnelly

Ignatius Donnelly was a Midwestern land promoter and politician who wrote popular novels. He was responsible for three of the most widespread myths of modern life. His book *Atlantis: The Antediluvian World* is the standard work on Atlantis. Though it is riddled with errors, the book is the main "proof" offered for the existence of the submerged continent.

In a second book, *Ragnorak: The Age of Fire and Gravel*, Donnelly expounded the theory that violent cosmic catastrophes caused the geologic features of the Earth. This idea has now been expanded by Velikovsky and others (see "The Book of Cataclysms" in the chapter "The Occult Bible"). Donnelly's third pet theory, that Francis Bacon really wrote Shakespeare, is also still among us.

Donnelly's is an American success story. He was born in Philadelphia in 1831, studied law, and moved West to Minnesota in the 1850s. He lived well off the land-boom and narrowly escaped bankruptcy when it ended. Meanwhile, he involved himself in frontier politics, in both the Republican and Democratic parties, and he was lieutenant governor of Minnesota for a time. During the 1860s and 1870s he represented Minnesota in the House of Representatives. He died in 1901.

Donnelly spent much of his later life on the lecture circuit, a major form of entertainment a century ago. His favorite lecture topics were Atlantis and social reform. In his later life he increasingly began to speak out against the monopolies, race prejudice, and other evils of the capitalist system. However, his writings too often betray the very prejudices against which he spoke.

Donnelly's contemporaries considered him a harmless, perhaps slightly lunatic, idealist. But he was destined to have a more lasting effect on history than most of his detractors. His Atlantean theory is now "mainstream" occultism. Edgar Cayce, Ruth Montgomery, and any number of other astrologers, witches, and gurus claim that they have been to Atlantis. Most of these people also maintain that there are, at present, an exceptionally large number of reincarnated Atlanteans living on the Earth today. You could be one, too.

Arthur Conan Doyle

Many people today believe that in the late nineteenth and early twentieth centuries there lived in London a brilliant, lonely, intellectual cocaine addict named Sherlock Holmes, who turned his incisive mind to the business of detection in peace and espionage in wartime, all for the preservation of democracy. Sherlock Holmes proves that fiction can create reality. Most people today have a far clearer idea of him than they have of, say, Oscar Wilde.

Holmes was the projection of the extraordinary mind of Arthur Conan Doyle, who was a writer of popular fiction and also became a famous spokesman for the Spiritualist Movement. Conan Doyle had a remarkable personality. In some ways he resembled Dr. Watson. Both believed in hard work, manliness, courage, patriotism, and other such solid virtues; both were bluff, straightforward and somewhat naive.

But Conan Doyle had some elements of Holmes in his character too. He developed remarkable reasoning ability as he developed Sherlock's character. He was even called in on police cases and succeeded in solving several baffling ones.

All of this made wonderful copy, and by 1891 Conan Doyle was famous. It helped a lot that "A Scandal in Bohemia" was quite close in plot to the current court scandals about the Prince of Wales. After that, Conan Doyle was tied for life to Sherlock Holmes. Doyle tried to kill him off several times, but the public always demanded that he be resurrected, and Conan Doyle always obliged at last. Thus Holmes saw the Britons through the Boer War and the First World War, and (after Conan Doyle's death) through World War II and Korea as well.

Conan Doyle seems to have become a serious student of the occult in 1893, shortly after his father died and his wife Louise learned she had tuberculosis, at that time an incurable disease. In November 1893 he joined the Society for Psychical Research. With the other members of the society, Conan Doyle investigated such mediums as Daniel Dunglas Home and Florrie Cook (see chapter two).

He began attending séances regularly, a practice he was to continue all his life. The Doyle children were raised on séances just as most of their contemporaries were raised on prayers. In his later years, Doyle devoted more and more of his time and considerable wealth to spreading the psychic gospel. He lectured widely in America and Europe. He was a great celebrity. He bought a succession of grand houses for himself and his family and continued to make unpopular occult pronouncements that embarrassed his millions of respectable fans. Indeed, he was so frequently tricked by mediums and professional magicians that he lost most of his credibility as an observer for the Society for Psychical Research.

As he grew older, however, Conan Doyle began to be regarded with greater indulgence. Sherlock Holmes had been projected by means of film into the minds of millions all over the world; Conan Doyle filmed several shorts of himself talking about the life beyond and asked that they be shown with the Holmes films. But in spite of all Conan Doyle's efforts, Sherlock Holmes always got better press. Doyle was regarded as a harmless eccentric, a resident national potty uncle. He died in 1930 at the age of seventy-one.

Conan Doyle wrote dozens of stories other than the Sherlock Holmes tales. Many of them were on occult subjects. He was adept at creating genuine terror, and his psychic stories succeed very well in convincing the reader.

In *The Leather Funnel*, Conan Doyle deals with the art of psychometry, the ability to receive psychic impressions from objects. In *The Lost World*, Conan Doyle had his characters journey into a jungle that mysteriously moved back in time; it was populated by horrible prehistoric monsters and apemen.

Conan Doyle also wrote science fiction stories and war adventure stories, all of which were widely read. He can be said to have influenced almost every writer of any kind of fiction today. An amazing number of writers list Sherlock Holmes as among their favorite childhood heroes.

Among Conan Doyle's writings on occult themes are *The Black Doctor, and Other Tales of Terror and Mystery* (1919); *The Case for Spirit Photography* (1922); *The Early Christian Church and Modern Spiritualism* (still available from Psychic Press, London); *The Edge of the Unknown* (1930); *The History of Spiritualism* (1926); *The Land of Mist* (1926); and *The Lost World* (1912). With the single exception noted, Conan Doyle's occult fiction is not in print, though some libraries have old volumes. Sherlock Holmes is, of course, available everywhere.

Gustave Flaubert

Flaubert was one of the greatest French novelists of the nineteenth century. His most influential works were *Madame Bovary* (1856), *The Sentimental Education* (1869), and *Three Tales* (1877). Flaubert was also the author of *Salammbo*, an Egyptian-mystery-temple novel that was as popular in its own time as *Madame Bovary* and *The Sentimental Education*.

Flaubert was born in 1821 in Rouen, into a doctor's family. He spent much of his youth reading Romantic novels and imagining himself to be a Byronic hero. Though his parents wanted him to study law, the law made Flaubert develop a sensitive nervous disorder. He then retired to write.

Salammbo was the result of a long trip to the Middle East, which Flaubert took with a friend from November 1849 to February 1851. Their travels took them to Egypt, Syria, Jerusalem, Turkey, and Greece. *Salammbo* is set in none of these places, but Flaubert soaked up the feel of Greek and Roman times from the numerous ruins that he visited. He returned to North Africa on a research trip in 1858, to consult with various archeologists who had excavated Carthage. *Salammbo* was finally published in November 1862.

Few books convey the nineteenth century lust for exotic oriental splendors better than *Salammbo*. The action takes place in Carthage during the interval between the first and second Punic Wars. The plot is a love story between Matho, a Libyan general, and Salammbo, the voluptuous daughter of Hamilcar and sister of Hannibal. Salammbo is a priestess in the temple of the moon goddess Tanit and has all the frigid seductiveness commonly associated with that heavenly body.

The novel is richly detailed, with some of the most colorful battle scenes in literature (the secret is the elephants). The exotica is much more believable from the pen of a good writer than it is from the multitude of hacks who also turned out oriental-temple fantasies in the nineteenth century. *Salammbo* is also historically accurate. (It is not, however, Flaubert's best work.)

Salammbo is available from Penguin Books (1977) in a translation by A.J. Krailsheimer.

Joan Grant

Joan Grant is the author of respectable middle-class family novels with a psychic gimmick: Grant claims she is not writing fiction at all but is merely remembering her past incarnations. Her "Far Memory" books are conveniently summarized in *Far Memory*, her autobiography.

Joan Grant's reincarnations have marked for her a clear path of spiritual development, obviously intended to make her a historical romance writer. Why else was she incarnated in the most popular novelistic-historical eras? She suffered under the Spanish Inquisition, helped rule ancient Egypt, and so forth.

Grant's books are very preachy, full of such platitudes as this one, in which Ra-ab prays over the boy Senusert (the future Pharaoh):

> Anubis! Teach me to refresh myself from the waters of memory so that I may understand the mind of this child, and help him to grow in your image. Let him desire above all things to become one with the Gods, and to remember that only the wise can teach the foolish, that only the strong can give courage to the weak,; but that he who is never foolish learns no wisdom, and he who has known no weakness can feel no strength. (From *Lord of the Horizon*)

The books are obviously slanted to an audience of housewives. They glorify domestic bliss. In *Lord of the Horizon*, for example, the Pharaohs and their families resemble those of American and European suburbia. They worry a lot about where their teenage children are.

By remarkable coincidence, the nuns and abbesses in *Life as Carola* behave just as the sisters in Ann Radcliffe's *The Mysteries of Udolpho* did. This is what her publishers refer to as "the unmistakable ring of authenticity."

Joan Grant's other books include *Eyes of Horus, So Moses was Born, Scarlet Feather,* and *Return to Elysium*. All these, and her autobiography, *Far Memory*, are available from Corgi Books.

Nathaniel Hawthorne

Hawthorne was one of the greatest American writers and one of the few writers of occult fiction whose work is studied as literature. His stories are firmly in the Romantic and Gothic tradition in the way that they use occultism primarily to creat a melancholic mood. But Hawthorne's characters are American Puritans. They believe literally in devils, angels, and in the spiritual warfare between them.

Critics tend to associate the same string of adjectives with Hawthorne's work as they do with Poe's: dark, brooding, mysterious, grim, fantastic. But Hawthorne is never morbid or heavy-handed, and he was the more graceful writer, a fact Poe himself recognized.

Hawthorne was born in 1804 in Salem, Massachusetts, of an old New England family. Among his schoolmates were Henry Wadsworth Longfellow and Franklin Pierce.

Hawthorne's first published work appeared in 1828, and he wrote steadily until his death in 1864. Most of his short stories first appeared in such periodicals as *The Token, The New England Magazine*, and *Atlantic Monthly*. The first collection of his stories was *Twice Told Tales*, which appeared in 1837. Hawthorne's work was critically successful and highly praised by other writers, but he made little money by his pen.

In 1850 Hawthorne published *The Scarlet Letter*, his best-known novel. Henry James said that it "has hung an ineffaceable image on the portrait gallery, the reserved inner cabinet, of literature."

In *The Scarlet Letter*, Hawthorne explored the effects of sexual and moral guilt on individuals and society. Hester Prynne, the heroine, has borne an illegitimate child by an unknown lover. She is imprisoned and forced to wear on her clothing a large red *A* for the rest of her life. She is doomed as an adultress, a fallen woman. Her secret lover, meanwhile, has gone free. But he is doomed by his own sense of guilt. Although the book contains much mysticism and depends on a supranormal event for its conclusion, it is more of a Christian novel than an occult one.

Hawthorne's other major novel was *The House of Seven Gables*, which first appeared in 1851. In a preface, Hawthorne insisted that this work was a "romance," as opposed to a "novel." The difference is, according to Hawthorne, that in *Seven Gables* he was concerned with narrative rather than moral.

The House of Seven Gables is the prototypical haunted house. Its builder, Colonel Pyncheon, had caused a certain Matthew Maule to be hanged for witchcraft. Maule cursed Pyncheon, and the curse lingered about the house for years. The gloomy effects of the curse bring out some of Hawthorne's best descriptive writing.

Hawthorne's works are available in a number of editions, both paperback and hardbound, and are certain to be found at the public library. W.W. Norton publishes annotated editions of both *The Scarlet Letter* and *The House of Seven Gables*. *The Complete Short Stories of Nathaniel Hawthorne* (Doubleday, 1959) is a one-volume edition of his shorter pieces.

Robert Heinlein

Although Heinlein is a science-fiction rather than occult writer, he belongs here because of the influence his semireligious novel *Stranger in a Strange Land* has among occultists. The book appeared in the sixties, just in time to become a "counterculture" bestseller.

Stranger in a Strange Land is hardly counterculture in its message. Its values are law and order, patriotism, and pulling oneself up by the bootstraps—the old American conservative ideal. The story is set in the space-age world of the future, however, which is perhaps why the thinking seems advanced.

Stranger in a Strange Land is the story of how Valentine Michael Smith, a boy raised on Mars though of human parentage, returns to Earth and becomes a Messiah. In the process of his rise, he acquires a stable of women and murders a few enemies (both of which seem to be okay to Heinlein). Much of the book consists of dull sermonizing by Smith's mentor, an aging lawyer.

Heinlein's problem is a familiar one among fantasy writers: the tendency to begin believing one's own fictions. In Heinlein's case this is especially ironic. In his "future history" stories, he mocked just that kind of credulity in depicting the rise of a prophet, Nehemiah Scudder.

L. Ron Hubbard

Hubbard began his career as a writer of pulp science fiction. Most of his short stories were published in *Astounding Science Fiction*, which in the 1940s and 1950s was in its glory days under the editorship of John Campbell, Jr. As a writer of short stories, Hubbard was respectable but not outstanding (his competition at *Astounding Science Fiction* included Arthur C. Clarke, Robert Heinlein, and Alfred Bester). Then Hubbard invented dianetics and came into his own (see chapter five).

Hubbard's writings on dianetics and Scientology are of literary interest because they are so typical of their period. He founded his religion of the future during the era of the Korean War and Joseph McCarthy. Americans were speaking of themselves as "the leaders of the Free World," by virtue of their independence and superior technology. At the same time, Americans were becoming terrified of subversion from within the country; *brainwashing* became part of the vocabulary. Hubbard's writings reflect both these fears and these hopes. He presented a "scientific" theory that claimed humans were technologically perfectible. The only thing that stood in their way was the Enemy Within (which in Hubbard's system was called an engram rather than a Commie). As any popular writer must, he gave the people what they wanted.

Evidently, the people still want what Hubbard as to offer. It remains to be seen whether Hubbard will become the Messiah of the occult movement, but he is a strong candidate. His followers, he claims, number in the millions. So does his personal wealth. No contemporary writer has succeeded better than he in going from fantasy to faith.

Joris K. Huysmans

Joris Karl Huysmans belonged to a circle of French writers and artists who experimented with occultism at the end of the nineteenth century.

He was born in 1848 in Paris. His parents were Dutch. He was given the French names of Charles Marie Georges Huysmans, but he began using the names Joris Karl when he began to write fiction.

Huysmans attended the University of Paris, but he spent most of his time in cafes, where the talk often turned to the occult. He was drafted into the French National Guard in 1870 and served as a military aide at Versailles during the period of the Paris Commune.

In the 1880s he began to study occultism seriously under the direction of Stanislaus de Gaita, Henriette Maillat, Sar Peladan, and others. He became very deeply involved in occult practices. He witnessed several Black Masses, and wrote the introduction to Jules Bois's *Satanisme et la magie*, a book that influenced Crowley and later Satanists. For years, Huysmans believed himself to be the target of psychic attacks from Stanislaus de Gaita, with whom he had quarreled.

Huysmans's novels are both philosophical and sentimental. He attempted to resolve some profound issues, such as the relationship of magic to spirituality and naturalism. But his novels remain more Roman Catholic than occult, and at last he resolved his intellectual difficulties by reconverting to Roman Catholicism. He never lost his interest in the occult; but in his later works, psychic and mystic manifestations are explained in religious terms. In 1901 Huysmans became an oblate in a Benedictine Abbey. Although his order was disbanded, he continued to think of himself as a monk. He was made an officer in the Legion of Honor in his old age. He died in 1907.

Huysmans's major works were translated into English and were influential in forming the popular idea of Satanism, which became fashionable again after the First World War. His books are available in paperback from Dover (*Against the Grain, Là-bas*) and Penguin (*Down Stream and Other Works; Against Nature*).

Joseph Sheridan LeFanu

Although his work is not read much today, LeFanu was one of the most influential writers of occult fiction. He was often called "the Irish Poe" or "the Irish Wilkie Collins," and was just as important to the development of the horror story as either one.

Joseph Sheridan LeFanu was born in Dublin in 1814 into a prominent family. Richard Brinsley Sheridan, the great dramatist, was his father's uncle. LeFanu was educated at Trinity College, Dublin. Although qualified to practice law, he preferred to write for a living. He had a private income, which must have made this decision easier.

In 1839 LeFanu bought two newspapers and part of a third and consolidated them into the *Evening Mail*. He was owner and editor-in-chief of this paper for the rest of his life.

He married in 1844. The marriage was a very happy one and when his wife died in 1858 he was shattered. He became known as a recluse; his mind turned to melancholy. Some critics say that in his later years LeFanu was insane. He was obsessed with death and grief, and after 1863 he began writing melancholy supernatural novels, which were tremendously popular. They show the strong influence of Poe, Collins, and H. Rider Haggard.

LeFanu's most notable character was Dr. Hesselius, the "Mr. Know-it-All" of the nineteenth century. The mysterious doctor of science who knows everything soon became a standard literary character. Algernon Blackwood's John Silence and Arthur Machen's Dr. Reymond are two examples of this fictional prototype.

LeFanu's best-known story was "Green Tea," which he called "the case history of a schizophrenic." In the story, the Reverend Dr. Jennings, under the influence of something in his tea, begins to be haunted by an apelike demon. The demon interrupts him at his prayers, utters blasphemies, and eventually drives the cleric to suicide.

The themes of "Green Tea" are LeFanu's favorite ones: drugs, fear of madness, and the "inner vision." The elevated style of the visionary passages reflects LeFanu's interest in the ideas of Swedenborg.

All his work is sexually repressed. He was fascinated by all aspects of female psychology, especially lesbianism and "nervous disorders," but his female characters are pale, childlike, and almost sexless. The male characters, too, often show weak, childish characteristics.

LeFanu's work is beginning to be brought out of its undeserved obscurity. *Best Ghost Stories of J. Sheridan LeFanu* and *Uncle Silas* are published by Dover Books.

Matthew G. ("Monk") Lewis

Monk Lewis was one of the first bestselling authors of the Industrial Age. He got his nickname from his Gothic novel, *Ambrosio, or The Monk*, which appeared in 1795, when he was twenty.

Matthew Gregory Lewis was born in 1775 into an upper-middle-class home. His father owned several estates in Jamaica. Lewis was educated as a young gentleman: sent to Westminster School and then on a tour of the Continent.

In 1792 he went to Weimar, Germany, to study and met Goethe, the leading German Romantic writer. In 1794 he was appointed an attache to the British Embassy at The Hague. While there, he wrote his bestselling novel.

The Monk has been one of the most influential books of occult fiction. Its atmosphere of sinister depravity was consciously imitated by such writers as LeFanu, Wilkie Collins, and Poe.

The cleric of the title is Ambrosio, a fanatically holy, impassioned, silver-tongued orator whose fiery sermons and dark, brooding good looks have spellbound the ladies of Madrid. (Ambrosio and his kind are also the literary ancestors of Father Damien in *The Exorcist*.)

Ambrosio impresses one lady in particular. She is an enchanting witch-temptress with the unlikely name of Matilda. By disguising herself as a novice monk, Matilda gains access to Ambrosio's inner chamber. After intense spiritual struggle and moral anguish, Ambrosio allows himself to be lured into Matilda's naked embrace.

Alas, Ambrosio's lust, once aroused, does not confine itself to Matilda, but fastens on the lovely, delicate, saintly Antonia, whom he determines to ravish. Antonia is also loved by a young nobleman whose sister has mysteriously disappeared into the dungeons of the Spanish Inquisition, due to machinations of the evil abbess of her convent. There are several subplots in this vein.

Although Lewis's style is rather florid for modern tastes, *The Monk* is still better reading than most of its thousands of imitators.

Lewis's other occult fiction works included *Tales of Terror* (1788) and *Tales of Wonder* (1801). He was also a playwright; his play *The Castle Spectre* was a hit at Drury Lane, London, in 1798.

Lewis's father died in 1812, leaving the estates in Jamaica to his son. Monk felt unable to enjoy his wealth, knowing it came from the labor of slaves. He sailed to Jamaica in 1815 to insure that blacks on his estates would be generously treated. He returned to Europe in 1816 and went back to Jamaica in 1818. He died at sea on the way back to England.

The Monk is available in several paperback editions, including those by Avon (1975) and Oxford University Press (1973).

H.P. Lovecraft

H.P. Lovecraft, a science-fiction writer, was responsible for many of the present links between occult and science fiction. However, he never had a wide following during his lifetime. He lived very quietly in Providence, Rhode Island, "publishing" many of his stories by circulating copies of them among his friends. He wrote fifty sci-fi stories between 1920 and his death in 1937. All his stories are horror tales as well.

Twelve of the stories are about the Cthulhu Mythos, a body of legend that Lovecraft invented and encouraged other sci-fi writers to expand upon. His challenge was taken up by Lin Carter, August Derleth, Robert Howard, Colin Wilson, and Robert Block, among others. Since these include some of the most widely read sci-fi and occult authors, it shouldn't surprise anyone that the Cthulhu Mythos is now passing for actual truth. Lovecraft himself has been elevated to the status of a prophet. The relatively early age of his death—forty-seven—makes some speak of him as a martyr. This view of Lovecraft is, not surprisingly, propagated through the fiction of Howard, Carter, Derleth, et al.

Derleth summarizes the myth in "The House in the Valley," a story that was read in manuscript and edited by Lovecraft.

> . . . the first inhabitants of outer space were great beings, not in human shape, who were called the Elder Gods and lived on Betelguese, at a remote time. Against these certain elemental Ancient Ones, also called the Great Old Ones, had rebelled—Azathoth, Yogi-Sothoth, the amphibious Cthulhu, the bat-like Hastur the Unspeakable, Lloigor, Zhar, Ithaqua, the wind-walker, and the earth beings, Nyarlathotep and Shub-Niggurath; but their rebellion failing, they were cast out and banished by the Elder Gods—locked away on far planets and stars under the seal of the Elder Gods. . . .
>
> Since this initial rebellion—which was basically in a legend pattern paralleling the rebellion of Satan and his followers against the arch-angels of heaven—the Great Old Ones had continually sought to regain their power to war against the Elder Gods, and there have grown up on earth and other planets certain cultists and followers—like the Abominable Snowmen, the Dholes, the Deep Ones, and many others, all dedicated to serve the Ancient Ones, and often succeeded in removing the Elder Seal to free the forces of ancient evil, which had then to be put down again either by direct intervention of the Elder Gods or by the alert watchfulness of human beings armed against them.

Lovecraft's "keystone" story of the Cthulhu Mythos was "The Festival." In that story, the narrator, responding to the "call" of his forefathers, returns to the town of Kingsport, where he is taken to a Yuletide festival of the most ancient, horrifying, pre-Druid sort. "The Festival" contained many elements already common to occult fiction: underground secret passages; entrance to the nether world through a church (as old as the Grail legends); the Yulerite; the underground river of death (as old as the Greek myths); the sacred birds who carry the initiates into the inner chamber (as old as the Egyptians).

"The Festival" also begins the Cthulhu tradition of listing the "sacred books," forbidden occult texts such as Joseph Glanvil's *Saducismus Triumphus* (1681) and, especially, the *Necronomicon* "by the mad Arab Abdul Alhazred." At least some of the Cthulhu books were actual Renaissance occult manuscripts. There is nothing in the Cthulhu stories, however, to indicate that Lovecraft and his followers actually read these ancient texts. The book names are listed simply to add mystery demonic vibrations, and an air of authority.

No "secrets of the ancients" are necessary to explain how the Cthulhu myth reached Lovecraft. The myth is directly descended from nineteenth-century horror writers such as Poe and LeFanu, as well as from Ambrose Bierce and Robert W. Chambers. For example, Bierce invented a place called Carcosa, "where the black stars hang in the heavens." Carcosa was picked up by Chambers in "The King in Yellow," and he called it Aldebaran of the Hyades. According to Lovecraft, Aldebaran of the Hyades is the place where the Great Old One Hastur has been exiled.

The Cthulhu myth was also influenced by William Hope Hodgson's *The House on the Borderland* and by the writings of Ignatius Donnelly. Lovecraft, in a careful, deliberate manner, chose for his myth those elements that seemed the most powerful both emotionally and symbolically.

It is impossible to calculate the influence of the Cthulhu stories on occult belief. Cthulhu is very suspiciously like the aquatic gods from outer space whose existence is so crucial to Erich von Däniken and to the believers in Sirius. At least one Cthulhu story, Derleth's "The Sandwin Compact," relates the Elder Gods to Easter Island; Lovecraft's "The Festival" relates the gods to the dog star, Sirius. R'lyeh, the Atlantic underwater home of Cthulhu, is little more than a sunken Atlantis, presumably the same city visited by the yellow submarine in the *Illuminatus* trilogy (Robert Anton Wilson and Robert Shea). It is also the home of television's "Man from Atlantis."

Pyramidologists too owe something to Lovecraft. He was among the first to put into fictional form the idea that the secrets of the ancients were buried in a tunnel connecting the pyramids with the Temple of the Sphinx. ("Imprisoned with the Pharaohs").

Lovecraft also refined the tradition of psychological horror, begun by LeFanu and Poe. He wrote after the universal acceptance of the idea of the subconscious, and this is the single greatest factor that separates his work from theirs. Poe's and LeFanu's characters hear voices in their opium dreams; Lovecraft's characters receive messages from inside their own psyches.

Lovecraft often leaves us in doubt as to the sanity of the narrator. This technique had been widely used, and it is a tribute to Lovecraft's writing ability that so many people nevertheless accept the Cthulhu stories as fact.

Lovecraft's stories, as well as those of Derleth, Bloch, and other Lovecraft disciples, were originally published by Arkham House, a firm founded specifically for that purpose. (Arkham was the name of the New England village most saturated with vibrations of Cthulhu.) Now Lovecraft's work has been issued in paperback by Ballantine Books. The following titles are available: *At the Mountains of Madness* (1975); *The Doom that Came to Sarnath* (1976); *The Dream Quest of the Unknown Kadath* (1976); *The Horror in the Museum and other Fiction* (1976), *The Lurker at the Threshold* (1976), *Lurking Fear and other Stories* (1975); *Tales of the Cthulhu Mythos* (1975); and *The Tomb* (1975).

Edward Bulwer-Lytton

Bulwer-Lytton is mostly remembered today as the author of *The Last Days of Pompeii,* a book that was highly influential in forming the nineteenth-century British and American conception of Rome. Lytton was also the author of such bestselling romantic novels as *Pelham* (1828), *Paul Clifford* (1830), and *Devereux* (1829). He was also a politician, who considered himself a reformer and was a friend of Disraeli.

Lytton was born in 1803 into a "good" family. His father died when Edward was very young and the boy was raised by his mother.

From his earliest childhood, he immersed himself in books, especially those of Sir Walter Scott. His hero was Byron. He even went so far, after he had entered society, to have a brief affair with Lady Caroline Lamb, who had scandalized polite society by vamping Lord Byron fifteen years before. Lady Caroline and others to whom the Byronic myth was important made Bulwer-Lytton very fashionable. He dressed and acted the part of the society dandy. He was a good fencer and boxer. He even fought a duel.

In due course Lytton embarked on a disastrous marriage of which his mother did not approve, and so he was deprived of his private income. He wrote his first novels to make money, and was successful in doing so.

We do not know at what point Lytton's interest in occultism led him to actually practice it. He was certainly familiar with Eliphas Lévi, whom he read in French. His fantastic occult and horror stories included "Zanoni"; "The Tale of a Dreamer" (a long poem); "The Haunters and the Haunted"; and "The Pilgrims of the Rhine."

Lytton's idea of "black" magic was not very grim or evil. It resembled the magic practiced by the theatrically inclined members of the Order of the

Golden Dawn. The majority of Bulwer-Lytton's occult stories were published at the height of the spiritualism craze. So his "mysticism" seems pale, and even a bit ridiculous, to us today. Sir Leslie Stephen, a later Victorian critic, wrote that Lytton's "attempts at the mysterious too often remind us of a spirit-rapping rather than excite the thrill of supernatural awe." Stephen was writing, of course, after the public had been exposed to the work of Poe and LeFanu, in comparison to which Bulwer-Lytton's writings seem tame.

Lytton's books are very hard to find today. Dover Books may have plans to reissue "Zanoni" since it has reissued many other nineteenth-century occult works. The *Last Days of Pompeii* can be found in some public libraries.

Arthur Machen

Arthur Machen's most influential story, "The Bowmen," was published in *The Evening News* (London) on September 29, 1914.

On September 28, the British army had retreated after the Battle of Mons. In "The Bowmen," Machen imagined St. George appearing to the beleaguered English troops. St. George was accompanied by a column of angels, who were dressed as English longbowmen of the seventeenth century.

As soon as "The Bowmen" appeared, the newspapers began printing stories confirming it. Hundreds of soldiers who had been at Mons swore that they had seen the angels. The Angels of Mons are now accepted as fact by many occultists; they are brought forth as "evidence" of extraterrestrial intervention. Machen always insisted the story was nothing but fiction.

Machen's interest in the occult began in his boyhood. He was born and raised in Wales, in the village of Caerleon-upon-Usk, one of the seats of King Arthur's Court. As a young man, he moved to London. After teaching school and working in a bookshop, he began to write for a living.

The Great God Pan, Machen's first major work, was published in 1895. Like Algernon Blackwood a few years later, Machen posited a world in which Pan was not dead but still intervened in the affairs of humans, occasionally spiriting them away to another world.

Machen's other occult stories during this period included "The Inmost Light" and "The White Powder."

Other books by Maden include *The Great Return*, about the meaning of the Holy Grail, and *The Secret Glory* (1922). *The Secret Glory* anticipates much later work by such writers as Aldous Huxley in attempting to define and describe the nature of religious experience in the modern world.

Machen died in 1947, very poor. However, his last four years were lightened by a small salary, which came from a fundraising effort by Max Beerbohm, T.S. Eliot, and George Bernard Shaw. Except for their generosity, Machen would have ended his life in a workhouse.

Machen's books are available in most public libraries. Pinnacle Books publishes a paperback collection of Machen called *Tales of Horror and the Supernatural.*

Edgar Allen Poe

Poe is one writer of popular fiction whose work has weathered changing public taste. He strongly influenced the development of the short-story form and was the inventor of the modern detective story. But he is most remembered for his ability to create horror.

Poe was born in Boston in 1809. He had a very insecure childhood. His parents, who were actors, separated before Edgar was two, and his mother died soon afterward. Edgar was adopted by John Allen, a Richmond, Virginia, merchant. He was not happy with his foster parents—apparently, his foster father never let him forget his adopted status.

However, the Allens gave Edgar a good education. He was sent to school in England, where he studied the classics. He then entered the University of Virginia. While he was there he fell in love, took up drinking and gambling, and annoyed his foster father. The girl married someone else; the money ran out; and Mr. Allen lost patience. So Edgar left school and went to Boston. He got a job as a clerk, published his first book, *Tamerlane and Other Poems*, and eventually joined the Army.

After his foster mother died in 1829, Edgar had a reconciliation with Mr. Allen, who used his influence to obtain a West Point appointment for Edgar. He got expelled quickly.

By 1833, Poe had begun writing for a living. He published a few short stories in various magazines and in 1835, he became an editor for the *Southern Literary Messenger* of Richmond. During this period Poe married Virginia Clemm, his fourteen-year-old cousin. Her mother lived with them. There is much controversy surrounding Poe's sex life, which may not have existed. At any rate, the marriage seems to have been mostly one of convenience.

The next few years were spent in New York, Baltimore, Philadelphia, and Richmond, in a succession of writing and editing jobs. Poe was always fairly poor. In 1845 came the event that made him famous—the publication of "The Raven," which may still be the best-known poem in America.

Poe had acquired a fashionable following. He enjoyed being the center of romantic society gossip. He wrote reviews, sometimes vicious ones, for *Godey's Lady's Book* and other publications. After Virginia's death in 1847, he renewed his engagement to his first love, who was now a widow. But the marriage never took place. Poe died in 1849 after going out on a drinking binge and being found unconscious on a Baltimore sidewalk. He was buried next to his wife and her mother.

The popular image of Poe is often confused with the narrative voice of his stories. This voice belongs to a gloomy, embittered misanthrope who frequently takes opium. Poe took opium once in a while for medicinal purposes, as did nearly everyone else in America at the time. But he was not an opium addict.

There is more substantial evidence for the charge that he was an alcoholic. He was often observed to behave drunkenly after ingesting a very small amount of liquor. His alcoholism might also account for his strange, fluctuating behavior. To some he was a charming Southern gentleman; to others he was vicious, spiteful, and judgmental. He had ardent defenders as well as bitter critics. The criticism was partly deserved because of Poe's vindictive reviews, often directed at better writers than himself.

Unquestionably, Poe experienced frequent depression, for it saturates his work. The general *atmosphere* of Poe's writing is far more impressive as a literary achievement than individual passages or lines are. Indeed, there were many times when Poe wrote rather badly. But he knew how to set a mood, build suspense, and then stun his readers with a blood-curdling ending.

Poe's best stories are "Ligeia," "The Masque of the Red Death," "The Telltale Heart," "The Pit and the Pendulum," and "The Fall of the House of Usher." Although these stories contain many occult elements, their atmosphere is more important than their philosophy. Even when Poe introduced an occult element, such as the reappearance of a dead lover in "Ligeia," his emphasis was always on the mental state of the narrator rather than on the apparition. This was one of Poe's most effective—and influential—devices, to leave the reader guessing as to the narrator's sanity, and thus as to the reality of the story's events.

In "Ligeia," we are not even sure that the woman is real. The narrator cannot remember her last name or where he met her. Poe describes her as a Greek statue, one who appeared "in the radiance of an opium dream." He devotes two long paragraphs to her eyes, "those shining, divine orbs." Ligeia is vastly learned: she has "traversed . . . all the wide areas of moral, physical, and mathematical science." And by this time we have begun to suspect that Ligeia is the projection of the narrator's mind, an all-knowing Earth Mother Goddess image. Poe seems to confirm it. "Without Ligeia I was but as a child groping benighted."

Poe's best stories can be read as allegories, in which the narrator's disordered mind both projects and represents the disordered universe that surrounds it. In "The Fall of the House of Usher," for instance, the house represents the mind, as it does in dreams. The narrator approaches the house "with an utter depression of soul which I can compare to no other earthly sensation more properly than to the after-dream of a reveller upon opium." The occupant of the House of Usher is an old boyhood friend about whom the narrator now knows little. The reader realizes, consciously or otherwise, that the narrator is approaching his own past as he rides up to the house. The narrator's description of the house reflects his feelings about himself.

> No portion of the masonry had fallen; and there appeared to be a wild inconsistency between its still perfect adaptation of parts and the crumbling condition of the individual stones. . . . The eye of the scrutinizing observer might have discovered a barely perceptible fissure, which, extending from the roof of the building in front, made its way down the wall in a zigzag direction. . . .

It is along this fissure that the House of Usher splits asunder at the end of the story. The split comes after the narrator has reviewed the events of his boyhood and buried a woman who has haunted him. We don't know, when the lady reappears, if it is the lady or the strong memory of her that is refusing to die. Thus "The Fall of the House of Usher" is a tale of mental breakdown.

Similarly, the woman Ligeia could be said to represent the creative aspects of the human mind. The story "Ligeia," then, becomes an allegory of the loss of creative powers and their reappearance in another form.

It is not necessary, of course, to read Poe's stories as allegories. They are highly convincing just as tales of terror. But the reason they stick so firmly in the mind of the reader is that they contain many levels of meaning.

Poe dealt with the moral universe from the point of view of individual psychology. This is what makes his work "modern." Unlike previous Gothic writers, Poe avoided sentimentality. He dealt directly with nightmares, madness, and illusion. Poe's work gave new direction to supernatural fiction because he recognized that the worst terrors lay inside the human psyche.

Ann Radcliffe

Ann Radcliffe's novel *The Mysteries of Udolpho* (1794) was one of the first important Gothic novels. It was enormously popular. Mrs. Radcliffe deserves much of the credit for the creation of the dark, brooding, Romantic hero, the character later played so successfully in real life by Lord Byron. (*Udolpho* was one of the favorite books of Byron's youth.) *The Mysteries of Udolpho* influenced much literature that was far better than itself, such as Keats's *Eve of St. Agnes*.

Very little is known about Ann Radcliffe's personal life. She received the usual education for middle-class women of her time: music, painting, embroidery, French, and Italian. She was married to William Radcliffe at twenty-three. Thereafter, she was supposedly condemned by her class to a life of enforced idleness.

She began writing ghost stories to fill the time while her husband was away at work (he was the editor of a weekly newspaper). Her first stories were "The Castles of Athlin" and "Dunbayne," and she published them anonymously.

After *The Mysteries of Udolpho* made her name famous, she became even more reticent about her private life. So we do not know what events may have led her to create the characters she did. But we do know that she had read Walpole's *The Castle of Otranto* and many of its imitators. *Udolpho* was not an original story, but it did add many new elements to the Gothic formula.

Among the elements invented or embroidered by Mrs. Radcliffe were: the heroine married for money and was then imprisoned; the dungeons; the convent abbess guarding a secret of identity; the evil stepfather; the band of highborn desperadoes terrorizing the countryside: and, of course, the handsome, tall, slim, dark hero. Mrs. Radcliffe's style was more effusive than that of previous Gothic writers. She tried to evoke grandeur in her descriptions of the landscape and lofty thoughts in her descriptions of the heroine's suffering.

Mrs. Radcliffe followed *Udolpho* with a second best seller, *The Italian*. Both of these novels are available in paperback editions from Oxford University Press.

Tuesday Lobsang Rampa

The case of Tuesday Lobsang Rampa is a wonderful example of reality being stranger than fiction. In this case, it is difficult to tell them apart.

Tuesday Lobsang Rampa is a Tibetan monk. He was brought up in the Chakpori Lamasery, the Temple of Tibetan Medicine. There he studied clairvoyance, levitation, and the healing arts. As a young boy, he was given a special operation. The surgery opened the pineal gland, the so-called "third eye." As a result, Rampa could see other people's auras and read their minds. At twenty, he was already a Recognized Incarnation, a kind of Tibetan saint.

That was the story handed out by Rampa's publisher when his first book, *The Third Eye*, was released in 1956. *The Third Eye* is a very readable piece of pulp. Its hero, the young Rampa, is an appealing, mischievous lad. Life in the lamasery is strict, rigid, bare. The food is plain and unvarying. The students are awakened in the middle of the night to attend useless religious services, made to take ice-cold baths, and whipped severely for the smallest misbehavior. At one point, Rampa is singled out for his excellence and invited to the head lama's quarters for man-to-man discussions and decent food.

In short, life at Chakpori Lamasery rather resembles that of a shabby English boarding school.

The Third Eye became a bestseller despite some skeptics who did not believe its author to be an authentic Tibetan monk. These detractors managed to dig up evidence that Rampa was actually one Cyril Hodgkins, a mild-mannered civil servant. The neighbors reported he was a dull, fussy little man. He had travelled in the East as a child, his father having held some minor foreign-service post. He had attended a boarding school, where he was noted for telling tall stories about his exotic oriental adventures, which no one ever believed.

Then one day, Hodgkins was up in a tree, pruning, and a branch broke off. He fell and was knocked unconscious—or killed. When he came to he was T. Lobsang Rampa, a Tibetan monk. Or he thought he was. Or he decided to let people think he thought he was.

After recovering from the shock of reincarnating into so insignificant a body, Lobsang Rampa began writing *The Third Eye*. Whatever the blow on the head did for Hodgkins, it turned him, at least briefly, into a writer.

Alas, the blow's effects did not last. Rampa has since published a great many more books. Each one further discredits his claims to lamahood.

In *Doctor from Lhasa*, Rampa told of his wartime adventures fighting Communists and Japanese. He supposedly served as a flying doctor in the army of Chiang Kai-shek. The book, alas, contains details that prove he knows little about either medicine or aviation. *The Rampa Story* and *The Cave of the Ancients* expanded further on the theme of how Rampa developed his occult powers. As one might expect, he had visited Atlantis and peeked at the Akashic Record.

After three or four books, the story wore thin for most people. Rampa's style lost the little vigor it had in *The Third Eye*. His "secret wisdom" turned out to be a kind of positive-mental-attitude brand of Eastern religion. His philosophy is to breathe deeply, think beautiful thoughts, communicate with the universe, and hate Commies.

Rampa's brand of oriental fantasy has since been depicted much more successfully by TV and movies. His descriptions of Chinese and Tibetan self-defense are absurd to a society whose rock stars visit gurus in the Himalayas and where aikido, tai chi, and other martial arts are widely practiced.

Today, Rampa makes his living not only from the sale of his books but also from the sale of records and tapes of his lectures. He also distributes "touch-stones," which have all sorts of mystical properties. Whether the fellow is Tuesday Lobsang Rampa or Cyril Hodgkins, he hasn't suffered from being hit on the head.

T. Lobsang Rampa's books are all published in paperback by Corgi Books, London. Titles include *The Third Eye, Doctor from Lhasa, The Rampa Story, The Cave of the Ancients, Living with the Lama, You-Forever, Wisdom of the Ancients, The Saffron Robe,* and *Beyond the Tenth*. *The Third Eye* and *The*

Cave of the Ancients are also available in Ballantine paperback editions (optimistically labelled "nonfiction").

Mary Shelley

Mary Shelley was the daughter of William Godwin, a leading radical reformer and writer, and of Mary Wollstonecraft, the feminist pioneer and author of *A Vindication of the Rights of Women* (1798). Wollstonecraft died as the result of Mary's birth. The child grew up among the writers and intellectuals who had been her mother's admirers, Robert Southey, Charles Lamb, Thomas Paine, and William Blake among them.

In 1801 Godwin married Mrs. Mary Jane Clairmont. Mary never got along with her stepmother, or with her two children, Charles and Jane. Her home life was miserable.

When she was seventeen, Mary eloped to France with Percy Bysshe Shelley. (He was already married—hence the need for flight.) The lovers were accompanied by Jane Clairmont, who began calling herself Claire.

Claire's attachment to the Shelley household has been the cause for much speculation. Claire, Mary, and Shelley had a strange triangular relationship which was later complicated by Claire's slavish attachment to Byron (whose charms were not lost on Mary, either). Scholars seldom have such lascivious material with which to work; the multiple liaisons of the Shelley-Byron households have kept scholars busy ever since.

In the summer of 1816, Byron, Claire, Shelley, and Mary were all living in Geneva, Switzerland. Byron and Shelley met for the first time that summer. One rainy night, Byron suggested that they each write a ghost story, as a friendly competition. Mary's entry was *Frankenstein, or The Modern Prometheus*. (Byron wrote his "Prometheus" that summer, and Shelley began thinking about "Prometheus Unbound." Whatever went on in Geneva seems to have had a liberating effect.)

Frankenstein was published in 1817, a few months before Mary's twentieth birthday. The book was an immediate success, which Mary was not able to enjoy to the fullest because of a series of personal tragedies.

She had been pregnant when she eloped with Shelley; the baby was born prematurely and died shortly thereafter. In January 1816 she gave birth to William; in September 1817 she had a daughter, Clara. Both children died in Italy, Clara in 1818 and William in 1819.

Mary had another son in 1819. There followed two years of happiness, during which she completed a second novel, *Valperga*. On July 8, 1822, the greatest tragedy of all took place—Percy Shelley drowned. By the age of twenty-four, Mary Godwin Shelley had eloped with a married man, had four children, published two novels, one of them a bestseller, watched three of her children die, and become a widow. She never remarried.

Instead she dedicated herself to the glorification of Shelley's memory and to the hereditary interests of Percy Florence Shelley, her son.

After her husband's death, Mary supported herself by her writing. She also received a small allowance from Sir Timothy Shelley, her father-in-law, who had been estranged from his son since the elopement. (The first Mrs. Shelley having been drowned, Mary Godwin and Percy Shelley had been legally married in 1816.)

In 1826, Mary published *The Last Man*, the story of the only human left after the destruction of the world by plague. Her other books include an edition of Shelley's *Posthumous Poems* (1824); *Perkin Warbeck* (1830); *Lodore* (1835); and *Falkner* (1837), as well as various short stories, verses, essays, and biographies. She died in 1851.

Frankenstein ensured Mary Shelley's place in literary history. Thanks to film and television, its plot may be the most familiar one in English. The book's idea has even entered common speech, a "Frankenstein's monster" being any project that backfires on its creator.

Victor Frankenstein, a scientist, has one overriding ambition: to create life. He succeeds, but the monster he invents kills all the people dearest to him: his little brother William, then two friends, then his bride.

Mary Shelley's monster is both frightening and pitiful. Brought into the world through no choice of its own, it is completely alone. No other like creature exists. The monster is the embodiment of the book's despairing epigraph, from Milton's *Paradise Lost*: "Did I request thee, Maker, from my clay/ To mould me Man, did I solicit thee/ From darkness to promote me?"

The monster is both Satan and Adam; Frankenstein is both Satan and God (the Creator). Throughout, Shelley uses the imagery of *Paradise Lost*. Frankenstein's creation of the monster is the original sin; it is the desire to eat of the tree of knowledge. At the end of the book, Frankenstein tells Walton, the Arctic explorer who has rescued him, "You seek for knowledge and wisdom, as I once did, and I ardently hope that the gratification of your wishes may not be a serpent to sting you, as mine has been."

Frankenstein has political and economic overtones as well, reflecting the influence of Shelley's father. The novel appeared at the beginning of the Industrial Age. Mary Shelley and other Romantic writers were among the first to recognize that technology might be a monster that turns on its human creators.

Frankenstein is available in a number of paperback editions, such as the 1965 New American Library "Signet Classics" edition. An edition of *The Last Man* (University of Nebraska Press, 1965) can be found at many libraries. Mary Shelley's other books are not readily available.

Isaac Bashevis Singer

Isaac Bashevis Singer writes in Yiddish, a disappearing language, about a world that has disappeared, the nineteenth-century *shtetl*, or Jewish village. Many of his characters lead medieval village lives and retain their medieval outlook. Devils, demons, and angels are real to them. The village Kabbalists are sages and (sometimes) saints. Singer thus portrays occultism as it was practiced by the rural masses everywhere in Europe before the Industrial Revolution. The Jews, fiercely persecuted and isolated by law from the mainstream of European life, retained their village culture until well into the twentieth century.

Singer was born in Warsaw, Poland, in 1904, into an Orthodox family. He read no secular books until he was twelve years old. Against family expectations, both Isaac and his older brother, Israel Joshua, became writers instead of rabbis. They further shocked their parents by becoming part of the "Jewish Enlightenment," a Westernizing movement among Jewish intellectuals.

Singer's grasp of village life comes not only from stories he heard as a child but from a long visit that he made during World War I to Bilgoray, his mother's village. His uncle was the rabbi of Bilgoray, as his father had been before him. Like the *shtetls* in Singer's stories, Bilgoray had changed very little since the seventeenth century. It was a world that was to be destroyed by Hitler.

Singer emigrated to the U.S. in 1935 and has lived in New York ever since. In 1944 he began working as a journalist for the *Jewish Daily Forward,* where his writing still appears in Yiddish. Singer's work has been translated into English by Jacob Sloan, Isaac Rosefeld, and Saul Bellow, among others. He has won wide critical acclaim, even more from his English readers than from his more conservative Yiddish readers. The latter have been upset by his "obsession" with eroticism, violence, and superstition. In 1978, Singer was awarded the Nobel Prize for Literature.

Singer's first novel, *Satan in Goray,* appeared in English in 1955. The novel is set in a seventeenth-century *shtetl* in Eastern Europe, an area repeatedly destroyed by Cossack pogroms against the Jews.

Some of the people of Goray have begun believing in Sabbatai Zevi, who claims he is the Messiah. (The Kabbalists have calculated that the Messiah will come in the year 1665–66 and end the exile of the Jews.) The Sabbatians take over Goray's prayer house; the people disregard rabbinical law in daily expectation of the end of their suffering. The movement is shattered when Sabbatai Zevi converts (on threat of death). The folly of the cultists is exposed; they learn not to be misled by their own false hopes.

Devils and demons are the main characters in many of Singer's short stories. In "The Gentleman from Cracow," the devil appears as a rich young nobleman who scatters largesse among the villagers of Frampol. The villagers experience greed, lust, and finally the destruction of their whole village.

In "Shiddah and Kuziba," Singer portrays the evil ones with much sympathy. The main characters are a she-devil and her son. They live under the surface of the Earth and must flee constantly from the encroachments of humans. "The Last Demon" is a devil who has been assigned to the village of Tishevitz. He is a thoroughly Jewish demon ("I've heard there are Gentile demons, but I don't know any, nor do I wish to know them"). When the Nazis destroy the village, the demon is the lone survivor. The story is a good example of Singer's ability to be very funny and very poignant at the same time.

Although he has chosen to portray a preindustrial world Singer is a modern writer who uses folklore, legend, and superstition to present modern fictional themes, such as existential despair.

Singer has stated that he believes in the reality of a psychic world, even though most psychics are liars and con artists (types Singer portrays remarkably well). Skepticism pervades his writing, but he does not mock the ignorance of his characters. Their concern with demons, evil forces, angels, and miracles is foolish and amusing, but it is also proof of the power of the spiritual dimension in everyday life.

Though Singer includes occult themes in almost every story, it would be insulting to label him an "occult writer." Similarly, though he is certainly both Jewish and a writer, and though all his characters and settings are Jewish, it would be misleading to label him a "Jewish writer." His work is far broader in scope and appeal.

Most of Singer's work has been translated into English and is available in paperback editions. Bantam Books has published *The Family Moskat* and *The Magician of Lublin*. Avon Books has published *Gimpel the Fool and Other Stories, Satan in Goray, The Slave,* and *The Spinoza of Market Street*. New American Library (Signet Classics) has brought out *In My Father's Court* and *Short Friday and Other Stories*. Noonday Books publishes all of the above titles. A collection of *Selected Short Stories* is available in paperback from Modern Library (Random House).

Jonathan Swift

Jonathan Swift was one of the greatest prose writers in English. An Anglican churchman, he became dean of St. Patrick's Cathedral in Dublin in 1713. Although he was a political conservative, the Irish regard him as a national hero for his pamphleteering in favor of Irish resistance. In the 1720s, he was the chief defender of Irish liberty in England.

Swift is best known for his satire *Gulliver's Travels*. Most of us read a watered-down version of Part I, "A Voyage to Lilliput," in elementary school. *Gulliver's Travels* is not at all a children's story, however; it is a savage, very funny attack on human society in Swift's day.

Jonathan Swift did not write any occult fiction, though other forms of popular fiction, especially sci-fi, owe much to *Gulliver's Travels*. The novel helped establish the form of the fantasy-adventure novel.

However, Swift is here primarily because he is quoted by Immanuel Velikovsky, among others, as a prophet of the new age of science. To support his planetary theories, Velikovsky quotes "a scholar and pamphleteer, Jonathan Swift" and his remarkable utterances about the revolutions of the satellites of Mars. Velikovsky concludes,

> Whether or not Swift borrowed his knowledge of the existence of the two trabants of Mars from some ancient astrological work the ancient poets knew of the existence of the satellites of Mars

The section so pompously invoked and illogically applied by Velikovsky comes from Part III of *Gulliver's Travels*, "A Voyage to Laputa." "A Voyage to Laputa" is a hilarious satire on so-called "science" and "higher mathematics" as practiced in Swift's time, a parody of the Velikovskys of the eighteenth century.

The relevant passage is the one in which the gullible Gulliver is taken to the Grand Academy of Lagado, an association of learned men of science whose research contributes to government policy on agriculture and economy, thus ruining the country utterly.

The mad scientists of Lagado engage in a variety of worthless projects, such as extracting sunbeams from cucumbers, reducing human excrement to its original food, and teaching the blind to mix paints by smell instead of by color.

The work of a dignitary called "the universal Artist" especially impressed Gulliver:

> He told us, he had been Thirty Years employing his thoughts for the Improvement of human Life. He had two large Rooms full of wonderful Curiosities, and Fifty Men at work. Some were condensing air into a dry tangible Substance, by extracting the Nitre, and letting the aqueous or fluid Particles percolate: Others softening Marble for Pillows and Pin-cushions; other petrifying the Hoofs of a living Horse to preserve them from foundring. The Artist himself was at that Time busy upon two great Designs: The first, to sow Land with Chaff, wherein he affirmed the true seminal Virtue to be contained, as he demonstrated by several Experiments which I was not skillful enough to comprehend. The other was, by a certain Composition of Gums, Minerals, and Vegetables outwardly applied, to prevent the Growth of Wool upon two young Lambs; and he hoped in a reasonable Time to propagate the Breed of naked sheep all over the Kingdom.

The Academy of Lagado is the academic arm of a malevolent scientifc government controlled from Laputa, an island that floats on hot air. The Laputans dispute over mathematics, astronomy, and music while brutally oppressing their subjects on the mainland below. The Laputan astronomers have discovered the two lesser satellites that revolved around Mars.

> . . . whereof the innermost is distant from the Center of the Primary Planet exactly three of his Diameters, and the outermost five; the former revolves in the Space of ten Hours, and the latter in Twenty-one and an Half; so that the Squares of their periodical Times, are very near in the same Proportion with the Cubes of their Distance from the Center of Mars; which evidently shews them to be governed by the same Laws of Gravitation, that influences the other heavenly Bodies.

Swift based the theories of Laputa on the absurd speculations of the "scientists" of his time, not on ancient astrological texts. "Laputa" skillfully ridicules pseudoscience linking it to madness and political irresponsibility How ironic, then, to find Swift quoted in support of the very theories he ridiculed.

Robert Anton Wilson

Robert Anton Wilson's books are evidence of just how slick the pulps have become, not just in style of writing but also in cover art, titling, and subtitling. His latest book has one of the catchiest titles of recent years. It's called *Cosmic Trigger* and is subtitled *The Final Secret of the Illuminati*. The cover asks, "Have we always shared this planet with beings that remain invisible to us?" (We have known the answer to that one at least since the invention of the microscope.) The book even has an introduction by Timothy Leary.

Cosmic Trigger is an autobiographical account of Wilson's fascination with the Illuminati, the secret, invisible society that supposedly has controlled the evolution of our planet since prehistory. In *Cosmic Trigger* Wilson helps spread the Sirius myth, described in "The Occult Bible" chapter. He also strengthens the web of myths growing around the assassinations of John F. Kennedy and Martin Luther King and the moon walks.

Who is Robert Anton Wilson that he should be writing our myths for us? In *Cosmic Trigger* he outlines the main events of his life. He was born in 1932 in Brooklyn of an Irish Catholic family. He spent his twenties going to psychiatrists. He married, bought a home in Yellow Springs, Ohio, and started taking drugs at the age of thirty.

In the intervening years he has worked as an editor and freelance writer. He presents all the proper credentials for the sixties cultural hero: he was a friend of Alan Watts; he met Leary at the Millbrook ashram; and he worked from 1966 to 1971 editing the letters in the "Playboy Forum."

In 1975, Wilson and Robert Shea entered the occult fiction market with the *Illuminatus* trilogy (*The Eye in the Pyramid, The Golden Apple,* and *Leviathan*).

The *Illuminatus* books are crammed with the myths and stock characters of the sixties. The "illumination" referred to is that of drugs and the fires of the Revolution. The hero pauses for the obligatory fond recall of the 1968 convention, is busted by a fat slob of a Texas cop, and even goes to Atlantis in a yellow submarine.

Other salient features of the *Illuminatus* books are the hips, thighs, breasts, nipples, and wet crotches of the female Adepts, who reach illumination mostly by stroking, petting, cooing, sniffing, massaging, licking, fondling—well, you get the idea. The hero is the sort of man who reads *Playboy*.

In his effusive introduction to *Cosmic Trigger,* Timothy Leary ranks the *Illuminatus* trilogy with Pynchon's *Gravity's Rainbow.* Contact with beings from Sirius has not helped the doctor's literary judgment. The *Illuminatus* books are not great fiction. They are not even good fiction, since they lack any substance. But they are what's known as "a good read"—nothing too profound to digest.

The best term to describe the style is "mind-blowing." Rules of the "mind-blowing" style seem to include: (1) change the subject every time you think the reader will be bored or wonder if it makes sense; (2) have the hero take drugs; (3) throw in a fuck scene; (4) use as many names and events of the '60s as you can, as buzz words for those who don't care to follow the actual narrative; (5) throw in a fuck scene; (6) don't let the hero think any thoughts more profound than *you* think on acid; (7) have the hero take more drugs; (8) have the hero get beat up and vomit; (9) give the hero a gun; and (10) throw in a fuck scene.

Cosmic Trigger is sold on bookstands with the three *Illuminatus* books and has similar cover art and type. They want you to buy all four, but if you can afford only one, get *Cosmic Trigger.* The book contains much of the same information (about Sirius, JFK, etc.), but with several bonuses. My favorite passages are the transcript of the message received from Sirius by Timothy Leary and the corporate flow-charts showing how the Illuminati message has passed through history (through the Freemasons and Rosicrucians and George Washington).

It will be interesting to see where Robert Anton Wilson goes from here. With the glorious examples of T. Lobsang Rampa, L. Ron Hubbard, and others before him, he may decide to become another occult guru and live well for the rest of his life. The way he talks about Timothy Leary, as if Leary were already martyred to the new faith, makes me wonder if he doesn't see himself as, perhaps, the Apostle Paul. Keep an eye out for Illuminati correspondence-courses—no, occult weekend retreats held in geodesic domes, featuring meditation sessions with dope and bunnies.

Appendix

Directory of Occult and Related Organizations

No attempt has been made to rate the following organizations. For a valuable, detailed guide, see Hans Holzer's *The Directory of the Occult* (Chicago: Regnery, 1974). Holzer's directory is an official publication of the New York Committee for the Investigation of Paranormal Occurrences. It has been of great help not only in preparing this appendix, but also in gathering material for this book.

Academy of Atlantis
12001 Wilshire Boulevard, Los Angeles, California
School specializing in material on Atlantis. Courses in yoga and related subjects. Leaders: Larry Fanning, medium Donna Marshall.

Aetherius Society
6202 Afton Place, Los Angeles, California
Organization led by George King, who regularly receives communications from Venus. Jesus Christ speaks through him.

Agasha Temple of Wisdom, Inc.
460 North Western Avenue, Los Angeles, California 90004
Spiritualist temple led by trance medium Richard Zenor.

American Society of Psychical Research
5 West 73rd Street, New York, New York 10023
Publishes *Journal of Psychic Research*. Maintains research library in New York. Full and student memberships available.

Amerisyche
141 Arsenal Street, Watertown, New York 13601
Name stands for American Society for Astropsychical Research. Publishes newsletter.

AMORC
San Jose, California 95114
Well-known Rosicrucian lodge. Circulates pamphlets and offers correspondence courses.

Anthroposophical Society
Offices in most major United States cities. For information, write Rudolf Steiner Information Center, 211 Madison Avenue, New York, New York.

The Aquarian Family
802 Holcomb Street, Watertown, New York 13601
A Wicca clan. Also runs mail- and phone-order shop specializing in robes, amulets, and other witchcraft accessories.

Arica Institute, Inc.
9916 Santa Monica Boulevard, Beverly Hills, California
Centers also located in Chicago, Honolulu, Los Angeles, and New York. Calls itself a "system of scientific mysticism."

Association for Research and Enlightenment
P.O. Box 595, Virginia Beach, Virginia 23451
Disseminates information about late prophet Edgar Cayce; maintains Cayce's healing files.

Atlanta Institute of Metaphysics
1625 Monroe Drive, Atlanta, Georgia 30324
School and center run by Mr. and Mrs. Peter Calhoun.

Chapel of the Living Presence
528 Lewis Road, Limerick, Pennsylvania 19468
Study group run by Medium Mildred Gourlay, who receives messages from dead U.S. Presidents.

Chicago Psychic Center, Inc.
451 West South Boulevard, Oak Park, Illinois 60302
Organization run by Clifford Royce.

Church of All Worlds
Post Office Box 2953, St. Louis, Missouri 63130
A "neo-Pagan" organization founded on the principles of Robert Heinlein's *Stranger in a Strange Land*. (See article on Heinlein in chapter eight.) Publishes newsletter, the *Green Egg*.

Church of the Eternal Source
P.O. Box 7091, Burbank, California 91510
Practices ancient Egyptian rites.

Church of Humanity
4503 Glenwick Lane, Dallas, Texas 75205
Church led by the Reverend Russ Michael.

Church of the Satanic Brotherhood
P.O. Box 325, Columbus–Worthington, Ohio 43085
Satanist group led by John DeHaven.

Church of Scientology
30 West 74th Street, New York, New York 10023
Organization founded by L. Ron Hubbard. See the entries on Hubbard in chapters five and eight.

Church of Wicca
1908 Verde Street, Bakersfield, California 93304

Dawn Horse Communion
Star Route 2 Avenue, Middleton, California 95462
Community devoted to Bubba Free John. See the entry on him in chapter five.

Divine Light Mission
P.O. Box 6495, Denver, Colorado 80206
Organization devoted to Guru Maharaj Ji. See the entry on him in chapter five.

Eckankar
P.O. Box 5325, Las Vegas, Nevada 89102
Offices and centers in major cities. Metaphysical organization founded by the late Paul Twitchell to teach "the ancient science of soul travel."

ESP Research Associates
1750 Tower Building, Little Rock, Arkansas 72201
Lecture and study center led by Medium Harold Sherman.

est (Erhard Seminars Training)
1750 Union Street, San Francisco, California 94123
See article on Werner Erhard in chapter five.

Esoteric Philosophy Center
523 Lovett Boulevard, Houston, Texas

The Farm
Summertown, Tennessee 38483
A self-sufficient rural community of about 650 people, led by Stephen Gaskin. Major industries include agriculture, childbearing, book publishing, and music.

The Fellowship of Isis
Huntington Castle, Clonegal, Enniscorthy, Eire

Feraferia
P.O. Box 691, Altadena, California 91001
Pagan organization led by Fred Adams. Publishes *Korythalia,* a pagan magazine.

Foundation for Research on the Nature of Man
Box 6848 College Station, Durham, North Carolina 27708
Maintains Institute for Parapsychology; publishes *The Journal of Parapsychology.*

The Fountainhead
P.O. Box 50426, Tucson, Arizona 85703
Center for lectures and seminars.

Gnostic Study Center
1414 Lorell Avenue, Minneapolis, Minnesota 55400
See Llewellyn Publications.

Institute for Realization of Personal Potential
916 Howard Avenue, New Orleans, Louisiana 70113

Institute of Metaphysics
P.O. Box 640, Yucca Valley, California 92284

Integral Yoga Institute
Satchidananda Ashram
P.O. Box 108, Pomfret Center, Connecticut 06259
Organization led by Swami Satchidananda. See entry on him in chapter five.

International Society for Krishna Consciousness
Srisri Radha Krsna Temple
3764 Watseka Avenue, Los Angeles, California 90034
The Hare Krishna Movement. Centers in most major cities.

Kundalini Research Foundation
10 East 39th Street, New York, New York 10016

Lama Foundation
Box 444, San Cristobal, New Mexico 87564
Self-sufficient rural community devoted to esoteric and Eastern thought. Publishers of *Be Here Now*, by Baba Ram Dass.

Light Affiliates
Box 431, South Burnaby, British Columbia, Canada
Publishes newsletter.

Light of Truth Church
P.O. Box 3125, Pasadena, California 91103
Pagan group headed by Nelson H. White

Llewellyn Publications
Gnostic Study Center
1414 Lorell Avenue, Minneapolis, Minnesota 55400
Small publishing group headed by Carl Weschke. Organizes Gnostic festivals, witchcraft conventions, study courses. Publishes *Gnostica* magazine, books.

Lotus Metaphysical Center, Inc.
128 N.E. Eighty-second Terrace, Miami, Florida 33138
Center led by British medium Noel Street.

Meher Baba House
186 West 4th Street, New York, New York
See entry on Meher Baba in chapter five.

Naropa Institute
1441 Broadway, Boulder, Colorado 80302
Offers instruction in spiritual disciplines (including Tibetan Buddhism) and sponsors Shambhala Publications. For more information, see the entry on Chögyam Trungpa in chapter five.

National Academy of Applied Awareness
6255 Sunset Boulevard, Hollywood, California 90028
Led by the medium and healer Leagh Caverhill.

National Spiritualist Association of Churches
11811 Watertown Plank Road, Milwaukee, Wisconsin 53226
Provides lists of mediums, churches, and local spiritualist associations. The most reliable place to contact a medium.

Optimum Center
4500 Mountrose, Houston, Texas 77006
Publishes *The Cosmic Echo,* a newsletter.

Ordo Templi Ashtart
Post Office Box 3341, Pasadena, California 91103
Hermetic-Rosicrucian order sponsored by the Church of Hermetic Science. Publishes magazine, *The Seventh Ray*. Lodges in Los Angeles, Pasadena, and Pittsburgh.

The Pagan Way
Post Office Box 2015, Wilmington, Delaware 19899

The Parapsychology Foundation
29 West 57th Street, New York, New York 10019
Publishes *Parapsychology Review*; maintains research library.

Parapsychology Research Foundation of the South
6131 Hurst Street, New Orleans, Louisiana 70118

Promethean Tranquility Center
Madeleine Morris
Box 4307-TE, Inglewood, California 90309

Psi Newsletter
c/o Department of Psychology and Parapsychology
Andhra University, Waltair, India

Psychedelic Venus Church
Post Office Box 4163, Sather Gate Station, Berkeley, California 94704
Pagan group with erotic rituals. Holzer rates it "not recommended."

Psychical Research Foundation, Inc.
Duke Station, Durham, North Carolina 27708
Investigates survival after death. Publishes a bulletin, *Theta*.

Sabean Society of Chicago
2553 North Halsted Street, Chicago, Illinois 60614
Pagan-magical organization run by psychic Frederico de Arechaga.

School of Wicca
Route 2, Salem, Missouri 65560
School run by Gavin and Yvonne Frost.

School of Witchcraft
69 Strathmore Village Drive, South Setauket, Long Island, New York 11720
School run by Phyllis Ammarati.

Self-Realization Fellowship
3880 San Raphael Avenue, Los Angeles, California 90065
Founded by Paramahansa Yogananda. For further information, see entry on Babaji in chapter five.

Siddha Yoga Center
324 West 86th Street, New York, New York 10024
Organization devoted to *gurukripa*, as practiced by Swami Muktananda. See entry on him in chapter five.

Silva Mind Control
P.O. Box 1149, Laredo, Texas 78040
Teaches how to correct disturbing behavior patterns through biofeedback, visualization exercises, etc. Theory owes much to Scientology.

Society of Psychic Awareness and Research
1120 South Mayfield Avenue, Chicago, Illinois 60644
Publishes newsletter.

Spiritual Frontiers Fellowship, Inc.
800 Custer Avenue, Evanston, Illinois 60202
Founded by medium Arthur Ford. Explores connections between psychical research and the Christian church.

Students International Meditation Society
1015 Gayley Avenue, Los Angeles, California 90024
One of the principal arms of the Transcendental Meditation group. For more information, see the entry on Maharishi Mahesh Yogi in chapter five.

Triune Science of Being Awareness Center
3497 Cahuenga Boulevard, Los Angeles, California 90068
Courses and lectures on a variety of occult subjects.

Unarius
P.O. Box 1042, El Cajon, California 92022
Members communicate with Beings of Light from Venus, Orion, and distant planets.

Unification Church of America
4 West 43rd Street, New York, New York
Organization founded by the Reverend Sun Myung Moon. See the entry on him in chapter five.

United Lodge of Theosophists
347 East 72nd Street, New York, New York,
Offers lectures and courses. For more information on Theosophy, see chapter seven.

Index